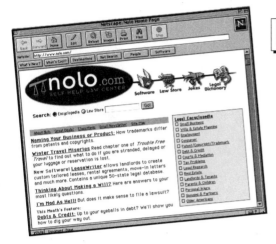

THIRD NATIONAL EDITION

# EVERY LANDLORD'S

**LEASES & RENTAL AGREEMENTS**
**DEPOSITS · RENT RULES · LIABILITY**
**DISCRIMINATION · PROPERTY MANAGERS**
**PRIVACY · REPAIRS & MAINTENANCE · EVICTIONS**

# LEGAL GUIDE

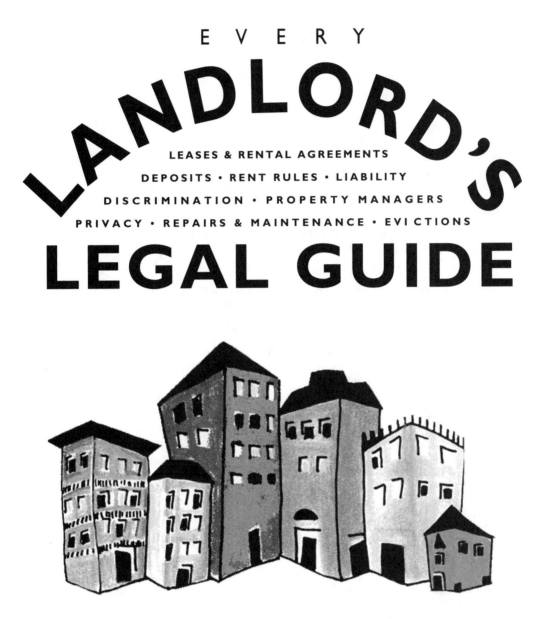

## BY MARCIA STEWART & ATTORNEYS RALPH WARNER & JANET PORTMAN

**nolo**.com
LAW FOR ALL

## Your Responsibility When Using a Self-Help Law Book

We've done our best to give you useful and accurate information in this book. But laws and procedures change frequently and are subject to differing interpretations. If you want legal advice backed by a guarantee, see a lawyer. If you use this book, it's your responsibility to make sure that the facts and general advice contained in it are applicable to your situation.

## Keeping Up to Date

To keep its books up to date, Nolo issues new printings and new editions periodically. New printings reflect minor legal changes and technical corrections. New editions contain major legal changes, major text additions or major reorganizations. To find out if a later printing or edition of any Nolo book is available, call Nolo at 510-549-1976 or check our Website at www.nolo.com.

To stay current, follow the "Update" service at our Website at www.nolo.com. In another effort to help you use Nolo's latest materials, we offer a 35% discount off the purchase of the new edition of your Nolo book when you turn in the cover of an earlier edition. (See the "Special Upgrade Offer" in the back of the book.)

This book was last revised in: July 1999.

|  |  |
| --- | --- |
| Third Edition | |
| Second Printing | JULY 1999 |
| Illustrations | LINDA ALLISON |
| Cover Design | JACKIE MANCUSO |
| Layout Design | TERRI HEARSH |
| Production | STEPHANIE HAROLDE |
| Index | THÉRÈSE SHERE |
| Proofreading | JOE SADUSKY |
| Printing | CONSOLIDATED PRINTERS, INC. |

Stewart, Marcia.
    Every landlord's legal guide : leases & rental agreements,
deposits, rent rules, liability, discrimination, property managers,
repairs & maintenance, evictions  /  by Marcia Stewart &
Ralph Warner & Janet Portman.  -- 3rd national ed.
    p.    cm.
    Includes index.
    ISBN 0-87337-471-1
    1. Landlord and tenant--United States--Popular works.  2. Leases-
-United States--Popular works.  3. Rent--United States--Popular
works.  I. Warner, Ralph E.   II. Portman, Janet.   III. Title.
KF590.Z9S74   1998
346.7304'34--dc21

98-13909
CIP

# Acknowledgments

We couldn't have written this book without the assistance and support of many people.

We'd like to especially acknowledge David Brown, author of Nolo Press's California *Landlords' Law Books,* who contributed many creative ideas to this book.

Nolo's Landlords' Team deserves much of the credit for this book. Our sincerest thanks to the Team members who made this work a pleasure:

Jackie Mancuso for her wonderful cover of this book, and for her patience and friendship in seeing this book through. Terri Hearsh for her terrific design work on the third edition

Mary Randolph, a fantastic editor whose sharp pen and cheerful spirit were invaluable

Patti Gima for her tremendous legal research and database design help

Stan Jacobsen, for his research assistance and willingness and competence to take on any task, and

Jaleh Doane for her creative marketing and copy ideas.

Many other Nolo people contributed to this book. Thanks also to:

Leslie Norwood and Naomi Starkman for their meticulous legal research

Ely Newman who did a great job designing the Legal Forms Disk

Nolo editors Barbara Kate Repa and Robin Leonard whose expertise and friendship contributed greatly to this book

Stephanie Harolde for help preparing the manuscript

Yvonne Schwartz for her early research assistance, and

All the other wonderful Nolo people who contributed in many different ways to this book, especially Nolo editors and authors Shae Irving, Steve Elias and Tony Mancuso.

Thanks to the staff and members of the National Apartment Association and the Joint Legislative Committee of the NAA and the Multi-Housing Council, especially Clarine Nardi Riddle and Barbara Vassallo, who generously shared their expertise regarding many of the issues in this book.

Michael Mansel of Insurance Associates in Walnut Creek, California, offered invaluable suggestions on the insurance sections of this book.

Norman Bates of Liability Consultants in Framingham, Massachusetts, gave useful suggestions and data on liability for crime.

Nadeen Green of *Apartment Guides* made helpful suggestions on screening tenants and discrimination.

Patrick Connor of Connor Associates provided useful advice on environmental hazards.

Gary Witt, Director of Municipal Government Affairs for the Arizona Multi-Housing Association, supplied up-to-date information and analysis of the ever-changing issue of occupancy standards.

The Volunteer Legal Services program of the Bar Association of San Francisco, California, offered practical suggestions and legal analyses on discrimination issues.

Finally, thanks to Linda Allison for her clever illustrations.

# About the Authors

**Marcia Stewart** brings her background in writing and editing on consumer issues to her job as a legal editor at Nolo.com. She is an expert on landlord-tenant law, buying and selling houses, and other issues of interest to consumers. She is the co-author of *Every Tenant's Legal Guide, Renters' Rights, Quick and Legal Leases* and *Rental Agreements* and the editor of Nolo's *LeaseWriter* software for landlords. Marcia received a Master's degree in Public Policy from the University of California at Berkeley and has written and edited a wide variety of consumer publications for government agencies and private businesses.

**Ralph Warner** is the co-founder and Publisher of Nolo.com. He is the author of a number of self-help law titles, including *Everybody's Guide to Small Claims Court, The Partnership Book* (with Clifford) and many landlord/tenant and real estate publications. Ralph is a lawyer who became fed-up with the legal system and as a result he has dedicated his professional life to making it more accessible and affordable to all Americans.

**Janet Portman**, an attorney and Nolo editor, received undergraduate and graduate degrees from Stanford and a law degree from the University of Santa Clara. She is an expert on landlord-tenant law and the co-author of *Every Tenant's Legal Guide* and *Renters' Rights*. As an attorney, she specialized in criminal defense, conducting trials and preparing and arguing appeals before the Court of Appeal and the California Supreme Court. Janet is the editor of several Nolo books, including *Legal Research: How to Find and Understand the Law* and *How to Seal Your Juvenile and Criminal Records*.

# Table of Contents

## 7 Getting the Tenant Moved In

## 8 Co-Tenants, Sublets and Assignments

## 9 Landlord's Duty to Repair and Maintain the Premises

## 10 Landlord's Liability for Dangerous Conditions

## 11 Landlord's Liability for Evironmental Health Hazards

## 12 Landlord's Liability for Criminal Acts and Activities

## 13 Landlord's Right of Entry and Tenants' Privacy

## 14 Ending a Tenancy

## 15 Returning Security Deposits

## 16 Problems With Tenants: How to Resolve Disputes Without a Lawyer

# Appendix I:
### State Laws and Agencies

# Appendix II:
### Tear-Out Forms

# Index

# Introduction

Face it: Few businesses on Earth are as regulated—some would say over-regulated—as is renting residential real property. Today a landlord either knows and follows the law or doesn't stay in business long.

Fortunately, armed with the knowledge in this book, you can cope with the law and get on with the real business of earning a decent return on your investment. Our approach involves three steps:

1. **Know the law.** This book covers most key laws affecting landlords in all 50 states—from meeting your repair and maintenance responsibilities to complying with tenants' privacy rights. In areas where more research may be needed, we show you how to do it.

2. **Adopt policies that exceed the letter of the law.** Like any good business, you'll do best with a customer-friendly approach that guards your legal interests at the same time your customers (tenants) feel that your practices are fair and reasonable. In the long run, this approach will help you attract the best possible tenants—which will almost guarantee success. Once you understand what the law requires (for example, how and when a departing tenant's deposit must be returned), it's usually easy to adopt procedures that almost effortlessly meet or even exceed legal requirements.

3. **Establish a relationship with an experienced landlord-tenant lawyer.** Inevitably, legal questions and problems will come up. Before, not after, you get into legal hot water, you need to line up a lawyer. The lawyer should be willing to help you help yourself as much as possible and be readily available when you need more help.

## A. How to Use This Book

In writing this book, our first goal was to clearly explain what the law requires of a landlord. But beyond that—and perhaps more important—we have been mindful that law doesn't exist in a

vacuum. It is always interpreted and applied by real people coping with real problems. We have labored mightily to explain legal rules in a real-world context.

We have also tried to suggest ways that you, as a conscientious landlord, can both comply with the law while at the same time making a decent profit. Stripped down to one sentence, we believe this involves choosing tenants carefully, keeping good tenants happy, teaching mediocre tenants how to improve and getting rid of bad tenants by applying policies that are strict, fair and legal.

**Note:** This book doesn't cover mobile homes, condominiums, hotels or commercial property.

## Guide to Icons Used in This Book

 This icon lets you know where you can read more about the particular issue or topic discussed in the text.

 This icon refers you to related information in another chapter of this book.

 This is a caution to slow down and consider potential problems.

 This icon means that you may be able to skip some material that doesn't apply to your situation.

 The form discussed in the text is on the Legal Forms Disk included with this book and a tear-out copy is in Appendix II.

 This icon alerts you to a practical tip or good idea.

 A rent control ordinance may address the issue discussed in the text.

 This icon lets you know when you probably need the advice of a lawyer who specializes in landlord-tenant law.

## Get a Little Help From Your Friends

Many landlords have discovered the value of belonging to a local or state association of rental property owners. These organizations, which range from small, volunteer-run groups to substantial organizations with paid staff and lobbyists, offer a wide variety of support and services to their members. Here are some services that may be available from your landlords' association:

- legal information and updates through newsletters, publications, seminars and other means
- tenant screening and credit check services
- training and practical advice on compliance with legal responsibilities, and
- a place to meet other rental property owners and exchange information and ideas.

If you can't find an association of rental property owners in your phone book, ask other landlords for references. You can also contact the National Apartment Association (NAA), a national organization whose members include many individual state associations:

National Apartment Association
201 North Union Street, Suite 200
Alexandria, Virginia 22314
703-518-6141

The National Multi-Housing Council, a national organization of many of the country's largest landlords, may also be helpful:

National Multi-Housing Council
1850 M Street, Suite 540, NW
Washington, DC 20036
202-659-3381

## B. Using the Forms Disk

The sample forms in the Appendices are included on a 3½" floppy disk in the back of the book. This forms disk is formatted for the PC (MS-DOS), and can be used by any PC running Windows or DOS. If you use a Mac, you must have a Super Disk drive and PC Exchange, or a similar utility, to use this disk. These files can be opened, filled in and printed out with your word processing program or text editor.

⚠ **The disk does not contain software and you do not need to install any files.** The forms disk contains only files that can be opened and edited using a word processor. This is not a software program. See below and the README.TXT file included on the disk for additional instructions on how to use these files.

## How to View the README File

If you do not know how to view the file README.TXT, insert the forms disk into your computer's floppy disk drive and follow these instructions:

- **Windows 95 and 98:** (1) On your PC's desktop, double-click the My Computer icon; (2) double-click the icon for the floppy disk drive into which the forms disk was inserted; (3) double-click the file README.TXT.
- **Windows 3.1:** (1) Open File Manager; (2) double-click the icon for the floppy disk drive into which the forms disk was inserted; (3) double-click the file README.TXT.
- **Macintosh:** (1) On your Mac desktop, double-click the icon for the floppy disk that you inserted; (2) double-click on the file README.TXT.
- **DOS:** At the DOS prompt, type EDIT A:README.TXT and press the Enter key.

While the README file is open, print it out by using the Print command in the File menu.

## 1. Copying the Disk Files Onto Your Computer

Before you do anything else, copy the files from the forms disk onto your hard disk. Then work on these copies only. This way the original files and instructions will be untouched and can be used again. Instructions on how to copy files are provided below. In accordance with U.S. copyright laws, remember that copies of the disk and its files are for your personal use only.

Insert the forms disk and do the following:

### a. Windows 95 and 98 Users

(These instructions assume that the A: drive is the source you want to copy from and that the C: drive is the location you want to copy the files to.)

Step 1. Double-click the My Computer icon to open the My Computer window.

Step 2. Double-click the A: drive icon in the My Computer window to open the drive window.

Step 3. First, choose Select All from the Edit menu (Ctrl+A). Then choose Copy from the Edit menu (Ctrl+C). Then close the drive window.

Step 4. Double-click the My Computer icon to open the My Computer window.

Step 5. Double-click the C: drive icon in the My Computer window to open the drive window.

Step 6. Choose New... from the File menu, then choose Folder to create a new, untitled folder on the C drive.

Step 7. Type "Landlord Forms" to rename the untitled folder.

Step 8. Double-click on the "Landlord Forms" folder icon to open that folder.

Step 9. Choose Paste from the Edit menu (Ctrl+V).

### b. Windows 3.1 Users

(These instructions assume that the A: drive is the source you want to copy from and that the C: drive is the location you want to copy the files to.)

Step 1. Open File Manager.

Step 2. Double-click the A: drive icon at the top of the File Manager window.

Step 3. Choose Select Files... from the File menu to open the Select Files dialog box.

Step 4. First, click the Select button to select all the files on the floppy disk. Then click the Close button to close the Select Files dialog box.

Step 5. Choose Copy... from the File menu to open the Copy dialog box.

Step 6. In the TO box, type C:\LANDLORD and click OK. Click OK again when you're asked if you want to copy the selected files to the C:\LANDLORD directory.

### c. Macintosh Users

Step 1. If the LANDLORD folder is open, close it.

Step 2. Click on the LANDLORD disk icon and drag it onto the icon of your hard disk.

Step 3. Read the message to make sure you want to go ahead, then click OK.

### d. DOS Users

(These instructions assume that the A: drive is the source you want to copy from and that the C: drive is the location you want to copy the files to.)

Step 1. To create a directory named "ML_FORMS" on your C: hard disk drive, type the following at the DOS prompt:
   C: <ENTER>
   CD\ <ENTER>
   MD LANDLORD<ENTER>

Step 2. To change to the LANDLORD directory you just created, type:
   CD LANDLORD<ENTER>

Step 3. To copy all the files from the floppy disk (in your A: drive) to the current directory, at the C:\ML_FORMS> prompt, type:
   XCOPY A:\*.* /s <ENTER>

All of the files in all directories on the floppy disk will be copied to the LANDLORD directory on your C: drive.

## 2.  Creating Your Documents With the Forms Disk Files

This disk contains all forms in two file types (or formats):

- the standard ASCII text format (TXT), and
- rich text format (RTF).

For example, the form for the Consent to Assignment of Lease discussed in Chapter 8 is on the files CONLEASE.RTF and CONLEASE.TXT.

ASCII text files can be read by every word processor or text editor including DOS Edit, all flavors of MS Word and WordPerfect (including Macintosh), Windows Notepad, Write and WordPad, and Macintosh SimpleText and TeachText.

RTF files have the same text as the ASCII files, but have additional formatting. They can be read by most recent word processing programs including all versions of MS Word for Windows and Macintosh, WordPad for Windows 95 and 98, and recent versions of WordPerfect for Windows and Macintosh.

To use a form on the disk to create your documents you must: (1) open a file in your word processor or text editor; (2) edit the form by filling in the required information; (3) print it out; (4) save your revised file.

The following are general instructions on how to do this. However, each word processor uses different commands to open, format, save and print documents. Please read your word processor's manual for specific instructions on performing these tasks.

DO NOT CALL NOLO'S TECHNICAL SUPPORT IF YOU HAVE QUESTIONS ON HOW TO USE YOUR WORD PROCESSOR.

### Step 1:  Opening a File

To open a file in your word processor, you need to start your word processing program and open the file from within the program. This process usually entails going to the File menu and choosing the Open command. This opens a dialog box where you will tell the program (1) the type of file you want to open (either *.TXT or *.RTF) and (2) the location and name of the file (you will need to navigate through the directory tree to get to the folder/directory on your hard disk that you created and copied the disk's files to). If these directions are unclear you will need to look through the manual for your word processing program—Nolo's technical support department will NOT be able to help you with the use of your word processing program.

### Which File Format Should You Use?

If you are not sure which file format to use with your word processor, try opening the RTF files first. Rich text files (RTF) contain most of the formatting included in the sample forms found in this book and in Appendix B. Most current Windows and Macintosh word processing programs, such as Microsoft Word or WordPerfect, can read RTF files.

If you are unable to open the RTF file in your word processor, or a bunch of "garbage" characters appear on screen when you do, then use the TXT files instead. All word processors and text editors can read TXT files, which contain only text, tabs and carriage returns; all other formatting and special characters have been stripped.

Windows and Mac users can also open a file more directly by double-clicking on it. Use File Manager (Windows 3.1), My Computer or Windows Explorer (Windows 95 and 98) or the Finder (Macintosh) to go to the folder/directory you created and copied the disk's files to. Then, double-click on the specific file you want to open. If you click on an RTF file and you have a program installed that "understands" RTF, your word processor should launch and load the file that you double-clicked on. If the file isn't loaded, or if it contains a bunch of garbage characters, use your word processor's Open command, as described above, to open the TXT file instead. If you directly double-click on a TXT file, it will load into a basic text editor like Notepad or SimpleText rather than your word processor.

### Step 2: Editing Your Document

Fill in the appropriate information according to the instructions and sample agreements in the book. Underlines are used to indicate where you need to enter your information, frequently followed by instructions in brackets. Be sure to delete the underlines and instructions from your edited document and, if necessary, renumber the clauses. If you do not know how to use your word processor to edit a document, you will need to look through the manual for your word processing program—Nolo's technical support department will NOT be able to help you with the use of your word processing program.

---

### Editing Forms That Have Optional or Alternative Text

Some of the forms have short, blank lines before text. These blank lines indicate:

- optional text, which you choose whether to include or exclude
- alternative text, where you select one alternative to include and exclude the other alternatives.

If you are using the tear-out forms in the Appendix, you simply mark the appropriate check box to make your choice.

If you are using the forms disk, however, we recommend that instead of marking the blank lines, you do the following:

**Optional text**. If you *don't want* to include optional text, just delete it from your document.

If you *do want* to include optional text, just leave it in your document.

In either case, delete the blank line itself as well as the italicized instructions that the text is optional.

**Alternative text**. First delete all the alternatives that you do not want to include.

Then delete the remaining blank line, as well as the italicized instructions that you need to select one of the alternatives provided.

### Step 3: Printing Out the Document

Use your word processor's or text editor's Print command to print out your document. If you do not know how to use your word processor to print a document, you will need to look through the manual for your word processing program—Nolo's technical support department will NOT be able to help you with the use of your word processing program.

### Step 4: Saving Your Document

After filling in the form, use the "Save As" command to save and rename the file. Because all the files are "read-only" and you will not be able to use the "Save" command. This is for your protection. IF YOU SAVE THE FILE WITHOUT RENAMING IT, THE UNDERLINES THAT INDICATE WHERE YOU NEED TO ENTER YOUR INFORMATION WILL BE LOST AND YOU WILL NOT BE ABLE TO CREATE A NEW DOCUMENT WITH THIS FILE WITHOUT RE-COPYING THE ORIGINAL FILE FROM THE FLOPPY DISK. MAKE SURE NEVER TO EDIT THE ORIGINAL FILE ON YOUR FLOPPY.

If you do not know how to use your word processor to save a document, you will need to look through the manual for your word processing program—Nolo's technical support department will NOT be able to help you with the use of your word processing program

■

# Chapter 1

# Screening Tenants:
# Your Most Important Decision

C hoosing tenants is the most important decision any landlord makes, and to do it well you need a reliable system. Follow the steps in this chapter to maximize your chances of selecting tenants who will pay their rent on time, keep their units in good condition and not cause you any legal or practical problems later.

**Before you advertise your property for rent, make a number of basic decisions**—including how much rent to charge, whether to offer a fixed-term lease or a month-to-month tenancy, how many tenants can occupy each rental unit, how big a security deposit to require and whether you'll allow pets. Making these important decisions should dovetail with writing your lease or rental agreement (see Chapter 2).

## A. Avoiding Illegal Discrimination

Federal and state antidiscrimination laws limit what you can say and do in the tenant selection process. Because the topic of discrimination is so important we devote a whole chapter to it later in the book (Chapter 5), including legal reasons for refusing to rent to a tenant and how to avoid discrimination in your tenant selection process. You should read Chapter 5 before you run an ad or interview prospective tenants. For now, keep in mind three important points:

1. **You are legally free to choose among prospective tenants as long as your decisions are based on legitimate business criteria.** You are entitled to reject people with bad credit histories, income that you reasonably regard as insufficient to pay the rent, or past behavior —such as property damage or consistent late rent payments—that makes someone a bad risk. A valid occupancy limit that is clearly tied to health and safety or legitimate business needs can also be a legal basis for refusing tenants. It goes without saying that you may legally refuse to rent to someone who can't come up with the security deposit or meet some other condition of the tenancy.

2. **Antidiscrimination laws specify clearly illegal reasons to refuse to rent to a tenant.** Federal law prohibits discrimination on the basis of race, religion, national origin, gender, age, familial status, physical or mental disability (including recovering alcoholics and people with a past drug addiction). Many states and cities also prohibit discrimination based on marital status or sexual orientation.

3. **Consistency is crucial when dealing with prospective tenants.** If you don't treat all tenants more or less equally—for example, if you arbitrarily set tougher standards for renting to a member of a racial minority—you are violating federal laws and opening yourself up to lawsuits.

## B. How to Advertise Rental Property

You can advertise rental property in many ways:

- putting an "Apartment for Rent" sign in front of the building or in one of the windows
- taking out newspaper ads
- posting flyers on neighborhood bulletin boards, such as the local laundromat or coffee shop
- listing with a homefinders' or apartment-finding service that provides a centralized listing of rental units for a particular geographic area
- listing with a local real estate office that handles rentals
- hiring a property management company which will advertise your rentals as part of the management fee
- posting a notice with a university, alumni or corporate housing office
- buying ads in apartment rental guides or magazines, or
- posting a notice with an online service such as Rent.Net (www.rent.net) which represents one million apartment units in the United States and Canada.

What will work best depends on a number of factors, including the characteristics of the particular property, its location, your budget and whether you

are in a hurry to rent. Many smaller landlords find that instead of advertising widely and having to screen many potential tenants in an effort to sort the good from the bad, it makes better sense to market their rentals through word-of-mouth—telling friends, colleagues, neighbors and current tenants. After all, people who already live in your property will want decent neighbors. For example, if you know a vacancy is coming up, you might visit or send a note to all tenants whom you or your manager think well of. Ask them to tell friends at work, the gym or in other activities.

If you do advertise your units, try to target your ads as narrowly as possible to produce the pool of prospective tenants you want. For example, if you rent primarily to college students, your best bet is the campus newspaper or housing office.

To stay out of legal hot water when you advertise, just follow these simple rules:

**Describe the rental unit accurately.** Your ad should be easy to understand and scrupulously honest. Also, as a practical matter, you should avoid abbreviations and real estate jargon in your ad. Include basic details, such as:

- rent
- size—particularly number of bedrooms and baths
- location—either the general neighborhood or street address
- lease or month-to-month rental agreement
- special features—such as fenced-in yard, view, washer/dryer, fireplace, remodeled kitchen, furnished, garage parking, doorman, hardwood floors or wall-to-wall carpeting

- phone number for more details (unless you're going to show the unit only at an open house and don't want to take calls), and
- date and time of any open house.

Read other ads to get good ideas. Some landlords find that writing a very detailed ad cuts down on the time they spend answering questions on the phone or taking calls from inappropriate tenants.

**If you have any important rules (legal and non-discriminatory), such as no pets, put them in your ad.** Letting prospective tenants know about your important policies can save you or your manager from talking to a lot of unsuitable people. For example, your ad might say that credit will be checked carefully in order to discourage applicants who have a history of paying rent late. However, it's optional, because the wording of your ad does not legally obligate you to rent on any particular terms. In other words, just because your ad doesn't specify "no pets," you are not obligated to rent to someone with two Dobermans.

**Be sure your ad can't be construed as discriminatory.** The best way to do this is to focus only on the rental property—not on any particular type of tenant. Specifically, ads should never mention sex, race, religion, disability or age (unless yours is really legally sanctioned senior citizens housing). And ads should never imply through words, photographs or illustrations that you prefer to rent to people because of their age, sex or race. For example, an ad in an environmental or church newsletter that contains a drawing of a recognizably white (or black or Asian) couple with no children might open you to an accusation of discrimination based on race, age and familial status (prohibiting children).

**Quote an honest price in your ad.** If a tenant who is otherwise acceptable (has a good credit history, impeccable references and meets all the criteria laid out in Section E, below, shows up promptly and agrees to all the terms set out in your ad, you may violate false advertising laws if you arbitrarily raise the price. This doesn't mean you are always legally required to rent at your advertised price, however. If a tenant asks for more services or different lease terms that you feel require more rent, it's fine to bargain and raise your price, as long as your proposed increase doesn't violate local rent control laws.

**Don't advertise something you don't have.** Some large landlords, management companies and rental services have advertised units that weren't really available in order to produce a large number of prospective tenants who could then be directed to higher priced or inferior units. Such bait-and-switch advertising is clearly illegal under consumer fraud laws, and many property owners have been prosecuted for such practices. So if you advertise a sunny two-bedroom apartment next to a rose garden for $500 a month, make sure that the second bedroom isn't a closet, the rose garden isn't a beetle-infested bush and the $500 isn't the first week's rent.

Keep in mind that even if you aren't prosecuted for breaking fraud laws, your advertising promises can still come back to haunt you. A tenant who is robbed or attacked in what you advertised as a "high-security building" may sue you for medical bills, lost earnings and pain and suffering. (See Chapter 12 for details.)

## C. Renting Property That's Still Occupied

Often, you can wait until the old tenant moves out to show a rental unit to prospective tenants. This gives you the chance to refurbish the unit and avoids problems such as promising the place to a new tenant, only to have the existing tenant not move out on time or leave the place a mess.

To eliminate any gap in rent, however, you may want to show a rental unit while its current tenants are still there. This can create a conflict; in most states, you have a right to show the still-occupied property to prospective tenants, but your current tenants are still entitled to their privacy. (For details on access rules, see Chapter 13.)

To minimize disturbing your current tenant, follow these guidelines:

- Before implementing your plans to find a new tenant discuss them with outgoing tenants, so you can be as accommodating as possible.

- Give current tenants as much notice as possible before entering and showing a rental unit to prospective tenants. State law usually requires at least one or two days. (See Chapter 13 for details.)
- Try to limit the number of times you show the unit in a given week, and make sure your current tenants agree to any evening and weekend visits.
- Consider reducing the rent slightly for the existing tenant if showing the unit really will be an imposition.
- If possible, avoid putting a sign on the rental property itself, since this almost guarantees that your existing tenants will be bothered by strangers. Or, if you can't avoid putting up a sign, make sure any sign clearly warns against disturbing the occupant and includes a telephone number for information. Something on the order of "For Rent: Shown by Appointment Only. Call 555-1700. DO NOT DISTURB OCCUPANTS" should work fine.

If, despite your best efforts to protect their privacy, the current tenants are uncooperative or hostile, wait until they leave before showing the unit. Also, if the current tenant is a complete slob or has damaged the place, you'll be far better off to apply paint and elbow grease before trying to re-rent it.

## D. Dealing With Prospective Tenants

It's good business, as well as a sound way to protect yourself from future legal problems, to carefully screen prospective tenants.

### 1. Take Phone Calls From Prospective Tenants

➡️ If you show rental property only at open houses and don't list a phone number in your ads, skip ahead to Section 2.

## Getting a Unit Ready for Prospective Tenants

It goes without saying that a clean rental unit in good repair will rent more easily than a rundown hovel. And, in the long run, it pays to keep your rental competitive. Before showing a rental unit, make sure the basics are covered:

- Clean all rooms and furnishings, floors, walls and ceilings—it's especially important that the bathroom and kitchen are spotless.
- Remove all clutter from closets, cupboards and surfaces.
- Take care of any insect or rodent infestations.
- Make sure that the appliances and fixtures work. Repair leaky faucets and frayed cords, and check the unit for anything that might cause injury or violate health and safety codes. (Chapter 9 discusses state and local health and safety laws.)
- Cut the grass, trim shrubbery and remove all trash and debris on the grounds.
- Update old fixtures and appliances, and repaint and replace the carpets if necessary.

If the previous tenant left the place in good shape, you may not need to do much cleaning before showing it to prospective tenants. To make this more likely, be sure to send outgoing tenants a move-out letter describing your specific cleaning requirements and conditions for returning the tenant's security deposit. (Chapter 15 discusses move-out letters.)

When prospective tenants call about the rental, it's best to describe all your general requirements—rent, deposits, pet policy, move-in date and the like—and any special rules and regulations up front. This helps you avoid wasting time showing the unit to someone who simply can't qualify—for example, someone who can't come up with the security deposit. Describing your general requirements and rules up front can also help avoid charges of discrimination, which can occur when a member of a racial minority or a single parent is told key facts so late in the process that she jumps to the conclusion that you've made up new requirements just to keep her out.

Also be sure to tell prospective tenants about the kind of personal information they'll be expected to supply on an application, including phone numbers of previous landlords and credit and personal references.

**Show the property to and accept applications from everyone who's interested.** Even if, after talking to someone on the phone, you doubt that a particular tenant can qualify, it's best to politely take all applications. Refusing to take an application may unnecessarily anger a prospective tenant, and may make the applicant more likely to look into the possibility of filing a discrimination complaint. Make decisions about who will rent the property later. Be sure to keep copies of all applications. (See discussion of recordkeeping in Section F, below.)

## 2. Have Interested Tenants Complete a Rental Application

To avoid legal problems and choose the best tenant, ask all prospective tenants to fill out a written rental application that includes information on the applicant's employment, income and credit; Social Security and driver's license numbers; past evictions or bankruptcies; and references.

A sample Rental Application is shown below.

The Legal Forms Disk includes a copy of the Rental Application. You'll also find a blank tear-out version in Appendix II at the back of this book.

Before giving prospective tenants a Rental Application, complete the box at the top, filling in the property address and any deposit or credit check fee tenants must pay before moving in.

Here are some basic guidelines for accepting rental applications:

- Each prospective tenant—everyone age 18 or older who wants to live in your rental property—should completely fill out a written

# Rental Application

*Separate application required from each applicant age 18 or older.*

---

### THIS SECTION TO BE COMPLETED BY LANDLORD

Address of Property to Be Rented: ___178 West 81st St., Apt. 4F___

Rental Term: ☐ month-to-month ☒ lease from ___March 1, 199X___ to ___February 28, 199X___

**Amounts Due Prior to Occupancy**

| | |
|---|---|
| First month's rent ................................................................ $ | 1,500 |
| Security deposit ................................................................... $ | 1,500 |
| Credit check fee ................................................................... $ | 30 |
| Other (specify): ___Broker's fee___ $ | 1,500 |
| TOTAL ...................................... $ | 4,530 |

---

## Applicant

Full Name—include all names you use(d): ___Hannah Silver___

Home Phone: (609) 555-3789          Work Phone: (609) 555-4567

Social Security Number: 123-000-4567          Driver's License Number/State: NJD123456

Vehicle Make: Toyota          Model: Tercel          Color: White          Year: 1994

License Plate Number/State: NJ1234567

## Additional Occupants

List everyone, including children, who will live with you:

| Full Name | Relationship to Applicant |
|---|---|
| Dennis Olson | Husband |
| | |
| | |
| | |

## Rental History

Current Address: ___39 Maple St., Princeton, NJ, 08540___

Dates Lived at Address: ___May 1990–date___          Reason for Leaving: ___New job in NYC___

Landlord/Manager: ___Jane Tucker___          Landlord/Manager's Phone: (609 555-7523

Previous Address: ___1215 Middlebrook Lane, Princeton, NJ, 08540___

Dates Lived at Address: ___June 1987-May 1990___          Reason for Leaving: ___Better apartment___

Landlord/Manager: ___Ed Palermo___          Landlord/Manager's Phone: (609) 555-3711

Previous Address: 1527 Highland Dr., New Brunswick, NJ, 08444

Dates Lived at Address: Jan. 1986–June 1987    Reason for Leaving: Wanted to live closer to work

Landlord/Manager: Millie & Joe Lewis    Landlord/Manager's Phone: (609) 555-9999

## Employment History

Name and Address of Current Employer: Argonworks, 54 Nassau St., Princeton, NJ

Phone: (609) 555-2333

Name of Supervisor: Tom Schmidt    Supervisor's Phone: (609) 555-2333

Dates Employed at This Job: 1983–date    Position or Title: Marketing Director

Name and Address of Previous Employer: Princeton Times

13 Junction Rd., Princeton, NJ    Phone: (609) 555-1111

Name of Supervisor: Dory Krossber    Supervisor's Phone: (609) 555-2366

Dates Employed at This Job: June 1982–Feb. 1983    Position or Title: Marketing Assistant

## Income

1. Your gross monthly employment income (before deductions): $ 5,000

2. Average monthly amounts of other income (specify sources): $

Note: This does not include my husband's income. See his application.

TOTAL: $ 5,000

## Credit and Financial Information

| Bank/Financial Accounts | Account Number | Bank/Institution | Branch |
|---|---|---|---|
| Savings Account: | 1222345 | N.J. Federal | Trenton, N.J. |
| Checking Account: | 789101 | Princeton S&L | Princeton, N.J. |
| Money Market or Similar Account: | 234789 | City Bank | Princeton, N.J. |

| Credit Accounts & Loans | Type of Account (Auto loan, Visa, etc.) | Account Number | Name of Creditor | Amount Owed | Monthly Payment |
|---|---|---|---|---|---|
| Major Credit Card: | Visa | 123456 | City Bank | $1,000 | $500 |
| Major Credit Card: | Dept. Store | 45789 | Macy | $500 | $500 |
| Loan (mortgage, car, student loan, etc.): | | | | | |
| Other Major Obligation: | | | | | |

**Miscellaneous**

Describe the number and type of pets you want to have in the rental property:     None now, but

we might want to get a cat some time

Describe water-filled furniture you want to have in the rental property:

Do you smoke?    ☐ yes  ☒ no

Have you ever:    Filed for bankruptcy? ☐ yes  ☒ no       Been sued? ☐ yes  ☒ no

Been evicted? ☐ yes  ☒ no           Been convicted of a crime? ☐ yes  ☒ no

Explain any "yes" listed above:

**References and Emergency Contact**

Personal Reference:    Joan Stanley                    Relationship:    Friend, coworker

Address:    785 Spruce St., Princeton, NJ, 08540

Phone: (609)  555-4578

Personal Reference:    Marnie Swatt                   Relationship:    Friend

Address:    82 East 59th St., #12B, NYC

Phone: ( 212 )  555-8765

Contact in Emergency:    Connie & Martin Silver        Relationship:    Parents

Address:    7852 Pierce St., Somerset, NJ, 08321

Phone: (609)  555-7878

I certify that all the information given above is true and correct and understand that my lease or rental agreement may be terminated if I have made any false or incomplete statement in this application. I authorize verification of the information provided in this application from my credit sources, credit bureaus, current and previous landlords and employers, and personal references.

February 15, 199X          *Hannah Silver*

Date                         Applicant

Notes (Landlord/Manager):

application. This is true whether you're renting to a married couple or to unrelated roommates, a complete stranger or the cousin of your current tenant.

- Always make sure that prospective tenants complete the entire Rental Application, including Social Security number, current employment and emergency contacts. You may need this information later to track down a tenant who skips town leaving unpaid rent or abandoned property.
- Be sure all potential tenants sign the Rental Application, authorizing you to verify the information and references and to run a credit report. (Some employers and others require written authorization before they will talk to you.) You may also want to prepare a separate authorization, so that you don't need to copy the entire application and send it off every time a bank or employer wants proof that the tenant authorized you to verify the information. See the sample Consent to Background and Reference Check, below.

The Legal Forms Disk includes a copy of the Consent to Background and Reference Check. Appendix II includes a blank, tear-out copy.

- Consider asking prospective tenants to show you their driver's license or other photo identification as a way to verify that the applicant is using his real name.

When you talk to prospective tenants, stick to questions on the application. Avoid asking questions that may discriminate, specifically any inquiries as to the person's birthplace, age, religion, marital status or children, physical or mental condition or arrests that did not result in conviction. (See Chapter 5 for details on antidiscrimination laws.)

**Take your time to evaluate applications.**
Landlords are often faced with anxious, sometimes desperate people who need a place to live immediately. On a weekend or holiday, especially when it's impossible to check references, a prospective tenant may tell you a terrific hard-luck story as to why normal credit- and reference-checking rules should be ignored in their case and why

---

### Consent to Background and Reference Check

I authorize __Jan Gold_____

to obtain information about me from my credit sources, current and previous landlords and employers

and personal references. I authorize my credit sources, credit bureaus, current and previous landlords

and employers, and personal references to disclose to _____Jan Gold_____

_____ such information about me as

__Jan Gold_____ may request.


__Michael Clark_____
Name

__123 State Street, Chicago, Illinois_____
Address

__312-555-9876_____
Phone Number

__February 2, 199X_____     __Michael Clark_____
Date                              Applicant

...e allowed to move right in. Don't
...ple who have planned so poorly that
...lly have to sleep in the street if they
...your place that day are likely to come up
with similar emergencies when it comes time to pay
the rent. Taking the time to screen out bad tenants
will save you lots of problems later on.

**Never, never let anyone stay in your property on
a temporary basis.** Even if you haven't signed a
rental agreement or accepted rent, you give someone
the legally protected status of a tenant by giving
that person a key or allowing him or her to move in
as much as a toothbrush. Then, if the person won't
leave voluntarily, you will have to file an eviction
lawsuit. (Chapter 8 discusses the legal rights of
occupants you haven't approved.)

---

### Fill Your Accessible Units

The National Accessible Apartment Clearinghouse
maintains a Web site that connects owners of
already accessible residential units with disabled
tenants seeking housing: www.aptsforrent.com/
naac. To register your unit, visit their Website;
contact them at 201 North Union Street, Suite
200, Alexandria, VA 22314; FAX 703-518-6191;
or call 800-421-1221. The service is free to landlords and tenants.

---

## E. Checking References, Credit History and More

If an application looks good, your next step is to
follow up thoroughly. The time and money you
spend are some of the most cost-effective expendi-
tures you'll ever make.

**Be consistent in your screening.** You risk a
charge of illegal discrimination if you screen
certain categories of applicants more stringently
than others. Make it your policy, for example, to
always require credit reports; don't just get a credit
report for a single parent or older applicants.

(Chapter 5 discusses legal reasons to refuse to rent
to a tenant.)

Here are six steps of a very thorough screening
process. You should always go through at least the
first three to check out the applicant's previous
landlords, income and employment, and run a
credit check.

## 1. Check With Previous Landlords and Other References

Always call previous landlords or managers for
references—even if you have a written letter of
reference from a previous landlord. It's worth the
cost of a long-distance phone call to weed out a
tenant who may cause problems down the road.
Also call previous employers and personal references
listed on the application.

To organize the information you gather from
these calls, use the Tenant References form which
lists key questions to ask previous landlords,
managers and other references. A sample is shown
below.

**Check out pets, too.** If the prospective tenant
has a dog or cat, be sure to ask previous
landlords if the pet caused any damage or problems
for other tenants or neighbors. It's also a good idea
to meet the dog or cat, so you can make sure that
it's well-groomed and well-behaved, before you
make a final decision. You must, however, accommodate a mentally or physically disabled applicant
whose pet serves as a support animal—no matter
how mangy looking the pet might be. For more
information on renting to tenants with pets, see
Chapter 2, Section C, Clause 14.

## Tenant References

Name of Applicant: Michael Clark

Address of Rental Unit: 123 State Street, Chicago, Illinois

**Previous Landlord or Manager**

Contact (name, property owner or manager, address of rental unit): _____

Kate Steiner, 345 Mercer St., Chicago, (312) 555-5432

Date: February 4, 199X

**Questions**

When did tenant rent from you (move-in and move-out dates)? December 1994 to date

What was the monthly rent? $750

Did tenant pay rent on time? A week late a few times

Was tenant considerate of neighbors—that is, no loud parties and fair, careful use of common areas? _____
Yes, considerate

Did tenant have any pets? If so, were there any problems? Yes, he had a cat, contrary to rental
agreement

Did tenant make any unreasonable demands or complaints? No

Why did tenant leave? He wants to live someplace that allows pets

Did tenant give the proper amount of notice before leaving? Yes

Did tenant leave the place in good condition? Did you need to use the security deposit to cover damage?
No problems

Any particular problems you'd like to mention? No

Would you rent to this person again? Yes, but without pets

Other Comments: _____

**Employment Verification**

Contact (name, company, position): _____ Brett Field, Manager, Chicago Car Company _____

Date: _____ February 5, 199X _____

Salary: _____ $30,000 _____ Dates of Employment: _____ March 1993 to date _____

Comments: _____ No problems. Fine employee. Michael is responsible and hard-working. _____

**Personal Reference**

Contact (name and relationship to applicant): _____ Sandy Cameron, friend _____

Date: _____ February 5, 199X _____ How long have you known the applicant? _____ five years _____

Would you recommend this person as a prospective tenant? _____ yes _____

Comments: _____ Michael is very neat and responsible. He's reliable and will be a great tenant. _____

**Credit and Financial Information**

Mostly fine—see attached credit report

**Notes, Including Reason for Rejecting Applicant**

Applicant had a history of late rent payments, and kept a cat, contrary to the rental agreement.

Be sure to take notes of all your conversations and keep them on file. You may note your reasons for refusing an individual on this form—for example, negative credit information, insufficient income or your inability to verify information. You'll want to record this information so that you can survive a fair housing challenge if a disappointed applicant files a discrimination complaint against you. Also, as explained below in Section F, you may have to divulge this information to a rejected applicant.

The Legal Forms Disk includes the Tenant References screening form and Appendix II includes a blank tear-out copy of the form.

Occasionally, you may encounter a former landlord who is unwilling to provide key information. This reluctance may have nothing to do with the prospective tenant, but instead reflects an exaggerated fear of lawsuits. And as landlords learn that their negative remarks about former tenants can be disclosed to rejected applicants if they request it (see Section F), one can expect that they will become even more circumspect. But if a former landlord seems willing to talk, an approach that often works is to try to keep the person on the line long enough to verify the dates of the applicant's tenancy. If you get minimal cooperation, you might say something like this: "I assume your reluctance to talk about Julie has to do with one or more negative things that occurred while she was your tenant." If the former landlord doesn't say anything, you have all the answer you need. If she says instead "No, I don't talk about any former tenants—actually, Julie was fairly decent," you have broken the ice and can probably follow up with a few general questions.

## 2.  Verify Income and Employment

Obviously, you want to make sure that all tenants have the income to pay the rent each month. Call the prospective tenant's employer to verify income and length of employment. Make notes on the Tenant References form, discussed above.

Before providing this information, some employers require written authorization from the employee. You will need to mail or fax them a signed copy of the release included at the bottom of the Rental Application form or the separate Consent to Background and Reference Check form (Section D). If for any reason you question the income information you get by telephone—for example, you suspect a buddy of the applicant is exaggerating on his behalf—you may also ask applicants for copies of recent paycheck stubs.

It's also reasonable to require documentation of other sources of income, such as Social Security, disability, workers' compensation, welfare, child support or alimony. To evaluate the financial resources of a self-employed person or someone who's not employed, ask for copies of tax returns or bank statements.

How much income is enough? Think twice before renting to someone if the rent will take more than one-third of their income, especially if they have a lot of debts.

## 3.  Obtain a Credit Report

Private credit reporting agencies collect and sell credit files and other information about tenants. Many landlords find it essential to check a prospective tenant's credit history with at least one credit reporting agency to see how responsible the person is managing money.

## a.  How to Get a Credit Report

A credit report contains a gold mine of information for a prospective landlord. You can find out, for example, if a particular person has ever filed for bankruptcy or has been:

- late or delinquent in paying rent or bills, including student or car loans
- convicted of a crime, or, in many states, even arrested
- evicted (your legal right to get information on evictions, however, may vary from state to state)

- involved in another type of lawsuit such as a personal injury claim, or
- financially active enough to establish a credit history.

Information covers the past seven to ten years. To run a credit check, you'll need a prospective tenant's name, address and Social Security number.

If you own many rental properties and need credit reports frequently, consider joining one of the three largest credit reporting agencies—Equifax, Trans Union or Experian (formerly TRW)—which charge about $20 to $30 in annual fees plus $10–$15 per report. You can find their numbers and those of other tenant-screening companies in the Yellow Pages or on the Internet under "Credit Reporting Agencies." Your state or local apartment association may also offer credit reporting services. With some credit reporting agencies, you can obtain an oral credit report the same day it's requested, and a written one within a day or two.

If you do not rent to someone because of negative information in a credit report, or you charge someone a higher rent because of such information, you must give the prospective tenant the name and address of the agency that reported the negative information. This is a requirement of the federal Fair Credit Reporting Act. (15 U.S.Code §§ 1681 and following.) You must also tell the person that he has a right to obtain a copy of the file from the agency that reported the negative information, by requesting it within 60 days of being told that your rejection was based on the individual's credit report.

## b. Credit Check Fees

It's legal in most states to charge prospective tenants a fee for the cost of the credit report itself and your time and trouble. Any credit check fee should be reasonably related to the cost of the credit check—$20 to $30 is common.

Many landlords don't charge credit check fees, preferring to absorb the cost as they would any other cost of business. For low-end units, charging an extra fee can be a barrier to getting tenants in the first place, and a tenant who pays such a fee but is later rejected is likely to be annoyed and possibly more apt to try to concoct a discriminatory reason for the denial.

The Rental Application form in this book informs prospective tenants of your credit check fee. Be sure prospective tenants know the purpose of a credit check fee and understand that this fee is not a holding deposit and does not guarantee the rental unit. (Chapter 4 discusses holding deposits.)

Also, if you expect a large number of applicants, you'd be wise not to accept fees from everyone. Instead, read over the applications first and do a credit check only on those who are genuine contenders (for example, exclude and reject those whose income doesn't reach your minimum rent-to-income ratio). That way, you won't waste your time (and prospective tenants' money) collecting fees from unqualified applicants.

**It is illegal to charge a credit check fee if you do not use it for the stated purpose and pocket it instead.** Return any credit check fees you don't use for that purpose.

## c. Investigative or Background Reports

Some credit reporting companies also gather and sell background reports about a person's character, general reputation, personal characteristics or mode of living. If you order a background check on a prospective tenant, it will be considered an "investigative consumer report" under federal law (the Fair Credit Reporting Act, 15 U.S.Code §§ 1681 and following) and you must tell the applicant, within three days of requesting the report, that the report may be made and that it will concern his character, reputation, personal characteristics and criminal history. You must also tell the applicant that more information about the nature and scope of the report will be provided upon request; and if asked, you must provide this information within five days.

If you turn down the applicant based wholly or in part on information in the report, you must tell the applicant that the application was denied based on information in the report, and give the applicant the name and address of the agency that prepared the report.

### d. What You're Looking For

In general, be leery of applicants with lots of debts—so that their monthly payments plus the rent obligation exceed 40% of their income. Also, look at the person's bill-paying habits, and of course pay attention to lawsuits and evictions.

Sometimes, your only choice is to rent to someone with poor or fair credit. If that's your situation, you might have the following requirements:

- good references from previous landlords and employer
- require someone more creditworthy to co-sign the lease (Chapter 2 includes a co-signer agreement)
- make sure you get a good-sized deposit, as much as you can collect under state law (see Chapter 4), and
- look at what steps the person has taken to improve credit—for example, enrolling in a debt counseling group.

If the person has no credit history—for example, a student or recent graduate—you may reject them or consider requiring a cosigner before agreeing to rent to them.

## 4. Verify Bank Account Information

If an individual's credit history raises questions about financial stability, you may want to double-check the bank accounts listed on the rental application. If so, you'll probably need an authorization form such as the one included at the bottom of the Rental Application, or the separate Consent to Background and Reference Check (discussed in Section D, above). Banks differ as to the type of information they will provide over the phone. Generally, banks will at most only confirm that an individual has an account there and that it is in good standing.

⚠ **Be wary of an applicant who has no checking or savings account.** Tenants who offer to pay cash or with a money order should be viewed with extreme caution. Perhaps the individual bounced so many checks that the bank dropped the account or

the income comes from a shady or illegitimate source—for example, from drug dealing.

## 5. Review Court Records

If your prospective tenant has lived in the area, you may want to review local court records to see if collection or eviction lawsuits have ever been filed against them. Checking court records may seem like overkill, since some of this information may be available on credit reports, but it's an invaluable tool, and not a violation of antidiscrimination laws as long as you check the records of every applicant. Because court records are kept for many years, this kind of information can supplement references from recent landlords. Call the local court that handles eviction cases for details, including the cost of checking court records. In most places, it runs about $50.

---

### Visiting the Homes of Prospective Tenants

Some landlords like to visit prospective tenants at their home to see how well they maintain a place. If you find this a valuable part of your screening process, and have the time and energy to do it, be sure you get the prospective tenants' permission first. Don't just drop by unexpectedly. Some landlords fabricate a reason for the visit ("I forgot to have you sign something"), but it's better to be honest regarding the purpose of your visit.

---

## 6. Use Megan's Law to Check State Databases

Not surprisingly, most landlords do not want tenants with criminal records, particularly convictions for violent crimes or crimes against children. Checking a prospective tenant's credit report, as we recommend above, is one way to find out about a person's criminal history. Self-reporting is another: Rental applications, such as the one in this book, typically ask whether the prospective tenant has ever been convicted of a crime, and, if so, to provide details.

"Megan's Law" may be able to assist you in confirming that some of the information provided in the rental application and revealed in the credit report is complete and correct. Named after a young girl who was killed by a convicted child molester who lived in her neighborhood, this 1996 federal crime prevention law charged the FBI with keeping a nationwide database of persons convicted of sexual offenses against minors and violent sexual offenses against anyone (42 U.S.C. §§ 14701 and following). Every state but Washington, DC has its own version of Megan's Law. These laws typically require certain convicted sexual offenders to register with local law enforcement officials, who keep a database on their whereabouts.

Unfortunately, the states are not consistent when it comes to using and distributing the database information. Notification procedures and the public's access rights vary widely:

- **Widespread notification/easy access.** A few states, such as Arizona and Texas, are "wide open"—they permit local law enforcement to automatically notify neighbors of the presence of sexual offenders on the database, by way of either letters, flyers or notices published in local newspapers. Alternately, some states, such as California and Colorado, make the information available to anyone who chooses to access the database.
- **Selected notification/limited access.** Other states, including Connecticut and Florida, take a more restrictive approach, allowing law enforcement to release the information only if they deem it necessary. Or, states such as Vermont permit public access only to persons who demonstrate a legitimate need to know the names of convicted sexual offenders.
- **Restricted notification/narrow access.** Finally, many states, such as Michigan, Minnesota and Ohio are quite restrictive, permitting notifica-

tion only to certain individuals or officials, and allowing access only to them.

For information on your state's Megan's Law, call your local law enforcement agency or your state's office of consumer protection (see the list in Appendix I.)

**Megan's Law databases may be incomplete or incorrect.** The database will depend on the rigor with which states enforce their ex-offender registration requirements. In some states, databases will include convictions from the entire state and beyond, whereas others will be limited to local counties.

If your state does not provide an accessible database that you can use when you screen, you may not learn of a person's past conviction for sexual offenses until *after* he registers his new address (yours) with the state's data collection agency. When he does so, you may get the flyer or phone call, but he'll already be a tenant. The fallout from angry neighbors and the negative publicity for your business can be dreadful. See Chapter 17, Section D, for suggestions on what to do if you find out one of your current tenants is a convicted sexual offender.

## F. Choosing—And Rejecting— An Applicant

After you've collected applications and done some screening, you can start sifting through the applicants. Start by eliminating the worst risks—people with negative references from previous landlords, a history of nonpayment of rent or poor credit or previous evictions. Chapter 5 discusses legal reasons for refusing to rent to a tenant, including convictions for criminal offenses. You'll want to arrange and preserve your information for two reasons: so that you can survive a fair housing challenge, if a disappointed applicant files a complaint; and so that you can comply with your legal duties to divulge your reasons for rejecting an applicant.

### 1. Information in Your Records

Be sure to note your reasons for rejection—such as poor credit history, pets (if you don't accept pets) or a negative reference from a previous landlord—on the Tenant References form or other paper so that you have a paper trail if an applicant asks for the reason for his rejection or accuses you of illegal discrimination. You want to be able to back up your reason for rejecting the person. Keep organized files of applications, credit reports and other materials and notes on prospective tenants for at least three years after you rent a particular unit. Keep in mind that if a rejected applicant files a complaint with a fair housing agency or files a lawsuit, your file will be made available to the applicant's lawyers. Knowing that, choose your words carefully, avoiding the obvious (slurs and exaggerations) and being scrupulously truthful.

### 2. How to Reject an Applicant

If you reject an applicant based on information from a third party, such as a bank, credit report, former landlord or employer, federal law requires you to make the information available to the applicant upon request. The federal requirements do not apply if you reject an applicant based on your review of his application or after you interview the applicant. For example, an applicant who wants a pet and is rejected because you have a no pets policy is not entitled to the disclosure procedures explained below.

Exactly what you must disclose, and how to do it, depends on the source of the information you have used to reject the applicant. The law doesn't require you to communicate an applicant's right to disclosure in writing, but it's a good idea to do so (and to keep a copy of the rejection letter in your files). That way, you'll have irrefutable proof that you complied with the law if you're ever challenged in court.

**Any source other than a credit bureau.** If you reject an applicant based on negative information from a previous landlord, bank, court clerk or court record, store, employer or personal reference, you must tell the applicant at the time you reject him that he has a right to send you a written request for disclosure of that information within 60 days after

learning of your decision. If a disappointed applicant sends you a request, you must disclose "the nature of the information" that led to your decision within a reasonable time. These are new requirements of the federal Fair Credit Reporting Act, effective September 30, 1997 (15 U.S.Code §§ 1681 and following.) An example of a rejection letter based on third party information from a source other than a credit bureau is shown below.

Unfortunately, the statute itself does not specify how much detail you must divulge. You may be able to relate that you simply received negative information from one of the applicant's personal references; or you may need to come clean with the dirty details ("John Smith told me that your housekeeping habits were a disaster and you were frequently overdrawn on your checking account"). Judges who are asked to rule on this issue will ultimately provide guidance; in the meantime, we suggest using the most general approach you feel you can get away with.

### Sample Applicant Rejection Letter

June 5, 199X

Ryan Holmes
34 Fourth Street
Cleveland, Ohio 44130

Dear Mr. Holmes

I regret to inform you that your application to rent the apartment at 89A West Shady Lane, Cleveland, has been turned down, based on information received from a source other than a consumer credit reporting agency. As specified by federal law, you have a right to learn the nature of this information if you make a request to us within 60 days of the date of this letter.

Sincerely,

*Carey Full*

Carey Full, Manager

**Credit reports.** If you do not rent to someone (or you charge a higher rent) because of an insufficient credit report or negative information in the report, you must give the applicant the name and address of the agency that reported the negative information or furnished the insufficient report. You must tell the applicant that the credit reporting company did not make the decision not to rent to them, and that the bureau cannot explain why the applicant was rejected. Tell the person that he has a right to obtain a free copy of his file from the agency that reported the negative information by requesting it within 60 days of being told that your rejection was based on the credit report. Finally, you have to tell applicants that they can dispute the report's accuracy and add their own "consumer statement" to their report.

**Background or "investigative consumer report."** If you reject an applicant based wholly or in part on information in a background report, you must tell the applicant that the application was denied based on information in the report, and give the applicant the name and address of the agency that prepared the report.

Assuming you choose the best-qualified candidate (based on income, credit history and references), you have no legal problem. But what if you have a number of more or less equally qualified applicants? The best response is to use an objective tie-breaker: Give the nod to the person who applied first. If you cannot determine who applied first, strive to find some aspect of one applicant's credit history or references that objectively establishes that person as the best applicant. Be extra careful not to always select a person of the same age, sex or ethnicity. For example, if you are a larger landlord who is frequently faced with tough choices and who always avoids an equally qualified minority or disabled applicant, you are guilty of discrimination.

**State laws may impose additional disclosure requirements.** Check with your state or local consumer protection agency or your attorney general's office. (See "State Consumer Protection Offices" in Appendix I.)

## Rating Applicants on a Numerical Scale

To substantiate your claim that you are fair to all applicants, you may be tempted to devise a numerical rating system—for example, ten points for an excellent credit report, 20 points for an excellent past landlord reference and the like. While this type of rating system may simplify your task, it has two significant drawbacks:

- Every landlord is entitled to rely on gut feelings regarding a potential tenant (as long as these are not illegally discriminatory—see Chapter 5). You can decline to rent to an applicant you feel, instinctively, is a creep. You can decline to rent to him in spite of stellar recommendations or a solid financial report. Use of a numerical rating system should not limit your exercise of good sense.

- If a rejected tenant sues you, you will have to hand over your rating sheet. It will be easier to explain your decision by referring to the whole picture, rather than defending every "point" allocated in your system. You do want to be able to point to the many specific background checks you performed and used to arrive at your decision, but you do not want to lock yourself into a numerical straight jacket that you will be asked to defend.

## G. Finder's Fees and Holding Deposits

Almost every landlord requires tenants to give a substantial security deposit. The laws concerning how much can be charged and when deposits must be returned are discussed in Chapters 4 and 15. Here we discuss some other fees and deposits.

### 1. Finder's Fees

You may legitimately charge a prospective tenant for the cost of performing a credit check. (See Section E3, above.) Less legitimate, however, is the practice of some landlords, especially in cities with a tight rental market, of collecting a nonrefundable "finder's fee" or "move-in fee" just for renting the place to a tenant. Whether it's a flat fee or a percentage of the rent, we recommend against finder's fees. First, a finder's fee may be illegal in some cities and states (particularly those with rent control). Second, it's just a way of squeezing a little more money out of the tenant—and tenants will resent it. If you think the unit is worth more, raise the price.

### 2. Holding Deposits

If you make a deal with a tenant but don't actually sign a lease or rental agreement, you may want a cash deposit to hold the rental unit while you do a credit check or call the tenant's references. Or, if the tenant needs to borrow money (or wait for a paycheck) cover the rent and security deposit. You might want a few hundred dollars cash to hold the place until the tenant pays balance. And some tenants may want to reserve a unit while continuing to look for a better one.

Is this a wise course? Accepting a deposit to hold a rental unit open for someone is legal in some states, but almost always unwise. Holding deposits do you little or no good from a business point of view, and all too often result in misunderstandings or even legal fights.

EXAMPLE: A landlord, Jim, takes a deposit of several hundred dollars from a prospective tenant, Michael. What exactly is Jim promising Michael in return? To rent him the apartment? To rent Michael the apartment only if his credit checks out to Jim's satisfaction? To rent to Michael only if he comes up with the rest of the money before Jim rents to someone who offers the first month's rent and deposit? If Jim and Michael disagree about the answers to any of these questions, it can lead to needless and result in a small claims court lawsuit alleging breach of contract.

Another prime reason to avoid holding deposits is that the laws of most states are unclear as to what portion of a holding deposit you can keep if a would-be tenant decides not to rent or doesn't come up with the remaining rent and deposit money, or if the tenant's credit doesn't check out to your satisfaction.

In California, for example the basic rule is that a landlord can keep an amount that bears a "reasonable" relation to the landlord's costs—for example, for more advertising and for prorated rent during the time the property was held vacant. A landlord who keeps a larger amount may be sued for breach of contract. A few states, including Washington, require landlords to provide a receipt for any holding deposit and a written statement of the conditions under which it is refundable.

If, contrary to our advice, you decide to take a holding deposit, it is essential that both you and your prospective tenant have a clear understanding. The only way to accomplish this is to write your agreement down, including:

- the amount of the holding deposit
- your name and that of the applicant
- the address of the rental property
- the dates you will hold the rental property vacant
- the term of the rental agreement or lease
- conditions for renting the applicant the available unit—for example, satisfactory references and credit history and full payment of first month's rent and security deposit
- what happens to the holding deposit if the applicant signs the rental agreement or lease—usually, it will be applied to the first month's rent, and
- amount of the holding deposit you will keep if the applicant doesn't sign a rental agreement or lease—for example, an amount equal to the prorated daily rent for each day the rental unit was off the market plus a small charge to cover your inconvenience.

A sample Receipt and Holding Deposit Agreement which covers each of these items is shown below. You can adapt this to your own situation.

The Legal Forms Disk includes the Receipt and Holding Deposit Agreement and Appendix II includes a blank tear-out copy of the form.

# Receipt and Holding Deposit Agreement

This will acknowledge receipt of the sum of $__500__ by __Jim Chow__

_____ ("Landlord") from __Hannah Silver__

_____ ("Applicant") as a holding deposit to

hold vacant the rental property at ____178 West 81st St., #4F, New York City____

_____,

until __February 20, 199X__ at __5 P.M.__. The property will be rented to Applicant

on a __one-year__ basis at a rent of $__2,000__ per month, if Applicant

signs Landlord's written __lease__ and pays Landlord the

first month's rent and a $__$1,500__ security deposit on or before that date, in which

event the holding deposit will be applied to the first month's rent.

This Agreement depends upon Landlord receiving a satisfactory report of Applicant's

references and credit history. Landlord and Applicant agree that if Applicant fails to sign

the Agreement and pay the remaining rent and security deposit, Landlord may retain of

this holding deposit a sum equal to the prorated daily rent of $__67__ per day

plus a $__35__ charge to compensate Landlord for the inconvenience.


February 16, 199X        _Hannah Silver_____

Date                     Applicant

February 16, 199X        _Jim Chow_____

Date                     Landlord

# Preparing Leases and Rental Agreements

The rental agreement or lease that you and your tenant sign forms the contractual basis of your relationship. Taken together with the laws of your state—and, in a few areas, local and federal laws—it sets out almost all the legal rules you and your tenant must follow.

Your rental agreement or lease is also an immensely practical document, full of crucial business details, such as how long the tenant can occupy your property and the amount of the rent.

Given their importance, there's no question that you need to create effective and legal agreements with your tenants. This chapter shows you how by providing clearly written, fair and effective tear-out lease and rental agreement forms, along with clear explanations of each clause.

Why use our lease or rental agreement, when you probably already use a printed form that seems adequate? There are several good reasons:

1. Our agreements are based on careful research of every state's landlord-tenant laws. Many pre-printed forms ignore state-by-state differences.

2. Our agreements are as legally accurate and up-to-date as we can make them. We don't use the illegal or unenforceable clauses that pepper many pre-printed agreements. Some forms still include clauses that courts threw out years ago or are so one-sided as to be unenforceable.

3. Our agreements are clearly written in plain English, and easy for you and your tenants to understand. We believe strongly that it's to everyone's advantage to have a written agreement that clearly informs tenants of their responsibilities and rights. Using legal gobbledygook is as counterproductive as it is unnecessary.

4. You can easily tailor our agreements to fit your own situation. Throughout the chapter, we suggest ways to modify clauses in certain circumstances. We'll also caution you about the types of modifications likely to get you into legal hot water.

**Don't use our forms if the rent is subsidized by the government.** You may need to use a special government lease if you rent subsidized housing. (See Chapter 5 for more on public housing.)

# A. Which Is Better, a Lease or a Rental Agreement?

One of the key decisions you need to make is whether to use a lease or a rental agreement. To decide which is better for you, read what follows and carefully evaluate your own situation.

## 1. Month-to-Month Rental Agreement

A written rental agreement provides for a tenancy for a short period of time. The law refers to these agreements as periodic, or month-to-month tenancies, although it is often legally possible to base them on other time periods—for example, if the rent were due every two weeks.

A month-to-month tenancy is automatically renewed each month unless you or your tenant gives the other the proper amount of written notice (typically 30 days) to terminate the agreement. The rental agreements in this book are month-to-month, although you can change them to a different interval.

Month-to-month rental agreements give landlords more flexibility than leases. You may increase the rent or change other terms of the tenancy on relatively short notice (subject to any restrictions of local rent control ordinances). You may also end the tenancy at any time (again, subject to any rent control restrictions), as long as you give the required amount of advance warning. (Chapter 14 discusses notice requirements to change or end a month-to-month tenancy. Chapter 3 covers rent control.) Not surprisingly, many landlords prefer to rent from month-to-month, particularly in urban areas with tight rental markets where new tenants can often be found in a few days and rents are trending upwards.

On the flip side, a month-to-month tenancy probably means more tenant turnover. Tenants who may legally move out with only 30 days' notice may be more inclined to do so than tenants who make a longer commitment. Some landlords base their rental business strategy on painstakingly seeking high-quality long-term renters. If you're one of those, or if you live in an area where it's difficult to fill vacancies, you will probably want tenants to commit for a longer period, such as a year. But, as discussed below, although a fixed-term lease may encourage tenants to stay longer, it is no guarantee against turnover.

## 2. Fixed-Term Lease

A lease is a contract that obligates both you and the tenant for a set period of time—usually a year. With a fixed-term lease, you can't raise the rent or change other terms of the tenancy until the lease runs out, unless the lease itself allows future changes or the tenant agrees in writing.

In addition, you usually can't ask a tenant to move out or prevail in an eviction lawsuit before the lease term expires unless the tenant fails to pay the rent or violates another significant term of the lease or the law, such as repeatedly making too much noise, damaging the rental unit or selling drugs on your property. (Chapter 17 discusses evictions for lease violations.) This restriction can sometimes be problematic if you end up with a tenant you would like to be rid of but don't have sufficient cause to evict.

To take but one example, if you wish to sell the property halfway into the lease, the existence of long-term tenants—especially if they are paying less than the market rate—may be a negative factor. The new owner usually purchases all the obligations of the previous owner, including the obligation to honor existing leases. Of course, the opposite can also be true—if you have good, long-term tenants paying a fair rent, it may be very attractive to potential new owners.

At the end of the lease term, you have several options. You can:

- decline to renew the lease, except in the few areas where rent control requirements prohibit it
- sign a new lease for a set period, or
- do nothing—which means, under the law of most states, your lease will usually turn into a month-to-month tenancy if you continue to accept monthly rent from the tenant.

Chapter 14 discusses in detail how fixed-term leases end.

Although leases restrict your flexibility, there's often a big plus to having long-term tenants. Some tenants make a serious personal commitment when they enter into a long-term lease, in part because they think they'll be liable for several months' rent if they leave early. And people who plan to be with you over the long term are often more likely to respect your property and the rights of other tenants, making the management of your rental units far easier and more pleasant.

**A lease guarantees less income security than you think.** As experienced landlords know well, it's usually not hard for a determined tenant to break a lease and avoid paying all of the money theoretically owed for the unused portion of the lease term. A few states allow tenants to break a lease without penalty in specific circumstances, such as a change in employment. And many states require landlords to "mitigate" (minimize) the loss they suffer as a result of a broken lease—meaning that if a tenant moves out early, you must try to find another suitable tenant at the same or a greater rent. If you re-rent the unit immediately (or if a judge believes it could have been re-rented with a reasonable effort), the lease-breaking tenant is off the hook—except, perhaps, for a small obligation to pay for the few days or weeks the unit was vacant plus any costs you incurred in re-renting it. (Chapter 14 discusses your responsibility to mitigate damages if the tenant leaves early.)

As mentioned, you'll probably prefer to use leases in areas where there is a high vacancy rate or it is difficult to find tenants for one season of the year. For example, if you are renting near a college that is in session for only nine months a year, or in a vacation area that is deserted for months, you are far better off with a year's lease. This is especially true if you have the market clout to charge a large deposit, so that a tenant who wants to leave early has an incentive to find someone to take over the tenancy.

The Legal Forms Disk includes copies of the Month-to-Month Residential Rental Agreement and the Fixed-Term Residential Lease. Appendix II includes blank tear-out versions of these forms. Both the disk and tear-out bersions are in English and in Spanish.

**Always put your agreement in writing.** Oral leases or rental agreements are perfectly legal for month-to-month tenancies and in most states for leases of a year or less. If you have an oral lease for a term exceeding one year, it becomes an oral month-to-month agreement after the first year is up. While oral agreements are easy and informal, it is never wise to use one. As time passes, people's memories (even yours) have a funny habit of becoming unreliable. You can almost count on tenants claiming that you made, but didn't keep, certain oral promises—for example, to repaint their kitchen or not increase their rent. Tenants may also forget key agreements, such as no subletting. And other issues, like how deposits may be used, probably aren't covered at all. Oral leases are especially dangerous because they require that both parties accurately remember one important term—the length of the lease—over a considerable time. If something goes wrong with an oral rental agreement or lease, you and your tenants are all too likely to end up in court, arguing over who said what to whom, when and in what context.

---

| Leases and Rental Agreements in a Nutshell | |
| --- | --- |
| **Leases** | **Rental Agreements** |
| You can't raise the rent or change other terms of the tenancy until the lease ends. | You may increase rent or change other terms of the tenancy on relatively short notice (subject to any restrictions of local rent control ordinances). |
| You usually can't end tenancy before the lease term expires, unless the tenant doesn't pay rent or violates another term of the lease. | You or the tenant may end the tenancy at any time (subject to any rent control restrictions), or by giving the required amount of written notice, typically 30 days. |

## B. Using the Forms in This Book

The fill-in-the-blank lease and rental agreements in this book are available in two forms:

- as files you can use with your word processor, on the Legal Forms Disk enclosed with the book
- as tear-out forms in Appendix II at the back of the book.

When you're ready to fill out a lease or rental agreement, go to Section C of this chapter for step-by-step instructions. The instructions explain how to fill in the blanks and also refer you to the chapter that discusses important issues that relate to your choices. Before you complete any clause for the first time, read the detailed discussion about it in the appropriate chapter. For example, before you complete Clause 5, which covers rent, be sure to read Chapter 3. Even if you have been a landlord for many years, reviewing the changing world of landlord-tenant law will be worthwhile.

You may want to modify our lease and rental agreement forms in some situations. The instructions suggest possible modifications for some of the clauses. If you make extensive changes on your own, however, you may wish to have your work reviewed by an experienced landlords' lawyer. (See

Chapter 18.) Also, see the Introduction to this book for advice on editing the forms on disk.

Don't be tempted to try to cram too many details into the lease or rental agreement. Instead, send new tenants a "move-in letter" that dovetails with the lease or rental agreement and highlights important terms of the tenancy—for example, how and where to report maintenance problems. You may also use a move-in letter to cover issues not included in the lease or rental agreement—for example, rules for use of a pool or laundry room or procedures for returning security deposits. (Chapter 7 covers move-in letters.)

**You may need to modify the forms if required by local ordinance.** Local rent control ordinances may require that your lease or rental agreement include specific information—for example, the address of the local rent control board. Check your local ordinance for more information and modify our forms accordingly.

**Help tenants understand the lease or rental agreement before they sign it.** Too many landlords thrust a lease or rental agreement at tenants and expect them to sign it unread. Far better to encourage tenants to ask questions about anything that's unclear, or actually review each clause with new tenants. It will save you lots of hassles later on.

If English is not the tenant's first language, give the tenant a written translation. (This book includes a Spanish version of our lease and rental agreement forms.) Some states require this; California, for example, requires landlords to notify Spanish-speaking tenants, in Spanish, of the right to request a Spanish version. But even if it's not legally required, you want your tenants to know and follow the rules. And it's a great way to establish rapport.

## C. Completing the Lease or Rental Agreement Form

This section explains each clause in the lease and rental agreement forms provided in this book.

Except for the important difference in the term of the tenancy (see Clause 4 in the forms), leases and written rental agreements are so similar that they are sometimes hard to tell apart. Both cover the basic terms of the tenancy (such as amount of rent and date due). Except where indicated below, the clauses are identical for the lease and rental agreement.

### How to Prepare Attachment Pages

Although we have tried to leave adequate blank space on the forms, it's possible that you may run out of room in completing a particular clause, or you may want to add a clause. Space is obviously no problem if you use the Legal Forms Disk. But if you need to add anything to the tear-out copies of the lease or rental agreement forms, take the following steps:

1. At the first place that you run out of room, begin your entry and then write "Continued on Attachment 1." Similarly, if there is another place where you run out of room, add as much material as you can and then write "Continued on Attachment 2," and so on. Use a separate Attachment each time you need more space.

2. Make your own Attachment form, using a sheet of blank white paper. At the top of the form, fill in the proper number—that is, "Attachment 1" for the first attachment, and so on.

3. Begin each attachment with the number of the clause you're continuing or adding. Then add "a continuation of" if you're continuing a clause, or "an addition to" if you're adding a clause.

4. Type or print the additional information on the Attachment.

5. Both you and each tenant should sign the page at the end of the added material.

6. Staple the Attachment page to the lease or rental agreement.

## CLAUSE 1.  IDENTIFICATION OF LANDLORD AND TENANT

This Agreement is entered into between _____ _____ ("Tenant") and _____ _____ ("Landlord"). Each Tenant is jointly and severally liable for the payment of rent and performance of all other terms of this Agreement.

Every lease or rental agreement must identify the tenant and the landlord or the property owner— often called the "parties" to the agreement. The term "Agreement" (a synonym for contract) refers to either the lease or rental agreement.

Any competent adult—at least 18 years of age— may be a party to a lease or rental agreement. A teenager who is slightly under age 18 may also be a party to a lease in most states if he or she has achieved legal adult status through a court order (called emancipation), military service or marriage.

The last sentence of Clause 1 states that if you have more than one tenant, they (the co-tenants) are all "jointly and severally" liable for paying rent and abiding by the terms of the agreement. This essential bit of legalese simply means that each tenant is legally responsible for the whole rent and complying with the agreement. You can legally seek full compensation from any one of the tenants should the others skip out or be unable to pay, or evict all of the tenants even if just one has broken the terms of the lease—for example, by seriously damaging the property. Chapter 8 provides more detail on the concept of joint and several liability and discusses the legal obligations of co-tenants.

### How to Fill in Clause 1:

Fill in the names of all tenants—adults who will live in the premises, including both members of a couple. Doing this makes everyone who signs responsible for all terms, including the full amount of the rent. Chapter 8 discusses why it's crucial that everyone who lives in your rental unit sign the lease or rental agreement. Also, make sure the tenant's name matches his or her legal documents, such as a driver's license. You may set a reasonable limit on the number of people per rental unit as discussed in Chapter 5.

In the last blank, list the names of all landlords or property owners.

## CLAUSE 2.  IDENTIFICATION OF PREMISES

Subject to the terms and conditions in this Agreement, Landlord rents to Tenant, and Tenant rents from Landlord, for residential purposes only, the premises located at _____, ("the premises"), together with the following furnishings and appliances: _____ _____. Rental of the premises also includes _____ _____.

Clause 2 identifies the address of property being rented ("the premises") and provides details on furnishings and extras such as a parking space. The words "for residential purposes only" are to prevent a tenant from using the property for conducting a business that might affect your insurance or violate zoning laws.

### How to Fill in Clause 2:

Fill in the address of the unit or house you are renting. If there is an apartment or building number, specify that as well as the city and state.

Add as much detail as necessary to clarify what's included in—or excluded from—the rental premises, such as kitchen appliances. If the rental unit is fully furnished, state that here and provide detailed information on the Landlord-Tenant Checklist included in Chapter 7.

In some circumstances, you may want to elaborate on exactly what the premises do or do not include. For example, if the rental unit includes a parking space, storage in the garage or basement, or other use of the property, such as a gardening shed in the backyard or the use of a barn in rural areas, specifically include it in your description of the premises. (See "How to Prepare Attachment Pages" at the beginning of this section.)

## Possible Modifications to Clause 2:

If a particular part of the rental property that might be assumed to be included is *not* being rented, such as a garage or storage shed you wish to use yourself or rent to someone else, explicitly exclude it from your description of the premises.

## CLAUSE 3. LIMITS ON USE AND OCCUPANCY

The premises are to be used only as a private residence for Tenant(s) listed in Clause 1 of this Agreement, and their minor children. Occupancy by guests for more than _____ is prohibited without Landlord's written consent and will be considered a breach of this Agreement.

Clause 3 states that the rental unit is only the residence of the tenants and their minor children. It lets the tenants know they may not move anyone else in as a permanent resident without your consent. The value of this clause is that a tenant who tries to move in a relative or friend for a longer period has clearly violated a defined standard, which gives you grounds for eviction. (New York landlords, however, are subject to the "Roommates Law," RPL § 235-f, which allows tenants to move-in relatives and other qualified individuals. The number of total occupants is still restricted, however, by any local statutes governing overcrowding.)

Clause 3 also includes a time limit for guest stays. Even if you do not plan to strictly enforce restrictions on guests, this provision will be very handy if a tenant tries to move in a friend or relative for a month or two, calling her a guest. It will give you the leverage you need to ask the guest to leave, request that the guest become a tenant with an appropriate increase in rent or, if necessary, evict the tenant for violating this lease provision. To avoid discrimination charges, don't make restrictions on guests that are based on the age or sex of the occupant or guest. Chapter 8 discusses guests in more detail.

## Investigate Before Letting a Tenant Run a Home Business

Over 20 million Americans run a business from their house or apartment. If a tenant asks you to modify Clause 2 to allow him to operate a business, you have some checking to do—even if you are inclined to say yes.

For one, you'll need to check local zoning laws for restrictions on home-based businesses, including the type of businesses allowed (if any), the amount of car and truck traffic the business can generate, outside signs, on-street parking, the number of employees and the percentage of floor space devoted to the business. In Los Angeles, for example, dentists, physicians (except for psychiatrists) and unlicensed massage therapists may not operate home offices. In addition, photo labs and recording studios are banned. And if your rental unit is in a planned unit or a condominium development, check the CC&Rs of the management association.

You'll also want to consult your insurance company as to whether you'll need a more expensive policy to cover potential liability of employees or guests. In many places, a home office for occasional use will not be a problem. But if the tenant wants to operate a business, especially one with people and deliveries coming and going, such as a therapy practice, jewelry importer or small business consulting firm, you should seriously consider whether neighboring tenants will be inconvenienced. (Where will visitors park, for example?)

You may also want to require that the tenant maintain certain types of liability insurance, so that you won't wind up paying if someone gets hurt on the rental property—for example, a business customer who trips and falls on the front steps.

Finally, be aware that if you allow a residence to be used as a commercial site, your property may need to meet the accessibility requirements of the federal Americans with Disabilities Act (ADA). For more information on the ADA, contact the Department of Justice, Office on the Americans with Disabilities Act, Civil Rights Division, in Washington, D.C., at 202-514-0301.

### How to Fill in Clause 3:

Fill in the number of days you allow guests to stay without your consent. We suggest you allow up to ten days in any six-month period, but of course you may want to modify this based on your own experience.

⚠️ **Don't discriminate against families with children.** You can legally establish reasonable space-to-people ratios, but you cannot use over-crowding as an excuse for refusing to rent to tenants with children. Space rules are available in your local or state housing code. Discrimination against families with children is illegal, except in housing reserved for senior citizens only. Just as important as adopting a reasonable people-to-square-foot standard in the first place is the maintenance of a consistent occupancy policy. If you allow three adults to live in a two-bedroom apartment, you had better let a couple with a child live in the same type of unit, or you are leaving yourself open to charges that you are illegally discriminating. (Chapter 5 covers discrimination and occupancy standards.)

### CLAUSE 4. TERM OF THE TENANCY

This clause sets out the key difference between a lease and a rental agreement: how long a rent-paying tenant is entitled to stay.

#### a. Lease Provision

The term of the rental will begin on _____, 199__, and end on _____, 199__. If Tenant vacates before the term ends, Tenant will be liable for the balance of the rent for the remainder of the term.

The lease form sets a definite date for the beginning and expiration of the lease and obligates both you and the tenant for a specific term.

Most leases run for one year. This makes sense, because it allows you to raise the rent at reasonably frequent intervals if market conditions allow. Leases may be shorter (six months) or longer (24 months)

—this, of course, is up to you and the tenants. A long period—two, three or even five years—can be appropriate, for example, if you're renting out your own house because you're taking a two-year sabbatical or if the tenant plans to make major repairs or remodel your property.

Chapter 14 discusses tenant's liability for breaking a lease, what exactly happens at the end of a lease, monetary consequences if a tenant "holds over" or fails to leave after the lease ends, termination of fixed-term leases and your duty to mitigate damages. It also covers notice requirements. You may want to specify some of these issues in the lease or rental agreement or in a move-in letter you send new tenants (see Chapter 7).

### How to Fill in Clause 4 (Lease):

In the blanks, fill in the starting date and the expiration date.

### Possible Modifications to Clause 4 (Lease):

If you want to provide for a periodic rent increase, perhaps tied to a consumer price index or your operating expenses, you'll need to add language to this effect. Without this type of built-in increase, you can't increase the rent until the lease ends.

⚠️ **Avoid liquidated damages provisions.** Some pre-printed forms (not ours) include what lawyers quaintly call a "liquidated damages" clause. This means that if a tenant moves out before the lease expires, he is supposed to pay you a pre-determined amount of money (damages) caused by his early departure. Unless the amount of liquidated damages is low, this approach is likely to be illegal. Under the laws of most states, a tenant who moves out before the lease expires is legally responsible to pay only for the actual losses he caused. If a suitable new tenant moves in immediately, this may be little or nothing. And, in most states, you are legally obligated to minimize your losses by trying to find a new tenant as soon as possible. Chapter 14 provides details on your responsibility to mitigate damages.

### b. Rental Agreement Provision

The rental will begin on _____, 199___, and continue on a month-to-month basis. Landlord may terminate the tenancy or modify the terms of this Agreement by giving the Tenant _____ days written notice. Tenant may terminate the tenancy by giving the Landlord _____ days written notice.

The rental agreement provides for a month-to-month tenancy and specifies how much written notice you must give a tenant to change or end a tenancy, and how much notice the tenant must provide you before moving out.

### How to Fill in Clause 4 (Rental Agreement):

In the first blank, fill in the date the tenancy will begin.

In the next two blanks, fill in the amount of written notice you'll need to give tenants to end or change a tenancy, and the amount of notice tenants must provide to end a tenancy. In most cases, to comply with the law of your state, this will be 30 days for both landlord and tenant in a month-to-month tenancy. (See State Laws on Notice Required to Change or Terminate a Tenancy, in Appendix I for details.)

### Possible Modifications to Clause 4 (Rental Agreement):

This rental agreement is month-to-month, although you can change it to a different interval as long as you don't go below the minimum notice period required by your state's law. If you do, be aware that notice requirements to change or end a tenancy may also need to differ from those required for standard month-to-month rental agreements, since state law often requires that all key notice periods be the same.

**Your right to terminate or change the terms of a tenancy, even one from month-to-month, can be limited by a rent control ordinance.** Such ordinances not only limit rent and other terms of tenancies, but also require the landlord to have a good reason to terminate a tenancy. (We discuss rent control in Chapter 3.)

### CLAUSE 5. PAYMENT OF RENT

*Regular monthly rent.*
Tenant will pay to Landlord a monthly rent of $_____, payable in advance on the first day of each month, except when that day falls on a weekend or legal holiday, in which case rent is due on the next business day. Rent will be paid in the following manner unless Landlord designates otherwise:

*Delivery of payment.*
Rent will be paid:
☐ by mail, to _____
☐ in person, at _____

*Form of payment.*
Landlord will accept payment in these forms:
☐ personal check made payable to

_____
☐ cashier's check made payable to

_____
☐ credit card
☐ money order
☐ cash

*Pro-rated first month's rent.*
For the period from Tenant's move-in date, _____, 199___, through the end of the month, Tenant will pay to Landlord the pro-rated monthly rent of $ _____. This amount will be paid on or before the date the Tenant moves in.

This clause provides details on the amount of rent and when, where and how it's paid. It requires the tenant to pay rent monthly on the first day of the month, unless the first day falls on a weekend or a legal holiday, in which case rent is due on the next business day. (Extending the rent due date for holidays is legally required in some states and is a general rule in most.)

We discuss how to set a legal rent and where and how rent is due in Chapter 3. Before you fill in the blanks, please read that chapter.

### How to Fill in Clause 5:

**Regular monthly rent.** In the first blank, state the amount of monthly rent. Unless your premises are subject to a local rent control ordinance, you can legally charge as much rent as you want (or more practically speaking, as much as a tenant will pay).

**Delivery of payment.** Next, specify to whom and where the rent is to be paid—by mail (most common) or in person (if so, specify the address, such as your office or to your manager at the rental unit).

**Form of payment.** Note all the forms of payment you'll accept, such as personal check and money order.

**Pro-rated first month's rent.** If the tenant moves in before the regular rental period—let's say in the middle of the month, and you want rent due on the first of every month—you can specify the pro-rated amount due for the first partial month. To figure out pro-rated rent, divide the monthly rent by 30 days and multiply by the number of days in the first rental period. That will avoid confusion about what you expect to be paid. Enter the move-in date, such as "June 21, 199X," and the amount of pro-rated monthly rent.

EXAMPLE: Meg rents an apartment for $900 per month with rent due on the first of the month. She moves in on June 21, so she should pay ten days' pro-rated rent of $300 when she moves in. ($900/30=$30X10 days=$300.) The full $900 rent check is due on July 1.

If the tenant is moving in on the first of the month, or the same day rent is due, write in "N/A" or "Not Applicable" in the section on pro-rated rent.

### Possible Modifications to Clause 5:

Here are a few common ways to modify Clause 5:

**Rent due date.** You can establish a rent due date different from the first of the month, such as the day of the month on which the tenant moves in. For example, if the tenant moved in on July 10, rent would be due on the tenth of each month, a system which of course saves the trouble of pro-rating the first month's rent.

**Frequency of rent payments.** You are not legally required to have your tenant pay rent on a monthly basis. You can modify the clause and require that the rent be paid twice a month, each week or by whatever schedule suits you.

If your property is under rent control, check your local ordinance to see if you must provide any specific information about rent control rules in the lease or rental agreement.

SURPRISE! MY RENT CHECK A DAY EARLY...

## CLAUSE 6.  LATE CHARGES

If Tenant fails to pay the rent in full before the end of the _____ day after it's due, Tenant will pay Landlord a late charge as follows: _____

_____

_____.

Landlord does not waive the right to insist on payment of the rent in full on the date it is due.

Landlords routinely charge a late fee if rent is not paid on time. This clause spells out details on your policy on late fees. A few states have statutes that put precise limits on the amount of late fees or when they can be collected. For advice on setting a late charge policy, see Chapter 3.

### How to Fill in Clause 6:

In the first blank, specify when you will start charging a late fee. You can charge a late fee the first day rent is late, but many landlords don't charge a late fee until the rent is two or three days late.

Next, fill in details on your late rent fee, such as the daily charge and any maximum fee.

### Possible Modifications to Clause 6:

If you decide not to charge a late fee (something we consider highly unwise), you may simply delete this clause, or write the words "N/A" or "Not Applicable" on it.

## CLAUSE 7.  RETURNED CHECK AND OTHER BANK CHARGES

If any check offered by Tenant to Landlord in payment of rent or any other amount due under this Agreement is returned for lack of sufficient funds, a "stop payment" or any other reason, Tenant will pay Landlord a returned check charge of $ _____.

As with late charges, any bounced-check charges you require must be reasonable. Generally, you should charge no more than the amount your bank charges you for a returned check, probably $10 to $20 per returned item, plus a few dollars for your trouble.

Chapter 3 covers returned check charges.

### How to Fill in Clause 7:

In the blank, fill in the amount of the returned check charge. If you won't accept checks, fill in "N/A" or "Not Applicable."

## CLAUSE 8.  SECURITY DEPOSIT

On signing this Agreement, Tenant will pay to Landlord the sum of $_____ as a security deposit. Tenant may not, without Landlord's prior written consent, apply this security deposit to the last month's rent or to any other sum due under this Agreement. Within _____ after Tenant has vacated the premises, returned keys and provided Landlord with a forwarding address, Landlord will return the deposit in full or give Tenant an itemized written statement of the reasons for, and the dollar amount of, any of the security deposit retained by Landlord, along with a check for any deposit balance.

The use and return of security deposits is a frequent source of disputes between landlords and tenants. To avoid confusion and legal hassles, this clause is clear on the subject, including:

- the dollar amount of the deposit
- the fact that the deposit may not be used for the last month's rent without your prior approval, and
- when the deposit will be returned, along with an itemized statement of deductions.

Chapters 4 and 15 cover the basic information you need to complete Clause 8, including state rules on how large a deposit you can require, when you must return it and the type of itemization you must provide a tenant when deductions are made.

## State-Mandated Additions to Security Deposit Clause

| State | Add this language to general security deposit clause: |
|---|---|
| **Alaska** | "Landlord will retain only that portion of Tenant's security deposit necessary to pay accrued rent or compensate Landlord for damages suffered by reason of Tenant's failure to maintain the dwelling unit." |
| **Florida** | "The security deposit will be held in [a separate or Landlord's] [interest-bearing or non-interest bearing] account at: [name and address of depository].<br><br>"Interest will be paid on this account as follows: [rate, time of payments].<br><br>"A copy of Florida Statutes § 83.49(3), explaining how and when the security deposit will be returned, is attached as required by law." [A copy for you to attach is included in Appendix I of this book.] |
| **Georgia** | "The security deposit will be held in account no. _____ at: [name and address of depository]." |
| **Kentucky** | "The security deposit will be held in account no. _____ at: [name and address of depository]." |
| **Maryland** | "Tenant has the right to receive from Landlord a written list of all existing damages if Tenant makes a written request within 15 days of Tenant's occupancy." |
| **Michigan** | "The security deposit will be held in an account at: [name and address of depository]."<br><br>You must also add the following paragraph in 12-point boldface type or type that is at least four points larger than the body of the agreement:<br><br>"To the Tenant: You must notify your landlord in writing within 4 days after you move of a forwarding address where you can be reached and where you will receive mail; otherwise your landlord shall be relieved of sending you an itemized list of damages and the penalties adherent to that failure." |
| **North Carolina** | "The security deposit will be held in account no. _____ at: [name and address of depository] or by [name and address of insurance company providing bond for security deposit]." |
| **Tennessee** | "The security deposit will be held in account no. _____ at: [name and address of depository]." |
| **Washington** | "The security deposit will be held in an account at: [name and address of depository]."<br><br>"Landlord may withhold only that portion of the security deposit necessary to (1) remedy any default in the payment of rent, (2) repair damage to the premises, except ordinary wear and tear, caused by Tenant, and (3) clean the premises if necessary." |

### How to Fill in Clause 8:

Once you decide how much security deposit you can charge (see "State Laws on Security Deposit Limits" in Chapter 4), fill in the amount in the first blank. Unless there's a lower limit, we suggest about two months as your rent deposit, assuming your potential tenants can afford that much. In no case is it wise to charge much less than one month's rent.

Next, fill in the time period when you will return the deposit. (See "Deadlines for Landlords to Itemize and Return Security Deposits" in Chapter 15.) If there is no statutory deadline for returning the deposit, we recommend three to four weeks as a reasonable time to return a tenant's deposit. Establishing a fairly short period (even if the law of your state allows more time) will discourage anxious tenants from repeatedly bugging you or your manager for their deposit refund.

### Possible Modifications to Clause 8:

The laws of several states require you to give tenants written information on various aspects of the security deposit, including where the security deposit is being held, interest payments, and the terms of and conditions under which the security deposit may be withheld. The chart, "State-Mandated Additions to Security Deposit Clause," lists specific clauses you should add to Clause 8. (See "How to Prepare Attachment Pages," at the beginning of this section.)

Even if it's not required, you may want to provide additional details on security deposits in your lease or rental agreement. Here are optional clauses you may add to the end of Clause 8.

The security deposit will be held at:
_____ *(name and address of financial institution)* _____ .

Landlord will pay Tenant interest on all security deposits as follows: _____ *(interest terms)* _____ .

Landlord may withhold only that portion of Tenant's security deposit necessary to: (1) remedy any default by Tenant in the payment of rent; (2) repair damage to the premises, except for ordinary wear and tear caused by Tenant; (3) clean the premises if necessary, and (4) compensate Landlord for any other losses as allowed by state law.

## Nonrefundable Fees

We don't recommend nonrefundable fees—for one thing, they are illegal in many states. (See Chapter 4.) If you do collect a nonrefundable fee —for example, for cleaning or pets—be sure your lease or rental agreement is clear on the subject.

### CLAUSE 9.  UTILITIES

Tenant will pay all utility charges, except for the following, which will be paid by Landlord:

_____

_____ .

This clause helps prevent misunderstandings as to who's responsible for paying utilities. Normally, landlords pay for garbage (and sometimes water, if there is a yard) to help make sure that the premises are well-maintained. Tenants usually pay for other services, such as phone, gas and electricity.

## How to Fill in Clause 9:

In the blank, fill in the utilities you—not the tenants—will be responsible for paying. If you will not be paying for any utilities, simply write in "N/A" or "Not Applicable."

### Disclose Shared Utility Arrangements

If there are not separate gas and electric meters for each unit, or a tenant's meter measures gas or electricity used in areas outside his unit (such as a water heater that serves several apartments or lighting in a common area), you should disclose this in your lease or rental agreement. Simply add details to Clause 20, Disclosures, preparing an attachment page if necessary. This type of disclosure is required by law in some states, and is only fair in any case. The best solution is to put in a separate meter for the areas served outside the tenant's unit. If you don't do that, you should:

- pay for the utilities for the tenant's meter yourself by placing that utility in your name
- reduce the tenant's rent to compensate for payment of utility usage outside of their unit (this will probably cost you more in the long run than if you either added a new meter or simply paid for the utilities yourself), or
- sign a separate written agreement with the tenant, under which the tenant specifically agrees to pay for others' utilities too.

## CLAUSE 10. ASSIGNMENT AND SUBLETTING

Tenant will not sublet any part of the premises or assign this Agreement without the prior written consent of Landlord.

Clause 10 is an antisubletting clause, breach of which is grounds for eviction. It prevents a tenant from subleasing during a vacation—letting someone stay in his place and pay rent while he's gone for an extended period of time—or renting out a room to someone unless you specifically agree.

Clause 10 is also designed to prevent assignments, a legal term that means your tenant transfers her entire tenancy to someone else. Practically, you need this clause to prevent your tenant from leaving in the middle of the month or lease term and moving in a replacement—maybe someone you wouldn't choose to rent to—without your consent.

By including Clause 10 in your lease or rental agreement, you have the option not to accept the person your tenant proposes to take over the lease. Under the law of most states, however, you should realize that if a tenant who wishes to leave early provides you with another suitable tenant, you can't both unreasonably refuse to rent to this person and hold the tenant financially liable for breaking the lease.

Chapter 8 discusses sublets and assignments in detail. Chapter 14 discusses what happens when a tenant breaks a lease.

## How to Fill in Clause 10:

You don't need to add anything to this clause in most situations. There may be local laws, however, that do apply.

## CLAUSE 11. TENANT'S MAINTENANCE RESPONSIBILITIES

Tenant will: (1) keep the premises clean, sanitary and in good condition and, upon termination of the tenancy, return the premises to Landlord in a condition identical to that which existed when Tenant took occupancy, except for ordinary wear and tear; (2) immediately notify Landlord of any defects or dangerous conditions in and about the premises of which Tenant becomes aware; and (3) reimburse Landlord, on demand by Landlord, for the cost of any repairs to the premises damaged by Tenant or Tenant's guests or business invitees through misuse or neglect.

Tenant has examined the premises, including appliances, fixtures, carpets, drapes and paint, and has found them to be in good, safe and clean condition and repair, except as noted in the Landlord-Tenant Checklist.

Clause 11 makes the tenant responsible for keeping the rental premises clean and sanitary. This clause also makes it clear that if the tenant damages the premises (for example, by breaking a window or scratching hardwood floors), it's his responsibility for the damage.

It is the law in some states (and wise in all) to notify tenants in writing of procedures for making complaints and repair requests. Clause 11 requires the tenant to alert you to defective or dangerous conditions.

Before the tenant moves in, you and the tenant should inspect the rental unit and fill out the Landlord-Tenant Checklist in Chapter 7, describing what is in the unit and noting any problems.

Chapter 9 provides details on landlords' and tenants' repair and maintenance responsibilities, recommends a system for tenants to request repairs, and offers practical advice on maintaining your rental property. Chapter 9 also covers tenant options (such as rent withholding) should you fail to maintain your property and keep it in good repair.

### How to Fill in Clause 11:

You do not need to add anything to this clause.

⚠ **Don't fail to maintain the property.** In most states, language you stick in a lease or rental agreement saying a tenant gives up his right to habitable housing won't be effective. By law, you have to provide habitable housing, no matter what the agreement says. If your tenants or their guests suffer injury or property damage as a result of poorly-maintained property, you may be held responsible for paying for the loss. See Chapters 10, 11 and 12 for liability-related issues.

## Renters' Insurance

It is becoming increasingly popular, especially in high-end rentals, to require tenants to obtain renters' insurance. It covers losses to the tenant's belongings as a result of fire or theft. Often called a "Tenant's Package Policy," renters' insurance also covers the tenant if his negligence causes injury to other people or property damage (to his property or to yours). Besides protecting the tenant from personal liability, renters' insurance benefits you, too: If damage caused by the tenant could be covered by either his insurance policy or yours—for example, the tenant starts a fire when he leaves the stove on—a claim made on the tenant's policy will affect his premiums, not yours.

If you decide to require insurance, insert a clause like the following at the end of your lease or rental agreement, under Clause 22, Additional Provisions. This will help assure that the tenant purchases and maintains a renters' insurance policy throughout his tenancy.

Landlords who are subject to rent control may not be able to require renters' insurance. In New York State, the Division of Housing and Community Renewal has stated that requiring renters' insurance constitutes a form of additional rent, in violation of the ordinance. Check with your rent control board for the law in your city.

---

Renters' Insurance
Within ten days of the signing of this Agreement, Tenant will obtain renters' insurance and provide proof of purchase to Landlord. Tenant further agrees to maintain the policy throughout the duration of the tenancy, and to furnish proof of insurance on a ☐ yearly ☐ semi-annual basis.

## CLAUSE 12. REPAIRS AND ALTERATIONS BY TENANT

a. Except as provided by law, or as authorized by the prior written consent of Landlord, Tenant will not make any repairs or alterations to the premises, including nailing holes in the walls or painting the rental unit.

b. Tenant will not, without Landlord's prior written consent, alter, re-key or install any locks to the premises or install or alter any burglar alarm system. Tenant will provide Landlord with a key or keys capable of unlocking all such re-keyed or new locks as well as instructions on how to disarm any altered or new burglar alarm system.

Clause 12 makes it clear that the tenant may not make alterations and repairs without your consent, including painting or nailing holes in the walls.

And to make sure you can take advantage of your legal right of entry in an emergency situation, Clause 12 specifically forbids the tenant from re-keying the locks or installing a burglar alarm system without your consent. If you do grant permission, make sure your tenant gives you duplicate keys or the name and phone number of the alarm company or instructions on how to disarm the alarm system so that you can enter in case of emergency. (See Chapter 12 for more information on your responsibility to provide secure premises, and Chapter 13 for information on your right to enter rental property in an emergency.)

The "except as provided by law" language in Clause 12 is a reference to the fact that, in certain situations and in certain states, tenants have a narrowly defined right to alter or repair the premises, regardless of what you've said in the lease or rental agreement. Examples include:

- **Alterations by a disabled person, such as lowering counter tops for a wheelchair-bound tenant.** Under the federal Fair Housing Acts, a disabled person may modify her living space to the extent necessary to make the space safe and comfortable, as long as the modifications will not make the unit unac-

ceptable to the next tenant, or if the disabled tenant agrees to undo the modification when she leaves. (See Chapter 5 for details.)

- **Use of the "repair and deduct" procedure.** In most states, tenants have the right to repair defects or damage that make the premises uninhabitable or substantially interfere with the tenant's safe use or enjoyment of the premises. Usually, the tenant must first notify you of the problem and give you a reasonable amount of time to fix it. (See Chapter 9 for more on this topic.)

- **Specific alterations allowed by state statutes.** In Connecticut, for example, tenants may install removable interior storm windows without the landlord's prior consent. (Conn. Gen. Statutes § 47a-13a.) In Virginia (Va. Gen. Statutes § 55-248.18.B) and Texas (Texas Security Devices Act, Texas Property Code §§ 92.151-170), tenants may install burglary prevention devices. Check your state statutes or call your local rental property association for more information on these types of laws.

### How to Fill in Clause 12:

If you do not want the tenant to make any repairs without your permission, you do not need to add anything to this clause.

You may, however, want to go further and specifically prohibit certain repairs or alterations by adding details in Clause 12. For example, you may want to make it clear that any "fixtures"—a legal term that describes any addition that is attached to the structure, such as bolted-on bookcases or built-in dishwashers—are your property and may not be removed by the tenant without your permission. See "How to Prepare Attachment Pages" at the beginning of this section.

If you do authorize the tenant to make any repairs, provide enough detail so that the tenant knows exactly what is expected, how much repairs can cost and who will pay. For example, if you decide to allow the tenant to take over the repair of any broken windows, routine plumbing jobs or landscaping, give specific descriptions and limits to the tasks. Chapter 9 includes a detailed discussion of delegating repair and maintenance responsibilities and a sample agreement form regarding tenant alterations and improvements.

⚠️ **If you want the tenant to perform maintenance work for you in exchange for reduced rent, don't write it into the lease or rental agreement**. Instead, use a separate employment agreement and pay the tenant for her services. That way, if she doesn't perform, you still have the full rent and you can simply cancel the employment contract.

## CLAUSE 13.  VIOLATING LAWS AND CAUSING DISTURBANCES

Tenant is entitled to quiet enjoyment of the premises. Tenant and guests or invitees will not use the premises or adjacent areas in such a way as to: (1) violate any law or ordinance, including laws prohibiting the use, possession or sale of illegal drugs; (2) commit waste (severe property damage); or (3) create a nuisance by annoying, disturbing, inconveniencing or interfering with the quiet enjoyment and peace and quiet of any other tenant or nearby resident.

This type of clause is found in most form leases and rental agreements. It prohibits tenants (and their guests) from violating the law, damaging your property or disturbing other tenants or nearby residents. Although this clause contains some legal jargon, it's probably best to leave it as is, since courts have much experience in working with terms like waste and nuisance (defined below).

This clause also refers to tenants' right to "quiet enjoyment" of the premises. As courts define it, the "covenant of quiet enjoyment" amounts to an implied promise that you will not act (or fail to act) in a way that seriously interferes with or destroys the ability of the tenant to use the rented premises—for example, by allowing garbage to pile up, tolerating a major rodent infestation or failing to control a tenant whose constant loud music makes it impossible for other tenants to sleep.

If you want more specific rules—for example, no loud music played after midnight—add them to Clause 18: Rules and Regulations, or to Clause 22: Additional Provisions.

### How to Fill in Clause 13:

You do not need to add anything to this clause.

### Waste and Nuisance: What Are They?

In legalese, committing **waste** means causing severe damage to real estate, including a house or an apartment unit—damage that goes way beyond ordinary wear and tear. Punching holes in walls, pulling out sinks and fixtures and knocking down doors are examples of waste.

**Nuisance** means behavior that prevents tenants and neighbors from fully enjoying the use of their homes, and results in a substantial danger to their health and safety. Continuous loud noise and foul odors are examples of legal nuisances that may disturb nearby neighbors. So, too, are selling drugs or engaging in other illegal activities that greatly disturb neighbors.

## CLAUSE 14.  PETS

No animal, bird or other pet will be kept on the premises, except properly trained dogs needed by blind, deaf or disabled persons and _____, under the following conditions: _____ _____.

This clause is designed to prevent tenants from keeping pets without your written permission. This is not necessarily to say that you will want to apply a flat "no-pets" rule. (Many landlords, in fact, report that pet-owning tenants are more appreciative, stable and responsible than the norm.) But it does provide you with a legal mechanism designed to keep your premises from being waist-deep in Irish wolfhounds. Without this sort of provision, particularly in a fixed-term lease that can't be terminated early save for a clear violation of one of its provisions, there's little to prevent your tenant from keeping dangerous or nonhousebroken pets on your property, except for city ordinances prohibiting tigers and the like.

You have the right to prohibit all pets, or to restrict the types of pets you allow, with the exception of trained dogs used by blind, deaf or physically or mentally disabled people.

### How to Fill in Clause 14:

If you do not allow pets, put the word "None" in the blanks.

If you allow pets, be sure to identify the type and number of pets in the first blank—for example, "one cat" or "one dog under 20 pounds." It's also wise to spell out your pet rules in the second blank—or in an attachment—for example, you may want to specify that the tenants will keep the grounds and street free of all animal waste, and that cats and dogs be spayed or neutered, licensed and up-to-date on vaccinations. (Your Rules and Regulations may be another place to do this. See Clause 18.)

⚠️ **Enforce no-pets clauses.** When faced with tenants who violate no-pets clauses, landlords often ignore the situation for a long time, then try to enforce it later if friction develops over some other matter. This could backfire. In general, if you know a tenant has breached the lease or rental agreement (for example, by keeping a pet), and do nothing about it for a long time, you risk having legally waived your right to object. Better to adopt a policy you plan to stick to and then preserve your right to object, by promptly giving any offending tenant an informal written notice to get rid of the animal—see the warning letter in Chapter 16 for an example. Then follow through with a termination notice, subject to any rent control law requirements.

### Renting to Pet Owners

Project Open Door, an ambitious program of the San Francisco Society for the Prevention of Cruelty to Animals (SPCA), is one of several humane societies across the country that seeks to show landlords how to make renting to pet-owning tenants a satisfying and profitable experience. The SPCA offers landlords:

- checklists to help screen pet-owning tenants
- pet policies that can be incorporated into a lease or rental agreement
- free mediation if landlords and tenants have pet-related problems after moving in, such as neighbor complaints.

For more information, contact the San Francisco SPCA at 2500 16th St., San Francisco, CA 94103, 415-554-3000.

Also, see *Dog Law*, by Mary Randolph (Nolo Press), for more information on renting to pet owners.

## Should You Require a Separate Security Deposit for Pets?

Some landlords allow pets but require the tenant to pay a separate deposit to cover any damages caused by the pet. The laws of a few states specifically allow separate, nonrefundable pet deposits. In others, charging a designated pet deposit is legal only if the total amount you charge for deposits does not exceed the state maximum for all deposits. (See Chapter 4 for details on security deposits.)

Even where allowed, separate pet deposits can often be a bad idea because they limit how you can use that part of the security deposit. For example, if the pet is well-behaved, but the tenant trashes your unit, you can't use the pet portion of the deposit to clean up after the human. If you want to protect your property from damage done by a pet, you are probably better off charging a slightly higher rent or security deposit to start with (assuming you are not restricted by rent control or the upper security deposit limits).

It is illegal to charge an extra pet deposit for people with trained guide dogs, signal dogs or service dogs.

## CLAUSE 15. LANDLORD'S RIGHT TO ACCESS

Landlord or Landlord's agents may enter the premises in the event of an emergency, to make repairs or improvements or to show the premises to prospective buyers or tenants. Landlord may also enter the premises to conduct an annual inspection to check for safety or maintenance problems. Except in cases of emergency, Tenant's abandonment of the premises, court order, or where it is impractical to do so, Landlord shall give Tenant _____ notice before entering.

Clause 15 makes it clear to the tenant that you have a legal right of access to the property to make repairs or to show the premises for sale or rental,

provided you give the tenant reasonable notice. In most states, 24 hours is presumed to be a reasonable amount of notice. A few states require longer notice period. (Chapter 13 provides details on landlord's right to enter rental property and notice requirements.)

### How to Fill in Clause 15:

In the blank, indicate the amount of notice you will provide the tenant before entering, at least the minimum required in your state. If your state law simply requires "reasonable" notice or has no notice requirement, we suggest you provide at least 24 hours' notice.

**Be scrupulous in respecting your tenants' privacy.** Deeply ingrained in almost every American is the idea that "My home is my castle." Landlords and managers, understandably concerned with efficiently managing their property, sometimes overlook how important privacy is. This is a mistake, since it often needlessly increases tensions with tenants and makes it harder to accomplish the long-term goal of cutting costs by retaining long-term tenants. Far better to go to a little extra time and trouble to truly respect tenants' privacy by giving them plenty of notice of your intent to enter.

## CLAUSE 16. EXTENDED ABSENCES BY TENANT

Tenant will notify Landlord in advance if Tenant will be away from the premises for _____ or more consecutive days. During such absence, Landlord may enter the premises at times reasonably necessary to maintain the property and inspect for needed repairs.

This clause requires that the tenants notify you when leaving your property for an extended time. It gives you the authority to enter the rental unit during the tenant's absence to maintain the property as necessary and to inspect for damage and needed repairs. (Chapter 13 discusses your legal right to enter during a tenant's extended absence.)

### How to Fill in Clause 16:

In the blank, fill in the time frame that you think is reasonable. Ten or fourteen days is common.

### CLAUSE 17. POSSESSION OF THE PREMISES

**a. Tenant's failure to take possession.**
If, after signing this Agreement, Tenant fails to take possession of the premises, Tenant will still be responsible for paying rent and complying with all other terms of this Agreement.

**b. Landlord's failure to deliver possession.**
If Landlord is unable to deliver possession of the premises to Tenant for any reason not within Landlord's control, including, but not limited to, partial or complete destruction of the premises, Tenant will have the right to terminate this Agreement upon proper notice as required by law. In such event, Landlord's liability to Tenant will be limited to the return of all sums previously paid by Tenant to Landlord.

The first part of this clause (part a) explains that a tenant who chooses not to move in after signing the lease or rental agreement will still be required to pay rent and satisfy other conditions of the agreement. This does not mean, however, that you can sit back and expect to collect rent for the entire lease or rental agreement term. As we explain in Chapter 14, you generally must take reasonably prompt steps to re-rent the premises, and you must credit the rent you collect against the first tenant's rent obligation.

The second part of the clause (part b) protects you if you're unable, for reasons beyond your control, to turn over possession after having signed the agreement or lease—for example, if a fire spreads from next door and destroys the premises or contracted repairs aren't done on time. It limits your financial liability to the new tenant to the return of any prepaid rent and security deposits (the "sums previously paid" in the language of the clause).

**⚠ Clause 17 may not limit your liability if you cannot deliver possession because the old tenant is still on the premises—even if he is the subject of an eviction which you ultimately win.** When a holdover tenant prevents the new tenant from moving in, landlords are often sued by the new tenant for not only the return of any prepaid rent and security deposits, but also the costs of temporary housing, storage costs and other losses. In some states, an attempt in the lease to limit the new tenant's recovery to the return of prepaid sums alone would not hold up in court. To protect yourself, you will want to shift some of the financial liability to the holdover tenant. You'll have a stronger chance of doing this if the old tenant has given written notice of his intent to move out. (See Clause 4, above, which requires written notice.)

### How to Fill in Clause 17:

You do not need to add anything to this clause.

**💡 Don't re-rent until you are positive that the unit will be available.** If you have any reason to suspect that your current tenant will not vacate when the lease or rental agreement is up, think twice before signing a new lease or agreement or even promising the rental unit to the next tenant. If the current occupant is leaving of her own will or appears to have another dwelling lined up (perhaps you have received a query from the new landlord), chances are that she will leave as planned. On the other hand, if you declined to renew the lease or rental agreement and there are bad feelings between you, or you suspect that the tenant has fallen on hard times and has not obtained replacement housing—and certainly if she is the subject of an eviction—you are asking for trouble if you promise the unit to someone else.

## CLAUSE 18. TENANT RULES AND REGULATIONS

☐ Tenants acknowledge receipt of, and have read a copy of, tenant rules and regulations, which are attached to and incorporated into this Agreement by this reference.

Many landlords don't worry about detailed rules and regulations, especially when they rent single-family homes or duplexes. However, in large multi-tenant buildings, rules are usually important to control the use of common areas and equipment—both for the convenience, safety and welfare of the tenants and as a way to protect your property from damage. Rules and regulations also help avoid confusion and misunderstandings about day-to-day issues such as garbage disposal and use of recreation areas.

Not every minor rule needs to be incorporated in your lease or rental agreement. But it is a good idea to specifically incorporate important ones (especially those that are likely to be ignored by some tenants). Doing so gives you the authority to evict a tenant who persists in seriously violating your code of tenant rules and regulations. Also, to avoid charges of illegal discrimination, rules and regulations should apply equally to all tenants in your rental property.

Because tenant rules and regulations are often lengthy and may be revised occasionally, we suggest you prepare a separate attachment. (See "How to Prepare Attachment Pages" at the beginning of this section.) Be sure the rules and regulations (including any revisions) are dated on each page and signed by both you and the tenant.

### How to Fill in Clause 18:

If you have a set of Tenant Rules and Regulations, check the box. If you do not, simply delete this clause, or put a line through it or write the words "N/A" or "Not Applicable."

---

### What's Covered in Tenant Rules and Regulations

Tenant rules and regulations typically cover issues such as:

- elevator safety and use
- pool rules
- garbage disposal and recycling
- vehicles and parking regulations—for examples, restrictions of repairs on the premises or types of vehicles (such as no RVs), or where guests can park
- lock-out and lost key charges
- pet rules
- security system use
- no smoking in common areas
- specific details on what's considered excessive noise
- dangerous materials—nothing flammable or explosive should be on the premises
- storage of bikes, baby strollers and other equipment in halls, stairways and other common areas
- specific landlord and tenant maintenance responsibilities (such as stopped-up toilets or garbage disposals, broken windows, rodent and pest control, lawn and yard maintenance)
- use of the grounds
- maintenance of balconies and decks—for instance, no drying clothes on balconies
- display of signs in windows
- laundry room rules
- waterbeds.

## CLAUSE 19. PAYMENT OF COURT COSTS AND ATTORNEY FEES IN A LAWSUIT

In any action or legal proceeding to enforce any part of this Agreement, the prevailing party ☐ shall not/ ☐ shall recover reasonable attorney fees and court costs.

Many landlords assume that if they sue a tenant and win, the court will order the losing tenant to pay the landlord's court costs (filing fees, service of process charges, deposition costs and so on) and attorney fees. In some states and under certain conditions, this is true. For example, an Arizona landlord who wins an eviction lawsuit is eligible to receive costs and fees even if the lease does not have a "costs and fees" clause in it. (Ariz. Rev. Stat. §§ 33-1315, 12-341.01.) But in most states, a court will order the losing tenant to pay your attorney fees and court costs only if a written agreement specifically provides for it.

If, however, you have an "attorney fees" clause in your lease, all this changes. If you hire a lawyer to bring a lawsuit concerning the lease and win, the judge will order your tenant to pay your court costs and attorney fees. (In rare instances, a court will order the loser to pay costs and fees on its own if it finds that the behavior of the losing party was particularly outrageous—for example, filing a totally frivolous lawsuit.)

But there's another important issue you may need to know about. By law in many states, an attorney fees clause in a lease or rental agreement works both ways, even if you haven't written it that way. That is, if the lease only states that you are entitled to attorney fees if you win a lawsuit, your tenants will be entitled to collect their attorney fees from you if they prevail. The amount you would be ordered to pay would be whatever the judge decides is reasonable.

So, especially if you live in a state that will read a "one-way" attorney fees clause as a two-way street, give some thought to whether you want to bind both of you to paying for the winner's costs and fees. Remember, if you can't actually collect a judgment containing attorney fees from an evicted tenant (which often happens), the clause will not help you. But if the tenant prevails, you will be stuck paying his court costs and attorney fees. In addition, the presence of a two-way clause will make it easier for a tenant to secure a willing lawyer for even a doubtful claim, because the source of the lawyer's fee (you, if you lose) will often appear more financially solid than if the client were paying the bill himself.

Especially if you intend to do all or most of your own legal work in any potential eviction or other lawsuit, you will almost surely be better off not to allow for attorney fees. Why? Because if the tenant wins, you will have to pay her fees; but if you win, she will owe you nothing since you didn't hire an attorney. You can't even recover for the long hours you spent preparing for and handling the case.

### How to Fill in Clause 19:

If you don't want to allow for attorney fees, check the first box before the words "shall not" and cross out (or delete on the disk) the words "shall."

If you want to be entitled to attorney fees and costs if you win—and you're willing to pay them if you lose—check the second box before the words "shall recover" and cross out (or delete on the disk) the words "shall not."

**Attorney fee clauses don't cover all legal disputes.** They cover fees only for lawsuits that concern the meaning or implementation of a rental agreement or lease—for example, a dispute about rent, security deposits, or your right to access (assuming that the rental document includes these subjects.) An attorney fee clause would not apply in a personal injury or discrimination lawsuit.

### CLAUSE 20. DISCLOSURES

Tenant acknowledges that Landlord has made the following disclosures regarding the premises:

☐ Disclosure of Information on Lead-Based Paint and/or Lead-Based Paint Hazards

☐ Other disclosures:

_____

_____

_____

Federal, state *and* local laws may require you to make certain disclosures before a new tenant signs a lease or rental agreement or moves in. Some disclosures that may be required include:

- the name of the owner and the person authorized to receive legal papers such as a property manager (see Clause 21)
- any known lead-based paint hazards in the rental premises (Chapter 11 provides complete details on disclosing environmental health hazards such as lead, including the specific form you must use)
- the name and address of the bank where security deposits are held, and the rate of interest and its payment to the tenant (see Clause 8)
- hidden (not obvious) aspects of the rental property that could cause injury or substantially interfere with tenants' safe enjoyment and use of the dwelling—for example, a warning that the building walls contains asbestos insulation, which could be dangerous if anyone made a hole in the wall. (Chapters 10, 11 and 12 discuss landlord's liability for dangerous conditions)

- planned condominium conversions (discussed in Chapter 14).

Here are some specific disclosures required by some state laws. This is not an exhaustive list:

- property located near former military ordnance (Cal. Civ. Code §1940.7)
- tenant's gas or electric meter serves areas outside of the rental unit (Cal. Civ. Code § 1940.9) and (Ill. Rev. Stat. ch. 765, § 735/1.2, § 740/5)
- full explanation of utility rates, charges and services (Iowa Code Ann. § 562A.13(4))
- details on installation and maintenance of smoke detectors (N.Y. Cons. Laws Mult. Dwell. § 68(4)(c); Cons. Laws Mult. Res. § 15(4)(c)), (Or. Rev. State. § 479.270) and (Wash. Rev. Code Ann. § 59.18.060(11)).
- existence of a state Department of Justice database that the tenant can access to learn if an individual is a registered sexual offender living within a community and zip code (buildings with four or less units only) (Cal Civ. Code § 2079.10a)
- availability of fire protection in building over three stories high (Fla. Statutes Annotated § 83.50)
- rental unit has been flooded within the past five years (Ga. Code Ann. § 44-7-20) and (Okla. Stat. tit. 41, § 113a)
- landlord's excise tax number, so that tenants may file for a low-income tax credit (Haw. Rev. Stat. § 521-43)
- outstanding inspection orders, condemnation orders or declarations that the property is unfit. Citations for violations that do not involve threats to tenant health or safety must be summarized and posted in an obvious place, and the original must be available for review by the tenant. (Minn. Stat. § 504.246(a), (b)).

Rent control ordinances typically include additional disclosures, such as the name and address of the government agency or elected board that administers the ordinance. (Chapter 3 discusses rent control.)

### How to Fill in Clause 20:

If your rental property was built before 1978, you must meet federal lead disclosure requirements, so check the first box, and follow the advice in Chapter 11.

If you are legally required to make other disclosures as described above, check the second box and provide details in the blank space, adding additional pages as necessary. (See "How to Prepare Attachment Pages" at the beginning of this section.)

⚠️ **Some problems need to be fixed, not merely disclosed**. Warning your tenants about a hidden defect does not absolve you of legal responsibility if the condition makes the dwelling uninhabitable or unreasonably dangerous. For example, you are courting liability if you rent an apartment with a gas heater that you know might blow up, even if you warn the tenant that the heater is faulty. Nor can you simply warn your tenants about prior crime on the premises and then fail to do anything (like installing deadbolts or hiring security) to promote safety. Chapters 10, 11 and 12 discuss problems that are proper subjects of warnings and those that ought to be fixed.

### CLAUSE 21. AUTHORITY TO RECEIVE LEGAL PAPERS

The Landlord, any person managing the premises, and anyone designated by the Landlord are authorized to accept service of process and receive other notices and demands, which may be delivered to:

☐ The Landlord, at the following address:

_____

☐ The manager, at the following address:

_____

☐ The following person, at the following address:

_____

It's the law in many states, and a good idea in all, to give your tenants information about everyone who you have authorized to receive notices and legal papers, such as a tenant's notice that she is ending the tenancy or a tenant's court documents as part of an eviction defense. Of course, you may want to handle all of this yourself or delegate it to a manager or management company. Make sure the person you designate to receive legal papers is almost always available to receive tenant notices and legal papers. In some states, such as Virginia and Hawaii, any nonresident owner must designate an agent who is a resident of or has a business office in the state (island in Hawaii's case).

Be sure to keep your tenants up-to-date on any changes in this information.

### How to Fill in Clause 21:

Provide your name and street address or the name and address of someone else you authorize to receive notices and legal papers on your behalf, such as a property manager.

⚠️ **Do you trust your manager?** It's unwise to have a manager you wouldn't trust to receive legal papers on your behalf. You don't, for example, want a careless apartment manager to throw away notice of a lawsuit against you without informing you. That could result in a judgment against you and a lien against your property in a lawsuit you didn't even know about. (For more information on using property managers, see Chapter 6.)

### CLAUSE 22. ADDITIONAL PROVISIONS

Additional provisions are as follows: _____

_____

_____.

In this clause, you may list any additional provisions or agreements that are unique to you and the particular tenant signing the lease or rental agreement, such as a provision that prohibits smoking in the tenant's apartment or in the common areas.

If you don't have a separate Rules and Regulations clause (see Clause 18, above), you may spell out a few rules under this clause—for example, regarding lost key charges or use of a pool on the property.

### How to Fill in Clause 22:

List additional provisions or rules here or in an attachment. (See "How to Prepare Attachment Pages" at the beginning of this section.) If there are no additional provisions, write "N/A" or "Not Applicable."

**There is no legal or practical imperative to put every small detail you want to communicate to the tenant into your lease or rental agreement.** Instead, prepare a welcoming, but no-nonsense "move-in letter" that dovetails with the lease or rental agreement and highlights important terms of the tenancy—for example, how and where to report maintenance problems. You may also use a move-in letter to cover issues not included in the lease or rental agreement—for example, rules for use of a laundry room. (Chapter 7 covers move-in letters.)

**Do not include exculpatory clauses or hold harmless clauses.** Many form leases include provisions which attempt to absolve you in advance from responsibility for all damages, injuries or losses, including those caused by your legal misdeeds. These clauses come in two varieties:

• Exculpatory: "If there's a problem, you won't hold me responsible," and

• Hold-harmless: "If there's a problem traceable to me, you're responsible."

Many exculpatory clauses are blatantly illegal and will not be upheld in court. (Chapter 10 discusses exculpatory clauses.) If a tenant is injured because of a dangerous condition you failed to fix for several months, no boilerplate lease language will protect you from civil and possibly even criminal charges.

## CLAUSE 23.  VALIDITY OF EACH PART

If any portion of this Agreement is held to be invalid, its invalidity will not affect the validity or enforceability of any other provision of this Agreement.

This clause is known as a "savings" clause, and it is commonly used in contracts. It means that, in the unlikely event that one of the other clauses in this lease or rental agreement is found to be invalid by a court, the remainder of the agreement will remain in force.

### How to Fill in Clause 23:

You do not need to add anything to this clause.

## CLAUSE 24.  GROUNDS FOR TERMINATION OF TENANCY

The failure of Tenant or Tenant's guests or invitees to comply with any term of this Agreement, or the misrepresentation of any material fact on Tenant's Rental Application, is grounds for termination of the tenancy, with appropriate notice to Tenant and procedures as required by law.

This clause states that any violation of the lease or rental agreement by the tenant, or by the tenant's business or social guests, is grounds for terminating the tenancy, according to the procedures established by your state or local laws. Making the tenant responsible for the actions of his guests can be extremely important—for example, if you discover that the tenant's family or friends are dealing illegal drugs on the premises or have damaged the property. Chapter 17 discusses terminations and evictions for tenant violation of a lease or rental agreement.

This clause also tells the tenant that if he has made false statements on the rental application concerning an important fact—such as his prior criminal history—you may evict.

**How to Fill in Clause 24:**

You do not need to add anything to this clause.

### CLAUSE 25. ENTIRE AGREEMENT

This document constitutes the entire Agreement between the parties, and no promises or representations, other than those contained here and those implied by law, have been made by Landlord or Tenant. Any modifications to this Agreement must be in writing signed by Landlord and Tenant.

This clause establishes that the lease or rental agreement and any attachments (such as rules and regulations) constitute the entire agreement between you and your tenant. It means that oral promises (by you or the tenant) to do something different with respect to any aspect of the rental are not binding. Any changes or additions must be in writing. (Chapter 14 discusses how to modify signed rental agreements and leases.)

**How to Fill in Clause 25:**

You do not need to add anything to this clause.

## D. Changing a Lease or Rental Agreement

If you want to make minor changes to your lease or rental agreement, the process is simple. To add or delete language, all you do is write in the desired changes or cross out the unwanted portion, and have everyone who is going to sign the document initial and date the changes. If you use the forms on disk, you should enter the changes and print out a clean copy for everyone to sign.

If the proposed changes are fairly lengthy, however, and you don't use the forms on disk you will need to prepare an amendment page (lawyers use the word "addendum") to the original document.

Chapter 14 discusses how to do this and includes a sample amendment form which you can tear out, copy and use to make changes or insert additions before you sign a lease or rental agreement. Chapter 14 also provides details on notice and procedures for changing a lease or rental agreement after you have begun your tenancy.

## E. Signing a Lease or Rental Agreement

At the end of the lease or rental agreement, there's space to include your signature, street address and phone number, or that of the person you authorize as your agent, such as a property manager. There's also space for the tenants' signatures and phone numbers. Again, as stressed in Clause 1, make sure all adults living in the rental unit, including both members of a couple, sign the lease or rental agreement. And check that the tenant's name and signature match his or her driver's license or other legal document. If the tenant has a cosigner, you'll need to add a line for the cosigner's signature or use a separate form. (Cosigners are discussed below.)

If you alter our form by writing or typing in changes, be sure that you and all tenants initial the changes when you sign the document, so as to forestall any possibility that a tenant will claim you unilaterally inserted changes after he or she signed. (See Section D, above.)

Give the tenant a copy of the signed lease or rental agreement.

⚠ **Don't sign a lease until all terms are final and the tenant understands what's expected.** All of your expectations should be written into the lease or rental agreement (or any attachments, such as Rules and Regulations) before you and the tenant sign the document. Never sign an incomplete document assuming last-minute changes can be made later. And be sure your tenant clearly understands the lease or rental agreement before signing (this may mean you'll need to review it clause by clause). Chapter 7 discusses how to get your new tenancy off to the right start.

## F. About Cosigners

Some landlords require cosigners on rental agreements and leases, especially when renting to students who depend on parents for much of their income. The cosigner signs a separate agreement or the rental agreement or lease, under which she agrees to be jointly and severally liable with the tenant for the tenant's obligations—that is, to cover any rent or damage-repair costs the tenant fails to pay. (Clause 1 discusses the concept of joint and several liability.) The cosigner retains responsibility regardless of whether the tenant sublets or assigns his agreement. (Clause 11 discusses sublets and assignments and Chapter 8 covers these issues in detail.)

In practice, a cosigner's promise to guarantee the tenant's rent obligation may have less value than at first you might think. This is because the threat of eviction is the primary factor that motivates a tenant to pay the rent, and obviously you cannot evict a cosigner. Also, since the cosigner must be sued separately in either a regular civil lawsuit or in small

claims court, actually doing so—for example, if a tenant stiffs you for a month's rent—may be more trouble than it's worth. This is especially true if the cosigner lives in another state, since the amount of money you are out will rarely justify hiring a lawyer and collecting a judgment.

In sum, the benefits of having a lease or rental agreement cosigned by someone who won't be living on the property are largely psychological. But these benefits may still be worth something: A tenant who thinks you can (and will) sue the cosigner—who is usually a relative or close friend—may be less likely to default on the rent. Similarly, a cosigner asked to pay the tenant's debts may persuade the tenant to pay.

If you decide to accept a cosigner, you may want to have that person fill out a separate rental application and agree to a credit check—after all, a cosigner who has no resources or connection to the tenant will be completely useless. Should the tenant and her prospective cosigner object to these inquiries and costs, you may wonder how serious they are about the guarantor's willingness to stand behind the tenant. Once you are satisfied that the cosigner can genuinely backup the tenant, add a line at the end of the lease for the dated signature, phone and address of the cosigner or use the cosigner agreement form we provide here.

A sample Cosigner Agreement is shown below. Simply fill in your name and your tenant's and cosigner's names, the address of the rental unit and the date you signed the agreement with the tenant.

💾 The Legal Forms Disk includes a Cosigner Agreement form and Appendix II includes a blank tear-out version of this form.

⚠ **If you change the lease, have the cosigner sign the new version.** Generally speaking, a cosigner is bound only to the terms of the exact lease or rental agreement he cosigns. If you later change a significant term, add a new tenant or otherwise create a new contract, the original cosigner will probably be off the hook, unless you again get him to sign.

## Cosigner Agreement

1. This Agreement is entered into on _____September 1_____, 199 _X_ , between _____Marty Nelson_____ ("Tenant"), _____Alex Stevens_____ ("Landlord") and _____Sandy Cole_____ ("Cosigner").

2. Tenant has leased from Landlord the premises located at _____137 Howell St., Houston,_____ _____Texas_____ ("Premises"). Landlord and Tenant signed a lease or rental agreement specifying the terms and conditions of this rental on _____September 1_____, 199 _X_ . A copy of the lease or rental agreement is attached to this Agreement.

3. Cosigner agrees to be jointly and severally liable with Tenant for Tenant's obligations arising out of the lease or rental agreement described in Paragraph 2, including but not limited to unpaid rent, property damage and cleaning and repair costs that exceed Tenant's security deposit. Cosigner further agrees that Landlord will have no obligation to report to Cosigner should Tenant fail to abide by the terms of the lease or rental agreement. (For example, if Tenant fails to pay the rent on time or damages the premises, Landlord has no duty to warn or inform Cosigner, and may demand that Cosigner pay for these obligations immediately.)

4. If Tenant assigns or subleases the Premises, Cosigner shall remain liable under the terms of this Agreement for the performance of the assignee or sublessee, unless Landlord relieves Cosigner by express written termination of this Agreement.

5. If Landlord and Cosigner are involved in any legal proceeding arising out of this Agreement, the prevailing party shall recover reasonable attorney fees, court costs and any costs reasonably necessary to collect a judgment.

_____September 1, 199X_____        _Alex Stevens_____
Date                          Landlord/Manager

_____September 1, 199X_____        _Marty Nelson_____
Date                          Tenant

_____September 1, 199X_____        _Sandy Cole_____
Date                          Cosigner

# Month-to-Month Residential Rental Agreement

### Clause 1. Identification of Landlord and Tenant

This Agreement is entered into between _____Marty Nelson_____

_____ ("Tenant") and

_____Alex Stevens_____ ("Landlord"). Each

Tenant is jointly and severally liable for the payment of rent and performance of all other terms of

this Agreement.

### Clause 2. Identification of Premises

Subject to the terms and conditions in this Agreement, Landlord rents to Tenant, and Tenant rents

from Landlord, for residential purposes only, the premises located at _____137 Howell St.,____

_Houston, Texas_____ ("the premises"),

together with the following furnishings and appliances: _____

_____.

Rental of the premises also includes _____

_____.

### Clause 3. Limits on Use and Occupancy

The premises are to be used only as a private residence for Tenant(s) listed in Clause 1 of this

Agreement, and their minor children. Occupancy by guests for more than _ten days every six months_

is prohibited without Landlord's written consent and will be considered a breach of this Agreement.

### Clause 4. Term of the Tenancy

The rental will begin on ___September 15_____, 199_X_, and continue on a month-to-month

basis. Landlord may terminate the tenancy or modify the terms of this Agreement by giving the

Tenant ___30_____ days written notice. Tenant may terminate the tenancy by giving the

Landlord _30_____ days written notice.

### Clause 5. Payment of Rent

_Regular monthly rent._

Tenant will pay to Landlord a monthly rent of $_____900_____ , payable in advance on the first

day of each month, except when that day falls on a weekend or legal holiday, in which case rent is

due on the next business day. Rent will be paid in the following manner unless Landlord designates

otherwise:

*Delivery of payment.*

Rent will be paid:

☒ by mail, to _Alex Stevens, 28 Franklin St., Houston, Texas, 77002_

☐ in person, at _____

*Form of payment.*

Landlord will accept payment in these forms:

☒ personal check made payable to _____ Alex Stevens

☒ cashier's check made payable to _____ Alex Stevens

☐ credit card

☒ money order

☐ cash

*Prorated first month's rent.*

For the period from Tenant's move-in date, _____September 15_____, 199_X_, through the

end of the month, Tenant will pay to Landlord the prorated monthly rent of $_____450_____.

This amount will be paid on or before the date the Tenant moves in.

## Clause 6. Late Charges

If Tenant fails to pay the rent in full before the end of the _____third_____ day after it's due, Tenant

will pay Landlord a late charge as follows: _____$10 plus $5 for each additional day that the_

_rent remains unpaid. The total late charge for any one month will not exceed $45_____.

Landlord does not waive the right to insist on payment of the rent in full on the date it is due.

## Clause 7. Returned Check and Other Bank Charges

If any check offered by Tenant to Landlord in payment of rent or any other amount due under this

Agreement is returned for lack of sufficient funds, a "stop payment" or any other reason, Tenant will

pay Landlord a returned check charge of $_____15_____.

## Clause 8. Security Deposit

On signing this Agreement, Tenant will pay to Landlord the sum of $_____1,800_____ as a security

deposit. Tenant may not, without Landlord's prior written consent, apply this security deposit to the

last month's rent or to any other sum due under this Agreement. Within _____30 days_____

after Tenant has vacated the premises, returned keys and provided Landlord with a forwarding

address, Landlord will return the deposit in full or give Tenant an itemized written statement of the

reasons for, and the dollar amount of, any of the security deposit retained by Landlord, along with a

check for any deposit balance.

*[optional clauses here, if any]*

**Clause 9. Utilities**

Tenant will pay all utility charges, except for the following, which will be paid by Landlord:

garbage and water

_____ .

**Clause 10. Assignment and Subletting**

Tenant will not sublet any part of the premises or assign this Agreement without the prior written consent of Landlord.

**Clause 11. Tenant's Maintenance Responsibilities**

Tenant will: (1) keep the premises clean, sanitary and in good condition and, upon termination of the tenancy, return the premises to Landlord in a condition identical to that which existed when Tenant took occupancy, except for ordinary wear and tear; (2) immediately notify Landlord of any defects or dangerous conditions in and about the premises of which Tenant becomes aware; and (3) reimburse Landlord, on demand by Landlord, for the cost of any repairs to the premises damaged by Tenant or Tenant's guests or business invitees through misuse or neglect.

Tenant has examined the premises, including appliances, fixtures, carpets, drapes and paint, and has found them to be in good, safe and clean condition and repair, except as noted in the Landlord-Tenant Checklist.

### Clause 12. Repairs and Alterations by Tenant

a. Except as provided by law, or as authorized by the prior written consent of Landlord, Tenant will not make any repairs or alterations to the premises, including nailing holes in the walls or painting the rental unit.

b. Tenant will not, without Landlord's prior written consent, alter, re-key or install any locks to the premises or install or alter any burglar alarm system. Tenant will provide Landlord with a key or keys capable of unlocking all such re-keyed or new locks as well as instructions on how to disarm any altered or new burglar alarm system.

### Clause 13. Violating Laws and Causing Disturbances

Tenant is entitled to quiet enjoyment of the premises. Tenant and guests or invitees will not use the premises or adjacent areas in such a way as to: (1) violate any law or ordinance, including laws prohibiting the use, possession or sale of illegal drugs; (2) commit waste (severe property damage); or (3) create a nuisance by annoying, disturbing, inconveniencing or interfering with the quiet enjoyment and peace and quiet of any other tenant or nearby resident.

### Clause 14. Pets

No animal, bird or other pet will be kept on the premises, even temporarily, except properly trained dogs needed by blind, deaf or disabled persons and _____ under the following conditions: _____

_____ .

### Clause 15. Landlord's Right to Access

Landlord or Landlord's agents may enter the premises in the event of an emergency, to make repairs or improvements or to show the premises to prospective buyers or tenants. Landlord may also enter the premises to conduct an annual inspection to check for safety or maintenance problems. Except in cases of emergency, Tenant's abandonment of the premises, court order, or where it is impractical to do so, Landlord shall give Tenant _____ 24 hours _____ notice before entering.

### Clause 16. Extended Absences by Tenant

Tenant will notify Landlord in advance if Tenant will be away from the premises for _____ seven _____ or more consecutive days. During such absence, Landlord may enter the premises at times reasonably necessary to maintain the property and inspect for needed repairs.

### Clause 17. Possession of the Premises

*a. Tenant's failure to take possession.*

If, after signing this Agreement, Tenant fails to take possession of the premises, Tenant will still be responsible for paying rent and complying with all other terms of this Agreement.

*b. Landlord's failure to deliver possession.*

If Landlord is unable to deliver possession of the premises to Tenant for any reason not within Landlord's control, including, but not limited to, partial or complete destruction of the premises, Tenant will have the right to terminate this Agreement upon proper notice as required by law. In such event, Landlord's liability to Tenant will be limited to the return of all sums previously paid by Tenant to Landlord.

### Clause 18. Tenant Rules and Regulations

☐ Tenant acknowledges receipt of, and has read a copy of, tenant rules and regulations, which are attached to and incorporated into this Agreement by this reference.

### Clause 19. Payment of Court Costs and Attorney Fees in a Lawsuit

In any action or legal proceeding to enforce any part of this Agreement, the prevailing party

☐ shall not / ☒ shall recover reasonable attorney fees and court costs.

### Clause 20.  Disclosures

Tenant acknowledges that Landlord has made the following disclosures regarding the premises:

☐ Disclosure of Information on Lead-Based Paint and/or Lead-Based Paint Hazards

☐ Other disclosures:

_____

_____

_____

### Clause 21. Authority to Receive Legal Papers

The Landlord, any person managing the premises and anyone designated by the Landlord are authorized to accept service of process and receive other notices and demands, which may be delivered to:

☒ The Landlord, at the following address: ___*28 Franklin St., Houston, Texas, 77002*___

_____

☐ The manager, at the following address: _____

_____

☐ The following person, at the following address: _____

_____

**Clause 22. Additional Provisions**

Additional provisions are as follows: _____

_____

_____

_____

_____

_____

_____

_____

**Clause 23. Validity of Each Part**

If any portion of this Agreement is held to be invalid, its invalidity will not affect the validity or enforceability of any other provision of this Agreement.

**Clause 24. Grounds for Termination of Tenancy**

The failure of Tenant or Tenant's guests or invitees to comply with any term of this Agreement, or the misrepresentation of any material fact on Tenant's Rental Application, is grounds for termination of the tenancy, with appropriate notice to Tenant and procedures as required by law.

**Clause 25. Entire Agreement**

This document constitutes the entire Agreement between the parties, and no promises or representations, other than those contained here and those implied by law, have been made by Landlord or Tenant. Any modifications to this Agreement must be in writing signed by Landlord and Tenant.

| | | |
|---|---|---|
| _Sept. 1, 199X_ | _Alex Steven_ | Landlord |
| Date | Landlord or Landlord's Agent | Title |
| _28 Franklin St._ | | |
| Street Address | | |
| _Houston, Texas 77002_ | | _713-555-1578_ |
| City, State & Zip | | Phone |
| _Sept. 1, 199X_ | _Marty Nelson_ | _713-555-8751_ |
| Date | Tenant | Phone |
| | | |
| Date | Tenant | Phone |
| | | |
| Date | Tenant | Phone |

# Chapter 3

# Basic Rent Rules

To state the obvious, one of your foremost concerns as a landlord is receiving your rent—on time and without hassle. It follows that you need a good grasp of the legal rules governing rent. This chapter outlines basic state and local rent laws affecting how much you can charge, as well as where, when and how rent is due. It also covers rules regarding grace periods, late rent, returned check charges and rent increases.

## Avoiding Rent Disputes

Here are three guidelines that can help you and your tenants have a smooth relationship when it comes to an area of utmost interest to both of you: rent.

1. Clearly spell out rent rules in your lease or rental agreement as well as in a move-in letter to new tenants.
2. Be fair and consistent about enforcing your rent rules.
3. If rent isn't paid on time, follow through with a legal notice telling the tenant to pay or move—the first legal step in a possible eviction—as soon as possible.

Related topics covered in this book include:
- Lease and rental agreement provisions relating to rent: Chapter 2
- Collecting deposits and potential problems with calling a deposit "last month's rent": Chapter 4
- Compensating a manager with reduced rent: Chapter 6
- Highlighting rent rules in a move-in letter to new tenants and collecting the first month's rent: Chapter 7
- Co-tenants' obligations for rent: Chapter 8
- How a landlord's responsibility to maintain the premises in good condition relates to a tenant's duty to pay rent: Chapter 9

- Tenants' obligation to pay rent when breaking a lease: Chapter 14
- Accepting rent after a 30-day notice is given: Chapter 14
- Evicting a tenant for nonpayment of rent: Chapter 17.

## A. How Much Can You Charge?

In most states, the law doesn't limit how much rent you can charge; you are free to charge what the market will bear. However, in some cities and counties, rent control ordinances do closely govern how much rent a landlord can legally charge. (Rent control is discussed in Section B.)

If you aren't subject to rent control, it's up to you to determine how much your rental unit is worth. To do this, you may wish to check newspaper want ads for rents of comparable properties in your area, and perhaps visit a few places that

sound similar to yours. Local property management companies, real estate offices that handle rental property and apartment-finding services can also provide useful advice. In addition, local apartment associations—or other landlords you meet at association functions—are a good source of pricing information.

Many wise landlords choose to charge just slightly less than the going rate as part of a policy designed to find and keep excellent tenants. As with any business arrangement, it usually pays in the long run to have your tenants feel they are getting a good deal. In exchange, you hope the tenants will be responsive to your business needs. This doesn't always work, of course, but tenants who feel their rent is fair are less likely to complain over trifling matters and more likely to stay for an extended period. Certainly, tenants who think you are trying to squeeze every last nickel out of them won't think twice before calling you about a clogged toilet at 11 p.m.

# B. Rent Control

➡️ Unless you own property in California, the District of Columbia, Maryland, New Jersey or New York, you aren't affected by rent control. You can skip ahead to Section C.

Communities in only five states—California, the District of Columbia, Maryland, New Jersey and New York—have laws that limit the amount of rent landlords may charge. Typically, only a few cities or counties in each state have enacted local rent control ordinances (also called rent stabilization, maximum rent regulation or a similar term), but often these are some of the state's largest cities—for example, San Francisco, Los Angeles, New York City and Newark all have some form of rent control. In "Selected Rent Control Ordinances" in Appendix I, you'll find summaries of the rent control ordinances of Los Angeles, Oakland, San Jose, Washington D.C., Newark and New York City.

## The Rent Control Board

In most cities, rent control rests in the hands of a rent control board of five to ten people. Board members often decide annual rent increase, fines and other important issues. (In many areas, the law itself limits how and when the rent may be raised.) In some cities, members are elected by voters; in others, the mayor or city council appoints them.

The actual rent control ordinance is a product of the local legislative body—the city council or county board of supervisors. But the rent control board is in charge of interpreting the provisions of the law, which can give the board significant power over landlords and tenants.

Rent control laws commonly regulate much more than rent. For example, owners of rent-controlled properties must follow specific eviction procedures. Because local ordinances are often quite complicated and vary widely, this book cannot provide details on each city's program. Instead, we provide a general description of what rent control ordinances cover and an outline of seven big-city ordinances.

If you own rental property in a city that has rent control, you should always have a current copy of the ordinance and any regulations interpreting it. And be sure to keep up to date; cities change their rent control laws frequently, and court decisions also affect them. It's a good idea to subscribe to publications of the local property owners' association, and pay attention to local politics to keep abreast of changes in your rent control ordinance and court decisions that may affect you.

⚠️ **Know the law or pay the price.** Local governments typically levy fines—sometimes heavy ones—for rent control violations. Violation of a rent control law may also give a tenant a legal ground on which to win an eviction lawsuit. Depending on the circumstances, tenants may also be able to sue you.

## 1. Property Subject to Rent Control

Not all rental housing within a rent-controlled city is subject to rent control. Generally, new buildings as well as owner-occupied buildings with two (or sometimes even three or four) units or fewer are exempt from rent control ordinances. Some cities also exempt rentals in single-family houses and luxury units that rent for more than a certain amount. For example, in Los Angeles a one-bedroom apartment that rents for over a specified rent per month is not subject to rent control; in San Francisco, tenants in a landlord-occupied single-family home are not covered by the ordinance's protections; and rentals of single-family homes in Los Angeles and San Jose are exempt from rent control.

## 2. Limits on Rent

Rent control ordinances typically set a base rent for each rental unit. The base rent usually takes into account several different factors, including the rent that was charged before rent control took effect, operation and upkeep expenses, inflation and housing supply and demand. The ordinances allow the base rent to be increased under certain circumstances or at certain times.

### a. Rent Increases for Existing Tenants

Most local ordinances build in some mechanism for rent increases. Here are just a few common examples:

**Annual increases.** Some ordinances automatically allow a specific percentage rent increase each year. The amount of the increase may be set by the rent control board, or may be a fixed percentage, a percentage tied to a local or national consumer price index, or even a percentage of the tenants' household income.

**Increased expenses.** Some rent control boards have the power to adjust rents of individual units based on certain cost factors, such as increased taxes or maintenance or capital improvements. The landlord may need to request permission from the rent control board before upping the rent.

**The tenant's consent.** In some cities, landlords may increase rent under certain circumstances only if the tenants voluntarily agree to the increase—or don't protest it.

A word of caution: Even if you are otherwise entitled to raise the rent under the terms of your rent control ordinance, the rent board may be able to deny you permission if you haven't adequately repaired and maintained your rental units.

### b. Rent Increases When a Tenant Moves

In most rent control areas, landlords may raise rent—either as much as they want or by a specified percentage—when a tenant moves out (and a new one moves in) or when a tenant renews a lease. This feature, called "vacancy decontrol," "vacancy rent ceiling adjustment," or similar term, is built into many local ordinances.

In practice, it means that rent control applies to a particular rental unit only as long as a particular tenant (or tenants) stays there. If that tenant voluntarily leaves, or, in some cities, is evicted for a legal or "just" cause (discussed below), the rental unit is subject to rent control again after the new (and presumably higher) rent is established.

> **EXAMPLE:** Marla has lived in Edward's apartment building for seven years. During that time, Edward has been allowed to raise the rent only by the modest amount authorized by the local rent board each year. Meanwhile, the market value of the apartment has gone up significantly. When Marla finally moves out, Edward is free to charge the next tenant the market rate. But once set, that tenant's rent will also be subject to the rent control rules, and Edward will again be limited to small annual increases as approved by the rent control board.

In some cities, no rent increase is allowed at all, even when a tenant moves out. Check your ordinance.

---

### Your Right to Go Out of Business

It's not uncommon for landlords in rent-controlled cities to decide to get out of the residential rental business entirely. To do so, however, they must evict tenants, who will protest that the eviction violates the rent control ordinance.

No rent control ordinance can force you to continue with your business against your will. However, if you withdraw rental units from the market, you must typically meet strict standards regarding the necessity of doing so. Rent control boards do not want landlords to use going out of business as a ruse for evicting long-term tenants, only to start up again with a fresh batch of tenants whose rents will invariably be substantially higher.

If you decide to go out of business and must evict tenants, check your ordinance carefully. It may require you to offer tenants relocation assistance, and may impose a minimum time period during which you may not resume business. If you own multiple units, the rent control ordinance may prohibit you from withdrawing only a portion of the units; and if the premises are torn down and new units constructed, the ordinance may insist that you offer former tenants a right of first refusal. State law may also address these issues. Contact your local landlords' association or rent control board for details on the specifics.

---

## 3. Legal or "Just Cause" Evictions

For rent control to work—especially if the ordinance allows rents to rise when a tenant leaves—it must place some restrictions on tenancy terminations. Otherwise, landlords who wanted to create a vacancy so they could raise the rent would be free to throw out tenants, undermining the whole system. Recognizing this, many local ordinances require landlords to have a legal or just cause—that is, a good reason—to terminate and, if the tenant doesn't leave on his own, evict.

Just cause is usually limited to a few reasons provided in the ordinance. If you really need to evict a tenant, you should have no problem finding your reason on the approved list. Here are a few typical examples of a legal or just cause to evict a tenant:

- The tenant violates a significant term of the lease or rental agreement—for example, by failing to pay rent or causing substantial damage to the premises. However, in many situations, you're legally required to first give the tenant a chance to correct the problem. (See Chapter 17.)
- The landlord wants to move into the rental unit, or give it to an immediate family member.
- The landlord wants to substantially remodel the property which requires the tenant to move out.
- The tenant creates a nuisance—for example, by repeatedly disturbing other tenants or engaging in illegal activity, such as drug dealing, on the premises.

Rent control ordinances often affect renewals as well as terminations midway through the rental term. Unless you can point to a just cause for tossing a tenant out, you may need to renew a lease or rental agreement under the same terms and conditions.

---

## 4. Registration of Rental Units

Some rent control ordinances require landlords to register their properties with the local rent control agency. This allows the rent board to keep track of the city's rental units, and the registration fees provide operating funds.

## 5. Deposits and Notice Requirements

Rent control ordinances may impose rules regarding security deposits or interest payments and the type of notice you must give tenants when you want to raise the rent or terminate a tenancy. The requirements of these local ordinances are in addition to any state law requirements. For example, state law may require a 30-day notice for a rent increase. A local rent control law might also require the notice to tell the tenant that the rent control board can verify that the new rental amount is legal under the ordinance.

### Where to Get Information About Rent Control

- **Your city rent control board.** It can supply you with a copy of the current local ordinance, and possibly also with a brochure explaining the ordinance. Check your phone book for the address and phone number of your local rent control board or contact your mayor or city manager's office. "Selected Rent Control Ordinances" in Appendix I gives the addresses and phone numbers for the boards of seven major cities.
- **Your state or local apartment owners' association.** Virtually every city with a rent control ordinance has an active property owners' association. In New York City, for example, the Rent Stabilization Association of N.Y. gives members information and help on rent matters and offers mediation for tenant complaints.
- **Local attorneys who specialize in landlord/ tenant law.** Check the Yellow Pages or ask another landlord. (Chapter 18 discusses how to find and work with a lawyer.)

## C. When Rent Is Due

Most leases and rental agreements, including the ones in this book, call for rent to be paid monthly, in advance, on the first day of the month. (See Clause 5 of the form agreements in Chapter 2.)

### 1. First Day, Last Day or In-Between?

The first of the month is a customary and convenient due date for rent, at least in part because many tenants get their paychecks on the last workday of the month. Also, the approach of a new month can, in itself, help remind people to pay monthly bills due on the first. With luck, your tenant will learn to associate flipping the calendar page with paying the rent on time.

It is perfectly legal to require rent to be paid on a different day of the month, and may make sense if the tenant is paid at odd times. Some landlords make the rent payable each month on the date the tenant first moved in. Generally, it's easier to prorate rent for a short first month and then require that rent be paid on the first of the next month. But if you have only a few tenants, and don't mind having different tenants paying you on different days of the month, it makes no legal difference.

**Special rules for tenants who receive public assistance.** Some states make special provisions for rent due dates for public assistance recipients. Public assistance recipients in Hawaii, for example, may choose to establish a due date that is on or before the third day after the day they usually receive their public assistance check.

Whatever you decide, be sure to put it in your lease or rental agreement. If you don't, state law may do it for you. In several states, for month-to-month rental agreements, rent is due in equal monthly installments at the beginning of each month, unless otherwise agreed.

In a few states, however, rent is not due until the end of the term unless the lease or rental agreement says otherwise. You would probably never deliberately allow a tenant who moved in on the first day of the month to wait to pay rent until the 31st. Make sure you don't accidentally allow it.

See "When Rent Is Due," below.

---

### When Rent Is Due

If you don't specify otherwise, state law makes the rent due on these days:

**1st of the month, in advance**

| | | |
|---|---|---|
| Alaska | Kansas | Oklahoma |
| Arizona | Kentucky | Oregon |
| Connecticut | Montana | Rhode Island |
| Delaware | Nebraska | South Carolina |
| Florida | Nevada | Tennessee |
| Hawaii | New Mexico | Virginia |
| Iowa | | |

**Last day of the month**

| | | |
|---|---|---|
| California | Michigan | South Dakota |
| Indiana | | |

Citations for these state laws are listed in "State Rent Rules" in Appendix I. States that are not listed have no statute on the subject.

---

### Collecting Rent More Than Once a Month

If you wish, you and the tenant can agree that the rent be paid twice a month, each week, or on whatever schedule suits you. The most common variation on the standard monthly payment arrangement is having rent paid twice a month. This is a particularly good idea if you have tenants who have relatively low-paying jobs and get paid twice a month, because they may have difficulty saving the needed portion of their mid-month check until the first of the month.

---

## 2. When the Due Date Falls on a Weekend or Holiday

The lease and rental agreements in this book state that when the rent due date falls on a weekend day or legal holiday, the tenant must pay it by the next business day. (See Clause 5 of the form agreements in Chapter 2.)

This is legally required in some states; it is the general rule in most. If you want to insist that the tenant always get the rent check to you on the first, no matter what, you'll have to check the law in your state to make sure it's allowed. It's probably not worth the trouble.

## 3. Grace Periods for Late Rent

Lots of tenants are absolutely convinced that if rent is due on the first, but they pay by the 5th (or sometimes the 7th or even the 10th) of the month, they have legally paid their rent on time because they are within a legal grace period. This is simply not true. It is your legal right to insist that rent be paid on the day it is due, and you should use your lease or rental agreement and move-in letter to disabuse tenants of this bogus notion.

In practice, many landlords do not get upset about late rent or charge a late fee (discussed in Section E), until the rent is a few days past due. And your state law may require you to give tenants a few days to come up with the rent before you can send a termination notice. (This is discussed in Chapter 17.) Even so, your best approach is to consistently stress to tenants that rent must be paid on the due date.

In our opinion, if you wait more than three or five days to collect your rent, you are running your business unwisely, and just extending the time a non-paying tenant can stay. Be firm, but fair. Any other policy will get you into a morass of special cases and exceptions and will cost you a bundle in the long run. If you allow exceptions only in extreme circumstances (see Section G), tenants will learn not to try and sell you sob stories.

### Evictions for Nonpayment of Rent

Failure to pay rent on time is by far the most common reason landlords go to court and evict tenants. First, however, a landlord must give the tenant a written notice, demanding that the tenant either pay within a few days or move out. How long the tenant is allowed to stay depends on state law; in most places, it's about three to five days.

In most instances, the tenant who receives this kind of notice pays up, and that's the end of it. But if the tenant doesn't pay the rent (or move), you can file an eviction lawsuit. (Chapter 17 explains the kinds of termination notices that landlords must use when tenants are behind on the rent, and includes a brief summary of evictions. Appendix I includes details on state laws on termination for nonpayment of rent.)

If you find yourself delivering too may pay-the-rent-or-leave notices to a particular tenant, you may want to end the tenancy—even if the tenant always comes up with the rent at the last minute.

## D. Where and How Rent Is Due

You should specify in your lease or rental agreement where the tenant should pay the rent and how you want it paid—for example, by check or money order only. (See Clause 5 of the form agreements in Chapter 2.)

### 1. Where Rent Must Be Paid

You have several options for where the tenant pays you rent:

**By mail.** Allowing tenants to mail you the rent check is the most common method of payment, by a long shot. It's pretty convenient for everyone, and you can make it even easier by giving tenants pre-addressed (and stamped, if you're feeling generous) envelopes. The small amount you spend on postage and supplies may save you money in the long run, because you'll get paid more quickly.

**At home.** You can send someone to each unit, every month, to pick up the rent. But this more old-fashioned way of collecting the rent isn't well suited to modern life, when in most households it's hard to find someone at home during the day. It may be useful, however, if you think face-to-face contact might prompt a tenant to come up with the rent more quickly.

**At your office.** Requiring the rent to be paid personally at your place of business or manager's office is feasible only if you have an on-site office. Asking tenants to drive across town is both unreasonable and counterproductive, because inevitably some of them just won't get around to it. This approach does have certain advantages. It makes the tenant responsible for getting the rent to the you at a certain time or place, and avoids issues such as whether or not a rent check was lost or delayed in the mail. It also guarantees at least a bit of personal contact with your tenants, and a chance to air little problems before they become big ones.

If your lease or rental agreement doesn't specify where you want tenants to pay you rent, state law may decide. Under statutes in several states (see "Where Rent Is Due," below), rent is payable at the dwelling unit unless otherwise agreed.

### Where Rent Is Due

Unless your lease or rental agreement says otherwise, you must pick up the rent at the rental unit according to statutes in these states:

| | | |
|---|---|---|
| Alaska | Kentucky | Oregon |
| Arizona | Nebraska | Rhode Island |
| Connecticut | New Mexico | South Carolina |
| Iowa | Oklahoma | Tennessee |
| Kansas | | |

Citations for these state laws are listed in "State Rent Rules" in Appendix I.

## New Ways to Pay the Rent

More and more owners, especially those with large numbers of rental units, are looking for ways to insure that rent payments are quick and reliable. Here are two common methods:

**Credit card.** If you have enough tenants to make it worthwhile, explore the option of accepting credit cards. You must pay a fee—a percentage of the amount charged—for the privilege, but the cost may be justified if it results in more on-time payments and less hassle for you and tenants. Keep in mind that you'll need to have someone in your on-site office to process the credit card payments and give tenants receipts. And if your tenant population is affluent enough, consider requiring automatic credit card debits.

**Automatic debit.** You can get tenants' permission to have rent payments debited automatically each month from the tenant's bank account and transferred into your account. Tenants may be leery of this idea, however, and it's not worth insisting on.

## 2. Form of Rent Payment

You should also specify in your lease or rental agreement how rent must be paid: by cash, check or money order. (See Clause 5 of the form agreements in Chapter 2.)

For most landlords, rental checks are routine. If a tenant doesn't have a checking account or has bounced too many checks, you may want to require a certified check or money order.

You should never accept post-dated checks. The most obvious reason is that the check may never be good. You have absolutely no assurance that necessary funds will ever be deposited in the account. In addition, a post-dated check may, legally, be considered a "note" promising to pay on a certain date. In some states, if you accept such a note (check), you have no right to bring an eviction action while the note is pending. Far better to tell the tenant that rent must be paid in full on time and to give the tenant a late notice if it isn't.

**⚠ Don't accept cash unless you have no choice.** You are a likely target for robbery if word gets out that you are taking in large amounts of cash once or twice a month. And if you accept cash knowing that the tenant earned it from an illegal act, such as drug dealing, the government could seize it from you. (Chapter 12 discusses federal and state forfeiture laws.) If you do accept cash, be sure to provide a written, dated receipt stating the tenant's name and the amount of rent paid. Such a receipt is required by law in a few states, and it's a good idea everywhere.

## 3. Changing Where and How Rent Is Due

If you've been burned by bounced checks from a particular tenant, you may want to decree that from now on, you'll accept nothing less than a certified check or money order, and that rent may be paid only during certain hours at the manager's office.

Be careful. It may be illegal to suddenly change your terms for payment of rent without proper notice to the tenant—unless you are simply enforcing an existing term. For example, if your rental agreement states that you accept only money orders, you are on solid ground when you tell a check-bouncing tenant that you'll no longer accept her checks, and that your previous practice of doing so was merely an accommodation not required under the rental agreement.

If, however, your lease or rental agreement doesn't say where and how rent is to be paid, your past practice may legally control how rent is paid until you properly notify the tenant of a change. If you want to require tenants to pay rent at your office, for example, you must formally change a month-to-month rental agreement, typically with a written 30-day notice. If you rent under a lease, you will have to wait until the lease runs out.

## E. Late Charges and Discounts for Early Payments

If you're faced with a tenant who hasn't paid rent on the due date, you probably don't want to immediately hand out a formal notice telling the tenant to pay the rent or leave. After all, it's not going to do anything positive for your relationship with the tenant, who may have just forgotten to drop the check in a mailbox. But how else can you motivate tenants to pay rent on time?

A fairly common and sensible practice is to charge a reasonable late fee, and highlight your late fee policy in your lease or rental agreement and move-in letter to new tenants. (See Clause 6 of the form agreements in Chapter 2.)

Some states have statutes that put precise limits on late fees. (See "State Law Restrictions on Late Fees," below.) But even if your state doesn't have specific rules, you are still bound by general legal principles that prohibit unreasonably high fees. Courts in some states have ruled that contracts that provide for unreasonably high late charges are not enforceable—which means that if a tenant fights you in court (either in an eviction lawsuit or a separate case brought by the tenant), you could lose. And obviously, excessive late fees generate tenant hostility, anyway.

**Some rent control ordinances also regulate late fees.** Check any rent control ordinances applicable to your properties.

Unless your state imposes more specific statutory rules on late fee, you should be on safe ground if you adhere to these principles:

**The late fee should not apply until at least three to five days after the due date.** Imposing a stiff late charge if the rent is only one or two days late may not be upheld in court.

**The total late charge should not exceed 4%–5% of the rent.** That's $30 to $38 on a $750-per-month rental. State law in Maine sets a 4% limit and Maryland and North Carolina both set 5% limits on late charges. Even in states with no statutory limits,

a higher late charge, such as 10%, might not be upheld in court.

**If the late fee increases each day the rent is late, it should be moderate and have an upper limit.** A late charge that increases without limit each day could be considered interest charged at an illegal ("usurious") rate. State laws set the maximum allowable rate of interest, typically less than 10%, that may be charged for a debt. (Ten dollars a day on a $1,000-per-month rent is 3,650% annual interest.) A more acceptable late charge would be $10 for the first day rent is late, plus $5 for each additional day, up to a maximum of 5% of the rental amount.

**Don't try to disguise excessive late charges by giving a "discount" for early payment.** For one thing, this kind of "discount" is illegal in some states. One landlord we know concluded he couldn't get away with charging a $50 late charge on a $425 rent payment, so instead, he designed a rental agree-

SORRY. WE'RE LATE WITH THE RENT... ITS SO HARD GETTING EVERYBODY TOGETHER.

ment calling for a rent of $475 with a $50 discount if the rent was not more than three days late. Ingenious as this ploy sounds, it is unlikely to stand up in court, unless the discount for timely payment is very modest. Giving a relatively large discount is in effect the same as charging an excessive late fee, and a judge is likely to see it as such.

Anyway, fooling around with late charges is wasted energy. If you want more rent for your unit, raise the rent (unless you live in a rent control area). If you are concerned about tenants paying on time—and who isn't—put your energy into choosing responsible tenants. (See Chapter 1 for advice.)

If you have a tenant with a month-to-month tenancy who drives you nuts with late rent payments, and a reasonable late charge doesn't resolve the situation, terminate the tenancy with the appropriate notice.

## State Law Restrictions on Late Fees

|  |  |
| --- | --- |
| **California** | Pre-set late fees are invalid. |
| **Connecticut** | Landlords may not charge late fee until nine days after rent is due. |
| **Delaware** | To charge a late fee, landlord must maintain an office in the county where the rental unit is located at which tenants can pay rent. If a landlord doesn't have a local office for this purpose, tenant has three extra days (beyond the due date) to pay rent before the landlord can charge a late fee. Late fee cannot exceed 5% of rent and cannot be imposed until the rent is more than five days late. |
| **Maine** | Late fees cannot exceed 4% of the amount due for 30 days. Landlord must notify tenants, in writing, of any late fee at the start of the tenancy, and cannot impose it until rent is 15 days late |
| **Maryland** | Late fees can't exceed 5% of the rent due. |
| **Massachusetts** | Late fees, including interest on late rent, may not be imposed until the rent is 30 days late. |
| **New Jersey** | Landlord must wait five days before charging a late fee. |
| **New Mexico** | Late fee may not exceed 10% of the rent specified per rental period. Landlord must notify the tenant of the charge no later than the end of the next rental period. |
| **North Carolina** | Late fee cannot be higher than $15 or 5% of the rental payment, whichever is greater, and may not be imposed until the tenant is five days late paying rent. |
| **Oklahoma** | Pre-set late fees are invalid. |
| **Oregon** | Landlord must wait four days after the rent due date to assess late fee, and must disclose the late fee policy in the rental agreement. A flat late fee must be "reasonable." A daily late fee may not be more than 6% of a reasonable late fee, and cannot add up to more than 5% of the monthly rent. |
| **Tennessee** | Landlord can't charge late fee until five days have passed. Fee can't exceed 10% of the amount past due. |

Citations to these state laws on late rent fees are in "State Rent Rules" in Appendix I. States not listed here do not have statutes governing late rent charges, but case law may address the issue.

## F.  Returned Check Charges

It's legal to charge the tenant an extra fee if a rent check bounces. (See Clause 7 of the form agreements in Chapter 2.) If you're having a lot of trouble with bounced checks, you may want to change your policy to accept only money orders for rent. (See Section D, above.)

Like late charges, bounced check charges must be reasonable. You should charge no more than the amount your bank charges you for a returned check charge, probably $10 to $20 per returned item, plus a few dollars for your trouble.

It is a poor idea to let your bank redeposit rent checks that bounce. Instead, tell the bank to return bad checks to you immediately. Getting a bounced check back quickly alerts you to the fact that the rent is unpaid much sooner than if the check is resubmitted and returned for nonpayment a second time. You can use this time to ask the tenant to make the check good immediately. If the tenant doesn't come through, you can promptly serve the necessary paperwork to end the tenancy.

If a tenant habitually gives you bad checks, give the tenant a notice demanding that he pay the rent or move. If the tenant doesn't make the check good by the deadline, you can start eviction proceedings.

**Laws in some states allow landlords to charge interest on a bounced check, regardless of whether your lease or rental agreement says anything about late check charges.** For example, California landlords may charge 10% per year interest on a bounced check—thus, on a $1,000 rent check that isn't made good for a month, a California landlord can demand an additional $8.34 (California Civil Code §3289(b)). Your state's consumer protection office should be able to tell you whether your state has a similar law. (See "State Consumer Protection Offices" in Appendix I.)

## G. Partial or Delayed Rent Payments

On occasion, a tenant suffering a temporary financial setback will offer something less than the full month's rent, with a promise to catch up as the month proceeds, or at the first of the next month. Although generally this is a bad business practice, you may nevertheless wish to make an exception where the tenant's financial problems truly appear to be temporary and you have known the person for a long time.

If you do give a tenant a little more time to pay some or all of the rent, establish a schedule, in writing, for when the rent will be paid. Then monitor the situation carefully. Otherwise, the tenant may try to delay payment indefinitely, or make such small and infrequent payments that the account is never bought current. A signed agreement—say for a one-week extension—lets both you and the tenant know what's expected. If you give the tenant two weeks to catch up and she doesn't, the written agreement precludes any argument that you had really said "two to three weeks." A sample Agreement for Delayed or Partial Rent Payments is shown below.

The Legal Forms Disk includes the Agreement for Delayed or Partial Rent Payments. A blank tear-out copy is in Appendix II.

If the tenant does not pay the rest of the rent when promised, you can, and should, follow through with the appropriate steps to terminate the tenancy, as discussed in Chapter 17.

## H. Raising the Rent

Except in cities with rent control, your freedom to raise rent depends primarily on whether the tenant has a lease or a month-to-month rental agreement.

---

**Agreement for Delayed or Partial Rent Payments**

This Agreement is made between _____Betty Wong_____ "Tenant(s),"

and _John Lewis_____ "Landlord/Manager."

1. _Betty Wong_____ "Tenant(s)" has/have paid

   _one-half of her $500 rent for apartment #2 at 111 Billy St., Phoenix, Arizona_

   _____

   on _March 1_____, 199_X_, which was due _March 1_____, 199_X_.

2. _John Lewis_____ (Landlord/Manager)

   agrees to accept all the remainder of the rent on or before _March 15_____, 199_X_,

   and to hold off on any legal proceeding to evict _Betty Wong_____

   _____ (Tenant(s)) until that date.

_March 2, 199X_____      _John Lewis_____
Date                            Landlord/Manager

**_March 2, 199X_____**      **_Betty  Wong_____**
Date                            Tenant

_____      _____
Date                            Tenant

_____      _____
Date                            Tenant

---

## 1. When You Can Raise Rent

For the most part, a lease fixes the terms of tenancy for the length of the lease. You can't change the terms of the lease until the end of the lease period unless the lease itself allows it or the tenant agrees. When the lease expires, you can present the tenant with a new lease that has a higher rent or other changed terms. It's always safest to give tenants at least a month or two notice of any rent increase before negotiating a new lease.

In contrast, you can raise the rent in a periodic tenancy just by giving the tenant proper written notice, typically 30 days for a month-to-month tenancy. (If you collect rent every 15 days, you probably have to give your tenant only 15 days' notice.) State law may override these general rules, however. In a few states, landlords must provide 45 or 60 days' notice to raise the rent for a month-to-month tenancy. See "Notice Required to Change or Terminate a Month-to-Month Tenancy" in Appendix I and the Chapter 14 discussion of changing terms during the tenancy.) You'll need to consult your state statutes for the specific information you must provide in a rent increase notice, how you must deliver it to the tenant and any rights tenants have to dispute rent increases.

 Local rent control laws also affect rent increase notices.

## 2. How Much Can You Raise the Rent?

In areas without rent control, there is no limit on the amount you can increase the rent of a month-to-month or other periodic tenant. Similarly, there is no restriction on the period of time between rent increases. You can legally raise the rent as much and as often as good business dictates. Of course, common sense should tell you that if your tenants think your increases are unfair, you may end up with vacant units or a hostile group of tenants looking for ways to make you miserable. As a courtesy, you may wish to tell your tenants of the rent increase personally, perhaps explaining the reasons—although reasons aren't legally necessary, except in areas covered by rent control.

## 3. Avoiding Tenant Charges of Retaliation or Discrimination

You can't legally raise a tenant's rent as retaliation—for example, in response to a legitimate complaint or rent-withholding action (see Chapter 9) or in a discriminatory manner (see Chapter 5). The laws in many states actually presume retaliation if you increase rent soon—typically, within three to six months—after a tenant's complaint of defective conditions. See the Chapter 16 discussion of general ways to avoid tenant charges of retaliation. "State Laws Prohibiting Landlord Retaliation" in Appendix I lists state-by-state details.

One way to protect yourself from charges that ordinary rent increases are retaliatory or discriminatory is to adopt a sensible rent-increase policy and stick to it.

For example, many landlords raise rent once a year in an amount that more or less reflects the increase in the Consumer Price Index. Other landlords use a more complicated formula that takes into account other rents in the area, as well as such factors as increased costs of maintenance or

rehabilitation. They make sure to inform their tenants about the rent increase in advance and apply the increase uniformly to all their tenants. Usually, this protects the landlord against any claim of a retaliatory rent increase by a tenant who has coincidentally made a legitimate complaint about the condition of the premises.

> **EXAMPLE:** Lois owns two multi-unit complexes. In one of them, she raises rents uniformly, at the same time, for all tenants. In the other apartment building, where she fears tenants hit with rent increases all at once will organize and generate unrest, Lois does things differently: She raises each tenant's rent in accordance with the Consumer Price Index on the yearly anniversary of the date each tenant moved in. Either way, Lois is safe from being judged to have retaliatorily increased rents, even if a rent increase to a particular tenant follows on the heels of a complaint.

Of course, any rent increase given to a tenant who has made a complaint should be reasonable—in relation to the previous rent, what you charge other similarly situated tenants, and rents for comparable property in the area—or you are asking for legal trouble.

> **EXAMPLE:** Lonnie has no organized plan for increasing rents in his 20-unit building, but simply raises them when he needs money. On November 1, he raises the rent for one of his tenants, Teresa, without remembering her recent complaint about her heater. Teresa is the only one to receive a rent increase in November. She has a strong retaliatory rent-increase case against Lonnie, simply because an increase that seemed to single her out coincided with her exercise of a legal right. If the increase made her rent higher than those for comparable units in the building, she will have an even better case. ∎

Chapter **4**

# Security Deposits

Most landlords quite sensibly ask for a security deposit before entrusting hundreds of thousands of dollars worth of real estate to a tenant. But it's easy to get into legal trouble over deposits, because they are strictly regulated by state law, and sometimes also by city ordinance.

The law of most states dictates how large a deposit you can require, how you can use it, when you must return it and more. Many states require you to put deposits in a separate account and pay interest on them. You cannot escape these requirements by putting different terms in a lease or rental agreement. You may face substantial financial penalties for violating state laws on security deposits.

This chapter explains how to set up a clear, fair system of setting, collecting and holding deposits. It may exceed the minimum legal requirements affecting your property, but it will ultimately work to your advantage, resulting in easier turnovers, better tenant relations and fewer legal hassles.

---

### Where to Get More Information on Security Deposits

If you have any questions of what's allowed in your state, you should get a current copy of your state's security deposit law (statute) or an up-to-date summary from a landlords' association. Start by referring to the "Citations for State Laws on Security Deposits" in Appendix I. Then read the statute at a public library, law library or online. (See Chapter 18 for information on using the law library and accessing state statutes online.)

---

In addition, be sure to check local ordinances in all areas where you own property. Cities, particularly those with rent control, may add their own rules on security deposits, such as a limit on the amount you can charge or a requirement that you pay interest on deposits.

**⚠ This discussion is limited to security deposit statutes.** Some states—Alabama, Idaho, Louisiana, West Virginia, Wisconsin and Wyoming— do not have statutes on security deposits. That doesn't mean that there is no law on the subject. Court decisions (what lawyers call "case law") in your state may set out quite specific requirements for refundability of deposits, whether they should be held in interest-bearing accounts and the like. This book doesn't cover all this case law, but you may need to check it out yourself. To find out whether courts in your state have made decisions you need to be aware of, contact your state or local property owners' association or do some legal research on your own.

Related topics covered in this book include:
- Charging prospective tenants credit check fees, finder's fees or holding deposits: Chapter 1
- Writing clear lease and rental agreement provisions on security deposits: Chapter 2
- Highlighting security deposit rules and procedures in move-in and move-out letters to the tenant: Chapters 7 and 15
- Returning deposits and deducting for cleaning, damage and unpaid rent; how to handle legal disputes involving deposits: Chapter 15.

## A. Purpose and Use of Security Deposits

All states allow you to collect a security deposit when a tenant moves in and hold it until the tenant leaves. The general purpose of a security deposit is to assure that a tenant pays rent when due and keeps the rental unit in good condition. Rent you collect in advance for the first month is not considered part of the security deposit.

State laws typically control the amount you can charge (see Section B) and how and when you must return security deposits. When a tenant moves out, you will have a set amount of time (usually from 14 to 30 days, depending on the state) to either return the tenant's entire deposit or provide an itemized statement of deductions and refund any deposit balance.

Although state laws vary, you can generally withhold all or part of the deposit to pay for:

1. Unpaid rent

2. Repairing damage to the premises (except for "ordinary wear and tear") caused by the tenant, a family member or guest

3. Cleaning necessary to restore the rental unit to its condition at the beginning of the tenancy (over and above "ordinary wear and tear")

4. Restoring or replacing rental unit property taken by the tenant.

States typically also allow you to use a deposit to cover the tenant's obligations under the lease or rental agreement, which may include payment of utility charges.

You don't necessarily need to wait until a tenant moves out to tap into their security deposit. You may, for example, use some of the tenant's security deposit during the tenancy—for example, because the tenant broke something and didn't fix it or pay for it. In this case, you should require the tenant to replenish the security deposit.

> **EXAMPLE:** Millie pays her landlord Maury a $1,000 security deposit when she moves in. Six months later, Millie goes on vacation, leaving the water running. By the time Maury is notified, the overflow has damaged the paint on the ceiling below. Maury repaints the ceiling at a cost of $250, taking the money out of Millie's security deposit. Maury is entitled to ask Millie to replace that money, so that her deposit remains $1,000.

To protect yourself and avoid misunderstandings with tenants, make sure your lease or rental agreement is clear on the use of security deposits and the tenant's obligations. (See Clause 8 of the form agreements in Chapter 2.)

## Security Deposit Exemptions for Small Landlords

These states exempt some landlords and rental properties from all or portions of state security deposit laws:

| State | Exemption |
|---|---|
| **Alaska** | Any rental unit where the rent exceeds $2,000 per month |
| **Arkansas** | Landlord who owns five or fewer rental units, unless these units are managed by a third party for a fee |
| **Georgia** | Landlord who owns ten or fewer rental units, unless these units are managed by an outside party |
| **Illinois** | Landlord who owns four or fewer dwelling units |
| **Maine** | Rental unit which is part of structure with five or fewer units, one of which is occupied by landlord |
| **New Hampshire** | Landlord who leases a single-family residence and owns no other rental property or landlord who leases rental units in an owner-occupied building of five units or less. (Exemption does not apply to any individual unit in owner-occupied building that is occupied by a person 60 years of age or older) |
| **New Jersey** | Owner-occupied building with two or less units where tenant fails to provide 30 days' written notice to landlord invoking provisions of act. |
| **New York** | Landlord who rents out fewer than six rental units |
| **Tennessee** | Rental properties outside of Davidson, Knox, Hamilton and Shelby Counties |

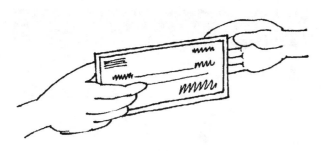

## B. Dollar Limits on Deposits

Many states limit the amount you can collect as a deposit to an amount equal to one or two months of rent. And the limit within each state sometimes varies depending on various factors such as:

- age of the tenant (senior citizens may have a lower deposit ceiling)
- whether or not the rental unit is furnished
- whether you have a month-to-month rental agreement or a long-term lease, and
- whether or not you have a pet or waterbed.

For details, see "State Laws on Security Deposit Limits," below.

In some states, the rent you collect in advance for the last month is not considered part of the security deposit limit, while in others it is. (Section D covers last month's rent.) Also, see Section F which covers nonrefundable fees you may charge in addition to security deposits.

⚠ **An inconsistent security deposit policy is an invitation to a lawsuit.** Even if your motives are good—for example, you require a smaller deposit from a student tenant—you risk a charge of illegal discrimination by other tenants who did not get the same break. Chapter 5 explains fair housing laws and their impact on your business practices.

## C. How Much Deposit Should You Charge?

Normally, the best advice is to charge as much as the market will bear, within any legal limits. The more the tenant has at stake, the better the chance your property will be respected. And, the larger the deposit, the more financial protection you will have if a tenant leaves owing you rent.

The market, however, often keeps the practical limit on deposits lower than the maximum allowed by law. Your common sense and your business sense need to work together in setting security deposits. Here are a number of considerations to keep in mind:

- **Charge the full limit in high-risk situations**— for example, where there's a lot of tenant turnover, if the tenant has a pet and you're concerned about damage, or if the tenant's credit is shaky and you're worried about unpaid rent.
- **Consider the psychological advantage of a higher rent rather than a high deposit.** Many tenants would rather pay a slightly higher rent than an enormous deposit. Also, many acceptable, solvent tenants have a hard time coming up with several months' rent, especially if they are still in a rental and are awaiting the return of a previous security deposit. And, remember, unlike the security deposit, the extra rent is not refundable.

EXAMPLE: Lenora rents out a three-bedroom furnished house in San Francisco for $2,000 a month. Because total deposits on furnished property in California can legally be three times the monthly rent, Lenora could charge up to $6,000. This is in addition to the first month's rent of $2,000 that Lenora can (and should) insist on before turning the property over to a tenant. But, realistically, Lenora would probably have difficulty finding a tenant if she insisted on receiving a $6,000 deposit plus the first month's rent, for a total of $8,000. So she decides to charge only one month's rent for the deposit but to increase the monthly rent. That gives Lenora the protection she feels she needs without imposing an enormous initial financial burden on her tenants.

# State Laws on Security Deposit Limits

Here's the limit each state sets on the amount of security deposit you can charge. "No statutory limit" means that the state does not specify the amount you can charge. For the specific law in your state, see "Citations for State Laws on Security Deposits" in Appendix I. Also, be sure to check rent control or rent regulation rules for any deposit limits.

| State | Limit | State | Limit |
|-------|-------|-------|-------|
| Alabama | No statutory limit | Mississippi | No statutory limit |
| Alaska | Two months' rent, except where rent exceeds $2,000 per month | Missouri | Two months' rent |
| | | Montana | No statutory limit |
| Arizona | One and one-half months' rent (unless tenant voluntarily agrees to pay more) | Nebraska | One month's rent (no pets); one and one-quarter months' rent (pets) |
| Arkansas | Two months' rent | Nevada | Three months' rent |
| California | Two months' rent (unfurnished, no waterbed); two and one-half months' rent (unfurnished, tenant has waterbed); three months' rent (furnished, no waterbed); three and one-half months' rent (furnished, tenant has waterbed) | New Hampshire | One month's rent or $100, whichever is greater |
| | | New Jersey | One and one-half month's rent |
| | | New Mexico | One month's rent (for rental agreement less than one year); no limit for leases of one year or more |
| Colorado | No statutory limit | New York | No statutory limit |
| Connecticut | Two months' rent (tenant under 62 years of age); one month's rent (tenant 62 years of age or older) | North Carolina | One and one-half months' rent for month-to-month rental agreements; two months' rent if term is longer than two months |
| Delaware | One month's rent on leases for one year or more; no limit for month-to-month rental agreements | North Dakota | One month's rent (or $1,500 if tenant has a pet) |
| | | Ohio | No statutory limit |
| District of Columbia | One month's rent | Oklahoma | No statutory limit |
| | | Oregon | No statutory limit |
| Florida | No statutory limit | Pennsylvania | Two months' rent for first year of renting; one month's rent during the second and subsequent years of renting |
| Georgia | No statutory limit | | |
| Hawaii | One month's rent | | |
| Idaho | No statutory limit | Rhode Island | One month's rent |
| Illinois | No statutory limit | South Carolina | No statutory limit |
| Indiana | No statutory limit | South Dakota | One month's rent (higher deposit may be charged if special conditions pose a danger to maintenance of the premises) |
| Iowa | Two months' rent | | |
| Kansas | One month's rent (unfurnished, no pets); one and one-half months' rent (unfurnished with pets or furnished with no pets) | | |
| | | Tennessee | No statutory limit |
| | | Texas | No statutory limit |
| Kentucky | No statutory limit | Utah | No statutory limit |
| Louisiana | 30 days' rent | Vermont | No statutory limit |
| Maine | Two months' rent | Virginia | Two months' rent |
| Maryland | Two months' rent or $50, whichever is greater | Washington | No statutory limit |
| Massachusetts | Two months' rent | West Virginia | No statutory limit |
| Michigan | One and one-half months' rent | Wisconsin | No statutory limit |
| Minnesota | No statutory limit | Wyoming | No statutory limit |

- **Single-family homes call for a bigger deposit.**
Unlike multi-unit residences, where close-by
neighbors or a manager can spot, report and
quickly stop any destruction of the premises,
the single-family home is somewhat of an
island. The condition of the interior and even
the exterior may be hard to assess. And, of
course, the cost of repairing damage to a
house is likely to be higher than for an apartment. Unless you live next door or can frequently check the condition of a single-family
rental, a substantial security deposit is a good
idea.

- **Gain a marketing advantage by allowing a
deposit to be paid in installments.** If rentals
are plentiful in your area, with comparable
units renting at about the same price, you
might give yourself a competitive edge by
allowing the tenant to pay the deposit in
several installments over a few months, rather
than one lump sum.

- **Charge less than one month's rent to discourage tenants from considering the deposit as
simply the last month's rent.** Many landlords
have found that charging a little less than the
last month's rent results in fewer tenants
assuming (incorrectly) that the deposit is
simply an advance payment for their last
month's rent. (Section D, below, covers the
topic of last month's rent.)

**Require renters' insurance as an alternative
to a high security deposit.** If you're worried
about damage, but don't think you can raise the
deposit any higher, require renters' insurance.
Renters' insurance, which may cover damage done
by the tenant or guests, gives your property an
extra measure of protection. While you're at it,
evaluate your own insurance policy to make sure it
is adequate. Insurance is discussed in Chapter 10. If
the tenant's security deposit is inadequate to cover
any damage and there is no renters' insurance (or it
won't cover the loss), you may be able to collect
from your own carrier.

# D. Last Month's Rent

It's a common—but often unwise—practice to
collect a sum of money called "last month's rent"
from a tenant who's moving in. Landlords tend to
treat this money as just another security deposit,
and use it to cover not only the last month's rent
but also other expenses such as repairs or cleaning.
   Problems can arise when:
- you try to use the last month's rent to cover
repairs or cleaning, or
- the rent goes up—and you want to top off
the last month's rent.
We'll look at these situations below.

## 1. Applying Last Month's Rent to Damage or Cleaning

If you collect a sum of money labeled last month's
rent and your tenant is leaving (voluntarily or involuntarily), chances are that he will not write a rent
check for the last month. After all, he's already paid
for that last month, right? Surprisingly, many tenants
do pay for the last month anyway, often forgetting
that they have pre-paid. What happens to that last
month's rent?
   Ideally, the tenant will leave the place clean and
in good repair, enabling you to refund the entire
last month's rent and all or most of the tenant's
security deposit. But if the tenant leaves the place a
mess, most states allow you to treat "last month's
rent" as part of the security deposit and use all or
part of it for cleaning or to repair or replace damaged
items.

EXAMPLE: Katie required her tenant Joe to pay
a security deposit of one month's rent, plus last
month's rent. Her state law allowed a landlord
to use all advance deposits to cover a tenant's
unpaid rent or damage, regardless of what the
landlord called the deposit. When Joe moved
out, he didn't owe any back rent, but he left his
apartment a shambles. Katie was entitled to use
the entire deposit, including that labeled last
month's rent, to cover the damage.

A few states, such as Massachusetts and New York, restrict the use of money labeled as "last month's rent" to its stated purpose: the rent for the last month of your occupancy. In these states, if you use any of last month's rent to repair the cabinet the tenant broke, you're violating the law.

EXAMPLE: Mike collected a security deposit of one month's rent, plus last month's rent, from his tenant Amy. Mike's state required that landlords use money collected for the last month as last month's rent only, not for cleaning or repairs. When Amy moved out, she didn't owe any rent but she, too, left her apartment a mess. Mike had to refund Amy's last month's rent and, when the remaining security deposit proved too little to cover the damage Amy had caused, Mike had to sue Amy in small claims court for the excess.

In general, it's a bad idea to call any part of the deposit "last month's rent." Why? Because if your state restricts your use of the money, you've unnecessarily hobbled yourself. And if your state considers last month's rent part of the security deposit, you haven't gained anything. You may have even put yourself at a disadvantage, because you've given the tenant the impression that the last month's rent is taken care of. You would be better off if the tenant paid the last month's rent when it came due, leaving the entire security deposit available to cover cleaning and repairs.

EXAMPLE 1: Fernando rents out a $600-per-month apartment in a state where the security deposit limit is two months' rent. Fernando charged his tenant, Liz, a total deposit of $1,200, calling $600 a security deposit and $600 last month's rent. Liz, used this last month's rent for the last month when she gave her notice to Fernando. This left Fernando with the $600 security deposit. Unfortunately, when Liz moved out, she left $700 worth of damages, sticking Fernando with a $100 loss.

EXAMPLE 2: Learning something from this unhappy experience, Fernando charged his next tenant a simple $1,200 security deposit, not limiting any part of it to last month's rent. This time, when the tenant moved out, after paying his last month's rent as legally required, the whole $1,200 was available to cover the cost of any repairs or cleaning.

## 2. If You Increase Rent

Avoiding the term "last month's rent" also keeps things simpler if you raise the rent, but not the deposit, before the tenant's last month of occupancy. If you have collected the last month's rent in advance, and the rent at the end of your tenancy is the same as when your tenant moved in, your tenant is paid up. However, if the rent has increased, but you have not asked your tenant to top off the last month's rent, questions arise. Does the tenant owe you for the difference? If so, can you take money from the tenant's security deposit to make it up?

Unfortunately, there are no clear answers. But because landlords in every state are allowed to ask tenants to top off the last month's rent at the time they increase the rent, judges would probably allow you to go after it at the end of the tenancy, too. Whether you get the difference from your security deposit or sue the tenant in small claims court is somewhat academic.

EXAMPLE: When Rose moved in, the rent was $800 a month, and she paid this much in advance as last month's rent, plus an additional $800 security deposit. Over the years the landlord, Artie, has raised the rent to $1,000. Rose does not pay any rent during the last month of her tenancy, figuring that the $800 she paid up front will cover it. Artie, however, thinks that Rose should pay the $200 difference. Artie and Rose may end up in small claims court fighting over who owes what. They could have avoided the problem by discussing the issue of last month's rent when Rose's tenancy began.

### 3. How to Avoid Problems

To minimize confusion and disputes, we suggest that you avoid labeling any part of the security deposit last month's rent and get issues involving last month's rent straight with your tenant at the outset.

Clause 8 of the form agreements in Chapter 2 makes it clear that the tenant may not apply the security deposit to the last month's rent. Even with this type of clause, a tenant who's leaving may ask to use the security deposit for the last month's rent. Chapter 15 discusses how to handle these types of requests.

## E. Interest and Accounts on Deposits

In most states, you don't have to pay tenants interest on deposits, or put them in a separate bank account. In other words, you can simply put the money in your personal bank account and use it, as long as you have it available when the tenant moves out.

### 1. Separate Accounts

Several states require you to put security deposits in a separate account, sometimes called a "trust" account, rather than mixing the funds with your personal or business accounts. Some states require landlords to give tenants information on the location of this separate trust account at the start of the tenancy, usually as part of the lease or rental agreement. The idea is that by isolating these funds, it is more likely that you will have the money available whenever the tenant moves out and becomes entitled to it. In addition, separating these deposits makes it easier to trace them if a tenant claims that they were not handled properly. You are not required to set up separate accounts for every tenant. If you keep one account, be sure to maintain careful records of each tenant's contribution.

### 2. Interest

Several states require landlords to pay tenants interest on security deposits. Of course, you may find that it helps your relationship with your tenants to pay interest on deposits, even if this is not a legal requirement. It's up to you.

Even among the states that require interest, there are many variations. A few states, such as Illinois, don't require small landlords (less than 25 rental units) to pay interest on deposits. Others, such as Iowa, allow the landlord to keep the interest earned during the first five years of tenancy.

State laws typically establish detailed requirements, including:

- The interest rate to be paid. Usually it's a little lower than the bank actually pays, so the landlord's costs and trouble of setting up the account are covered.
- When interest payments must be made. The most common laws require payments to be made at termination of tenancy or also made annually.
- Notification landlords must give tenants as to where and how the security deposit is being held and the rate of interest. (See Clause 8 of the form agreements in Chapter 2 for details on states that require this type of notification.)

Chicago, Los Angeles and several other cities (typically those with rent control) require landlords to pay or credit tenants with interest on security deposits, even if the state law does not impose this duty. A few cities require that the funds be kept in separate interest-bearing accounts.

## States That Require Landlords to Maintain a Separate Account for Security Deposits

| | |
|---|---|
| **Alaska** | "Wherever practicable," deposit must be held in trust account or by escrow agent. |
| **Connecticut** | |
| **Delaware** | |
| **District of Columbia** | |
| **Florida*** | Instead of keeping separate account, landlord can post surety bond. |
| **Georgia*** | Instead of keeping separate account, landlord can post surety bond. |
| **Iowa** | |
| **Kentucky*** | |
| **Maine** | Deposit must be unavailable to landlord's creditors. |
| **Maryland** | Deposit must be held in Maryland banking or savings institution. |
| **Massachusetts** | Deposit must be held in Massachusetts and be unavailable to landlord's creditors. |
| **Michigan*** | |
| **New Hampshire** | |
| **New Jersey** | |
| **New York*** | |
| **North Carolina*** | |
| **North Dakota** | |
| **Oklahoma** | |
| **Pennsylvania** | |
| **Tennessee*** | |
| **Washington** | |

* Landlords must give tenants written information on where the security deposit is being held.

## States That Require Landlords to Pay Interest on Deposits

| | | |
|---|---|---|
| Connecticut | Maryland | New York |
| District of Columbia | Massachusetts | North Dakota |
| | Minnesota | Ohio |
| Florida* | New Hampshire | Pennsylvania |
| Illinois | New Jersey | Virginia |
| Iowa* | New Mexico | |

For details, see "States That Require Landlords to Pay Interest on Deposits" in Appendix I.

* Interest payments are not required, but when they are made, certain conditions apply.

## F. Nonrefundable Deposits and Fees

In general, state laws are often muddled on the subject of nonrefundable deposits and fees. A few states, such as California, specifically prohibit landlords from charging any fee or deposit that is not refundable. Some states specifically allow landlords to collect a fee that is not refundable—such as for pets or cleaning. (See "States That Allow Nonrefundable Fees," below.) While most of these states don't require terms to be spelled out in the lease or rental agreement, it's still a good idea to do so, in order to avoid disputes with your tenant.

Generally, it's best to avoid the legal uncertainties and not try to collect any nonrefundable fees from tenants. It's much simpler just to consider the expenses these fees cover as part of your overhead, and figure them into the rent. By avoiding nonrefundable fees, you'll prevent a lot of time-consuming disputes with tenants.

If you have a specific concern about a particular tenant—for example, you're afraid a tenant's pet will damage the carpets or furniture—just ask for a higher security deposit. That way, you're covered if the pet causes damage, and if it doesn't, the tenant won't have to shell out unnecessarily.

Charging a set fee can actually backfire. If you collect $50 for cleaning, for example, but when the tenant moves out the unit needs $100 worth of cleaning, you're stuck. You've already charged for cleaning, and the tenant could make a good argument that you're not entitled to take anything more out of the security deposit for cleaning.

If, despite our advice, you want to charge a nonrefundable fee, check your state's law to find what (if any) kinds of nonrefundable fees are allowed. Then, make sure your lease or rental agreement is clear on the subject.

---

### States That Allow Nonrefundable Fees

The following states have statutes that permit at least certain types of nonrefundable fees, such as for cleaning or pets:

| | | |
|---|---|---|
| Arizona | Nevada | Oregon |
| Florida | New Jersey | Utah |
| Georgia | North Carolina | Washington |

Citations to these security deposit statutes appear in the Appendix.

In states that have no statute on the subject, the legality of nonrefundable fees and deposits is determined in court. For example, courts in Texas and Michigan have ruled that a landlord and tenant may agree that certain fees will be nonrefundable. (*Holmes v. Canlen Management Corp.*, 542 S.W.2d 199 (1976); *Stutelberg v. Practical Management Co.*, 245 N.W.2d 737 (1976).)

If this issue is of concern to you, you'll have to do some legal research.

---

## G. How to Increase Deposits

Especially if you rent to a tenant for many years, you may want to increase the amount of the security deposit. The legality of doing this depends on the situation.

**Leases**: If you have a fixed-term lease, you may not raise the security deposit during the term of the lease, unless the lease allows it. Security deposits may be increased, however, when the lease is renewed or becomes a month-to-month tenancy.

**Written rental agreements:** With a month-to-month tenancy, you can increase a security deposit the same way you raise the rent, typically by giving the tenant a written notice 30 days in advance of the change. (See the discussion in Chapter 3.) Of course, you can increase the security deposit without also increasing the rent as long as you don't exceed the maximum legal amount.

> EXAMPLE: Jules rents out an apartment for $750 a month in a state that limits security deposits to one month's rent. If he raises the rent to $1,000, the maximum deposit he may collect goes up to $1,000. But the deposit does not go up automatically. To raise the deposit amount, Jules must give the tenant the required notice.

Local rent control ordinances typically restrict your right to raise deposits as well as to raise rents. (See Chapter 3, Section B, for more on rent control.)

## H. Handling Deposits When You Buy or Sell Rental Property

When you sell rental property, what should you do with the deposits you've already collected? After all, when the tenant moves out, she'll be entitled to her deposit back. Who owes her the money? In most states, whoever happens to be the landlord at the time a tenancy ends is legally responsible for complying with state laws requiring return of security deposits. That means that you may need to hand over the deposits to the new owner. Read your state's statutes carefully as to how this transfer is handled, including any requirements that tenants be notified of the new owner's name, address and phone number.

If you buy rental property, make sure you know the total dollar amount of security deposits. For a multi-unit building, it could be tens of thousands of dollars. ■

Chapter **5**

# Discrimination

Not so long ago, a landlord could refuse to rent to an applicant, or could evict a tenant, for almost any reason—because of skin color, or religion, or because the tenant had children or was elderly or disabled. Some landlords even discriminated against single women, believing that they would be incapable of paying the rent or would have too many overnight guests.

So that all Americans would have the right to live where they chose, Congress and state legislatures passed laws prohibiting housing discrimination. Most notable of these are the federal Fair Housing Acts, which outlaw discrimination based on race or color, national origin, religion, sex, familial status or disability. Many states and cities have laws making it illegal to discriminate based on additional factors, such as marital status or sexual orientation. Courts play a role, too, by interpreting and applying anti-discrimination laws. It is safe to say that unless you have a legitimate business reason to reject a prospective tenant (for example, poor credit history), you risk a fair housing complaint and a potentially costly lawsuit.

While most modern landlords would never intentionally violate an antidiscrimination law, it's not always easy to determine what's legal or illegal, especially in the area of advertising, where well-meaning attempts to appeal to potential renters may have the unintended effect of alienating others, resulting in an unfair housing complaint. Also, your well-intentioned attempts to accommodate the needs or wishes of your tenants can sometimes, ironically, be used as the basis for an unfair housing complaint. (For example, a landlord who advertised the presence of a toddlers' wading pool, but who did not make it clear that children were also welcome at the full-sized pool, found himself fighting and eventually settling a complaint that he discriminated against families.)

The discussion in this chapter is intended to not only explain the law, but to steer you away from hidden discrimination traps. It explains:

- legal reasons to turn down prospective tenants, such as a bad credit history or too many people for the size of the rental unit (Sections A and D)
- protected categories (such as race and religion) identified by federal and state laws prohibiting housing discrimination (Sections B and C)
- precautions to ensure that managers don't violate housing discrimination laws (Section E)
- legal penalties for housing discrimination, including tenant lawsuits in state and federal courts (Section F), and
- whether your insurance policy is likely to cover the cost of defending a discrimination claim, and the cost of the judgment if you lose the case (Section G).

Chapter 1 also discusses how to avoid discrimination in advertising your property, accepting applications and screening potential tenants.

## A. Legal Reasons for Refusing to Rent to a Tenant

The most important decision you make, save possibly for deciding whether to purchase rental property in the first place, is your choice of tenants. Chapter 1 recommends a system for carefully screening potential tenants in order to select people who will pay rent on time, maintain your property and not cause you any problems. Here we focus more closely on making sure that your screening process does not precipitate a costly charge of discrimination.

Remember that only certain kinds of discrimination in rental housing are illegal, such as selecting tenants on the basis of religion or race (see Section C). You are legally free to choose among prospective tenants as long as your decisions are based on valid and objective business criteria, such as the person's ability to pay the rent and properly maintain the property. For example, you may legally refuse to rent to prospective tenants with bad credit histories, unsteady employment histories or even low incomes that you reasonably regard as insufficient to pay the rent. Why? Because these criteria for tenant selection are reasonably related to your right to run your business in a competent, profitable manner (sometimes called your "legitimate business interests"). And if a person who fits one or more obvious "bad tenant risk" criteria happens to be a member of a minority group, you are still on safe legal ground as long as:

- You are consistent in your screening and treat all tenants more or less equally—for example, you always require a credit report for prospective tenants.
- You are not applying a generalization about people of a certain group to an individual.
- You can document your legal reasons for not renting to a prospective tenant.

But pay attention to the fact that judges, tenants' lawyers and government agencies that administer and enforce fair housing laws know full well that some landlords try to make up and document legal reasons to discriminate, when the real reason is that they just don't like people with a particular racial, ethnic or religious background. So, if you refuse to rent to a person who happens to be African-American, has children or speaks only Spanish, be sure you document your legitimate business reason specific to that individual (such as insufficient income or a history of eviction for nonpayment of rent). Be prepared to show that your tenant advertising, screening and selection processes have been based on objective criteria and that a more qualified applicant has always gotten the rental unit.

This section discusses some of the common legal reasons you may use to choose or reject applicants based on your business interests. A valid occupancy limitation (such as overcrowding) can also be a legal basis for a refusal, but since this issue is fairly complicated, we have devoted a separate section to the subject. (See Section D.)

**To protect yourself in advance, always note your reasons for rejecting a tenant on the application.** A tenant you properly reject may

nevertheless file a discrimination complaint with a fair housing agency. (See Section F for details on the complaint procedure.) Recognizing this, you want to be able to prove that you had a valid business reason for refusing to rent to the particular person, such as negative references from a previous landlord. This means you need to routinely document your good reasons for rejecting all potential tenants before anyone files a discrimination claim. (We discuss how to document why you chose—or rejected—a particular tenant in Chapter 1.)

## Objective Criteria— What Do They Look Like?

"Objective criteria" are tenancy requirements that are established before the applicant even walks in the door, and are unaffected by the personal value judgments of the person asking the question. For example, a requirement that an applicant must never have been evicted for nonpayment of rent is "objective" because it is a matter of history and can be satisfied by a clear "yes" or "no." "Subjective criteria," on the other hand, have no pre-established correct answers, and the results of the questions will vary depending on the person who poses the question—for example, a requirement that the applicant present "a good appearance" has no predetermined "right" answer and will be answered differently by each person who asks the question. Subjective criteria are always suspicious in a housing context because their very looseness allows them to mask deliberate illegal discrimination.

So much for theory. Here are a few examples of allowable, objective criteria for choosing tenants:

- two positive references from previous landlords
- sufficient income to pay the rent
- signed waiver allowing you to investigate applicant's credit history.

## 1. Poor Credit Record or Income

You can legitimately refuse to rent to a prospective tenant who has a history of nonpayment of rent or whom you reasonably believe would be unable to pay rent in the future.

Here's some advice on how to avoid charges of discrimination when choosing tenants on the basis of income or credit history.

**Do a credit check on every prospective tenant and base your selection on the results of that credit check.** Accepting or rejecting tenants based on objective criteria tied to a credit report is the best way to protect yourself against an accusation that you're using a bad credit history as an excuse to illegally discriminate against certain prospective tenants. For example, if you establish rules saying you won't rent to someone with bad credit or who is evicted by a previous landlord for nonpayment of rent (information commonly found in credit reports), be sure you apply this policy to all tenants. Chapter 1 shows you how to check a prospective tenant's credit history and find out whether an applicant has ever been evicted, gone through bankruptcy or been convicted of a crime.

**Avoid rigid point systems that rank prospective tenants on the basis of financial stability and other factors.** Some landlords evaluate prospective tenants by giving each one a certain number of points at the outset, with deductions for bad credit and negative references and additional points for extremely good ones. Points are also awarded based on length of employment and income. The person with the highest score gets the nod. Point systems give the illusion of objectivity, but because the weight you give each factor is, after all, subjective, they can still leave you open to charges of discrimination.

**Don't discriminate against married or unmarried couples by counting only one spouse's or partner's income.** Always consider the income of persons living together, married or unmarried, in order to avoid the accusation of marital status discrimination (discussed in Section C7) or sex discrimination (discussed in Section C5).

**If your state prohibits discrimination based on personal characteristics or traits, don't give too much weight to years spent at the same job, which can arguably discriminate against certain occupations.** For example, software designers and programmers commonly move from one employer to another.

## 2. Negative References From Previous Landlords

You can legally refuse to rent to someone based on what a previous landlord or manager has to say—for example, that the tenant was consistently late paying rent, broke the lease or left the place a shambles. (Chapter 1 discusses how to check references with previous landlords and managers.)

## 3. Civil Lawsuits Involving a Tenant

Credit reports typically indicate whether the applicant has been involved in civil lawsuits, such as an eviction or breach of contract suit. For many landlords, an eviction lawsuit is a red flag. Can you reject a tenant on this basis? It depends.

If a former landlord has filed—and won—an eviction lawsuit against the applicant, you have solid grounds to reject this person. Be careful, however, if the credit report indicates that the applicant, not the former landlord, won the eviction suit: A tenant who has been vindicated in a court of law has not done anything wrong, even though you may suspect that the person is a troublemaker who just got lucky. If you reject someone simply because an eviction lawsuit was filed against them, and if you live in a state that prohibits discrimination on the basis of someone's personal characteristic or trait, you are risking a charge that you are discriminating. In most situations, however, if the applicant is truly a poor prospect, the information you get from prior landlords and employers will confirm your suspicions and you can reject the applicant on these more solid grounds (negative references).

The credit report may also indicate that the applicant is now, or has been, involved in another type of civil lawsuit—for example, a custody fight, a personal injury claim, or a dispute with an auto repair shop. If the legal matter has nothing to do with the applicant's rental history, ability to pay the rent or satisfy your other tenancy requirements, you may be on shaky ground if you base a rejection solely on that basis.

## 4. Criminal History

Understandably, many landlords wish to check an applicant's criminal history, and credit reports will often include this information. Can you reject an applicant because of a conviction for drunk driving, or murder or drug use? What if there was an arrest but no conviction?

**Convictions.** If an applicant has been convicted for criminal offenses, you are probably, with one exception, entitled to reject him on that basis. After all, a conviction indicates that the applicant was not, at least in that instance, a law-abiding individual, which is a legitimate criterion for prospective tenants or managers. The exception, however, involves convictions for past drug use: As explained in Section C4 below, past drug addiction is considered a disability under the Fair Housing Amendments Act, and you may not refuse to rent to someone on that basis—even if the addiction resulted in a conviction. People with convictions for the sale or manufacture of drugs, or current drug users, are not, however, protected under federal law.

**Arrests.** A more difficult problem is posed by the person who has an arrest record but no conviction. Under our legal system, a person is presumed not guilty until the prosecution proves its case or the arrestee pleads guilty. So, is it illegal to deny housing to someone whose arrest did not result in a conviction? Because "arrestees" are not, unlike members of a race or religion, protected under federal or state law, you could probably reject an applicant with an arrest history without too much fear of legal consequences. But there is an easy way to avoid even the slightest risk: Chances are that a previously arrested applicant who is *truly* a bad risk will have plenty of other facts in his or her background (like poor credit or negative references) that will clearly justify your rejection. In short, if you do a thorough check on each applicant, you'll get enough information on which to base your decision.

## 5. Incomplete or Inaccurate Rental Application

Your carefully designed application form will do its job only if the applicant provides you with all the necessary information. Obviously, if you can reject applicants on the basis of negative references or a bad credit history, you can reject them for failing to allow you to check their background, or if you catch them in a lie.

## 6. Inability to Meet Legal Terms of Lease or Rental Agreement

It goes without saying that you may legally refuse to rent to someone who can can't come up with the security deposit or meet some other condition of the tenancy, such as the length of the lease.

## 7. Pets

You can legally refuse to rent to people with pets and you can restrict the types of pets you accept. You can also, strictly speaking, let some tenants keep a pet and say no to others—because pet owners, unlike members of a religion or race, are not as a group protected by antidiscrimination laws. However, from a practical point of view, an inconsistent pet policy is a bad idea because it can only result in angry, resentful tenants. Also, if the pet owner you reject is someone in a protected category and you have let someone outside of that category rent with a pet, you are courting a discrimination lawsuit.

Keep in mind that you cannot refuse to rent to someone with an animal if that animal is a properly trained dog for a blind, deaf or physically or mentally disabled person. (Clause 14 of the form lease and rental agreements in Chapter 2 discusses pet policies and legal issues.)

# B. Sources of Antidiscrimination Laws

This section reviews the sources of antidiscrimination laws—the federal Fair Housing Act of 1968 and the federal Fair Housing Amendments Act of 1988 (throughout this chapter, we refer to these laws as the federal Acts), and state and local antidiscrimination laws. Section C, which follows, discusses specific types of discrimination that will almost surely get you into trouble with a federal, state or local housing agency.

## 1. The Federal Fair Housing Acts

The Fair Housing Act and Fair Housing Amendments Act (42 United States Code §§ 3601-3619, 3631), which are enforced by the U.S. Department of Housing and Urban Development (HUD), addresses many types of housing discrimination. It applies to all aspects of the landlord-tenant relationship throughout the U.S.

### a. Types of Discrimination Prohibited

The Fair Housing Act prohibits discrimination on the following grounds (called protected categories):
- Race or color or religion (Section C1)
- National origin (Section C2)
- Familial status—includes families with children under the age of 18 and pregnant women (Section C3)
- Disability or handicap (Section C4)
- Sex, including sexual harassment (Section C5).

Although the federal Acts use certain words to describe illegal discrimination (such as "national origin"), the Department of Housing and Urban Development and the courts are not limited to the precise language of the Acts. For instance, sexual harassment is a violation of law because it qualifies as discrimination on the basis of sex—even though the term "sexual harassment" is not used in the text of the law itself.

### How Fair Housing Groups Uncover Discrimination

Landlords who turn away prospective tenants on the basis of race, ethnic background or other group characteristics obviously never come out and admit what they're doing. Commonly, a landlord falsely tells a person who's a member of a racial minority that no rentals are available, or that the prospective tenant's income and credit history aren't good enough. From a legal point of view, this can be a dangerous—and potentially expensive—tactic. Here's why. Both HUD and private fair-housing groups are adept at uncovering this discriminatory practice by having "testers" apply to landlords for vacant housing. Typically, a tester who is African-American or Hispanic will fill out a rental application, listing certain occupational, income and credit information. Then, a white tester will apply for the same housing, listing information very similar—or sometimes not as good—as that given by the minority applicant.

A landlord who offers to rent to a white tester, and rejects—without valid reason—a minority applicant who has the same (or better) qualifications, is very likely to be found to be guilty of discrimination. Such incidents have resulted in many hefty lawsuit settlements. Fortunately, it's possible to avoid the morass of legal liability for discrimination by adopting tenant screening policies that don't discriminate, and applying them even-handedly.

### b. Aspects of Landlord-Tenant Relationship Covered

The federal Acts essentially prohibit landlords from taking any of the following actions based on race, color, religion, national origin, familial status, disability or sex:

- advertising or making any statement that indicates a limitation or preference based on race, religion or any other protected category
- falsely denying that a rental unit is available
- setting more restrictive standards for selecting tenants
- refusing to rent to members of certain groups
- before or during the tenancy, setting different terms, conditions, or privileges for rental of a dwelling unit, such as requiring larger deposits of some tenants, or adopting an inconsistent policy of responding to late rent payments
- during the tenancy, providing different housing services or facilities, such as making a community center or other common area available only to selected tenants, or
- terminating a tenancy for a discriminatory reason.

An individual who suspects discrimination may file a complaint with HUD or a state or local fair housing agency, or sue you in federal or state court. (See Section F, below.)

### c. Exempt Property

The following types of property are exempt from the federal Acts:

- owner-occupied buildings with four or fewer units
- single-family housing rented without the use of discriminatory advertising or without a real estate broker
- certain types of housing operated by religious organizations and private clubs that limit occupancy to their own members, and
- with respect to age discrimination only, housing reserved exclusively for senior citizens,

that is intended for and solely occupied by persons 62 years of age or older or households with at least one person 55 years of age or older. To qualify as "55 and older housing," at least 80% of the units in the housing facility must be occupied by at least one person 55 years or older.

**State and local laws may cover federally exempt units.** Even though your property may be exempt under federal law, similar state or local anti-housing-discrimination laws may nevertheless cover your rental units. For example, owner-occupied buildings with four or fewer units are exempt under federal law, but not under California law.

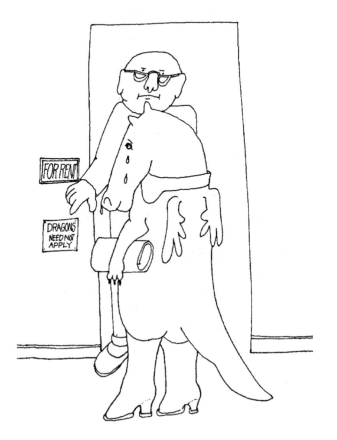

# HUD Regional Offices

For more information on the rules and regulations of the Fair Housing Act, contact one of HUD's regional offices listed below, call HUD's Fair Housing Information Clearinghouse at 800-343-3442 or check the HUD Website at www.hud.gov.

### Region I - Boston

*(Connecticut, Maine, Massachusetts, New Hampshire, Rhode Island, Vermont)*

Boston Federal Office Building, 10 Causeway St.
Boston, Massachusetts 02222-1092
617-565-5236

### Region II - New York

*(New Jersey, New York)*

26 Federal Plaza
New York, New York 10278-0068
212-264-4771

### Region III - Philadelphia

*(Delaware, District of Columbia, Maryland, Pennsylvania, Virginia, West Virginia)*

100 Penn Square East
Philadelphia, Pennsylvania 19107-3380
215-656-0600

### Region IV - Atlanta

*(Alabama, Florida, Georgia, Kentucky, Mississippi, North Carolina, South Carolina, Tennessee, Puerto Rico, Virgin Islands)*

Richard B. Russell Federal Building,
75 Spring Street, S.W.
Atlanta, Georgia 30303-3388
404-331-4576

### Region V - Chicago

*(Illinois, Indiana, Michigan, Minnesota, Ohio, Wisconsin)*

Ralph H. Metcalfe Federal Building,
77 West Jackson Blvd.
Chicago, Illinois 60604-3507
312-353-6236

### Region VI - Fort Worth

*(Arkansas, Louisiana, New Mexico, Oklahoma, Texas)*

1600 Throckmorton, P.O. Box 2905
Fort Worth, Texas 76113-2905
817-978-9000

### Region VII - Kansas City

*(Iowa, Kansas, Missouri, Nebraska)*

Gateway Tower 11
400 State Avenue
Kansas City, Kansas 66101-2406
913-551-5419

### Region VIII - Denver

*(Colorado, Montana, North Dakota, South Dakota, Utah, Wyoming)*

633 17th St.
Denver, Colorado 80202-3607
303-672-5258

### Region IX - San Francisco

*(Arizona, California, Hawaii, Nevada, Guam, American Samoa)*

450 Golden Gate Avenue
San Francisco, California 94102-3448
415-436-6532

### Region X - Seattle

*(Alaska, Idaho, Oregon, Washington)*

Suite 200 Seattle Federal Building
909 1st Ave.
Seattle, Washington 98104-1000
206-220-5205

## 2. State and Local Antidiscrimination Laws

Most state and local laws prohibiting housing discrimination echo federal antidiscrimination law in that they outlaw discrimination based on race or color, national origin, religion, familial status, disability and sex. (If your state law doesn't track federal law group-by-group, it makes little difference—you're still bound by the more-inclusive federal law.) But state and local laws often go in the other direction—they may provide more detail and may also forbid some kinds of discrimination—such as discrimination based on marital status—that aren't covered by federal law. For example, in states that prohibit discrimination based on marital status, it would be illegal to refuse to rent to divorced people.

For information on state and local housing discrimination laws, contact your state fair housing agency. See the list of State Fair Housing Agencies in Appendix I.

# C. Types of Illegal Discrimination

In the sections that follow, we'll look at each of the categories of illegal discrimination and explore their obvious and not-so-obvious meaning.

## 1. Race or Religion

Fortunately, the amount of overt racial and religious discrimination has lessened over the last several decades. This is not to say, however, that discrimination doesn't exist, especially in subtle forms. And unfortunately, HUD may see "discrimination" where your intent was completely well-intentioned. Below, we'll look at some of the common examples of both intentional (but subtle) discrimination and unintended discrimination.

### a. Intentional, Subtle Discrimination

It goes without saying that you should not overtly treat tenants differently because of their race or religion—for example, renting only to members of your own religion or race is obviously illegal. Deliberate discrimination should not be cavalierly dismissed, however, as a thing of the past practiced by insensitive oafs. Unexpected situations can test your willingness to comply with equal treatment laws and can reveal subtle forms of intentional discrimination that are just as illegal as blatant discrimination. Consider the following scenario:

EXAMPLE: Several tenants in Creekside Apartments reserved the common room for a religious occasion. Creekside management learned that the tenants were members of a white supremacist religion that believes in the inferiority of all non-whites and non-Christians. Creekside was appalled at the thought of these ideas being discussed on its premises, and denied the group the use of the common room. The tenants who were members of this group filed a discrimination complaint with HUD on the basis of freedom of religion. HUD supported the religious group and forced Creekside to make the common room available. Creekside wisely sent all tenants a memo stating that making the common room available reflects management's intent to comply with fair housing laws and not their endorsement of the principles urged by any group that uses the room.

As the above example illustrates, religions that are outside the mainstream are protected under the federal Acts.

### b. Unintended Discrimination

In Chapter 1, we discussed the unintended discriminatory messages that are conveyed when advertisements feature statements such as "safe Christian community," or "Sunday quiet times enforced." (Both ads may be understood as suggesting that only Christians are welcome as tenants.) The same considerations apply to your dealings with your tenants after they have moved in. Conscientious landlords should carefully review tenant rules, signs, newsletters and all communications to make sure that they cannot be construed in any way to benefit, support or discriminate against any racial or religious group. The examples and advice we give below may seem "politically correct" in the extreme, but take our word for it, they are based on actual fair housing complaints and deserve to be taken seriously.

- The apartment complex newsletter invites everyone to a "Christmas party" held by the management. Non-Christian tenants might feel that this event is not intended for them and therefore that they have been discriminated against. A better approach: Call it a "Holiday Party" and invite everyone.

- Management extends the use of the common room to tenants for "birthday parties, anniversaries and Christmas and Easter parties." A better idea: Invite your tenants to use the common room for special celebrations, rather than list specific Christian holidays.

- In an effort to accommodate your Spanish-speaking tenants, you translate your move-in letter and house rules into Spanish. Regarding the use of alcohol in the common areas, the Spanish version begins, "Unlike Mexico, where drinking is practiced in public places, alcoholic beverages may not be consumed in common areas...." Because to many people this phrase implies an ethnic generalization, it may well become the basis for a fair housing complaint.

- The metropolitan area where you own residential rental property contains large numbers of both Spanish-speaking and Cantonese-speaking people. Advertising in only Spanish, or translating your lease into only Cantonese, will likely constitute a fair housing violation because it suggests that members of the other group are not welcome. Of course, if you advertise only in English, you are not violating fair housing laws.

## 2. National Origin

Like discrimination based on race or religion, discrimination based on national origin is illegal, whether it's practiced openly and deliberately or unintentionally. Even if you are motivated by a valid business concern, but choose tenants in a way that singles out people of a particular nationality, it's still illegal. Let's see how a misguided attempt to choose financially stable, long-term tenants can amount to discrimination against a nationality.

You may legally reject a tenant who has a shadowy financial background and has broken prior leases by suddenly leaving the property. (Section A, above, discusses these types of objective criteria for choosing tenants.) Now, it is common knowledge that many people who are illegally in this country do not have verifiable financial histories. Furthermore, they can be picked up and deported at any moment, which would leave you, the landlord, with an abandoned apartment and no rental income. In order to save the cost of a reference check, can you simply ask all Hispanic applicants for immigration papers or proof of citizenship?

The answer is no, and the reason lies in the impact this practice will have upon Hispanics as a whole (or any other group you treat this way). If you make it a practice to ask only Hispanics for their immigration papers, you can be sure that a legal Hispanic (who after all is the only one likely to complain to HUD) will interpret your actions as sending a negative message to Hispanics in general: Hispanics are not welcome because you assume all of them are poor and living in the country illegally. A fair housing agency or court of law would probably agree that this sort of selective "let me see your papers" policy is illegal discrimination.

On the other hand, if you require all prospective tenants to supply satisfactory proof of their identity and eligibility to work (as well as meeting your other criteria), you will get the needed information but in a nondiscriminatory way.

For advice on verifying the legal status of prospective tenants, contact the Immigration and Naturalization Service (INS) at 800-755-0777. For a local INS office, check the phone book under U.S. Department of Justice.

**If you ask one person a question, ask everyone.** It cannot be emphasized enough that questions on a prospective tenant's legal status must be put to all applicants, not just the ones whom you suspect are illegal, and not just the ones who are applying to live in one of your buildings in a certain part of town.

## 3. Familial Status

Discrimination on the basis of familial status includes not only openly refusing to rent to families with children or to pregnant women, but also trying to accomplish the same goal by setting overly restrictive space requirements (limiting the maximum number of people permitted to occupy a rental unit), thereby preventing families with children from occupying smaller units.

Section D, below, discusses how to establish reasonable occupancy standards. The fact that you can legally adopt occupancy standards, however, doesn't mean you can use "overcrowding" as a euphemism for refusing to rent to tenants with children, if you would rent to the same number of adults. A few landlords have adopted criteria that for all practical purposes forbid children under the guise of preventing overcrowding—for example, allowing only one person per bedroom, with a couple counting as one person. Under these criteria, a landlord would rent a two-bedroom unit to a husband and wife and their one child, but would not rent the same unit to a mother with two children. This practice, which has the effect of keeping all (or most) children out of a landlord's property, would surely be found illegal in court and would result in monetary penalties.

It would also be illegal to allow children only on ground floors, or to designate certain apartments as separate adult units and family units.

It is essential to maintain a consistent occupancy policy. If you allow three adults to live in a two-bedroom apartment, you had better let a couple with a child (or a single mother with two children) live in the same type of unit, or you leave yourself open to charges that you are illegally discriminating.

EXAMPLE: Jackson owned and managed two identical one-bedroom units in a duplex, one of which he rented out to three flight attendants who were rarely there at the same time. When the other unit became vacant, Jackson advertised it as a one-bedroom, two-person apartment. Harry and Sue Jones and their teenage daughter were turned away because they exceeded Jackson's occupancy limit of two people. The Jones family, learning that the companion unit was rented to three people, filed a complaint with HUD, whose investigator questioned Jackson regarding the inconsistency of his occupancy policy. Jackson was convinced that he was in the wrong, and agreed to rent to the Jones family and to compensate them for the humiliation they had suffered as a result of being refused.

Finally, do not inquire as to the age and sex of any children who will be sharing the same bedroom. This is their parents' business, not yours.

## 4. Disability

The Fair Housing Amendments Act prohibits discrimination against people who:

- have a physical or mental disability that substantially limits one or more major life activities—including, but not limited to hearing, mobility and visual impairments, chronic alcoholism (but only if it is being addressed through a recovery program), mental illness, HIV-positive status, AIDS, AIDS-Related Complex and mental retardation
- have a history or record of such a disability, or
- are regarded by others as though they have such a disability.

You may be shocked to see what is—and what is not—considered a disability. Although it may seem odd, alcoholism is classed as a protected disability. Does this mean that you must rent to a drunk? What about past, and current, drug addiction? Let's look at each of these issues.

## a. Recovering Alcoholics

You may encounter an applicant, let's call him Ted, who passes all your criteria for selecting tenants but whose personal history includes a disquieting note: Employers and past landlords let you know that Ted has a serious drinking problem that he is dealing with by attending AA meetings. As far as you can tell, Ted has not lost a job or a place to live due to his drinking problem. Can you refuse to rent to Ted for fear that he will drink away the rent, exhibit loud or inappropriate behavior or damage your property? No, you cannot, unless you can point to specific acts of misbehavior or financial shakiness that would sink any applicant, regardless of the underlying cause. Your fear alone that this might happen (however well-founded) will not legally support your refusal to rent to Ted.

In a nutshell, you may not refuse to rent to what HUD calls a "recovering alcoholic" simply because of his status as an alcoholic—you must be able to point to specific facts other than his status as an alcoholic in recovery that render him unfit as a tenant.

> **EXAMPLE:** Patsy applied for an apartment one morning and spoke with Carol, the manager. Patsy said she would have to return that afternoon to complete the application form because she was due at her regular Alcoholics Anonymous meeting. Carol decided on the spot that she did not want Patsy for a tenant, and she told Patsy that the unit "had just been rented," which was a lie. (Patsy continued to see the newspaper ad for the unit.) Patsy filed a complaint with HUD, alleging that she was an alcoholic who had been discriminated against.

Because Carol could not point to any reason for turning Patsy away other than her assumption that Patsy, as a recovering alcoholic, would be a bad tenant, the judge awarded Patsy several thousand dollars in damages.

Unfortunately, HUD has not been very helpful in explaining what steps an alcoholic must take in order to quality as "recovering." Regular attendance at AA meetings and counseling probably qualify, but an alcoholic who is less conscientious may not make the grade. In any event, you as the landlord are hardly in a position to investigate and verify an applicant's personal habits and medical history. So how can you choose tenants without risking a violation of law?

The answer lies in putting your energies into a thorough background check that will yield information that can unquestionably support a rejection at the rental office. If the applicant, recovering or not, is truly a bad risk, you'll discover facts (like job firings, bad credit or past rental property damage) independent of the thorny problem of whether the person has entered the "recovery" stage of his alcoholism. And if you have a current tenant whom you suspect of alcoholism, use the same approach —focus on his behavior as a tenant, regardless of his status as an alcoholic. If the tenant damages your property or interferes with your other tenants' ability to quietly enjoy their property, he is a candidate for eviction regardless of whether he is in or out of recovery, just as would any tenant who exhibited this behavior. Consider the following scenario, which is what Carol should have done:

> **EXAMPLE:** Same facts as above, except that Carol went ahead and took an application from Patsy later that day and checked her references. Patsy's former landlord told Carol that Patsy had refused to pay for damage from a fire she had negligently caused; Patsy's employment history showed a pattern of short-lived jobs and decreasing wages. Carol noted this information on Patsy's application form and, as she would have done for any applicant with a similar

background, Carol rejected Patsy. Patsy filed a complaint with HUD, again claiming discrimination on the basis of her alcoholism. When the HUD investigator asked to see Patsy's application and questioned Carol about her application criteria for all applicants, he concluded that the rejection had been based on legally sound business reasons and was not, therefore, a fair housing violation.

### b. Drug Users

Under the Fair Housing Amendments Act, a person who has a past drug addiction is classed as someone who has a record of a disability and, as such, is protected under the fair housing law. You may not refuse to rent to someone solely because he is an ex-addict, even if that person has felony convictions for drug use. Put another way, your fear that the person will resume his illegal drug use is not sufficient grounds to reject the applicant. If you do a thorough background check, however, and discover a rental or employment history that would defeat any applicant, you may reject the person as long as it is clear that the rejection is based on these legal reasons.

On the other hand, someone who currently and illegally uses drugs is breaking the law, and you may certainly refuse to rent to him—particularly if you suspect the person is dealing drugs. (See Chapter 12 for a discussion of legal problems you face by allowing current drug users to live in your property.) Also, if the applicant has felony convictions for dealing or manufacturing illegal drugs, as distinct from convictions for possession of drugs for personal use, you may use that history as a basis of refusal.

### c. Mental or Emotional Impairments

Like alcoholics or past drug users, applicants and tenants who had, or have (or appear to have) mental or emotional impairments must be evaluated and treated by the landlord and manager on the basis of their financial stability and histories as tenants, not on the basis of their mental health status. Unless you can point to specific instances of past behavior that would make a prospective tenant dangerous to others, or you have other valid business criteria for rejecting the person, a refusal to rent could result in a fair housing complaint.

### d. No "Approved List" of Disabilities

The physical and mental disabilities that are covered by the Fair Housing Acts range from the obvious (wheelchair use and sensory disabilities) to those that may not be so apparent. The law reaches to past drug users and to those who are HIV-positive (*Bragdon v. Abbott*, U.S. Supreme Ct. No. 97-156).

The list of groups protected by the law is not, however, set in stone. What may seem to you like an individual's hypochondria or personal quirk may become a legally accepted disability if tested in court. For example, tenants with hypertension (which may lead to more serious medical problems) have been known to ask for protection under the fair housing laws, as have tenants suffering from "building material sensitivity" (sensitivities to vapors emitted from paint, upholstery and rugs). Similarly, tenants who have a sensitivity or problem that is widespread throughout the population, such as asthma or allergies, may also win coverage under the fair housing laws. Contact your local HUD office to find out whether the courts have extended fair housing protections in these situations.

### e. Questions and Actions That May Be Considered to Discriminate Against the Disabled

You may not ask a prospective tenant if she has a disability or illness, and may not ask to see medical records. If it is obvious that someone is disabled—for example, the person is in a wheelchair or wears a hearing aid—it is illegal to inquire how severely he is disabled.

Unfortunately, even the most innocuous, well-meaning question or remark can get you into trouble, especially if you decide not to rent to the person. What you might consider polite conversation may be taken as a probing question designed to discourage an applicant.

EXAMPLE: Sam, a Vietnam veteran, was the owner of Belleview Apartments. Jim, who appeared to be the same age as Sam and who used a wheelchair, applied for an apartment. Thinking that Jim might have been injured in the Vietnam War, Sam questioned Jim about the circumstances of his disability, intending only to pass the time and put Jim at ease. When Jim was not offered the apartment—he did not meet the financial criteria that Sam applied to all applicants—he filed a complaint with HUD, alleging discrimination based on his disability. Sam was unable to convince the HUD investigator that his questions were not intended to be discriminatory and, on the advice of his attorney, Sam settled the case for several thousand dollars.

Your well-intentioned actions, as well as your words, can become the basis of a fair housing complaint. You are not allowed to "steer" applicants to units that you, however innocently, think would be more appropriate. For example, if you have two units for rent—one on the ground floor and one three stories up—do not fail to show both units to the applicant who is movement-impaired, however reasonable you think it would be for the person to consider only the ground floor unit.

## f. The Rights of Disabled Tenants to Live in an Accessible Place

You must also concern yourself with the fair housing laws after you have rented a home to a disabled person. The Fair Housing Amendments Act requires that landlords

- **accommodate** the needs of disabled tenants, at the landlord's own expense (42 U.S. Code § 3604(f)(B) (1988), and
- allow disabled tenants to make reasonable **modifications** of their living unit or common areas at their expense if that is what is needed for the person to comfortably and safely live in the unit. (42 U.S. Code § 3604(f)(3)(A) (1988).)

We'll look briefly at each of these requirements.

**Accommodations.** You are expected to adjust your rules, procedures or services in order to give a person with a disability an equal opportunity to use and enjoy a dwelling unit or a common space. Accommodations include such things as:

- Parking—if you provide parking in the first place, providing a close-in, spacious parking space for a wheelchair-bound tenant
- Service animals—allowing a guide dog, hearing dog or service dog in a residence that otherwise disallows pets

- Rent payment—allowing a special rent payment plan for a tenant whose finances are managed by someone else or by a government agency
- Reading problems—arranging to read all communications from management to a blind tenant, and
- Phobias—for example, providing a tub and clothesline for a mentally ill tenant whose anxiety about machines makes her unable to use the washer and dryer.

Does your duty to accommodate disabled tenants mean that you must bend every rule and change every procedure at the tenant's request? Generally speaking, the answer is "No." You are expected to accommodate "reasonable" requests, but need not undertake changes that would seriously impair your ability to run your business. For example, if a wheelchair-bound applicant prefers the third-story apartment in a walk-up building constructed in 1926 to the one on the ground floor, you do not have to rip the building apart to install an elevator.

**Modifications.** Where your duty to accommodate the needs of disabled tenants ends, your obligation to allow the tenant to modify living space may begin. A disabled person has the right to modify his living space to the extent necessary to make it safe and comfortable, as long as the modifications will not make the unit unacceptable to the next tenant, or the disabled tenant agrees to undo the modification when he leaves. Examples of modifications undertaken by a disabled tenant include:

- lowering counter tops for a wheelchair-bound tenant
- installing special faucets or door handles for persons with limited hand use
- modifying kitchen appliances to accommodate a blind tenant, and
- installing a ramp to allow a wheelchair-bound tenant to negotiate two steps up to a raised lobby or corridor.

You are not obliged to allow a disabled tenant to modify his unit at will, without prior approval. You are entitled to ask for a reasonable description of the proposed modifications, proof that they will be done in a workmanlike manner and evidence that the tenant is obtaining any necessary building permits. Moreover, if a tenant proposes to modify the unit in such a way that will require restoration when the tenant leaves (such as the repositioning of lowered kitchen counters), you may require that the tenant pay into an interest-bearing escrow account the amount estimated for the restoration. (The interest belongs to the tenant.)

## New Buildings and the Disabled

The Fair Housing Amendments Act (42 U.S. Code § 3604(f)(3)(C) and 3604(f)(7)) imposes requirements on new buildings of four or more units that were first occupied after March 1991. All ground floor units and every unit in an elevator building must be designed or constructed so that:

- the main building is accessible and on an accessible route
- the public and common areas are "readily accessible to and usable by" the disabled, including parking areas (a good rule of thumb is to reserve 2% of the spaces)
- entryway doorways have 36" of free space *plus* shoulder and elbow room; and interior doorways are at least 32" wide
- interior living spaces have wheelchair-accessible routes throughout, with changes in floor height of no more than 1/4"
- light switches, outlets, thermostats and other environmental controls are within the legal "reach range" (15" to 48" from the ground)
- bathroom walls are sufficiently reinforced to allow the safe installation of "grab bars," and
- kitchens and bathrooms are large enough to allow a wheelchair to maneuver within the room (40" turning radius minimum) and have sinks and appliances positioned to allow side or front use.

**Verification.** If a tenant asks for an accommodation or wants to modify his dwelling to accommodate a disability, you may ask for substantiation (from the tenant's physician, for example) that the person does, indeed, need the proposed accommodations or modifications in order to live safely and comfortably on your rental property. You may not ask for proof that the tenant or applicant is impaired, or for details of that impairment.

## 5. Sex and Sexual Harassment

You may not refuse to rent to a person on the basis of gender—for example, you cannot refuse to rent to a single woman solely because she is female. Neither may you impose special rules on someone because of their gender—for example, limiting upper-story apartments to single females.

Illegal sex discrimination also includes sexual harassment—refusing to rent to a person who resists your sexual advances, or making life difficult for a tenant who has resisted such advances.

What is sexual harassment in a rental housing context? Courts have defined it as:

- a pattern of persistent, unwanted attention of a sexual nature, including the making of sexual remarks and physical advances, or a single instance of highly egregious behavior. A manager's persistent requests for social contact, or constant remarks concerning a tenant's appearance or behavior could constitute sexual harassment, as could a single extraordinarily offensive remark, or
- a situation in which a tenant's rights are conditioned upon the acceptance of the owner's or manager's attentions. For example, a manager who refuses to fix the plumbing until the tenant agrees to a date is guilty of sexual harassment. This type of harassment may be established on the basis of only one incident.

EXAMPLE: Oscar, the resident manager of Northside Apartments, was attracted to Martha, his tenant, and asked her repeatedly for a date.

Martha always turned Oscar down and asked that he leave her alone. Oscar didn't back off, and began hanging around the pool whenever Martha used it. Oscar watched Martha intently and made suggestive remarks about her to the other tenants. Martha stopped using the pool and filed a sexual harassment complaint with HUD, claiming that Oscar's unwanted attentions made it impossible for her to use and enjoy the pool and even to comfortably live at Northside. Oscar refused to consider a settlement when the HUD investigator spoke to him and Martha about his actions. As a result, HUD pursued the case in court, where a federal judge ordered Oscar to leave Martha alone and awarded several thousand dollars in damages to Martha.

**Sexual harassment awards under the Civil Rights Act have no limits.** Owners and managers who engage in sexual harassment risk being found liable under either the Fair Housing Act or Title VII of the 1964 Civil Rights Act, which also prohibits sexual discrimination. The Fair Housing Act limits the dollar amount of damages that can be levied against the defendant (see Section F, below), but there are no limits to the amount of punitive damages that can be awarded in Title VII actions. Punitive damages are generally not covered by insurance, and it is far from clear whether even actual damages in a discrimination case (that is, non-punitive damages, such as pain and suffering) will be covered, either. See Section G, below, for a discussion of insurance coverage in discrimination cases.

## 6. Age

The federal fair housing law does not expressly use the word "age," but nevertheless discrimination on the basis of age is definitely included within the ban against discrimination on the basis of familial status. Many states and localities, however, have laws that directly address the issue of age.

We are reminded often that ours is an aging society. With the increase in the number of older adults comes the need for appropriate housing. Some older tenants may not, however, be able to live completely independently—for example, they may rely on the regular assistance of a nearby adult child or friend. Can you, as the landlord, refuse to rent to an older person solely because you fear that her frailty or dimming memory will pose a threat to the health or safety of the rest of your tenants? Or, can you favor younger tenants over equally qualified elderly tenants because you would like your property to have a youthful appearance?

The answer to these questions is "No." You may feel that your worry about elderly tenants is well-founded, but unless you can point to an actual incident or to facts that will substantiate your concern, you cannot reject an elderly applicant on the basis of your fears alone. For example, you could turn away an older applicant if you learned from a prior landlord or employer that the person regularly forgot to lock the doors, failed to manage his income so that he was often late in paying rent or demonstrated an inability to undertake basic house-keeping chores. In other words, if the applicant has demonstrated that he or she is unable to live alone, your regular and thorough background check should supply you with those facts, which are legally defensible reasons to refuse to rent. As for your stylistic preference for youthful tenants, this is age discrimination in its purest form and it will never survive a fair housing complaint.

**EXAMPLE 1:** Nora's 80-year-old mother Ethel decided that it was time to find a smaller place and move closer to her daughter. Ethel sold her home and applied for a one-bedroom apartment at Coral Shores. Ethel had impeccable references from neighbors and employers and an outstanding credit history. Nonetheless, Mike, the manager of Coral Shores, was concerned about Ethel's age. Fearful that Ethel might forget to turn off the stove, lose her key or do any number of other dangerous things, Mike decided on the spot not to rent to her. Ethel filed a fair housing complaint, which she won on the basis of age discrimination.

Learning from his experience with Ethel, Mike, the manager at Coral Shores, became more conscientious in screening tenants. The following example shows how he avoided another lawsuit on age discrimination.

**EXAMPLE 2:** William was an elderly gentleman who decided to sell the family home and rent an apartment after his wife passed away. He applied for an apartment at Coral Shores. Since William had no "prior rental history," Mike, the manager, drove to William's old neighborhood and spoke with several of his former neighbors. Mike also called William's personal references. From these sources, Mike learned that William had been unable to take care of himself the last few years, having been completely dependent on his wife. Mike also learned that, since his wife's death, William had made several desperate calls to neighbors and family when he had

been unable to extinguish a negligently started kitchen fire, find his keys and maintain basic levels of cleanliness in his house. Mike noted these findings on William's application and declined to rent to him on the basis of these specific facts.

The issue of age discrimination may also arise during a well-established tenancy. You may have a tenant who has lived alone competently for years but who, with advancing age, appears to be gradually losing the ability to live safely by himself. Determining the point when the tenant should no longer live alone is a judgment call that will vary with every situation, and we cannot provide a checklist of "failings" that will suffice for everyone. There is, however, one universal ground rule that will, by now, sound pretty familiar: You cannot take action merely on the basis of the person's age or because you fear what that person might do. You must be able to point to real, serious violations of the criteria that apply to all tenants before you can evict or take action against an elderly tenant.

⚠ **Elderly tenants may also qualify as disabled tenants, who are entitled to accommodation under the law.** An elderly tenant who, because of her age, cannot meet one of your policies may be entitled to special treatment because she also qualifies as a disabled person. (See the discussion of discrimination on the basis of disability in Section C4, above.) In other words, you may not be able to use an elderly tenant's inability to abide by one of the terms of the tenancy as the basis of an eviction —instead, you may be expected to adjust your policy in order to accommodate her disability. For example, an elderly tenant who is chronically late with the rent because of her sporadic disorientation might be entitled to a grace period, or a friendly reminder when the rent is due; whereas a non-disabled tenant who is chronically late with the rent is not entitled to such special treatment. And if an elderly tenant can't negotiate the stairs, the legal solution is a ramp, not an eviction notice.

## Renting to Minors

You may wonder whether the prohibition against age discrimination applies to minors (in most states, people under age 18). A minor applicant who is legally "emancipated"—is legally married, or has a court order of emancipation or is in the military —has the same status as an adult. This means you will need to treat the applicant like any other adult. In short, if the applicant satisfies the rental criteria that you apply to everyone, a refusal to rent to a minor could form the basis of a fair housing complaint. On the other hand, if the applicant is not emancipated, she lacks the legal capacity to enter into a legally binding rental agreement with you.

## 7. Marital Status

Federal law does not prohibit discrimination on the basis of marital status (oddly, being married isn't included within the federal concept of "familial status"). Consequently in most states you may legally refuse to rent to applicants on the grounds that they are (or are not) married. The issue comes up when a landlord chooses a married couple over a single applicant, or when an unmarried couple applies for a rental (or a current tenant wants to move in a special friend).

Some states have addressed these situations. About 20 states ban discrimination on the basis of marital status, but most of these extend protection to married couples only. In these states, landlords cannot legally prefer single, platonic roommates (or one-person tenancies) over married couples. What about the reverse—preferring married couples over single roommates or a single tenant? Courts in Maryland, Minnesota, New York and Washington have ruled that the term "marital status" only protects single people from being treated differently than married people, and vice versa.

Now then, what about the remaining possibility—an unmarried couple? In only a few states—California, Massachusetts, Michigan and New Jersey—does the term "marital status" refer to unmarried couples. If you own rental property in these four states, can you reject unmarried couples solely because they aren't married? It depends on your reasons. If you refuse to rent to unmarried couples on the grounds that cohabitation violates your religious beliefs and you live in California, Massachusetts or Michigan, the answer is no.

**Unmarried couples may be protected by a city or county ordinance prohibiting discrimination on the basis of sexual orientation.** Although usually passed to protect the housing rights of gay and lesbian tenants, most local laws forbidding discrimination based on sexual orientation also protect unmarried heterosexual couples as well. In addition, unmarried people may be able to challenge a landlord's refusal to rent to them on the basis of sex discrimination, which is covered by the federal Acts.

---

### Where Living Together Is a Crime

In a few states, it's illegal for an unmarried couple to live together. Although these anti-cohabitation laws are rarely enforced, they give legal backing to landlords who want to deny housing to unmarried couples.

| | | |
|---|---|---|
| Arizona | Mississippi | South Carolina |
| Florida | New Mexico | Virginia |
| Idaho | North Carolina | |

Also, Georgia, Rhode Island and Utah still consider fornication to be a crime, so cohabitation is probably illegal in these states, too, unless the couple insists they are roommates, not lovers—something it is very hard for a landlord to prove or disprove.

---

## 8. Sexual Orientation

Federal law doesn't specifically prohibit housing discrimination based on sexual orientation, but several states have such laws, including California, Connecticut, the District of Columbia, Massachusetts, Minnesota, New Jersey, Rhode Island, Vermont and Wisconsin. In addition, many cities prohibit discrimination against gays and lesbians, including Atlanta, Chicago, Detroit, Miami, New York, Pittsburgh, St. Louis and Seattle.

## 9. Source of Income

In a few states, including California, New Jersey and North Dakota, you may not refuse to rent to a person simply because he is receiving public assistance. You may, however, refuse to rent to persons whose available incomes fall below a certain level, as long as you apply that standard across the board. (See Section A1 for advice on choosing tenants on the basis of income.)

## 10. Arbitrary Discrimination

After reading the above material outlining the types of illegal discrimination, you may be tempted to assume that it is legal to discriminate for any reason not mentioned by name in a state or federal law. For example, because none of the civil rights laws specifically prohibits discrimination against men with beards or long hair, you might conclude that such discrimination is permissible. This is not always true.

For example, even though California's Unruh Civil Rights Act (California Civil Code §§ 51-53, 54.1-54.8) contains only the words "sex, race, color, religion, ancestry, or national origin" to describe types of discrimination that are illegal, the courts have ruled that these categories are just examples of illegal discrimination. The courts in California have construed the Unruh Act to forbid all discrimination on the basis of one's personal characteristic or trait.

# Low-Income Tenants

Many tenants with low incomes qualify for federally subsidized housing assistance, the most common being the Section 8 program of the federal Department of Housing and Urban Development (HUD). ("Section 8" refers to Section 8 of the United States Housing Act of 1937, 42 U.S. Code § 1437f.) That program pays part of the rent directly to you. The local housing authority, you and the tenant enter into a one-year agreement, which includes a written lease supplied by the county housing authority. The tenant pays a percentage of his monthly income to you, and the housing authority pays you the difference between the tenant's contribution and what it determines is the market rent each month.

Landlords have traditionally been able to choose not to participate in the Section 8 program without fear of violating the federal fair housing laws. However, as the federal government's ability to provide sufficient housing diminishes, legislators are looking to the private sector to fill the void—and one way to do this is to require landlords to accept Section 8. Your ability to categorically reject Section 8 tenants is being questioned in New Jersey (*Franklin Tower One v. N.M.*, New Jersey Supreme Court No. 45,037) and California (Senate Bill 1730). Landlords in these states should keep informed of developments by checking with local HUD offices.

Section 8 offers several advantages:

- The larger part of the rent is paid on time every month by the housing authority, and the tenant's portion is low enough so that he shouldn't have too much trouble paying on time either.

- If the tenant doesn't pay the rent and you have to evict him, the housing authority guarantees the tenant's unpaid portion, and also guarantees payment for damage to the property by the tenant, up to a certain limit.

Section 8's disadvantages are that:

- The housing authority's determination of what is market rent is often low.

- You are locked into a tenancy agreement for one year, and can't terminate the tenancy except for nonpayment of rent or other serious breach of the lease. (Evictions based on grounds other than nonpayment of rent or other serious breaches are difficult.)

Although you have the right to refuse to rent to Section 8 tenants without violating any antidiscrimination laws, you do not appear to have the liberty of deciding to rent to only a select number of Section 8 tenants. The government has adopted a "take one, take all" policy, which pressures you into accepting every Section 8 applicant once you have accepted one, regardless of your desire to have a mix of Section 8/non-Section 8 tenants.

Call the housing authority in the county where your property is located if you wish to participate in the Section 8 program. They will refer eligible applicants to you and will prepare the necessary documents (including the lease) if you decide to rent to an eligible applicant. Be sure to get a copy from HUD of the Section 8 rules and procedures that all participating landlords must use; often, they vary significantly from your state or local law.

Even if you live in a state that does not specifically outlaw arbitrary discrimination, there is a very strong practical reason why you should not engage in arbitrary discrimination—for example, based an obesity, occupation or style of dress. Because fair housing law includes numerous protected categories —race, sex, religion, etc.—chances are that a disappointed applicant can fit himself or herself into at least one of the protected categories and file a discrimination claim. Even if the applicant does not ultimately win his or her claim, the time, aggravation and expense caused by his attempt will be costly to the landlord.

> **EXAMPLE:** Jane, a lawyer, applied for an apartment and returned her application to Lee, the landlord. Lee had spent the better part of the last year fighting a frivolous lawsuit brought by a former tenant (who was also a lawyer), and the thought of renting to another lawyer was more than Lee could bear. Jane's credit, rental and personal references were excellent, but she was turned away.
>
> One of Lee's tenants told Jane that Lee had refused her solely because she was a lawyer. This made Jane angry and she decided to get even. Although her state did not have a law prohibiting arbitrary discrimination, that didn't stop Jane. She filed a fair housing complaint alleging that she had been turned away because she was single, female and Jewish. The complaint was ultimately dismissed, but not before it had cost Lee a bundle of time and energy to defend.

## D. Valid Occupancy Limits

Your ability to limit the number of people per rental unit is one of the most hotly debated issues in the rental housing industry. Like most controversial topics, it has two sides, each with a valid point. No one disputes the wisdom of enforcing building codes that specify minimum square footage per occupant for reasons of health and safety. But it is another matter altogether when even relatively small families—especially those with children—are excluded from a large segment of the rental market because landlords arbitrarily set unreasonable occupancy policies.

The law allows you to establish an occupancy policy that is truly tied to health and safety needs. In addition, you can adopt standards that are driven by a legitimate business reason or necessity, such as the capacities of your plumbing or electrical systems. (See Section 3.) Your personal preferences (such as an exaggerated desire to reduce wear and tear by limiting the number of occupants, or to ensure a quiet uncrowded environment for upscale older tenants), however, do not constitute a legitimate business reason.

If your occupancy policy limits the number of tenants for any reason other than health, safety and legitimate business needs, you risk charges of discrimination against families, known in legalese as "familial status" discrimination. (Occupancy policies that cross over the line into discrimination towards families are discussed in Section C.)

The federal government has taken the lead in establishing occupancy standards through passage of the Fair Housing Amendments Act and by means of regulations from the Department of Housing and Urban Development (HUD). But states and localities may also set their own occupancy standards, as long as they are no more restrictive than the federal standard. In other words, a city or state can establish an occupancy standard that allows more people per unit than the federal standard, but not fewer. If you violate the federal occupancy law and a rejected tenant complains, you will have to answer to the federal agency that administers the law (HUD) or to a judge in federal or state court. Violations of state occupancy standards will get you into trouble with the state housing authority; and violations of the local law will expose you to liability under the local authority.

## Minimum and Maximum Numbers of Occupants

Two kinds of laws affect your occupancy standards:

- **Minimum occupancy standards.** The federal, state and local occupancy standards discussed in this section establish the minimum number of occupants you must allow in a particular unit. If you set a lower occupancy limit, you may be accused of violating a fair housing law.
- **Maximum occupancy limits.** State and local health and safety codes may set maximum limits on the number of tenants, based purely on the size of the unit and number of bedrooms and bathrooms.

Finding out whether your occupancy policy is legal is not always a simple matter. You must answer three questions for each rental situation:

1. How many people must you allow in that particular unit under the federal standard?
2. How many people must you allow in that unit under the state standard?
3. How many people must you allow in that unit under the local standard?

Once you know the answers to each of these questions, the rest is easy: To avoid a federal, state or local fair housing complaint, simply apply the occupancy standard that is the least restrictive—that is, the one that allows the most people. If you don't follow the least restrictive standard, be prepared to show that your policy (allowing fewer people) is motivated by reasons of health or safety or a legitimate business reason.

Unfortunately, getting the answers to the three questions is often difficult. This section will attempt to methodically guide you through the process by explaining:

- federal occupancy standards (Section D1)
- common state occupancy standards and local laws on the subject (Section D2)
- how to calculate the number of occupants that must be allowed for each rental unit (Section D3), and
- "legitimate business reasons" that might support a more restrictive policy than the law allows (Section D3).

## 1. The Federal Occupancy Standard

Federal law allows you to establish "reasonable" restrictions on the number of persons per dwelling. These restrictions must be motivated by legitimate business reasons or the need to preserve the health and safety of the occupants.

The Department of Housing and Urban Development, or HUD, interprets federal law by means of memos, guidelines and regulations. Unfortunately, HUD has never been very helpful when it comes to explaining what a "reasonable" restriction on persons per dwelling might be. HUD has simply said that a policy of two persons per bedroom will, as a general rule, be considered reasonable, but that other factors will also be considered when determining whether a landlord was illegally discriminating by limiting the number of people in a rental unit. Because the number of bedrooms is not the only factor, the federal test has become known as the "two-per-bedroom-plus" standard. These other factors include:

- the size of the bedrooms and rental unit—if the unit or the bedrooms are small, you may take that into account
- age of the children—babies do not have the same space requirements as teenagers, and you may take that into account
- configuration of the rental unit—if a room could serve as a bedroom, but there is no access to a bathroom except through another bedroom, you might be able to designate that room a "non-bedroom" and limit the number of occupants accordingly
- physical limitations of the building—for example, limitation of the sewerage or electrical system

- state and local building codes that impose their own set of minimum space requirements per occupant, and
- prior discrimination complaints against the landlord—if you must respond to a fair housing complaint, you will be at a disadvantage if you are known to repeatedly violate antidiscrimination laws.

The flexibility of the federal standard helps landlords because it lets them take into account all the particulars of a given situation. But it also means that you cannot set an occupancy limit for a unit and know for certain that it will pass the federal test. The legal occupancy maximum cannot be determined until you analyze every applicant. For example, if you decide that the family with a newborn needs less space than one with a teenager, the occupancy limit for the same unit will be different for each family.

As you might imagine, a federal "standard" that changes according to the make-up of every applicant has proven very difficult and confusing to apply. HUD once discarded the test for a few months, but now the standard is definitely in place, and you must do your best to apply it conscientiously.

Begin by multiplying the number of bedrooms times two, and then think about the factors listed above. For example, is one of the bedrooms so small as to be unsuitable for two people? On the other hand, could a room that you might think of as a den be usable as another bedroom? Could a couple with a baby in a bassinet comfortably occupy a bedroom that would be unsuitable for three adults? As you can see, use of the two-per-bedroom-plus standard may result in an occupancy limit that might be below or above twice the number of bedrooms.

EXAMPLE: Murray owned a large, old house that had been remodeled into two apartments. The upstairs unit had large rooms, two bedrooms and two bathrooms. The lower apartment was considerably smaller, with one bedroom and one bath.

*The Upstairs.* Murray was approached by a family of five—three young children and two adults. He realized that the large bedroom could safely sleep three children, so he figured that the five people in this family came within the federal standards.

*The Downstairs.* The first applicants for the lower apartment were three adults. Murray told them that the occupancy limit was two. Later, a couple with a newborn applied for the apartment. Realizing that a bassinet could easily fit into the bedroom, Murray adjusted his occupancy limit and rented to the couple.

## 2. Common State and Local Occupancy Standards

Even if you are okay under the federal standard, you can't relax just yet. Remember, states and localities can set their own occupancy standards, as long as they are more generous than the federal government. You must comply with any state or local standard or (if a complaint is filed) risk prosecution by the state or local agency that administers the standard.

First, obviously you need to see whether any state or local standard applies to you. Check with your local and state housing authority for information. (See Chapter 9 for advice on finding state and local housing agencies, or call the U.S. Department of Housing and Urban Development (HUD) office. Section B of this chapter includes a list of HUD offices.)

For many of you, we can help a little with the task of finding and understanding your state or local occupancy law. Thirty-two states have adopted all or part of the "two-per-bedroom plus" standard, either by statute or by decisions of their housing authorities. (See the chart below and check your state and local laws for exact requirements.) States that are not listed in the chart either do not have any statewide laws or have laws more generous than the HUD standard.

**Remember, you must apply the most generous standard—federal, state or local—in determining how many people may occupy a particular rental unit.** If you are unsure of the result, it is always safer to err on the side of more, rather than fewer, occupants.

### States That Have Adopted All or Part of the Federal "Two-per-Bedroom-Plus" Standard

| | | |
|---|---|---|
| Arizona (in statute)[1] | Kentucky[1] | Pennsylvania |
| California[2] | Louisiana | Rhode Island |
| Colorado[1] | Maryland | South Carolina[1] |
| Delaware | Massachusetts | Tennessee |
| Florida[1] | Missouri[1] | Texas (in statute)[5] |
| Georgia[1] | New Mexico[3] | Utah |
| Hawaii | New York[3] | Virginia |
| Illinois | Ohio | West Virginia |
| Indiana | Oklahoma[4] | Wisconsin[3] |
| Iowa[1] | Oregon[3] | Wyoming[3] |
| Kansas[1] | | |

[1] Some cities or counties in these states have ordinances also.

[2] California has a state guideline of "two per bedroom and one more occupant" (who need not be a child). Localities can have ordinances also.

[3] New Mexico, New York, Oregon, Wisconsin and Wyoming have a standard that is roughly "two per bedroom," but these states did not copy the rest of the federal standard (involving age of unit, age of children and so on, discussed below in Section 3). New York City may fashion its own laws.

[4] The Oklahoma statute does not count children born to the tenants during the term of the lease.

[5] The Texas statute specifies a maximum occupancy of three persons per bedroom to prevent overcrowding, but the state uses a minimum standard of two per bedroom plus a child under the age of six months to evaluate fair housing discrimination complaints.

## 3. Legitimate Reasons for a More Restrictive Occupancy Policy

What if you decide that your particular rental unit ought to be occupied by fewer than the most generous number you got when you calculated the occupancy under the federal, state and local laws? If you set an occupancy limit that is lower than the legal standard, you must be prepared to defend it with a legitimate business reason. This term is impossible to describe in the abstract, since its meaning will vary with the circumstances of every rental property. Here are some examples of legitimate business reasons that have been advanced by landlords who have established occupancy limits lower than the government standard.

- **Limitations of the infrastructure.** The plumbing or electrical systems cannot accommodate more than a certain amount of use.
- **Limitations of the facilities.** Common areas and facilities (such as laundry rooms and hallways) would be overcrowded if more occupants were allowed.
- **Dilapidation that common sense tells you would result from more people living in the structure.** (*Pfaff v. U.S. Department of Housing and Urban Development,* 88 F.3d 739 (1996).)

If your occupancy policy is lower than the most generous applicable legal standard, be prepared for an uphill fight. It is very difficult to establish a "winning" legitimate business reason that justifies a lower occupancy standard. You will need to carefully assess whether it's worth your time and money to fight the complaint. (Section F, below, describes the complaint process.) In order to establish that your lower occupancy policy is based upon legitimate business reasons and is therefore legal, you'll need to convince a fair housing judge that:

- changing the limiting factor (such as rewiring the rental unit's electrical system to accommodate more use) is impractical from a business perspective, or

- common sense, your business experience and the practice of landlords in your area support your lower number, and
- limiting the number of occupants is the only practical way to address the limiting factor.

Here are some examples of situations in which landlords have argued that their occupancy policy, which was lower than that allowed by the most generous applicable law, should nonetheless survive a fair housing challenge. In both cases, the landlord argued that the limitations of the septic system justified a more restrictive occupancy standard. In the first example, the landlord prevailed. In the second example, the landlord failed to establish that his occupancy policy was based upon legitimate business reasons.

EXAMPLE 1: John and Mary Evans advertised the small two-bedroom cottage on their property as suitable for two people only. Their occupancy limit was based on the limitations of the septic system, which could legally accommodate no more than four people (the Evanses and two tenants in the cottage). John and Mary declined to rent to a family of four, who then filed a fair housing complaint. At the conciliation meeting arranged by the housing authority, John and Mary presented an engineer's report on the limitations of the septic system. The report estimated that it would cost many thousands of dollars to expand the septic system to accommodate more than four people on the property. The hearing officer accepted the Evanses' explanation and decided not to take the complaint further.

EXAMPLE 2: The occupancy policy for all the units at Westside Terrace was three persons per apartment, even for the two-bedroom units. A family of four applied for one of the two-bedrooms and was turned down. When the family filed a complaint with HUD, the owner of Westside Terrace justified the policy on the grounds that the building's infrastructure—its sewage capacities, pipes and common areas—

could not support as many people as would result from allowing four persons in the two-bedroom apartment units. Westside also presented evidence that it would be prohibitively expensive to upgrade these facilities. The judge heard evidence from structural and sanitary engineers which indicated that these facilities were capable of handling that number of people and had done so many times in the past. HUD decided that Westside's restrictive occupancy policy was not based on legitimate business needs, and ruled against it.

## E. Managers and Discrimination

If you hire a manager, particularly one who selects tenants, make certain that he fully understands and abides by laws against housing discrimination. Even an innocent owner whose agent or manager discriminates without the owner's knowledge, or who sexually harasses a tenant, can be sued and found liable. On the other hand, if you use an independent management company (which is a true independent contractor, rather than an employee such as a resident manager), the possibility that you will be liable for their discriminatory acts is greatly decreased. (See Chapter 6 on landlord liability for a manager's conduct and strategies for avoiding problems in this area.)

You should always let your tenants know that you, as well as your manager, intend to abide by the law, and that you want to know about and will address any fair housing problems that may arise. While this will not shield you from liability if you are sued due to your manager's conduct, it might (if you are lucky) result in the tenant's initial complaint being made to you, not a fair housing agency. If you hear about a manager's discriminatory act and can resolve a complaint before it gets into "official channels," you will have saved yourself a lot of time, trouble and money.

One way to alert your tenants and prospective tenants to your commitment to the fair housing laws is to write all ads, applications and other material given to prospective tenants to include a section containing your antidiscrimination stance. Prepare a written policy statement as to the law and your intention to abide by it. Post this statement in the manager's office or somewhere on the premises and give a copy to all prospective tenants. See the following sample statement.

### Sample Statement on Equal Opportunity in Housing

FROM: Shady Dell Apartments

TO: All Tenants and Applicants

It is the policy of the owner and manager of Shady Dell Apartments to rent our units without regard to a tenant's race, ethnic background, sex, age, religion, marital or family status, physical disability or sexual orientation. As part of our commitment to provide equal opportunity in housing, we comply with all federal, state and local laws prohibiting discrimination. If you have any questions or complaints regarding our rental policy, call the owner at (phone number).

If, despite your best efforts, you even suspect your manager may use unlawful discriminatory practices to select or deal with tenants—whether on purpose or inadvertently—you should immediately resume control of the situation yourself. Alternatively, this may be the time to shield yourself from potential liability and engage the services of an independent management company, who in most cases will be responsible for its employees' actions.

⚠ **Never give managers or rental agents the authority to offer their own rent concessions or "deals" to selected tenants or applicants.** If you want to offer inducements—a discount for signing an extended lease or one free month for tenants who begin renting in the month of March—do so on a consistent basis. Make sure offers are available to all tenants who meet the requirements of the special deal. Otherwise, a tenant who gets a worse deal from your manager than his identically-situated neighbor is sure to complain—and if he is a member of a group protected by fair housing laws, he's got the makings of a case against you.

## F. Unlawful Discrimination Complaints

A landlord accused of unlawfully discriminating against a prospective or current tenant may end up before a state or federal housing agency, or in state or federal court. Here's a brief description of the legal process involved in each arena and the consequences of discrimination charges.

**Get expert help to defend a housing discrimination lawsuit.** With the exception of a suit brought in small claims court, you should see an attorney if a tenant sues you or files an administrative complaint against you for discrimination. For more information on small claims courts, see *Everybody's Guide to Small Claims Court* (National Edition), by Ralph Warner (Nolo Press). For advice on finding and working with an attorney or doing your own legal research, see Chapter 18.

### 1. When a Tenant Complains to a Fair Housing Agency

A prospective or current tenant may file a discrimination complaint with either HUD or the state or local agency charged with overseeing fair housing complaints. A federal HUD complaint must be filed within one year of the alleged violation, but state statutes may set shorter time periods. If the complaint is filed with HUD, the agency should (but doesn't always) conduct an investigation within 180 days. (Time periods for state housing agencies vary.)

After HUD investigates the complaint (and this is true of most state agencies as well), it will either dismiss the complaint or attempt to reach a conciliation agreement (compromise) between you and the person filing the complaint. For example, a tenant might agree to drop his complaint in exchange for a sum of money or your written promise to rent him an apartment, or, if he's a current tenant, to stop discriminatory practices.

If conciliation is unsuccessful, the fair housing agency will hold an administrative hearing (a trial before a judge but without a jury) to determine whether discrimination has occurred. If the administrative law judge decides that a fair housing violation occurred, he or she will direct that the violation be corrected in the ways described below in Section F3.

HUD litigation is typically long and laborious. It is not unusual for cases to take up to ten years before they are concluded.

### 2. When a Tenant Sues in Federal or State Court

A tenant may also file suit in federal court or state court. This can be done even after filing an administrative complaint (as long as he has not signed a conciliation agreement or a HUD administrative hearing has not started). If the tenant goes to federal court, he must do so within two years of the alleged violation.

In a typical federal lawsuit, the aggrieved tenant (or would-be tenant) has gone to a private lawyer immediately after the alleged discriminatory incident. The attorney prepares a complaint and also asks the court for an expedited hearing, hoping to get an order from the court directing the landlord to cease the discriminatory practice. These orders are called "temporary restraining orders," and they are granted if the plaintiff (the tenant) can convince the judge that he has a good chance of winning and will suffer irreparable harm if immediate relief isn't granted. The order remains in place until a more formal hearing is held. Open-and-shut cases of discrimination often settle at the temporary restraining order stage.

### 3. Penalties for Discrimination

If a state or federal court or housing agency finds that discrimination has taken place, it may order you to:

- rent a particular unit to the person who was discriminated against
- pay the tenant for "actual" or "compensating" damages, including any additional rent the tenant had to pay elsewhere as a result of being turned down, and damages for humiliation or emotional distress
- pay the tenant punitive damages (extra money as punishment for especially outrageous discrimination) and the tenant's attorney fees
- in the case of a disability violation, retrofit your property or set up an escrow fund to be used for retrofitting in the future
- pay a civil penalty to the federal government. The maximum penalty under the federal Fair Housing Acts is $11,000 for a first violation and $55,000 for a third violation within seven years. Many states have comparable penalties.

Even if you are ultimately vindicated, the costs of defending a discrimination claim can be devastating. Your insurance policy may cover the dollar costs, but it cannot compensate you for lost time and aggravation. Careful attention to the discrimination rules described in this chapter and Chapter 1 will, we hope, save you from this fate.

⚠ **If you are the subject of a fair housing complaint, do not take the matter "into your own hands."** It is illegal to retaliate against, threaten, coerce, intimidate or interfere with anyone who either files a complaint with HUD, cooperates in the investigation of such a complaint or exercises a fair housing right.

## G. Insurance Coverage in Discrimination Claims

If you find yourself the subject of a fair housing claim, will your insurance policy cover the cost of defending the claim and, if you lose, the cost of the settlement or judgment? The answers to these questions depend entirely on two highly variable factors: the wording of your insurance policy and the decisions of the courts in your state in similar cases. In short, there are no answers that will apply to everyone, but we can alert you to the issues that arise in every situation. At the very least, knowing how insurance companies are likely to approve or deny defense and judgment costs in discrimination claims should help you as you evaluate your own policy.

Chapter 10 discusses broad types of liability insurance, coverage for managers and other employees and coverage for injuries suffered as a result of defective conditions on the property.

Most owners of residential rental property carry a comprehensive liability insurance policy, which typically includes business liability coverage. With this type of coverage, the insurance company agrees to pay on your behalf all sums that you are legally obligated to pay as damages "for bodily injury, property damage or personal injury caused by an occurrence to which this insurance applies." The policy will generally define the three key terms "bodily injury," "occurrence" and "personal injury." The definitions will determine whether the insurance company will help you with a discrimination claim.

⚠ **Find out if your policy covers administrative claims (complaints to fair housing agencies such as HUD).** Insurance companies in Colorado, Delaware, Illinois, Louisiana, Wisconsin and elsewhere have successfully argued that their duties to defend and cover you extend only to lawsuits, not agency claims. Ask your agent.

**The Insurance Company's Duty to Defend: Broader Than the Duty to Cover**

When you purchase liability insurance, you buy two things: the promise of the insurance company to defend you if you are sued for an act that arguably falls within the coverage of the policy, and its promise to pay the settlement or damage award if you lose. But sometimes (as is the case in fair housing claims) it is unclear whether, assuming you lose the case, your policy covers the conduct that gave rise to the claim. When this happens, your insurance company will usually defend you, but it may reserve the right to argue about whether it is obligated to pay the damages if the case is lost.

## 1. Definition of "Bodily Injury"

Discrimination complaints rarely include a claim that the victim suffered a physical injury at the hands of the landlord or manager. It is far more likely that the tenant or applicant will sue for the emotional distress caused by the humiliation of the discriminatory act.

"Bodily injury" does not usually include emotional distress. Courts in a few states, however, including New Jersey, Louisiana and Maryland, have held that bodily injury does include emotional distress. If your state does not include emotional distress in the concept of bodily injury, an insurance company may be able to successfully argue that a discrimination complaint is not covered by the policy.

## 2. Definition of "Personal Injury"

Insurance policies also typically provide coverage for "personal injury," or an injury that arises out of the conduct of your business. Personal injuries typi-

cally include false arrest, libel, slander and violation of privacy rights; they also include "wrongful entry or eviction or other invasions of the right of private occupancy." As you can see from this definition, personal injuries include items that are neither bodily injuries nor accidental. And the definition includes some offenses, like libel, that seem somewhat similar to discrimination.

Nevertheless, an insurance company may argue that a discrimination claim isn't covered under a policy's definition of "personal injury."

Very few courts have addressed this question, let alone answered it, but of those that have, the answers have been quite mixed. For example, coverage has been denied on the grounds that "discrimination" is a specific wrong and, had the insurance company intended to cover discrimination, it would have specifically mentioned it. Coverage for discrimination claims by prospective tenants (such as applicants who have been turned away) has been denied on the theory that "the right of private occupancy" is a right enjoyed only by current, not would-be, tenants. Still other courts, realizing that the language in the policy is far from clear, have been willing to resolve the question in favor of the insured, and have ordered the insurance company to at least defend the lawsuit.

In sum, there are at least three ways that insurance companies can deny coverage, if not also the defense of a fair housing claim and award: They can claim that the discriminatory act resulted in emotional distress, which is not a type of bodily injury; they can argue that an act of discrimination was intentional, and thus not an accidental occurrence to which the policy applies; and they can argue that discrimination is not one of the personal injuries that are covered by the policy. We suggest that you give the matter some thought when choosing a broker and negotiating your policy; but by far the best use of your energy is to make sure that your business practices do not expose you to these claims in the first place.

## Discrimination and Public Policy

An insurance company will occasionally argue that it should not have to cover a landlord's intentional acts of discrimination because discrimination is an evil act that someone should not be able to insure against. While this argument has some persuasive aspects—discrimination is, indeed, contrary to public policy—it falls apart when you acknowledge that all sorts of other intentional bad acts (like libel and slander) are perfectly insurable. Courts have not been persuaded by the "public policy" argument.

## 3. Definition of "Occurrence"

Your insurance company will defend and pay out on a claim if it is caused by an occurrence to which the policy applies. An "occurrence" is typically defined as an accident, whose results are neither expected nor intended from the standpoint of the insured (the property owner).

It doesn't take much brainwork to see how an insurance company can argue that an act of discrimination—like turning away a minority applicant—cannot be considered an "occurrence" because it is by definition intentional, not accidental. Courts in Louisiana, Oregon and South Dakota have ruled in favor of insurance companies on this issue, and courts in other states have ruled similarly when the question has come up in employment discrimination cases.

## Insurance Coverage You Can Count On

Insurance companies have, predictably, denied that general business liability policies cover discrimination and sexual harassment claims. But all the major insurers now offer separate policies that cover discrimination and harassment claims.

These "Employment Related Practices" policies are quite expensive, especially in California and Texas (where most claims are filed). You can, however, get a significantly lower rate if you show the company that you have taken steps to reduce the risk that you will be sued—such as instituting an affirmative action program, employing a human resources advisor or preparing and abiding by a fair housing employee handbook.

Another less expensive route is to buy defense coverage only. That covers the cost of hiring a lawyer to defend you against a fair housing claim, but doesn't pay the cost of any settlement you make or a jury award against you. Ask your broker for details.

■

Chapter **6**

# Property Managers

Many landlords hire a resident manager to handle all the day-to-day details of running an apartment building, including fielding tenants' routine repair requests and collecting the rent. Landlords who own several rental properties (large or small) may contract with a property management firm in addition to, or in place of, a resident manager. Hiring a manager can free you from many of the time-consuming (and tiresome) aspects of being a residential landlord. But it can also create some headaches of its own: lots of paperwork for the IRS, worries about liability for a manager's acts, and the responsibility of finding, hiring and supervising an employee. This chapter explains how to weigh all these factors and how to minimize complications if you do decide to get some management help.

In some states, you may not have a choice—you may be required, by law, to hire a manager. California, for example, requires a resident manager on the premises of any apartment complex with sixteen or more units. (Cal. Code of Regulations, Title 25, § 42.) Check with your state or local rental property owners' association to see if your state requires resident managers, or do your own research on the subject. (Chapter 18 shows how to do legal research.)

*The Employer's Legal Handbook,* by Fred S. Steingold (Nolo Press), is a complete guide to the latest workplace laws and regulations. It covers everything you need to know about hiring and firing employees, personnel policies, employee benefits, discrimination and other laws affecting small business practices.

## A. Hiring Your Own Resident Manager

If you put some thought into writing a job description, and some effort into recruiting and hiring a good manager, you'll avoid problems down the road. Don't hurry the process, or jump into an informal arrangement with a tenant who offers to help

out if you'll take a little off the rent—you'll almost surely regret it.

### 1. Decide the Manager's Duties, Hours and Pay

Why do you want to hire a manager? You need to answer this question in some detail as your first step in the hiring process. Here are the key issues you need to decide:

**What are the manager's responsibilities?** The Property Manager Agreement (Section B, below) includes a list of duties you may want to delegate, such as selecting tenants, collecting rents and hiring and paying repair people. Finding an on-site manager who can handle all these aspects of the job, however, is a tall order—so tall that many owners restrict the on-site manager's job to handling routine repairs and maintenance chores. Listing the job duties and skills you're looking for in a manager will make the hiring process more objective and will give you ready standards to measure which applicants are most qualified.

**Is the job full- or part-time?** How many hours do you anticipate the manager working? What hours do you expect the manager to be on the rental property or available (for example, by beeper)?

**Will the manager live on the rental property or out?** If you just want someone to collect the rent and handle minor repairs, they don't necessarily need to live in. Obviously, you need a vacant apartment for a resident manager.

**How much do you plan to pay the manager?** You may pay an hourly wage, generally ranging from $10 to $20 per hour, or a flat salary with hourly additions for special tasks such as yard work. How much you pay depends on the manager's responsibilities, the number of hours, time of day and regularity of the schedule, benefits and the going rate in your community. You can get an idea how much managers are paid by asking other landlords or checking want ads for managers. (See Section C5, below, for guidance on minimum wage requirements.) Offering slightly above the going rate in your area should allow you to hire the best, most experienced candidates. If you do this, you might want to try and tap into the local grapevine of experienced managers to see if maybe you can snag someone who wants to move up.

**Should you give the manager reduced rent?** Some landlords prefer giving a resident manager reduced rent in exchange for management services, rather than paying a separate salary. This isn't a good idea—for one thing, reduced rent alone won't work for a full-time manager. Reduced rent in exchange for being a manager can be a particular problem in rent control areas, since you may not be able to adjust rent easily. If you later have to fire a manager who is compensated by reduced rent, you may run into problems when you insist that the ex-manager go back to paying the full rent. But if the tenant-manager pays the full rent and receives a separate salary, there will be no question that he is still obligated to pay the full rent, as he has done all along. (See Sections G and H for advice on firing or evicting a manager.)

Your obligations as an employer are the same whether you compensate the manager with reduced rent or a paycheck—for example, you must still pay Social Security and payroll taxes as discussed in Section C. Also, it can be confusing under wages and hours and overtime laws.

## Illegal Discrimination in Hiring

Federal, state and local laws prohibit many kinds of discrimination in hiring. The federal laws, Title VII of the Civil Rights Act and the Americans with Disabilities Act, apply only if you employ 15 or more people; many state laws kick in if you have just five employees.

Pay attention to these laws even if they do not specifically bind your business. Doing so will not hinder you from making a decision based on sound business reasons—skills, experience, references. The laws only forbid making a decision based on a factor that isn't reasonably related to the applicant's ability to do the job. Following them will protect you from accusations of discrimination.

Here are some of the factors on which these laws make it illegal to discriminate: race, color, gender, religious beliefs, national origin, age (if the person is 40 or older) and disability. Several states and cities also prohibit discrimination based on marital status or sexual orientation.

Much of the advice in Chapter 5, which deals with illegal discrimination against tenants, will also be of help when you're hiring a manager.

➡️ If you already know someone, such as a current tenant, who you think will be perfect for the manager's job, skip ahead to Section 5.

## 2. Advertise the Job

Next, determine the best way to advertise the position. Some landlords find great managers via word-of-mouth by talking to tenants, friends and relatives. Others run a newspaper ad, use an employment agency or advertise online. What will work best depends on your particular property and needs. In writing an ad, stick to the job skills needed and the basic responsibilities—for example, "Fifty-unit apartment complex seeks full-time resident manager with experience in selecting tenants, collecting rent and apartment maintenance."

If you do advertise, it's usually best to have interested applicants call for information, rather than come in for an interview without prior screening.

## 3. Screen Potential Managers Over the Phone

When people call about the manager's job, be ready to describe the responsibilities, pay and hours. Then ask some questions yourself—you'll be able to quickly eliminate unlikely candidates and avoid wasting time interviewing inappropriate people. Use the phone call to get information on potential employees, including their:

- experience and qualifications
- interest in the position and type of work
- current employment, and
- ability to work at the proposed pay and schedule.

Jot notes of your conversation.

## 4. Interview Strong Candidates

Limit your interviews to people you're really interested in hiring as manager. There's no point meeting with someone who's unqualified or unsuitable for the job. When setting interviews, ask potential managers to bring a resume with relevant experience and names and phone numbers of four or five references.

A face-to-face meeting provides the opportunity to get in-depth information about a person's background, work experience and ability to handle the manager's job, and allows you to assess an individual's personality and style.

Before you begin interviewing, write down questions focusing on the job duties and the applicant's skills and experience. To avoid potential charges of discrimination, ask everyone the same questions and don't ask questions that are not clearly job-related—for example, the applicant's medical condition, religion or plans for having children.

Here are some examples of questions that are appropriate to ask potential managers:

- "Tell me about your previous jobs managing rental properties."
- "How much experience do you have collecting rents? Doing general repairs? Keeping records of tenants' complaints of repair problems?"
- "What have you liked most about previous manager jobs? What have you liked least?"
- "What kinds of problems have you encountered as a property manager? How did you solve them?"
- "Why do you want this job?"

You might also ask some more direct questions, like:

- "What would you do if a tenant who had paid rent on time for six months asked for a ten-day extension because money was short as a result of a family problem?"
- "What would you do if a tenant called you at 11 p.m. with a complaint about a clogged sink?"

## Character Traits of a Good Manager

Look for a person who is:

- **Honest and responsible.** This is specially important if the manager will be entitled to receive legal documents and papers on your behalf (see Section F).
- **Patient.** Predictably, dealing with tenants, repair people and guests will have its share of hassles. A person with a short fuse is a definite liability.
- **Financially responsible.** This should be demonstrated by a good credit history.
- **Personable yet professional.** Good communication skills are a must, both with you and your current and prospective tenants and any other workers the manager may supervise (for example, a cleaning crew).
- **Fastidious about keeping the building and common areas neat, clean and secure.**
- **Meticulous about maintaining records.** This is particularly important if collecting rent will be part of the job.
- **Fair and free of biases.** This is a must if the manager will be showing apartments, taking rental applications or selecting tenants.
- **Unafraid of minor confrontations with tenants.** This is particularly important if the manager will be collecting overdue rents and delivering eviction notices, and handling disputes between tenants (for example, complaints over noise).

**Don't offer the job yet.** Even if an applicant seems perfect, hold off on making an offer. You'll need at least to review his or her application and check references. These issues are covered in Steps 6, 7 and 8, below.

## 5. Get a Completed Application

If your manager will also be a tenant, make sure he or she (like all other tenants) completes a rental application (as discussed in Chapter 1) and that you check references and other information carefully. Be sure the applicant signs a form authorizing you to check credit history and references. This can be either part of the application form itself or a separate document.

If your manager is not also a tenant, prepare your own application (you can use the Rental Application in Chapter 1 and cross out what's not relevant) or ask prospective managers to bring a resume with their employment and educational background.

**When you check a prospective manager's application or resume, be sure to look for holes—dates when the person didn't indicate an employer.** The applicant may be covering up a bad reference. Insist that the applicant explain any gaps in employment history.

## 6. Check References

No matter how wonderful someone appears in person or on paper, it's essential to contact former employers. Ideally, you should talk with at least two former employers or supervisors with whom the applicant held similar positions.

Before calling any references, make a list of key questions. Ask about the applicant's previous job responsibilities, character and personality traits, strengths and weaknesses and reasons for leaving the job. Review your interview notes for issues you want to explore more—for example, if you sense that the potential manager really doesn't seem organized enough to handle all the details of the manager's job, ask about it. Take your time and get all the information you need to determine whether the applicant is the best person for the job.

Employers are often reluctant to say anything negative about a former employee for fear of being hit by a lawsuit for defamation. Many may refuse to give any information other than the dates the person worked and the position held. It may be helpful to send the former employer a copy of the applicant's signed consent to disclosure of employment information. If a former employer is not forthcoming, you'll need to learn to read between the lines. (See the form in Chapter 1.) If a former employer is neutral, offers only faint praise or over-praises a person for one aspect of a job only— "always on time"—he may be hiding negative information. Ask former employers: "Would you hire this person back if you could?" The response may be telling. If a reference isn't glowing and doesn't cover all aspects of the job, check several other references—or hire someone else.

## 7. Check Credit History and Background

Checking an individual's credit history is especially important if you want a manager to handle money. Someone with large debts may be especially tempted to skim money from your business. And a prospective manager with sloppy personal finances is probably not a good choice for managing rental property. Before you order a credit report, be sure you get the applicant's consent.

You may also wish to ask a credit bureau to do a background report. Investigators will talk to friends, neighbors and employers and get information about the applicant's character, reputation and lifestyle. A report like this is considered an "investigative consumer report" under the Fair Credit Reporting Act, 15 U.S. Code §§ 1681 and following. If you decide to order a background report, you must:

- inform the applicant, in writing, within three days of your requesting the report
- include a statement of the applicant's right to make a written request—to you or the credit agency—for a description of the nature and scope of the investigation you have requested, and
- provide that description within five days of receiving the applicant's request.

## 8. Check Criminal and Driving Records

A property manager occupies a position of trust, often having access to tenants' apartments as well as to your money. Obviously, it's essential that the manager not present a danger to tenants. You may want to check an applicant's criminal history; credit reports often include this information. Another consideration is your personal liability—if a manager commits a crime, you may be held responsible. (See Chapter 12.)

Our best advice is check carefully and consider the type, seriousness and dates of any prior convictions and how they relate to the job. Nolo's *The Employer's Legal Handbook* includes information on state laws on obtaining and using information on arrest and conviction records when making employment decisions.

If a manager will be driving your car or truck, be sure your insurance covers someone driving your vehicle as part of their employment. (Chapter 10 covers insurance.)

### Drug Tests and Managers

You have a legal right to fire a manager or reject an applicant who uses, possesses or distributes illegal drugs. However, testing to weed out drug users may conflict with workers' rights to privacy. The laws on drug testing vary widely from state to state and are changing quickly as legislators and judges struggle to strike a balance between workers' rights and the legitimate needs of business.

For more information on drug tests, see *The Employer's Legal Handbook,* by Fred S. Steingold (Nolo Press). For information on how to set up a drug testing program, contact the Institute for a Drug-Free Workplace at 202-842-7400.

## 9. Offer the Position and Put Your Agreement in Writing

Once you make your decision and offer someone the manager's job, you may need to do some negotiations. The potential employee may, for example, want a higher salary, different hours, more vacation, a different rental unit or a later starting date than you offer. It may take some compromises to establish mutually agreeable work arrangements. When all terms and conditions of employment are mutually agreed upon, you and the manager should complete a Property Manager Agreement (discussed in Section B).

We recommend that when you hire a tenant as a manager, you sign two separate agreements:

- An employment agreement that covers manager responsibilities, hours and pay that can be terminated at any time for any reason by either party. See Section B, below.
- A month-to-month rental agreement that can be terminated by either of you with the amount of written notice, typically 30 days, required under state law.

### How to Reject Applicants

It used to be a matter of simple courtesy to inform unsuccessful applicants that you'd hired someone else for the job. Sending a quick but civil rejection letter cut down on post-interview calls, too. You didn't owe them an explanation, however, and were usually better off saying as little as possible.

Is this approach still legal? It depends on why you have rejected the applicant. If your reasons come from information that the applicant himself has provided, or if the applicant simply doesn't have the qualifications for the job, you can still use the courteous-but-minimalist approach. For example, if the applicant tells you that she has never managed real estate property (but experience is one of your job criteria), or if the interview reveals that the applicant obviously doesn't have the "people skills" the position requires, you can (if you wish) simply say that you have chosen someone more qualified for the job.

However, if your rejection is based on information in a credit report, you must comply with new federal requirements. Under amendments to the Fair Credit Reporting Act, 15 U.S. Code §§ 1681 and following, effective September 30, 1997, your rejection letter must include:

- the name, address and phone number of the credit bureau you used
- a statement that the credit bureau did not make the rejection decision and cannot provide the reasons for the rejection
- a statement of the applicant's right to obtain a free copy of the report from the credit bureau if he requests it within 60 days of your rejection, and
- a statement telling the applicant that he can dispute the accuracy of the report as provided by Section 1681 of the Act (he can demand a reinvestigation and the insertion of a statement of dispute).

## Why Do You Need a Written Agreement?

Landlords and resident managers often agree orally on the manager's responsibilities and compensation, never signing a written agreement.

Even though oral agreements are usually legal and binding, they are not advisable. Memories fade, and you and your employee may have different recollections of what you've agreed to. If a dispute arises between you and the manager, the exact terms of an oral agreement are difficult or impossible to prove if you end up arguing about them in court. It is a far better business practice to put your understanding in writing.

**Don't promise long-term job security.** When you hire someone, don't give assurances that you may not be able to honor and that may give an applicant a false sense of security. Your best protection is to make sure your Property Manager Agreement emphasizes your right to fire an employee at will—and have the applicant acknowledge this in writing. (See Clause 6 of the agreement in Section B, below.) This means you'll have the right to terminate the employment at any time for any reason that doesn't violate the law. (See Section G for information on how to fire a manager.)

## B. How to Prepare a Property Manager Agreement

Below is an example of a sound written agreement that spells out the manager's responsibilities, hourly wage or salary, hours, schedule and other terms. The step-by-step instructions that follow take you through the process of completing your own agreement.

The Legal Forms Disk includes a copy of the Property Manager Agreement which you can modify to fit your exact needs. Appendix II includes a blank tear-out form.

### 1. Parties

Here, you provide details about you and the manager and the location of the rental property, and state that the rental agreement is a separate document.

### 2. Beginning Date

Fill in the month, day and year of the manager's first day of work.

### 3. Responsibilities

This form includes a broad checklist of managerial duties, such as rent collection, maintenance and repair. Check all the boxes that apply to your situation. In the space provided, spell out what is required, with as much detail as possible, particularly regarding maintenance responsibilities. (Read Chapter 9 for details on your repair and maintenance responsibilities.)

To make sure your manager doesn't act illegally on the job, also prepare a more detailed set of instructions to give to the manager when he or she starts work. We show you how in Section E, below.

### 4. Hours and Schedule

Before filling this section in, check with your state department of labor or employment for wage and hour laws that may affect the number of hours you can schedule a manager to work in a day or days in a week. Don't expect a manager to be on call 24 hours a day. In most circumstances, you must pay overtime after 40 hours per week. (Section C5, below, covers overtime.)

### 5. Payment Terms

Here you state how much and when you pay your manager. Specify the interval and dates on which you will pay the manager. For example, if the payment is weekly, specify the day. If payment is once each month, state the date, such as "the first of the month." If the payment is twice each month, indicate the dates, such as *"the 15th and the 30th, or the last previous weekday if either date falls on a weekend."*

---

### Should You Pay Benefits?

No law requires you to pay a manager for vacations, holiday and sick pay, premium pay for weekend or holiday work (unless it's for overtime) or fringe benefits such as health insurance. You may, however, want to provide your manager with some extras, if you can afford to do so.

---

## 6. Ending the Manager's Employment

This clause gives you the right to fire a manager any time for any legal reason. It makes clear that you are not guaranteeing a year's, or even a month's, employment to your new hire. You can legally fire your manager any time for any or no reason—as long as it's not for an illegal reason. (See Section G.)

## 7. Additional Agreements and Amendments

Here you provide details about any areas of the manager's employment that weren't covered elsewhere in the agreement, such as the number of vacation or sick days, or any paid holidays the manager is entitled to each year, or how you plan to reimburse managers for the cost of materials they purchase for repairs.

The last part of this section is fairly standard in written agreements. It states that this is your entire agreement about the manager's employment, and

that any changes to the agreement must be in writing.

Together, these provisions prevent you or your manager from later claiming that additional oral or written promises were made, but just not included in the written agreement.

⚠ **Make changes in writing.** If you later change the terms of your agreement, write the new terms down and have each person sign.

## 8. Place of Execution

Here you specify the city and state in which you signed the agreement. If there's any legal problem with the agreement later, it may be resolved by the courts where it was signed. Be advised, however, that the laws where the work is to be performed may be applied instead. So if, for example, you sign the Property Manager Agreement at your office in Maryland, but your rental property and the manager's work place is in nearby Washington, D.C., the different laws of Washington, D.C., may be applied by a court.

# Property Manager Agreement

## 1. Parties

This Agreement is between ___Jacqueline Marsh___,

Owner of residential real property at ___175 Donner Avenue, Brooklyn, New York___,

_____, and

___Bradley Finch___,

Manager of the property. Manager will be renting unit ___Number 5___ of the property under

a separate written rental agreement that is in no way contingent upon or related to this agreement.

## 2. Beginning Date

Manager will begin work on ___April 10, 199X___.

## 3. Responsibilities

Manager's duties are set forth below:

### Renting Units

[X] answer phone inquiries about vacancies

[X] show vacant units

[X] accept rental applications

[ ] select tenants

[X] accept initial rents and deposits

[ ] other (specify) _____

[ ] _____

### Vacant Apartments

[X] inspect unit when tenant moves in

[X] inspect unit when tenant moves out

[ ] clean unit after tenant moves out, including:

    [ ] floors, carpets and rugs

    [ ] walls, baseboards, ceilings, lights and built-in shelves

    [ ] kitchen cabinets, countertops, sinks, stove, oven and refrigerator

    [ ] bathtubs, showers, toilets and plumbing fixtures

    [ ] doors, windows, window coverings and mini-blinds

    [ ] other (specify) _____

    [ ] _____

**Rent Collection**

- [X] collect rents when due
- [X] sign rent receipts
- [X] maintain rent-collection records
- [X] collect late rents and charges
- [X] inform Owner of late rents
- [X] prepare late rent notices
- [X] serve late rent notices on tenants
- [X] serve rent increase and tenancy termination notices
- [X] deposit rent collections in bank
- [ ] other (specify) _____
- [ ] _____

**Maintenance**

- [ ] vacuum and clean hallways and entryways
- [X] replace lightbulbs in common areas
- [ ] drain water heaters
- [X] clean stairs, decks, patios, facade and sidewalks
- [X] clean garage oils on pavement
- [ ] mow lawns
- [ ] rake leaves
- [ ] trim bushes
- [X] clean up garbage and debris on grounds
- [X] shovel snow from sidewalks and driveways or arrange for snow removal
- [ ] other (specify) _____
- [ ] _____

**Repairs**

- [X] accept tenant complaints and repair requests
- [X] inform Owner of maintenance and repair needs
- [X] maintain written log of tenant complaints
- [X] handle routine maintenance and repairs, including:
  - [X] plumbing stoppages
  - [X] garbage disposal stoppages/repairs
  - [X] faucet leaks/washer replacement
  - [X] toilet tank repairs
  - [X] toilet seat replacement

[X] stove burner repair/replacement

[X] stove hinges/knobs replacement

[X] dishwasher repair

[X] light switch and outlet repair/replacement

[ ] heater thermostat repair

[ ] window repair/replacement

[ ] painting (interior)

[ ] painting (exterior)

[X] replacement of keys

[ ] other (specify)

[ ] _____

## Other Responsibilities

_____

_____

_____

_____

## 4. Hours and Schedule

Manager will be available to tenants during the following days and times: _____Monday through Friday, 3 p.m.-6 p.m._____. If the hours required to carry out any duties may reasonably be expected to exceed ____30____ hours in any week, Manager shall notify Owner and obtain Owner's consent before working such extra hours, except in the event of an emergency. Extra hours worked due to an emergency must be reported to Owner within 24 hours.

## 5. Payment Terms

a. Manager will be paid:

[ ] $ _____ per hour

[ ] $ _____ per week

[X] $ __1,200_____ per month

[ ] Other: _____

b. Manager will be paid on the specified intervals and dates:

[ ] Once a week on every _____

[ ] Twice a month on _____

[X] Once a month on ____the first of the month____

[ ] Other: _____

**6. Ending the Manager's Employment**

Owner may terminate Manager's employment at any time, and Manager may quit at any time.

**7. Additional Agreements and Amendments**

a. Owner and Manager additionally agree that: _____

_____

_____

_____

_____

_____

_____

_____

_____

_____

_____

_____

b. All agreements between Owner and Manager relating to the work specified in this Agreement are incorporated in this Agreement. Any modification to the Agreement must be in writing and signed by both parties.

**8. Place of Execution**

Signed at ___Brooklyn_____, ___New York_____
                    City                                          State

___April 3, 199X___            _Jacqueline Marsh_____
Date                            Owner

___April 3, 199X___            _Bradley Finch_____
Date                            Manager

## C. Your Legal Obligations as an Employer

Whether or not you compensate a manager with reduced rent or a regular salary, you have specific legal obligations as an employer, such as following laws governing minimum wage and overtime. If you don't pay Social Security and meet your other legal obligations as an employer, you may face substantial financial penalties.

**Start out by getting IRS Publication 334 (Tax Guide for Small Businesses), which provides details about the records you must keep on your employees.** Contact the IRS at 800-829-3676 or www.irs.ustreas.gov to obtain a free copy of this and other IRS publications. *Tax Savvy for Small Business*, by Frederick W. Daily (Nolo Press), covers strategies that will help you minimize taxes and stay out of legal trouble, including how to deduct business expenses, write off or depreciate long-term business assets, keep the kinds of records that will satisfy the IRS, get a tax break from business losses and handle a small business audit.

### Most Resident Managers Are Employees, Not Independent Contractors

A resident manager will probably be considered your employee by the IRS and other government agencies. Employees are guaranteed a number of workplace rights that are not guaranteed to people who work as independent contractors. To be considered an independent contractor, a person must offer services to the public at large and work under an arrangement in which he or she controls both the outcome of the project and the means and methods of accomplishing it. Most tenant-managers are legally considered to be employees because the property owner who hires them sets the hours and responsibilities and determines the particulars of the job. Only if a manager works for several different landlords might he or she qualify for independent contractor status.

### 1. Employer Identification Number

As an employer, you need a federal identification number for tax purposes. If you are a sole proprietor without employees, you can use your Social Security number. Otherwise, you need to get an "employer identification number" (EIN) from the IRS. To obtain an EIN, complete Form SS-4 (Application for Employer Identification Number), available free from the IRS. Call the IRS at 800-829-3676.

### 2. Income Taxes

The IRS considers the manager's compensation as taxable income to the manager. For that reason, your manager must fill out a federal W-4 form (Employee Withholding Allowance Certificate) when hired. You must deduct federal taxes from each paycheck (and state taxes if required), and turn over the withheld funds each quarter to the IRS and the appropriate state tax agency. You must provide the manager with a W-2 form (Wage and Tax Statement) for the previous year's earnings by January 31. The W-2 form lists the employee's gross wages and provides a breakdown of any taxes that you withheld.

### 3. Social Security and Medicare Taxes

Every employer must pay to the IRS a "payroll tax," currently equal to 7.65% of the employee's gross compensation—or paycheck amount before deductions. You must also deduct an additional 7.65% from the employee's wages and turn it over (with the payroll tax) to the IRS quarterly. These Federal Insurance Contributions Act (FICA) taxes go toward the employee's future Social Security and Medicare benefits.

If you compensate your manager with reduced rent, you must still pay the FICA payroll tax. For example, an apartment owner who compensates a manager with a rent-free $500/month apartment must pay 7.65% of $500, or $38.25, in payroll taxes each month. The manager is responsible for paying another 7.65% ($38.25) to the IRS.

⚠ **Always pay payroll taxes on time.** If you don't, the IRS will find you—and you could be forced out of business by the huge penalties and interest charges it will add to the delinquent bill. And unlike most other debts, you must pay back payroll taxes even if you go through bankruptcy.

## Help With Paperwork

Employers are responsible for a certain amount of paperwork and recordkeeping such as time and pay records. If you hate paperwork, your accountant or bookkeeper can probably handle it for you. Or, a reputable payroll tax service that offers a tax notification service will calculate the correct amount of Social Security, unemployment, workers' compensation and other taxes due, produce the check to pay your manager and the taxes and notify you when the taxes are due.

Payroll services can be cost-effective even if you employ only one or two people. But when you look for one, it pays to shop around. To get cost quotes, check the Yellow Pages under Payroll Service or Bookkeeping Service. Avoid services that charge set-up fees—basically, a fee for putting your information into the computer—or extra fees to prepare W-2 forms or quarterly and annual tax returns.

## 4. Unemployment Taxes

A manager who is laid off, quits for good reason, or is fired for anything less than gross incompetence or dishonesty is entitled to unemployment benefits.

These benefits are financed by unemployment taxes paid by employers. You must pay a federal unemployment tax (FUTA) at a rate of 6.2% of the first $7,000 of the employee's wages for the year. In addition to contributing to FUTA, you may also be responsible for contributing to an unemployment insurance fund in your state.

Contact the IRS for information on FUTA and a local office of your state department of labor or employment or the government agency that oversees your state income tax program for state tax requirements.

## 5. Minimum Wage and Overtime

However you pay your manager—by the hour, with a regular salary, or by a rent reduction—you should monitor the number of hours worked to make sure you're complying with the federal Fair Labor Standards Act (FLSA) (29 U.S.Code §§201 and following) and any state minimum wage laws.

The federal minimum hourly wage is currently $5.15. If your state's minimum wage is higher than the federal rate, you must pay the higher rate.

If you compensate your manager by a rent reduction, you may not be able to count the full amount of the rent reduction in complying with minimum wage laws.

Wage and hour laws also require employers to pay time-and-a-half if an employee works more than 40 hours a week (with a few exceptions).

**For information on minimum wage laws, overtime rules and recordkeeping requirements**, contact the nearest office of the U.S. Labor Department's Wage and Hour Division or a local office of your state's department of labor or employment. *The Employer's Legal Handbook*, by Fred S. Steingold (Nolo Press), also provides detailed advice on these issues.

## Equal Pay for Equal Work

You must provide equal pay and benefits to men and women who do the same job or jobs that require equal skills, effort and responsibility. This is required by the Equal Pay Act, an amendment to the FLSA.

## 6. Workers' Compensation Insurance

Workers' compensation provides replacement income and pays medical expenses for employees who are injured or become ill as a result of their job. It's a no-fault system—an injured employee is entitled to receive benefits whether or not you provided a safe workplace and whether or not the manager's own carelessness contributed to the injury. (You are, of course, required by federal and state laws to provide a reasonably safe workplace.) But you, too, receive some protection because the manager is limited to fixed types of compensation—basically, partial wage replacement and payment of medical bills. Employees may also get money for retraining or special equipment if they are "permanently disabled." The manager can't get paid for pain and suffering or mental anguish.

To cover the costs of workers' compensation benefits for employees, you'll need to purchase a special insurance policy—either through a state fund or a private insurance company. Each state has its own workers' compensation statute. Most states set a minimum number of employees (generally five or more) before coverage is required.

Most wise landlords obtain workers' compensation insurance, whether or not it's required. If you don't, and you're sued by a manager who is injured on the job—for example, by falling down the stairs while performing maintenance, or even by a violent tenant—you face the possibility of a lawsuit for a large amount of money.

Contact your state workers' compensation office for information on coverage and costs.

## 7. Immigration Laws

When you hire someone, even someone who was born and raised in the city where your rental property is located, you must review documents such as a passport or naturalization certificate that proves the employee's identity and employment eligibility. You and each new employee are required to complete INS Form I-9, Employment Eligibility Verification. These rules come from the Immigration Reform and Control Act (IRCA), a federal law that prohibits hiring undocumented workers. The law, enforced by the Immigration and Naturalization Service (INS), prohibits hiring workers who don't have government authorization to work in the U.S.

For more information, contact the nearest office of the Immigration and Naturalization Service, listed in the telephone book under U.S. Department of Justice, or call 800-755-0777. Ask for a copy of the free INS publication Handbook for Employers: Instructions for Completing Form I-9.

## 8. New Hire Reporting Form

Within a short time after you hire someone—20 days or less—you must file a New Hire Reporting Form with a designated state agency. The information on the form becomes part of the National Directory of New Hires, used primarily to locate parents so that child support orders can be enforced. Government agencies also use the data to prevent improper payment of workers' compensation and unemployment benefits or public assistance benefits. Your state department of labor or employment should be able to tell you how to get the forms and where to send them.

# D. Management Companies

Property management companies are often used by owners of large apartment complexes and by absentee owners too far away from the property to be directly involved in everyday details. Property management companies generally take care of renting units, collecting rent, taking tenant complaints, arranging repairs and maintenance and evicting troublesome tenants. Of course, some of these responsibilities may be shared with or delegated to resident managers who, in some instances, may work for the management company.

A variety of relationships between owners and management companies are possible, depending on your wishes and how the particular management company chooses to do business. For example, if you own one or more big buildings, the management company will probably recommend hiring a resident manager. But if your rental property has only a few units, or you own a number of small buildings spread over a good-sized geographical area, the management company will probably suggest simply responding to tenant requests and complaints from its central office.

One advantage of working with a management company is that you avoid all the legal hassles of being an employer: paying payroll taxes, buying workers' compensation insurance, withholding income tax. The management company is an independent contractor, not an employee. It hires and pays the people who do the work. Typically, you sign a contract spelling out the management company's duties and fees. Most companies charge a fixed percentage—about 5% to 10%—of the total rent collected. (The salary of any resident manager is additional.) This gives the company a good incentive to keep the building filled with rent-paying tenants.

Another advantage is that management companies are usually well informed about the law, keep good records and are adept at staying out of legal hot water in such areas as discrimination, invasion of privacy and returning deposits.

The primary disadvantage of hiring a management company is the expense. For example, if you pay a management company 10% of the $14,000 you collect in rent each month from tenants in a 20-unit building, this amounts to $1,400 a month and $16,800 per year. While many companies charge less than 10%, it's still quite an expense. Also, if the management company works from a central office with no one on-site, tenants may feel that management is too distant and unconcerned with their day-to-day needs.

Management companies have their own contracts, which you should read thoroughly and understand before signing. Be sure you understand how the company is paid and its exact responsibilities.

## Questions to Ask When You Hire a Management Company

- Who are its clients: owners of single-family houses, small apartments or large apartment complexes? Look for a company with experience handling property like yours. Also ask for client references, and check to see whether other landlords are satisfied with the management company. (Don't forget to ask these landlords how their tenants feel about the service they get. Unhappy tenants are bad business.)
- What services are provided?
- What are the costs?
- Will the management company take tenant calls 24 hours a day, seven days a week?
- Is the company located fairly close to your property?
- Are employees trained in landlord-tenant law? Will the company consult an attorney qualified in landlord-tenant matters if problems arise, such as disputes over rent?
- If your property is under rent control, are company personnel familiar with the rent control law?
- Can you terminate the management agreement without cause on reasonable notice?

## E. Your Liability for a Manager's Acts

Depending on the circumstances, you may be legally responsible for the acts of a manager or management company. For example, you could be sued and found liable if your manager or management company:

- refuses to rent to a qualified tenant (who is a member of a minority group or has children) or otherwise violates antidiscrimination laws (see Chapter 5)
- sexually harasses a tenant (see Chapter 5)
- makes illegal deductions from the security deposit of a tenant who has moved out, or does not return the departing tenant's deposit within the time limit set by your state law (see Chapters 4 and 15)
- ignores a dangerous condition, such as substandard wiring that results in an electrical fire, causing injury or damage to the tenant (see Chapter 10), or security problems that result in a criminal assault on a tenant (see Chapter 12), or
- invades a tenant's privacy by flagrant and damaging gossip or trespass (see Chapter 13).

Also see Chapter 12 for a discussion of your responsibilities for your manager's criminal acts.

In short, a landlord who knows the law but has a manager (or management company) who doesn't could wind up in a lawsuit brought by prospective or former tenants.

Here's how to protect your tenants and yourself:

**Choose your manager carefully.** Legally, you have a duty to protect your tenants from injury caused by employees you know or should know pose a risk of harm to others. If someone gets hurt or has property stolen or damaged by a manager whose background you didn't check carefully, you could be sued, so it's crucial that you be especially vigilant when hiring a manager who will have easy access to rental units. (See Section A, above, for advice on checking references and background of prospective managers.)

**Make sure your manager is familiar with the basics of landlord-tenant law, especially if your manager will be selecting tenants or serving eviction notices.** One approach is to give your manager a copy of this book to read and refer to. In addition, you'll want to provide detailed instructions that cover likely trouble areas, such as the legal rules prohibiting discrimination in tenant selection. Below is a sample set of instructions for a manager with fairly broad authority; you can tailor them to fit your situation. You'll also need to add any requirements that are imposed by the laws in your state—for example, stricter notice requirements to enter rental property than are outlined in the sample instructions. Have the manager sign a copy of the instructions and give it to you.

**Keep an eye on your manager, and listen to tenants' concerns and complaints.** Encourage your tenants to report problems to you. If you hear about or suspect problems—for example, poor maintenance of the building or sexual harassment—do your own investigating. For example, when you have a vacancy, have someone you suspect the manager might discriminate against apply for a vacancy. How does your manager treat the applicant? Would you want to defend a lawsuit brought by the prospective tenant? Try to resolve problems and get rid of a bad manager before problems accelerate and you end up with an expensive tenants' lawsuit.

**Make sure your insurance covers illegal acts of your employees.** No matter how thorough your precautions, you may still be liable for your manager's illegal acts—even if your manager commits an illegal act in direct violation of your instructions. To really protect yourself, purchase a good landlord's insurance policy. (See Chapter 10.)

## Sample Instructions to Manager

Dear New Manager:

Welcome to your new position as resident manager. Here are important instructions to guide you as you perform your duties under our management agreement. Please read them carefully and keep them for future reference.

1. Discrimination in rental housing on the basis of race, religion, sex, familial status, age, national or ethnic origin or disability is illegal—whether you are accepting rental applications for vacant apartments or dealing with current residents. Your duties are to advertise and accept rental applications in a nondiscriminatory manner. This includes allowing all individuals to fill out applications and offering the unit on the same terms to all applicants. After you have collected all applications, please notify me at the phone number listed below. I will sort through the applications, set up interviews and decide whom to accept.

2. Tenants have a right to feel comfortable and relaxed in and near their homes. To be sure all do, please avoid any comments, actions or physical contact that could be considered offensive, even by those whom you might see as being overly sensitive on the issue. Remember, sexual harassment is against the law and will not be tolerated.

3. Do not issue any rent-increase or termination notices without my prior approval.

4. Treat all tenants who complain about defects, even trivial defects or ones you believe to be nonexistent, with respect. Enter all tenant complaints into the logbook I have supplied to you on the day they are made. Respond to tenant complaints about the building or apartment units immediately in emergencies, or if the complaint involves security, and respond to other complaints within 24 hours. If you cannot correct (or arrange to correct) any problem or defect yourself, please telephone me immediately.

5. Except in serious life- or property-threatening emergencies, never enter (or allow anyone else to enter) a tenant's apartment without consent or in his or her absence, unless you have given written notice at least 24 hours in advance, either delivered personally or, if that's not possible, posted on the door. If you have given the tenant 24-hour written notice, you may enter in the tenant's absence during ordinary business hours to do repairs or maintenance work, unless the tenant objects. If the tenant objects, do not enter, but instead call me.

6. When a tenant moves in, and again when he or she moves out, inspect the unit. If possible, have the tenant accompany you. On each occasion, both you and the tenant should complete and sign a Landlord-Tenant Checklist form. Also take a series of Polaroid pictures.

7. If you think a tenant has moved out and abandoned the apartment, do not enter it. Telephone me first.

## Sample Instructions to Manager (continued)

8.  Once a tenant has vacated an apartment and given you the key, keep track of all costs necessary to repair damages in excess of ordinary wear and tear. Give me a copy of this list, along with a notation of the amount of any back rent, the before and after Landlord-Tenant Checklist forms and the departing tenant's forwarding address. Please make sure I see this material within a week after the tenant moves out, preferably sooner. I will mail the itemization and any security deposit balance to the tenant.

9.  If you have any other problems or questions, please do not hesitate to call me. Leave a message on my answering machine if I am not at home.

Sincerely,

*Terry Herendeen*

Terry Herendeen, Owner

1111 Maiden Lane, Omaha, Nebraska 54001

402-555-1234

I have received a copy of this memorandum and have read and understood it.

Dated:   *April 7, 199X*

*Barbara Louis*
Barbara Louis, Manager

## The High Cost of a Bad Manager: Sexual Harassment in Housing

If tenants complain about illegal acts by a manager, pay attention. The owners of a Fairfield, California, apartment complex learned this lesson the hard way—by paying more than a million dollars to settle a tenants' lawsuit.

The tenants, mostly single mothers, were tormented by an apartment manager who spied on them, opened their mail and sexually harassed them. They were afraid to complain, for fear of eviction. When they did complain to the building's owners, they refused to take any action—and the manager stepped up his harassment in retaliation.

Finally, tenants banded together and sued, and the details of the manager's outrageous and illegal conduct were exposed. The owners settled the case before trial for $1.6 million.

## F. Notifying Tenants of the Manager

In many states, you are legally required to give tenants the manager's name and address and tell them that the manager is authorized to accept legal documents on your behalf, such as termination of tenancy notices or court documents in an eviction lawsuit.

We recommend that you give tenants this information in writing, whether or not your state's law requires it. It is included in our lease and rental agreements (see Clause 21 in Chapter 2), but don't forget to notify tenants who moved in before you hired the manager.

Two sample disclosure notices are shown below. You should give each tenant a copy and post another in a prominent place in the building.

Be sure your Property Manager Agreement, discussed in Section B, above, notes the manager's authority in this regard. You can put details in the last section, Additional Agreements and Amendments.

## Emergency Procedures

It's an excellent idea to prepare a written set of emergency procedures for the manager, including:

- names and phone numbers of nearest hospital and poison control center
- ambulance, police and fire departments and a local taxi company
- what to do in case of an earthquake, flood, hurricane, tornado or other disaster, including how to shut off the gas, electricity and water.

## Sample Disclosure Notices

### Notice: Address of Manager of Premises

Muhammad Azziz, 1234 Market Street, Apartment 1, Boston, Mass., is authorized to manage the residential premises at 1234 Market Street, Boston, Mass. If you have any complaints about the condition of your unit or common areas, please notify Mr. Azziz immediately. He is authorized to act for and on behalf of the owner of the premises for the purpose of receiving all notices and demands from you, including legal papers (process).

### Notice: Address of Owner of Premises

Rebecca Epstein, 12345 Embarcadero Road, Boston, Mass., is the owner of the premises at 1234 Market Street, Boston, Mass.

## G. Firing a Manager

Unless you have made a commitment (oral or written contract) to employ a manager for a specific period of time, you have the right to terminate her employment at any time. But you cannot do it for an illegal reason, such as:

- race, age or gender discrimination, or
- retaliation against the manager for calling your illegal acts to the attention of authorities.

EXAMPLE: You order your manager to dump 20 gallons of fuel oil at the back of your property. Instead, the manager complains to a local environmental regulatory agency, which fines you. If you now fire the manager, you will be vulnerable to a lawsuit for illegal termination.

To head off the possibility of a wrongful termination lawsuit, be prepared to show a good reason for the firing. It's almost essential to back up a firing with written records documenting your reasons. Reasons that may support a firing include:

- performing poorly on the job—for example, not depositing rent checks promptly, or continually failing to respond to tenant complaints
- refusing to follow instructions—for example, allowing tenants to pay rent late, despite your instructions to the contrary
- possessing a weapon at work
- being dishonest or stealing money or property from you or your tenants
- endangering the health or safety of tenants
- engaging in criminal activity, such as drug dealing
- arguing or fighting with tenants
- behaving violently at work, or
- unlawfully discriminating or harassing prospective or current tenants.

Ideally, a firing shouldn't come suddenly or as a surprise. Give your manager ongoing feedback about job performance and impose progressive discipline, such as an oral or written warning, before termination. Do a six-month performance review (and more often, if necessary) and keep copies. Solicit comments from tenants twice a year (as mentioned earlier) and if comments are negative, keep copies.

---

### Handling Requests for References

One of your biggest problems after a manager quits or has been fired may be what to tell other landlords or employers who inquire about the former manager. You may be tugged in several directions:

- You want to tell the truth—good, bad or neutral—about the former manager.
- You want to help the former manager find another job for which he is better suited.
- You don't want to be sued for libel or slander because you say something negative.

Legally, you're better off saying as little as possible, rather than saying anything negative. Just say that it's your policy not to comment on former managers. Besides, if you politely say, "I would rather not discuss Mr. Jones," the caller will get the idea.

---

## H. Evicting a Manager

If you fire a manager, you may often want the ex-employee to move out of your property, particularly if there is a special manager's unit or the firing has generated (or resulted from) ill will. How easy it will be to get the fired manager out depends primarily on whether or not you have separate management and rental agreements.

 In many cases, you'll want the eviction lawsuit to be handled by an attorney who specializes in landlord-tenant law.

If you and the tenant-manager signed separate management and rental agreements (discussed in Section A), firing the manager does not affect the tenancy. The ex-manager will have to keep paying rent but will no longer work as manager. Evicting the former manager is just like evicting any other tenant. You will have to give a normal termination notice, typically 30 days for month-to-month tenancies, subject to any applicable rent control restrictions. If the tenant has a separate fixed-term lease, you cannot terminate the tenancy until the lease expires.

We do not recommend using a single management/rental agreement. Among other reasons, it may be difficult to evict the ex-manager in this situation. ■

Chapter **7**

# Getting the Tenant Moved In

Legal disputes between landlords and tenants have gained a reputation for being almost as emotional as divorce court battles. Many disputes are unnecessary and could be avoided if—right from the very beginning—tenants knew their legal rights and responsibilities. A clearly written lease or rental agreement, signed by all adult occupants, is the key to starting a tenancy. (See Chapter 2.) But there's more to establishing a positive attitude when new tenants move in. You should also:

- Inspect the property, fill out a Landlord-Tenant Checklist with the tenant and photograph the rental unit.
- Prepare a move-in letter highlighting important terms of the tenancy and your expectations.

---

### States That Require a Landlord-Tenant Checklist

The following states require landlords to give new tenants a written statement on the condition of the rental premises at move-in time, including a comprehensive list of existing damages.

Check the statutes for the exact requirements in your state, including the type of inspection required at the end of the tenancy. (See "Citations for State Laws on Security Deposits" in Appendix I.)

| | | |
|---|---|---|
| Arizona | Maryland | North Dakota |
| Georgia | Massachusetts | Virginia |
| Hawaii | Michigan | Washington |
| Kentucky | Montana | |

---

## A. Inspect the Rental Unit

To eliminate the possibility of all sorts of future arguments, it is absolutely essential that you (or your representative) and prospective tenants (together, if possible) check the place over for damage and obvious wear and tear before the tenant moves in. The best way to document what you find is to jointly fill out a Landlord-Tenant Checklist form.

In some states, the law requires you to give new tenants a written statement on the condition of the premises at move-in time, including a comprehensive list of existing damage. (See "States That Require a Landlord-Tenant Checklist," above.) Tenants in many of these states have the right to inspect the premises as to the accuracy of the landlord's list, and to note any problems. But even if this procedure is not legally required, you should follow it to avert later problems.

## 1. Fill Out the Landlord-Tenant Checklist

A Landlord-Tenant Checklist, inventorying the condition of the rental property at the beginning and end of the tenancy, is an excellent device to protect both you and your tenant when the tenant moves out and wants the security deposit returned. Without some record as to the condition of the unit, you and the tenant are all too likely to get into arguments about things like whether the kitchen linoleum was already stained, the garbage disposal was broken, the stove was filthy or the bathroom mirror was already cracked when the tenant moved in.

The checklist provides good evidence as to why you withheld all or part of a security deposit. And coupled with a system to regularly keep track of the rental property's condition, the checklist will also be extremely useful to you if a tenant withholds rent, breaks the lease and moves out or sues you outright, claiming the unit needs substantial repairs. (See Chapter 9 for instructions and forms that will let you stay updated on the condition of your rental properties.)

A sample Landlord-Tenant Checklist is shown below.

The Legal Forms Disk includes the Landlord-Tenant Checklist. A blank, tear-out copy is in the Appendix.

# Landlord-Tenant Checklist

## GENERAL CONDITION OF RENTAL UNIT AND PREMISES

572 Fourth St.                                                     Apt. 11      Washington, D.C.

Street Address                                                    Unit Number   City

| | Condition on Arrival | Condition on Departure | Estimated Cost of Repair/Replacement |
|---|---|---|---|
| **LIVING ROOM** | | | |
| Floors & Floor Coverings | OK | | |
| Drapes & Window Coverings | Mini-blinds discolored | | |
| Walls & Ceilings | OK | | |
| Light Fixtures | OK | | |
| Windows, Screens & Doors | Window rattles | | |
| Front Door & Locks | OK | | |
| Fireplace | N/A | | |
| Other | | | |
| Other | | | |
| **KITCHEN** | | | |
| Floors & Floor Coverings | Cigarette burn hole | | |
| Walls & Ceilings | OK | | |
| Light Fixtures | OK | | |
| Cabinets | OK | | |
| Counters | Stained | | |
| Stove/Oven | Burners filthy (grease) | | |
| Refrigerator | OK | | |
| Dishwasher | OK | | |
| Garbage Disposal | N/A | | |
| Sink & Plumbing | OK | | |
| Windows, Screens & Doors | OK | | |
| Other | | | |
| Other | | | |
| **DINING ROOM** | | | |
| Floors & Floor Covering | OK | | |
| Walls & Ceilings | Crack in ceiling | | |
| Light Fixtures | OK | | |
| Windows, Screens & Doors | OK | | |
| Other | | | |

| | Condition on Arrival | | Condition on Departure | | Estimated Cost of Repair/Replacement |
|---|---|---|---|---|---|
| **BATHROOM(S)** | Bath 1 | Bath 2 | Bath 1 | Bath 2 | |
| Floors & Floor Coverings | OK | | | | |
| Walls & Ceilings | OK | | | | |
| Windows, Screens & Doors | OK | | | | |
| Light Fixtures | OK | | | | |
| Bathtub/Shower | Tub chipped | | | | |
| Sink & Counters | OK | | | | |
| Toilet | Base of toilet very dirty | | | | |
| Other | | | | | |
| Other | | | | | |
| **BEDROOM(S)** | Bdrm 1 | Bdrm 2 | Bdrm 3 | Bdrm 1 | Bdrm 2 | Bdrm 3 | |
| Floors & Floor Coverings | OK | OK | | | | |
| Windows, Screens & Doors | OK | OK | | | | |
| Walls & Ceilings | OK | OK | | | | |
| Light Fixtures | Dented | OK | | | | |
| Other | Mildew in closet | | | | | |
| Other | | | | | | |
| Other | | | | | | |
| Other | | | | | | |
| **OTHER AREAS** | | | | | |
| Heating System | OK | | | | |
| Air Conditioning | OK | | | | |
| Lawn/Garden | OK | | | | |
| Stairs and Hallway | OK | | | | |
| Patio, Terrace, Deck, etc. | N/A | | | | |
| Basement | OK | | | | |
| Parking Area | OK | | | | |
| Other | | | | | |
| Other | | | | | |
| Other | | | | | |
| Other | | | | | |
| Other | | | | | |

☒ Tenants acknowledge that all smoke detectors and fire extinguishers were tested in their presence and found to be in working order, and that the testing procedure was explained to them. Tenants agree to test all detectors at least once a month and to report any problems to Landlord/Manager in writing. Tenants agree to replace all smoke detector batteries as necessary.

## FURNISHED PROPERTY

| | Condition on Arrival | Condition on Departure | Estimated Cost of Repair/Replacement |
|---|---|---|---|
| **LIVING ROOM** | | | |
| Coffee Table | Two scratches on top | | |
| End Tables | OK | | |
| Lamps | OK | | |
| Chairs | OK | | |
| Sofa | OK | | |
| Other | | | |
| Other | | | |
| **KITCHEN** | | | |
| Broiler Pan | N/A | | |
| Ice Trays | N/A | | |
| Other | | | |
| Other | | | |
| **DINING AREA** | | | |
| Chairs | OK | | |
| Stools | N/A | | |
| Table | Leg bent slightly | | |
| Other | | | |
| Other | | | |
| **BATHROOM(S)** | Bath 1    Bath 2 | Bath 1    Bath 2 | |
| Mirrors | OK | | |
| Shower Curtain | Torn | | |
| Hamper | N/A | | |
| Other | | | |
| **BEDROOM(S)** | Bdrm 1    Bdrm 2    Bdrm 3 | Bdrm 1    Bdrm 2    Bdrm 3 | |
| Beds (single) | OK    N/A | | |
| Beds (double) | N/A    OK | | |
| Chairs | OK    OK | | |
| Chests | N/A    N/A | | |
| Dressing Tables | OK    N/A | | |
| Lamps | OK    OK | | |
| Mirrors | OK    OK | | |
| Night Tables | OK    N/A | | |
| Other | | | |

| | Condition on Arrival | Condition on Departure | Estimated Cost of Repair/Replacement |
|---|---|---|---|
| Other | | | |
| **OTHER AREAS** | | | |
| Bookcases | N/A | | |
| Desks | N/A | | |
| Pictures | Hallway picture frame chipped | | |
| Other | | | |
| Other | | | |

Use this space to provide any additional explanation:

_____

_____

_____

_____

_____

_____

_____

_____

_____

_____

_____

_____

Landlord-Tenant Checklist completed on moving in on _____ May 1 _____, 199 _X_, and approved by:

_Bernard Cohen_____ and _____Maria Crouse_____
Landlord/Manager                                    Tenant

                                              _____Sandra Martino_____
                                              Tenant

                                              _____
                                              Tenant

Landlord-Tenant Checklist completed on moving out on _____, 199____, and approved by:

_____ and _____
Landlord/Manager                          Tenant

                                              _____
                                              Tenant

                                              _____
                                              Tenant

You and the tenant should fill out the checklist together. If that's impossible, complete the form and then give it to the tenant to review. The tenant should note any disagreement and return it to you.

The checklist is in two parts. The first side covers the general condition of each room. The second side covers furnishings, such as a living room lamp or bathroom shower curtain.

You will be filling out the first column—*Condition on Arrival*—before the tenant moves in. The last two columns—*Condition on Departure* and *Estimated Cost of Repair or Replacement*—are for use when the tenant moves out and you inspect the unit again. At that time the checklist will document your need to make deductions from the security deposit for repairs or cleaning, or to replace missing items. (See Chapter 15 for details on returning security deposits.)

## a. General Condition of Rental Unit and Premises

In the *Condition on Arrival* column, make a note—as specific as possible—on items that are not working or are dirty, scratched or simply in bad condition. For example, don't simply note that the refrigerator "needs fixing" if an ice maker doesn't work—it's just as easy to write "ice maker broken, should not be used." If the tenant uses the ice maker anyway and causes water damage, he cannot claim that you failed to tell him. Be sure to note any mildew, pest or rodent problems.

Mark "OK" next to items that are in satisfactory condition—basically, clean, safe, sanitary and in good working order.

If your rental unit does not have a particular item listed, such as a dishwasher or kitchen broiler pan, put "N/A" (not applicable) in the *Condition on Arrival* column.

⚠️ **Make repairs and clean thoroughly before a new tenant moves in.** To get the tenancy off to the best start, and avoid all kinds of hassles over repairs, handle problems before the start of a new tenancy. You must fix certain defects—such as a broken heater or leaking roof—under state and local housing codes. (Chapter 9 discusses landlords' repair and maintenance responsibilities.) You may often be able to cover your repair and cleaning costs by deducting expenses from the outgoing tenant's security deposit. Chapter 15 discusses how you may use security deposits for this purpose.

## b. Furnishings

The second part of the checklist covers furnishings, such as lamps or shower curtains. Obviously, you can simply mark "Not Applicable" or "N/A" in most of these boxes if your unit is not furnished.

If your rental property has rooms or furnishings not listed on the checklist, note them in "Other Areas" or cross out something that you don't have and write in the changes. If you are renting out a large house or apartment or providing many furnishings, be sure to include this information. You can easily make changes using the checklist on the Legal Forms Disk. Or you may attach a separate sheet of paper. Just make a separate list for additional items and staple it to the checklist.

## 2. Sign the Checklist

After you and your new tenant agree on all of the particulars of the rental unit, you each should sign and date every page of the checklist, including any attachments. Keep the original and give the tenant a copy. If the tenant filled out the checklist on his own, make sure you review his comments, note any disagreement and return a copy to him. You should make the checklist part of your lease or rental agreement, as we recommend in Chapter 2, Section C, Clause 11.

Be sure the tenant also checks the box on the bottom of the second page of the checklist stating that the smoke detector and fire extinguisher— required for new occupancies in many states and cities—were tested in his presence and shown to be in working order. This section on the checklist also requires the tenant to test the smoke detector monthly and to replace the battery when necessary. By doing this, you'll limit your liability if the smoke detector fails and results in fire damage or injury. (See Chapter 9 for details on your responsibility to maintain the property and Chapter 10 for a discussion of your liability for injuries to tenants.)

**Be sure to keep the checklist up to date if you repair, replace, add or remove items or furnishings after the tenant moves in.** Both you and the tenant should initial and date any changes.

## B. Photograph the Rental Unit

Taking photos or videotapes of the unit before a new tenant moves in is another excellent way to avoid disputes over security deposit deductions. In addition to the checklist, you'll be able to compare "before" and "after" pictures when the tenant leaves. This should help refresh your tenant's memory, which may result in her being more reasonable. Certainly, if you end up in mediation or court for not returning the full security deposit, being able to document your point of view with photos will be invaluable. In addition, photos or a video can also help if you have to sue a former tenant for cleaning and repair costs above the deposit amount.

It's best to take "before" photographs with a Polaroid camera that develops pictures on the spot. This will allow both you and the tenant to date and sign the pictures, each keeping a set. Otherwise, use a camera that automatically imprints the date on each photo. If you don't have access to either type of camera, photograph the tenant or yourself during the inspection. Then develop the pictures promptly and sign and date them on the back. If you're doing the inspection on your own, bring a copy of that day's newspaper and photograph the front page as part of one of the photos.

If you make a video, get the tenant on tape stating the date and time so that you can prove when the video was made.

You should repeat this process when the tenant leaves, as part of your standard move-out procedure. Chapter 15 discusses inspecting the unit when a tenant leaves.

## C. Send New Tenants a Move-In Letter

A move-in letter should dovetail with the lease or rental agreement and provide basic information such as the manager's phone numbers (day and night) and office hours. You can also use a move-in letter to explain any procedures and rules that are too detailed or numerous to include in your lease or rental agreement—for example, how and where to report maintenance problems, details on garbage disposal and recycling and location and use of laundry rooms. Consider including a brief list of maintenance do's and don'ts as part of the move-in letter—for example, how to avoid overloading circuits and proper use of the garbage disposal. (Alternatively, large landlords may use a set of Rules and Regulations to cover some of these issues. See Clause 18 of the form agreements in Chapter 2.)

# Move-In Letter

September 1, 199X
Date

Frank O'Hara
Tenant

139 Porter Street
Street address

Madison, Wisconsin 53704
City and State

Dear Frank ,
　　　　　　　　Tenant

Welcome to Apartment 45 B at Happy Hill Apartments

_____ (address of rental unit). We hope you will enjoy living here. This letter

is to explain what you can expect from the management and what we'll be looking for from you:

**1. Rent:** There is no grace period for the payment of rent. (See Clauses 5 and 6 of your rental agreement for

details, including late charges.) Also, we don't accept post-dated checks. .

**2. New roommates:** If you want someone to move in as a roommate, please contact us first. If your rental unit

is big enough to accommodate another person, we will arrange for the new person to fill out a rental application. If

it's approved, all of you will need to sign a new rental agreement. Depending on the situation, there may be a rent

increase to add a roommate. .

**3. Notice to end tenancy:** To terminate your month-to-month tenancy, you must give at least 30 days' written

notice. We have a written form available for this purpose. We may also terminate the tenancy, or change its terms,

on 30 days' written notice. If you give less than 30 days' notice, you will still be financially responsible for rent for
the balance of the 30-day period.

**4. Deposits:** Your security deposit will be applied to costs of cleaning, damages or unpaid rent after you move out.

You may not apply any part of the deposit toward any part of your rent in the last month of your tenancy. (See

Clause 8 of your rental agreement.) .

**5. Manager:** Sophie Beauchamp (Apartment #15, phone 555-1234) is your resident manager. You should pay

your rent to her and promptly let her know of any maintenance or repair problems (see #7, below) and any other

questions or problems. She's in her office every day from 8 a.m. to 10 a.m. and from 4 p.m. to 6 p.m. and can be
reached by phone at other times.

**6. Landlord-Tenant Checklist:** By now, Sophie Beauchamp should have taken you on a walk-through of your

apartment to check the condition of all walls, drapes, carpets and appliances and to test the smoke alarms and

fire extinguisher. These are all listed on the Landlord-Tenant Checklist, which you should have reviewed carefully

and signed. When you move out, we will ask you to check each item against its original condition as described on

the Checklist. .

**7. Maintenance/Repair Problems:** <u>We are determined to maintain a clean, safe building in which all systems are in good repair. To help us make repairs promptly, we will give you Maintenance/Repair Request forms to report to the manager any problems in your apartment, such as a broken garbage disposal, or on the building or grounds, such a burned-out light in the garage. (Extra copies are available from the manager.) In an emergency, or when it's not convenient to use this form, please call the manager at 555-1234.</u>

**8. Semi-Annual Safety and Maintenance Update:** <u>To help us keep your unit and the common areas in excellent condition, we'll ask you to fill out a form every six months updating any problems on the premises or in your rental unit. This will allow you to report any potential safety hazards or other problems that otherwise might be overlooked.</u>

**9. Annual Safety Inspection:** <u>Once a year, we will ask to inspect the condition and furnishings of your rental unit and update the Landlord-Tenant Checklist. In keeping with state law, we will give you reasonable notice before the inspection, and you are encouraged to be present for it.</u>

**10. Insurance:** <u>We highly recommend that you purchase renters' insurance. The building property insurance policy will not cover the replacement of your personal belongings if they are lost due to fire, theft or accident. In addition, you could be found liable if someone is injured on the premises you rent as a result of your negligence. If you damage the building itself—for example, if you start a fire in the kitchen and it spreads—you could be responsible for large repair bills.</u>

**11. Moving Out:** <u>It's a little early to bring up moving out, but please be aware that we have a list of items that should be cleaned before we conduct a move-out inspection. If you decide to move, please ask the manager for a copy of our Move-Out Letter, explaining our procedures for inspection and returning your deposit.</u>

**12. Telephone Number Changes:** <u>Please notify us if your home or work phone number changes, so we can reach you promptly in an emergency.</u>

Please let us know if you have any questions.

Sincerely,

<u>September 1, 199X</u>      *Tom Guiliano*
Date                  Owner

I have read and received a copy of this statement.

<u>September 1, 199X</u>      *Frank O'Hara*
Date                  Tenant

Because every situation is different, we cannot supply you with a generic move-in letter that will work for everyone. We can, however, give you a template for a move-in letter that you can easily fill in with your own details, using the Legal Forms Disk. You can use the sample shown above as a model in preparing your own move-in letter.

We recommend that you make a copy of each tenant's move-in letter for yourself and ask him to sign the last page, indicating that he has read it. (As an extra precaution, ask him to initial each page.) Although this step may seem paranoid now, you won't think so later if a tenant sues you over something he claims you never told him (like the importance of purchasing renters' insurance).

Be sure to update the move-in letter from time to time as necessary.

## D. Cash Rent and Security Deposit Checks

Every landlord's nightmare is a new tenant whose first rent or deposit check bounces and who must be dislodged with time-consuming and expensive legal proceedings.

To avoid this, never sign a rental agreement, or let a tenant move furniture into your property or take a key until you have the tenant's cash, certified check or money order for the first month's rent and security deposit. An alternative is to cash the tenant's check at the bank before the move-in date. (While you have the tenant's first check, photocopy it for your records. The information on it can be helpful if you ever need to sue to collect a judgment from the tenant.) Be sure to give the tenant a signed receipt for the deposit.

Clause 5 of the form lease and rental agreements in Chapter 2 requires tenants to pay rent on the first day of each month. If the move-in date is other than the first day of the month, rent is prorated between that day and the end of that month.

## E. Organize Your Tenant Records

A good system to record all significant tenant complaints and repair requests will provide a valuable paper trail should disputes develop later—for example, regarding your right to enter a tenant's unit to make repairs or the time it took for you to fix a problem. Without good records, the outcome of a dispute may come down to your word against your tenant's—always a precarious situation.

Set up a file folder on each property with individual files for each tenant. Include the following documents:

- tenant's rental application, references, credit report and background information, including information about any co-signers
- a signed lease or rental agreement, plus any changes made along the way
- Landlord-Tenant Checklist and photos or video made at move-in, and
- signed move-in letter.

After a tenant moves in, add these documents to the individual's file:

- your written requests for entry
- rent increase notices
- records of repair requests, and details of how and when they were handled. If you keep repair records on the computer, you should regularly print out and save files from past months; if you have a master system to record all requests and complaints in one log, you would save that log separately, not necessarily put it in every tenant's file.
- safety and maintenance updates and inspection reports, and
- correspondence and other relevant information.

Your computer can also be a valuable tool to keep track of tenants. Set up a simple database for each tenant with spaces for the following information:

- address or unit number
- move-in date
- home phone number
- name, address and phone number of employer
- credit information, including up-to-date information as to where tenant banks
- monthly rent amount and rent due date
- amount and purpose of deposits plus any information your state requires on location of deposit and interest payments

- vehicle make, model, color, year and license plate number
- emergency contacts, and
- whatever else is important to you.

Once you enter the information into your database, you can sort the list by address or other variables and easily print labels for rent increases or other notices.

There are several commercial computer programs that allow you to keep track of every aspect of your business, from the tracking of rents to the follow-up on repair requests. Especially if you own many rental properties, these programs are well worth the cost. ■

Chapter **8**

# Co-Tenants, Sublets and Assignments

onscientious landlords go to a lot of trouble to screen prospective tenants. However, all your sensible precautions will be of little avail if unapproved tenants simply move in at the invitation of existing tenants. Not only is it possible that you'll have difficulty getting these tenants to pay rent or maintain the rental unit, but if they fail to do so, you may have an extra tough time evicting them.

This chapter helps you analyze your options when your tenant asks questions like these:

- "Can I sublet my apartment?"
- "May I get someone else to take over the rest of my lease?"
- "Is it okay if I move in a roommate?"

We also advise you on what to do when your tenant attempts to do any of the above *without* consulting you. Because, as with so many of life's problematic situations, the best defense is a good offense, we prepare you in advance for these situations by suggesting that you protect your interests from the outset by using lease clauses that limit occupants and require your permission for subleasing or assigning. In particular, this chapter explains:

- why everyone living in a rental unit should sign a lease or rental agreement
- the legal differences between sublets and assignments
- your right (and legal and practical limitations) to prohibit sublets and assignments
- how to add a tenant to an existing tenancy, and
- how to deal with repeated overnight guests.

Related topics covered in this book include:
- Limiting how long tenants' guests may stay: Chapter 2 (Clause 3)
- Requiring your written consent in advance for any sublet, assignment of the lease or rental agreement, or for any additional people to move in: Chapter 2 (Clauses 1, 3 and 10).
- Your duty to re-rent the property if a tenant neither sublets nor assigns, but simply breaks the lease: Chapter 14

- Returning security deposits when one tenant leaves but the others stay: Chapter 15.

**New York tenants may have special rights.** By virtue of New York's Roommates Law, " (RPL § 235-f), New York tenants have the right to bring in certain additional roommates without obtaining the landlord's prior approval and subject only to any applicable local laws on overcrowding. If you own rental property in New York, be sure you understand this law before setting restrictions on tenants and roommates. See Chapter 18 for advice on doing legal research.

## A. Co-Tenants

When two or more people rent property together, and all sign the same rental agreement or lease—or enter into the same oral rental agreement and move in at the same time—they are co-tenants. Each co-tenant shares the same rights and responsibilities for the rent and other terms of the lease or rental agreement. In addition, each co-tenant is legally responsible to the landlord to carry out all of the terms of the lease, including being obligated to pay the entire rent and 100% of any damages to the premises if the others fail to pay their share.

### 1. Obligation for Rent

Among themselves, co-tenants may split the rent equally or unequally, depending on their own personal arrangement. However, any co-tenant who signs a lease or rental agreement with you is independently liable for all of the rent. Landlords often remind co-tenants of this obligation by inserting into the lease a chunk of legalese which says that the tenants are "jointly and severally" liable for paying rent and adhering to terms of the agreement (see "Joint and Several Liability," below). If one tenant can't pay his share a particular month, or simply moves out, the other tenant(s) must still pay the full rent during the rental period.

## Joint and Several Liability

"Joint and several" refers to the sharing of obligations and liabilities among two or more people—both as a group and as individuals. When two or more tenants are "jointly and severally liable," you can choose to hold all of them, or just one of them, responsible to pay rent and to abide by the rules of the tenancy.

That means you may demand the entire rent from just one tenant, should the others skip out, or evict all of the tenants even if just one has broken the terms of the lease.

Clause 1 of the form lease and rental agreements in Chapter 2 makes co-tenants jointly and severally liable. Co-tenants are jointly and severally liable for rent and other obligations—even if your lease or rental agreement does not include this clause. Nonetheless, we recommend you include a "jointly and severally liable" clause to alert tenants to this responsibility.

EXAMPLE: James and Helen sign a month-to-month rental agreement for an $800 apartment rented by Blue Oak Properties. They agree between themselves to each pay half of the rent. After three months, James moves out without notifying Helen or Blue Oak. As one of two co-tenants, Helen is still legally obligated to pay Blue Oak all the rent (although she might be able to recover James's share by suing him).

Blue Oak has three options if Helen can't pay the rent:

- Blue Oak can give Helen a written notice to pay up or leave (called a Notice to Pay Rent or Quit in most states), and follow through with an eviction lawsuit if Helen fails to pay the entire rent or move within the required amount of time (usually three to five days).
- If Helen offers to pay part of the rent, Blue Oak can legally accept it, but should make it clear that Helen is still responsible for the entire rent. It's important to make this clear, since it's common for one co-tenant to offer only "my portion" of the rent, when in fact each co-tenant (roommate) is liable for the entire rent. (See Chapter 3 for a discussion of accepting partial rent payments.)
- If Helen wants to stay, and finds a new co-tenant with a decent credit history, Blue Oak may not be able to withhold its approval of the new person and still hold Helen to her obligation to pay 100% of the rent. If Blue Oak accepts a new person, it should, however, have him become a co-tenant by signing a rental agreement. (See Section B, below.)
- If Helen wants to stay and proposes a co-tenant who proves to be unacceptable to Blue Oak (because the applicant does not meet Blue Oak's usual credit or income specifications for every new tenant), Blue Oak may say "No" and evict Helen if Helen is unable to pay the entire rent.

## 2. Violations of the Lease or Rental Agreement

In addition to paying rent, each tenant is responsible for any co-tenant's action that violates any term of the lease or rental agreement—for example, each co-tenant is liable if one of them seriously damages the property, or moves in an extra roommate or a dog, contrary to the lease or rental agreement. This means you can hold all co-tenants responsible and can terminate the entire tenancy with the appropriate notice, even though some of the co-tenants objected to the dog or weren't consulted by the prime offender.

If you must evict a tenant for a breach other than for nonpayment of rent (in which case you would evict all the tenants), you must decide whether to evict only the offending co-tenant or all of them. Your decision will depend on the circumstances. You have no legal obligation to evict a blameless co-tenant (for example, one who has no control over a dog-owning co-tenant). Practically, of course, you'll want to be sure the innocent tenant can still shoulder the rent after his problem roommate is gone. On the other hand, because co-tenants are "jointly and severally liable" (see Section 1, above) you also have the legal right to evict all co-tenants (even those who claim not to have caused the difficulty) and start over. Chapter 17 provides an overview of evictions.

## Special Rules for Married Couples

We strongly recommend that everyone who lives in a rental unit—including both members of a married couple—be required to sign the lease or rental agreement. This underscores your expectation that each individual is responsible ("jointly and severally liable") for the rent and the proper use of the rental property.

If, however, you neglect to have either the husband or wife sign the lease, that person may still be directly responsible to you. That's because in some states, a spouse is financially responsible for the necessities of life of the other, including rent.

But rather than counting on your state's law for protection, just put both names on the lease or rental agreement and make them each co-tenants. (And if one of your tenants gets married during the lease term, prepare a new agreement and have both bride and groom sign it.)

## 3. Disagreements Among Co-Tenants

Usually, co-tenants make only an oral agreement among themselves concerning how they will split the rent, occupy bedrooms and generally share their joint living space. For all sorts of reasons, roommate arrangements may go awry. If you have been a landlord for a while, you surely know all about co-tenants who play the stereo too loud, are slobs, pay their share of the rent late, have too many overnight guests or create some other problem that their roommates can't abide. If the situation gets bad enough, the tenants may start arguing about who should leave, whether one co-tenant can keep another out of the apartment or who is responsible for what part of the rent.

The best advice we can give landlords who face serious disagreements among co-tenants is this: Don't get involved in spats between co-tenants, as a mediator or otherwise. The reasons for our advice are both practical and legal.

On the practical side, you probably do not have the time to get to the bottom of financial or personal disputes; and even if you do, you have no ability to enforce any decisions among your tenants. (How could you enforce a ruling that one tenant must occupy the smaller of the two bedrooms?)

On the legal side, too, you are largely helpless. For example, you cannot threaten eviction if a tenant violates an agreement with the other tenant and occupies the larger bedroom, unless you put that particular "offense" into the lease as a ground for eviction. And since it's impossible to design a lease that will predict and list every possible roommate disagreement, attempting to use a legal solution will be of little help.

If one or more co-tenants approach you about a dispute, explain that they must resolve any disagreements among themselves. Remind them that they are each legally obligated to pay the entire rent, and that you are not affected by any rent-sharing agreements they have made among themselves. If one co-tenant asks you to change the locks to keep another co-tenant out, tell the tenant that you cannot legally do that—unless a court has issued an order that the particular tenant stay out.

The wisdom of remaining aloof during tenants' squabbles stops at the point that you fear for the physical safety of one of your tenants. Call the police immediately if you hear or witness violence

## When Couples Separate

Landlords need to be alert to the special emotional and possibly legal situations presented by a couple who rent the premises together and undergo a nasty break-up. Whether they are married or living together, dealing with feuding lovers is never easy. Here are some issues to consider:

- Especially if the couple is married, one tenant may not have the legal right to deprive the other of a place to live without a court order. If violence—or even the threat of it—is involved, the fearful spouse (usually the woman) is entitled to get a quick court order restraining the other partner from coming near her, either as part of a divorce filing or, in some states, separately. To help facilitate this, you might check out how to get a restraining order (there is usually a non-lawyer procedure) and make this information available to affected tenants. For advice, call the police department, your local courthouse, a women's shelter or an advocacy organization for women.

- If one married tenant changes the locks without your consent to keep the other out, you probably have no legal liability. (If your lease or rental agreement—like the one in this book—prohibits changing the locks without the landlord's permission, you probably have grounds for eviction.) But you should not normally participate in acts that will keep one member of a married couple out (say by changing the locks yourself) without a court restraining order, which specifically bars the other member of the couple from coming near the remaining tenant.

- When it comes to unmarried couples, you should know if your state or municipality grants any legal status to long-term relationships between people who are not married (these can take the form of either common-law marriages or domestic partner laws). If so, the law may treat people in these relationships similarly to married couples.

- When unmarried couples—whether of the same or opposite sex—separate, the law treats them as roommates. But in many states, a fearful member of an unmarried couple can qualify for a civil restraining order banning the other from the joint home, using a procedure similar to that available to married couples.

between tenants, or if a reliable source tells you about it. If you have any reasonable factual basis to believe that a tenant intends to harm another tenant, you may also have a legal duty to warn the intended victim (who probably already knows) and begin proceedings to evict the aggressor. Failure to sensibly intervene where violence is threatened might result in a finding of liability if the aggressor carries through with the threat. (See a related discussion of assaults by one tenant against another tenant in Chapter 12. The fact that the parties are co-tenants instead of tenants in different rental units would be immaterial to a court when determining liability.)

In the meantime, if one tenant fears violence from a co-tenant, consider taking the following steps:

- Suggest mediation if you think there is a potential for a reasoned resolution. (Chapter 16 discusses how to find low-cost local mediation services.)
- Contact the local police department or court clerk's office on behalf of the intended victim for information on obtaining a temporary restraining order, and urge the victim to apply for one. If the judge decides that the situation merits it, he or she will issue an order forbidding the aggressor tenant from coming near the other.
- Evict the aggressor or all co-tenants on the lease. If you choose to allow a blameless tenant to stay, keep in mind the remaining tenant's ability to pay the rent may be severely curtailed by the absence of a paying co-tenant.

EXAMPLE: Andy and his roommate Bill began their tenancy on friendly terms. Unfortunately, it soon became clear that their personal habits were completely at odds. Their arguments regarding housekeeping, guests and their financial obligations to contribute to the rent escalated to a physical fight. As a result, they each asked their landlord, Anita, to evict the other.

After listening to Andy's and Bill's complaints, Anita referred them to a local mediation service, and they agreed to participate. The mediator's influence worked for a while, but Andy and Bill were soon back at loud, unpleasant shouting matches. Anita initiated eviction proceedings against both, on the grounds that their disruptive behavior interfered with the rights of the other tenants to the quiet enjoyment of their homes.

## 4. When a Co-Tenant Leaves

When a co-tenant leaves and someone is proposed as a substitute, you want three things to happen:

- The departing tenant should sign a Termination of Lease statement.
- You should investigate the proposed new tenant, beginning with the application process (like any new tenancy).
- The remaining tenant(s), including the replacement tenant, should sign a new lease or rental agreement.

These steps are all discussed in Section B.

There are three reasons for formally "resetting the stage" this way: (1) to ensure that you continue to receive the entire rent, (2) to ensure that any new tenant meets your criteria for selecting tenants, and (3) to avoid the specter of the return—or attempted return—of the departed tenant who claims that he never *really* intended to leave.

**The rent.** Although the departing tenant will still be technically liable for the rent until you formally release him from the lease or rental agreement (except where he has given timely written notice), this may not be worth much if he has left for parts unknown. And, although the remaining tenants (individually and as a group) are liable for the rent too, they may not be able (or willing) to pay the departing tenant's share. You are almost always better off signing a lease with a new tenant if he is acceptable. (Section B discusses this in detail.)

**Who is entitled to live in the rental unit.** As an added advantage, formally terminating a co-tenant's lease or rental agreement and preparing a new one, signed by the remaining tenant(s) and any replacement tenant, will make it clear that the outgoing tenant is no longer entitled to possession of the property. Although you do not want to become entangled in your tenants' personal lives, you also want to avoid being dragged into disputes regarding who is entitled to a key and the use of your rental property.

But what happens if despite your vigilance, a new tenant moves in without your permission who isn't acceptable to you? Assuming you see no reason to change your mind, you have a right to evict all co-tenants under the terms of the clause in your lease or rental agreement that prohibits unauthorized sublets. (See Section D, below.)

## B. What to Do When a Tenant Wants to Sublet or Assign

Ideally, you want to rent to tenants who will stay a long time, or at least the entire term of the lease. But despite your best efforts, you will encounter tenants who, for various reasons, such as a job-related move, will want to leave before the expiration of their lease. Sometimes, of course, these tenants simply disappear. Other tenants, out of regard for their promise, or to recover as much as possible of their deposit, or maybe just out of concern that you will pursue them or damage their credit rating, will want to leave "legally" by supplying a stand-in for the balance of the term.

What should you do if a tenant approaches you with a request to move out, substituting another tenant in her place? Because our lease and rental agreements (Clause 10) prohibit sublets or assignments without your written consent, you have some flexibility. This section discusses your options.

### 1.  Create a New Tenancy

In most situations, your best bet when confronted with a tenant who wants to sublease or assign is to

simply insist that the tenancy terminate and a new one begin—with the proposed "subtenant" or "assignee" as the new prime tenant.

Suppose a tenant wants to sublet her apartment for six months while she is out of the area, or assign the last four months of her lease because she has to move for employment reasons. If the proposed new tenant passes your standard screening process, agree to take the tenant—on the condition that the proposed new tenant sign a new lease and become a prime tenant. This gives you the most direct legal relationship with the substitute. In other words, simply treat your tenant's wish to sublet or assign as a wish to get out from under the lease early, with a candidate for the next occupant at the ready.

The way to accomplish this is to first release your original tenant from her obligations under the lease (see the sample Termination of Lease, below). Then begin the new tenancy with the substitute in the same way that you begin any tenancy: sign a lease, present a move-in letter, and so on.

What are the pros and cons of this approach as compared to accepting a subtenancy or assignment? Here are a few:

- **Subtenancy.** If you allow a subtenancy, you have no direct legal relationship with the new tenant (see Section 2, below). Practically, this means that if you should need to sue her for damage to the property or failure to pay rent, you cannot do it directly; you must involve the original tenant.

- **Assignment.** If you allow the tenant to assign the lease, the new tenant (the assignee) steps into the original tenant's legal shoes and (unlike a subtenant) has a complete legal relationship with you. In short, you can take legal action directly against the assignee in any dispute. In addition, you get one significant advantage: If the new tenant fails to pay the rent, the old one is still legally responsible to do so. (See Section 2, below.) So why prefer a new tenancy? Simply because insisting on a regular tenancy will do away with any misunderstanding about who is liable. If disagreements later arise concerning liability for damages or rent, the new tenant knows exactly where she stands.

## Only Landlords Can Evict Tenants

A co-tenant may not terminate another co-tenant's tenancy. Termination and eviction are available only to landlords.

But a tenant who rents out part of his premises to another (called a subtenant) has considerably more power. If you allow this kind of subtenancy, realize that you have allowed your tenant to be a "landlord" as well (he's your tenant *and* the subtenant's landlord). And in his role as landlord to a subtenant, he *does* have the right to terminate and evict the subtenant.

Most owners want to control when and if the local police show up on their property to enforce eviction decrees. For this reason alone, it behooves you to prohibit "tenancies within tenancies" by insisting that every occupant become a full-fledged co-tenant.

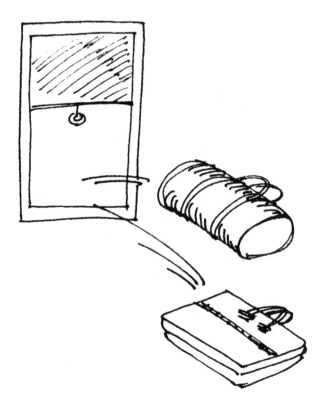

The sample Termination of Lease below will terminate the original tenancy so that you can rent the property to the new tenant. Then, if and when the first tenant wants to return and the second voluntarily leaves, you can again rent to the first, using a new lease.

 You will find a Termination of Lease on the Legal Forms Disk and a blank tear-out copy in Appendix II.

## Common Terms

**Prime tenant.** We use this term to refer to the original tenant—someone you chose from a pool of applicants and who has signed a lease or rental agreement. This is our shortcut term—it has no legal meaning.

Here are common terms that do have accepted, legal meaning:

**Tenant.** Someone who has signed a lease or a rental contract, or who has gained the status of a tenant because the landlord has accepted his presence on the property or has accepted rent from him.

**Co-tenants.** Two or more tenants who rent the same property under the same lease or rental agreement. As far as the landlord is concerned, each is 100% responsible for carrying out the agreement (in legal slang, "jointly and severally liable"), including paying all the rent. (See Section A.)

**Subtenant.** Someone who subleases (rents) all or part of the premises from a tenant (not the landlord).

**Assignment.** The transfer by a tenant of all his rights of tenancy to another tenant (the "assignee"). Unlike a subtenant, an assignee rents directly from the landlord.

**Roommates.** Two or more people, usually unrelated, living under the same roof and sharing rent and expenses. (See Section C.) A roommate is usually a co-tenant, but in some situations may be a subtenant.

---

**Termination of Lease**

Robert Chin _____ ("Landlord")

and _____ Carl Mosk _____

("Tenant") agree that the lease they entered into on November 1, 199X _____, for premises at

_____ 56 Alpine Terrace, Hamilton, Tennessee _____, will terminate

on _____ January 5, 199X _____ .


_____ December 28, 199X _____      *Robert Chin* _____
Date                                    Landlord


_____ December 28, 199X _____      *Carl Mosk* _____
Date                                    Tenant

---

In most cases, tenants should be happy that you're letting them off the hook. But what if the original tenant really does want to return and is uneasy about having you rent to the new tenant directly, because he fears the second person may not honor her promise to leave? Your answer should normally be a polite version of "That's your problem." Think of it this way: Your tenant is admitting that he doesn't completely trust the new tenant to move out on demand, even though he selected her. You don't want to be in the middle of this type of situation. It's better that the original tenant bear the brunt of any problem—if there is one—than you.

## 2. Allow a Sublet or Assignment

Although you are almost always better off starting a new, independent tenancy with a proposed stand-in tenant, there are situations in which you may want to agree to a subtenancy or assignment.

## Co-Tenants Can Sublet and Assign, Too

The legal principles that apply to tenants who want to sublet or assign also apply to a co-tenant who wants to do the same thing. For example, it is not unusual for one of several roommates to want to sublet for a period of time, or assign the remainder of the lease. If you followed our advice and insisted that all roommates be official co-tenants on the lease, you are well-positioned to react to the co-tenant's request, just as you would if the request came from a lone tenant.

You might, for example, want to accommodate —and keep—an exceptional, long-term tenant who has every intention of returning and whose judgment and integrity you have always trusted. If the proposed stand-in meets your normal tenant criteria, you may decide that it is worth the risk of a subtenancy or assignment in order to keep the prime tenant.

Another good reason is a desire to have a sure source of funds in the background. This might come up if you have a prime tenant who is financially sound and trustworthy, but a proposed stand-in who is less secure but acceptable in every other respect. By agreeing to a sublet or assignment, you have someone in the background (the prime tenant) still responsible for the rent. The risk you incur by agreeing to set up a subtenancy or assignment and the hassle that comes with dealing with more than one person may be worth what you gain in keeping a sure and reliable source of funds on the hook.

EXAMPLE: The Smith family rented a duplex for a term of two years but, after 18 months, the father's employer transferred him to another city. Mr. Smith asked Bob, the landlord, to agree to an assignment of the balance of the lease to Mr. Smith's 19-year old son, who wanted to finish out his school year at the local college.

Knowing that the son was a decent and conscientious young man, Bob agreed, but did not insist that Mr. Smith terminate his tenancy.

Bob realized that keeping Dad in the picture was insurance against the unlikely but possible event that the son would not be able to keep up with the rental payments. Another way Bob could accomplish this same goal would be to end the old lease and create a new one with Mr. Smith's son, but require that Dad also sign it as a guarantor. (See discussion of co-signers in Chapter 2.)

If you would prefer not to allow a subtenancy or assignment, but the original tenant presses you, don't reject a proposed subtenant or assignee unless you have a good business reason. In a few states, including California and Florida, you may not unreasonably withhold your consent when asked to allow a sublet or assignment, no matter what the lease or rental agreement says. See "The Landlord's Duty to Re-Rent the Premises" table in Chapter 14 for state-by-state details. In broad terms, this requirement means that you must use the same criteria in evaluating the proposed stand-in that you used when choosing the prime tenant.

You can stay out of trouble by evaluating the proposed tenant by exactly the same standards that you use in evaluating any other new tenant: financial stability, credit history, references and other criteria described in Chapter 1. If the would-be subtenant or assignee passes your tests, great; rent to him or her. If he fails the test that you apply to all potential tenants, you will be legally justified in saying "No."

Then, if the prime tenant goes ahead and breaks the lease, leaving you with lost rents and re-rental expenses, you can sue. You should be able to show a judge that you fairly considered (but objectively rejected) the proposed new tenant as part of your duty to try to limit (mitigate) your losses. But if the prime tenant convinces the judge that you unreasonably turned down an acceptable substitute tenant, chances are you'll lose.

⚠ **Don't discriminate illegally.** If you turn down a proposed subtenant or assignee for an illegal reason (racial discrimination, for example), you are vulnerable to a lawsuit under federal laws and some state and local laws (see Chapter 5 for an extended discussion of illegal discrimination).

## a. Sublets

A *subtenant* is someone who rents all or part of the property from a tenant and does not sign a rental agreement or lease with you. A subtenant either:

- rents (sublets) an entire dwelling from a tenant who moves out temporarily—for example, for the summer, or
- rents one or more rooms from the tenant, who continues to live in the unit. (See Section C discussion of roommates.)

The key to subtenant relationships is that the original tenant retains the primary relationship with you and continues to exercise some control over the rental property, either by occupying part of the unit or by reserving the right to retake possession at a later date. The prime tenant functions as the subtenant's landlord. The subtenant is responsible to the prime tenant for the rent, which is usually whatever figure they have agreed to between themselves. The prime tenant, in turn, is responsible to the landlord for the rent. The written or oral agreement by which a tenant rents to a subtenant is called a *sublease*, because it is under the primary lease.

Subtenancies are often a pain in the neck for landlords. Besides the obvious hassles of dealing with people coming and going, landlords in some states are limited by law to the kinds of lawsuits they can bring against subtenants. In these states, and for reasons that stretch back to age-old principles of English law, landlords and subtenants can sue each other to correct behavior that is contrary to the lease, but they cannot sue for money damages. This means, for instance, that a subtenant may go to court to force you to maintain habitable housing, but you could not sue that subtenant for money damages if he left the place a mess and the security deposit was insufficient to cover your loss (you

would have to sue the original tenant). If you have an excellent long-term tenant who really wants to return after subleasing for a few months, you may want to risk it.

⚠ **Don't accept rent from a subtenant.** Repeatedly taking rent from a subtenant, plus taking other actions that indicate that you have basically forgotten about the prime tenant, might turn a subtenancy into a tenancy—and take the prime tenant off the hook for rent.

---

### Leases vs. Rental Agreements

Our discussion of subleasing and assigning assumes that there is an underlying lease for a term of one year or more. If there is a long amount of time remaining on a lease, both landlord and tenant will be very concerned about a number of issues, including a tenant's obligation for remaining rent and the landlord's duty to find a new tenant and limit (mitigate) his losses.

By contrast, a month-to-month tenancy lasts no more than 30 days. When a tenant wants to leave before the end of the 30 days (to sublet and return, say, on day 28, or to assign the rental agreement and not return at all), the short amount of time (and rent money) remaining on the rental agreement may make a landlord less willing to accept the substitute.

You should not be any less thorough in checking the background of a proposed subtenant or assignee of a rental agreement, however. In theory the amount of money at stake may be less than that involved in a lease, since the tenancy usually can be terminated with 30 days notice for any reason. In reality, however, other considerations (such as the health and safety of other tenants, or the possibility of accepting a tenacious bad apple who proves difficult and expensive to evict) suggest the need for the same background checking that is used in evaluating any new tenant. (Chapter 1 discusses how to screen tenants.)

## Comparing Subleases and Assignments

|  | Sublease | Assignment |
| --- | --- | --- |
| **Rent** | New tenant (subtenant) is liable to the prime tenant, not to the landlord. Prime tenant is liable to landlord. | New tenant (assignee) is liable to the landlord. Old tenant is liable if new tenant doesn't pay. |
| **Damage to premises** | Prime tenant is liable for damage caused by new tenant. | Absent an agreement to the contrary, prime tenant is not liable for damage caused by new tenant. |
| **Violations of lease** | Landlord can't sue new tenant for money losses caused by violating lease, because new tenant never signed lease. New tenant can't sue landlord for lease violations, either. | New tenant and landlord are bound by all terms in lease except those that were purely personal to the landlord or old tenant. |
| **Eviction** | Landlord can sue to evict new tenant for any reason old tenant could have been evicted. But to evict subtenant, landlord must also evict old tenant. | Landlord can sue to evict new tenant for any reason old tenant could have been evicted. |

## b. Assignments

From a landlord's point of view, assignments are usually preferable to subleases. With an assignment, you have more control over the tenant because you have a direct legal relationship with the assignee.

An *assignee* is a person to whom the prime tenant has turned over the entire lease. In most states, this means simply that the prime tenant has moved out permanently. The assignee not only moves into the premises formerly occupied by the prime tenant, but into her legal shoes as well. Unlike a subtenant, whose legal relationship is with the prime tenant, not you, the assignee rents directly from you. If things go wrong with respect to behavior or money matters under the lease, the assignee can sue or be sued by the landlord.

Assignment doesn't, however, completely sever the legal relationship between you and the original tenant. Oddly enough, the original tenant remains responsible for the rent if the assignee fails to pay. Absent an agreement to the contrary, however, the prime tenant is not liable for damage to the premises caused by the assignee. (The Consent to Assignment of Lease form, discussed below, protects you by incorporating this promise.)

Generally, the landlord and assignee are bound by promises made in the lease signed by the original tenant. For example, the lease provision in which the landlord agreed to return the security deposit in a certain manner is still in effect; it now benefits the assignee. And the assignee must honor the previous tenant's promise to abide by the lease's noise rules and use restrictions. Only in very unusual situations, where a lease provision is purely personal, is it not transferred. For example, a promise by a tenant to do a landlord's shopping in exchange for a rent reduction would not automatically pass to an assignee.

### Laws That Lock In the Tenant

Legislatures in some states have tried to protect landlords from tenants who want to break a lease. In California, for example, the landlord can "lock in" the tenant—that is, continue to legally expect rent to be paid as it comes due without the duty to look for another tenant. (During this time, the landlord must not "retake" the property, so that the original tenant can, at any time during the lease term, come back.)

Two conditions are necessary before a California landlord may "lock in" a tenant:

- The lease must include a provision that the landlord will not unreasonably withhold consent to an assignment, and
- The tenant must have abandoned the lease without producing an acceptable substitute.

While this sounds good, it has big practical limitations. The biggest one is leaving the property vacant while you track down, sue and collect from the departing tenant. Most owners would rather collect rent from a good current tenant than someone far away, who may be difficult, if not impossible, to sue. So despite this law, a lease-breaking tenant usually escapes with everything but the deposit.

**Liability for injuries remains the same.** If a subtenant or assignee is injured on your property, the question of whether you are liable will be the same as if the injured person were the original tenant. Chapters 10, 11 and 12 discuss liability-related issues.

### How to Assign a Lease

Typically, to accomplish an assignment the landlord and the tenant write "Assigned to John Doe" on the lease at each place where the prime tenant's name appears. The new tenant, John Doe, then signs at each place where the original tenant signed. If this is all that's done, the prime tenant remains liable for the rent, but not for damage to the property.

We suggest that a formal "Consent to Assignment of Lease" document also be used, such as the sample shown below. Using this form protects you in two additional respects:

- It educates the prime tenant to the fact that he will remain liable for the rent if the assignee defaults, and
- It obligates the prime tenant to cover damages to the property beyond normal wear and tear if the assignee refuses or is unable to do so.

You will find a Consent to Assignment of Lease form on the Legal Forms Disk and a blank, tear-out copy in Appendix II.

## C. When a Tenant Brings in a Roommate

Suppose now that love (or poverty) strikes your tenant and he wants to move in a roommate. Assuming your lease or rental agreement restricts the number of people who can occupy the unit (as ours does in Clause 3), the tenant must get your written permission for additional tenants.

### 1. Giving Permission for a New Roommate

Although you may be motivated to accommodate your tenant's friend, your decision to allow a new co-tenant should be based principally on whether

# Consent to Assignment of Lease

Carolyn Friedman ("Landlord") and

Joel Oliver ("Tenant") and

Sam Parker ("Assignee")

agree as follows:

1. Tenant has leased the premises at 5 Fulton, Indianapolis, Indiana _____ from Landlord.

2. The lease was signed on April 1 , 199 X , and will expire on March 31 , 199 X .

3. Tenant is assigning the balance of Tenant's lease to Assignee, beginning on November 1 , 199 X , and ending on March 31 , 199 X .

4. Tenant's financial responsibilities under the terms of the lease are not ended by virtue of this assignment. Specifically, Tenant understands that:

   a. If Assignee defaults and fails to pay the rent as provided in the lease, namely on the first of the month , Tenant will be obligated to do so within three days of being notified by Landlord; and

   b. If Assignee damages the property beyond normal wear and tear and fails or refuses to pay for repairs or replacement, Tenant will be obligated to do so.

5. As of the effective date of the assignment, Tenant permanently gives up the right to occupy the premises.

6. Assignee is bound by every term and condition in the lease that is the subject of this assignment.


October 1, 199X     Carolyn Friedman
Date     Landlord

October 1, 199X     Joel Oliver
Date     Tenant

October 1, 199X     Sam Parker
Date     Assignee

or not you believe the new person will be a decent tenant. After all, if the original tenant moves out at some later date (maybe even because the new person is so awful), you will remain stuck with this person. So always have the proposed new tenant complete a rental application (see Chapter 1) and follow your normal screening procedures. If the new person meets your standards (a good credit record and references), and there is enough space in the unit, you will probably want to say yes. (See Chapter 5 for overcrowding standards that you may lawfully impose.)

**Don't give spouses the third degree.** The one exception to the rule of checking new tenants carefully has to do with spouses. If the new tenant is a spouse and there's no problem with overcrowding, be very careful before you say no. Refusal without a good, solid reason could be considered illegal discrimination based on marital status. (See Chapter 5, discussion of discrimination.) In short, it's fine to check the person out, but say no only if you discover a real problem.

## 2. Preparing a New Rental Agreement or Lease

If you allow a new person to move in, make sure he becomes a full co-tenant by preparing a new lease or rental agreement—possibly with some changed terms, such as the amount of rent—for signature by all tenants. (Chapter 14 discusses how.) Do this before the new person moves in to avoid the possibility of a legally confused situation. (See Section B discussion of subtenants.)

We suggest that you send a letter to the original tenant and the new tenant as soon as you decide to allow the newcomer to move in. A sample Letter to Original Tenant and New Co-Tenant is shown below.

You will find a Letter to Original Tenant and New Co-Tenant on the Legal Forms Disk, and a blank tear-out copy in Appendix II.

## 3. Raising the Rent

When an additional tenant comes in, it is both reasonable and legal (in either a lease or a rental agreement situation) for you to raise the rent (and/or the security deposit), unless you live in an area covered by a rent control law that prohibits you from doing so. (Chapter 3 discusses rent rules and rent control.) Obviously, from your point of view, more people living in a residence means more wear and tear and higher maintenance costs in the long run. Also, as long as your increase is reasonable, it should not be a big issue with existing occupants, who, after all, will now have someone else to pay part of the total rent.

**Make rent policy clear in advance.** To avoid making tenants feel that you invented a rent increase policy at the last minute to unfairly extract extra money, it's a good idea to establish in advance

## Letter to Original Tenant and New Co-Tenant

_July 22, 199X_
Date


Dear _Abby Rivas_ and
      New co-tenant

      _Phoebe Viorst_ ,
      Original tenant or tenants


As the landlord of _239 Maple Street_

_____ (address) , I am pleased that

_Abby_ (new co-tenant)

has proved to be an acceptable applicant and will be joining _Phoebe_

_____ (original tenant or tenants) as a co-tenant. Before

_Abby_ (new co-tenant)

moves in, everyone must sign a new lease that will cover your rights and responsibilities. Please

contact me at the address or phone number below at your earliest convenience so that we can

arrange a time for us to meet and sign a new lease. Do not begin the process of moving in until we

have signed a lease.


Sincerely yours,

_Sam Stone_
Landlord
_1234 Central Avenue_
Street address
_Sun City, Minnesota_
City and State
_612-555-4567_
Phone

your rent policies for units occupied by more than one person. A move-in letter (see Chapter 7) is a good place to do this. That way, your request for higher rent when an additional roommate moves in will simply be in line with what you charge everyone who occupies a unit of a certain size with a certain number of people.

Just as you may want to take this opportunity to raise the rent, you may also want to increase the amount of the security deposit. (Chapter 4 discusses security deposits.) Again, however, if the property is subject to rent control, you may need to petition the local rent control board for permission to increase the rent based on an increased number of occupants.

## D. Guests and New Occupants You Haven't Approved

Our form rental agreement and lease include a clause requiring your written consent for guests to stay overnight more than a reasonable amount of time. We recommend that you allow guests to stay up to ten days in any six-month period without your written permission. (See Clause 3 of the form lease and rental agreements in Chapter 2.) The value of this clause is that a tenant who tries to move someone in for a longer period has clearly violated a defined standard, which gives you grounds for eviction.

When deciding when and whether to enforce this clause, you'll need to use a good amount of common sense. Obviously, the tenant whose boyfriend regularly spends two or three nights a week will quickly use up the ten-day allotment. However, it would be unrealistic to expect the boyfriend (assuming he has his own apartment) to become a co-tenant, and you may not object to the arrangement at all. In short, you'll want to turn a blind eye.

At the same time, you may well want to keep your lease or rental agreement clause restricting guests, in the event that an occasional arrangement starts to become too permanent. But don't be surprised if a tenant claims that your prior willingness

to disregard the clause limiting guests means you gave up the right to enforce it. The best way to counter this claim is to be as consistent as you can. (Don't let one tenant have a guest five nights a week and balk when another does so for two.) As long as you are reasonably consistent, a court will likely side with you if push comes to shove and you decide to evict a tenant who completely refuses to obey your rules.

If a tenant simply moves a roommate in on the sly—despite the fact that your lease or rental agreement prohibits it—or it appears that a "guest" has moved in clothing and furniture and begun to receive mail at your property, it's best to take decisive action right away. If you think your tenant is reasonable, send a letter telling the tenant that the new roommate or longtime guest must move out immediately. (You can use the Warning Letter for Lease or Rental Agreement Violation in Chapter 16 for this purpose.) But if you feel that the tenant will not respond to an informal notice, use a formal termination notice as explained in Chapter 17. If you allow the situation to continue, the danger is strong that the roommate will turn into a subtenant—one you obviously haven't screened or approved of. This can have significant negative consequences: While a subtenant doesn't have all the rights of a tenant, she is entitled, in an eviction proceeding, to the same legal protection as a tenant (see Section B2, above). And she may even turn into a de facto prime tenant if the original tenant suddenly moves out.

**Get help to evict unwanted occupants.** If you want to get rid of an unacceptable new occupant, initiate legal proceedings quickly. Technically, these proceedings are not an eviction (only tenants can be evicted), but instead either a criminal complaint for trespassing or a civil suit aimed at ridding the property of a squatter. If you are faced with this situation, you will probably need to consult a lawyer for advice.

Again, your best choice is to insist that the roommate or guest fill out a formal application. Assuming he checks out, you may also increase the rent or the security deposit, unless that's prohibited by any applicable rent control ordinance.

If you do not want to rent to the guest or roommate and if that person remains on the premises, make it immediately clear in writing that you will evict all occupants based on breach of the occupancy terms of the lease if the person doesn't leave immediately.

**Avoid discrimination against guests.** In many states and cities, you cannot legally object to a tenant's frequent overnight guests based on your religious or moral views. (See Chapter 5.) For example, it is illegal to discriminate against unmarried couples, including gay or lesbian couples, in many states and cities. In short, our advice is to worry about your tenants' business practices, not their personal ones. ■

# Chapter 9

# Landlord's Duty to Repair and Maintain the Premises

Landlords in virtually every state are required by law to provide rental property that meets basic structural, health and safety standards—although some states set more stringent requirements than others. Every landlord needs to know that if he doesn't meet his duties, tenants may legally respond in a variety of ways. Depending on the state, tenants may have the legal right to:

- reduce or withhold rent
- pay for repairs themselves and deduct the cost from the rent
- sue you, or
- move out without notice.

This chapter describes landlords' and tenants' rights and responsibilities for repair and maintenance under state and local housing laws and judicial decisions. It also provides practical advice on how to stay on top of your repair and maintenance needs and minimize financial losses and legal problems with tenants.

The recommendations in this chapter reflect our belief that you will be better off in the long run if you offer and maintain housing in excellent condition—that is, you go beyond satisfying the letter of the law. Those of you in states with less stringent repair and maintenance responsibilities may question our advice that you meet higher standards. Although from a purely legal standpoint you may have a point, it's important to understand that our reasons for suggesting that you do an excellent job of maintaining your property are eminently practical. Here's why:

- For most landlords, particularly those in urban areas or in larger states, chances are a state or local housing code sets high standards. Comfortably exceeding these standards will help you avoid expensive legal trouble.
- Tenants who are given an added measure of care are likely to be more satisfied—and, as a result, easier to deal with. More importantly, happy tenants are likely to stay longer, resulting in fewer turnovers and interruptions of your stream of income.

- Landlords who know that they are well within their state's legal requirements can be confident that their housing is not likely to be found wanting if they are challenged by a disgruntled tenant. You can negotiate from a position of strength (and get more sleep at night), since you know you are likely to win if a dispute ends up in court.
- Landlords who maintain their property well are far less likely to face the risk of tenant lawsuits based on habitability problems or injuries resulting from defective conditions. A good record in this regard can, of course, translate into lower insurance premiums.

Related topics in this book include:
- Writing clear lease and rental agreement provisions for repair and maintenance: Chapter 2
- Setting valid occupancy limits: Chapter 5
- Delegating maintenance and repair responsibilities to a manager: Chapter 6
- Highlighting repair and maintenance procedures in a move-in letter to new tenants and using a Landlord-Tenant Checklist to keep track of the condition of the premises before and after the tenant moves in: Chapter 7
- Landlord's liability for a tenant's injuries caused by defective housing conditions: Chapter 10
- Landlord's responsibility for cleaning up environmental hazards, such as asbestos and lead: Chapter 11
- Landlord's responsibilities to protect tenants from criminal assault, and to protect neighbors from illegal activities of tenants: Chapter 12
- Conducting a final inspection of the rental unit for cleaning and damage repair before the tenant moves out: Chapter 15
- How to research state laws, local ordinances and court cases on landlord repair and maintenance responsibilities: Chapter 18.

## A. The Implied Warranty of Habitability

The cornerstone of landlord responsibility for repairing and maintaining rental premises is a legal doctrine called the implied warranty of habitability. Landlords who are subject to the implied warranty are legally required to offer livable premises when they originally rent an apartment or unit and to maintain them in that condition throughout the rental term.

Nearly every state has, by judicial decision or statute, adopted the implied warranty of habitability. Only Alabama, Arkansas and Colorado have not adopted this warranty. Landlords in these states retain some repair and maintenance responsibilities, however, because of the covenant of quiet enjoyment, a common law requirement discussed in Section B below. In addition, local laws in these three states, particularly those in urban areas, may specify health and safety requirements that essentially amount to a requirement that rental housing be habitable.

We begin our discussion of your obligations to repair and maintain by explaining the content of the implied warranty of habitability. Later on in this chapter, we explain consequences to landlords who have not lived up to its requirements. (Tenant remedies, such as rent withholding and termination of the lease, are discussed in Sections C and D, below.)

### 1. Legal Basis of the Implied Warranty of Habitability

The implied warranty of habitability has its origins in a court case decided in 1970 in Washington, D.C. (*Javins v. First National Realty Corp.*, 428 F.2d 1071 (DC Cir. 1970)). In the *Javins* case, a landlord sued to evict his tenants for nonpayment of rent, and the tenants countered by pointing to 1,500 housing code violations that the landlord had refused to fix. The court ruled in favor of the tenants, by allowing the amount of their unpaid rent to be applied to repairs of the building, and refusing to let the landlord evict the tenants. In making his decision, the judge pointed to two sources for the notion that landlords should offer and maintain their property in a habitable way:

- local building codes that specify minimum requirements for heat, water, plumbing and other essential services, and
- widely-held common law notions of what constitutes decent housing.

All of the states that have adopted the implied warranty of habitability, either by court action or statute, have apparently done so using one or the other of these two approaches. Unfortunately, however, many states have not made it clear which source (building codes or court decisions) was the basis for the implied warranty. This has important consequences for the landlord, since the source of the warranty determines the landlord's responsibilities and the legal remedies available to tenants.

### 2. Local or State Housing Laws as Basis of Implied Warranty

Cities and counties (and sometimes entire states) adopt building or housing codes to protect the health and safety of residential tenants. These codes regulate structural aspects of buildings and usually set specific space and occupancy standards, such as the minimum size of sleeping rooms. They also establish minimum requirements for light and ventilation, sanitation and sewage disposal, heating, water supply (such as how hot the water must be), fire protection and wiring (such as the number of electrical outlets per room).

In addition, housing codes typically make property owners responsible for keeping common areas (or parts of the premises which the owner controls) in a clean, sanitary and safe condition.

Courts in some states, including Idaho, West Virginia and the District of Columbia, have decided that the implied warranty of habitability requires no more (or less) than the requirements specified in the state and local housing codes. Landlords who live in states with this approach enjoy the luxury of knowing that they can find out the exact details of their repair and maintenance responsibilities. In states taking this approach, substantial compliance with the housing codes (rather than literal, 100% compliance) is generally viewed as being sufficient. In short, the tenant may usually withhold rent (as did the defendants in the *Javins* case), successfully defend against an eviction action and pursue other remedies discussed in Sections C and D only for significant violations of the codes that affect their health and welfare.

## Who's Responsible for Habitability Problems?

It is important to understand the difference between being legally obligated for the habitability of rental property and financially responsible to keep it fit. In most situations—for example, when a unit is rented in the first place—the owner is on the hook for both responsibilities. What happens, however, if the tenant does something to make the property unfit—for example, by negligently breaking the water main? If damage beyond regular wear and tear is caused by a tenant or his guest, the financial burden of fixing it properly falls on the tenant. The landlord, however, remains responsible for seeing that the work gets done and the property returned to a habitable state. In this situation, the landlord could rightly bill the tenant for the repair. (Clause 11 of the form lease and rental agreements in Chapter 2 alerts the tenant to this responsibility.) If, however, the damage is done by a third party (such as a vandal or burglar), or if it is the result of normal wear and tear, the landlord bears the burden of fixing and paying for the damage. (See Section B, below, for more details on tenants' repair and maintenance responsibilities.)

## 3. Court Decisions as the Basis of the Implied Warranty

In many states, including California, Iowa, New York and Vermont, the implied warranty of habitability is considered by courts to be independent of any housing code. Under this approach, the legal question is not merely whether the building meets specific state or local housing codes, but whether it is "fit for human occupation," or "fit and habitable." Although a breach of the housing code does not automatically determine that a unit is uninhabitable (nor does compliance alone mean that it is habitable), usually a substantial housing code violation will also qualify as a breach of the warranty of habitability.

The independence of the implied warranty of habitability from the housing code has particular importance to landlords because it:

- imposes duties of maintenance or repair on the landlord in situations where the housing or building codes are poorly written or non-existent, and
- allows a court to require *more* of a landlord than the letter of the law as contained in the housing or building codes.

EXAMPLE: The city building code where Russell owned a few small apartment buildings required residential rental properties to have a kitchen sink, but said nothing about a separate kitchen. Russell assumed that he would not have to provide a separate room or other kitchen facilities, except for the sink. He was dismayed to learn that the law in his state, developed in court cases over the years, also required that, to be habitable, a unit must contain a separate and sanitary cooking area.

As you might expect, understanding how courts have interpreted the "fit" and "habitable" concepts is much more difficult than understanding the code-specified square footage requirements or minimum hot water temperatures typical of housing codes.

Nevertheless, it's possible to identify key requirements, as follows.

### a. Basic Definition of "Fit" and "Habitable"

There are some aspects of rental housing that are covered by virtually every implied warranty law based on court decisions. These include:

- the maintenance of all common areas, such as hallways and stairways, in a safe and clean condition
- the maintenance of electrical, plumbing, sanitary, heating ventilating, air-conditioning and elevators that are supplied by the landlord or that are required to be supplied by him
- supplying water, hot water and heat in reasonable amounts at reasonable times, and
- providing trash receptacles and arranging for their removal.

### b. Geographic Variations

Whether housing is "fit" and "habitable" depends substantially on the weather, the terrain and where the rental property is located. Thus, features or services that might be considered nonessential extras in some parts of the country are legally viewed as components of fit and habitable housing in others. For example:

- In climates that experience severe winters, storm windows or shutters may be considered basic equipment.
- Housing in wet, rainy areas needs to be protected from the damp. In Oregon, for example, courts have specifically made the landlord responsible for waterproofing.
- In areas especially prone to insect infestations, landlords may be required to provide extermination services. In Florida, the landlord must exterminate bedbugs, mice, roaches and ants.

### c. Habitability Is an Evolving Concept

Having its roots in the decisions of judges, the implied warranty of habitability is obviously not a frozen legal idea. The meaning of the phrase has evolved significantly even in the 25 years since its widespread adoption, as living conditions have changed and technology has advanced. Here are two recent trends:

- Courts are likely to consider the prevalence of crime in urban areas when determining what constitutes habitable housing. Good locks, security personnel, exterior lighting and secure common areas may, in some cities, be seen as an absolute necessity, as important to the tenants as are water and heat. Chapter 12 discusses your need to provide adequate security, and the consequences for failure to do so.
- The discovery that lead-based paint and asbestos building materials pose significant health hazards has suggested to some courts that buildings containing these materials are not fit for habitation. (See Chapter 11 for a detailed discussion of landlord liability for environmental hazards.)

## Local Housing Codes and Nuisances

Local housing codes prohibit something called "nuisances," broadly defined by statutes as whatever is dangerous to human life or detrimental to health, as determined by the public health officer—for example, overcrowding a room with occupants, providing insufficient ventilation or illumination or inadequate sewage or plumbing facilities, or allowing drug dealing on the premises. A landlord found to have created or tolerated a nuisance will be subject to the code's enforcement and penalty provisions.

The local ordinances also prohibit "attractive nuisances." These are conditions that would tend to attract inquisitive children, such as abandoned vehicles, wells and shafts, basements, abandoned equipment or appliances, excavations and unsafe fences, structures or foliage. If children are hurt while playing in or on an attractive nuisance, you may be held liable.

## B. How to Meet Your Legal Responsibilities

A conscientious landlord, no matter where he lives, can meet repair and maintenance responsibilities by following the steps outlined below.

### 1. Know and Comply With Local Housing Codes

Every landlord needs to know what the local housing codes call for in the way of structural requirements, facilities and essential services, such as plumbing and heat. Your local building or housing authority, and health or fire department, can provide this information.

Be sure to find out about all ordinances affecting your repair and maintenance responsibilities—for

example, many cities require the installation of smoke detectors in residential units, or security items, such as viewing devices in doors that open onto a hallway. Some cities also make owners responsible for the prevention of infestation and, if necessary, the extermination of insects, rodents and other pests.

## Exemptions for Older Buildings

When a housing code changes, it doesn't necessarily mean that all existing buildings are illegal because they are not "up to code." Especially when it comes to items that would involve major structural changes, lawmakers will often exempt certain older buildings. They do it by writing a "grandfather clause" into the code, exempting all buildings constructed before a certain date (sometimes that date is the same as when the new code takes effect, but not always). Such exemptions will often not apply to renovations or remodeling, meaning that, over the years, you may eventually have to comply with these new rules. Contact your local housing authority for information on any "grandfather clauses" that may apply to your rental property.

There are, however, many types of code changes—for example, those involving locks, peepholes and smoke detectors—that must be made regardless of the age of the building and irrespective of the fact that the owner wasn't intending to remodel or renovate.

### 2. Know and Comply With State Housing Laws

Legislatures in most states have also enacted general laws governing landlords' repair and maintenance responsibilities, which in many instances require you to make all repairs and do whatever is necessary to put and keep the premises in a fit and habitable condition. In addition, some state legislatures have written more detailed laws in response to geographic and weather conditions as described above. And, as with local housing laws, some state laws require smoke detectors and the extermination of rodents and insects or specify security measures involving locks and keys.

You should get a copy of and carefully read your state housing laws, because landlords who fail to comply with state housing laws face problems similar to those resulting from violating local housing codes. Appendix I includes citations for the major state laws affecting landlords. You'll need to look through these statutes in a law library or online, if your state has posted its codes. (See Chapter 18 for a list of states that have posted their codes, and for advice on using the law library.) If you're using an index, check your statutes under headings such as Landlord Obligations to Maintain Premises. You might also contact your state consumer protection agency for pamphlets or brochures that describe landlords' repair and maintenance responsibilities in less legalistic terms. (Appendix I includes a list of state consumer protection agencies, and notes those which provide free informational brochures for landlords and tenants.)

⚠️ **Rural property owners alert:** Checking state housing laws is particularly important to landlords who live in communities—such as some rural and unincorporated areas—where there may be no local ordinance (or a very limited one). In these areas, state law, and court cases decided under state law, will be the only guide to the implied warranty of habitability.

Checking out state law and local housing ordinances, and complying with all requirements, should adequately protect landlords from any tenant claim of uninhabitability. (Sections C and D of this chapter discuss tenant remedies for violation of state housing laws.) But if such a claim is raised, you may want to do further research by looking at how courts have interpreted housing law in your state. See Chapter 18 for legal research tips.

## Enforcement of Housing Codes

Local housing authorities, such as a building, health or fire department, may discover code violations through routine inspections or in response to a tenant complaint. If title to a property changes hands, an inspection will often accompany the sale; and if the property is used as collateral for a loan, the lender will usually require an inspection. Local authorities may cite rental properties that are unsafe, dangerous or hazardous—for example, due to lack of adequate heating facilities, trash in the hallways, hazardous electrical wiring, leaking roof, broken toilet or other defective conditions.

The local enforcement agency typically requires the property owner to remedy (within a certain amount of time, such as five business days) all violations found. If you fail to make any repairs demanded by local officials within the time allowed, the city or county may bring a civil lawsuit against you. Moreover, in many cities, failure to comply with cited violations of local housing laws is a criminal misdemeanor punishable by hefty fines or even imprisonment. In some cases, local officials may require that the building be vacated, with the landlord providing tenants with temporary housing, until the violation is corrected.

Tenants may also point to a violation of a local code if they do not pay the rent, or attempt to pay less, on the grounds that the premises are substandard. If you sue a tenant for eviction on the basis of nonpayment of rent, the tenant may use housing code violations as the justification for her action.

## Common Myths About Repairs and Maintenance

Many landlords (and tenants) are under the mistaken impression that every time a rental unit turns over, certain cosmetic changes, such as a new paint job, are required. The actual condition of the rental unit determines what's necessary in terms of repair and maintenance. Some changes may be called for during the tenancy, rather than at the end.

**Paint.** No state law requires you to repaint the interior every so often (local ordinances may, however). So long as the paint isn't creating a habitability problem—for example, paint that's so thick around a window that the window can't be opened—it should comply with the law. Lead-based paint, however, may create all sorts of legal problems—for example, if a child becomes ill from eating lead-based paint chips, a court may find you liable because of your carelessness. (We discuss negligence and liability for lead poisoning in Chapter 11.)

**Drapes and Carpets.** So long as drapes and carpets are not sufficiently damp or mildewy to constitute a health hazard, and so long as carpets don't have dangerous holes that could cause someone to trip and fall, you aren't legally required to replace them.

**Windows.** A tenant is responsible for a broken window only if she or her guest intentionally or carelessly broke it. If a burglar, vandal or neighborhood child broke a window, however, you are responsible for fixing it.

**Keys.** You may need to re-key every rental unit for each new tenant. In fact, this is the law in Texas and in many cities. Regardless of whether it's legally required, re-keying ought to be the practice of every careful rental property owner in order to reduce the chances of break-ins. See Chapter 12 for a thorough discussion of liability for crime on the premises.

## 3. Understand the Covenant of Quiet Enjoyment

Only Alabama, Arkansas and Colorado have not legally embraced the implied warranty of habitability, either by judicial decision or statute. Landlords in these three states are not required to offer housing that is fit and habitable at the time it is rented. But they are not completely off the hook as to repair and maintenance responsibilities. First, as noted above, there may be local ordinances or state building or safety laws that impose duties similar to the implied warranty. Second, landlords in all 50 states are subject to the age-old common law requirement applicable that the landlord not breach the "covenant of quiet enjoyment." As courts define it, this amounts to an implied promise that you will not act (or fail to act) in a way that interferes with or destroys the ability of the tenant to use the rented premises.

Examples of violations of the covenant of quiet enjoyment include:

- tolerating a nuisance, such as allowing garbage to pile up or a major rodent infestation
- failing to provide sufficient working electrical outlets, so that tenants cannot use appliances, and
- failing to fix a leaky roof, which deprives a tenant of the use of his rented space.

Although the covenant of quiet enjoyment is not as far-reaching as the implied warranty of habitability—that is, landlords can get away with more in Alabama, Arkansas and Colorado—the remedies available to tenants are substantially the same in both cases. Moreover, the tenant who can show that the covenant has been broken can simply refuse to pay rent and move out, claiming that the interference was tantamount to eviction. This is called "constructive eviction." Sections C and D discuss tenant remedies.

## 4. Don't Try to Evade Your Legal Responsibilities

Some landlords have attempted to get around the implied warranty of habitability by advancing one or both of the following theories:

- **Tenant waiver.** Landlords may argue that, if the housing was substandard when the lease or rental agreement began, or it became so during the tenancy, the fact that the tenant nevertheless moved in (or stayed) indicated that he *waived* the protections of the implied warranty.

- **Landlord disclaimer.** Some lease or rental agreements include a clause stating that the landlord will not satisfy the implied warranty's requirements. You may argue that a tenant who signs a lease with this type of clause has effectively absolved you from the responsibility of the implied warranty of habitability.

In a rare showing of unanimity, courts almost everywhere have rejected these two legal theories. Except for a handful of states, including Maine and Texas, neither a tenant waiver (at the beginning of the tenancy or during its life) nor disclaimer in the lease will relieve you of the responsibility to provide housing that begins—and remains—fit and habitable.

You may, however, legally delegate some repair and maintenance responsibilities to tenants. Many states have specific rules regarding the types of repairs that can be delegated, and you need to use common sense when deciding whether to entrust particular jobs to tenants. (See Section F, below.)

⚠ **Choose your lease or rental agreement carefully.** Be especially leery of preprinted "form" leases available in stationery stores or generic software programs. They are usually not designed for the laws of each state, and as a result they often include clauses that are illegal in many states and localities. To be on solid ground, consult your state and local laws and use the lease or rental agreement included in this book. (See Chapter 2.)

## 5. Make Sure You—And Your Tenant— Know the Tenant's Obligations

Cities and states that impose landlord maintenance and repair responsibilities typically specify tenant obligations to maintain a dwelling unit. If a dwelling is rendered uninhabitable due to the tenant's failure to keep up his end of the bargain, the tenant will have a difficult, if not impossible, time convincing a judge that he is not a suitable candidate for eviction and the repair bill. (If the tenant won't pay up, you can deduct the expense from the security deposit.)

State and local housing laws generally require the tenant to:

**Keep the rental unit as clean and safe as the condition of the premises permits.** For example, if the kitchen has a rough, unfinished wooden floor that is hard to keep clean, you should not expect it to be shiny and spotless—but a tenant with a new tile floor would be expected to do a decent job. If she doesn't, and you have to do a major clean-up when she moves out, you may legitimately deduct its cost from her security deposit.

**Dispose of garbage, rubbish and other waste in a clean and safe manner.** For instance, if mice or ants invaded the kitchen because your tenant forgot to take out the garbage before he left on a two-week vacation, the tenant would be responsible for paying any necessary extermination costs.

**Keep plumbing fixtures as clean as their condition permits.** For example, bathtub caulking that has sprouted mold and mildew will render the tub unusable (or at least disgusting). Since it could have been prevented by proper cleaning, the tenant is responsible. On the other hand, if the bathroom has no fan and the window has been painted shut, the bathroom will be hard to air out; resulting mildew might be your responsibility.

**Use electrical, plumbing, sanitary, heating, ventilating, air-conditioning and other facilities and other systems, including elevators, properly.** Examples of abuse by tenants include overloading electrical outlets and flushing large objects down the toilet.

**Fix things the tenant breaks or damages.** If a tenant causes a serious habitability problem on your property—for example, carelessly breaking the heater—she is responsible. You can insist that she pay for the repair. Legally, she can't just decide to live without heat for a while to save money. If she drags her feet, you can use her security deposit to pay for it, and if that isn't enough, sue her besides. You can't, however, charge her for problems caused by normal wear and tear—for example, a carpet that has worn out from use.

In addition to these basics, some states set additional tenant responsibilities, such as requiring that tenants inform the landlord, as soon as practicable, of defective conditions of the premises that the tenant believes to be unknown to the landlord and that the tenant believes is the landlord's duty to repair.

To protect yourself (and to notify your tenant of what's required), make sure your lease or rental agreement spells out these basic tenant obligations—to maintain the dwelling unit and notify the landlord of defects—regardless of whether or not they are required by law in your state. (See Clause 11 of the form agreements in Chapter 2. Also, see Clause

13, which specifically prohibits tenant's damage to the property and disturbing neighbors.)

## 6. Repair What You Provide or Promise

State and local housing laws typically deal with basic living conditions only—heat, water and plumbing, for example. They do not usually deal with "amenities"—features that are not essential but make living a little easier. Examples are drapes, washing machines, swimming pools, saunas, parking places, intercoms and dishwashers. Although housing laws clearly do not require you to furnish these things, a landlord who does may nevertheless be legally required to maintain or repair them. The reason for this is simple: By providing amenities, the law concludes that you promise to maintain them. This promise might be express (in the lease) or implied.

When the lease or rental agreement says that you will repair or maintain certain items, such as appliances, the promise is express. When you (or a manager or rental agent) says something that seems to indicate that you will be responsible for repairing or maintaining an item or facility, the promise is implied. Implied promises are also found where you have, over time, repeatedly repaired or maintained certain aspects of the rental, thus establishing a practice of repair that the tenant may rely upon. Here are some typical examples of implied promises.

EXAMPLE 1: Tina sees Joel's ad for an apartment, which says "heated swimming pool." After Tina moves in, Joel stops heating the pool regularly, because his utility costs have risen. Joel has violated his implied promise to keep the pool heated. Joel might want to avoid ad language that commits him to such things if he wants more flexibility.

EXAMPLE 2: When Joel's rental agent shows Tom around the building, she goes out of her way to show off the laundry room, saying, "Here's the terrific laundry room—it's for the use of all the tenants." Tom rents the apartment. Later, all the washing machines break down, but Joel won't fix them. Joel has violated his implied promise to maintain the laundry room appliances in working order.

EXAMPLE 3: Tina's apartment has a built-in dishwasher. When she rented the apartment, neither the lease nor the landlord said anything about the dishwasher or who was responsible for repairing it. The dishwasher has broken down a few times and whenever Tina asked Joel to fix it, he did. By doing so, Joel has established a "usage" or "practice" that the landlord—not the tenant—is responsible for repairing the dishwasher.

If you violate an express or implied promise relating to the condition of the premises, the tenant may sue you (usually in small claims court) for money damages for breach of contract, and may be able to pursue other legal remedies discussed below.

---

### Make the Tenant Financially Liable for Damage to Your Property

Be sure your lease or rental agreement makes the tenant financially responsible for repair of damage caused by the tenant's negligence or misuse. (See Clause 11 of the form agreements in Chapter 2.) That means that where the tenant or his friends or family cause damage—for example, a broken window, a toilet clogged with children's toys or a freezer that no longer works because the tenant defrosted it with a carving knife—it's the tenant's responsibility to make the repairs or to reimburse you for doing so. If a tenant refuses to repair or pay for the damage he caused, you can use the security deposit to cover the bill, then demand that the tenant bring the deposit up to its original level (if he refuses, he's a candidate for termination and eviction). Or you can sue, perhaps in small claims court, for the cost of the repairs. Chapter 16 discusses small claims court.

---

## 7. Set Up a Responsive Maintenance System—And Stick to It

Landlords who fail to maintain the premises face various financial losses and legal problems, both from tenants—who may withhold rent and pursue other legal remedies—and from government agencies that enforce housing codes. Your best bet to avoid problems in the first place is to design a maintenance program that meets housing laws *and* satisfies the question "Is this building safe, sound and fit for people to live in?" And in doing so, you should be mindful of your larger goal—to attract and keep reliable tenants who will stay as long as possible. Viewed this way, excellent repair and maintenance policies that go far beyond what the law requires may nevertheless be a bargain.

Sections G and H recommend a system for tenants to regularly report on repair and maintenance problems, and explain how your prompt response and good recordkeeping will keep you out of legal trouble.

## C. Tenant Responses to Unfit Premises: Paying Less Rent

If you fail to live up to your legal duty to maintain your property, your tenants may have a variety of legal responses, each one designed to pressure you into compliance. Hopefully, you will run your business in such a way that your tenants will have no reason to take legal action. But even the most conscientious landlord may encounter a tenant who attempts to avoid his responsibility to pay the rent by claiming that the premises are unfit. If you are a victim of a scam like this, you'll need to know how to defend yourself.

Your tenants' options will probably include one or more of what we call the "big sticks" in a tenant's self-help arsenal. These include:

- withholding the rent
- repairing the problem (or having it repaired by a professional) and deducting the cost from the rent

- calling state or local building or health inspectors
- moving out, or
- paying the rent and then suing you for the difference between the rent the tenant paid and the value of the defective premises.

If you haven't fixed a serious problem that truly makes the rental unit uninhabitable—rats in the kitchen, for example—you can expect that a savvy tenant will use one or more of these options. In this section, we'll explain the two options that involve paying less rent; in Section D, below, we'll explain the others.

When a tenant pays you less than the stated rent, it can make an enormous impact on your business. Accordingly, tenants cannot use these options unless three conditions are met:

1. **The problem is serious, not just annoying, and imperils the tenant's health or safety.** Not every building code violation or annoying defect in a rental home (like the water heater's ability to reach only 107 degrees F, short of the code-specified 110 degrees) justifies use of a "big stick" against the landlord.

2. **The tenant told you about the problem, gave you a reasonable opportunity to get it fixed, or the minimum amount of time required by state law, but you failed to fix it.** In some states, you are given a statutorily specified amount of time (ten days to three weeks is common); in others, you must respond within a reasonable time under the circumstances.

3. **The tenant (or a guest) did not cause the problem, either deliberately or through carelessness or neglect.** If so, the tenant's use of one of the self-help options won't be upheld.

## 1. Rent Withholding

If you have not met the responsibility of keeping your property livable, your tenant may be able to stop paying rent until the repairs are made. Called rent withholding or rent escrowing, 32 states have established this option by statute; additional states

(such as Washington, D.C.) authorize the same by court decision, and some cities have ordinances allowing it. (See "Tenants' Options in Your State.") Rent withholding can be done *only* in states or cities that have specifically embraced it.

The term "withholding" is actually a bit misleading, since in some states and cities a tenant can't simply keep the rent money until you fix the problem. Instead, tenants often have to deposit the withheld rent with a court or a neutral third party or escrow account set up by a local court or housing agency until the repairs are accomplished.

Before a tenant can properly withhold the rent, three requirements must be met:

- The lack of maintenance or repair has made the dwelling unlivable.
- The problems were not caused by the tenant or his guest, either deliberately or through neglect.

and

- You've been told about the problem and haven't fixed it within a reasonable time or the minimum amount required by state law.

MRS. MARTIN. I'VE DECIDED TO WITHHOLD MY RENT UNTIL THAT "DRIP" IS FIXED...

## Tenants' Options in Your State

In every state, tenants can call the housing or building inspector and sue you in small claims court if your rental unit is defective. In every state but Alabama, Arkansas and Colorado, tenants have the option of moving out. This table lists states which give tenants additional options.

| State | Withhold the rent | Repair and deduct | State | Withhold the rent | Repair and deduct |
|---|---|---|---|---|---|
| Alabama | | | New Jersey | ✔ | |
| Alaska | ✔ | ✔ | New Mexico | ✔ | ✔ |
| Arizona | ✔ | ✔ | New York | ✔ | ✔ |
| Arkansas | | | North Carolina | | |
| California | ✔ | ✔ | North Dakota | | |
| Colorado | | | Ohio | ✔ | |
| Connecticut | ✔ | ✔ | Oklahoma | | ✔ |
| Delaware | | ✔ | Oregon | ✔ | ✔ |
| District of Columbia | | | Pennsylvania | ✔ | |
| Florida | ✔ | | Rhode Island | ✔ | ✔ |
| Georgia | ✔ | | South Carolina | ✔ | ✔ |
| Hawaii | ✔ | ✔ | South Dakota | ✔ | ✔ |
| Idaho | | | Tennessee | | ✔ |
| Illinois | ✔ | | Texas | | ✔ |
| Indiana | | | Utah | | |
| Iowa | ✔ | ✔ | Vermont | ✔ | ✔ |
| Kansas | ✔ | | Virginia | ✔ | |
| Kentucky | ✔ | ✔ | Washington | ✔ | ✔ |
| Louisiana | | ✔ | West Virginia | | |
| Maine | ✔ | ✔ | Wisconsin | ✔* | |
| Maryland | ✔ | | Wyoming | | |
| Massachusetts | ✔ | ✔ | | | |
| Michigan | ✔ | ✔ | | | |
| Minnesota | ✔ | ✔ | | | |
| Mississippi | | ✔ | | | |
| Missouri | ✔ | ✔ | | | |
| Montana | ✔ | ✔ | | | |
| Nebraska | ✔ | ✔ | | | |
| Nevada | ✔ | ✔ | | | |
| New Hampshire | ✔ | | | | |

* Wisconsin tenants may withhold rent only for lead and asbestos problems.

Citations to the state statutes are listed in "State Laws on Rent Withholding and Repair and Deduct Remedies" in Appendix I.

**Important:** This table reflects statutes passed by the state legislatures and some court decisions. But your local government courts may authorize methods similar to these.

In addition, under most rent withholding laws, tenants cannot withhold rent if they are behind in the rent or in violation of an important lease clause. In short, tenants who use this drastic measure need to be squeaky clean.

---

### Illegal Lease Clauses: Don't Limit Your Tenant's Right to Withhold the Rent Under State Law

Some landlords insert clauses in their leases and rental agreements purporting to prohibit a tenant from withholding the rent, even if a property is uninhabitable. In many states, the rent withholding law itself makes this practice flatly illegal. But even where a state statute or court decision does not specifically disallow this side-step, these clauses may be tossed out if a tenant nevertheless withholds rent and you attempt to evict him for nonpayment of rent. Why? Because a judge will approve a tenant's waiver of his right to withhold rent only if his "waiver" has been the subject of real negotiations between him and you, and not something you have insisted upon unilaterally. If you gave your tenant a pre-printed lease (with a habitability waiver) and told him to take it or leave it, a judge is likely to decide that the so-called "waiver" was in fact imposed by you and, consequently, invalid. In short, your attempt to take away the right to use this option may be worthless.

---

### a.   Typical Rent Withholding Requirements

If rent withholding is allowed in your state or city, read the law to find out:

- what circumstances justify rent withholding (normally, only significant health and safety problems justify the use of the remedy, but statutes vary as to the particulars)
- whether the tenant must give you a certain amount of notice (ten to 30 days are typical)

and time to fix the defect, or whether the notice and response time simply be "reasonable" under the circumstances

- whether the tenant must ask a local court for permission to withhold rent, providing compelling reasons why the rental is not livable, and follow specific procedures, and
- whether the tenant must place the unpaid rent in a separate bank account or deposit it with a court or local housing agency and how this is done.

We explain how to find and look up your state's law in the library and online in Chapter 18.

### b.   What Happens to the Rent?

While repairs are being made, the tenant may continue to pay the entire rent to the court or housing authority, or may be directed to pay some rent to you and the balance to the court or housing authority. If the rent money is being held by a court or housing authority, you can sometimes ask for release of some of the withheld rent to pay for repairs. When the dwelling is certified as fit by the local housing inspectors or the court, any money in the account is returned to you, minus court costs and inspection fees.

If your state's withholding law does not require the tenant to escrow the rent and a court has not been involved, the tenant may make his own arrangements as to what to do with the money. Careful tenants (who want to prove that they are not withholding rent simply because they do not have the money) will devise their own escrow set-up, by placing the rent in an attorney's trust account or a separate bank account dedicated solely for that purpose.

Once you have made the repairs, you'll undoubtedly expect full payment of the withheld rent. But don't be surprised if your tenant argues that he should be compensated for having had to live in substandard conditions. He may want a retroactive reduction in rent, starting from the time that the premises became uninhabitable. (Some states limit tenants to a reduction starting from the time you were notified of the problem.) Reducing the rent is also known in legalese as rent "abatement" or "recoupment."

Your tenant may press for a retroactive rent abatement through a court process or through negotiation with you. The following section describes how a judge will determine how much you should compensate your tenant for the inconvenience of having lived in a substandard rental unit. If a court is not involved, you and the tenant can use this same system in your own negotiations.

### c. Determining the Value of a Defective Rental Unit

How does a judge determine the difference between the withheld rent and what a defective, unlivable unit was really worth? There are two widely-used ways:

**Figuring the market value.** In some states, statutes or court cases say that if you've left the unit in a defective condition, all you're entitled to is the fair market value of the premises in that condition. For example, if an apartment with a broken heater normally rented for $1,200 per month, but was worth only $600 without operable heating, you would be entitled to only $600 a month from the escrowed funds. Of course, the difficulty with this approach—as with many things in law—is that it is staggeringly unrealistic. An apartment with no heat in winter has *no* market value, because no one would rent it. As you can see, how much a unit is worth in a defective condition is extremely hard to determine.

**By percentage reduction**. Another slightly more sensible approach is to start by asking what part of the unit is affected by the defect, and then to calculate the percentage of the rent attributable to that part. For example, if the roof leaked into the living room of a $900 a month apartment, rendering the room unusable, a tenant might reduce the rent by the percentage of the rent attributable to the living room. If the living room were the main living space and the other rooms were too small to live in

comfortably, the percentage of loss would be much greater than it would be in more spacious apartments. Obviously, this approach is far from an exact science, either.

EXAMPLE: When Henry and Sue moved into their apartment, it was a neat and well-maintained. Soon after, the building was sold to an out-of-state owner, who hired an off-site manager to handle repairs and maintenance. Gradually, the premises began to deteriorate. At the beginning of May, 15 months into their two-year lease, Henry and Sue could count several violations of the building code, including the landlord's failure to maintain the common areas, remove the garbage promptly and fix a broken water heater.

Henry and Sue sent numerous requests for repairs to their landlord over a two-month period, during which they gritted their teeth and put up with the situation. Finally they had enough and checked out their state's rent withholding law. They learned a tenant could pay rent into an escrow account set up by their local court. Henry and Sue went ahead and deposited their rent into this account.

- During the time that they lived in these uninhabitable conditions, Henry and Sue were not required to pay full rent. Using the "market value" approach, the court decided that their defective rental was worth half its stated rent. Accordingly, since the landlord owed them a refund for portions of their rent for May and June, Henry and Sue would be paid this amount from the escrow account.

- The balance of the rent in the account would be released to the landlord (less the costs of the escrow and the tenants' attorney fees), but only when the building inspector certified to the court that the building was up to code and fit for human habitation.

- Henry and Sue could continue to pay 50% of the rent until needed repairs were made and certified by the building inspector.

## Rogue Rent Withholding: Without Legal Authority

In states that don't permit withholding, either by statute or court decision, tenants may nevertheless attempt to reduce the rent on their own. For example, if the water heater is broken and you haven't fixed it despite repeated requests, your tenant may decide to pay a few hundred dollars less per month, figuring that a cold-water flat is only worth that much.

Can you terminate and evict a tenant who gives you a short rent check in a state that has not authorized rent withholding? In some states, the answer is yes. In others, however, a tenant's partial withholding may survive an eviction lawsuit, especially if the defects were significant and your failure to fix them flagrant and long-standing. The wise course is not to gamble—if you lose the eviction lawsuit, you may get hit with the tenant's court costs and attorney fees. Attend to maintenance problems before they escalate into rent wars.

## 2. Repair and Deduct

If you let your rental property fall below the fit and habitable standard, tenants in many states may be able to use a legal procedure called "repair and deduct." It works like this: Under certain conditions the tenant can, without your permission and without filing a lawsuit, have the defect repaired and subtract the cost of the repairs from the following month's rent. The repair and deduct remedy is available only if state or local law has authorized it. (See "Tenant Options in Your State.")

Like the rent withholding option described above, the repair and deduct remedy cannot be invoked at whim. Instead, most states have established specific criteria a tenant must meet before legally qualifying to use the repair and deduct procedures: The defect must be either inexpensive, involve an essential service, or both (depending on the wording of the statute); and the subject of the repair must clearly be the landlord's responsibility. Let's look more closely at these requirements.

### a. Repairs Must Qualify

Some states allow the repair and deduct remedy for minor repairs only, such as a leaky faucet or stopped-up sink. In most states there is a dollar limit or a specific percentage of the month's rent—for example, $100 or less than one-half the monthly rent, whichever is greater.

Other states allow tenants to use the repair and deduct remedy only for essential services, such as the procuring of heat and water. For example, in Massachusetts, a tenant can spend up to four months' rent, but only for health code violations certified by an inspector. (Mass. Gen. Laws ch. 111, § 127L.) Some states allow the remedy to be used in either situation.

> EXAMPLE: On a chilly November evening, the pilot light for Larry's heater failed. He called his building manager, who promised to fix it soon. After calling the manager several more times to no avail and suffering through three frigid days with no heat, Larry called a heater repair person, who came promptly and replaced the broken mechanism for $150. Since Larry lives in a state that allows the repair and deduct remedy, Larry deducted $150 from his next rent check and gave his manager the repair bill.

### b. Repairs Must Be Your Responsibility

A tenant cannot use the rent deduction method to fix a defect or problem that was caused by the careless or intentional act of the tenant or a guest of the tenant. Thus, a tenant cannot use this remedy to replace a window he broke himself. Also, since in most states the tenant is required to keep the dwelling as clean and orderly as the premises permit, he cannot use the remedy if the problem is traceable to his carelessness or unreasonable use of the property.

### c. You Must Be Notified of the Problem

Before using the repair and deduct remedy, the tenant must notify you of the problem. He need not, however, inform you that he intends to utilize the remedy if you fail to respond. Each state has its own procedures and timeline for notification. Generally, the tenant's notice must be in writing. However, in some states the law simply requires that the tenant give the landlord or manager "reasonable" notice of the problem (this could be orally or in writing).

### d. You Must Be Given Time to Fix the Problem

Statutes often give you a specified amount of time to make needed repairs before a tenant can legally use the repair and deduct remedy. For non-emergency repairs, this is typically within ten to 14 days of being notified by the tenant in writing. In the case of an emergency (such as a hole in the roof or a defective heater in winter), you must respond promptly. However, in some states no time limits are given; instead, you must make the repairs in a reasonable time.

### e. How Much Rent Can the Tenant Deduct?

In states that allow the repair and deduct remedy, the amount the tenant deducts is always limited to the actual and reasonable amount spent on the repair. In addition, many states impose a dollar limit on tenants' repairs. In Hawaii, for example, the tenant may withhold up to $300 or up to one month's rent; in Arizona, the amount the tenant withholds must be less than $150 or an amount equal to one-half the periodic rent, whichever is greater. And in California, a tenant is limited to deducting one month's rent to make repairs. Another restriction is added in Washington, where the tenant must accept the lowest bid for the job. In most states, tenants must present an itemized accounting for the work when using this remedy and presenting less than a full month's rent.

### f. Repeated Use of the Repair and Deduct Remedy

Many states limit how often tenants may pursue this option—for example, no more than once or twice in any 12-month period. Just because a tenant has used up his ability to utilize the remedy does not mean, however, that a landlord who has refused to fix a problem can ignore it. The tenant can still invoke any of the other remedies described in this chapter: rent withholding, filing a lawsuit in small claims court or moving out.

### g. The Price of Repair and Deduct

A tenant's use of the repair and deduct remedy can have unpleasant consequences. The tenant may not hire a skilled, reasonably priced repair person who does the job just as you would have done. Consequently, the chances for a needlessly expensive job or a shoddy one are great. Careful adherence to the high quality maintenance system described below in Sections G and H should help you avoid this fate.

EXAMPLE: When Matt opened the cupboard underneath his bathroom sink, he saw that the flexible hose connecting the pipe nipple to the sink was leaking. He turned off the water and called his landlord, Lee, who promised to attend to the problem right away. After three days without a bathroom sink, Matt called a plumber, who replaced the hose for $100. Matt deducted this amount from his next rent check. Lee thought no more about this until he got a frantic call from the tenant in the apartment beneath Matt's. She described her ceiling as looking like a giant, dripping sponge. Lee called his regular plumber to check the problem out. His plumber told Lee that the repair on

Matt's sink had been done negligently, resulting in a major leak into the walls. If Lee had called his own plumber, the job would have been done right in the first place, saving Lee lots of money and hassle.

## 3.  Your Options If a Tenant Withholds, Reduces or Repairs and Deducts Rent

When confronted with a tenant who does not pay all or part of the rent, many landlords almost reflexively turn to a lawyer to bring an eviction lawsuit. But even if you eventually get the tenant evicted (and you may not if the judge finds the tenant's rent withholding was justified), it is usually only after considerable cost. This is appropriate in some circumstances, especially when the tenant is clearly wrong and simply throwing legal sand in the air in an effort to obscure the fact that he can't or won't pay rent. But it's important to realize that tenants can fall into at least two other categories:

- Tenants who have some right on their side— that is, the needed repairs or maintenance should have been done more promptly, and
- Tenants who sincerely thought they had the right to withhold or repair and deduct rent, but have overreacted to the problem or have just done the wrong thing under the law.

How you react when a tenant reduces, repairs and deducts or withholds rent should depend on which category the tenant fits into. The following sections look at your options depending on the three categories: obvious troublemakers, mistaken but sincere tenants who are worth salvaging and tenants who had some justification for using the remedy they chose.

### a.  Obvious Troublemakers

If you keep your rental properties in good shape and properly handle repair and maintenance problems, your best bet may be to promptly and legally terminate the tenancy of any tenant who pays you

less or no rent. (Chapter 17 provides an overview of evictions in these situations.)

If you're heading for court, you may need to consult a lawyer or do some legal research first on your state's laws on evictions. If you do end up in court, be prepared to prove the following:

- The claimed defect was nonexistent and nothing justified the tenant's failure to pay the rent.
- The tenant caused the defect himself in order to avoid paying rent.
- The claimed defect was not really serious or substantial enough to give the tenant the right to pursue a particular remedy, such as rent withholding.
- Even if the defect was substantial, you were never given adequate notice and a chance to fix it. (At this point you should present a detailed complaint procedure to the court as we recommend in Section G. You should show, if possible, that the tenant didn't follow your complaint procedure.)
- The tenant failed to comply with some other aspect of the rent withholding law. For example, in states that require the tenant to place the withheld rent in escrow with the court, a tenant's failure to do so may defeat her attempt to use the procedure at all. A tenant who repeatedly failed to use the escrow procedure might be a candidate for eviction.

**If in doubt, hold off on eviction.** Sometimes it's hard to know if a tenant is truly a bad apple or just badly confused as to her legal rights. Until you are sure the tenant fits into the first category (had absolutely no good reason to reduce, withhold or repair and deduct rent), don't try to evict the tenant. Under the law of virtually every state, retaliatory evictions are penalized, often severely—that is, you may not evict a tenant in retaliation for his asserting a particular right, such as the right to withhold rent or complain to governmental authorities about health or safety problems. See Chapter 16 for a discussion of how to avoid tenant charges of retaliation.

## b. Mistaken But Sincere Tenants

If you think the tenant is wrong, but sincere—that is, she probably isn't trying to make up an excuse for not paying rent, but nevertheless is clearly not legally eligible to abate, withhold rent or repair and deduct—your best course is usually to try and work things out with the tenant in a face-to-face meeting. If, for example, the tenant used the repair and deduct remedy, but you were never given adequate legal notice (and would have had the problem fixed for $50 less if you had been), it may make sense to accept the tenant's solution but make sure the tenant knows how to notify you of the problems in the future. It may be painful to make this sort of compromise, but not nearly as bad as trying to evict the tenant and risking that a judge might even agree with her course of action.

The chances for resolving a conflict will be greater if you have a compromise system in place when you need it. When you find yourself dealing with a tenant who is not an obvious candidate for eviction (and especially if the tenant has some right on her side, as discussed below), consider taking the following steps:

1. Meet with the tenant (or tenants) and negotiate. You should be interested in establishing a good solution to avoid problems in the future and not in determining who was "right."
2. If negotiation fails, suggest mediation by a neutral third party. Check out how this works in advance so you can move quickly should the need arise again.
3. Put your solution in writing.
4. If the process indicates a larger problem with tenant dissatisfaction, encourage the tenant or tenants to meet with you regularly to solve it.

In many cases, it may be possible for you and the tenant to come to a mutually acceptable agreement using this system. On your end, this might mean promptly having the necessary work done and better maintaining the unit in the future. You might also give the tenant a prorated reduction in rent for the period between the time the tenant notified you of the defect and the time it was corrected. In exchange, the tenant might promise to promptly notify you of problems before resorting to the same tactic in the future.

> **EXAMPLE:** A leaky roof during a rainy month deprives a tenant, Steve, of the use of one of his two bedrooms. If Steve gave his landlord, Joe, notice of the leak, and Joe did not take care of the problem quickly, Steve might be justified in deducting $300 from the $800 rent for that month. However, if Steve didn't tell Joe of the problem until the next month's rent was due, a compromise might be reached where Steve bears part of the responsibility, by agreeing to deduct only $100 from the rent.

The first step in working towards a compromise with the tenant who uses rent abatement, withholding or repair and deduct, is to call him. If you're reluctant to call, you might want to try a letter. See the sample letter below suggesting a compromise on rent withholding.

**Chapter 16 recommends ways to negotiate with tenants over legal disputes such as rent withholding.** Chapter 16 includes a section on mediation, and covers other options, such as small claims court, if you can't work something out with the tenant.

## c. Tenants Who Are Partially Right

Sometimes, despite your best efforts to keep on top of repair and maintenance issues, a repair job falls through the cracks. It could happen while you are on vacation and your back-up system doesn't work, or maybe you simply need a better manager. If, in all fairness, a tenant was justified in using rent withholding or repair and deduct, admit it and take steps to rectify the situation. For example, after getting the necessary work done, you might try to make use of the compromise procedure outlined above. Once the immediate problem is behind you, treat what happened as an opportunity to review, revise and improve your maintenance and repair procedures:

- **Complaint procedure.** Do you have a complaint system that makes it easy for tenants to communicate their concerns? Are complaint forms readily available and easy to use?
- **Tenant education.** Do your tenants know that you intend to respond quickly to repair and maintenance problems? Do you need to remind all tenants, via a tenant notice or newsletter, of your complaint procedure?
- **Management response.** Does management respond reasonably quickly to a tenant's request for repairs?

In Section G below, we give detailed suggestions of how to set up and implement a maintenance program designed to identify repair needs before they become repair problems.

## D. Tenant Responses: Calling Inspectors, Filing Lawsuits and Moving Out

Tenants who are faced with unfit rentals are not limited to withholding rent or repairing the defects themselves. Other options that do not involve paying less rent include calling government inspectors, breaking the lease and moving out and suing in small claims court.

### 1. Reporting Code Violations to Housing Inspectors

A tenant may complain to a local building, health or fire department about problems such as inoperable plumbing, a leaky roof or bad wiring. If an inspector comes out and discovers code violations, you will be given an order to correct the problem. Fines and penalties usually follow if you fail to comply within a certain amount of time (often five to 30 business days). If there's still no response, the city or county may sue you. In many cities, your failure to

promptly fix cited violations of local housing laws is a misdemeanor (minor crime) punishable by hefty fines or even imprisonment. In rare cases, especially if tenants' health is imperiled, local officials may even require that the building be vacated.

In many areas, getting reported to a building inspector is a very big deal—an inspector who finds lots of problems can force you to clear them up immediately. But there is wide variation as to the effectiveness of building inspectors. In New Orleans, for example, there are very few inspectors compared to the number of tenant complaints, and courts are largely unable to follow up on the properties that are cited. But chances are that if the complaint procedure proves ineffective, your tenant will turn to a more effective option, such as one of the ones listed below.

### Severe Code Violations Will Close Your Building

If a judge decides that a building's condition substantially endangers the health and safety of its tenants, and repairs are so extensive they can't be made while tenants inhabit the building, the result may be an order to vacate the building. You usually won't have a chance to come to the court hearing to object to this dire consequence—your tenants will simply be told to get out, sometimes within hours.

In some states, you must pay for comparable temporary housing nearby. Some statutes also make you cover moving expenses and utility connection charges and give the original tenant the first chance to move back in when the repairs are completed. To find out whether you'll be liable for relocation expenses, check your state statutes (listed in "Landlord-Tenant Statutes" in Appendix I). If you go to the law library, try a more direct approach. Look in the index to your state's codes, under "Landlord-Tenant," for subheadings such as "Relocation Assistance" or "Padlock Orders." (See Chapter 18 for general advice on using the law library.)

## Sample Letter Suggesting Compromise on Rent Withholding

May 3, 199X

Tyrone McNab
Villa Arms, Apt. 4
123 Main Street
Cleveland, Ohio  44130

Dear Mr. McNab:

I am writing you in the hope we can work out a fair compromise to the problems that led you to withhold rent. You have rented a unit at the Villa Arms for the last three years and we have never had a problem before. Let's try to resolve it.

To review briefly, on May 1, Marvin, my resident manager at Villa Arms, told me that you were temporarily withholding your rent because of several defective conditions in your apartment. Marvin said you had asked him to correct these problems a week ago, but he hasn't as yet attended to them. Marvin states that you listed these defects as some peeling paint on the interior wall of your bedroom, a leaky kitchen water faucet, a running toilet, a small hole in the living room carpet and a cracked kitchen window.

I have instructed Marvin to promptly arrange with you for a convenient time to allow him into your apartment to repair all these problems. I am sure these repairs would already have been accomplished by now except for the fact that Hank, our regular repair person, has been out sick for the last ten days.

I understand that these problems are annoying and significant to you, and I acknowledge that they should have been attended to more promptly. However, I do not believe that they justify rent withholding under state law. Rent withholding is allowed only when the defects make the premises unfit for habitation. I do not think, however, that in the long run either one of us would be well served by stubbornly standing on our rights or resorting to a court fight. My first wish is to come to an amicable understanding with you that we can live with and use to avoid problems like this in the future.

Because of the inconvenience you have suffered as a result of the problems in your apartment, I am prepared to offer you a pro-rated rebate on your rent for ten days, this being the estimated length of time it will have taken Marvin to remedy the problems from the day of your complaint. As your monthly rent is $600, equal to $20 per day, I am agreeable to your paying only $400 rent this month.

If this is not acceptable to you, please call me at 555-1234 during the day. If you would like to discuss any aspect of the situation in more detail, I would be pleased to meet with you at your convenience. I will expect to receive your check for $400, or a call from you, before May 10.

Sincerely,
*Sandra Schmidt*
Sandra Schmidt

## 2. Lawsuits by the Tenant

A consumer who purchases a defective product—be it a car, a hair dryer or a steak dinner—is justified in expecting a minimum level of quality, and is entitled to compensation if the product is seriously flawed. Tenants are consumers, too, and may remain in possession of the premises and still sue you for the following:

- partial or total refund of rent paid while the housing conditions were substandard
- the value, or repair costs, of property lost or damaged as a result of the defect—for example, furniture ruined by water leaking through the roof
- compensation for personal injuries—including pain and suffering—caused by the defect (Chapter 10 discusses liability), and
- attorney fees (Chapter 18 discusses attorney fees).

In some states, tenants may also seek a court order—similar to a rent withholding scheme—directing you to repair the defects, with rent reduced until you show proof to the court that the defects have been remedied.

⚠ **You may not retaliate against a tenant who files a lawsuit and stays in the property.** (See Chapter 16 for a discussion of retaliatory eviction.) It may seem inconsistent for a tenant to take the extreme step of suing you and expecting to remain on the property. Nevertheless, a tenant who sues and stays is exercising a legal right. Retaliation, such as delivering a rent increase or a termination notice, is illegal and will give the tenant yet another ground on which to sue.

## 3. Moving Out

If a tenant's dwelling isn't habitable and you haven't fixed it, he also has the right to move out—either temporarily or permanently. These drastic measures are justified only when there are truly serious problems, such as the lack of essential services or the total or partial destruction of the premises. Tenants may also use these options if environmental health hazards such as lead paint dust (discussed in Chapter 11) make the unit uninhabitable.

### a. Failure to Keep the Unit Habitable

The 47 states that require you to provide habitable housing allow tenants to move out if you don't do your job. Depending on the circumstances, tenants may move out permanently, by terminating the lease or rental agreement, or temporarily. This approach is borrowed directly from consumer protection laws. Just as the purchaser of a seriously defective car may sue to undo the contract or return the car for a refund, tenants can consider the housing contract terminated and simply return the rental unit to you if the housing is unlivable.

The law, of course, has a convoluted phrase to describe this simple concept. It's called "constructive eviction," which means that, by supplying unlivable housing, you have for all practical purposes "evicted" the tenant. A tenant who has been constructively evicted (that is, he has a valid reason to move out) has no further responsibility for rent.

Your state statute may have specific details, such as the type of notice tenants must provide before moving out because of a major repair problem. You may have anywhere from five to 21 days to fix the problem, depending on the state, and sometimes the seriousness of the situation. Check your state law for details.

**Temporary moves.** In many states, if you fail to provide heat or other essential services, tenants may procure reasonable substitute housing during the period of your noncompliance. They may recover the costs (as long as they're reasonable) of substitute housing up to an amount equal to the rent.

**Permanent moves.** A tenant who moves out permanently because of habitability problems may also be entitled to money from you to compensate them for out-of-pocket losses. For example, the tenant may be able to recover for moving expenses and the cost of a hotel for a few days until they find a new place. Also, if the conditions were substandard during prior months when the tenant did pay the full rent, you may be sued for the difference between the value of the defective dwelling and the rent paid. In addition, if the tenant is unable to find comparable housing for the same rent, and ends up paying more rent than they would have under the old lease, you may be on the hook for the difference.

EXAMPLE: Susan signed a one year's lease for a beachfront apartment. She thought it was a great deal because the monthly rent of $700 was considerably less than similar properties in the neighborhood. Susan's dream of an apartment began to turn into a nightmare when she discovered, soon after moving in, that the bedroom was full of mildew that attacked every surface and interfered with her breathing. After numerous complaints to the landlord, which were ignored, Susan moved out at the end of four months, and rented a comparable apartment nearby for $800. She then sued the landlord for the following:

- *Compensation for the months she had endured the defective conditions.* Susan asked for the difference between the agreed-upon rent and the real value of the apartment (the apartment with its defects), times four (the number of months she paid rent).
- *The benefit of her bargain.* Susan pointed out that the rent for the first apartment was a real bargain, and that she had been unable to find a similar apartment for anything less than $800 per month. She asked for the added rent she will have to pay ($100) times eight, the number of months left on her original lease.
- *Moving costs.* Susan asked for the $250 cost of hiring a moving company to transport her belongings to her new home.

After hearing Susan's arguments and the landlord's feeble defense, the judge decided that Susan was entitled to:

- *Compensation for past problems.* The mildew problem, which had forced Susan to sleep in the living room, had essentially reduced the one-bedroom apartment to a studio apartment, which would have rented for $400 per month. Accordingly, Susan was entitled to a refund of $300 for each of the four months, or $1,200.
- *The benefit of her bargain.* The judge acknowledged that a similar apartment, such as the one she rented when she moved out, cost $100 more per month than the one she had originally rented, and awarded her that amount per month times eight, or $800.
- *Moving costs.* The judge ruled that Susan's moving costs of $250 were reasonable, and ordered the landlord to pay them.

## b. Damage to the Premises

A tenant whose home is significantly damaged—either by natural disaster or any other reason beyond his responsibility or control—has the right to consider the lease at an end and to move out. Depending on the circumstances of the damage, however, everyone may not be able to simply walk away from the lease or rental agreement with no financial consequences. A tenant may have the legal right to your assistance with substitute housing or living expenses. Obviously, the tenant whose rental unit is destroyed by a natural disaster has less reason to expect resettlement assistance from you than one whose home is destroyed by fire caused by your botching an electrical repair job. And the tenant whose home burns down because he left the stove on all night will probably find himself at the other end of a lawsuit.

**Natural or third-party disasters**. State laws vary on the extent of your responsibility depending on the cause of the damage. If a fire, flood, tornado, earthquake or other natural disaster renders the dwelling unlivable, or if a third party is the cause of the destruction (for instance, a fire due to an arsonist), your best bet is to look to your insurance policy for help in repairing or rebuilding the unit and to assist your tenants in resettlement. While waiting for the insurance coverage to kick in, give month-to-month tenants a termination notice (typically 30 days' notice is required). In some cases, you may be required by law to pay the tenant for substitute housing for 30 days. With tenants who have a lease, you may be obligated to pay for substitute housing for a longer period until the tenant finds a comparable replacement. To be prudent, raise the issue of tenant assistance with your insurance broker at the time the policy is purchased so that you know exactly where you stand if a disaster strikes.

**Destruction that is traceable to the landlord.** If it can be shown that you or your employees were even partially responsible for the damage, your legal responsibility to the tenant is likely to increase. You may be expected to cover a longer period of temporary housing and, if the substitute housing is more expensive, you may be stuck with paying the difference between the new rent and the old rent. The insurance issue will also take on a different cast: Some policies exclude coverage for natural disasters, but include (as is standard) coverage for the owner's negligent acts. The facts surrounding the property damage or destruction, applicable state law and the wording of your insurance policy will determine how each situation is handled.

If a tenant moves out due to damage or destruction of the premises, for whatever cause, it will be important for you and the tenant to sign a written termination of the rental agreement or lease once the tenant is relocated. (See the sample termination of lease in Chapter 8.) This allows you to proceed with the repair or rebuilding without the pressure of tenants waiting to move in immediately. If you want to re-rent to the same tenant, a new lease or rental agreement can be drawn up at that time.

## E. Minor Repairs

If you're like most landlords, what really drives you nuts are hassles over leaky faucets, temperamental appliances, worn carpets, noisy heaters, hot water heaters that produce too little hot water and dozens of other aggravating complaints. You are much more likely to face tenants' minor complaints than major problems that make a unit unlivable. To avoid hassles with tenants over minor repairs, you may delegate responsibility to a tenant—particularly one who is especially reliable and handy. (Section F, below, shows how to delegate minor repairs and maintenance.)

You have different legal duties depending on whether a problem is major (affecting the habitability of the rental unit) or minor. Major jobs are yours, period. Minor repair and maintenance includes:

- Small plumbing jobs, like replacing washers and cleaning drains
- System upkeep, like changing heating filters
- Structural upkeep, like replacing excessively worn flooring
- Small repair jobs like fixing broken light fixtures or replacing the grout around bathtub tile, and
- Routine repairs to and maintenance of common areas, such as pools, spas and laundry rooms.

Most often, minor repairs are your job. But you are not required to keep the rental premises looking just like new—ordinary wear and tear does not have to be repaired during a tenancy. (When the tenant moves out, however, the cost of dealing with ordinary wear and tear will fall on you and cannot come out of the security deposit. See Chapter 15.) And if the tenant or one of his guests caused it, carelessly or intentionally, the tenant is responsible for repairing it—or, if your lease or rental agreement prohibits him from doing so, paying you to do it.

If the tenant had nothing to do with the repair problem, and it's not a cosmetic issue, chances go way up that you are responsible, for one of the following reasons:

- A state or local building code requires you to keep the damaged item (for example, a kitchen sink) in good repair.
- A state or local law specifically makes it your responsibility.

- Your lease or rental agreement provision or advertisement describes or lists particular items, such as hot tubs, trash compactors and air conditioners; by implication, this makes you responsible for maintaining or repairing them.
- You made explicit promises when showing the unit—for example, regarding the security or air conditioning system.
- You made an implied promise to provide a particular feature, such as a whirlpool bathtub; or because you have fixed or maintained it in the past.

Each of these reasons is discussed below. If you're not sure whether or not a minor repair or maintenance problem is your responsibility, scan the discussion to find out.

## 1. Building Codes

States (and sometimes cities) write building codes that cover structural requirements, such as roofs, flooring and windows, and essential services, such as and hot water and heat. If your tenant's repair request involves a violation of the building code, you may be facing a habitability problem, as discussed above in Section A. But building codes often cover other, less essential, details as well. For example, codes may specify a minimum number of electrical outlets per room; if a broken circuit breaker means that there are fewer working outlets, the consequence is probably not an unfit dwelling, but you are still legally required to fix the problem.

## 2. Landlord-Tenant Laws

Some state laws place responsibility for specific minor repairs and maintenance on the landlord. A common example is providing garbage receptacles and arranging for garbage pick-up. Many states have their own special rules. In Alaska, for example, the law makes landlords responsible for maintaining vacuum cleaners, dishwashers and other appliances supplied by them. (Alaska Stat. § 34.03.100 and following.)

In many states, renters of single-family residences may agree to take on responsibilities that would otherwise belong to the landlord, such as disposing of garbage. For details, check your state's landlord-tenant codes under "Landlord-Tenant Statutes," which are listed in Appendix I.

## 3. Promises in the Lease or Rental Agreement

When it comes to legal responsibility for repairs, your own lease or rental agreement is often just as important (or more so) than building codes or state laws. If your written agreement describes or lists items such as drapes, washing machines, swimming pools, saunas, parking places, intercoms or dishwashers, you must provide them in decent repair. And the promise to provide them carries with it the implied promise to maintain them.

## 4. Promises in Ads

If an advertisement for your unit described or listed a feature, such as a cable TV hookup, especially if the feature is emphasized, you must follow through with these promises, even if your written rental agreement says nothing about appliances. Items such as dishwashers, clothes washers and dryers, garbage disposals, microwave ovens, security gates and Jacuzzis must be repaired by you if they break through no fault of the tenant.

EXAMPLE: Tina sees Joel's ad for an apartment, which says "heated swimming pool." After Tina moves in, Joel stops heating the pool regularly, because his utility costs have risen. Joel has violated his promise to keep the pool heated.

The promise doesn't have to be in words.

**EXAMPLE:** Tom's real estate agent showed him a glossy color photo of an available apartment, which featured a smiling resident using an intercom to welcome a guest. The apartment Tom rented did not have a working intercom, and he complained to the management, arguing that the advertisement implied that all units were so equipped. The landlord realized that he would have to fix the intercom.

## 5. Promises Made Before You Rented the Unit

It's a rare landlord or manager who refrains from even the slightest bit of puffing when showing a rental to a prospective tenant. It's hard to refrain from announcing rosy plans for amenities or services that haven't yet materialized ("We plan to re-do this kitchen—you'll love the snappy way that trash compactor will work!"). Whenever you make promises

like these, even if they're not in writing, your tenant can legally hold you to them.

> **EXAMPLE:** When Joel's rental agent shows Tom around the building, she goes out of her way to show off the laundry room, saying, "Here's the laundry room—we have two machines now, but will be adding two more soon." Tom rents the apartment. Two months go by and Joel still hasn't added the new machines. Joel has violated his promise to equip the laundry room with four machines.

## 6. Implied Promises

Suppose your rental agreement doesn't mention a garbage disposal and neither did any of your advertising. And you never pointed it out when showing the unit. But there is a garbage disposal and it was working when the tenant moved in. Now the garbage disposal is broken—do you have to fix it? Many courts will hold you legally responsible for maintaining all significant aspects of the rental unit. If you offer a unit that *already has* certain features —light fixtures that work, doors that open and close smoothly, faucets that don't leak, tile that doesn't fall off the wall—many judges reason that you have made an implied contract to keep them in workable order throughout the tenancy.

The flip side of this principle is that when your tenant has paid for a hamburger, the waiter—you— doesn't have to deliver a steak. In other words, if the rental was shabby when the tenant moved in, and you never gave the tenant reason to believe that it would be spruced up, he has no legal right to demand improvements—unless, of course, he can point to health hazards or code violations. As when you offer secondhand goods "as is" for a low price, legally your buyer/tenant is stuck with the deal.

Another factor that is evidence of an implied contract is your past conduct. If you have consistently fixed or maintained a particular feature of a rental, you have an implied obligation to continue doing so.

**EXAMPLE:** Tina's apartment has a built-in dishwasher. When she rented the apartment, neither the lease nor the landlord said anything about the dishwasher or who was responsible for repairing it. The dishwasher has broken down a few times and whenever Tina asked Joel to fix it, he did. By doing so, Joel has established a "practice" that he—not the tenant—is responsible for repairing the dishwasher.

## 7. The Consequences of Refusing to Attend to Minor Repairs

If you have determined that the repair problem is minor and falls fairly in your lap, it's wise to attend to it promptly. Although your tenant's health and safety may not be immediately imperiled (as is true with major repairs), you don't want to court disaster. For example, the repair may be minor now, but have the potential to become major and expensive; there may be a potential for injury and liability; or the problem may affect other renters, presenting the unpleasant possibility of a cadre of disgruntled tenants.

If you refuse to fix a minor problem that is your responsibility, your tenant has several options. He may

- fix it himself
- report you to the housing inspectors, if the problem involves a code violation
- attempt to use one of the legal options designed for habitability problems, such as rent withholding or repair and deduct
- break the lease and move out, or
- sue you, usually in small claims court.

Some of these responses are appropriate and others may not be—we'll explain why below. But keep in mind that even if a tenant improperly responds, your being in the right may be an illusory victory. Legal disputes—in court or out—are expensive and time-consuming. Unless the tenant is a whining prima-donna who demands constant, unnecessary repairs, it's usually wiser to fix the problem and nip the issue in the bud.

### a. Tenants Who Fix It Themselves

Your exasperated tenant might strap on his tool belt and fix the minor problem himself. If he's handy and has used the proper procedures and materials, you may come out ahead. But you have no way of gauging his expertise; and there is always the possibility that the tenant will do a slipshod job, either negligently or through spite.

**EXAMPLE:** Colin decided to replace a window that was broken by his son's basketball. He removed the shards of glass, fitted a new pane in place and caulked the circumference. He did not, however, paint the caulk; and a year later it had cracked, allowing rainwater to seep onto the windowsill and down the wall. His landlord Sarina was furious when she realized that she would have to replace the sill and the drywall, simply because Colin had not done a workman-like job. The cost of these repairs exceeded Colin's security deposit and Sarina had to sue him in small claims court for the balance, which she had a hard time collecting.

### b. Reporting Code Violations

If the minor repair problem constitutes a code violation, such as inadequate electrical outlets or low water pressure, your tenant may find an ally in the building or housing agency in charge of enforcing the code. Whether the tenant will get an effective response from the agency will depend on the seriousness of the violation, the workload of the agency and its ability to enforce its compliance orders. Since by definition the problem is minor, it's unlikely to get much action especially if code enforcement officials are already overworked. But his complaint will remain on file, which is a public record that may come back to haunt you.

**EXAMPLE:** Randall was a successful landlord who owned several properties. A rotten and poorly-supported deck at one of his apartment houses collapsed, killing one tenant and injuring several others. Randall was sued by the injured tenants and the family of the deceased for intentionally violating building codes when constructing the deck. Local news coverage made much of the fact that he had been cited numerous times for minor code violations; this publicity made it extremely difficult for him to get a fair trial. The jury found in favor of the plaintiffs and awarded them several million dollars. Because this tragedy was not the result of Randall's negligence, but rather an expected consequence of deliberately ignoring proper building procedures, Randall's insurance company refused to cover the award. Randall was forced to declare bankruptcy.

### c. Using Rent Withholding or Repair and Deduct

Tenants often make the mistake of using these powerful remedies, usually reserved for major, habitability problems, for minor repairs. If your tenant has done so, you should be able to terminate and evict for nonpayment of rent. (Terminations and evictions are covered in Chapter 17.) Be sure to read your state's statute or other authority carefully to make sure that there's no way your tenant can fit his action within your state's withholding or repair and deduct laws.

### d. Breaking the Lease

A disgruntled tenant may decide it's not worth putting up with your obduracy regarding minor repairs and may simply break the lease and move out. A defect that is truly minor does not justify this extreme step. But being in the right does you little good here—in most states, you'll have to take reasonable steps to re-rent and credit the new rent to the departed tenant's responsibility for the balance of the rent. The fact that he left because he didn't like the squeaky closet door does not relieve you of

this duty. (Your duty to "mitigate damages" is explained in Chapter 14.)

### e. Suing in Small Claims Court

Be it ever so minor, your tenant is entitled to get what he paid for—and if he doesn't, he might decide to sue in small claims court. Small claims court judges usually won't order you to paint, fix the dishwasher or repair the intercom. The judge may, however, order that the tenant be compensated in dollars for living in a rental unit with repair problems, on the theory that the tenant is not getting the benefit of what he's paying rent for—for example, a functioning dishwasher, presentable paint or a working air conditioner. You may be ordered to pay the tenant an amount that reflects the difference between his rent and the value of the unit with repair problems. (To calculate this amount, the judge will use one of the methods described above in section C.)

How much of a threat is a small claims suit likely to be? A judge is not going to adjust the rent because a little grout is missing from the bathroom tile. But if the dishwasher is broken, three faucets leak noisily and the bathroom door won't close, your tenant's chances of winning go way up.

## F. Delegating Landlord's Responsibilities to Tenants

You may want to delegate some repair and maintenance responsibilities to the tenants themselves—perhaps you live at a distance and the tenant is particularly responsible and handy. Is this legal? Courts in each state have faced this question and have come to several different conclusions. While we cannot offer a country-wide analysis of each state's position, here are the basics.

**Consider hiring a resident manager.** Many landlords hire a tenant-manager to handle day-to-day details of running their rental property.

Chapter 6 covers all aspects of hiring and working with a property manager, including setting repair and maintenance responsibilities.

## 1. Do Not Delegate Responsibility for Major Repairs and Maintenance to the Tenant

By law, housing must be habitable because society has decided that it is unacceptable for landlords to offer substandard dwellings. For this reason, the implied warranty of habitability and the covenant of quiet enjoyment cannot be waived by a tenant in most states. In other words, even though the tenant may be willing to live in substandard housing, society has decided that it will not tolerate such conditions.

It is a small but logical step to the next question of whether you can delegate to the tenant the responsibility of keeping the premises fit for habitation. Many courts have held that you cannot, fearing that the tenant will rarely be in the position, either practically or financially, to do the kinds of repairs that are often needed to bring a structure up to par.

Even if you do have the legal right, it is always a mistake to try and delegate to a tenant your responsibility for major maintenance of essential services, such as heat, plumbing or electricity or repairs involving the roof or other parts of the building structure. And remember, even inexpensive jobs can have enormous repercussions if done poorly. For instance, replacing an electrical outlet seems simple, but the results of an improper job (fire or electrocution) can be devastating. Think twice before entrusting sensitive jobs to people who are not experts.

## 2. How to Delegate Minor Repairs and Maintenance to Tenants

Delegating minor repairs is usually a different issue. Under the law of some states, and as a matter of

sensible practice in all states, you may delegate minor repairs and maintenance responsibilities to the tenant—such as mowing the lawn, trimming the bushes and sweeping the lobby—without making the tenant responsible for keeping the structure habitable. Practically speaking, however, you must be willing to check to see if the work is done properly. If you wish to delegate responsibilities to a tenant, be advised that, as far as any *other* tenants are concerned (and probably with respect to the living space of the tenant-repair person, too), your delegation of certain maintenance and repair duties to one tenant does not relieve you of the ultimate responsibility for meeting state and local health and safety laws.

Always remember that the implied warranty of habitability makes you responsible for maintenance of common areas—for example, cleaning hallways and mowing the lawn. If you transfer this duty to someone who fails to do it, the transfer will not shield you if you are haled into court for failure to maintain the premises. On the other hand, if you monitor the manner in which the job is being done and step in and get it done right if the tenant does a poor job, there should be no practical problems.

Repair and maintenance arrangements between landlords and tenants often lead to dissatisfaction—

typically the landlord feels that the tenant has neglected certain tasks, or the tenant feels that there is too much work for the money. When a court is asked to step in, the validity of the arrangement will typically be judged along the following lines:

- **Was it in writing?** Any agreement as to repairs or maintenance should be written and signed, either as part of the lease or rental agreement (See Clause 12 of the form agreements in Chapter 2), or as a separate employment agreement (see Section F3, below).

- **Was it a fair bargain?** You must adequately pay the tenant for the services provided. Often, this payment consists of a reduction in rent. A judge may look askance at a $50 reduction in monthly rent for 20 hours of work, which represents a pay scale well below the minimum wage.

- **Is it fair to other tenants?** Some courts will also inquire as to whether your agreement adversely affects your obligations to other tenants. For example, if your tenant-maintenance person does his job poorly or only now and then, the other tenants will have to live with his spotty performance.

- **Have you treated the delegation separately from your other duties as the landlord?** The agreement you have with your tenant has nothing to do with your other responsibilities. For example, if you and your tenant agree that she will do gardening work in exchange for a reduction in rent, and you feel that she is not doing a proper job, you may not respond by shutting off her water. (See discussion of retaliation and other prohibited landlord actions in Chapter 16.) The proper recourse is to discuss the problem with the tenant and, if it persists, to cancel the arrangement.

⚠ **Be careful delegating repairs involving hazardous materials.** The simplest repair may actually create an environmental health hazard, which may open you to liability on three fronts: You may be sued by the exposed tenant, sued by other tenants who might also be affected and cited by the relevant regulating agency for allowing an untrained or uncertified person to work on toxic materials. For example, preparing a surface for a seemingly innocuous paint job may actually involve the creation of lead-based paint dust; and the quick installation of a smoke alarm could involve the disturbance of an asbestos-filled ceiling. Handling and disposal of toxic materials is highly regulated and violations may subject you to significant fines. See Chapter 11 for more information on your responsibility for environmental hazards.

---

### Landlords May Be Able to Delegate More Repair Responsibilities to Single-Family Residences

In several states, including Alaska, Arizona, Hawaii, Iowa, Kansas, Kentucky, Montana, Nebraska, New Mexico and South Carolina, the landlord and tenant of a single-family dwelling may agree in writing that the tenant is to perform some of the landlord's statutory duties—to arrange for garbage receptacles and garbage disposal, running water, hot water and heat, in addition to making other specified repairs. States allowing this type of delegation typically require that the transaction be entered into in good faith—meaning that each side completely understands their rights and responsibilities, and neither pressures the other. In addition, the work must usually not be necessary to cure the landlord's failure to substantially comply with health and safety codes.

Although the possibility for delegation is greater in some single-family rental situations than it is in a multi-unit context, we caution owners of single-family rental properties to think carefully before entering into an arrangement of this type. Unless you are very sure about the skill and integrity of your tenant, the possibilities for shoddy work and disagreements are as great as they are in any rental situation, and indeed the consequences (poor work done to an entire house) may be greater.

### 3. Compensating a Tenant for Repair and Maintenance Work

Paying an on-site tenant to do repair and mainte-nance tasks, such as keeping hallways, elevators, or a laundry room clean or maintaining the landscap-ing is preferable to giving the tenant a reduction in rent for work performed. Why? Because if the job is not done right, you can simply cancel the employ-ment arrangement, rather than have to amend the lease or rental agreement in order to re-establish the original rent. By paying the tenant separately, there will be no question that he is still obligated to pay the full rent as he has done all along.

> ### You May Have to Pay Federal and State Tax on Your Tenant-Repair Person
>
> Paying your handy tenant $100 per month, or reducing his rent by this amount, in exchange for maintenance and repair duties may have impor-tant tax consequences for you. That person may be considered your "employee" (as distinguished from an independent contractor). If you "pay" the person more than a certain amount per year, either in cash or in the form of a rent reduction, you may be obliged to pay Social Security and meet other legal obligations as an employer. These obligations are covered in the Chapter 6 discussion of compensating a tenant-manager.

### 4. Landlord Liability for Tenant Repair and Maintenance Work

The delegation of basic repair and maintenance work to a tenant may not relieve you of liability if the repair is done poorly and someone is injured or property is damaged as a result. (Chapter 10 discusses your responsibility for injuries on the property.)

Of course, you could always try to recoup your losses by suing that tenant (called "seeking indem-nity" in legalese), but your chances of recovery will be slim unless your tenant has sufficient monetary assets. On the other hand, a maintenance or repair service will generally carry its own insurance (you should confirm this before you engage their services), and your manager should be a named insured on your insurance policy.

The cruelest cut of all could be the ability of the tenant-repair person to sue you if he is injured performing the repair tasks. The tenant could argue that you had no business entrusting a dangerous job to someone whose expertise was not proven—and, in some courts and in front of some juries, he might prevail. A carefully written exculpatory clause might shield you from liability in some situations, but you can never be 100% sure that the clause will be up-held in court. (Exculpatory clauses are explained in Chapter 10.)

> EXAMPLE: Clem, the landlord, hired Tom, the teenage son of a long-time tenant, for yard work. Part of Tom's job consisted of mowing the two front lawns, which were separated by a gravel walkway. Tom cut the first lawn and, without turning off the mower, pushed it over the gravel to the second lawn. Pieces of gravel were picked up by the blades and fired to the side, where they struck and partially blinded a child playing in the next yard. Clem was sued and faced an uphill battle with his insurance company as to whether Tom's negligence was covered under Clem's policy.

## G. Avoiding Problems by Adopting a Good Maintenance and Repair System

Your best defense against rent withholding hassles and other disputes with tenants is to establish and communicate a clear, easy-to-follow procedure for tenants to ask for repairs and to document all complaints, respond quickly when complaints are made and schedule annual safety inspections. And, if you employ a manager or management company, make sure they follow your guidelines as well.

## 1. Recommended Repair and Maintenance System

Follow these steps to avoid maintenance and repair problems with tenants:

1. Clearly set out your and the tenant's responsibilities for repair and maintenance in your lease or rental agreement. (See Clauses 11, 12 and 13 of the form agreements in Chapter 2.)

2. Use the written Landlord-Tenant Checklist form in Chapter 7 to check over the premises and fix any problems before new tenants move in.

3. Don't assume your tenants know how to handle routine maintenance problems such as a clogged toilet or drain. Make it a point to explain the basics when the tenant moves into the unit. In addition, include a brief list of maintenance do's and don'ts as part of your move-in materials. For example:
   • how to avoid overloading circuits
   • proper use of garbage disposal
   • location and use of fire extinguisher
   • problems tenant should definitely not try to handle, such as electrical repairs.

4. Encourage tenants to immediately report plumbing, heating, weatherproofing or other defects or safety or security problems—whether in the tenant's unit or in common areas such as hallways and parking garages. A Maintenance/Repair Request form (discussed in Section 3, below) is often useful in this regard.

5. Keep a written log (or have your property manager keep one) of all complaints (including those made orally). This should include a

box to indicate your immediate and any follow-up responses (and subsequent tenant communications), as well as a space to enter the date and brief details of when the problem was fixed. The Maintenance Repair/ Request form, below, can serve this purpose.

6. Keep a file for each rental unit with copies of all complaints and repair requests from tenants and your response. As a general rule, you should respond in writing to every tenant repair request (even if you also do so orally).

7. Handle repairs (especially urgent ones) as soon as possible, but definitely within the time any state law requires. (See Section 5, below.) Notify the tenant by phone and follow up in writing if repairs will take more than 48 hours, excluding weekends. Keep the tenant informed—for example, if you have problems scheduling a plumber, let your tenant know with a phone call or a note.

8. Twice a year, give your tenants a checklist on which to report any potential safety hazards or maintenance problems that might have been overlooked. See the Semi-Annual Safety and Maintenance Update, described below. Respond promptly and in writing to all requests, keeping copies in your file.

9. Once a year, inspect all rental units, using the Landlord-Tenant Checklist as a guide, below. (Keep copies of the filled-in checklist in your file.)

10. Especially for multi-unit projects, place conspicuous notices in several places around your property about your determination to operate a safe, well-maintained building, and list phone numbers for tenants to call with maintenance requests.

11. Remind tenants of your policies and procedures to keep your building in good repair in every written communication by printing it at the bottom of all routine notices, rent increases and other communications.

**Sample Notice to Tenants Regarding Complaint Procedure**

Tenants will be more likely to keep you apprised of maintenance and repair problems if you remind them that you are truly interested. A notice such as the following will be helpful:

Fair View Apartments wants to maintain all apartment units and common areas in excellent condition so that tenants enjoy safe and comfortable housing. If you have any questions, suggestions or requests regarding your unit, or the building, please direct them to the manager between 9 A.M. and 6 P.M., Monday through Saturday, either by calling 555-9876 or by dropping off a completed Maintenance/Repair Request form at the manager's office. In case of an emergency, please call 555-1234 at any time.

## 2. Benefits of Establishing a Repair and Maintenance System

In addition to a thorough and prompt system for responding to problems after they have been brought to your attention, you should establish a good, nonintrusive system of frequent and periodic maintenance inspections. In short, encouraging your tenants to report problems, and following the guidelines we suggest here will give you several advantages:

- **Prevention.** First, the system we recommend allows you to fix little problems before they grow into big ones. For example, you would want to replace the washer in the upstairs bathtub before the washer fails, the faucet can't be turned off and the tub overflows, ruining the floor and the ceiling of the lower unit.
- **Good tenant relations**. Communication with tenants who have legitimate concerns with the property creates a climate of cooperation

and trust that can work wonders in the long run. Making tenants happy and keeping them is really an investment in your business.

- **Rent withholding defense**. At least as important as damage prevention and good tenant relations, a responsive communication system provides you with an excellent defense when it comes to those few unreasonable tenants who seek to withhold or reduce rent for no reason other than their disinclination to pay. (In addition, if you need to establish as part of an eviction procedure that a claimed repair problem is phony, you may want to have the repair person who looked at the supposed "defect" come to court to testify as to why it was phony.) In short, you may still have to go to court to evict the tenant, but your carefully documented procedures will constitute a "paper trail" to help you accomplish this with a minimum of time and expense. And, a tenant who doesn't pay the rent because you "failed" to fix a problem will have a hard time making his case if you can show that he never availed himself of your repair procedures. If you make it your normal business practice to save all repair requests from tenants, the absence of a request is evidence that the tenant has made no complaints.
- **Limit legal liability.** Finally, an aggressive repair policy backed up by an excellent recordkeeping system can help reduce your potential liability to your tenants in lawsuits based on injuries suffered as a result of defective conditions on your property. There are two reasons for this. First, it is less likely that there will be injuries in the first place if your property is well-maintained. Second, in many situations an injured person must prove not only that they were hurt but that you were negligent (careless) in allowing the situation to develop. You may be able to defeat this claim by demonstrating that you actively sought out and quickly fixed all defects. (Landlord liability for injuries is discussed in Chapter 10.)

EXAMPLE: Geeta owns a 12-unit apartment complex and regularly encourages her tenants to request repairs in writing on a special form she's prepared. Several prominent signs, as well as reminders on all routine communications with tenants, urge tenants to report all problems. Most tenants do so. One month, Ravi simply doesn't pay his rent. After her phone calls are not answered, Geeta serves a Notice to Pay Rent or Quit. Still Ravi says nothing.

When Geeta files an eviction suit, Ravi claims he withheld rent because of a leaky roof and defective heater Geeta supposedly refused to repair. At trial, Geeta testifies that she routinely saves all tenants' filled-out forms for at least one year, and that she has no record of ever receiving a complaint from Ravi, even though she supplied him with blank forms and sent notices twice a year asking to be informed of any problems. She also submits her complaint log, which has a space to record oral requests. The judge has reason to doubt Ravi ever complained, and rules in Geeta's favor.

## 3. Resident's Maintenance/Repair Request Form

One way to assure that defects in the premises will be reported by conscientious tenants—while helping to refute bogus tenant claims about lack of repairs—is to include a clause in your lease or rental agreement requiring that tenants notify you of repair and maintenance needs. Make the point again and describe your process for handling repairs in your move-in letter to new tenants (see Chapter 7).

Many tenants will find it easiest (and most practical) to call you or your manager with a repair problem or complaint, particularly in urgent cases. Make sure you have an answering machine, voice mail or other service available at all times to accommodate tenant calls. Check your messages frequently when you're not available by phone.

We also suggest you provide all tenants with a Maintenance/Repair Request form. Give each tenant five or ten copies when they move in, explain how the form should be used to request specific repairs (see the sample, below). Be sure that tenants know to describe the problem in detail and to indicate the best time to make repairs. Make sure tenants know how to get more copies. Your manager (if any) should keep an ample supply of the Maintenance/ Repair Request form in her rental unit or office.

You (or your manager) should complete the entire Maintenance/Repair Request form or keep a separate log for every tenant complaint, including those made by phone. (See the discussion below.) Keep a copy of this form or your log in the tenant's file along with any other written communication. Be sure to keep good records of how and when you handled tenant complaints, including reasons for any delays and notes on conversations with tenants. For a sample, see the bottom of the Maintenance/ Repair Request form (labeled For Management Use, shown below). You might also jot down any other comments regarding repair or maintenance problems you observed while handling the tenant's complaint.

The Legal Forms Disk includes a copy of the Resident's Maintenance/Repair Request form, and Appendix II includes a blank, tear-out copy of the form.

## 4. Tracking Tenant Complaints

Most tenants will simply call you when they have a problem or complaint, rather than fill out a Maintenance/Repair Request form. For recordkeeping purposes we suggest you always fill out this form, regardless of whether the tenant does. And, in addition, it's also a good idea to keep a separate chronological log or calendar with similar information on tenant complaints. A faithfully kept log will qualify as a "business record," admissible as evidence in court, that you can use to establish that you normally record tenant communications when they are made. By implication, the *absence* of an entry is evidence that a complaint was *not* made. This argument can be important if your tenant has reduced

## Resident's Maintenance/Repair Request

Date: _____August 29, 199X_____

Address: _____392 Main St., #402, Houston, Texas_____

Resident's Name: _____Mary Griffin_____

Phone (home): ___555-4321_____ Phone (work): ___555-5679_____

Problem (be as specific as possible):_____Garbage disposal doesn't work____

_____

_____

_____

_____

_____

Best time to make repairs: _____After 6 p.m. or Saturday morning_____

_____

Other comments: _____

_____

_____

_____

I authorize entry into my unit to perform the maintenance or repair requested above, in my absence, unless stated otherwise above.

_Mary Griffin_____

Resident

. . . . . . . . . . . . . . . . . . . . . . . . . . . . . . . . . . . . . . . . . . . . .

FOR MANAGEMENT USE

Work done: _____Fixed garbage disposal (removed spoon)_____

Time spent: _____1/2_____ hours

Date completed: _____August 30_____, 199 _X_

Unable to complete on _____, 199____, because: _____

_____

Notes and comments: _____

_____August 30, 199X_____     _Hal Ortiz_____
Date                              Landlord/Manager

or withheld rent or broken the lease on the bogus claim that requests for maintenance or repairs went unanswered.

## 5.  Responding to Tenant Complaints

You should respond almost immediately to all complaints about defective conditions by talking to the tenant and following up (preferably in writing). Explain when repairs can be made or, if you don't yet know, tell the tenant that you will be back in touch promptly. This doesn't mean you have to jump through hoops to fix things that don't need fixing or to engage in heroic efforts to make routine repairs. It does mean you should take prompt action under the circumstances—for example, immediate action should normally be taken to cope with broken door locks or security problems. Similarly, a lack of heat or hot water (especially in winter in cold areas) and safety hazards such as broken steps or exposed electrical wires should be dealt with on an emergency basis.

One way to think about how to respond to repair problems is to classify them according to their consequences. Once you consider the results of *inaction,* your response time will be clear:

- **Personal security and safety problems = injured tenants = lawsuits.** Respond and get work done immediately if the potential for harm is very serious, even if this means calling a 24-hour repair service or having you or your manager get up in the middle of the night to put a piece of plywood over a broken ground floor window.
- **Major inconvenience to tenant=seriously unhappy tenant=tenant's self-help remedies (such as rent withholding) and vacancies.** Respond and attempt to get work done as soon as possible, or within 24 hours, if the problem is a major inconvenience to tenant, such as a plumbing or heating problem.
- **Minor problem = slightly annoyed tenant = bad feelings.** Respond in 48 hours (on business days) if not too serious.

Yes, these deadlines may seem tight and, occasionally, meeting them will cost you a few dollars extra, but in the long run you'll be way ahead.

If you're unable to take care of a repair right away, such as a dripping faucet, and if it isn't so serious that it requires immediate action, let the tenant know when the repair will be made. It's often best to do this orally (a message on the tenant's answering machine should serve), and follow up in writing by leaving a notice under the tenant's door. If there's a delay in handling the problem (maybe the part you need to fix the oven has to be ordered), explain why you won't be able to act immediately.

**Respect tenant's privacy.** To gain access to make repairs, the landlord can enter the rental premises only with the tenant's consent, or after having given reasonable notice, or the specific amount of notice required by state law, usually 24 hours. See Chapter 13 for rules and procedures for entering a tenant's home to make repairs and how to deal with tenants who make access inconvenient for you or your maintenance personnel.

The Legal Forms Disk includes a copy of the Time Estimate for Repair form, and Appendix II includes a blank, tear-out copy of the form.

**If you can't attend to a repair right away, avoid possible rent withholding.** Some landlords voluntarily offer a "rent rebate" if a problem can't be corrected in a timely fashion, especially if it's serious, such as a major heating or plumbing problem. A rebate builds good will and avoids rent withholding.

If, despite all your efforts to conscientiously find out about and make needed repairs on a timely basis, a tenant threatens to withhold rent, move out or pursue another legal remedy discussed in Sections C and D above, you should respond promptly in writing, telling him either:

a. when the repair will be made and the reasons why it is being delayed—for example, a replacement part may have to be ordered to

## Time Estimate for Repair

Stately Manor Apartments
_____

August 30, 199X
_____
Date

Mary Griffin
_____
Tenant

392 Main St., #402
_____
Street address

Houston, Texas
_____
City and State

Dear   Mary Griffin
_____,
                     Tenant

Thank you for promptly notifying us of the following problem with your unit:

Garbage disposal doesn't work
_____

_____

_____

_____

_____

_____

We expect to have the problem corrected on ___September 3_____, 199 _X_ , due to

the following:

Garbage disposal part is out of stock locally, but has been ordered and will be delivered in

a day or two.
_____

_____

_____

We regret any inconvenience this delay may cause. Please do not hesitate to point out any other

problems that may arise.

Sincerely,

_Hal Ortiz_
_____
Landlord/Manager

correct the running sound in a bathroom toilet, or

b. why you do not feel there is a legitimate problem that justifies rent withholding or other tenant action—for example, point out that the running sound may be annoying, but the toilet still flushes and is usable.

At this point, if you feel the tenant is sincere, you might also consider suggesting that you and the tenant mediate the dispute. (See Section D, above.) If you feel the tenant is trying to concoct a phony complaint to justify not paying the rent, take action to evict him.

## H. Tenant Updates and Landlord's Regular Safety and Maintenance Inspections

In addition to a thorough and prompt system for responding to problems after they have been brought to your attention, you should establish a good, nonintrusive system of frequent and periodic maintenance inspections. In short, encouraging your tenants to promptly report problems as they occur should not be your *sole* means of handling your maintenance and repair responsibilities. Here's why: If the tenant is not conscientious, or if he simply doesn't notice that something needs to be fixed, the best reporting system will not do you much good. To back it up, you need to force the tenant (and yourself) to take stock at specified intervals. In the sections, below, we'll explain the tenant update system, and the landlord's annual safety inspection. Make sure your lease or rental agreement and move-in letter cover these updates and inspections as well.

### Year 2000 Problems

Almost every landlord relies on an office computer and equipment, such as a security system or lighting system, that runs off a microchip (a mini-computer). Your business would be in a pretty mess if all of a sudden these date-sensitive computers began misreading the year by an entire century or simply crashed.

Odd as it sounds, that's what might happen when January 1, 2000 rolls around. That's because of the way most computers have been programmed to read a date: When the computer sees the date "01/01/00," it thinks that you're referring to *1900!* Some computers will proceed to make calculations based on this assumption, while others will simply be overwhelmed and will crash, taking your hard drive or building system with them.

There's more at stake here than just massive inconvenience. If a building system fails because of a crash, you could face high repair costs if equipment is damaged due to malfunctions. The failure of critical systems such as lighting and security could increase your risks of liability if tenants are injured or assaulted when your protective systems were down. (Landlords' liability for injuries and crime are covered in Chapters 10 and 12.)

Obviously, you need to take steps now to assess which items in your business rely on computers and chips and whether they are, in fact, vulnerable to Year 2000 problems.

The Building Owners and Managers Association [BOMA] publishes an excellent resource that will explain, step by step, the process of finding and remedying any problems. You can order *Meeting the Year 2000 Challenge: A Guide for Property Professionals* by calling BOMA at 800-426-6292. You can also order from BOMA's Web site (www.boma.org).

## Semi-Annual Safety and Maintenance Update

Please complete the following checklist and note any safety or maintenance problems in your unit or on the premises.

Please describe the specific problems and the rooms or areas involved. Here are some examples of the types of things we want to know about: garage roof leaks, excessive mildew in rear bedroom closet, fuses blow out frequently, door lock sticks, water comes out too hot in shower, exhaust fan above stove doesn't work, smoke alarm malfunctions, peeling paint and mice in basement. Please point out any potential safety and security problems in the neighborhood and anything you consider a serious nuisance.

Please indicate the approximate date when you first noticed the problem and list any other recommendations or suggestions for improvement.

Please return this form with this month's rent check. Thank you.—THE MANAGEMENT

Name: _____ Mary Griffin _____

Address: _____ 392 Main St., #402 _____

_____ Houston, Texas _____

Please indicate (and explain below) problems with:

☐ Floors and floor coverings _____

☐ Walls and ceilings _____

☐ Windows, screens and doors _____

☐ Window coverings (drapes, mini-blinds, etc.) _____

☐ Electrical system and light fixtures _____

☒ Plumbing (sinks, bathtub, shower or toilet) __Water pressure low in shower__

☐ Heating or air conditioning system_____

☒ Major appliances (stove, oven, dishwasher, refrigerator) _Exhaust fan doesn't work_

☐ Basement or attic _____

☒ Locks or security system __Front door lock sticks_____

☐ Smoke detector _____

☐ Fireplace _____

☐ Cupboards, cabinets and closets _____

☐ Furnishings (table, bed, mirrors, chairs) _____

☐ Laundry facilities _____

☐ Elevator _____

☐ Stairs and handrails _____

☐ Hallway, lobby and common areas _____

☐ Garage _____

☐ Patio, terrace or deck _____

☒ Lawn, fences and grounds_____ _Shrubs near back stairway need pruning_____

☐ Pool and recreational facilities _____

☐ Roof, exterior walls, and other structural _____

☐ Driveway and sidewalks_____

☐ Neighborhood _____

☒ Nuisances _____ _Tenant in #501 often plays stereo too loud_____

☐ Other _____

_____

Specifics of problems: _____

_____

_____

_____

_____

_____

Other comments: _____

_____

_____

_____

_____

_____

_February 1, 199X_____        _Mary Griffin_____
Date                                          Tenant

· · · · · · · · · · · · · · · · · · · · · · · · · · · · · · · · · · · · · · · · · ·

FOR MANAGEMENT USE

Action/Response: _____ _Fixed shower exhaust fan and sticking front door lock on February 15. Pruned_

_shrubs on February 21. Spoke with tenant in #501 about keeping stereo low on February 2._____

_____

_____

_____

_____

_____

_____

_February 22, 199X_____        _Terri Zimet_____
Date                                          Landlord/Manager

## 1. Tenant's Semi-Annual Safety and Maintenance Update

You can (nicely) insist that your tenants think about and report needed repairs by giving them a Semi-Annual Safety and Maintenance Update on which to list any problems in the rental unit or on the premises—whether it's low water pressure in the shower, peeling paint or noisy neighbors. Asking tenants to return this Update twice a year should also help you in court if you are up against a tenant who is raising a false implied warranty of habitability defense, particularly if the tenant did not note any problems on his most recently completed Update. As with the Maintenance/Repair Request form, be sure to note how you handled the problem on the bottom of the form. (See the sample Update below.)

The Legal Forms Disk includes a copy of the Semi-Annual Safety and Maintenance Update form, and Appendix II includes a blank, tear-out copy.

## 2. Landlord's Annual Safety Inspection

Sometimes even your pointed reminder (by use of the Semi-Annual Update) that safety and maintenance issues need to be brought to your attention will not do the trick: If your tenant can't recognize a problem even if it stares him in the face, you'll never hear about it either. In the end, you must get into the unit and inspect for yourself.

You should perform an annual "safety and maintenance inspection," as part of your system for repairing and maintaining the property. For example, you might make sure that items listed on the Semi-Annual Safety and Maintenance Update—such as smoke detectors, heating and plumbing systems and major appliances—are in fact safe and in working order. If a problem develops with one of these items, causing injury to a tenant, you may be able to defeat a claim that you were negligent by arguing that your periodic and recent inspection of the item

was all that a landlord should reasonably be expected to do. (Chapter 10 discusses in detail the consequences to a landlord if a tenant or guest is injured on the property.)

In many states you have the right to enter a tenant's home for the purpose of a safety inspection (See Chapter 13 discussion of landlord's right to entry and tenant privacy rules). This does not mean, however, that you can just let yourself in unannounced. All states that allow for inspections require advance notice: Some specify 24 hours; others simply state that the landlord must give "reasonable notice." To be on the safe side, check your state's statutes and, if all that is required is "reasonable notice," allow 24 hours at least.

What should you do if your tenant objects to your safety inspection? If your state allows landlords to enter for this purpose (and if you have given adequate notice and have not otherwise abused your right of entry by needlessly scheduling repeated inspections), the tenant's refusal is grounds for eviction. If your state does not allow the landlord to enter and inspect the dwelling against the tenant's will, you have a problem. Even if your own lease or rental agreement provision allows for inspections, the provision may be considered illegal and unenforceable. Also, evicting a tenant because she refused to allow such an inspection might constitute illegal retaliatory eviction.

There may be, however, a practical way around the obdurate tenant who bars the door. Point out that you take your responsibility to maintain the property very seriously. Remind her that you'll be checking for plumbing, heating, electrical and structural problems that she might not notice, which could develop into bigger problems later if you're not allowed to check them out. Most tenants will not object to yearly safety inspections if you're courteous about it—giving plenty of notice and trying to conduct the inspection at a time convenient for the tenant. (You might offer to inspect at a time when she is home, so that she can see for herself that you will not be nosing about her personal items.)

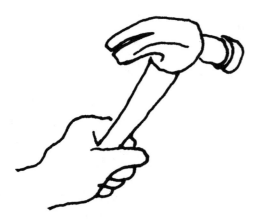

## I.  Tenants' Alterations and Improvements

Your lease or rental agreement probably includes a clause prohibiting tenants from making any alterations or improvements without your express, written consent. (See Clause 12 of our lease or rental agreement forms in Chapter 2.) For good reason, you'll want to make sure tenants don't change the light fixtures, replace the window coverings or install a built-in dishwasher unless you agree first.

But in spite of your wish that your tenants leave well enough alone, you're bound to encounter the tenant who goes ahead without your knowledge or consent. On the other hand, you may also hear from an upstanding tenant that she would, indeed, like your consent to her plan to install a bookshelf or closet system. To know how to deal with unauthorized alterations or straightforward requests, you'll need to understand some basic rules.

Disabled tenants have rights to modify their living space that may override your ban against alterations without your consent. See Chapter 5 for details.

## 1.  Improvements That Become Part of the Property

Anything your tenant attaches to a building, fence, deck or the ground itself (lawyers call such items "fixtures") belongs to you, absent an agreement saying it's the tenant's. This is an age-old legal principle, and for good measure it's wise to spell it out in your lease or rental agreement. This means when the tenant moves out, you are legally entitled to refuse her offer to remove the fixture and return the premises to its original state.

When a landlord and departing tenant haven't decided ahead of time as to who will own the fixture, the dispute often ends up in court. Judges use a variety of legal rules to determine whether an object—an appliance, flooring, shelving or plumbing—is something that the tenant can take with her or is a permanent fixture belonging to you. Here are some of the questions judges ask when separating portable from non-portable additions:

- **Did your tenant get your permission?** If the tenant never asked you for permission to install a closet organizer, or she did and got no for an answer, a judge is likely to rule for you—particularly if your lease or rental agreement prohibits alterations or improvements.
- **Did the tenant make any structural changes that affect the use or appearance of the**

# Agreement Regarding Tenant Alterations to Rental Unit

_____Iona Lott_____ (Landlord)

and _____Doug Diep_____ (Tenant)

agree as follows:

1. Tenant may make the following alterations to the rental unit at _____75A Cherry Street,_____

   Pleasantville, North Dakota._____:

   _1. Plant three rose bushes along walkway at side of residence._____

   _2. Install track lighting along west (ten-foot) kitchen wall._____

   _____

   _____

   _____

   _____

   _____.

2. Tenant will accomplish the work described in Paragraph 1 by using the following materials and

   procedures: _____1. Three bare-root roses, hybrid teas, purchased from Jackson-Perky and___

   ___planted in March._____

   _2. "Wallbright" track lighting system purchased from "Lamps and More," plus necessary___

   ___attachment hardware._____

   _____

   _____.

3. Tenant will do only the work outlined in Paragraph 1 using only the materials and procedures outlined
   in paragraph 2.

4. The alterations carried out by Tenant _(check either a or b)_:

   ☒ will become Landlord's property and are not to be removed by Tenant during or at the end of the
   tenancy

   ☐ will be considered Tenant's personal property, and as such may be removed by Tenant at any time
   up to the end of the tenancy. Tenant promises to return the premises to their original condition
   upon removing the improvement.

5. Landlord will reimburse Tenant only for the costs checked below:

   ☒ the cost of materials listed in paragraph 2

   ☒ labor costs at the rate of $ _____10_____ per hour for work done in a workmanlike
   manner acceptable to Landlord up to _____10_____ hours.

6. After receiving appropriate documentation of the cost of materials and labor, Landlord shall make any payment called for under paragraph 5 by:

[X] lump sum payment, within ____10____ days of receiving documentation of costs, or

[ ] by reducing Tenant's rent by $ _____ per month for the number of months necessary to cover the total amounts under the terms of this agreement.

7. If under Paragraph 4 of this contract the alterations are Tenant's personal property, Tenant must return the premises to their original condition upon removing the alterations. If Tenant fails to do this, Landlord will deduct the cost to restore the premises to their original condition from Tenant's security deposit. If the security deposit is insufficient to cover the costs of restoration, Landlord may take legal action, if necessary, to collect the balance.

8. If Tenant fails to remove an improvement that is his or her personal property on or before the end of the tenancy, it will be considered the property of Landlord, who may choose to keep the improvement (with no financial liability to Tenant), or remove it and charge Tenant for the costs of removal and restoration. Landlord may deduct any costs of removal and restoration from Tenant's security deposit. If the security deposit is insufficient to cover the costs of removal and restoration, Landlord may take legal action, if necessary, to collect the balance.

9. If Tenant removes an item that is Landlord's property, Tenant will owe Landlord the fair market value of the item removed plus any costs incurred by Landlord to restore the premises to their original condition.

10. If Landlord and Tenant are involved in any legal proceeding arising out of this agreement, the prevailing party shall recover reasonable attorney fees, court costs and any costs reasonably necessary to collect a judgment.

_February 10, 199X_          _Iona Lott_
Date                         Landlord

_February 10, 199X_          _Doug Diep_
Date                         Tenant

**property?** If so, chances are that the item will be deemed yours, because removing it will often leave an unsightly area or alter use of part of the property. For example, if a tenant modifies the kitchen counter to accommodate a built-in dishwasher and then takes the dishwasher with her, you will have to install another dishwasher of the same dimensions or re-build the space. The law doesn't impose this extra work on landlords, nor does it force you to let tenants do the return-to-original work themselves.

- **Is the object firmly attached to the property?** In general, additions and improvements that are nailed, screwed or cemented to the building are likely to be deemed "fixtures." For example, hollow-wall screws that anchor a bookcase might convert an otherwise free-standing unit belonging to the tenant to a fixture belonging to you. Similarly, closet rods bolted to the wall become part of the structure and would usually be counted as fixtures. On the other hand, shelving systems that are secured by isometric pressure (spring-loaded rods that press against the ceiling and floor) involve no actual attachment to the wall and for that reason are not likely to be classified as fixtures.

- **What did you and the tenant intend?** Courts will look at statements made by you and the tenant to determine whether there was any understanding as to her right to remove an improvement. In some circumstances, courts will even infer an agreement from your actions—for instance, if you stopped by and gave permission for her to install what you referred to as a portable air conditioner, or helped her lift it into place. By contrast, if the tenant removes light fixtures and, without your knowledge, installs a custom-made fixture that could not be used in any other space, it is unlikely that the tenant could convince a judge that she reasonably expected to take it with her at the end of her tenancy.

### Improvements That Plug or Screw In

The act of plugging in an appliance doesn't make the appliance a part of the premises. The same is true for simple connectors or fittings that join an appliance to an electrical or water source. For example, a refrigerator or free-standing stove remains the property of the tenant. Similarly, portable dishwashers that connect to the kitchen faucet by means of a coupling may be removed.

## 2. Responding to Improvement and Alteration Requests

If a tenant approaches you with a request to alter your property or install a new feature, chances are that your impulse will be to say no. But perhaps the request comes from an outstanding tenant whom you would like to accommodate and would hate to lose. Instead of adopting a rigid approach, consider these alternatives:

**Option One:** Is the improvement or alteration one that is easily undone? For example, if your tenant has a year's lease and you plan to re-paint when she leaves, you can easily fill and paint any small holes left behind when she removes the bookshelf bolted to the wall (and you can bill her for the spackling costs, as explained below). Knocking out a wall to install a wine closet is a more permanent change and not one you're likely to agree to.

**Option Two:** Is the improvement or alteration an enhancement to your property? For example, a wine closet might actually add value to your property. If so, depending on the terms of the agreement you reach with your tenant, you may actually come out ahead.

Before you accommodate your tenant's requests, decide which option makes sense in the circumstances and which you prefer. For example, you may have no use for an air conditioner attached to the window frame, and your tenant may want to take it with her. You'll need to make sure that she understands that she is responsible for restoring the window frame to its original condition, and that if her restoration attempts are less than acceptable, you will be justified in deducting from her security deposit the amount of money necessary to do the job right. (And if the deposit is insufficient, you can sue her in small claims court for the excess.) On the other hand, a custom-made window insulation system may enhance your property (and justify a higher rent later on) and won't do your tenant any good if she takes it with her. Be prepared to hear your tenant ask you to pay for at least some of it.

If you and the tenant reach an understanding, put it in writing. As shown in the sample agreement regarding tenant alterations above, you will want to carefully describe the project and materials, including:

- whether the improvement or alteration is permanent or portable
- the terms of the reimbursement, if any, and
- how and when you'll pay the tenant, if at all, for labor and materials.

Our agreement makes it clear that the tenant's failure to properly restore the premises, or remove an alteration that was to be permanent, will result in deductions from her security deposit or further legal action if necessary.

The Legal Forms Disk includes a copy of the Agreement Regarding Tenant Alterations to Rental Unit, and Appendix II includes a blank tear-out copy.

## J. Cable TV and Satellite Dishes

Major changes in technology have expanded entertainment services available from cable TV and satellite dishes. Tenants are often eager to take advantage of the offerings, but do not always realize that doing so usually involves an installation of a wire, cable or other piece of hardware. Unless you have provided the essential bit of technical equipment (or agree to its installation), your tenant must get permission, just as he must have your OK to attach a sundial or plant a rosebush.

### 1. Cable TV Access

The wonders of cable TV may already be in your rental property through coaxial cables that are strung along telephone poles or underground and into your building, with a single "plug" on the exterior of the building and branches to individual units. Tenants who want to sign up need only call the cable provider to activate the existing cable line to their unit.

If your building isn't wired for cable TV, tenants cannot force you to allow them to install a junction box and wiring through the building. Similarly, if your building is already hooked up to one cable company, and a tenant would prefer to buy the services of another, you're probably on solid ground to say no. Although an incumbent cable company can in theory share its wires with other providers, they typically don't want to make their hardware available to competitors. You are not obliged to allow a hodge-podge of wires through-out your building, either.

We doubt, however, that we have heard the last word on the issue of cable access. The Federal Communications Commission (FCC) will ultimately grapple with the problem and, to complicate matters further, the public utilities commissions of several states (including Arizona, Colorado, Connecticut, Indiana and New Jersey) have begun their own regulation-making process. To find out the current state of your rights to limit cable access, contact your state's public utilities commission.

Meanwhile, if you are not already wired, do some homework and find out whether there are multiple service providers in your area who will vie for your building's business. In a competitive situation, you might be offered incentives that make the deal hard to turn down.

## 2.  Satellite Dishes

Wireless communications have the potential to reach more people with less hardware than any cable system. But there is one, essential piece of equipment: A satellite dish with wires connecting it to the television set or computer.

You may be familiar with the car-sized dishes often seen in backyards or on roofs of houses—the pink flamingo of the new age. Recently, however, smaller and cheaper dishes, two feet or less in diameter, have shown up in appliance stores. Wires from the dishes can easily be run under a door or through an open window to an individual TV or computer. Predictably, tenants have bought dishes and attached them to roofs, window sills, balconies and railings. Landlords have reacted strongly, citing their unsightly looks and the potential for liability should a satellite dish fall and injure someone below.

On this subject, at least, the FCC has given some guidance. In December 1996, it ruled that renters have no right to install a dish. You can prevent the installation of a satellite dish for the same reason that you can prevent a tenant from erecting a flagpole on the patio: It's an alteration to the structure that is not allowed without your consent. ■

# Chapter 10

# Landlord's Liability for Dangerous Conditions

As a property owner, you are responsible for keeping your premises safe for tenants and guests. For example, you may be liable (legally responsible) for physical injuries caused by a broken step or defective wiring. Injured tenants can seek financial recovery for medical bills, lost earnings, pain and other physical suffering, permanent physical disability and disfigurement and emotional distress. Tenants can also look to you for the costs of property damage that results from faulty or unsafe conditions. In extreme cases, a single personal injury verdict against your business has the potential to wipe you out.

Contact your insurance company as soon as you know about a tenant's injury (your policy probably requires you to "immediately tender" any claim or *expected* claim). Your agent will tell you what to do, such as preparing a report on details of the accident.

A tenant who is injured on your property may have a good legal claim against you. That doesn't necessarily mean you'll end up in court. The majority of tenant claims against landlords are settled without trial—usually though negotiations with your insurance company. If your tenant does end up filing a personal injury lawsuit, you'll need to hire a lawyer.

So you can head off problems before they occur, this chapter provides an overview of the legal and practical issues involving landlord liability for tenant injuries, such as those suffered in slip or trip accidents. Most importantly, it offers suggestions on how to avoid injuries and liability through defensive and preventive repair and maintenance procedures.

Related topics covered in thos book include:

- Lease and rental agreement provisions covering landlords' and tenants' responsibilities for repairs, damage to premises and liability-related issues, such as disclosure of hidden defects: Chapter 2
- How to minimize your liability for your property manager's mistakes or illegal acts: Chapter 6
- How to comply with state and local housing laws and avoid safety and maintenance problems and potentially dangerous situations on your rental property: Chapter 9
- Your liability for environmental health hazards: Chapter 11
- Your liability for crime on the premises, including injuries or losses to tenants by strangers or other tenants, and liability for drug dealing on rental property: Chapter 12
- Your liability for non-physical injuries caused by intentional discrimination (Chapter 5), invasion of privacy (Chapter 13) and retaliatory conduct against the tenant (Chapter 17)
- How to choose a lawyer and pay for legal services: Chapter 18.

## A. Landlord Liability for Tenant Injuries

It isn't always easy to determine whether or not you are legally responsible for a tenant's injury. Basically, you may be liable for injuries resulting from your:

- negligence or unreasonably careless conduct
- violation of a health or safety law
- failure to make certain repairs
- failure to keep the premises habitable, or
- reckless or intentional acts.

And in rare instances, you may be liable because courts or the legislature in your state have decided that landlords are automatically liable for certain kinds of injuries, even though you haven't been careless.

Keep in mind that several of these legal theories may apply in your situation, and a tenant (and his lawyer) can use all of them when pressing a claim. The more plausible reasons a tenant can give for your liability, the better the tenant will do when negotiating with your insurance company or making a compelling case in court.

### 1. Negligence

A tenant who files a personal injury claim will most likely charge that you acted negligently—that is, acted carelessly, in a way that wasn't reasonable under the circumstances—and that the injury was caused by your carelessness.

Negligence is always determined in light of the unique facts of each situation. For example, it may be reasonable to put adequate lights in a dark, remote stairwell. If you don't, and a tenant is hurt because she couldn't see the steps and fell, your failure to install the lights might be negligence. On the other hand, extra lights in a lobby that's already well-lit would not be a reasonable expectation.

Whether or not you were negligent and are likely to be held responsible for a tenant's injury depends on answers to six questions. Your insurance adjuster (or a judge or jury, if the case goes to court) will consider these same questions when evaluating a tenant's claim.

### Question 1: Did you control the area where the tenant was hurt or the thing that hurt the tenant?

In most cases, you will be held responsible for an injury if you were legally obligated to maintain and repair the injury-causing factor. For example, you normally have control over a stairway in a common

area, and if its disrepair causes a tenant to fall, you will likely be held liable. You also have control over the building's utility systems. If a malfunction causes injury (like boiling water in a tenant's sink because of a broken thermostat), you will likewise be held responsible.

### Question 2: How likely was it that an accident would occur?

You may be responsible for an injury if a tenant can show that an accident was foreseeable. For example, common sense would tell anyone that loose hand-rails or stairs are likely to lead to accidents, but it would be unusual for injuries to result from peeling wallpaper or a thumbtack that's fallen from a bulletin board. If a freak accident does happen, chances are you will not be held liable.

### Question 3: How difficult or expensive would it have been for you to reduce the risk of injury?

The chances that you will be held responsible for an accident are greater if a reasonably priced response could have averted the accident. In other words, could something as simple as warning signs, a bright light or caution tape have prevented people from tripping over an unexpected step leading to the patio, or would major structural remodeling have been necessary to reduce the likelihood of injury? But if there is a great risk of very serious injury, you will be expected to spend money to avert it. For example, a high-rise deck with rotten support beams must be repaired, regardless of the cost, since there is a great risk of collapse and dreadful injuries to anyone on the deck. If you knew about the condition of the deck and failed to repair it, you would surely be held liable if an accident did occur.

## Question 4: Was a serious injury likely to result from the problem?

The amount of time and money you are expected to spend on making rental premises safe will also depend on the seriousness of the probable injury if you fail to do so. For example, if the umbrella on a poolside table wouldn't open, no one would expect it to cause serious injury. If a tenant is sunburned at the pool as a result, it's not likely that a judge would rule that you had the duty of keeping the tenant from getting burned. But if a major injury is the likely result of a dangerous situation—the pool ladder was broken, making it likely a tenant would fall as he climbed out—you are expected to take the situation more seriously and fix it faster.

The answers to these four questions should tell you (or an insurance adjuster or judge) whether or not there was a dangerous condition on your property that you had a legal duty to deal with. Lawyers call this having a "duty of due care."

Let's look at how these first four questions would get answered in a few possible scenarios.

EXAMPLE 1: Mark broke his leg when he tripped on a loose step on the stairway from the lobby to the first floor. Since the step had been loose for several months, chances are his landlord's insurance company would settle a claim like this.

Mark's position is strong because of the answers to the four questions:
1. Landlords are legally responsible for (in control of) the condition of the common stairways,
2. It was highly foreseeable to any reasonable person that someone would slip on a loose step.
3. Securing the step would have been simple and inexpensive.
4. The probable result of leaving the stair loose—falling and injuring oneself on the stairs—is a serious matter.

EXAMPLE 2: Lee slipped on a marble that had been dropped on the public sidewalk outside his apartment by another tenant's child just a few minutes earlier. Lee twisted his ankle and lost two weeks' work. Lee will have a tough time establishing that his landlord had a duty to protect him from this injury. Here's what the questions turn up:
1. Landlords have little control over the public sidewalk.
2. The likelihood of injury from something a tenant drops is fairly low.
3. The burden on a landlord to eliminate all possible problems at all times by constant inspecting or sweeping the sidewalk is unreasonable.
4. Finally, the seriousness of the likely injury as a result of not checking constantly is open to great debate.

EXAMPLE 3: James suffered a concussion when he hit his head on a dull-colored overhead beam in the apartment garage. When the injury occurred, he was standing in the back of his pickup, loading items onto the roof rack. Did his landlord have a duty to take precautions in this situation? Probably not, but the answers to the four questions are not so easy.
1. Landlords exercise control over the garage, and certainly have a responsibility to reasonably protect tenants from harm there.
2. The likelihood of injury from a beam is fairly slim, since most people don't stand on trucks, and those who do have the opportunity to see the beam and avoid it.
3. As to eliminating the condition that led to the injury, it's highly unlikely anyone would expect a landlord to rebuild the garage. But it's possible that a judge might think it reasonable to paint the beams a bright color and post warning signs, especially if lots of people put trucks and other large vehicles in the garage.
4. As to the seriousness of probable harm, injury from low beams is likely to be to the head, which is a serious matter.

In short, this situation is too close to call, but if an insurance adjuster or jury considered the case, they might decide that James was partially at fault (for not watching out for the beams) and reduce any award accordingly. (See Section B, below.)

If, based on these first four questions, you had a legal duty to deal with a condition on the premises that posed a danger to tenants, keep going. There are two more questions to consider.

### Question 5:  Did you fail to take reasonable steps to prevent an accident?

For example, if a stair was in a dangerous condition, was your failure to fix it unreasonable in the circumstances? Let's take the broken step that Mark (Example 1, above) tripped over. Obviously, leaving it broken for months is unreasonably careless—that is, negligent—under the circumstances.

But what if the step had torn loose only an hour earlier, when another tenant dragged a heavy footlocker up the staircase? Mark's landlord would probably concede that he had a duty to maintain the stairways, but would argue that the manager's daily sweeping and inspection of the stairs that same morning met that burden. In the absence of being notified of the problem, the landlord would probably claim that his inspection routine met his duty of keeping the stairs safe. If a jury agreed, Mark would not be able to establish that the landlord acted unreasonably under the circumstances.

### Question 6:  Did your failure to take reasonable steps to keep tenants safe cause an injury?

This last question establishes the crucial link between your negligence and a tenant's injury. Not every dangerous situation results in an accident. A tenant has to prove that his injury was the result of your carelessness, and not some other reason. Sometimes this is self-evident: One minute a tenant is fine, and the next minute she's slipped on a freshly waxed floor and has a broken arm. But it's not always so simple. For example, in the case of

the loose stair, the landlord might be able to show that the tenant barely lost his balance because of the loose stair and that he had really injured his ankle during a touch football game he'd just played.

Here's a final example, applying all six questions to a tenant's injury.

**EXAMPLE:** Scotty's apartment complex had a pool bordered by a concrete deck. On his way to the pool, Scotty slipped and fell, breaking his arm. The concrete where he fell was slick because the landlord had cleaned the pool and spilled some of the cleaning solution earlier that morning. The landlord's liability for Scotty's injury will depend on the answers to these six questions :

1. Did the landlord control the pool area and the cleaning solution? Absolutely. The pool was part of a common area, and the landlord had done the cleaning.

2. Was an accident like Scotty's foreseeable? Certainly. It's likely that a barefoot person heading for the pool would slip on slick cement.

3. Could the landlord have eliminated the dangerous condition without much effort or money? Of course. All that was necessary was to hose the deck down.

4. How serious was the probable injury? Falling on cement presents a high likelihood of broken bones, a serious injury.

   The answers to these four questions established that the landlord owed Scotty a duty of care.

5. Had his landlord also breached this duty? A jury would probably answer yes—and conclude that leaving spilled cleaning solution on the deck was an unreasonable thing to do.

6. Did the spilled cleaning solution cause Scotty's fall? This one is easy, because several people saw the accident and others could describe Scotty's robust fitness before the fall. Since Scotty himself hadn't been careless (see Section B, below), he had a pretty good case.

## Examples of Injuries From Landlord Negligence

Here are some examples of injuries for which tenants have recovered money damages due to the landlord's negligence:

- Tenant falls down a staircase due to a defective handrail.
- Tenant trips over a hole in the carpet on a common stairway not properly maintained by the landlord.
- Tenant injured and property damaged by fire resulting from an obviously defective heater or wiring.
- Tenant gets sick from pesticide sprayed in common areas and on exterior walls without advance notice.
- Tenant's child is scalded by water from a water heater with a broken thermostat.
- Tenant slips and falls on a puddle of oil-slicked rainwater in the garage.
- Tenant's guest injured when she slips on ultra-slick floor wax applied by the landlord's cleaning service.
- Tenant receives electrical burns when attempting to insert the stove's damaged plug into the wall outlet.
- Tenant slips and falls on wet grass cuttings left on a common walkway.

## Landlord Liability for Injuries to Guests and Trespassers

If you have acted negligently and a tenant's guest or even a trespasser is injured, will you be liable? The precise answer to these questions varies with each state. In a few states, including Alaska, California, Hawaii, Louisiana, Rhode Island and Washington, D.C., you're liable no matter why the injured person was on your property. As a general rule, however, you have a reduced duty of care when it comes to non-tenants, especially trespassers. For example, a tenant who is injured when falling from an unfenced porch will have a fairly strong case for charging you with negligence; but a trespasser, even an innocent one who has come to the wrong address, who falls off the same porch might have a harder time recovering from you.

While your state may require less of a duty of care to guests or trespassers, we recommend you consistently maintain high standards for the condition of your property. You have to maintain the highest standard for tenants, anyway.

## 2. Violation of a Health or Safety Law

Many state and local governments have enacted health and safety laws requiring smoke detectors,

sprinklers, inside-release security bars on windows, childproof fences around swimming pools and so on. To put real teeth behind these important laws, legislators (and sometimes the courts) have decided that a landlord who doesn't take reasonable steps to comply with certain health or safety statutes, will be legally considered negligent. And if that negligence results in an injury, the landlord is liable for it. A tenant doesn't need to prove that an accident was foreseeable or likely to be serious; nor does a tenant have to show that complying with the law would have been relatively inexpensive. The legal term for this rule is "negligence per se."

EXAMPLE: A local housing code specifies that all kitchens must have grounded power plugs. There are no grounded plugs in the kitchen of one of your rental units. As a result, a tenant is injured when using an appliance in an otherwise safe manner. In many states, the law would presume negligence on your part. If a tenant can show that the ungrounded plug caused injury, you will be held liable.

Bear in mind that you are only expected to take reasonable steps to comply with safety and health laws that fall within the negligence *per se* realm. For example, most states require landlords to supply smoke detectors. If you have supplied one but your tenant has disabled it, you won't be held responsible if a tenant is hurt by a fire that could have been stopped had the detector been left alone.

Your violation of a health or safety law may also indirectly cause an injury. For example, if you let the furnace deteriorate in violation of local law and a tenant is injured trying to repair it, you will probably be liable unless the tenant's repair efforts are extremely careless themselves.

EXAMPLE: The state housing code requires landlords to provide hot water. In the middle of the winter, a tenant's hot water heater has been broken for a week, despite his repeated complaints to the landlord. Finally, to give a sick child a hot bath, a tenant carries pots of steaming water from the stove to the bathtub. Doing this, he spills the hot water and burns himself seriously.

The tenant sues the landlord for failure to provide hot water as required by state law. If the case goes to court, it will be up to the jury to decide whether or not the landlord's failure to provide hot water caused the tenant's injury. Many juries would think that the tenant's response to the lack of hot water was a foreseeable one and, knowing this, the landlord's insurance company would probably be willing to offer a fair settlement.

## 3. Failure to Make Certain Repairs

For perfectly sensible reasons, many landlords do not want tenants to undertake even relatively simple tasks like painting, plastering or unclogging a drain. Leases and rental agreements (including the ones in this book) often prohibit tenants from making any repairs or alterations without the landlord's consent, or limit what a tenant can do. (If you do decide to allow tenants to perform maintenance tasks, be sure to do so with a clear, written agreement, as explained in Chapter 9.)

But in exchange for reserving the right to make all these repairs yourself, the law imposes a responsibility. If, after being told about a problem, you don't maintain or repair something a tenant is not to touch—for example, an electrical switch— and the tenant is injured as a result, you could be held liable. The legal reason is that you breached the contract (the lease) by not making the repairs. (You may be negligent as well; remember, there is nothing to stop a tenant from presenting multiple reasons why you should be held liable.)

EXAMPLE: The sash cords that opened the living room window in Shanna's apartment broke, making it necessary to support the entire weight of the window while raising or lowering it and securing it with a block of wood. Since Shanna's lease included a clause forbidding repairs of any nature, she reported the problem to Len, the owner. Despite his promises to repair the window, Len never got around to it. One hot summer evening Shanna attempted to raise the heavy window, but her hands slipped and the window came crashing down on her arm, breaking it. Shanna threatened to sue Len, claiming that he had negligently delayed the repair of the window, and furthermore that the lease clause forbidding any repairs by the tenant contractually obligated Len to attend to the problem in a reasonably prompt manner. Mindful of the strength of Shanna's arguments, and fearful that the jury would side with Shanna and give her a large award, Len's insurance company settled the case for several thousand dollars.

⚠️ **A landlord's duty to maintain premises can be a big factor in lawsuits based on security problems or environmental hazards.** Liability based on the landlord's retained control over aspects of the tenant's space are commonly seen in lawsuits over environmental hazards, such as those based on lead paint, asbestos and radon. For example, if you forbid repainting without your consent, you thereby obligate yourself to maintain the paint—and if it's lead paint that you either fail to monitor or handle negligently, you will be liable for the health problems that follow. (See Chapter 11.) Also, your control over door and window locks within a tenant's leased space can obligate you to provide truly secure and effective equipment, and can result in liability if a crime occurs because of the failure of these features. (See Chapter 12.)

## 4. Failure to Keep the Premises Habitable

One of a landlord's basic responsibilities is to keep the rental property in a "habitable" condition. (Chapter 9 discusses the implied warranty of habitability.)

Failure to maintain a habitable dwelling may make you liable for injuries caused by the substan-

dard conditions. For example, a tenant who is bitten by a rat in a vermin-infested building may argue that your failure to maintain a rat-free building constituted a breach of your duty to keep the place habitable, which in turn led to the injury. The tenant must show that you knew of the defect and had a reasonable amount of time to fix it.

This theory applies only when the defect is so serious that the rental unit is unfit for human habitation. For example, a large, jagged broken picture window would make the premises unfit for habitation in North Dakota in winter, but a torn screen door in southern California obviously would not. The North Dakota tenant who cut herself trying to cover the window with cardboard might sue under negligence and a violation of the implied warranty of habitability, while the California tenant would be limited to a theory of negligence.

EXAMPLE: Jose notified his landlord about the mice that he had seen several times in his kitchen. Despite Jose's repeated complaints, the landlord did nothing to eliminate the problem. When Jose reached into his cupboard for a box of cereal, he was bitten by a mouse. Jose sued his landlord for the medical treatment he required, including extremely painful rabies shots, and alleged that the landlord's failure to eradicate the rodent problem constituted a breach of the implied warranty of habitability, and that this breach was responsible for his injury. The jury agreed and gave Jose a large monetary award.

The injury sustained by Jose in the example above could also justify a claim that the injury resulted from the landlord's negligence. And, if Jose's landlord had failed to take reasonable steps to comply with a state or local statute concerning rodent control, the landlord might automatically be considered negligent. Finally, the owner may also be liable if the lease forbade Jose from make repairs, such as repairing improper sewage connections or changing the way garbage was stored. As you can see, sometimes there are several legal theories that will fit the facts and support a tenant's claim for damages.

## 5. Reckless or Intentional Acts

In the legal sense of the word, "recklessness" usually means extreme carelessness regarding an obvious defect or problem. A landlord who is aware of a long-existing and obviously dangerous defect but neglects to correct it may be guilty of recklessness, not just ordinary carelessness.

If you or an employee acted recklessly, a tenant's monetary recovery could be significant. This is because a jury has the power to award not only actual damages (which, as discussed in Section C, include medical bills, loss of earnings and pain and suffering) but also extra, "punitive" damages for outrageous or extremely careless behavior. Punitive damages are almost never given in simple negligence cases, but are given to punish recklessness and to send a sobering message to others who might behave similarly. In any situation the line between ordinary negligence and recklessness is wherever the unpredictable American jury thinks it should be. The size of the punitive award is likewise up to the jury.

The very unpredictability of punitive damage awards, should be considered when you (or, more likely, your insurance company) is negotiating with a tenant. You might prefer to settle the tenant's claim rather than risk letting an indignant jury award punitive damages.

EXAMPLE: The handrail along the stairs to the first floor of the apartment house Jack owned had been hanging loose for several months. Jack attempted to fix it two or three times by taping the supports to the wall. The tape did no good, however, and the railing was literally flapping in the breeze. One dark night when Hilda, one of Jack's tenants, reached for the railing, the entire thing came off in her hand, causing her to fall and break her hip.

Hilda sued Jack for her injuries. In her lawsuit, she pointed to the obviously ineffective measures that Jack had taken to deal with a clearly dangerous situation, and charged that he had acted with reckless disregard for the safety of his tenants. (Hilda also argued that Jack was negligent because of his unreasonable behavior and because he had violated a local ordinance regarding maintenance of handrails.) The jury agreed with Hilda and awarded her punitive damages.

Better yet, avoid situations that give rise to punitive damages, especially because many insurance companies do not cover punitive damages, as discussed in Section E, below.

## 6. Intentional Harm

If you or your manager struck and injured a tenant during an argument, that would be an intentional act for which you would be liable.

Less obvious, but no less serious, are emotional or psychological injuries which can, in extreme circumstances, also be inflicted intentionally. Intentional infliction of emotional distress may arise in these situations:

- **Sexual harassment.** Repeated, disturbing attentions of a sexual nature which leave a tenant fearful, humiliated and upset. (Chapter 5 discusses sexual harassment as a form of sex discrimination.)

EXAMPLE: Rita's landlord Mike took advantage of every opportunity to make suggestive comments about her looks and social life. When she asked him to stop, he replied that he was "just looking out for her," and he stepped up his unwanted attentions. Rita finally had enough, broke the lease and moved out. When Mike sued her for unpaid rent, she turned around and sued him for the emotional distress caused by his harassment. To his surprise, Mike was slapped with a multi-thousand dollar judgment, including punitive damages.

- **Assault.** Threatening or menacing someone without actually touching them is an assault, which can be enormously frightening and lead to psychological damage.
- **Repeated invasions of privacy.** Deliberately invading a tenant's privacy—by unauthorized entries, for example—may cause extreme worry and distress. (Chapter 13 covers tenants' privacy rights.)

## 7. The Law Makes Landlords Liable

In rare circumstances, you may be responsible for a tenant's injury even though you did your best to create and maintain a safe environment. In other words, even if you did your best to provide a safe premises—you were not negligent—you may be held responsible for a tenant's injuries. This legal principle is called "strict liability," or liability without fault. It's a very similar concept to "no fault" auto insurance—a person may collect without having to prove that the accident was the other person's fault.

In most states, strict liability is imposed by courts or lawmakers only when a hidden defect poses an unreasonably dangerous risk of harm to a group of persons unable to detect or avoid the danger. For example, Massachusetts landlords are subject to strict liability if tenants are poisoned by lead-based paint. In New York, strict liability has been applied to injuries from radon.

Louisiana is the only state that makes strict liability available for a wide range of tenant injuries, but the quirkiness of the law (a tenant must have been injured by an "original aspect" of the structure that has succumbed to "ruin" or significant damage) makes it little used in practice. Most injured Louisiana tenants sue their landlords for negligence.

---

### Incorporating or Forming a Limited Liability Company May Limit Your Personal Liability

The most important feature of a corporation or a limited liability company (known as an "LLC") is that, legally, they're a separate entity from the individuals who own or operate them. You may own all the stock of your corporation or LLC, and you may be its only employee, but—if you follow sensible organizational and operating procedures—you and your corporation or LLC are separate legal entities. This means that the corporation or LLC—not your personal bank account—is liable for any awards or settlements won by injured tenants. How to incorporate, which is usually more appropriate for larger landlords, is beyond the scope of this book. *The Legal Guide for Starting and Running a Small Business*, by Fred S. Steingold (Nolo Press), covers how to choose the best way to structure your business. *Form Your Own Limited Liability Company*, by Anthony Mancuso (Nolo Press), explains LLCs and shows you how to form one in your state.

---

## B. If a Tenant Is at Fault, Too

If tenant is partially to blame for his injury, your liability for the tenant's losses will be reduced accordingly.

### 1. Tenant Carelessness

If a tenant is also guilty of unreasonable carelessness—for example, he was drunk and, as a result, didn't (or couldn't) watch his step when he tripped on a loose tread on a poorly maintained stairway—in most states your liability will be proportionately reduced.

The legal principle is called "comparative negligence." Basically, this means that a tenant who is partially at fault can collect only part of the value of her losses. For example, if a judge or jury ruled that a tenant had suffered $10,000 in damages (such as medical costs or lost earnings) but that she was 20% at fault, she would recover only $8,000.

Comparative negligence is applied in different ways in different states. In some states (listed below), injured tenants can collect something no matter how careless they were—even if they were 99% at fault.

In many others, however, a tenant can recover only if her own carelessness was not too great. In Arkansas and Colorado, for example, a tenant will get something only if her carelessness was less than the landlord's. If it's equal to or greater than yours, the tenant will get nothing. In a majority of states, including New Jersey, Texas and Wisconsin, a tenant can recover if the tenant's negligence was *equal to* or lower than yours; so if the jury concludes that a tenant was equally at fault, she'll collect half her damages.

In a few states—Alabama, Maryland, North Carolina and Virginia—the doctrine of comparative negligence doesn't exist. A tenant who was even the least bit negligent can collect nothing.

---

### Generous Comparative Negligence States

In these states, injured tenants can collect something even if they were 99% at fault:

| | | |
|---|---|---|
| Alaska | Louisiana | New Mexico |
| Arizona | Maine | New York |
| California | Missouri | Rhode Island |
| Florida | Mississippi | Washington |
| Kentucky | | |

---

### 2. Tenant Risk-Taking

A tenant's carelessness is not the only factor affecting the outcome of a personal injury case. If a tenant deliberately chose to act in a way that caused or worsened his injury, another doctrine may apply. Called "assumption of risk," it refers to a tenant who knows the danger of a certain action and decides to take the chance anyway.

> **EXAMPLE:** In a hurry to get to work, a tenant takes a shortcut to the garage by using a walkway that he knows has uneven, broken pavement. The tenant disregards the sign posted by his landlord—"Use Front Walkway Only." If the tenant trips and hurts his knee, he'll have a hard time pinning blame on his landlord because he deliberately chose a known, dangerous route to the garage.

In some states, a tenant who is injured as a result of putting himself in harm's way may not be entitled to recover anything, even if your negligence contributed to the injury. In other states, a tenant's recovery will be diminished according to the extent that he appreciated the danger involved.

## C. How Much Money the Tenant May Be Entitled To

A tenant who was injured on your property and has convinced an insurance adjuster or jury that you are responsible, at least in part, can ask for monetary compensation, called "compensatory damages." Injured tenants can recover the money they have lost (wages) and spent (doctors' bills), plus compensation for physical pain and suffering, mental anguish and lost opportunities. Given the often quirky nature of American juries, these costs can be enormous.

**Medical care and related expenses**. A injured tenant can recover for doctors' and physical therapists' bills, including future care.

**Missed work time.** A tenant can sue for lost wages and income while out of work and undergoing medical treatment for injuries. He can also recover for expected losses due to continuing care.

**Pain and other physical suffering.** The type of injury the tenant has suffered and its expected duration will affect the amount awarded for pain and suffering. Insurance adjusters require objective corroboration of a tenant's level of discomfort, such as a doctor's prescription of strong anti-pain medication. And the longer a tenant's recovery period, the greater the pain and suffering.

**Permanent physical disability or disfigurement.** If the tenant's injury has clear long-lasting or permanent effects—such as scars, back or joint stiffness or a significant reduction in mobility—the amount of damages goes way up.

**Loss of family, social, career and educational experiences or opportunities.** A tenant who can demonstrate that the injury prevented a promotion or better job can ask for compensation representing the lost income.

**Emotional damages resulting from any of the above.** Emotional pain, including stress, embarrassment, depression and strains on family relationships may be compensated. Like pain and suffering, however, insurance adjusters require proof, such as evaluations from a therapist, physician or counselor.

**Punitive damages.** In some cases, injured tenants can collect more than compensatory damages. Punitive damages are awarded if a judge or jury decides that the landlord acted outrageously, either intentionally or with extreme carelessness. As a general rule, you won't be liable for punitive damages if you refrain from extreme neglect and intentional wrongs against tenants and others. (See Section A5, above, for more details on punitive damages.)

---

### Injuries Without Impact: Legal Nuisances

If you maintain a legal nuisance—a serious and persistent health or safety condition that adversely affects a tenant's (or neighbor's) enjoyment of the property—a tenant can seek damages, even if no physical injury occurs. For example, a tenant who is repeatedly plagued by the stench of garbage scattered about because you haven't provided enough garbage cans for the apartment building can sue for the annoyance and inconvenience of putting up with the smell. Similarly, a tenant or neighbor—or a group of them—may sue if you do nothing to evict a notorious drug-dealing tenant, whose dangerous associates genuinely frighten them. And as discussed in Chapter 5, a landlord may also be sued for the non-physical distress caused by illegal discrimination or harassment.

---

## D. How to Prevent Liability Problems

There are specific steps you can take to protect yourself from lawsuits and hefty insurance settlements and at the same time make your tenants' lives safer and happier.

**1. Regularly look for dangerous conditions on the property and fix them promptly—whether it's a structural problem, an environmental health hazard or any other dangerous condition.** Keep good records on the dates and details of your property inspections and any follow-up repairs done. Ask your tenants, manager, employees and insurance company to help you spot problems. When you become aware of a repair problem with an obvious potential for injury, put it on the top of your "to do" list. (Chapter 9 discusses inspections.)

**2. Scrupulously keep up to date on, and comply with, all state and local health, safety and building codes.** Once you establish basic compliance with these rules, you can't just forget about them. Since they change occasionally, you can stay current by reviewing them once a year. If your structure and operation are "up to code," you should avoid most lawsuits based on your violation of a statute. (Chapter 9 explains how to find all the relevant codes.)

**3. Maintain your rental property and reduce risk exposure as much as possible—for example, by providing sufficient lighting in hallways, parking garages and other common areas.** If there are problems that you cannot completely control and eliminate, such as the presence of environmental hazards, educate your tenants to the dangers and their need to follow safety procedures. (See Chapter 11.)

**4. Warn of dangers you can't fix.** Landlords have a duty to warn tenants and others about naturally occurring dangers (such as loose soil) and man-made dangers (like low doorways or steep stairs) that are hidden but which you know (or should know) about. Disclose hidden defects in your lease or rental agreement (see Clause 20 of the form agreements in Chapter 2), or include a section in a move-in letter (see Chapter 7), so that it can never be claimed that a tenant was not warned of a potentially dangerous condition. If appropriate, also post warning signs near the hazard.

EXAMPLE 1: Towering eucalyptus trees lined the side and back yards of the duplex owned by Jack and Edna. During windy weather, the trees often dropped entire strips of bark and even some branches. Realizing this, Jack and Edna warned their tenants to steer clear of the

trees during windy spells. As an extra precaution, Jack and Edna included a written warning to this effect in a move-in letter to new tenants and posted signs near the trees.

EXAMPLE 2: The sidewalk ramp leading to the front door of Sandra's duplex was painted white. The paint was non-porous and became extremely slippery when wet. The owner provided a railing and a warning sign, at both ends of the ramp, telling users that the surface was "Slippery When Wet" and directing them to use the handrail.

**5. Adopt a policy of soliciting and responding quickly to tenant complaints about potential safety problems and nuisances.** Back your policy up with a good recordkeeping system. (See Chapter 9 for advice.)

**6. Install and maintain basic security features, such as deadbolt locks, smoke detectors, fire extinguishers, window locks and outside lighting.** Candidly appraise the security situation around your property and provide heightened protection if the conditions warrant it. (See Chapter 12.)

**7. Be especially vigilant about dangers to children.** If children are drawn onto your property due to an irresistibly interesting (to children) but dangerous feature, such as a stack of building materials or an abandoned refrigerator or well (known in legal jargon as an "attractive nuisance"), you must exercise special care. Because young children can't read and all children tend to ignore warnings, you should place physical barriers between the children and the attractive feature. And if the danger is of the type that can be cleaned up or removed (like a pile of junk or an abandoned refrigerator), you should do so.

Laws sometimes regulate activities and conditions that have proved attractive and dangerous to children. By far the most common are local laws that require fencing around swimming pools and impose construction and height requirements on pool fences. It is very common for landlords to be found liable for tragic drownings when they have failed to comply with fencing requirements. Ordinances requiring the removal of doors from unused refrigerators and the fencing or removal of abandoned cars or piles of junk are also typical. These are prime examples of negligence *per se* (negligence that is presumed because the violation of the safety law allowed the injury), which is discussed in Section A, above.

---

### Landlord Liability for Play Structures Made by the Tenant

If you don't create a dangerous situation yourself, but allow a tenant to do so, you may also be legally liable. For example, a tree house that your tenant builds in the backyard, or a play structure that parents buy for their own children, might also attract other tenants' children or children from the neighborhood. If one of the neighborhood kids falls from the tree (or play structure) and is injured, you may be liable. The fact that the attractive nuisance, though not created by you, was allowed to remain on your property with your tacit consent, may be grounds for your liability.

---

Be sure to inform tenants of your concerns regarding specific aspects of your property that might be dangerous to children.

**EXAMPLE:** An apartment building owner took great pride in the fishpond in the courtyard. The yard was accessible to the general public, and neighborhood children frequently came to watch the fish. When one child fell in and nearly drowned, the child's parents sued the landlord. The landlord was found liable for the child's accident on the grounds of negligence—the landlord should have known that the fishpond was dangerous and that unsupervised children would come onto his property and could be injured by falling into the pond. In hindsight, the landlord should have gotten rid of the pond or fenced it off so that small children were kept out.

---

### Swimming Pools Can Mean Deep Trouble

If your property includes a swimming pool, you must take special care to make sure your tenants and their guests appreciate the dangers involved. Let tenants know that they are also responsible for proper supervision of their children. All the fencing in the world, for example, will not protect a young child who is left unattended inside a pool enclosure. Obviously, rules requiring adult supervision of young children and the need to walk carefully on wet, slippery surfaces should be part of any move-in letter and rules and regulations that are part of your lease or rental agreement. (Clause 18 of the form agreements in Chapter 2 discusses rules and regulations. Chapter 7 discusses move-in letters.) The rules (including a reminder that there is no lifeguard on duty) should be repeated on signs posted near the pool. Pool supply stores are a good source of pre-printed, easy-to-read signs.

---

**8. Be aware of threats to tenants' safety and security from third parties and other tenants.** Evict any tenant who is a serious nuisance to other tenants or neighbors. (See Chapter 12.)

**9. Educate your manager as to his or her responsibilities.** You may face substantial financial liability for your manager's actions. (See Chapter 6 for how to protect yourself from your manager's and management company's mistakes and illegal acts.)

**10. Supervise contractors.** If construction work is done on your property, make sure that the contractor in charge secures the site and removes or locks up dangerous tools or equipment when the site is left unattended. Remember, a pile of sand or a stack of sheet rock might look like work to an adult, but fun to a child. You might consider sending your tenants written notice of the intended project, suggesting that they take care during the construction period.

**11. Get a good liability insurance policy.** (See Section E, below.)

## Don't Use Exculpatory Clauses to Shield Yourself From Liability

Landlords used to be able to protect themselves from most lawsuits brought by tenants by inserting a clause in all leases and rental agreements that absolved the landlord of responsibility for all injuries suffered by a tenant, even those caused by the landlord's negligence. Known as "exculpatory clauses," these blanket provisions are now viewed with disfavor by courts in most states.

Because courts are so wary of exculpatory clauses, our general advice is not to use them, and to never use a broad, all-encompassing waiver. But there may be unusual situations when a narrowly-worded exculpatory clause would be appropriate— for example, if you have delegated appropriate repair and maintenance duties to a tenant (see Chapter 9 for tips on delegation of repairs), you may want to make it clear that the tenant is not to look to you if he injures himself in the course of his duties. (Remember, however, that an exculpatory clause will *not* shield you from liability if your tenant injures a third party.)

EXAMPLE: Sadie and Hal lived in one half of their duplex and rented out the second half. They offered Fred, their tenant, a trade-off whereby he would be responsible for the upkeep of the common walk-ways and gardens in exchange for a reduction in rent. As part of the bargain, Fred agreed to absolve Sadie and Hal of any liability if a defect in these areas caused him an injury. Because this agreement was the result of good-faith negotiations on both sides, each party received a benefit from the deal, and the landlords' delegated duties (gardening and general maintenance on a small piece of property affecting only them and their one tenant) could safely and reasonably be performed by their tenant, the agreement would likely be upheld if either side challenged it later in court.

When Fred hurt his back pushing the lawn-mower, he was bound by the exculpatory clause and could not sue Sadie and Hal for his injuries. But when Mac, a delivery person, slipped on wet grass cuttings that Fred left carelessly on the walk-way, both Fred and Sadie and Hal found themselves at the other end of Mac's personal injury claim.

# E. Liability and Other Types of Property Insurance

A well-designed insurance program can protect your rental property from losses caused by many types of perils, including damage to the property caused by fire, storms, burglary and vandalism. A comprehensive policy will also include liability insurance, covering injuries or losses suffered by others as the result of defective conditions on the property. Equally important, liability insurance covers the cost of settling personal injury claims, including lawyer's bills for defending personal injury lawsuits.

This section provides advice on choosing liability and other property insurance. For a more detailed discussion on insuring your rental property business, see *The Legal Guide for Starting and Running a Small Business*, by Fred S. Steingold (Nolo Press).

## 1. Choosing Liability Insurance Coverage

Here are some specific tips on choosing liability insurance, something all landlords should buy. Advice on property insurance in general and working with an insurance agent are covered in the sections below.

### a. Purchase High Levels of Liability Coverage

Liability policies are designed to cover you against lawsuit settlements and judgments up to the amount of the policy limit, including the cost of defending the lawsuit. They provide coverage for a host of common perils, such as tenants falling and getting injured on a defective staircase. Liability policies usually state a dollar limit per occurrence and an aggregate dollar limit for the policy year. For example, your policy may say that it will pay $300,000 per occurrence for personal injury or a total of $1 million in any one policy year.

Depending on the value of your property and the value of the assets you are seeking to protect, buying more coverage is a very good idea, especially in large metropolitan areas where personal injury damage awards can be very high.

### b. Purchase Commercial Liability Coverage

Make sure your liability policy covers not only physical injury but also lists libel, slander, discrimination, unlawful and retaliatory eviction and invasion of privacy suffered by tenants and guests.

As explained in Chapter 5, this kind of coverage can be very important in discrimination claims.

### c. Purchase Non-Owned Auto Liability Insurance

Be sure to carry liability insurance not only on your own vehicles but also on your manager's car or truck if it will be used for business purposes. Non-owned auto insurance will protect you from liability for accidents and injuries caused by your manager or other employee while running errands for you in their own vehicle.

### 2. Punitive Damages and Other Common Insurance Exclusions

Punitive damages are monetary awards that are intended to punish you for willful or malicious behavior, rather than to compensate the injured person.

As you might expect, the insurance industry would like to be able to exclude punitive damages from coverage, but they have never adopted a standard-form exclusion clause. (Insurance policies are typically made up of canned, commonly used clauses that are used by virtually every insurance company.) If an insurance policy does not specifically state whether punitive damages will be covered (and most do not), it will be up to the courts of the state where the policyholder lives to decide whether standard policy language covers punitive awards.

Not surprisingly, states have not been consistent in their treatment of this issue. In California, Colorado, Connecticut, Kansas, Minnesota, New York, Ohio and Washington, D.C., courts have held that punitive damages are not included within standard comprehensive liability policies. Oregon, Rhode Island, Tennessee and several others, however, have reached the opposite conclusion. Your insurance agent should be able to tell you whether the courts in your states have held that punitive damages are understood as falling within the standard language in your policy.

It's clear, however, that intentional harms or violations of penal statutes are not covered. Unfortunately, the inquiry does not end here, for it is often a matter of debate as to whether a particular act was intended (and therefore not insurable). While illegal discrimination, physical assaults, harassment or retaliation (by you or your manager) are often treated by insurers as intentional acts not covered by the policy, most liability insurers will at least pay for the defense of such lawsuits.

## 3. Some General Tips on Choosing Property Insurance

In choosing property coverage, there are four main questions to consider:

### a. What Business Property Is Insured?

Be sure your insurance covers all the property you want protected. In addition to the entire building, does your insurance cover additions under construction? Outdoor fixtures, such as pole lights? Washing machines and other appliances? Property used to maintain the building, such as gardening equipment and tools? Boilers and heavy equipment? Personal business property such as computers used in managing your rental business?

**Make sure your tenants know that your insurance does not cover loss or damage (caused by theft or fire) to their personal property.** Your tenants will need to purchase their own renters' insurance to cover their personal property. (See the discussion of renters' insurance in Chapter 2.) This does not mean, however, that you cannot be sued by your tenant (or his insurance company) if your negligence caused his loss. In this event, your insurance won't cover the loss of the tenant's personal belongings.

### b. What Perils Will Be Insured Against?

Be sure you know what kind of losses the policy covers. Coverage for damage caused by fire is common in the most basic policies, while damage from mud slides, windstorms and the weight of snow may be excluded. Earthquake insurance on the building itself and flood insurance are typically separate. They are often expensive and have a very high deductible, but they still are a good option if your building is highly susceptible to earthquake or flood damage. Whatever policy you decide on, read it carefully before you pay for it—you've suffered a loss.

**Be sure to check out "loss of rents**
This will reimburse you for the loss of rents from rental units that have been sidelined—for example, due to a fire or other calamity. This coverage will kick in even if you are able to move the tenant to another, vacant unit.

### c. How Much Insurance Should You Buy?

Obviously, the higher the amount of coverage, the higher the premiums. You don't want to waste money on insurance, but you do want to carry enough so that a loss wouldn't jeopardize your business.

Be sure to carry enough insurance on the building to rebuild it. But there's no need to insure the total value of your real property (the legal term that includes land and buildings), because land doesn't burn. Especially if you're in an area where land is very valuable, this is a big consideration. If you're in doubt as to how much it would cost you to rebuild, have an appraisal made so you know that your idea of value is realistic. Because the value of the building and other property may increase, it's wise to get a new appraisal every few years. Your insurance agent should be able to help you do this.

### d. Should You Buy Coverage for Replacement Cost?

Historically, in the event of a loss a basic fire insurance contract covered the actual cash value of the property, not its full replacement value. Today, policies are routinely available with replacement cost coverage. This is the coverage you want.

**Consider purchasing insurance to cover "code upgrades."** Plain "cost of replacement" coverage, which replaces the existing building should it be destroyed, won't be adequate should you need to bring an older building up to code after a fire or other damage. The problem is that legal requirements adopted since the building was constructed will normally require that a stronger, safer, more fire-resistant building be constructed. Doing this can cost far more than simply replacing the old building. To cope with this possibility, you want a policy that will not only replace the building but pay for all legally required upgrades. This coverage is called "Ordinance of Law Coverage," and it is almost never included in standard policies. You must ask for it.

## 4. Working With an Insurance Agent

Here are some tips for choosing an insurance agent:

**Find and work with a knowledgeable insurance agent—one who takes the time to analyze your business operations and come up with a sensible program for your business.** Get recommendations from people who own property similar to yours, or from real estate people with several years' experience—they will know who comes through and who doesn't. Working with an agent who knows your business is advantageous because that person is already a fair way along the learning curve when it comes to helping you select affordable and appropriate insurance.

**Steer clear of an agent who, without learning the specifics of your property and business, whips out a package policy and claims it will solve all your problems.** While there are some excellent packages available that may meet your needs, neither you nor your insurance agent will know for sure until the agent asks you a lot of questions and thoroughly understands your business. If the agent is unable or unwilling to tailor your coverage to your particular business, find someone else.

**Be frank with your agent when discussing your business.** Reveal all areas of unusual risk. If you fail to disclose all the facts, you may not get the coverage you need. Or, in some circumstances, the insurance company may later take the position that you misrepresented the nature of your operation and, for that reason, deny you coverage.

**Make sure you have a clear understanding of what your insurance policy covers and what's excluded.** Does the policy exclude damage from a leaking sprinkler system? From a boiler explosion? From an earthquake? If so, and these are risks you face, find out if they can be covered by paying a small extra premium.

**Insist on a highly rated carrier.** Insurance companies are rated according to their financial condition and size. The most recognized rater is the A.M. Best Company, which assigns letter ratings according to financial stability (A++ is the highest) and Roman Numeral ratings reflecting the size of a company's surplus (XV is the best). Since 80% of American companies receive an A rating or higher, you wouldn't want to choose a company rated less than that. As to surplus, you will be on solid ground to require an "X." Your local public library's business section or reference desk will likely have the *Best Key Rating Guide.* More information is on Best's Web site: www.ambest.com.

⚠️ **Consider insuring for the cost of rubble removal and engineering surveys.** Ruined buildings don't just disappear—they have to be completely demolished, carted away and disposed of—and you might have to hire an engineer to oversee the whole process. Your standard policy won't cover these costs, which can be astonishing—for example, you may have to comply with costly disposal procedures if there is lead paint or asbestos in the debris. You can buy an endorsement for a reasonable sum that will protect you.

📖 Landlords with managers and other employees may need workers' compensation insurance. See Chapter 6 for a discussion of workers' compensation.

### 5. Saving Money on Insurance

Few landlords can really afford to adequately insure themselves against every possible risk. You need to decide what types of insurance are really essential and how much coverage to buy. Many factors affect this decision including the condition and location of the rental property. While choosing insurance is not always an easy task, here are some guidelines that should help.

### a. Set Priorities

Beyond any required coverage for your business, ask these questions: What insurance do I really need? What types of property losses would threaten the viability of my business? What kinds of liability lawsuits might wipe me out? Use your answers to tailor your coverage to protect against these potentially disastrous losses. Get enough property and liability coverage to protect yourself from common claims. Buy insurance against serious risks where the insurance is reasonably priced.

### b. Select High Deductibles

Deductibles (the amount of money you must pay out-of-pocket before insurance coverage kicks in) are used primarily for real and personal property insurance, including motor vehicle collision coverage. The difference between the cost of a policy with a $250 deductible and one with a $500 or $1,000 or even higher deductible is significant—particularly if you add up the premium savings for five or ten years. Consider using money saved with a higher deductible to buy other types of insurance where it's really needed. For example, the amount you save by having a higher deductible might pay for loss of rents coverage.

### c. Reduce the Likelihood of Insurance Claims Through Preventive Measures

Good safety and security measures, such as regular property inspections, may eliminate the need for some types of insurance or lead to lower insurance rates. In addition to following the steps we recommend in Section D, ask your insurance agent what you can do to get a better rate.

Although how to protect against some types of risks may be obvious to you, how to protect against many others won't be. Get help from people who are experienced in identifying and dealing with risks. One excellent resource is your insurance company's safety inspector; your insurance agent can tell you whom to contact. Another good approach is to ask your tenants to identify all safety risks, no matter how small.

### d. Comparison Shop

No two companies charge exactly the same rates; you may be able to save a significant amount by shopping around. But be wary of unusually low prices—it may be a sign of a shaky company. Or it may be that you're unfairly comparing policies that provide very different types of coverage. Make sure you know what you're buying, and review your coverage and rates periodically.

*How to Win Your Personal Injury Claim,* by Joseph L. Matthews (Nolo Press), explains personal injury cases and how to work out a fair settlement without going to court.

*Everybody's Guide to Small Claims Court,* by Ralph Warner (Nolo Press), provides detailed advice on small claims court, which in most states, allows lawsuits for about $3,000 to $7,500.

*Represent Yourself in Court,* by Paul Bergman and Sara Berman-Barrett (Nolo Press), will help you prepare and present your case should you end up in court.

*Mediate Your Dispute,* by Peter Lovenheim (Nolo Press), gives detailed information on the mediation process.

*How to Sue for Up to $25,000 ... and Win!* by Roderick Duncan (Nolo Press), is a step-by-step guide to suing (and defending against lawsuits) in municipal court in California. ■

Chapter **11**

# Landlord's Liability for Evironmental Health Hazards

I n 1863, an English judge could write that "Fraud apart, there is no law against letting [leasing] a tumble-down house." But in 20th century America, it's no longer legal to be a slumlord. Landlords must exercise a duty of due care towards tenants and guests alike. As discussed in Chapter 9, this duty requires you to maintain the structural integrity of the rental property. If needed repairs are not made and, as a result of defective conditions, a tenant is injured, you may be found liable. (See Chapter 10.)

Here we focus on an additional responsibility that has been imposed on landlords in the last few decades—the duty to divulge and remedy environmental health hazards, including some not caused by you. Or, put bluntly, landlords are increasingly likely to be held liable for tenant health problems resulting from exposure to environmental hazards in the rental premises. This liability is based on many of the same legal theories discussed in Chapter 10, such as negligence and negligence *per se* (negligence that is automatic when a statute is broken).

This chapter provides an overview of the legal and practical issues involving landlord liability for environmental health hazards, specifically asbestos, lead, radon and carbon monoxide.

Related topics covered in this book include:
- How to make legally required disclosures of environmental hazards to tenants: Chapter 2
- Maintaining habitable property by complying with state and local housing laws and avoiding safety and maintenance problems: Chapter 9
- Landlord's liability for tenant's injuries from defective housing conditions: Chapter 10.

# A. Asbestos

Exposure to asbestos has long and definitively been linked to an increased risk of cancer, particularly for workers in the asbestos manufacturing industry or in construction jobs involving the use of asbestos materials. More recently, the danger of asbestos in people's homes has also been acknowledged.

Homes built before the mid-1970s often contain asbestos insulation around heating systems, in ceilings and in other areas. Until 1981, asbestos was also widely used in many other building materials, such as vinyl flooring and tiles. Asbestos that has begun to break down and enter the air—for example, when it is disturbed during regular maintenance or renovation work—has the potential to become a significant health problem to tenants.

Until quite recently, however, private owners of residential rental property had no legal obligation to test for the presence of asbestos. A landlord whose tenant developed an asbestos-related disease could successfully defend himself if he could convince the judge or jury that he did not know of the presence of asbestos on his rental property.

Landlord's protection from liability for asbestos exposure all but evaporated in 1995, when the U.S. Occupational Safety and Health Administration (OSHA) issued a 200-page regulation setting strict workplace standards for the testing, maintenance and disclosure of asbestos.

## 1. Landlord Liability for Asbestos Exposure: OSHA Regulations

OSHA's regulations require property owners in general industry, construction work and shipyards to install warning labels, train staff and notify people who work in areas that might contain asbestos. In certain situations, owners must actually test for asbestos.

Rental property owners are considered to be part of "general industry" as understood by OSHA, and must adhere to the regulations for general industry in their role as *employers of maintenance personnel.* This includes large landlords who employ maintenance staff (or managers who do maintenance work) and small-scale landlords who have no employees, but who do hire outside contractors for repair and maintenance jobs.

OSHA regulations apply to any building constructed before 1981, and apply even if the property owner doesn't plan to remodel or otherwise disturb the structure. Unless the owner rules out the presence of asbestos by having a licensed inspector test the property, it will be *presumed* that asbestos is present and the regulations will apply.

## a.  Levels of OSHA's Protective Requirements

OSHA protections vary according to the level of asbestos disturbed by the activity being done. For example, workers who are involved in the removal of large amounts of asbestos receive maximum protection, whereas those who merely perform superficial custodial tasks need less.

- **Asbestos exposure in custodial work.** Employees and contractors whose work involves direct contact with asbestos or materials that are presumed to include it—for example, certain types of floors and ceilings—or who clean in areas near asbestos, are subject to OSHA regulations designed for "general

industry." The cleaning service that washes asbestos tiles in the lobby of a pre-1981 building, or the handyman who installs smoke alarms that are embedded in acoustic-tile ceilings made with asbestos, would both fall within the custodial work category. OSHA's general industry regulations require custodial workers to receive two hours of instruction (including appropriate cleaning techniques) and to use special work procedures under the supervision of a trained superior. The "general industry" standard does not require testing for asbestos. Of course, if it is known that high levels of asbestos are present, even custodial tasks must be performed with appropriately higher levels of protection, such as special masks and clothing.

- **Asbestos exposure in renovation or repair work.** A stricter set of procedures is triggered by any intentional disturbance of asbestos or asbestos-containing materials (for example, in heating systems or ceilings). This invariably happens when asbestos materials are subject to repair or renovation. At this level of activity, the landlord must test for the presence of asbestos. OSHA's "construction standard" requires exposure assessment (air monitoring for asbestos), sixteen hours of worker training per year, oversight by a specially-trained person and respiratory protection in some situations. In addition, employers must conduct medical surveillance of certain employees and maintain specified records for many years. So, for example, your decision to replace that ugly, stained acoustic-tile ceiling would require, first, that the material be tested for asbestos, followed by worker training and protection measures that are appropriate to the level of exposure.

## b.  How OSHA Regulations Affect Tenants

You may still be wondering what OSHA's workplace regulations for asbestos have to do with your obligations to your tenants, who are not, after all, your employees or hired contractors. The answer, simply put, is that once the pesky genie is out of the bottle, you cannot put him back in. When you comply with OSHA's testing and maintenance requirements for your employees or contractors, and your professional tester discovers that asbestos is either airborne (or is about to become so), you cannot pretend that you do not know that a potential health hazard is present with respect to your tenants as well. The presence of asbestos, regardless of how you found out about it, becomes simply an undisclosed, hidden and dangerous defect that you are obligated to disclose to tenants and remedy under everyday common law principles. (The landlord's duty to disclose dangerous defects is discussed in Chapter 10.)

If asbestos is present on your property and can be shown to be the cause of a tenant's illness, you may be found liable on legal theories other than failing to disclose a known hidden defect. For example, landlords in Louisiana may be held liable under the theory of strict liability. Some states may consider the presence of airborne asbestos to be a breach of the implied warranty of habitability, which (depending on the state) would give the tenant the right to break the lease and move out without notice, pay less rent, withhold the entire rent or sue to force the landlord to bring the dwelling up to a habitable level. (Chapter 10 discusses various legal theories of landlord liability for tenant injuries.)

**⚠ There is no escaping OSHA's asbestos regulations under the theory that what you don't know about can't cause legal problems.** You may think that you can escape the clutches of OSHA's asbestos regulations by personally doing minor repair and maintenance and hiring independent contractors to do the major jobs. This may work for a while until you hire a law-abiding contractor who acknowledges his independent duty to protect his employees and performs asbestos testing. The results of the tests will, of course, become known to you because you'll see the report and pay the bill.

---

### Key Aspects of OSHA Asbestos Regulations

Our discussion of the impact of the OSHA regulations on residential rental property owners is not intended to give you all the necessary information to make renovations and otherwise conduct your business safely and within the requirements of the regulations. You'll need to get a copy of the actual regulations for that. (See "Asbestos Resources," below.) Briefly, however, you should at least know:

**Buildings affected.** The regulations apply to pre-1981 structures, and if a newer structure is found to contain asbestos, the regulations apply to it as well.

**Where asbestos is likely to be found.** The regulations cover two classes of materials: those that definitely contain asbestos (such as certain kinds of flooring and ceilings) and those that the law *presumes* to contain asbestos. The second class is extremely inclusive, describing, among other things, any surfacing material that is "sprayed, troweled on or otherwise applied." Under this definition, virtually every dwelling built before 1980 must be suspected of containing asbestos.

**What work is covered.** The regulations apply to custodial work and to renovation and repair work. Mere custodial work does not typically require the stringent training and precautions that are triggered by renovation work.

---

## 2. How You Can Limit Liability for Asbestos

Limiting your liability for asbestos-related injuries (to tenants and workers alike) begins with your understanding a fundamental point: Unless you perform detailed testing to rule out the presence of asbestos, every pre-1981 structure must be treated as if it does contain asbestos. Acknowledging that you must follow the OSHA procedures for custodial and renovation/repair work should trigger the following actions:

- Get a copy of the OSHA regulations, which explain in detail what we have touched upon here. (See "Asbestos Resources," below.)

- Realize that almost any repair and maintenance work you do—no matter how small—may involve asbestos materials. Test for the presence of asbestos in advance for the benefit of workers and tenants.

- Make disclosures to tenants if you learn of the presence of asbestos (see Chapter 2). For example, if there is asbestos in the walls but it is not a health problem, point out that it is not likely to pose a danger, and that you will monitor the situation.

- Where possible, don't disturb asbestos. The conventional wisdom is that unless the asbestos material has begun to break down and enter the air, it is usually best to leave it alone and monitor it. This may mean that it simply may not make economic sense to do certain types of remodeling jobs. Seek an expert's opinion before taking action.

- If you must disturb asbestos—for example, when stripping floor tiles in the lobby—warn all tenants before the work is started, giving them an opportunity to avoid the area. Use written notices to alert tenants and place cones and caution tape around the area. You might even consider temporarily relocating your tenants. The costs of a few days or weeks in alternate housing will pale compared to the expense, monetary and human, of responding to a personal injury lawsuit by an exposed tenant.

- If you learn that asbestos material is airborne (or is about to be), thus posing a health hazard, seek an expert's advice on how to remedy the situation. When removal is necessary, hire trained asbestos removal specialists, and check to make sure the debris is legally disposed of in approved hazardous waste disposal sites.

- Make sure tenants don't make repairs to or otherwise invade any spaces containing asbestos, such as walls and ceilings. This might consist of prohibiting tenants from hanging planters from the ceiling or otherwise making holes in the ceiling. (See Clause 12 of the form lease and rental agreement in Chapter 2, which prohibits tenant repairs.)

- Require your tenants to report any deterioration to you—for example, in sprayed-on acoustical plaster ceilings. (Chapter 9 discusses tenant repair and maintenance responsibilities and systems for tenants to report defective conditions on the property.)

- Monitor the asbestos situation as part of regular safety and maintenance procedures, discussed in Chapter 9.

**Asbestos Resources.** For further information on asbestos rules, inspections and control, contact the nearest office of the U.S. Occupational Safety and Health Administration (OSHA) or see their website at www.osha.gov.

Be sure to check into OSHA interactive computer software, called "Asbestos Advisor," that will walk you through questions designed to help identify asbestos in your property and suggest the most sensible solution.

## B. Lead

As we all know, exposure to lead-based paint and lead water pipes may lead to serious health problems, particularly in children. Brain damage, attention disorders and hyperactivity have all been associated with lead poisoning. Landlords who are found responsible for lead poisoning (even if they did not know of the presence of the lead) may face liability for a child's lifelong disability. Jury awards and settlements for lead poisoning are typically enormous, because they cover remedial treatment and education of a child for the rest of his life, and include an award for the estimated "loss of earning" capacity caused by the injury. The cost of a typical "slip and fall" injury pales in comparison to some of the multimillion dollar jury awards and settlements for lead poisoning.

Buildings constructed before 1978 are likely to contain some source of lead, be it lead-based paint, lead pipes or lead-based solder used on copper pipes. (In 1978, the federal government required the reduction of lead in house paint; lead pipes are generally only found in homes built before 1930, and lead-based solder in home plumbing systems was banned in 1988.) Pre-1950 housing in poor and urban neighborhoods that has been allowed to age and deteriorate is by far the greatest source of lead-based paint poisonings.

**WARNING**

## 1. Landlord Liability for Lead Poisoning: Title X

Because of the health problems caused by lead-paint poisoning, the Residential Lead-Based Paint Hazard Reduction Act was enacted in 1992, and is commonly referred to as Title X [Ten]. The goal of Title X is "lead hazard reduction," which means evaluating the risk of poisoning in each housing situation and taking the appropriate steps to reduce the hazard. The Occupational Safety and Health Administration (OSHA) and the Environmental Protection Agency (EPA) have written regulations explaining the law. Compliance with Title X became the law for all landlords as of December 6, 1996.

### a. Disclosure

You must inform tenants, before they sign or renew a lease or rental agreement, of any information you possess on lead paint hazards on the property, including individual rental units, common areas and garages, tool sheds, other outbuildings, signs, fences and play areas. If you have had your property tested (testing must be done only by state-certified lead inspectors; see "Lead Hazard Resources," below), a copy of the report, or a summary written by the inspector, must be shown to tenants.

With certain exceptions (listed below), every lease and rental agreement must include a disclosure page, even if you have not tested. You can use the one developed by the EPA, or you can design your own as long as it meets the EPA requirements (these are specified in the Code of Federal Regulations cited in "Further Reading," below.)

What about tenants who were your tenants before December 6, 1996—must you fill-out a disclosure form for them, too? Your compliance obligations depend on whether that tenant has a lease or is renting month to month.

- **Tenants with leases.** You need not comply until the lease ends and the tenant renews or stays on as a month-to-month tenant.
- **Month-to-month tenants.** You should have given month-to-month tenants a disclosure statement when you collected your first rent check dated on or after December 6, 1996.

The Legal Forms Disk includes the Disclosure of Information on Lead-Based Paint or Lead-Based Paint Hazards form and Appendix II includes a blank tear-out copy of the form (in Spanish and English).

## b.  Information

You must give all tenants the lead hazard information booklet "Protect Your Family From Lead In Your Home," written by the Environmental Protection Agency (EPA). (See "Lead Hazard Resources.") Appendix II includes a tear-out copy of the pamphlet (both in English and Spanish) which you may reproduce and attach to the lease. The graphics in the original pamphlet must be included.

State agencies may develop their own pamphlets that you can use, but they may not be used in place of the EPA version unless the EPA has approved them. California's pamphlet, Environmental Hazards: A Guide for Homeowners, Buyers, Landlords and Tenants has been approved.

## Lead Inspections

While inspections are not required by federal law, you may voluntarily arrange an inspection in order to certify that the property is lead-free and exempt from federal regulations. (See list of exemptions, below.) Also, if you take out a loan or buy insurance, your bank or insurance company may require a lead inspection.

Professional lead inspectors don't always inspect every unit in large, multifamily properties. Instead, they inspect a sampling of the units and apply their conclusions to the property as a whole. Giving your tenants the results and conclusions of a building-wide evaluation satisfies the law, even if a particular unit was not tested. If, however, you have specific information regarding a unit that is inconsistent with the building-wide evaluation, you must disclose it to the tenant.

## How Lead Poisoning Occurs

When the dangers of lead-based paint were first discovered, the ingestion of lead-based paint chips was considered the most common means of poisoning. While this source (or "vector") for lead poisoning certainly exists, it is now widely acknowledged that airborne lead-laden dust caused by the deterioration of exposed lead-based paint is the greater culprit. Falling on window sills, walls and floors, this dust makes its way into the human body when it is stirred up, becomes airborne and is inhaled, or when it is transmitted directly from hand to mouth. Exterior lead-based house paint is also a potential problem in that it can slough off walls directly into the soil and be tracked into the house.

An equally powerful source of lead-paint contamination is the dust that results from renovations or remodeling, including *unfortunately* those very projects undertaken to rid the premises of the lead-based paint.

Lead-based paint isn't the only culprit. For decades, American cars ran on leaded gas, spewing leaded exhaust into the air. Lead particles came to rest on the ground adjacent to roadways; ample evidence shows that the closer a piece of property is to heavily-traveled roads, the greater the presence of lead. Lead poisoning can also occur by drinking water that contains leached-out lead from lead pipes or from broken-down lead solder used in copper pipes.

Children between the ages of 18 months and five years are the most likely to become lead-based paint victims. Their poisoning is detected when they become ill or, increasingly, in routine examinations that check for elevated blood levels of lead.

## c.  Enforcement and Penalties

HUD and the EPA plan to enforce renters' rights to know about the presence of lead-based paint. They'll use "testers," like they do when looking for illegal discrimination (see Chapter 5). Posing as applicants, testers who get the rental will document whether landlords disclosed lead paint information when the lease or rental agreement was signed.

Landlords who fail to distribute the required information booklet, or who do not give tenants the disclosure statement, may receive one or more of the following penalties:

- a notice of noncompliance, the mildest form of reprimand
- a civil penalty, which can include fines of up to $11,000 per violation for willful and continuing noncompliance
- an order to pay an injured tenant up to three times his actual damages, or
- a criminal fine of up to $11,000 per violation.

Government testers will also be on the lookout for property owners who falsely claim that they have no knowledge of lead-based paint hazards on their property. Here's how it will likely come up: A tenant may complain to HUD if he becomes ill with lead poisoning after you told him that you knew of no lead-based paint hazards on your premises. If HUD decides to investigate whether, in fact, you knew about the hazard and failed to tell tenants, their investigators will get access to your records. They'll comb leasing, maintenance and repair files—virtually your entire business records. If HUD finds evidence that you knew (or had reason to know) of lead paint hazards, such as a contract from a painting firm that includes costs for lead paint removal or a loan document indicating the presence of lead paint, you will be hard pressed to explain why you've checked the box on the disclosure form stating that you have no reports or records regarding the presence of lead-based paint on your property.

Cities with high concentrations of homes with potential lead hazards will be initially targeted by HUD and the EPA. They include Baltimore, Boston, Buffalo, Chicago, Cleveland, Columbus (OH), Detroit, Houston, Indianapolis, Jersey City, Los Angeles, Minneapolis/St. Paul, New Orleans, New York City, Oakland (CA), Philadelphia, Pittsburgh, Providence, Richmond (VA), Rochester (NY), St. Louis, San Francisco, Savannah (GA), Washington DC and Youngstown (OH).

## Rental Properties Exempt From Federal Regulations

These rental properties are exempt from the federal regulations. State law may still apply:

- Housing for which a construction permit was obtained, or on which construction was started, after January 1, 1978. Older buildings that have been completely renovated since 1978 are *not* exempt, even if every painted surface was removed or replaced.
- Housing certified as lead-free by a state-accredited lead inspector. Lead-free means the absence of any lead paint, even paint that has been completely painted over and encapsulated.
- Lofts, efficiencies, studios and other "zero-bedroom" units, including dormitory housing and rentals in sorority and fraternity houses. University-owned apartments and married student housing are not exempted.
- Short-term vacation rentals of 100 days or less
- A single room rented in a residential home
- Housing designed for persons with disabilities (as explained in HUD's Fair Housing Accessibility Guidelines, 56 Code of Federal Regulations 9472, 3/6/91), *unless* any child less than six years old resides there or is expected to reside there
- Retirement communities (housing designed for seniors, where one or more tenant is at least 62 years old) *unless* children under the age of six are present or expected to live there.

The Residential Lead-Based Paint Hazard Reduction Act was enacted in 1992 to reduce the danger from lead paint. It is commonly referred to as Title X [Ten] (42 U.S. Code § 4852d). The Environmental Protection Agency (EPA) has written regulations that explain how landlords should implement lead hazard reduction (24 Code of Federal Regulations Part 35 and 40 Code of Federal Regulations Part 745). For more information, see "Lead Hazard Resources," below.

## 2. State Laws on Lead Affecting Landlords

Many states have also addressed the lead issue by prohibiting the use of lead-based paint in residences and requiring the careful maintenance of existing lead paint and lead-based building materials. Some states require property owners to disclose lead hazards to prospective tenants. If you are subject to a state statute, you must comply with it as well as the federal law.

### States with Lead Hazard Reduction Laws

| | | |
|---|---|---|
| Alabama | Kentucky | North Carolina |
| Arkansas | Louisiana | Ohio |
| California | Maine | Oklahoma |
| Colorado | Maryland | Oregon |
| Connecticut | Massachusetts | Rhode Island |
| Delaware | Michigan | South Carolina |
| District of | Minnesota | Tennessee |
| Columbia | Mississippi | Texas |
| Georgia | Missouri | Vermont |
| Hawaii | Nebraska | Virginia |
| Illinois | New Hampshire | West Virginia |
| Indiana | New Jersey | Wisconsin |
| Iowa | New York | |

For complete details on each state's law, see "State Lead Hazard Reduction Laws" in Appendix I.

If your state has its own lead hazard reduction law, you'll see that, like its federal cousin, it does not directly require you to test for lead. Does this mean that you need not conduct inspections? In at least one city, the answer is "No": In New York City, an appellate court has ruled that a local ordinance that requires a landlord to remove lead paint in excess of a certain level also means that every landlord in New York City has a duty to inspect for lead paint (*Juarez v. Wavecrest Management Team Ltd.*, 88 N.Y.2d 628 (1996)). The court found that the local requirement to remove lead paint makes sense only if there is an implied duty to inspect and detect the presence of lead paint. Courts in other cities or states could reach the same conclusion.

Also, many states are considering passage of legislation that would require testing of pre-1978 residential structures. The legislation most often considered is the Model Lead Exposure Reduction Act, also known as the "Model Act." The Act has been drafted by experts in the industry and is designed to be an all-purpose lead law that can be adopted in part or in full by any state. In addition to requiring testing, the Model Act would require landlords to remedy lead problems and disclose lead hazards to potential tenants and buyers.

### Leaded Mini-Blinds

Some imported mini-blinds from China, Taiwan, Indonesia and Mexico are likely to contain lead, but are not banned by the Consumer Product Safety Commission. If your property has leaded mini-blinds, you do not have to disclose this fact unless you know that the blinds have begun to deteriorate and produce lead dust. To avoid problems, use mini-blinds from other sources or different kinds of window coverings.

### 3. Why You Should Test for Lead

If you suspect that there might be lead lurking in your rental property's paint or water, you face a difficult choice:

- If you have the property tested and learn that lead is present, you'll know that your property has a hidden and dangerous defect. As a result, you must tell tenants and deal with the expensive lead problem or risk liability for injuries.

- On the other hand, if you don't test for lead you'll live with the nagging suspicion that your property might be making your tenants sick and damaging the development of their children.

It may be tempting to adopt the second, ostrich-like approach, and hope that all will work out OK. The odds may be with you for a while, but eventually this will prove to be a short-sighted solution. Here are seven reasons why:

1. Lead hazard control (see Section 4, below) is much less burdensome than going through a lawsuit, let alone living with the knowledge that a child's health has been damaged.

2. Even though the federal regulations do not require testing, ignorance of the condition of your property may not shield you from liability. At some point, some court is bound to rule that the danger of lead paint in older housing is so well-known that owners of older housing will be presumed to know of the danger. Should this "imputed knowledge" of the hazard ever be attributed to you, a jury will have a difficult time believing that you were truly ignorant. Moreover, an injured tenant may be able to show the court that it was likely that you were, in fact, apprised of the lead problem—through your attendance at seminars for landlords, subscriptions to periodicals aimed at property owners and even reading this book!

3. State law may make the question of knowledge a done deal. Under the Model Act now under consideration in many states, pre-1978 houses are presumed to contain lead paint. If your state adopts the Model Act or similar legislation, the issue of knowledge will be resolved against you, the property owner: If it can be shown that, in fact, your property does contain lead paint, you will be presumed to have known this fact, period. This puts the landlord in the position of failing to disclose a hidden defect—a garden-variety basis for recovery by an injured tenant.

4. Recognizing that children are the ones most at risk for lead poisoning, you cannot simply refuse to rent to tenants with children—this is illegal discrimination in all states. (See Chapter 5.)

5. You cannot count on a clause in your lease or rental agreement attempting to shift responsibility for lead-based injuries from you to the tenant to protect you. This type of clause (called an "exculpatory clause," in legalese) is viewed with disfavor by many states, especially when the intent is to avoid a policy of strong public concern. (See Chapter 10 for a discussion of exculpatory clauses.) Ironically, if you make liability for lead poisoning a subject of an exculpatory clause, and the clause is not upheld in court, you will have effectively established that you were aware of the lead problem. (Why else would you have written such a clause?)

6. If you attempt to refinance or sell your rental property, you will find that most major lenders will require lead testing before a loan is approved.

7. You can expect that your own insurance company may soon require lead testing as a condition of issuing a policy. Lead poisoning cases are incredibly expensive—for example, in two New York cases recently, injured tenants were awarded seven and ten million dollars. It is only a matter of time before the insurance industry nationwide realizes that it cannot continue to blindly insure all properties against lead poisoning. (Consider the reaction of the insurance industry to earthquakes and

wildfires in California, where coverage for these disasters is now often difficult to procure.)

In sum, as with many landlord problems discussed in this book, there is no effective way to hide a serious lead problem over the long run. Your best bet is to tackle it directly on your own terms, before you are forced to do so. The next section explains how to go about getting information on testing and reducing one of the most serious lead hazard risks—lead-based paint.

**⚠️ Your insurance company may not cover you if a tenant is injured by lead that you knew about and failed to deal with.** Insurance policies uniformly deny coverage for losses that you knew (or should have known) were likely. If you understand the effect of lead on the human body, once you know about the presence of lead on your property, you can reasonably expect poisonings. Facing a lawsuit without insurance will probably end your business.

**📖 Lead Hazard Resources.** Information on the evaluation and control of lead dust, and copies of the "Protect Your Family From Lead in Your Home" pamphlet, may be obtained from the regional offices of the federal EPA or by calling the National Lead Information Center at 800-424-LEAD. Information is also available from the EPA on its Web site: www.epa.gov or the National Lead Information Center Site: www.epa.gov/lead/nlic.htm. In addition, OSHA has developed interactive software, called "Asbestos Advisor." The program will ask you for the details of your renovation project and, based on your answers, make suggestions as to legal and safe renovation procedures. The software can be downloaded from OSHA'S Web site at www.osha.gov.

HUD issues a pamphlet entitled "Guidance on the Lead-Based Paint Disclosure Rule, Parts I and II," which may be obtained by contacting your nearest HUD office. (Chapter 5 includes a list of HUD regional offices.) You can also get this infor-

mation online from the HUD Lead Office website at www.hud.gov/lea/leahome.html.

HUD also maintains a "Lead Listing" of names, addresses and phone numbers of trained lead paint contractors (for testing and abatement) in every state. Call 202-755-1785 or access the list on the Web at www.leadlisting.org.

State housing departments will have information on state laws and regulations. Start by calling your state consumer protection agency. (See the list in Appendix I.)

## 4. How to Clean Up Lead-Based Paint

Lead is relatively easy to detect—you can buy home use kits that contain a simple swab, which turns color when drawn over a lead-based surface. Knowing how much lead is present, and how to best clean it up, however, are subjects for the experts. It is beyond the scope of this book to present detailed remediation or clean-up instructions, if only because each situation will require a specific response. We can, however, give you an overview of the current thinking on the issue.

The most important thing to understand when faced with a lead paint problem is that sometimes the wholesale removal of the paint, or even sanding and repainting, may not be the best solution. This is because these types of renovations often create and release tremendous amounts of lead dust, the deadliest vector for poisoning. Unless the job is done by trained personnel, the well-intentioned removal of lead paint may actually create a far bigger problem than originally existed. Several states now have training and licensing requirements for lead abatement professionals (see State Lead Hazard Reduction Laws in Appendix I).

Drastic measures may be needed when the underlying structure itself is so deteriorated that safety requires a from-the-bottom-up approach, but this is rarely the case. The most effective response to lead-based paint is usually a program consisting of these steps:

1. **Inspect for deteriorated paint.** Pay close attention to areas that get the most use (floors and window channels), and determine whether lead is present. An environmental engineer will be able to tell you how much lead is present at floor level and above, which will alert you as to whether your property exceeds the amounts allowable by law.

2. **Clean up lead-contaminated dust with a good vacuum cleaner and detergent that is specifically designed to pick up lead.** Regular household cleaners, even TSP, do not do a very effective job of capturing lead, nor will a standard vacuum cleaner be able to filter out the microscopic lead particles. Consider using a phosphate-based cleaner ("Leadisolve" is one such product) and buying or renting a "HEPA" vacuum (a "high efficiency particle arresting" vacuum, often available for rent from hardware stores or equipment rental agencies). If you are dealing with lead dust, wear a mask and disposable protective clothing.

3. **Repaint with non-lead-based paint to provide a strong, cleanable surface.**

4. **Educate your tenants on how to identify, control and clean up any lead dust that might still be present.** The EPA's lead hazard information booklet you are required to give to each resident under Title X will help you in this respect.

5. **Monitor lead dust situations.** Design your periodic safety inspections (discussed in Chapter 9) so that you keep on top of any deterioration of lead-based surfaces.

6. **Do as much as possible, within the recommendations of your experts, to prevent the accumulation of lead dust.** Theoretically, some lead dust problems might be containable by frequent, lead-specific and thorough cleaning, rather than repainting. There are some professional cleaning companies that specialize in lead dust cleaning. It is risky, however, to entrust that specialized housecleaning job to your tenants, even if you are prepared to give them the appropriate vacuum cleaners and detergents. You cannot, from a practical point of view, adequately monitor their housekeeping practices. Instead, prevent the accumulation of lead dust by painting over lead paint, if possible, even if this solution appears more costly than dust maintenance. It will certainly cost less than a lawsuit.

## C. Radon

Radon is a naturally occurring radioactive gas that is associated with lung cancer. It can enter and contaminate a house built on soil and rock containing uranium deposits or enter through water from private wells drilled in uranium-rich soil. Radon becomes a lethal health threat when it is trapped in tightly-sealed homes that have been insulated to keep in heat or have poor ventilation, when it escapes from building materials that have incorporated uranium-filled rocks and soils (like certain types of composite tiles or bricks) or is released into the air from aerated household water that has passed through underground concentrations of uranium. Problems occur most frequently in areas where rocky soil is relatively rich in uranium and in climates where occupants keep their windows tightly shut—to maintain heat in the winter and air conditioning in the summer.

The U.S. Environmental Protection Agency estimates that about six million American homes have unacceptably high levels of radon. Fortunately, there are usually simple, inexpensive ways to measure radon levels in buildings. Ventilation measures will effectively disperse the gas in most situations. These measures range from the obvious (open the windows and provide cross-ventilation) to the somewhat complex (sealing cracks in the foundation, or sucking radon out of the soil before it enters the foundation and venting it into the air above the door through a pipe). According to the EPA, a typical household radon problem can be solved for $500 to $2,500.

## State Laws on Radon

New Jersey and Florida have been at the forefront in addressing the radon problem. New Jersey has an extensive program that includes an information and outreach program. (N.J. Rev. Stat. §§ 26:2d-61, 26:2d-70 and 26:2d-71f.) Florida taxes new construction to raise funds for the development of a radon-resistant construction code, and it requires landlords to warn tenants about the known presence of radon. (Fla. Stat. § 404.056.)

Do you have to inspect for radon contamination? There are currently no laws that require a private landlord to detect and remedy the presence of radon. This does not necessarily mean, however, that under certain circumstances you would not be found liable for radon poisoning. For example, a trial court in New York has held a landlord strictly liable for radon poisoning—meaning that he was held responsible for the injury regardless of whether he tested or not. (*Kaplan v. Coulston*, 381 N.Y.S.2d 634 (1976).) (See Chapter 10 for a fuller explanation of the theory of strict liability.)

Whether to test for radon depends on the circumstances of each rental property. Your city planning department or your insurance broker may know about local geology and radon dangers. Certainly, owners of rental property in areas where radon levels are generally known to be dangerously high should test rental property. For the most professional results, hire an inspector certified by the EPA. Testing takes at least three days, and sometimes months. Do-it-yourself testing kits are also available. If you use one of these, make sure it says "Meets EPA Requirements."

If testing indicates high radon levels, be sure to warn tenants and correct the problem. If you own rental property in an area known to have radon problems, but don't test, warn tenants or take action, you may be sued on any number of legal theories, including negligence and a violation of the implied warranty of habitability.

**Radon Resources.** For information on the detection and removal of radon, contact the U.S. Environmental Protection Agency Radon Hotline at 800-767-7236. You can ask for a copy of the booklet, "Consumer's Guide to Radon Reduction," which includes a list of every state's agency or department in charge of radon reduction.

# D. Carbon Monoxide

Carbon monoxide (CO) is a colorless, odorless, lethal gas. Unlike radon, whose deadly effects work over time, CO can build up and kill within a matter of hours. And, unlike any of the environmental hazards discussed so far, CO cannot be covered up or managed.

When CO is inhaled, it enters the bloodstream and replaces oxygen. Dizziness, nausea, confusion and tiredness can result; high concentrations bring on unconsciousness, brain damage and death. It is possible for someone to be poisoned from CO while sleeping, without waking up. Needless to say, a CO problem must be dealt with immediately.

## 1. Sources of Carbon Monoxide

Carbon monoxide is a by-product of fuel combustion; electric appliances cannot produce it. Common home appliances, such as gas dryers, refrigerators, ranges, water heaters or space heaters; oil furnaces, fireplaces, charcoal grills and wood stoves all produce CO. Automobiles and gas gardening equipment also produce CO. If appliances or fireplaces are not vented properly, CO can build up within a home and poison the occupants. In tight, "energy-efficient" apartments, indoor accumulations are especially dangerous.

## 2. Preventing Carbon Monoxide Problems

If you have a regular maintenance program, you should be able to spot and fix the common malfunctions that cause CO buildup. But even the most careful service program cannot rule out unexpected problems like the blocking of a chimney by a bird's nest or the sudden failure of a machine part.

Fortunately, relatively inexpensive devices, similar to smoke detectors, can monitor CO levels and sound an alarm if they get too high. If you install one, make sure it is UL certified.

### Avoiding Carbon Monoxide Problems

- Check chimneys and appliance vents for blockages.
- In your rules and regulations, prohibit the indoor use of portable gas grills or charcoal grills.
- Warn tenants never to use a gas range, clothes dryer or oven for heating.
- Prohibit nonelectric space heaters, or specify that they must be inspected annually. Tenants can get recommendations from fuel suppliers.
- Check the pilot lights of gas appliances as part of your regular maintenance routine. They should show a clear blue flame; a yellow or orange flame may indicate a problem.

Unlike smoke detectors, which are required by many local ordinances, CO detectors are not legally required. But that doesn't mean that you wouldn't be wise to install one. Detectors that are connected to the interior wiring of the house and backed-up with emergency batteries are best.

## 3. Responsibility for Carbon Monoxide

Most CO hazards are caused by a malfunctioning appliance or a clogged vent, flue or chimney. It follows that the responsibility for preventing a CO buildup depends on who is responsible for the upkeep of the appliance.

**Appliances.** Appliances that are part of the rental, especially built-in units, are typically your responsibility, although the tenant is responsible for intentional or unreasonably careless damage. For example, if the pilot light on the gas stove that came with the rental is improperly calibrated and emits high amounts of CO, you must fix it. On the other hand, if your tenant brings in a portable oil space heater that malfunctions, that is his responsibility.

**Vents.** Vents, chimneys and flues are part of the structure, and their maintenance is typically your job. In single-family houses, however, it is not unusual for landlords and tenants to agree to shift maintenance responsibility to the tenant. As always, write down any maintenance jobs that you have delegated—if an accident occurs, you'll be able to prove that responsibility had been shifted to and accepted by the tenant. (Chapter 9 discusses the pros and cons of delegating repairs to tenants.)

**Carbon Monoxide Resources.** Local natural gas utility companies often have consumer information brochures available to their customers. You can also contact the American Gas Association for consumer pamphlets on carbon monoxide. It can be reached at 1615 Wilson Boulevard, Arlington, VA 22209, 703-841-8667.

## Electromagnetic Fields

Electromagnetic fields (EMFs) are the newest and the most controversial of the household "environmental hazards" that concern landlords.

Power lines, electrical wiring and appliances emit low-level electric and magnetic fields. The intensity of both fields are thousands of times lower than the natural fields generated by the electrical activity of the human heart, brain and muscles. The further away you are from the source of these fields, the weaker their force.

The controversy surrounding EMFs concerns whether or not exposure to them increases a person's chances of getting certain cancers—specifically, childhood leukemia. The National Academy of Sciences undertook a three-year review of hundreds of scientific papers and concluded, in November 1996, that exposure to these fields does not present a human health hazard. Then, in October 1998, another government-sponsored group of scientists looked at the same data and concluded that exposure to EMGs should be considered "possibly carcinogenic to humans."

On balance, however, there is very little solid scientific support for the fear that EMFs cause cancer. Your tenants probably have nothing to worry about if your rental property sits under or near a set of power lines. Besides, since you cannot insist that the power companies move their transmitters or block the emissions, you are not responsible for EMFs. But these realities won't stop some tenants from complaining. Does a worried tenant have any legal recourse against you?

Practically speaking, a tenant's only option is to move. If the tenant has a month-to-month rental agreement or the lease is up, she can easily move on without legal repercussions. But what about a tenant who decides mid-lease that the EMFs are intolerable? Legally, she would be justified in breaking a lease or rental agreement only if the property presents a significant threat to her health or safety. (Breaking a lease when the property is unfit is explained at length in Chapter 9.) Given the professional debate regarding the danger from EMFs, it is unclear whether that a court would decide that their presence makes your property unlivable.

**Electromagnetic Fields Resources.** The National Institute of Environmental Health Sciences and the U.S. Department of Energy publish an excellent booklet entitled "Questions and Answers About EMF (1995)." For a free copy, contact the U.S. Government Printing Office, Washington DC, 20402, 202-512-1800.

Chapter **12**

# Landlord's Liability for Criminal Acts and Activities

With crime—especially urban crime—on the increase in recent years, the public has clamored for more and better police protection and longer prison terms for those convicted of crimes. At the same time, it's become clear that the criminal justice system—the police, courts and prisons—primarily deals with crime after it takes place, and that fundamental crime prevention depends on an active, concerned citizenry.

But crime prevention isn't something that people only worry about in personal terms. Crime has also become a big issue for many rental property owners —and with good reason, since landlords in most states now have at least some degree of legal responsibility to provide secure housing. This means you must take reasonable steps to:

- protect tenants from would-be assailants, thieves and other criminals
- protect tenants from the criminal acts of fellow tenants
- warn tenants about dangerous situations they are aware of but cannot eliminate, and
- protect the neighborhood from tenants' illegal and noxious activities, such as drug dealing.

If you don't live up to these responsibilities, you may be liable for any injuries or losses that occur as a result.

This chapter discusses your legal duties under building codes, ordinances, statutes and, most frequently, court decisions, to protect your tenants *and* the larger neighborhood. It is our goal to provide practical advice on how to protect your tenants and the neighborhood from crime, limit your liability and avoid trouble before it finds you.

We can't overstate the importance of reading this chapter carefully. Landlords are sued more than any other group of business owners in the country, and the legal subspecialty of "premises liability" for criminal acts (suing landlords for injuries suffered by tenants at the hands of third-party criminals) is one of the fastest growing areas of law. Why are lawyers so eager to try to pin responsibility for the acts of criminals on landlords? The not-so-surprising answer is money: Horrific crimes such as rape and assault result in tremendous monetary awards and settlements, of which the plaintiffs' attorneys take a sizable chunk. The average settlement paid by the landlord's insurance company is $600,000, and the average jury award (when cases do go to trial) is $1.2 million. Only liability for lead poisoning (discussed in Chapter 11) rivals premises liability for astronomical settlement and jury award costs.

In short, if this book motivates you to do only two things, it should be to assess and address the security situation on your rental property and make sure your insurance policy provides maximum protection against the acts of criminals.

Related topics covered in this book include:

- How to choose the best tenants and avoid legal problems: Chapter 1
- Lease and rental agreement provisions prohibiting tenants' illegal activities and disturbances: Chapter 2
- How to avoid renting to convicted criminals without violating privacy and antidiscrimination laws: Chapter 5
- How to minimize danger to tenants from a manager by carefully checking applicants' backgrounds and references: Chapter 6
- Highlighting security procedures in a move-in letter to new tenants: Chapter 7
- Landlords' and tenants' responsibilities for repair and maintenance under state and local housing laws: Chapter 9
- Landlord's liability for a tenant's injuries from defective housing conditions: Chapter 10
- Landlord's right of entry and tenant's privacy: Chapter 13
- Evicting a tenant for drug dealing and other illegal activity: Chapter 17
- How to choose a lawyer and do legal research: Chapter 18.

---

### Troubled Property: Is It Time to Cut Your Losses?

Owners of property in high-crime areas may find it impossible to raise rents to cover the costs of providing secure housing and purchasing comprehensive insurance. Landlords often have a choice—operate a potentially dangerous building or sell out cheap. Although landlords seldom want to face it, the truth is that you may be better off selling troubled property at a loss than courting an excessive risk that you will be sued for criminal acts beyond your control. If you do continue to own high-crime property, consider ways to legally separate it from your other assets —for example, by establishing a separate corporation or limited liability company.

## A. Your Responsibility to Keep Tenants Safe

In virtually every state, landlords are expected to take reasonable precautions to protect tenants from foreseeable harm. No one expects you to build a moat around your rental property and provide round-the-clock armed security. But it's also true that, increasingly, you cannot simply turn over your keys and trust to the local constable and fate to assure your tenants' safety.

### 1. Basic Security Duties Imposed by State and Local Laws

In many areas of the country, local building and housing codes are rich with specific rules designed to protect tenants. For example, some city ordinances require peepholes, deadbolt locks and specific types of lighting on the rental property.

Only a few states have specific laws as to landlords' responsibilities to provide secure premises. For example:

- Under Florida law, landlords must provide locks and keep common areas in a "safe condition." A Florida tenant who was assaulted by someone who entered because of a broken back door lock was allowed to argue to a jury that the landlord was partially responsible. (*Paterson v. Deeb,* 472 So. 2d 1210 (Fla. Dist. Ct. 1985).)
- Texas has the most stringent law in the country. All Texas rental units must be equipped with keyless bolts and peepholes on all exterior doors and pin locks on sliding glass doors, as well as a handle latch or security bar. If a landlord doesn't supply this equipment, the tenant may do so and deduct the cost from the rent, or legally break the lease and move out. (Tex. Prop. Code §§ 92.151-170.)

On the other hand, many state and local laws offer little specific guidance. For example, they may require "clean and safe" or "secure" housing, without defining these terms. Courts in several states have ruled that these requirements apply only to the condition of the physical structure. In other words, "safe" stairways are those that will not collapse or otherwise cause injury, not those that are well-lit, protected and unlikely to be the site of a criminal incident.

But as the following examples show, some courts have taken a broader view of the term "safe."

EXAMPLE 1: The housing code in the city where Andrew owned rental property set minimum standards for apartment houses, including a requirement that all areas of rental property be kept clean and safe. The garage in Andrew's apartment house was poorly lit and accessible from the street because the automatic door worked excruciatingly slowly. Andrew added a few lights, but the garage was still far from bright. Andrew would be wise to spend the money to do the lighting job right and fix the garage door, since courts in Andrew's state had consistently held that conditions like these constituted a violation of the "clean and safe" requirement of the local housing code. If a tenant was assaulted by someone who gained entry through the substandard garage door, Andrew would likely be sued and found partially liable for the tenant's injuries.

EXAMPLE 2: Martin lived in a state that required rental housing to be maintained in a fit and habitable condition. Courts in his state had interpreted "fit and habitable" to mean, among other things, that dwellings should be reasonably secure from unwanted intrusions by people other than tenants or their guests. One evening Martin was assaulted in the elevator by someone who got into the building through the unlocked front door. Martin sued his landlord, Jim, and was able to show that the front door lock had been broken for a long time and that Jim had failed to fix it. The jury decided that Jim's failure to provide a secure front door

violated the implied warranty of habitability (discussed in Chapter 9), that he was aware of the problem and had plenty of time to fix it, and that the unsecured front door played a significant role in the assault. The jury awarded Martin several thousand dollars for his injuries, lost wages and pain and suffering.

How the courts in your state will interpret the tenant safety laws that apply to your rental property is difficult to predict, since courts inevitably have some discretion in their rulings and each situation presents unique facts. Some courts will interpret tenant safety laws more strictly than others. To be on the safe side, we recommend that you find and comply with all security laws that apply to you. For more information on the presence (or absence) of mandatory security regulations, contact your state or local housing agency (see Chapter 9) or rental property owners' association. In fact, carry your responsibilities out as generously as possible. A careful approach will protect your tenants *and* you, by helping to avoid a situation where you end up in court trying to explain why you cut corners when it came to taking steps to prevent crime.

---

### Violation of a Safety Statute May Be Negligence Per Se

If you violate a law designed to protect tenants' safety—like a local ordinance requiring the installation of deadbolts—the violation may constitute *negligence per se.* As we explain in Chapter 10, this is devastating for the landlord who is sued when a crime occurs: Unlike the landlord who is sued under a general negligence theory, the landlord who is sued under a *negligence per se* theory cannot argue that it was unreasonable to expect him to provide the security measure in question. (Section A2 of this chapter discusses negligence in general and its relation to crime on the premises.)

If you do not comply with specific equipment requirements, your tenants can complain to the agency in charge of enforcing the codes, often a local building or housing authority. If a tenant is injured as a result of your violation of a safety law—for example, an intruder enters the apartment building because of a lock that's been broken for weeks—you may be liable for tenant injuries. Your liability in this situation is explained in Chapter 10.

---

### The Implied Warranty of Habitability

State and local statutes and their interpretation by the courts are not the only source of security requirements for landlords. Many states recognize the implied warranty of habitability, a legal standard that requires landlords to offer and maintain housing that is "fit and habitable." (See Chapter 9 for a discussion of the implied warranty.) If you breach the implied warranty of habitability and the defect contributes substantially to the ability of an assailant to commit a crime against a tenant, you may be held liable for the resulting injuries.

---

## 2. Your General Responsibility of Due Care

In addition to complying with local and state laws that require basic security measures, you have a general duty to act reasonably under the circumstances—or, expressed in legal jargon, to "act with due care." If you don't take reasonable steps to maintain your premises, be it repairing an unsafe handrail or replacing a faulty thermostat, you will be considered negligent and may be liable for tenant injuries if they result from your carelessness. When it comes to security, too, courts in most states have ruled that landlords must take reasonable precautions to protect tenants from foreseeable criminal assaults and property crimes.

What precautions are reasonable depends on the situation. What does remain constant, however, are the six key questions discussed in Chapter 10 that explain how an insurance adjuster or court evaluates your negligence and assesses responsibility when a tenant suffers accidental injury.

**1. Did you control the area where the crime occurred?** You aren't expected to police the entire world. For example, a lobby, hallway or other common area is an area of high landlord control, which heightens your responsibility. However, you exert much less control over the sidewalk outside the front door, so it may be more difficult to minimize the chances of a crime occurring there.

**2. How likely was it that a crime would occur?** You are duty-bound to respond to the foreseeable, not the improbable. Have there been prior criminal incidents at a particular spot in the building? Elsewhere in the neighborhood? If you know that an offense is likely (because of a rash of break-ins or prior crime on the property), you have a heightened legal responsibility in most states to take reasonable steps to guard against future crime.

**3. How difficult or expensive would it have been to reduce the risk of crime?** If relatively cheap or simple measures could significantly lower the risk of crime, it is likely that a court would find that you had a duty to undertake them if their absence facilitated a crime, especially in an area where criminal activity is high. For instance, would reasonably inexpensive new locks and better lighting discourage thieves? How about better management practices, such as strict key control, locked tenant files, scrupulous employee screening and trained, alert on-site personnel? However, if the only solution to the problem is costly, such as structural remodeling or hiring a full-time doorman, it is doubtful that a court would expect it of you.

**4. How serious an injury was likely to result from the crime?** The consequences of a criminal incident (break-in, robbery, rape or murder) may be horrific.

Let's look at how these first four questions might be answered in three crime situations.

**EXAMPLE 1:** Sam was accosted outside the entryway to his duplex by a stranger who was lurking in the tall, overgrown bushes in the front yard next to the sidewalk. There had been many previous assaults in the area. Both the bushes and the lack of exterior floodlights near the entryway prevented Sam from seeing his assailant until it was too late. If Sam filed a claim with the landlord's liability insurance company, or sued the landlord, an adjuster or judge would probably conclude that the landlord was bound to take measures to protect Sam's safety, because:

1. The landlord controlled the common areas outside the duplex.
2. It was foreseeable that an assailant would lurk in the bushes and that another assault would occur.
3. The burden of trimming the shrubbery and installing lights was small in comparison to the risk of injury.
4. There are usually serious consequences from a criminal assault.

**EXAMPLE 2:** Caroline was assaulted in the house she rented by someone whom she let in, thinking that he was a gas company repairperson. There was a peephole in the front door, as required by law, which she could have used had she asked to see proof of his identification. When Caroline sued her landlord, the judge tossed the case out. Her case collapsed on question 1: The landlord had no control over Caroline foolishly opening the door to someone whom she could have safely questioned (and excluded) from inside.

**EXAMPLE 3:** Max was assaulted and robbed in the open parking lot next to his apartment house when he came home from work late one night. The landlord knew that several muggings had recently been reported in the neighborhood. The parking lot was thoroughly lit by bright floodlights, but it was not fenced and gated. Here's how the four questions got answered:

1. The lot was under the landlord's control.
2. An assault seemed reasonably foreseeable in view of the recent nearby muggings.
3. However, the burden of totally eliminating the danger (fencing the lot) would have been very expensive.
4. The seriousness of the probable injury was great.

When Max sued, the judge ruled in favor of the landlord, concluding that it wasn't reasonable to expect the landlord to fence and lock the parking lot. In a high-crime area in another state or where tenants had previously been assaulted in the parking lot, a judge's decision might be different.

If, based on these first four questions, you think you had a legal duty to deal with a condition on the premises that exposed tenants to the risk of crime, keep going. You have two more questions to answer.

**5. Did you fail to take reasonable steps to prevent a crime?** As ever, "reasonableness" is evaluated within the context of each situation. For example, returning to Sam (Example 1, above), the fact that the landlord let the bushes grow high and didn't replace the lights clearly was unreasonable. But suppose the landlord had cut the bushes back halfway and installed one light. Would that have been enough? It would be up to an insurance adjuster or a jury to decide.

"Reasonable precautions" in a crime-free neighborhood are not the same as those called for when three apartments in your building have been burglarized within the past month.

The greater the danger, the more you must do. If there is a risk of crime in the neighborhood of your rental property, and conditions on your property increase that risk to tenants, you may be held liable for damage and injuries caused by a criminal act. Your duty to keep tenants safe (and your liability) may be particularly enhanced if there have been prior criminal incidents on the property and you haven't taken steps to reduce the risk of future crimes.

EXAMPLE: Allison rented an apartment in Manor Arms after being shown the building by the resident manager. Nothing was said about recent criminal activity in the building. A month after moving in, Allison was assaulted by a man who stopped her in the hallway, claiming to be a building inspector. Unbeknownst to Allison, similar assaults had occurred in the building in the past six months, and the manager even had a composite drawing of the suspect done by the local police. Allison's assailant was captured and proved to be the person responsible for the earlier crimes.

Allison sued the building owners after their insurance carrier refused to offer her a reasonable settlement. In her lawsuit, Allison claimed that the owners were negligent (unreasonably careless) in failing to warn her of the specific danger posed by the repeat assailant and in failing to beef up their security (such as hiring a guard service) after the first assault. The jury agreed and awarded Allison a large sum of money.

Many courts have ruled that prior criminal activity in the neighborhood increases a landlord's duty to tenants only if the prior crimes were similar to the current one. For example, a string of car break-ins in the neighborhood will probably not obligate you to provide extra security measures to prevent apartment break-ins.

EXAMPLE: In New Jersey, a fight between two tenants in a downstairs apartment knocked loose their light fixture; later, another altercation between the same tenants resulted in a shotgun blast through the ceiling, injuring the upstairs tenant. The trial court found that the landlord was not negligent for failing to evict the rowdy tenants, and was not liable for the neighbor's injuries, because the second incident was not reasonably foreseeable as a result of the first. (*Williams v. Gorman,* 214 N.J. Super. 517 (1986).) Similar limitations on a landlord's liability have been drawn in California, Illinois, Massachusetts, Michigan and Missouri.

How much alike do two criminal incidents have to be in order to qualify as "similar?" What about a daytime burglary at a neighboring building followed by a nighttime rape in your building—in retrospect, will a judge decide that the rape was foreseeable because of the "similar" prior burglary? Who knows —the only thing we can say for sure is that you'll be more likely to avoid tragedy and liability by erring liberally on the side of caution and prevention.

**6. Did your failure to take reasonable steps to keep tenants safe contribute to the crime?** A tenant must be able to connect your failure to provide reasonable security with the criminal incident. It is often very difficult for tenants to convince a jury that the landlord's breach caused (or contributed to) the assault or burglary.

Think of it this way: If a tenant falls because the rotten front step on your apartment building collapsed, the collapse can be traced directly to your failure to maintain the property. But when an intruder enters through an unsecured front door, there's another ingredient: the burglar's independent decision to commit the crime. You are not responsible for the criminal's determination to break the law, and many juries simply won't place any responsibility on you, even if, for example, your failure to install a lock made the entry possible. To convince a jury otherwise, a tenant must emphasize that a crime of this nature was highly foreseeable and would probably have been prevented had you taken appropriate measures.

If a jury decides that you didn't meet the duty to keep tenants safe, and that this failure facilitated the crime, it will typically split the responsibility for the crime between you and the criminal. For example, jurors might decide that you were 60% at fault and the criminal 40%. You must compensate the injured tenant accordingly. Not surprisingly, the criminal's share is usually never collected.

In Sam's case (Example 1, above), he convinced the jury that, had the bushes been properly trimmed and the area well-lit, he could have seen the assailant or, more likely, the assailant wouldn't have chosen this exposed place to commit a crime. The jury found that the landlord was 70% at fault for Sam's injuries.

---

### How Much Money a Tenant Is Entitled To

To get financial compensation, an injured tenant must show that she was harmed by the criminal incident. Tragically, this is often quite obvious, and the only issue that lawyers argue about is the worth, in dollars, of dreadful injuries. Compensation may also be awarded for mental anguish and continuing psychological effects of the encounter. See Chapter 10 for more details on tenant compensation for injuries and losses.

---

Now let's look at two final, realistic cases, applying all six questions.

EXAMPLE 1: Elaine was assaulted and robbed by an intruder who entered her apartment through a sliding window that was closed but could not be locked. To determine whether or not the landlord would be liable, Elaine asked herself the six questions and came up with these answers:

1. The landlord controlled the window and was responsible for its operation.

2. This burglary was foreseeable, since there had been break-ins at the building in the past.
3. Installing a window lock was a minor burden.
4. The seriousness of foreseeable injury was high.
5. The landlord had done nothing to secure the window or otherwise prevent an intrusion.
6. The intruder could not have entered so easily and silently had the window been locked.

Putting these answers together, she concluded that the landlord owed her the duty to take reasonable steps to fix the problem. She filed a claim with the landlord's insurance company. but it failed to offer a fair settlement and Elaine's case went to trial. The jury decided that the landlord should have installed a window lock and that since the burglar might not have entered at all through a properly secured window, the landlord was partially responsible for Elaine's injuries. The jury fixed the value of her injuries at $500,000 and decided that the landlord was 80% responsible.

EXAMPLE 2: Nick was assaulted in the underground garage of his apartment building by someone who hid in the shadows. Nick's neighborhood had recently experienced several muggings and assaults. Nick couldn't identify the assailant, who was never caught. The automatic garage gate was broken and wouldn't close completely, allowing anyone to slip inside.

Nick decided that

1. The landlord controlled the garage
2. In view of the recent similar crimes in the neighborhood, an assault was foreseeable
3. Fixing the broken gate wouldn't have been a great financial burden, and
4. The likelihood of injury from an assault was high.

Nick concluded that the landlord owed him a duty of care in this situation. Nick then considered the last two questions. The garage door was broken, which constituted a breach of the landlord's duty. But the garage was also accessible from the interior of the building, making it possible that the assailant had been another tenant or a guest. Nick's case fell apart because the landlord's failure to provide a secure outside door hadn't necessarily contributed to the crime. If the assailant were another tenant or guest, the landlord's failure to fix the gate would have been completely unconnected to the crime. Nick probably would have had a winning case if he could have proved that the assailant got in through the broken gate.

---

### Install Basic Security and Use It Correctly

Your duty to provide basic security under the circumstances does not stop with the mere installation of appropriate equipment. Not only must the equipment work, but it must be used intelligently, as the following case illustrates:

A landlord in Indiana provided locking exterior and interior doors for a tenant's rental unit. The landlord regularly left a front door key for the mailman in an unlocked box at the entrance. The landlord was found liable for his tenant's injuries when an assailant used the key to enter the building and attack her on a stairwell. The court reasoned that, having provided a fair measure of security (the locks on the doors), the landlord was obligated to refrain from negligently allowing a criminal to enter locked doors. In other words, he had failed in his duty of due care by leaving a key in a place where an intruder could easily have found it. (*Nalls v. Blank*, 571 N.E.2d 1321 (Ind. App. 1991).)

Courts in Idaho, Illinois, Michigan, California and New York have reached similar conclusions.

---

## 3.  Your Promises

Knowing the security requirements of your local and state law and being generally familiar with how the courts in your state have ruled on cases holding landlords responsible for criminal acts against their tenants is a good start. Your next step is to understand how your responsibilities may be increased both by your own acts and promises.

### a.  Be Careful What You Advertise or Promise

The desire for secure housing is often foremost in the minds of prospective tenants, and landlords know that the promise of a safe environment is often a powerful marketing tool. In ads or during discussions with interested renters, you will naturally be inclined to point out security locks, outdoor lighting and burglar alarms, since these features may be as important to prospective tenants as a fine view or a swimming pool.

Take care, however, that your written or oral description of security measures are not exaggerated. Not only will you have begun the landlord-tenant relationship on a note of insincerity, but your descriptions of security may legally obligate you to actually provide what you have portrayed. And if you fail to do so, or fail to conscientiously maintain promised security measures in working order (such as outdoor lighting or an electronic gate on the parking garage), a court or jury may find this lack of security to be a material factor in a crime on the premises. In this case, you may well be held liable for a tenant's losses or injuries. And this is true even though you might not have been liable if you hadn't promised the specific security measures in the first place.

If you promise specific security features—such as a doorman, security patrols, interior cameras or an alarm system—you must either provide them or be liable (at least partially) for any criminal act that they would have prevented.

You won't be liable for failing to provide what was promised, however, unless this failure caused or contributed to the crime. Burned-out light bulbs in the parking lot won't mean anything if the burglar got in through an unlocked trap door on the roof.

EXAMPLE: The manager of Jeff's apartment building gave him a thorough tour of the "highly secure" building before he decided to move in. Jeff was particularly impressed with the security locks on the gates of the high fences at the front and rear of the property. Confident that the interior of the property was accessible only to tenants and their guests, Jeff didn't hesitate to take his kitchen garbage to the dumpsters at the rear of the building late one evening. There he was accosted by an intruder who got in through a rear gate which had a broken lock. Jeff's landlord was held liable because he had failed to maintain the sophisticated, effective locks that had been promised.

### Ads That Invite Lawsuits

Advertisements like the following will come back to haunt you if a crime occurs on your rental property:

- "No one gets past our mega-security systems. A highly trained guard is on duty at all times."
- "We provide highly safe, highly secure buildings."
- "You can count on us. We maintain the highest apartment security standards in the business."

## b. Be Especially Careful What Your Written Lease or Rental Agreement Promises

The simple rule of following through with what you promise, discussed above in the context of ads and oral promises, is even more crucial when it comes

to written provisions in your lease or accompanying documents. Why? Your lease is a contract, and if it includes a "24-hour security" promise or a commitment to have a doorman on duty at night, your tenants have a right to expect it. The fact that you have made the promise is preserved in black and white, in your own lease. If you have failed to follow through with the written promise, you will likely find that a court will hold you liable for criminal acts that injure your tenants or their property.

EXAMPLE: The information packet given to Mai when she moved into her apartment stressed the need to keep careful track of door keys: "If you lose your keys, call the management. and the lock will be changed immediately." When Mai lost her purse containing her keys, she immediately called the management company but couldn't reach them because it was after 5 p.m. and there was no after-hours emergency procedure. That evening, Mai was assaulted by someone who got into her apartment by using her lost key. Mai sued the owner and management company on the grounds that they had completely disregarded their own standard (to change the locks promptly) and so were partially responsible (along with the criminal) for the assailant's entry. The jury agreed and awarded Mai a large sum.

⚠ **Don't go overboard by specifying in your lease or rental agreement all the security measures you don't provide.** Some people believe that if they provide no security and say that a tenant is completely on her own, they can eliminate liability for the acts of criminals. True, making it clear that you provide little or no security probably can reduce your potential liability for tenant injuries as a result of criminal activity, but only as long as you have not attempted to excuse yourself from providing what is required by law. For example, if the local ordinance provides that exterior doors must have locks, you will increase—not decrease—your potential liability by failing to provide a front door lock.

### c. Be Careful to Maintain What You Have Already Provided

Sometimes your actions can obligate you as much as an oral or written statement. If you "silently" provide enhanced security measures (such as security locks or a nighttime guard)—that is, you make these features available without mentioning them in the lease, in advertisements or through oral promises —you may be bound to continue and maintain these features, even though you never explicitly promised to do so. Many landlords react with understandable frustration when their well-meaning (and expensive) efforts to protect their tenants actually have the effect of *increasing* their level of liability. But the answer to this frustration is not to cut back to the bare minimum for security. Instead, be practical and keep your eye on the long run: Over time, you are better off (legally safer) using proven security measures (thereby insuring contented, long-term tenants and fewer legal hassles) than you would be by offering the bare minimum and trusting to fate, the police and hopefully the savviness of the tenants to keep crime at bay. But at least from the point of view of future liability for criminal acts, the less you brag about your security measures, the better.

### d. Be Careful How You Handle Complaints

Complaints about a dangerous situation or a broken security item should be handled immediately, even if the problem occurs in the middle of the night or at some other inconvenient time. Failing to do this may saddle you with a higher level of legal liability should a tenant be injured by a criminal act while the security system is out of service or the window or door lock broken. Some courts will even see your receipt of the complaint as an implicit promise to do something about it. In short, if you get a

complaint about a broken security item—even one you didn't advertise—you should act immediately to:

1. Fix it, or,
2. If it's impossible to fix it for a few days or weeks, alert tenants to the problem and take other measures. For example, you might hire a security officer and close off other entrances for a few days if your front door security system fails and a necessary part is not immediately available.

Section B, below, provides more advice on how to respond to tenants' complaints about security.

---

### Keep Your Promises

Regardless of the exact wording of your promise, an offer to provide effective security can result in a finding of liability if you don't deliver and an assailant gains access as a result. In New York, California, Idaho, Illinois, Virginia, Ohio, Indiana and a number of other states, tenants have been able to successfully argue in court that since the failures of the promised security measures contributed significantly to the criminals' ability to gain entrance to the building, the landlord was partially responsible for their resulting injuries and losses.

---

## B. How to Protect Your Tenants From Criminal Acts

The job of maintaining rental units that are free from crime—both from the outside and, in the case of multi-unit buildings, from within—can be a monumental task. Sometimes, your duty to protect your tenants can even seem to conflict with your duty to respect your tenants' rights to privacy and autonomy. How will you know if the premises are safe unless you perform frequent inspections of individual rental units and the common areas? How will you know about the activities of your tenants unless you question them thoroughly regarding their background and livelihoods, or unless you watch them carefully?

Effective preventive measures are, in the long run, your best response to possible liabilities for tenant injuries and losses from criminal acts and activities. The most successful prevention techniques are not necessarily the most expensive—the cost of proper lighting, good locks, criminal-unfriendly landscaping designs and well-trained on-site personnel does not compare with the maintenance of a private security force. It should be noted, however, that sometimes more expensive measures are necessary—beyond the minimum response currently required by the laws or court decisions in your state. Nevertheless, it is our belief that a cost-cutting, minimalist response to security that skirts the letter of the law (or perhaps even falls short of meeting legal minimums) is likely to be more costly in the long run.

We can't overstate the value of prevention. The effort and money you spend today on effective crime-prevention measures will pale in comparison to the costs that may result from crime on the premises. These costs can include increased insurance premiums, jury verdicts in excess of your insurance coverage, expensive attorney fees, low morale among tenants and lost income due to rapid turnover of tenants. Of course, there is no way to measure the sorrow and guilt that will come with knowing that you, as the landlord, may share responsibility for a crime because you did not take reasonable steps to prevent its occurrence.

We recommend an eight-step preventive approach to effectively and reasonably protect your tenants, and, at the same time, reconcile your need to see and know (and thus to protect) with your duty to respect tenants' privacy:

**Step 1:** Meet or exceed basic legal requirements for safety devices, such as deadbolt locks, good lighting and window locks imposed by state and local housing codes. Keep your oral and written promises regarding security measures—such as an advertisement promising garage parking or security personnel—to a truthful minimum. (Section A discusses these crucial first steps.)

**Step 2:** Provide and maintain adequate security measures based on an analysis of the vulnerability of your property and neighborhood. (See Section B1, below.) If your tenants will pay more rent if you make the building safer, you are foolish not to do it.

**Step 3:** Tighten up management practices to make your tenants and property safer—for example, practice strict key control as described below. (See Section B2, below.)

**Step 4:** Educate your tenants about crime problems and prevention strategies. Make it absolutely clear that they—not you—are primarily responsible for their own protection. (See Section B3, below.)

**Step 5:** Don't hype your security measures. Provide a safe building, but don't brag about it. (Section B3 discusses the importance of being candid with your tenants. Section A, above, covers the dangers of failing to deliver on your security promises.)

**Step 6:** Conduct regular inspections of your rental properties to spot any security problems, and ask tenants for their suggestions. Quickly respond to your tenants' suggestions and complaints. If an important component of your security systems breaks, be prepared to fix it on an emergency basis and provide appropriate alternative security. (See Section B5.)

**Step 7:** Be aware of threats to tenants' security from the manager or other tenants and handle safety and security problems pronto, especially those involving drug dealing. (See Sections D and E.)

**Step 8:** Purchase adequate liability insurance to protect you from lawsuits related to crime on your rental property. (See the discussion of liability insurance in Chapter 10.)

These steps will not only limit the likelihood that criminal activity will occur on your property, but also reduce the risk that you will be found responsible if a criminal assault or robbery does occur there.

## 1. Provide Adequate Security Measures

If you want to improve the security of your property, approach the problem the way you would if you wanted to improve the way your property looks. For example, you might start a cosmetic face-lift by studying the property and making a list of possible improvements. (Tenants might also have good ideas at this stage of the process.) Next, you might hire a professional designer or landscaper as a consultant to help you copy other properties that have achieved the look you are after. Finally, before spending a fortune, you would measure the cost of any potential improvement project against both your available funds and any increase in the property's rental or sales value.

Personal inspection, attention to what has worked in nearby properties, professional advice (including input from the local police and your insurance company) and a cost/benefit analysis will also result in a sensible approach to providing safe housing. The steps are the same for all kinds of housing and neighborhoods—whether you rent a duplex or single-family home in a low-crime suburban area or a multiunit apartment building in a dangerous part of town.

### a. Start With Your Own Personal Inspection

Walk around your property and, as you assess the different areas, ask yourself two questions:

- Would I, or a member of my family, feel reasonably safe here, at night or alone? and,
- If I were a thief or assailant, how difficult would it be to get into the building or individual rental unit?

Schedule your assessment walks at different times of the day and night—you might see something at 11 p.m. that you wouldn't notice at 11 a.m.

At the very least, we recommend the following sensible security measures for every multi-unit rental property:

- Exterior lighting directed at entranceways and walkways should be activated by motion or on a timer. Do not rely on managers or tenants to manually operate exterior lights. The absence or failure of exterior lights is regarded by many security experts as the single most common failing that facilitates break-ins and crime.
- Make sure you have good, strong interior lights in hallways, stairwells, doorways and parking garages.
- Sturdy deadbolt door locks on individual rental units and solid window and patio door locks are essential, as are peepholes (with a wide-angle lens for viewing) at the front door of each unit. (Best to install two peepholes— one at eye-level for an adult and another at a

level appropriate for a child.) Lobby doors should have deadbolt locks.

- Solid metal window bars or grills over ground floor windows are often a good idea in higher-crime neighborhoods, but you may not always be able to install them because of restrictions of local fire codes. All grills or bars should have a release mechanism, allowing the tenant to open them from inside. Too many tenants have tragically died in fires because they could not escape an apartment with window bars or grills that had no release mechanism.
- Intercom and buzzer systems that allow the tenant to control the opening of the front door from the safety of his apartment are also obviously a good idea for many types of buildings.
- Landscaping needs to be designed and maintained so that it is neat and compact. Shrubs should be no higher than three feet and trees cleared to seven feet from the ground. Trees and shrubbery should not obscure entryways nor afford easy hiding places adjacent to doorways or windows.
- In some areas, a 24-hour doorman is essential and may do more to reduce crime outside your building than anything else. Spread over a large number of units, a doorman may cost less than you think. (See "Should You Use a Doorman or Security Guard?" below.)
- Driveways, garages and underground parking need to be well-lit and as secure (inaccessible to unauthorized entrants) as possible. Fences and automatic gates may be a virtual necessity in some areas.
- Elevators, where people are confined to a small space, are an ideal space for a fast-acting assailant. Limiting access to the elevators by requiring a pass key, and installing closed-circuit monitoring, reduce the chances that an assailant will choose this site.
- A 24-hour internal security system with cameras and someone monitoring them is an effective crime detector. Though these systems are expensive, in high crime areas many reasonably affluent tenants will bear the extra costs in exchange for the added protection. Also, keep in mind that these kinds of security systems may not deter a determined (or simply crazy) criminal.

## b. Consider the Neighborhood

The extent of your security measures depends somewhat on the nature of the neighborhood as well as the property itself. Keep up to date on crime in the area of your rental property. If there have been no incidents of crime in the neighborhood, you have less reason to equip your property with extensive security devices. On the other hand, residential crime is a spreading, not receding, problem, and you certainly do not want one of your tenants to be the first to be raped or robbed on your block. Especially if there have been criminal incidents in the neighborhood, talk to the neighbors and the police department about what measures have proven to be effective.

The physical aspects of the neighborhood, as well as its history, can be important indicators of the risk of crime on your property. Properties adjacent to late-night bars and convenience stores often experience more burglaries and assaults than housing that is removed from such establishments. In some cities, proximity to a freeway on-ramp (an effective avenue of escape) may increase the risk of crime.

## c. Get Advice From the Police, Your Insurance Company and Other Security Professionals

Increasingly, as the problems of urban crime escalate, the police will work with you to develop a sound security approach and educate tenants. Some local police departments will send an officer out to assess the vulnerability of your property and recommend security measures. Many police departments will train tenants in neighborhood watch techniques, such as how to recognize and report suspicious behavior.

Another professional resource that may not immediately come to mind is your own insurance company. Some companies will consult with their clients for free on ways to deter crime, having figured out that in the long run it is cheaper to offer preventive consultation services than to pay out huge awards to injured clients. For example, drawing on its experience with prior claims generated by security breaches, your insurance company might be able to tell you which equipment has (and has not!) proven to be effective in preventing break-ins and assaults.

Another resource for advice is the private "security industry." As the amount of residential crime has gone up, so too have the number of companies that specialize in providing security services. Listed in the telephone book under "Security Systems," these firms will typically provide an analysis of your situation before recommending specific equipment—whether it be bars on windows or an internal electronic surveillance system. Even if you do not ultimately engage their services, a professional evaluation may prove quite valuable as you design your own approach. As with other professional services, be sure to get several estimates and check references before selecting any security firm.

Be aware that security companies have a vested interest in getting you to buy products and services that may not be needed. If you own lots of rental properties, it may be worth your while to hire an independent security consultant for a disinterested evaluation. Call the International Association of Professional Security Consultants in Washington, D.C. at 202-466-7212, or check their Web site at www.iapsc.org.

## Should You Use a Doorman or Security Guard?

Security guards, or doormen, are appropriate in some situations—in big cities such as New York, they are practically essential. The presence of an alert human can make an empty lobby more inviting to a tenant and less attractive to a prospective criminal. But bear in mind that the security provided is only as good as the individual doing the job. If you hire a firm, choose carefully and insist on letters of reference and proof of insurance. You can also hire your own guard, but this tends to get complicated very quickly, since you will be responsible for his or her training and weapons used (if any). It is essential to remember that, even with the best-trained and most visible security personnel, you must continue to pay attention to other aspects of security.

EXAMPLE: An assailant studied an upscale apartment complex and waited until it was clear that large numbers of people were arriving for a party. When he entered the lobby, he told the guard that he, too, was headed for the party upstairs. Because the guard had not been given a list of invited guests and told to ask for identification from every party-goer, the assailant was allowed into the building, where he assaulted a tenant in the laundry room. Had the owner or manager instructed his tenants to supply the guard with lists of guests, and told the guard that no one should be admitted without confirmation, the unfortunate incident would not have happened. The landlord was held partially liable for the assaulted tenant's injuries.

## Do Not Rely on "Courtesy Officers"

Some rental property owners attempt to provide on-site security by renting to police officers who, in exchange for a reduction in rent, agree to be the resident "courtesy officer." The idea is to provide a professional "presence" on the property while not having to pay for a regular security service. While well-intentioned, using an officer/tenant in this way is a poor idea for these reasons:

- The fact that you have labeled the officer/tenant a "courtesy" officer does not change the fact that your tenants will look to him to provide real, consistent security protection. (In fact, since you are giving the officer a rent reduction, he is not working as a "courtesy" at all.) Moreover, a court will hold the police officer (and you) to the same standard of conduct as that applied to professional guard services, meaning that if this person falls short, your liability may even be higher than if you had no "courtesy officer."

- Since your officer/tenant can only provide "security" when he is home, the protection he supplies will obviously be episodic and unpredictable. Tenants will have no way of knowing when they can (and cannot) count on security coverage, and consequently may do things (like coming home late at night) under the mistaken impression that the officer/tenant is on the property.

- The value of your officer/tenant's services will be as good as his level of wakefulness and attention. You are essentially asking him to assume a second job when, in fact, he may be doing other things. For example, what if he wants to unwind after a hard day with a few beers? How good will his judgment and response time be under these circumstances?

Relying on a tenant who is paid to provide intermittent security makes you his employer, regardless of what you call him, meaning you'll have to pay Social Security, taxes and meet other employer obligations. (See the Chapter 6 discussion regarding tax issues and resident managers.) A security service, on the other hand, will typically be considered an independent contractor and take care of these bookkeeping details. More important, if a court finds your officer/tenant partially responsible for crime on the premises (by failing in his duties and allowing unauthorized access, for example), you will be liable as his employer. Independent contractors are generally responsible for their own lapses and should be insured (be sure you check). Of course, you may still be sued, but the chances of your being held liable will be reduced if an independent contractor provided the security service.

## 2. Initiate Good Management Practices

Physical safety devices and improvements aren't the only way you can improve security and decrease the chances of liability. Your business practices, including personnel policies, are crucial. They include:

- **Tenant information.** Keep tenant files in a locked cabinet. As an added precaution, identify tenant residences by your own code, so that no one but you and your manager can read a tenant's file and learn where he or she lives.

- **Employee discretion.** Impress upon your employees the need to preserve your tenants' privacy. If your tenant wants friends, family or bill collectors to know where she lives, she'll tell them, not you.

- **Train employees to avoid dangerous situations and correct worrisome ones.** Your prevention approach is only as good as the people who implement it. Managers and employees should be taught to rigorously abide by your safety rules and to report areas of concern. Consider sending employees to management courses on security offered by many landlord associations.

---

### Key Control

The security of your rental property depends in large part on the locks on rental unit doors and the keys to those doors. Don't let keys get into the wrong hands:

- Keep all duplicate keys in a locked area, identified by a code that only you and your manager know. Several types of locking key drawers and sophisticated key safes are available. Check ads in magazines that cater to the residential rental industry, or contact local locksmiths and security firms.

- Don't label keys with the rental unit number or name and address of the apartment building, and advise your tenants to take the same precaution.

- Strictly limit access to master keys by allowing only you and your manager to have them.

- Keep strict track of all keys provided to tenants and, if necessary, to your employees.

- Require tenants to return all keys at move-out.

- Re-key every time a new tenant moves in or loses a key.

- Give careful thought to the security problem of the front door lock: If the lock opens by an easy-to-copy key, there is no way to prevent a tenant from copying the key and giving it to others or using it after he moves out. Consider using locks that have hard-to-copy keys; or (with rental houses or small properties) re-key the front door when a tenant moves. There are also easy-to-alter card systems that allow you to change front door access on a regular basis or when a tenant moves. Again, locksmiths and security firms can advise you on options available.

- Only give keys to people you know and trust. If you have hired a contractor whom you do not know personally, open the unit for him and return to close up when he is done. Keep in mind that often even known and trusted contractors hire day laborers whose honesty is yet to be proven.

### 3. Educate Your Tenants About Security Problems and Crime Prevention

After you have identified the vulnerabilities of your particular neighborhood—for example, by talking to the police—don't keep this information to yourself, but make your tenants savvy to the realities of life in your neighborhood. It's best to do this at the start, when you first show the rental unit to prospective tenants. We recommend a two-step process:

- Alert tenants to the specific risks associated with living in your neighborhood (problems are worst Friday and Saturday night between 10 p.m. and 1 a.m.) and what they can do to minimize the chances of assault or theft (avoid being alone on the street or in outside parking lots late at night), and
- No matter how secure your building, warn tenants of the limitations of the security measures you have provided.

EXAMPLE: Paul recently moved into his apartment and had been told by the manager that doormen were on duty from 6 p.m. to 6 a.m. One afternoon, someone knocked on Paul's door and identified himself as a "building inspector" who needed to check his heating system. Realizing that the doorman was not on duty at this time to screen visitors, Paul demanded identification. When the alleged "building inspector" refused to show ID, Paul wouldn't open the door. Paul later found out someone in the neighborhood had been robbed, falling for the same ruse.

This two-fold approach allows you to cover your legal bases by both disclosing the risks and frankly informing the tenants that you have not (and cannot) insure their safety in all possible situations. If, despite your best efforts, a criminal incident does occur on your property, your candid disclosures regarding the safety problems of your neighborhood and the limitations of the existing security measures may help shield you from liability.

From the tenant's point of view, such disclosures serve to alert her to the need to be vigilant and to assume some responsibility for her own safety. If you do not disclose the limitations of the security you provide (or if you exaggerate) and a crime does occur, one of the first things your tenant will say (to the police, his lawyer and the jury) is that he was simply relying upon the protection you had assured him would be in place. (Section B, above, discusses the pitfalls of failing to deliver on your security promises.)

---

### When a Tenant Wants to Supply Additional Security

Some tenants may be dissatisfied with your security measures and may want to install additional locks or an alarm system to their rental unit or house at their expense. Clause 12 of the form lease and rental agreements (Chapter 2) forbids the tenant from re-keying or adding locks or a burglar alarm system without your written consent. Think carefully before you refuse your tenant permission to install extra protection: If a crime occurs that would have been foiled had the security item been in place, you will obviously be at a disadvantage before a judge or jury. If you allow a tenant to add additional security measures, make sure the tenant gives you duplicate keys and instructions on how to disarm the alarm system and the name and phone number of the alarm company, so that you can enter in case of emergency.

---

### a. Identify Specific Crime Problems and Issues

Give tenants information specific to your rental property. Here are some ideas:

- If there have been incidents of crime in the area (and especially in your building), inform your tenants (but be careful not to disclose the identity of the victim).

- Update your information on the security situation as necessary. For example, let tenants know if there has been an assault in or near the building by sending them a note and post a notice in the lobby, including the physical description of the assailant.
- If you have hired a professional security firm to evaluate your rental property, share the results of their investigation with your tenants.
- Encourage tenants to set up a neighborhood watch program. Many local police departments will come out and meet with citizens attempting to organize such a program.
- Encourage tenants to report any suspicious activities or security problems to you, such as loitering, large numbers of late-night guests or broken locks. (Chapter 9 recommends a system for handling tenant complaints.)

---

### Security for a House or Duplex

Single-family housing and duplexes require many of the same security measures as multi-unit rental property—for example, effective exterior lighting, strong door and window locks and secure parking. Houses and duplexes also present different opportunities to provide security than are usually appropriate in apartment buildings and other multifamily residences. For example, it may be wise to install a burglar alarm in a house or duplex that is hooked up to a security service.

Also, though yard maintenance may be the tenants' responsibility in a single-family house, you may need to supervise the job to make sure that bushes and trees are trimmed so as not to obscure entryways or provide convenient hiding spots for would-be criminals.

---

### b.  Explain the Limitations of Your Security Measures

An important component of your disclosures to tenants involves disabusing them of any notion that you are their guardian angel. Let them know where your security efforts end, and where their own good sense (and the local police force) must take over. Specifically:

- Point out each security measure—such as locking exterior gates, key locks on windows and peepholes in every front door—and explain how each measure works. It's best to do this in writing—either as part of a move-in letter to new tenants (see Chapter 7) or at the time a new security item is installed.
- Highlight particular aspects of the property that are, despite your efforts, vulnerable to the presence of would-be assailants or thieves. Say, for example, your apartment parking garage has a self-closing door. When you explain how this door works, you might also point out that it's not instantaneous. For example, a fast-moving person could, in most situations, slip into the garage behind an entering car despite the self-closing door. Pointing this out to your tenant may result in more careful attention to the rear-view mirror.
- Place signs in any potentially dangerous locations that will remind tenants of possible dangers and the need to be vigilant. For example, you might post a notice in the lobby asking tenants to securely lock the front door behind them.
- Suggest safety measures. For example, tenants arriving home after dark might call ahead and ask a neighbor to be an escort.

Giving your tenants information on how they, too, can take steps to protect themselves will also help if you are sued. If a tenant argues that you failed to inform him of a dangerous condition, you will be able to show that you have done all that could be expected of a reasonably conscientious landlord.

## 4. Maintain Your Property and Conduct Regular Inspections

Landlords are most often found liable for crime on their property when the criminal gained access through broken doors or locks. Not only is the best security equipment in the world useless if it has deteriorated or is broken, but the very fact that it's not working can be enough to result in a finding of landlord liability. By contrast, a jury is far less likely to fault a landlord who can show that reasonable security measures were in place and operational, but were unable to stop a determined criminal.

Inspect your property frequently, so that you discover and fix problems before an opportunistic criminal comes along. At the top of your list should be fixing burned-out exterior floodlights and broken locks and cutting back overgrown shrubbery that provides a convenient lurking spot for criminals.

Enlist your tenants to help you spot and correct security problems—both in their own rental unit and in common areas such as parking garages. Remember that the people who actually live in your rental property will generally know first about security hazards. One good approach is to post several notices in central locations, such as elevators and main lobbies, asking tenants to promptly report any security problems, such as broken locks or windows. If you rent a duplex or house, periodically meet with your tenants and discuss any changes in the neighborhood or the structure of the building.

Chapter 9 provides a detailed system for inspecting rental property and staying on top of repair and maintenance needs.

## 5. Respond to Your Tenants' Complaints Immediately

Respond immediately to your tenants' complaints about broken locks or concerns about security problems and suspicious activities. Keep in mind that a serious breach in your security measures has much greater potential liability consequences than a garden-variety maintenance problem. That's why we recommend a truly fast response when tenant safety is in question. For example, a stopped-up sink is certainly inconvenient to the tenant, and may result in rent withholding or repair and deduct measures if not fixed for a period of days or weeks (see Chapter 9), but it rarely justifies a four-alarm response by the landlord. On the other hand, a broken lock or disabled intercom system is an invitation to crime and needs to be addressed pronto. If you fail to do so, and a crime occurs, your chances of being held liable increase dramatically.

Consider the following all-too-common scenarios, and our suggested response:

- The glass panel next to the front door is accidentally broken late one afternoon by a departing workman. Conscious of the fact that this creates a major security problem, you call a 24-hour glass replacement service to get it replaced immediately.
- The intercom system fails due to a power surge following an electrical storm. You hire a 24-hour guard for the two days it takes to repair the circuitry.
- Several exterior floodlights are knocked out by vandals throwing rocks at 6 p.m. A tenant who had been encouraged by management to immediately report problems of this nature calls you. You alert the police and ask for an extra drive-by during the night, post signs in the lobby and the elevator, close off the darkened entrance and advise tenants to use an alternate, lighted entryway instead. The floodlights are repaired the next day and equipped with wire mesh screen protection.

Establishing complaint procedures will help prevent crime on your rental property by alerting you to security problems. Such procedures will also be of considerable value to you in limiting your liability, should you be sued by a tenant whose assailant gained access via a broken window lock that the tenant never told you about.

## Protect Yourself, Too

Landlords and managers need to take precautions for their own personal safety as well as for the safety of tenants. In addition to being subject to many of the same risks tenants face, there are added special considerations that come with your job. Regardless of whether or not you live on the rental property:

- Promptly deposit rent checks and money orders. If possible, do not accept cash.
- When you show a vacant apartment, consider bringing someone with you. A would-be assailant may be deterred by the presence of another person who could either overpower or identify him later. If you must show apartments by yourself, at least alert a family member or friend to the fact that you are showing a vacant unit, and when you expect to be done.
- Especially if your building is in a relatively high crime area, carry a small alarm device (such as beeper-sized box that emits a piercing alarm when its pin is removed), and consider carrying a cellular phone. Many cellular service providers offer "emergency only" service that is relatively inexpensive.
- Work on vacant units during the day and be alert to the fact that, although keeping the front door open (to the building or the unit) may be convenient as you go to and fro for materials and equipment, it is also an invitation to someone to walk right into the building.

## The Mesa Project: Team Approach to Security

Landlords, tenants and the police have teamed up in cities throughout the country, including ten cities in Arizona alone, to rid their apartment communities of crime. Called the "Mesa Project" after Mesa, Arizona, its city of origin, the program consists of an intensive training program for apartment managers, strict security requirements for participating properties and resident crime prevention education programs. A community that fulfills the Mesa Project requirements is certified as a Crime Free Multi-Housing Property, and owners can proudly display the colorful signs attesting to this fact. Moreover, management is allowed to use the police department logo on ads, business cards and letterheads. Communities that have participated in the program have reported a decided increase in stable tenants and a decrease in the number of police calls and criminal incidents. For information about the Mesa Crime-Free Multi-Housing Program, contact the Mesa, Arizona, Police Department at 602-644-2211.

## C. Protecting Tenants From Each Other

The sections above focus on your duty to take reasonable measures to avert foreseeable crime on the premises by unknown, third-party criminals. This section will explore your responsibility when one of the tenants themselves is responsible for criminal activity on the premises. (Physical disputes between tenants in the same household, or domestic disturbances within a family, are discussed in Chapter 8.)

Section D, below, discusses your liability for the criminal acts of a manager or other employee.

## 1. Your Responsibility for Tenants' Criminal Acts

Sometimes danger lurks within as well as beyond the gate. And you have a duty to take reasonable steps to protect tenants if another resident on the property threatens harm or property damage.

You should respond to a troublesome tenant in essentially the same way you would respond to a loose stair or broken front-door lock. If you know about a problem (or should know about it), you are expected to take reasonable steps to prevent foreseeable harm to other tenants. If you fail to do that, and a tenant is injured or robbed by another tenant, you may be sued and pay a hefty judgment.

### a. When You Must Act

Your liability for a tenant's illegal acts will likely increase if the problem tenant had done or threatened similar criminal conduct in the recent past, and you knew about it. In short, a tenant who is injured or robbed by another tenant will need to convince an insurance adjuster, judge or jury that:

- it was reasonable to expect you to know or discover the details of a tenant's past, and
- once known, you could have taken steps to control or evict the troublemaker.

Unless there's a clear history of serious problems with the offending tenant, landlords often win these cases.

EXAMPLE 1: Evelyn decided to rent an apartment to David, although she knew that he had been convicted of spousal abuse some years earlier. For several months David appeared to be a model tenant, until he hit another tenant, Chuck, in the laundry room over a disagreement as to who was next in line for the dryer. Chuck was unable to convince the jury that Evelyn should bear some responsibility for his injuries, because he could not show that the incident was foreseeable.

EXAMPLE 2: Mary rented an apartment to Carl, who appeared to be a nice young man with adequate references. Carl stated that he had no criminal convictions when he answered this standard question on the rental application. Several months later, Carl was arrested for the burglary and assault of another tenant in the building. At trial, it came out that Carl had recently been released from state prison for burglary and rape. Because Mary had no knowledge of his criminal past, she was not held liable for his actions.

On the other hand, tenants sometimes win if they can show that the landlord knew about a resident's tendency towards violence and failed to take reasonable precautions to safeguard the other tenants.

EXAMPLE: Bill received several complaints from his tenants about Carol, a tenant who had pushed another resident out of the elevator, slapped a child for making too much noise and verbally abused a tenant's guest for parking in Carol's space. Despite these warning signs, Bill didn't terminate Carol's tenancy or even speak with her about her behavior. When she picked a fight with a resident whom she accused of reading her newspaper and badly beat her up, Bill was held partly liable on the grounds that he knew of a potentially dangerous situation and failed to take appropriate steps to safeguard his tenants.

### b.    Using Megan's Law Information

Your state probably has a version of "Megan's Law," which requires certain convicted sexual offenders to register with local law enforcement, who keep a database on their whereabouts. As explained in Chapter 1, Section E, some states make it easy to get this information, while others restrict it to certain individuals and situations.

If you learn that a current tenant has a conviction for a sexual offense, you may want to terminate the tenancy. Your actual ability to do this is explained at length in Chapter 17, Section D. But suppose you have no legal grounds to evict? What are your obligations to your other tenants? And even if you are eventually able to evict, what should you do in the meantime?

Your response to this information should be governed by your answers to the now-familiar questions: How foreseeable is it that this tenant, with this past, will be a danger to my tenants? How difficult will it be to take steps to warn others of this danger? If the risk of danger is great—the tenant has recent and multiple burglary and rape convictions—your worry level will be higher than if, say, the conviction is old and involves conduct that might not be prosecuted today (for example, convictions for consensual intercourse between minors). How to warn other tenants is covered below in Subsection c.

### c.    What You Must Do

If you know about the potential for danger from another tenant you must do something about the problem tenant, such as warn other tenants or evict the troublemaker.

For example, suppose a tenant complains about his neighbor who bangs on the walls every time the tenant practices the violin during the afternoon—and the pounding is getting louder. The tenant can reasonably expect you to intervene and attempt to broker a solution—perhaps an adjustment of the violin-playing tenant's practice schedule or some heavy-duty earplugs for the neighbor. If the circumstances are more threatening—for example, one tenant brandishes a gun—you might be legally expected to call the police, post a security guard and warn other tenants pending the speedy eviction of the dangerous tenant.

To make this legal responsibility easier for landlords to meet, many states now make it relatively simple for landlords to evict troublemakers. These laws specify that harm or the threat of harm to other persons justifies a quick eviction. (See Chapter 17 for details on expedited eviction.)

Intervention and eviction of the troublemaker are the usual ways that landlords meet the duty to take care that residents don't harm other residents. But the law doesn't require you to have a crystal ball.

If you learn through your state's Megan's Law (discussed in Chapter 1) that a tenant has a conviction for a serious sexual offense, and you are unable to evict (as explained in Chapter 17, Section D) or eviction is pending, your warnings to other tenants should be as factual and noninflammatory as possible. The last thing you want is an angry mob gathering outside a tenant's door, demanding that he leave town (unfortunately, such scenes have happened). One approach might be to offer a financial incentive to encourage the tenant to vacate voluntarily. Quite frankly, there is no perfect answer, except to repeat again (as we do throughout this book) that careful screening of applicants (where many of these problems will surface) is the most important part of your business.

## Limits to the Landlord's Ability to Anticipate Trouble Among Tenants

Three cases illustrate the limits that courts have placed on landlord liability for crimes by tenants against other tenants.

One case concerned a schizophrenic youth who attacked another tenant in the hallway of the building where they both lived. The assailant had been repeatedly hospitalized and was regularly medicated for his schizophrenia. At the time of the attack, he was living with his parents and had gone off medication. The injured tenant sued the landlord for injuries he sustained during the assault. The court found that, although the landlord owed a duty to protect his tenants, it did not extend to protecting them from the type of injury involved. The court held that it would be "intolerable" to subject the schizophrenic tenant to scrutiny about his private affairs, and that, in any event, the landlord could hardly be in the position of guaranteeing that the man took his medication. (*Gill v. N.Y. Housing Authority*, 519 N.Y.S.2d 364 (1987).)

In a second New York case, in which two boys playing with BB guns injured a third, a court made a similar decision absolving the landlord of liability. The court ruled that, even if the landlord had known about the boys' activities, he could not be expected to monitor and police them. (*Johnson v. Slocum Realty Corporation*, 595 N.Y.S.2d 244 (1993).)

In Minnesota, a landlord rented a trailer to a man whom he knew (from a local newspaper article) was on parole for sexually molesting a minor. The landlord then rented a nearby house to a family with young children. He did not tell this family about their neighbor's past. When one of the children was molested by the tenant in the trailer, the family sued but did not collect. A very troubled judge wrote that the landlord did not have a duty to warn because the landlord did not know of an intended specific victim. (*N.W. by J.W. v. Anderson*, 478 N.W.2d 542 (1991).) In other states or before other judges, the outcome might not have been the same.

## 2. How to Protect Tenants From Each Other

As with your duty to protect tenants from crime at the hands of unknown, third-party assailants, your duty to keep the peace among your tenants is limited to what is *reasonably* foreseeable and to what a *reasonable* person in your position would do.

There are several practical steps that you can take both to avoid trouble among your tenants and, in the event that hostilities do erupt, to limit your exposure to lawsuits.

### a. Screen Tenants Carefully

You need to be especially aware of your potential liability if you know about a tenant's criminal past, yet fail to warn other tenants (who could reasonably be expected to be future victims) about the potential for danger.

Careful tenant selection is by far the best approach to choosing tenants who are likely to be law-abiding and peaceful citizens. Chapter 1 recommends a comprehensive system for screening prospective tenants, including checking applicants' credit reports, calling past landlords and employers and accessing information on "Megan's Law" state databases of sexual offenders where possible. Thorough screening will give you a fairly complete idea as to a prospective tenant's legitimate source of income and his or her temperament, and will help you select tenants who are not likely to cause you any legal or practical problems later.

Your questions about a tenant's past criminal activity, drug use or mental illness may be limited both legally and practically.

For details on questions that are legal—and illegal—to ask prospective tenants, see Chapter 5.

## b. Do Not Tolerate Tenants' Disruptive Behavior

In addition to choosing tenants carefully, be sure you establish a system to respond to tenants' complaints and concerns about other tenants or the manager, the way you handle repair complaints (see Chapter 9). A system of this kind will enable you to respond quickly to inappropriate tenant or manager behavior, and it will serve an additional, perhaps unexpected function: If a manager or tenant does, despite your best selection efforts, prove suddenly to be dangerous or unreliable and you are sued, and if you have complete business records that show that there were no prior complaints regarding his behavior, the absence of any complaints will bolster your claim that you acted reasonably under the circumstances (by continuing to rent to or hire the individual) because you had no inkling that trouble was likely.

If a tenant does cause trouble, act swiftly. You do not want to establish a police state, but you do want to emphasize your expectation that all tenants (and their families and guests) will conduct themselves in a law-abiding manner, or face the threat of prompt eviction. An explicit provision in your lease or rental agreement is the most effective way to make this point. (See Clause 13 of the form agreements in Chapter 2.)

Your response to a disruptive tenant should be carefully designed to fit the problem. Some situations call for prompt efforts to evict the troublemaker. If the tenant causes problems before you are able to get him out, and you are sued, you can at least argue that you acted as quickly as possible to get rid of him. On the other hand, if the behavior is disruptive, but not serious enough to sustain an eviction, a warning notice or mediation might be warranted as a first step—particularly if the tenant has not created other problems. In each situation, you will have to consider the seriousness of the risk and the likelihood that a court will uphold your attempt to evict. See Chapter 16 for information on handling disputes with tenants and Chapter 17 for an overview of eviction lawsuits.

# D. Your Responsibility for an Employee's Criminal Acts

The person you hire as your manager will occupy a critical position in your business. Your manager will interact with every tenant, and will often have access to their personal files *and* their homes. If your manager commits a crime—especially if you had any warning that this might occur—you are likely to be held liable. It follows that extreme caution must be exercised in your choice of a manager.

Whether you will be held legally liable for a manager's crimes will usually turn on whether you acted "reasonably under the circumstances" in hiring and supervising the manager. Let's take a closer look at what this means.

## 1. Checking Your Manager's Background

As we explained earlier in Chapter 6, it is essential to thoroughly check the background of your potential manager. If a manager commits a crime—for example, he robs or assaults a tenant—you are likely to be sued for negligent hiring. You may be found liable if:

- you failed to investigate your manager's background to the full extent allowed by the privacy laws in your state
- it can be shown that a proper investigation would have revealed a past criminal conviction that would have rendered the applicant unsuitable for the job, and
- the manager's offense against the tenant is one that is reasonably related to the past conviction.

EXAMPLE: Martin needed to hire a new manager for his large apartment complex when Sandy, his longtime manager, suddenly left. Pressured by the need to replace Sandy fast, Martin hired Jack without checking his background and information provided on the application form. Martin took Jack at his word when he said that he had no felony convictions. Several months later, Jack was arrested for stealing stereo equipment from a tenant's home that he had entered using the master key. Martin was successfully sued when the tenant learned that Jack had two prior felony convictions for burglary and grand theft.

## 2. Supervising Your Manager

As the manager's employer, you may also be held liable if your manager's negligence makes it possible for another person to commit a crime against a tenant. For example, if your manager develops lax key management practices, which results in the ability of a criminal to obtain and use a tenant's key, you will be held responsible on the grounds that you failed to properly supervise the manager.

Establishing a system for tenants to express concerns about the manager is one way to keep tabs on the situation. See Chapter 6 for further advice on the subject.

## E. Protecting Neighbors From Drug-Dealing Tenants

It's an understatement to say that tenants who engage in illegal activity on your property—by dealing drugs, storing stolen property, engaging in prostitution or participating in gang-related activity—present you with a host of problems. In this section, we focus on the most common problem (drug dealing), but our discussion applies equally to the other illegal activities.

## 1. The Cost of Renting to Drug-Dealing Tenants

Increasingly over the last decade, stricter laws and court decisions have made landlords liable when they fail to sufficiently monitor the activities of their tenants, especially if a tenant is found to be engaging in a continuing illegal activity such as drug deal-

ing. In addition, your failure to act quickly—for example, by failing to evict drug-dealing tenants—can result in these practical and legal problems:

- Good tenants who pay rent on time and maintain the rental property may be difficult to find and keep, and the value of your property will plummet.
- Good tenants, trying to avoid drug-dealing tenants, may be able to legally move out without notice and before a lease runs out. They will argue that the presence of the illegal activity has, for all practical purposes, evicted them, in that the problems associated with drug dealing prevent them from the "quiet enjoyment" of their home, or violate the implied warranty of habitability. In many states, the tenant will have a very strong case to break their lease. (See Clause 13 of the form agreements in Chapter 2 for a fuller discussion of the tenant's right to quiet enjoyment of the premises and Chapter 9 for details on the implied warranty of habitability.)
- Tenants injured or annoyed by drug dealers, both in the building and neighborhood, may sue you for violating anti-nuisance laws and building codes.
- Local, state or federal authorities may levy stiff fines and padlock penalties against you for allowing the illegal activity to continue.
- Law enforcement authorities may choose to pursue criminal penalties against both the tenants *and* you as landlord for knowingly allowing the activities to continue.
- As an extreme but relatively uncommon consequence, the presence of drug dealers may result in your rental property being confiscated under one of two powerful tools developed by society to deal with crime: public nuisance abatement laws and forfeiture laws.

⚠️ **Be vigilant or be sorry.** In some situations, fines are levied and property is seized with only the barest of knowledge on the landlord's part as to the nefarious activities of his tenants. Some landlords may suspect—or even know full well—

that illegal drug dealing is taking place on their rental property, but do nothing—either out of inertia, fear of reprisals from drug dealers or the attitude that they're unlikely to get in trouble. It clearly behooves landlords to learn how to *avoid* substantial fines or the risk of losing rental property by acting very quickly and decisively to eliminate drug dealing and other illegal activities on their property.

---

### Nice Properties Are Not Immune

If your rental property is in a safe neighborhood, you may think that drug crime is largely a problem in seedy neighborhoods. Think again. A study by the Crime Control Institute, a nonprofit group in Washington, D.C., found that smaller apartment complexes with some measure of security are preferred by drug dealers over large, unprotected housing units. The reason may surprise you: A drug dealer, as much as a law-abiding tenant, is interested in a safe, controlled environment. Also, remember that illegal drug use is spread widely throughout American society—the notion that drug use is a ghetto phenomenon is just plain wrong.

---

## 2. Government Lawsuits Against Landlords

The legal meaning of "nuisance" bears only a little resemblance to its meaning in everyday life. A legal nuisance is a pervasive, continuing and serious condition—like a pile of stinking garbage or a group of drug dealers—that threatens public health, safety or morals. In some states, it also includes obnoxious activity that is simply offensive (like excessive noise or open sexual conduct).

Every state has some type of abatement law, which allows the government, and sometimes the neighbors, to step in and stop the nuisance, often by court order and fines against the landlord. Using public nuisance abatement laws against crime-tolerant landlords is increasingly common in large cities with pervasive drug problems. In extreme cases, where the conduct giving rise to the nuisance complaint is illegal (drug dealing or prostitution, for example), landlords themselves face civil fines or criminal punishment for tolerating the behavior.

Public nuisance laws come in two forms: civil and criminal. The table below explains the differences between the two types.

Of special concern is the fact that even though it's the tenant's conduct that causes the nuisance, the punishment may be directed *at you, as the landlord.* Put another way, although you are not the drug dealer, you may be fined, deprived of the use of your property and even assessed criminal penalties. The best approach to the threat of nuisance lawsuits is vigilance and constant prevention. Subsection 6 suggests how you can accomplish these ends.

## 3. Governmental Use of Public Nuisance Abatement Laws

Not surprisingly, the use of public nuisance abatement statutes is most common in large cities plagued with pervasive drug problems. The basis for legal action against a property owner is that the owner is liable for creating a nuisance by allowing property to be used as a drug house, which injures and interferes with the rights of neighbors to use and enjoy their property. A drug house easily qualifies as a legal nuisance, given the crime problems it creates for people who live nearby.

EXAMPLE: Alma owned a duplex in Wisconsin. Despite repeated complaints from the neighbors that one of her tenants was conducting a drug operation in his home (and in spite of the tenant's two arrests for dealing from that address), Alma did nothing about the problem. Responding to pressure from fed-up neighbors, the local police finally took action and sued Alma to evict the tenant and close the duplex. Alma learned to her dismay that Wisconsin law actually defines drug houses as nuisances. (Wisconsin Statutes Annotated § 823.113.) Her tenants were evicted by the state police and the property was padlocked.

Each state has had to answer the question "How involved in tenants' illegal activities must the landlord be in order to be found responsible under the nuisance law?" On a theoretical legal level, the answers vary significantly:

- In Texas, landowners are held "strictly liable" for the nuisance activities of their tenants—that is, landlords will be held responsible (and will face the consequences) of drug-dealing tenants even if they did not know about the illegal activity. (Chapter 10 discusses the concept of strict liability.)

- In Tennessee, New York, Alabama and other states, however, the government must show that the landlord had *some* knowledge of the illegal activity before his property can be seized. Generally, landlords are given a short time in which to cure the problem before the ax falls and the property is seized.

In reality, since most landlords are acutely aware of their tenants' illegal behavior—having been informed by disgusted neighbors and overwhelmed law enforcement—even in states that require that you have clear actual knowledge of the situation, this "knowledge" standard is usually met. Or, put another way, it's a rare situation in which you can realistically claim that you didn't know about drug-dealing tenants.

| | Civil and Criminal Nuisance Laws | |
|---|---|---|
| | **Civil Nuisance Laws** | **Criminal Nuisance Laws** |
| **Activities the laws target** | Unhealthy, immoral or obnoxious behavior which may be, but is not necessarily, a violation of the criminal law as well | Criminal behavior |
| **Examples of targeted activities** | Excessive noise, piles of garbage and trash and inordinate amounts of foot or car traffic | Drug dealing, prostitution, gambling and gang activities |
| **Who can sue** | Public agencies such as city health departments, law enforcement agencies and, in many states, affected neighbors, who may band together and sue for large sums in small claims court. | Law enforcement agencies only |
| **How landlord's liability is determined** | "Preponderance of evidence" shows landlord intentionally tolerated the illegal activity, or was negligent or reckless in allowing it to occur | Prosecutor must prove guilt "beyond a reasonable doubt" and usually must show landlord had some knowledge of illegal activity |
| **Possible consequences to the landlord** | A court ordering the offending tenant, and sometimes the landlord, to compensate other tenants. If a health, fire or other enforcement agency brings the nuisance action based on many violations, it can result in a court order closing down the entire building. | Liability for money damages plus fines and imprisonment. Government may also close the property. |

## Know the Law

It is important to know the nuisance laws in your state. At the very least, it will alert you to the standard by which your actions (or inaction) will be judged should there be proceedings brought against you or your property. Chapter 18 gives tips on how to unearth the laws that apply to you.

## Designer Nuisance Laws

The public nuisance statutes in some states are fine-tuned to efficiently deal with offending tenants with a minimum of court entanglement.

- Laws in Rhode Island and Missouri specify that if the landlord is aware of certain illegal activity, including drug dealing, occurring on the premises, the lease is rendered void and the tenant must vacate. The landlord does not need to take any legal action—that is, file an eviction lawsuit—even if there isn't a criminal conviction for the tenant's offense. Of course, the physical removal of the tenant is still up to the landlord and the local sheriff.
- Florida's way to deal with drug dealing involves local administrative boards that receive complaints and hold hearings regarding alleged nuisances. These boards have the power to shut down the premises for up to one year.
- In Texas, 10% of the voters in any voting district may require the district attorney to call a public meeting regarding any alleged nuisance. The property owner is notified of the meeting, and the results of the meeting are forwarded to the district attorney, who may take steps to close the property.

### 4. Your Neighbors' Rights

Overworked and understaffed police and health departments are often unable to make a real dent in problem-plagued neighborhoods.

Determined tenants and neighbors have stepped into the breach, bringing their own lawsuits, seeking the elimination of the offensive behavior. Basically, tenants and neighbors may sue a landlord for failing to take steps to clean up the property, and seek:

- monetary compensation for each of them for having put up with the situation. Each neighbor generally sues for the maximum allowed in state small claims court ($3,000 to $7,500 in most states), and the landlord often pays the maximum to *each* one. (See the discussion of small claims courts in Chapter 16.)
- an order from the judge directing the landlord to evict the troublemakers, install security and repair the premises. Such orders are not available in all states.

Private use of nuisance abatement laws is not as common as governmental use, but the practice will probably grow as neighbors learn of the remedy and read about successful cases in the press. Landlords are not entirely defenseless when faced with these charges, since most statutes require that the owner have some knowledge, however slight, of the offending activity. However, common sense tells you that it will be quite difficult to assert your ignorance in the face of festering problems, repeated complaints and ineffective police raids. The best approach to the threat of nuisance lawsuits is vigilance and consistent prevention.

Many laws proscribing nuisances are "neighbor friendly"—that is, an offended neighbor doesn't need to have the resources of Scotland Yard to successfully use them. For example, in New York City a local ordinance allows neighbors within 200 feet of property used as a "bawdy house" or for other illegal activity to begin summary eviction proceedings against the tenants if the owner does not take steps to correct the problem after being given five days' notice. (New York City Administrative Code, §§ C16 and following.) A notable aspect of the ordinance is that the neighbors need not prove specific acts of illegality; all they need show is the ill repute of the premises or of those renting or using it. (*Kellner v. Cappellini,* 516 N.Y.S.2d 827 (NY City Civ. Ct. 1986).)

### Small (But Sometimes Mighty) Claims Court

The private enforcement of public nuisance laws has been creatively and successfully pursued in small claims courts in California and several other states, where groups of affected neighbors have brought multiple lawsuits targeted at drug houses.

In one case in Berkeley, California, after failing to get the police and city council to close down a crack house, neighbors sought damages stemming from the noxious activities associated with a crack house. Each of the 18 plaintiffs collected the maximum amount allowed in small claims court ($3,500 at the time), avoided the expense of hiring counsel and sent the landlord a very clear and expensive message. The problem was solved within a few weeks.

## 5. Federal and State Forfeiture Laws

Federal and state forfeiture proceedings—where the government *takes* your property because of the illegal activities of one or more tenants—are the most dramatic and devastating consequence of owning crime-ridden rental property. Forfeitures are relatively rare, and not something you are likely to encounter if you have followed the suggestions in this book for choosing decent tenants and maintaining safe and secure rental property. Nonetheless, you definitely need to understand what is involved, since the effects of a successful forfeiture proceeding are final and devastating: The government now owns your property. Compare this result to the other consequences we have discussed in this book: While damage awards in individual lawsuits may be significant and even astronomical, they do not deprive the owner of title to his property; and even abatement actions are generally temporary in effect.

Unlike the nuisance abatement laws, which depend upon the establishment of a pervasive and continuing pattern of illegal activity, forfeitures may be accomplished on the basis of a single incident. Also, unlike nuisance abatement laws, which temporarily deprive the you of the use of your property, the consequence of a forfeiture is the complete and final transfer of title to the government.

Most forfeiture laws extend to both the site of the illegal activity and the proceeds from the activity. If you know, or have reason to know, that a tenant's rent has been "earned" in the course of an illegal act, the rent money is itself forfeitable, irrespective of the site of the illegal act. A clever dealer may live in your nice, respectable building and conduct his trade elsewhere—but if he pays the rent with the money received in his drug transactions, the rent money will be forfeited if the government can show that you knew (or had reason to know) of its source.

It is harder for the government to prove that you knew of the source of the rental payments than it is to show that you knew that the premises had become a site for illegal activity—but it is not impossible. To protect yourself against a charge that you knew (or should have known) of the "dirty" source of your tenant's rental payments, your best bet is to be able to point to your careful background check (regarding the tenant's job, credit and bank account) that you performed before renting to the tenant. (See Chapter 1.) If you can show that there appeared to be a legitimate and sufficient source of income to cover the rent, it will be harder for the government to argue that it should have been obvious that the rent constituted ill-gotten gain. Your refusal to accept cash rent may help protect you from an assertion that the rent was the fruit of a drug transaction. Of course, if you do perform the background checks recommended in Chapter 1, you reduce the chances that you will unwittingly rent to a professional drug dealer.

> EXAMPLE: Sterling Properties hired a management firm to run several apartment buildings it owned in a high-crime area. At one of the complexes, there were repeated drug arrests and complaints from neighbors regarding incessant comings and goings of strange people at all hours. The government initiated forfeiture proceedings. Sterling opposed the forfeiture on the grounds that it had not been informed by its management company of the situation, and therefore it had no knowledge of the illegal activities of the tenants. The court held that the neighborhood was a virtual "anthill" of illegality, that any reasonable person would know of the involvement of the tenants and that the knowledge of the management company could be imputed to the owners. The building was forfeited and became the property of the United States government.

## a.  Federal Forfeiture Laws

On the federal level, the Comprehensive Drug Abuse Prevention and Control Act of 1970 (21 U.S.Code § 881) allows the government to seize property that has "facilitated" an illegal drug transaction, or that has been purchased or maintained with funds, such as rent payments, gained through illegal drug dealing.

The power of the federal government's forfeiture law must give any landlord pause. To initiate the proceedings, the government need only show that it is *reasonably probable* that illegal activities are occurring on the premises, and may do so by relying on circumstantial evidence and hearsay. You must then prove either that the property did not facilitate the crime, or that the tenants' activities were done without your knowledge or consent. Your deliberate blindness will be of no avail. To survive a forfeiture proceeding, you must show that you have done *all* that reasonably could be expected to prevent the illegal use of your property.

## b.  State Forfeiture Laws

Every state has adopted the Uniform Controlled Substances Act, modifying it to specify when property involved in crime can be seized.

The Uniform Controlled Substances Act specifies that land involved in drug transactions is *not* forfeitable. However, the statute provides that "containers" of drugs are forfeitable, and some states (including Washington and Michigan) have interpreted that term to include property interests—for example, the rental property where the drugs were kept. In many states, the Act has been changed to include rental or other property that has "facilitated" the illegal act.

Under every state's version of the Act, you must be shown to have "knowledge" of the illegal activity in order for forfeiture to occur, but statutes and court decisions have resulted in tremendous variation in the meaning of that term. In Florida and Rhode Island, the state need only show constructive knowledge of drug dealing—that is, what a reasonable person in the circumstances would conclude—whereas in South Dakota and Missouri, the state must prove that you actually knew of the drug problem. In Arizona, California, Idaho and Iowa, landowners are held accountable if it can be shown that they were negligent in not knowing of the drug-related activities of their tenants. In Texas, even a non-negligent, truly innocent landowner has no defense if his property is put to illegal use.

## 6. What You Can Do to Prevent Drug Lawsuits and Seizures

Carefully managing your property so as to minimize the possibility that tenants will be burglarized or assaulted (by strangers or other tenants) will go a long way toward preventing the development of situations that lead to abatement and nuisance actions. If you follow these steps, it is unlikely that a tenancy will deteriorate to the point that neighbors or the government feel it is necessary to step in and take over:

- Carefully screen potential renters.
- Keep the results of your background checks that show that your tenants' rent appeared to come from legitimate sources (jobs and bank accounts).
- Don't accept cash rental payments.

- Include a clause in your lease or rental agreement prohibiting drug dealing and other illegal activity and promptly evict tenants who violate the clause. Chapter 17 discusses expedited eviction procedures which make it easier to evict drug-dealing tenants.
- Make your presence and interest in keeping drug dealing out of the building or neighborhood known among your renters.
- Respond to tenant and neighbor complaints about drug dealing on the rental property.
- Be aware of heavy traffic in and out of the rental premises.
- Inspect rental premises and improve lighting and security.
- Get advice from police and security professionals *immediately* upon learning of a problem.
- Consult with security experts to determine whether you have done all that one could reasonably expect to discover and prevent illegal activity on your property. ■

Chapter **13**

# Landlord's Right of Entry and Tenants' Privacy

Next to disputes over rent or security deposits, one of the most common—and emotion-filled—misunderstandings between landlords and tenants involves conflicts between your right to enter the rental property and a tenant's right to be left alone at home. What is so unfortunate is that many of these problems are unnecessary. Most can be avoided if you adopt fair—and, of course, legal—policies to enter the tenant's unit and then clearly explain these policies to the tenant from the first day of your relationship. (And if you employ a manager or management company, make sure they also follow your guidelines.)

This chapter recommends a practical approach that should keep you out of legal hot water. If you want to go further and find out exactly how courts in your state have ruled on landlord's rights of entry, see the discussion of how to research court decisions in Chapter 18.

To make sure you and your tenant are operating on the same wavelengths, be sure your lease or rental agreement includes a clause explaining your rights and responsibilities regarding access to the property. (See Clause 15 of the form agreements in Chapter 2.)

 Related topics covered in this book include:
- Recommended lease and rental agreement clause for landlord's access to rental property: Chapter 2
- How to make sure your manager doesn't violate tenants' right of privacy: Chapter 6
- How to highlight access procedures in a move-in letter to new tenants: Chapter 7
- Tenants' right of privacy and landlord's policy on guests: Chapter 8
- Procedures for respecting tenants' right of privacy while handling tenant complaints about safety and maintenance problems and conducting an annual safety inspection: Chapter 9

- How to handle disputes with tenants through negotiation, mediation and other means: Chapter 16.

## A. General Rules of Entry

In most states, the tenant's duty to pay rent is conditioned on your proper repair and maintenance of the premises. This means that, of necessity, you have a legal responsibility to keep fairly close tabs on the condition of the property. For this reason, and because it makes good sense to allow landlords reasonable access to their property, nearly every state has, by judicial decision or statute, clearly recognized the right of a landlord to legally enter rented premises while a tenant is still in residence under certain broad circumstances, such as to deal with an emergency and when the tenant gives permission. (See Sections B and C.)

### 1. Allowable Reasons for Entry

About half the states have access laws specifying the circumstances under which landlords may legally enter rented premises. (See State Laws on Landlord's Access to Rental Property in Appendix I.) Most access laws allow landlords to enter rental units to make repairs and inspect the property (see Section D) and to show property to prospective tenants or buyers (see Section E).

### 2. Notice Requirements

State access laws typically specify the amount of notice required for landlord entry—usually 24 hours or two days (unless it is impracticable to do so—for example, in cases of emergency). A few states simply require the landlord to provide "reasonable" notice, often presumed to be 24 hours. (See "How Much Notice You Must Give Tenants," below.)

# How Much Notice You Must Give Tenants

This is a synopsis of state laws on the amount of notice landlords must give tenants before they enter. For details on reasons landlords may enter, and citations for state privacy laws, see "State Laws on Landlord's Access to Rental Property" in Appendix I.

| State | Amount of notice required for landlord to enter | State | Amount of notice required for landlord to enter |
|---|---|---|---|
| Alabama | No statute | Montana | 24 Hours |
| Alaska | 24 Hours | Nebraska | One Day |
| Arizona | Two Days | Nevada | 24 Hours |
| Arkansas | No statute | New Hampshire | Notice which is adequate under the circumstances |
| California | 24 Hours | | |
| Colorado | No statute | New Jersey | No statute |
| Connecticut | Reasonable notice | New Mexico | No notice requirements in statute |
| Delaware | Two Days | New York | No statute |
| District of Columbia | No statute | North Carolina | No statute |
| Florida | 12 Hours | North Dakota | Reasonable notice |
| Georgia | No statute | Ohio | 24 Hours |
| Hawaii | Two Days | Oklahoma | One Day |
| Idaho | No statute | Oregon | 24 Hours |
| Illinois | No statute | Pennsylvania | No statute |
| Indiana | No statute | Rhode Island | Two Days |
| Iowa | 24 Hours | South Carolina | 24 Hours |
| Kansas | Reasonable notice | South Dakota | No statute |
| Kentucky | Two Days | Tennessee | No notice requirements in statute |
| Louisiana | No statute | Texas | No statute |
| Maine | 24 Hours | Utah | No notice requirements in statute |
| Maryland | No statute | Vermont | 48 Hours |
| Massachusetts | No notice requirements in statute | Virginia | Reasonable notice |
| Michigan | No statute | Washington | Two Days |
| Minnesota | Reasonable notice | West Virginia | No statute |
| Mississippi | No statute | Wisconsin | Reasonable notice |
| Missouri | No statute | Wyoming | No statute |

## How to Respect Tenants' Privacy Rights

Step 1:  Know and comply with your state's law on landlord's access to rental property.

Step 2:  Include a lease or rental agreement clause that complies with the law and gives you reasonable rights of entry.

Step 3:  To avoid any uncertainty, highlight your policies on entry in a move-in letter to new tenants and other periodic communications.

Step 4:  Notify tenants whenever you plan to enter their rental unit.

Step 5:  Provide as much notice as possible before you enter, or at a minimum the amount of time required by state law.

Step 6:  Keep written records of your requests to enter rental units.

Step 7:  Protect yourself from a tenant's claim that you or your employee or independent contractor is a thief—for example, try to arrange repairs only when the tenant is home.

Step 8:  Meet—and possibly mediate—with any tenants who object to your reasonable access policies to come up with a mutual agreement regarding your entry.

Step 9:  Never force entry, short of a true emergency.

Step 10: Consider terminating the tenancy of any tenant who unreasonably restricts your right to enter the rental unit.

### a.  Must Notice Be in Writing?

State access laws do not uniformly require that notice be in writing, but it's a good idea to give written notice. If the tenant later claims that you didn't follow legal procedures regarding right to entry, your copy of a written notice that you mailed, left in the tenant's mailbox or posted on his door is proof that you notified him in advance of your in-

tention to enter. (It's also wise to document all oral requests for entry.) A sample letter requesting entry and a formal notice of intent to enter a dwelling unit are included in Section D, below.

### b.  Time of Day You May Enter

Most state access laws either do not specify the hours when a landlord may enter or simply allow entry at "reasonable" times, without setting specific hours and days. Weekdays between 9 a.m. and 6 p.m. would seem to be reasonable times, and perhaps Saturday mornings between 10 a.m. and 1 p.m. On the other hand, some statutes are more specific, such as California ("normal business hours") and Delaware (between 8 a.m. and 9 p.m.).

## 3. The Best Approach

If your state does not set specific rules regarding landlords' entry, this doesn't mean you can—or should—enter a tenant's home at any time for any reason. Once you rent residential property, you must respect it as your tenant's home. We recommend you provide as much notice as possible (in writing), try to arrange a mutually convenient time, and only enter for clearly legitimate business reasons, such as to make necessary repairs. Section D provides an expanded discussion of the best approach to entry. If it's not an emergency or clearly impractical, try to give at least 24 hours' notice, especially when entering a rental unit when the tenant is likely to be home. In some circumstances, less notice (say, ten or 15 hours) might be fine—for example, if you find out Thursday evening that an electrician is available Friday morning to put extra outlets in the tenant's apartment. Except for an emergency, less than four hours' notice is not ordinarily considered reasonable. Common sense suggests that you be considerate of your tenants' privacy and do your best to accommodate their schedules. You'll go a long way toward keeping tenants, and avoid disputes and legal problems by doing so.

## B. Entry in Case of Emergency

In all states, you can enter a rental unit without giving notice to respond to a true emergency—such as a fire or gas leak—that threatens life or property if not corrected immediately.

Here are some examples of emergency situations when it would be legal to enter without giving the tenant notice:

- Smoke is pouring out the tenant's window. You call the fire department and use your master key—or even break in if necessary—to try to deal with the fire.
- You see water coming out of the bottom of a tenant's back door. It's okay to enter and find the water leak.
- Your on-site manager hears screams coming from the apartment next door. He knocks on the apartment door, but no one answers. After calling the police, he uses his pass key to enter and see what's wrong.

On the other hand, your urge to repair a problem that's important but doesn't threaten life or property —say, a stopped-up drain that is not causing any damage—isn't a true emergency that would allow entry without proper notice.

If you do have to enter a tenant's apartment in an emergency, be sure to leave a note or call the tenant explaining the circumstances and the date and time you entered. Here's an example:

---

September 2, 199x

Dear Tammy,

Due to your oven being left on, I had to enter your apartment this afternoon around 3 o'clock. Apparently, you left your apartment while bread was still in the oven, and didn't return in time to take it out. Joe, your upstairs neighbor, called me and reported smoke and a strong burning smell coming from your kitchen window, which is below his. I entered your apartment and turned the oven off and removed the bread. Please be more careful next time.

Sincerely,

*Herb Layton*

Herb Layton

---

To facilitate your right of entry in an emergency, make sure your lease or rental agreement forbids tenants from re-keying, adding additional locks or installing a security system without your permission. (See Clause 12 of the form agreements in Chapter 2.) If you grant permission to change or add locks, make sure your tenant gives you duplicate keys. If you allow the tenant to install a security system, make sure you get the name and phone number of the alarm company or instructions on how to disarm the system in an emergency.

⚠ **Don't change locks.** If your tenant installs a lock without your permission, don't change the lock, even if you immediately give the tenant a key. This invites a lawsuit and false claims that you tried to lock the tenant out or stole the tenant's possessions. Section I discusses how to deal with tenants who unreasonably deny entry.

## C. Entry With the Permission of the Tenant

You can always enter rental property, even without notice, if the tenant agrees. If your need to enter is only occasional, you can probably rely on a friendly telephone call to the tenant asking for permission.

EXAMPLE: Because of corrosion problems with the pipes leading to water heaters, you want to check out all apartments in your building. You call your tenants, explain the situation, and arrange a mutually convenient date and time to inspect the pipes.

If the tenant agrees to let you enter his apartment or rental unit, but has been difficult and not always reliable in the past, you might even want to cover yourself by documenting the tenant's apparent co-operation. Send him a confirmatory thank-you note and keep a copy for yourself. If this note is met with unease or outright hostility, you should send the tenant a formal notice of your intent to enter. (See Section D, below.)

If you have a maintenance problem that needs regular attention—for example, a fussy heater or temperamental plumbing—you might want to work out a detailed agreement with the tenant covering entry.

⚠ **Don't be too insistent on entry.** If you pressure a tenant for permission to enter, perhaps implying or even threatening eviction if the tenant doesn't allow immediate or virtually unrestricted access, you may face a lawsuit for invasion of privacy.

## D. Entry to Make Repairs or Inspect the Property

Many states, either by statute or court decision, allow you and your repair person to enter the tenant's home to make necessary or agreed-upon repairs, alterations or improvements or to inspect the rental property.

### 1. Entry to Make Repairs

If you need to make a repair—for example, to fix a broken oven, replace the carpet or check the point of entry of a persistent ant infestation—you generally must enter only at reasonable times and you must give at least the required amount of notice, usually 24 hours. However, if this is impracticable—for example, a repair person is available on a few hours' notice—you will probably be on solid ground if you explain the situation to your tenant and then give shorter notice. Of course, if your tenant agrees to a shorter notice period, you have no problem. (See Section C, above.)

EXAMPLE: Amy told her landlord Tom that her bathroom sink was stopped up and draining very slowly. Tom called the plumber, who said that he had several large jobs in progress, but would be able to squeeze in Amy's repair at some point within the next few days. The plumber promised to call Tom before he came over. Tom relayed this information to Amy, telling her he would give her at least four hours' notice before the plumber came.

### 2. How to Give Tenants Notice of Entry

In many situations, the notice period will not be a problem, since your tenant will be delighted that you are making needed repairs and will cooperate with your entry requirements. However, as every experienced landlord knows, some tenants are uncooperative when it comes to providing reasonable access to make repairs, while at the same time demanding that repairs be made immediately. (Of course, if the time is really inconvenient for the tenant—you want to make a non-emergency repair the day your tenant is preparing dinner for her new in-laws—try to be accommodating and reschedule a more convenient appointment.)

Here's how to avoid having a tenant claim that you violated his legal right of privacy:

- Meet your state notice requirements; or, if there's no specified amount of notice, provide at least 24 hours' notice.

- Try to reach the tenant at home or at work to give the required amount of notice. Make sure you know how to reach the tenant during the day to give required notice.

- Provide written notice as much as possible—either a brief letter or a formal notice (see samples below).

- If you give notice orally, document this fact by keeping a log of your requests for entry.

- If you can't reach the tenant personally or by phone, and if your intended date of entry is too soon to enable you to send a letter, it's a good idea to post a note detailing your plan on the tenant's front door. If, despite all of these efforts, your tenant does not receive notice, you are probably on solid ground, in most states, to enter and do the repair, since you have done all that could reasonably be expected to comply with the notice requirements.

- Keep a copy of all requests for entry (written and oral) in your tenant's file, along with other communications, such as Maintenance/Repair Request forms (discussed in Chapter 9).

Section I, below, discusses how to handle tenants who unreasonably deny entry.

You will find a Notice of Intent to Enter Dwelling Unit on the Legal Forms Disk as well as a blank tear-out copy in Appendix II.

**Let the tenant know if your plans change.** A tenant may be justifiably annoyed if you or your repair person show up late or not at all—for example, if you're supposed to come at 2 p.m. and don't show up until 8 a.m. the next morning. If it isn't possible to come on time in the first place, call the tenant and explain the problem, and ask permission to enter later on. If the tenant denies permission, you'll have to give a second notice.

### Sample Letter Requesting Entry

January 5, 199X

Anna Rivera
123 East Avenue, Apartment 4
Rochester, New York 14610

Dear Ms. Rivera:

In response to your complaint regarding the garbage disposal in your apartment, I have arranged to have it repaired tomorrow, on Tuesday, January 6, at 2:00 P.M. I attempted to reach you today (both at your home and work phone numbers) and notify you of this repair appointment. Because I was unable to reach you by phone, I am leaving this note on your door.

Sincerely,
*Marlene Morgan*

## 3. Entry to Inspect for Needed Repairs

It's an excellent idea to inspect your rental properties at least once or twice a year. That way you can find small problems before they become big ones, and tenants can't claim that they didn't have an opportunity to report complaints to you. (Chapter 9 discusses inspections.)

The lease and rental agreements in this book (see Clause 17 in Chapter 2) give you the right to

## Notice of Intent to Enter Dwelling Unit

To: _Anna Rivera_
Tenant
_123 East Avenue, Apt. #4_
Street address
_Rochester, New York_
City and State

THIS NOTICE is to inform you that on _____ January 7, 199X _____,

[X] at approximately ___1:00___ ~~AM~~/PM the landlord, or the landlord's agent, will enter the premises for the following reason:

[X] To make or arrange for the following repairs or improvements:

_fix garbage disposal_

_____

_____

_____

_____

[ ] To show the premises to:

   [ ] a prospective tenant or purchaser

   [X] workers or contractors regarding the above repair or improvement

[ ] Other: _____

_____

_____

You are, of course, welcome to be present. If you have any questions or if the date or time is inconvenient, please notify me promptly at _____ 716-555-7899 _____.

                                          Phone number

_January 5, 199X_       _Marlene Morgan_
Date                Landlord/Manager

enter a tenant's unit—after giving reasonable notice—to make this kind of regular inspection.

If you don't have a clause on access in your lease or rental agreement, state law may give you the right anyway. All states with privacy statutes, except California and Utah, grant this right to inspect rental property. In other states, you must determine whether or not the courts in your state have addressed the issue of landlord inspections. (See Chapter 18 for information on doing legal research yourself.)

**⚠ Don't use the right to inspect improperly.** Don't use your right to access to harass or annoy the tenant. Repeated inspections absent a specific reason, even when proper notice is given, are an invitation to a lawsuit.

### 4. Entry During Tenant's Extended Absence

Several states with privacy statutes give landlords the specific legal right to enter the rental unit during a tenant's extended absence, often defined as seven days or more. You are allowed entry to maintain the property as necessary and to inspect for damage and needed repairs. For example, if you live in a cold-weather place, such as Connecticut, it makes sense to check the pipes in rental units to make sure they haven't burst when the tenant is away for winter vacation.

While many states do not address this issue, either by way of statute or court decision, you should be on safe legal ground to enter rental property during a tenant's extended absence, as long as there is a genuine need to protect the property from damage. You should enter only if something really needs to be done—that is something that the tenant would do if he were home, as part of his obligation to keep the property clean, safe and in good repair. (See Chapter 9, Section B, for a discussion of tenant repair and maintenance responsibilities.) For example, if the tenant leaves the windows wide open just before a driving rainstorm, you would be justified in entering to close them.

**💡 Require tenants to report extended absences.** To protect yourself and make sure your tenant knows what to expect, be sure your lease or rental agreement requires the tenant to inform you when he will be gone for an extended time, such as two weeks, and alerts him of your intent to enter the premises during these times if necessary. (See Clause 16 of the form agreements in Chapter 2.)

### How to Avoid Tenant Theft Claims

By planning ahead, you can minimize the chances that you or your repair persons will be accused of theft. Give plenty of notice of your entry—this gives the tenant the chance to hide valuables. Try to arrange repairs or visit the rental unit only when the tenant is home. If that's not possible, you or your manager should be present. Carefully check references of plumbers and other repair people, and only allow people whom you trust to enter alone.

## E. Entry to Show Property to Prospective Tenants or Buyers

Most states with access laws allow landlords to enter rented property to show it to prospective tenants toward the end of a tenancy or to prospective purchasers if you wish to sell the property. Follow the same notice procedures for entry to make repairs, discussed in Section D, above. As always, be sure your lease or rental agreement authorizes this type of entry. (See Clause 15 of the form agreements in Chapter 2.)

You can use the same Notice of Intent to Enter Dwelling Unit as the one used for entry to make repairs.

## 1. Showing Property to Prospective New Tenants

If you don't plan to renew a tenant's about-to-expire lease, or have given or received a notice terminating a month-to-month tenancy, you may show the premises to prospective new tenants during the last few weeks (or even months) of the outgoing tenant's stay. It is not a good idea, however, to show property if the current tenant is under the impression that his lease or rental agreement will be renewed, or if a dispute exists over whether the current tenant has a right to stay. If there's a chance the dispute will end up in court as an eviction lawsuit, the current tenant may be able to hang on for several weeks or even months. Insisting on showing the property in this situation only causes unnecessary friction at the same time that it's of little value, since you will be unable to tell the new tenants when they can move in.

The form lease and rental agreements in this book include a clause that may limit your liability if, for reasons beyond your control, you must delay a new tenant's move-in date after you've signed a lease or rental agreement. (See Clause 17 in Chapter 2.)

## 2. Showing Property to Prospective Buyers

You may also show your property—whether apartments in a multiple-unit building, a rented single-family house or condominium unit—to potential buyers or mortgage companies. Remember to give the required amount of notice to your tenant. It's also a good idea to tell the tenant the name and phone number of the realty company handling the property sale and the particular real estate agent or broker involved.

Problems usually occur when an overeager real estate salesperson shows up on the tenant's doorstep without warning, or calls on very short notice and asks to be let in to show the place to a possible buyer. In this situation, the tenant is within his right

to say "I'm busy right now—try again in a few days after we've set a time convenient for all of us." Naturally, this type of misunderstanding is not conducive to good landlord-tenant relations, not to mention a sale of the property. Make sure the real estate salespeople you deal with understand the law and respect your tenants' rights to advance notice.

## 3. Putting For Sale or For Rent Signs on the Property

Occasionally, friction is caused by landlords who put signs on tenants' homes, such as "For Sale" or "For Rent" signs in front of an apartment building or a rented single-family house. Even if the sign says "Don't Disturb the Occupant" and you are conscientious about giving notice before showing property, prospective buyers or renters may nonetheless disturb the tenant with unwelcome inquiries.

When thinking about this, it pays to put yourself in the tenant's shoes and realize that a tenant who likes where he is living will often feel threatened and insecure about a potential sale. A new owner may mean a rent increase or eviction notice if the new owner wants to move in herself. In this situation, if your tenant's privacy is ruined by repeated inquiries the tenant may even resort to suing you for invasion of privacy, just as if you personally had made repeated illegal entries.

To head off this possibility, consider not putting a For Sale sign on the property. In this age of computerized multiple-listing services and video house listings, signs aren't always necessary. Indeed, many real estate agents sell houses and other real estate without ever placing a For Sale sign on the property, except when an open house is in progress. If you or your real estate agent must put up a sign advertising sale or rental of the property, make sure it clearly warns against disturbing the occupant and includes a telephone number to call—for example, "Shown by Appointment Only" or "Inquire at 555-1357—Do Not Disturb Occupant Under Any Circumstances." If your real estate agent refuses to accommodate you, find a new one who will respect your tenants' privacy and keep you out of a lawsuit.

⚠ **Don't use a lockbox.** Under no circumstances should an owner of occupied rental property that is listed for sale allow the placing of a key-holding "lockbox" on the door. This is a metal box that attaches to the front door and contains the key to that door. It can be opened by a master key held by area real estate salespeople. Since a lockbox allows a salesperson to enter in disregard of notice requirements, it should not be used—period. A lockbox will leave you wide open to a tenant's lawsuit for invasion of privacy, and possibly liable for any property the tenant claims to have lost.

### 4. Getting the Tenant's Cooperation

Showing a house or apartment building occupied by a tenant isn't easy on anyone. At times, you will want to show the property on short notice. And you may even want to have an occasional open house on weekends. From your tenant's point of view, any actions you take to show the property to strangers may seem like an intolerable intrusion. Also, if you're selling the property, your tenant may feel threatened by the change in ownership.

Obviously, the best way to achieve your ends is with the cooperation of the tenant. One good plan is to meet with the tenant in advance and offer a reasonable rent reduction in exchange for cooperation—for example, two open houses a month and showing the unit on two-hour notice, as long as it doesn't occur more than five times a week. Depending on how much the tenant will be inconvenienced, 10% to 20% rent reduction might be reasonable. However, you should realize that this type of agreement is in force only so long as the tenant continues to go along with it. Technically, any written agreement changing the rent is really an amendment to the rental agreement, and rental agreement clauses under which tenants give up their privacy rights are typically void and unenforceable if it comes to a court fight. This may be one situation when an informal understanding that the rent be lowered so long as the tenant agrees to the frequent showings may be better than a written agreement.

## F. Entry After the Tenant Has Moved Out

To state the obvious, you may enter the premises at any time after the tenant has completely moved out. It doesn't matter whether the tenant left voluntarily after giving back the key, or involuntarily following a successful eviction lawsuit.

In addition, if you believe a tenant has abandoned the property—that is, skipped out without giving any notice or returning the key—you may legally enter.

## G. Entry by Others

This section describes situations when other people, such as municipal inspectors, may want entry to your rental property.

### 1. Health, Safety or Building Inspections

While your state may set guidelines for your entry to rental property, the rules are different when it comes to entry by state or local health, safety or building inspectors.

## a. Neighbor's Complaints

If inspectors have credible reasons to suspect that a tenant's rental unit violates housing codes or local standards—for example, a neighbor has complained about noxious smells coming from the tenant's home or about his 20 cats—they will usually knock on the tenant's door and ask permission to enter. Except in the case of genuine emergency, your tenant has the right to say no.

Inspectors have ways to get around tenant refusals. A logical first step (maybe even before they stop by the rental unit) is to ask you to let them in. Since you can usually enter on 24 hours' notice, this is probably the simplest approach. We recommend that you cooperate with all such requests for entry. If inspectors can't reach you, (or you don't cooperate), their next step will probably be to get a search warrant based on the information from the tenant's neighbor. The inspectors must first convince a judge that the source of their information—the neighbor—is reliable, and that there is a strong likelihood that public health or safety is at risk. Inspectors who believe that a tenant will refuse entry often bring along police officers who, armed with a search warrant, have the right to do whatever it takes to overcome the tenant's objections.

## b. Random Inspections

Fire, health and other municipal inspectors sometimes randomly inspect apartment buildings even if they don't suspect noncompliance. These inspections may be allowed under state law or local ordinance. (Most ordinances exempt single-family homes and condominiums.) Your tenant has the right to say no. But this will buy only a little time, since you will probably allow the inspection. If not, the inspector will almost surely have a judge issue a search warrant, allowing him to enter to check for fire or

safety violations. Again, if there is any expectation that your tenant may resist, a police officer will usually accompany the inspector.

### States With Municipal Inspections

Some cities in the following states have municipal inspection programs:

| | |
|---|---|
| California | New Jersey (statewide and |
| Colorado | additional city ordinances) |
| Florida | North Carolina |
| Illinois | Ohio |
| Indiana | Pennsylvania |
| Kansas | South Dakota |
| Louisiana | Texas |
| Minnesota | Utah |
| Missouri | Virginia (statewide) |
| | Washington |

To find out whether your city has such a program, call your city manager's or mayor's office.

An inspector who arrives when the tenant is not home may ask you to open the door on the spot, in violation of your state's privacy laws. If the inspector's come with a warrant, you can probably give consent, since even the tenant couldn't prevent entry. But if the inspector is there without a warrant, you probably cannot speak for the tenant and say "Come on in." However, the answer will depend on each state's interpretation of its laws regarding warrantless entries. Since municipal inspection programs are relatively new, few courts have decided the issue. Cautious landlords will ask an inspector without a warrant to enter after they have given the tenant the proper amount of notice, under their state's law or the terms of your their lease or rental agreement.

## c. Inspection Fees

Many cities impose fees for inspections, on a per unit or building basis or a sliding scale based on the number of your holdings. Some fees are imposed only if violations are found. If your ordinance imposes fees regardless of violations, you may pass the inspection cost on to the tenant in the form of a rent hike. It's not illegal to do this, and even in rent-controlled cities, the cost of an inspection might justify a rent increase. (See Chapter 3 for information on how you may legally increase rents.)

If your ordinance imposes a fee only when violations are found, you should not pass the cost on to the tenant if the non-compliance is not his fault. For example, if inspectors find that you failed to install state-mandated smoke alarms, you should pay for the inspection; but if the tenant has allowed garbage to pile up in violation of city health laws, the tenant should pay the inspector's bill.

## 2. Police

Even the police may not enter a tenant's rental unit unless they can show you or your tenant a recently issued search or arrest warrant, signed by a judge. The police do not need a search warrant, however, if they need to enter to prevent a catastrophe, such as an explosion, or if they are in hot pursuit of a fleeing criminal.

## 3. Your Right to Let Others In

You should not give others permission to enter a tenant's home. (Municipal inspections, however, may pose an exception.)

Occasionally, you or your resident manager will be faced with a very convincing stranger who will tell a heart-rending story:

- "I'm Nancy's boyfriend and I need to get my clothes out of her closet now that I'm moving to New York."
- "If I don't get my heart medicine that I left in this apartment, I'll die on the spot" or
- "I'm John's father and I just got in from the North Pole, where a polar bear ate my wallet, and I have no other place to stay."

The problem arises when you can't contact the tenant at work or elsewhere to ask whether it's okay to let the desperate individual in. This is one reason why you should always know how to reach your tenants during the day.

The story the desperate person tells you may be the truth, and chances are that if your tenant could be contacted, she would say "Yes, let Uncle Harry in immediately." But you can't know this, and it doesn't make sense to expose yourself to the potential liability involved should you get taken in by a clever con artist. There is always the chance that the person is really a smooth talker whom your tenant has a dozen good reasons to want kept out. You risk being legally responsible should your tenant's property be stolen or damaged. If you do let a stranger in without your tenant's permission, you may be sued for invasion of privacy for any loss your tenant suffers as a result.

In short, never let a stranger into your tenant's home without your tenant's permission. Even if you have been authorized to allow a certain person to enter, it is wise to ask for identification. Although this no-entry-without-authorization policy may sometimes be difficult to adhere to in the face of a convincing story, stick to it. You have much more to lose in admitting the wrong person to the tenant's home than you would have to gain by letting in someone who's "probably okay."

# H. Other Types of Invasions of Privacy

Entering a tenant's home without his knowledge or consent isn't the only way you can interfere with the tenant's privacy. Here are a few other common situations, with advice on how to handle them.

## 1. Giving Information About the Tenant to Strangers

As a landlord, you may be asked by strangers, including creditors, banks and prospective landlords, to provide credit or other information about your tenant. Did she pay the rent on time? Did she maintain the rental property? Cause any problems?

Basically, you have a legal right to give out normal business information about your tenant to people and businesses who ask and have a legitimate reason to know—for example, the tenant's bank when she applies for a loan or a prospective landlord who wants a reference. Resist your natural urge to be helpful, unless the tenant has given you written permission to release this sort of information. (We discuss release forms in Chapter 1.) You have nothing to gain, and possibly a lot to lose, if you give out information that your tenant feels constitutes a serious violation of her privacy.

And if you give out incorrect information—even if you believe it to be accurate—you can really be in a legal mess if the person to whom you disclose it relies on it to take some action that negatively affects your tenant.

> EXAMPLE: If you tell others that a tenant has filed for bankruptcy (and this isn't true), the tenant has grounds to sue you for defamation (libel or slander) if he is damaged as a result—for example, if he doesn't get a job.

Some landlords feel that they should communicate information to prospective landlords, especially if the tenant has failed to pay rent, maintain the premises or has created other serious problems. If you do give out this information, make sure you are absolutely factual and that the information you provide has been requested. If you go out of your way to give out negative information—for example, you try to blackball the tenant with other landlords in your area—you definitely risk legal liability for libeling your tenant.

⚠ **Beware of gossipy managers.** Many landlords have had serious problems with on-site managers who have gossiped about tenants who, for example, paid rent late, were served with an eviction notice, had overnight visitors or drank too much. This sort of gossip may seem innocent, but if

flagrant and damaging can be an invasion of privacy for which you can be liable. Impress on your managers their duty to keep confidential all sensitive information about tenants.

## 2. Calling or Visiting Tenants at Work

Should you need to call your tenant at work (say, to schedule a time to make repairs), try to be sensitive to whether it's permissible for him to receive personal calls. While some people work at desks with telephones and have bosses who don't get upset about occasional personal calls, others have jobs that are greatly disrupted by any phone call. A general rule seems to be that the more physical the type of the work, the more tyrannical employers are about prohibiting personal phone calls at work.

Under no circumstances should you continue to call a tenant at work who asks you not to do so. This is especially true when calling about late rent payments or other problems.

Never leave specific messages with your tenant's employer, especially those that could reflect negatively on her. A landlord who leaves a message like "Tell your deadbeat employee I'll evict her if she doesn't pay the rent" can expect at least a lot of bad feeling on the part of the tenant and, at worst, a lawsuit, especially if your conduct results in the tenant losing her job or a promotion.

As for visiting the tenant at work—say to collect late rent—this is something you should avoid unless invited. What it boils down to is that no matter what you think of your tenant, you should respect the sensitive nature of the tenant's relationship with her employer.

There may, however, be times you'll need to contact the tenant at work if you can't find the tenant at home after repeated tries—for example, to serve notice of a rent increase or an eviction notice.

### 3. Undue Restrictions on Guests

A few landlords, overly concerned about tenants moving new occupants into the property, go a little overboard in keeping tabs on the tenants' legitimate guests who stay overnight or for a few days. Often their leases, rental agreements or rules and regulations require a tenant to "register" any overnight guest.

Clause 3 of the form agreements (Chapter 2) limits guests' visits to no more than ten days in any six-month period, to avoid having a guest turn into an illegal subtenant. While you should be concerned about persons who begin as guests becoming permanent unauthorized residents, it is overkill to require a tenant to inform you of a guest whose stay is only for a day or two. Keep in mind that just because you rent your tenant her home, you don't have the right to restrict her social life or pass upon the propriety of her visitors' stays. Extreme behavior in this area—whether by you or a management employee—can be considered an invasion of privacy for which you may be held liable.

### 4. Spying on a Tenant

As a result of worrying too much about a tenant's visitors, a few landlords have attempted to interro-

gate tenants' visitors, knock on their tenants' doors at odd hours or too frequently in order to see who answers or even peek through windows. Needless to say, this sort of conduct can render you liable for punitive damages in an invasion of privacy lawsuit. As far as talking to tenants' guests is concerned, keep your conversations to pleasant hellos or non-threatening small talk.

---

### Watch Out for Drug Dealing on Your Property

It's crucial that you keep a careful eye on your tenants if you suspect they're engaging in drug dealing or other illegal behavior. Landlords have a responsibility to keep their properties safe—that includes keeping dealers out by carefully screening prospective tenants (see Chapter 1) and kicking them out pronto when they are discovered. Other tenants and neighbors, as well as government agencies, may bring costly lawsuits against landlords who allow drug dealing on their properties. Chapter 12 discusses your liability for drug-dealing tenants and how to avoid problems, while at the same time, respecting your tenants' legitimate expectations of privacy.

---

### 5. "Self-Help" Evictions

It is generally illegal for you to come on the rental property and do such things as take off windows and doors, turn off the utilities or change the locks. (Chapter 17, Section H, discusses illegal "self help" evictions.)

## I. What to Do When Tenants Unreasonably Deny Entry

Occasionally, even if you give a generous amount of notice and have a legitimate reason, a tenant may refuse to let you in. If you repeatedly encounter unreasonable refusals to let you or your employees enter the premise, you can probably legally enter anyway, provided you do so in a peaceful manner.

Never push or force your way in. Even if you have the right to be there, you can face liability for anything that goes wrong.

For practical reasons, don't enter alone. If you really need entry and the tenant isn't home, it's just common sense to bring someone along who can later act as a witness in case the tenant claims some of her property is missing.

Another problem landlords face is that some tenants have their locks changed. This is probably illegal, because it restricts your right of access in a true emergency or when you have given proper notice. As noted in Section B, above, your lease or rental agreement should require landlord key access, as well as notice of any change of locks or the installation of any burglar alarms. (See Clause 12, Chapter 2.)

If you have a serious conflict over access with an otherwise satisfactory tenant, a sensible first step is to meet with the tenant to see if the problem can be resolved. If you come to an understanding, follow up with a note to confirm your agreement. Here's an example:

---

This will confirm our conversation of ____ [date] ____ regarding access to your apartment at _____ [address] _____ for the purpose of making repairs. The management will give you 24 hours' [or two days'] advance written notice, and will enter only during business hours or weekdays. The person inspecting will knock first, then enter with a passkey if no one answers.

---

If this doesn't work, you may wish to try mediation by a neutral third party. It's an especially good way to resolve disputes when you want the tenant to stay. See Chapter 16 for details on finding and using a mediation service.

If attempts at compromise fail, you can terminate the tenancy. Unless your tenant has a long-term lease or lives in a rent control city that requires just cause for eviction, you can simply give the tenant a 30-day notice and terminate the tenancy, rather than put up with a problem tenant.

And in every state, you can usually evict the tenant, including those with long-term leases, for violating a term of the lease or rental agreement. To do this, you must comply with your state law as to reasons for entry and notice periods. (Chapter 17 provides an overview of evictions.) And your lease or rental agreement must contain an appropriate right-of-entry provision. The cause justifying eviction is the tenant's breach of that provision. (See Clause 15 in the form lease and rental agreements, Chapter 2). Keep copies of any correspondence and notes of your conversations with the tenant.

If you're heading for court, you may need to consult a lawyer or do some legal research on your state's laws on evictions. (Chapter 18 discusses legal research and lawyers.) If you do end up in court, be prepared to prove your entry was legal—as to purpose and amount of notice required. A good recordkeeping system is crucial in this regard.

## J. Tenants' Remedies If a Landlord Acts Illegally

Conscientious landlords should be receptive to a tenant's complaint that her privacy is being violated and work out an acceptable compromise. If you violate a tenant's right to privacy and you can't work out a compromise, the tenant may bring a lawsuit and ask for money damages. You may be held liable for your property manager's disrespect of the tenant's right of privacy even if you never knew about the manager's conduct. A tenant who can show a repeated pattern of illegal activity, or even one clear example of outrageous conduct, may be able to get a substantial recovery.

In most states, it's easy for a tenant to press her claim in small claims court without a lawyer. For details on small claims court procedures and the maximum amount for which someone can sue, see Chapter 16.

Depending on the circumstances, the tenant may be able sue you for:

- Trespass: entry without consent or proper authority
- Invasion of privacy: interfering with a tenant's right to be left alone
- Breach of implied covenant of quiet enjoyment: interfering with a tenant's right to undisturbed use of his home, or
- Infliction of emotional distress: doing any illegal act that you intend to cause serious emotional consequences to the tenant.

These types of lawsuits are beyond the scope of this book and require expert legal advice. (See Chapter 18 for advice on finding and working with a lawyer.)

Finally, you should know that repeated abuses by a landlord of a tenant's right of privacy may give a tenant under a lease a legal excuse to break it by moving out, without liability for further rent. ■

Chapter **14**

# Ending a Tenancy

Most tenancies end because the tenant leaves voluntarily. But little else is so uniform. Some tenants give proper legal notice and leave at the end of a lease term; others aren't so thoughtful and give inadequate notice, break the lease or just move out in the middle of the night. And, of course, some tenants fail to live up to their obligations for reasons they can't control—for example, a tenant dies during the tenancy.

Whether your rentals turn over a lot or your tenants tend to stay put for years, you should understand the important legal issues that arise at the end of a tenancy, including:

- the type of notice a landlord or tenant must provide to end a month-to-month tenancy
- your legal options if a tenant doesn't leave after receiving (or giving) a termination notice or after the lease has expired
- what happens if a tenant leaves without giving required notice
- the effect of a condominium conversion on a tenant's lease.

This chapter starts with a brief discussion of a related topic—how you may change a lease or rental agreement during a tenancy.

Related topics covered in this book include:
- How to advertise and rent property before a current tenant leaves: Chapter 1
- Writing clear lease and rental agreement provisions on notice required to end a tenancy: Chapter 2
- Raising the rent: Chapter 3
- Highlighting notice requirements in a move-in letter to the tenant: Chapter 7
- Handling tenant requests to sublet or assign the lease, and what to do when one co-tenant leaves: Chapter 8
- Preparing a move-out letter and returning security deposits when a tenant leaves: Chapter 15
- Terminating a tenancy when a tenant fails to leave after receiving a 30-day notice or violates the lease or rental agreement—for example, by not paying rent: Chapter 17.

## A. Changing Lease or Rental Agreement Terms

Once you sign a lease or rental agreement, it's a legal contract between you and your tenant. All changes should be in writing and signed by both of you.

If you use a lease, you cannot unilaterally change the terms of the tenancy for the length of the lease. For example, you can't raise the rent unless the lease allows it or the tenant agrees. If the tenant agrees to changes, however, simply follow the directions below for amending a rental agreement.

### 1. Amending a Month-to-Month Rental Agreement

You don't need a tenant's consent to change something in a month-to-month rental agreement. Legally, you need simply send the tenant a notice of the change. The most common reason landlords amend a rental agreement is to increase the rent. (Chapter 3 provides a detailed discussion of this issue.)

To change a month-to-month tenancy, most states require 30 days' notice, subject to any local rent control ordinances. (See Notice Required to Change or Terminate a Month-to-Month Tenancy in Appendix I for a list of each state's notice requirements.) You'll need to consult your state statutes for the specific information on how you must deliver a 30-day notice to the tenant. Most states allow you to deliver the notice by first-class mail.

**Contact the tenant and explain the changes.** It makes good personal and business sense for you or your manager to contact the tenant personally and tell him about a rent increase or other changes before you follow up with a written notice. If the tenant is opposed to your plan, your personal efforts will allow you to explain your reasons.

You don't generally need to re-do the entire rental agreement in order to make a change or two. It's just as legal and effective to attach a copy of the notice making the change to the rental agreement. However, you may want the change to appear on the written rental agreement itself.

If the change is small and simply alters part of an existing clause—such as increasing the rent or making the rent payable every 14 days instead of every 30 days—you can cross out the old language in the rental agreement, write in the new and sign in the margin next to the new words. Make sure the tenant also signs next to the change. Be sure to add the date, in case there is a dispute later as to when the change became effective.

If the changes are lengthy, you may either add an amendment page to the original document or prepare a new rental agreement, as discussed below. If an amendment is used, it should clearly refer to the agreement it's changing and be signed by the same people who signed the original agreement. See the sample amendment, below.

The Legal Forms Disk includes an Amendment to Lease or Rental Agreement form, and Appendix II includes a blank, tear-out version.

### 2. Preparing a New Rental Agreement

If you want to add a new clause or make several changes to your rental agreement, you will probably find it easiest to substitute a whole new agreement for the old one. This is simple to do if you use the lease or rental agreement on the Legal Forms Disk in this book. If you prepare an entire new agreement, be sure that you and the tenant both write "Canceled by mutual consent, effective (date)" on the old one, and sign it. All tenants should sign the new agreement. The new agreement should take effect on the date the old one is canceled. To avoid problems, be sure there is no time overlap between the old and new agreements, and do not allow any gap between the cancellation date of the old agreement and the effective date of the new one.

**A new tenant should mean a new agreement.** Even if a new tenant is filling out the rest of a former tenant's lease term under the same conditions, it is never wise to allow her to operate under the same lease or rental agreement. Start over and prepare a new agreement in the new tenant's name. See Chapter 8 for details on signing a new agreement when a new tenant moves in.

## B. How Month-to-Month Tenancies End

This section discusses how you or the tenant can end a month-to-month tenancy.

### 1. Giving Notice to the Tenant

If you want a tenant to move out, you can end a month-to-month tenancy simply by giving the proper amount of notice. No reasons are required in most states (New Hampshire and New Jersey are exceptions because landlords in these states must have a just or legally recognized reason to end a tenancy). In most places, all you need to do is give the tenant a simple written notice to move, allowing the tenant the minimum number of days required

## Amendment to Lease or Rental Agreement

This is an Amendment to the lease or rental agreement dated _____ March 1 _____, 199 _X_,

(the Agreement) between _____ Olivia Matthew _____

(Landlord) and _____ Steve Phillips _____

(Tenant) regarding property located at _____ 1578 Maple St., Seattle _____

_____ (the premises).

Landlord and Tenant agree to the following changes and/or additions to the Agreement:

1. Beginning on June 1, 199X, Tenant shall rent a one-car garage, adjacent to the main premises, from Landlord for the sum of $75 per month.

2. Tenant may keep one German shepherd dog on the premises. The dog shall be kept on a leash in the yard unless tenant is present. Tenant shall clean up all animal waste from the yard on a daily basis. Tenant agrees to repair any damages to the yard or premises caused by his dog, at Tenant's expense.

| May 20, 199X | Olivia Matthew, Landlord |
|---|---|
| Date | Landlord |
| May 20, 199X | Steve Phillips, Tenant |
| Date | Tenant |
| | |
| Date | Tenant |
| | |
| Date | Tenant |

by state law (typically 30), and stating the date on which the tenancy will end. (See Notice Required to Change or Terminate a Tenancy in Appendix I.) After that date, the tenant no longer has the legal right to occupy the premises.

In most states, a landlord who wants to terminate a month-to-month tenancy must provide the same amount of notice as a tenant—typically 30 days. (See subsection 2, below.) But this is not true everywhere. For example, in Georgia, landlords must give 60 days' notice to terminate a month-to-month tenancy, while tenants need only give 30 days' notice. State and local rent control laws can also impose notice requirements on landlords. Things are different if you want a tenant to move because he or she has violated a term of the rental agreement —for example, by failing to pay rent. If so, notice requirements are commonly greatly shortened, sometimes to as little as three days. (Chapter 17 discusses terminations and evictions.)

Each state, and even some cities, has its own very detailed rules and procedures for preparing and serving termination notices. For example, some states specify that the notice be printed in a certain size or style of typeface. If you don't follow these procedures, the notice terminating the tenancy may be invalid. It is impossible for this book to provide all specific forms and instructions. Consult a landlords' association or local rent control board and your state statutes for more information and sample forms. (Chapter 18 shows how to do your own legal research.) Your state consumer protection agency (see the list in Appendix I) may also have useful advice. Once you understand how much notice you must give, how the notice must be delivered and any other requirements, you'll be in good shape to handle this work yourself—usually with no lawyer needed.

## 2. How Much Notice the Tenant Must Give

In most states, the tenant who decides to move out must give you at least 30 days' notice. Some states allow less than 30 days' notice in certain situations— for example, because a tenant must leave early because of military orders or health problems. And in some states, tenants who pay rent more frequently than once a month can give notice to terminate that matches their rent payment interval—for example, tenants who pay rent every two weeks would have to give 14 days' notice.

To educate your tenants as to what they can expect, make sure your rental agreement includes your state's notice requirements for ending a tenancy. (See Clause 4 of the form agreements in Chapter 2.) It is also wise to list termination notice requirements in the move-in letter you send to new tenants. (See Chapter 7.)

For details on your state's rules, see Notice Required to Change or Terminate a Month-to-Month Tenancy in Appendix I.

### Restrictions to Ending a Tenancy

The general rules for terminating a tenancy described in this chapter don't apply in all situations:

- **Rent control ordinances.** Many rent control cities require "just cause" (a good reason) to end a tenancy, such as moving in a close relative. You will likely have to state your reason in the termination notice you give the tenant. (Chapter 3 discusses rent control.)
- **Discrimination.** It is illegal to end a tenancy because of a tenant's race, religion or other reason constituting illegal discrimination. (Chapter 5 discusses antidiscrimination laws.)
- **Retaliation.** You cannot legally terminate a tenancy to retaliate against a tenant for exercising any right under the law, such as the tenant's right to complain to governmental authorities about defective housing conditions. (Chapter 16 discusses how to avoid charges of retaliation.)

## Must Tenants Give Notice on the First of the Month?

In most states, a tenant can give notice at any time—in other words, they don't have to give notice so that the tenancy will end on the last day of the month. If a tenancy ends mid-month, the tenant will be paying rent until that date. For example, a tenant who pays rent on the first of the month, but gives notice on the tenth, will be obliged to pay for ten days' rent for the next month, even if the tenant moves out earlier.

The only exception to this general rule comes if your rental agreement requires that notice may be given only on a certain date, typically the date the rent is due. This means that if the tenant decides on the fifth that she needs to move, she'll have to wait until the first to give notice, and will be obliged to pay for the entire next month, even if she leaves earlier.

## 3. Insist on a Tenant's Written Notice of Intent to Move

In many states, a tenant's notice must be in writing and give the exact date the tenant plans to move out. Even if it is not required by law, it's a good idea to insist that the tenant give you notice in writing (as does Clause 4 of the form agreements in Chapter 2). Why bother?

Insisting on written notice will prove useful should the tenant not move as planned after you have signed a lease or rental agreement with a new tenant. The new tenant may sue you to recover the costs of temporary housing or storage fees for her belongings because you could not deliver possession of the unit. In turn, you will want to sue the old (holdover) tenant for causing the problem by failing to move out. You will have a much stronger case against the holdover tenant if you can produce a written promise to move on a specific date instead of your version of a conversation (which will undoubtedly be disputed by the tenant).

A sample Tenant's Notice of Intent to Move Out form is shown below. Give a copy of this form to any tenant who tells you he or she plans to move.

The Legal Forms Disk includes a copy of the Tenant's Notice of Intent to Move Out form. You'll also find a blank tear-out version in Appendix II.

## 4. Accepting Rent After a 30-Day Notice Is Given

If you accept rent for any period beyond the date the tenant told you he is moving out, this cancels the termination notice and creates a new month-to-month tenancy. This means you must give the tenant another 30-day notice to start the termination process again.

EXAMPLE: On April 15, George sends his landlord Yuri a 30-day notice of his intent to move out. A few weeks later, however, George changes his mind and decides to stay. He simply pays the usual $500 monthly rent on May 1. Without thinking, Yuri cashes the $500 check. Even though she's already re-rented to a new tenant who plans to move in on May 16th, Yuri is powerless to evict George unless she first gives him a legal (usually 30-day) notice to move. Unless the lease Yuri signed with the new tenant limits her liability, she will be liable to the new tenant for failing to put her in possession of the property as promised.

⚠ **If you collected "last month's rent" when the tenant moved in, do not accept rent for the last month of the tenancy.** You are legally obligated to use this money for the last month's rent. Accepting an additional month's rent may extend the tenant's tenancy.

## Tenant's Notice of Intent to Move Out

April 3, 199X
Date

Anne Sakamoto
Landlord

888 Mill Avenue
Street Address

Nashville, Tennessee 37126
City and State

Dear Ms. Sakamoto ,
Landlord

This is to notify you that I/we will be moving from 999 Brook Lane, Apartment Number 11

,

on May 3, 199X , 30 days from today.

This provides at least 30 days written notice as required in our

rental agreement.

Sincerely,

Patti Ellis
Tenant

Joe Ellis
Tenant

Tenant

If the tenant asks for more time but you don't want to continue the tenancy as before, you may want to give the tenant a few days or weeks more, at pro-rated rent. Prepare a written agreement to that effect and have the tenant sign it. See the sample letter extending the tenant's move-out date.

## 5. When the Tenant Doesn't Give the Required Notice

All too often, a tenant will send or give you a "too short" notice of intent to move. And it's not unheard of for a tenant to move out with no notice or with a wave as he hands you the keys.

A tenant who leaves without giving enough notice has lost the right to occupy the premises, but is still obligated to pay rent through the end of the required notice period. For example, if the notice period is 30 days, but the tenant moves out after telling you 20 days ago that he intended to move, he still owes you for the remaining ten days.

In most states, you have a legal duty to try to re-rent the property before you can charge the tenant for giving you too little notice, but few courts expect a landlord to accomplish this in less than a month. (This rule, called the landlord's duty to mitigate damages, is discussed in Section D3, below.)

## 6. When You or Your Tenant Violates the Rental Agreement

If you seriously violate the rental agreement and fail to fulfill your legal responsibilities—for example, by not correcting serious health or safety problems—a tenant may be able to legally move out with no written notice or by giving less notice than is other-wise required. Called a "constructive eviction," this doctrine typically applies only when living conditions are intolerable—for example, if the tenant has had no heat for an extended period in the winter, or if a tenant's use and enjoyment of the property has been substantially impaired because of drug dealing in the building.

---

### Sample Letter
### Extending Tenant's Move-Out Date

June 20, 199X

Hannah Lewis
777 Broadway Terrace, Apartment #3
Richmond, Virginia 23233

Dear Hannah:

On June 1, you gave me a 30-day notice of your intent to move out on July 1. You have since requested to extend your move-out to July 18 because of last-minute problems with closing escrow on your new house. This letter is to verify our understanding that you will move out on July 18, instead of July 1, and that you will pay pro-rated rent for 18 days (July 1 through July 18). Prorated rent for 18 days, based on your monthly rent of $900 or $30 per day, is $540.

Please sign below to indicate your agreement to these terms.

Sincerely,

*Fran Moore*

Fran Moore, Landlord

Agreed to by Hannah Lewis, Tenant:

Signature ___*Hanna Lewis*___

Date ___*June 20, 199X*___

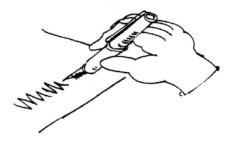

What exactly constitutes a constructive eviction varies slightly under the laws of different states. Generally, if a rental unit has serious habitability problems for anything but a very short time, the tenant may be entitled to move out without giving notice. The conditions that can cause constructive eviction are described in Chapters 9, 11 and 12.

Along the same lines, a landlord may terminate a tenancy (and evict, if necessary) if the tenant violates a lease or rental agreement—for example by failing to pay rent or seriously damaging the property—by giving less notice than is otherwise required to end a tenancy. Chapter 17 explains the situations in which landlords can quickly terminate for tenant misbehavior, and gives an overview of evictions.

## C. How Leases End

A lease lasts for a fixed term, typically one year. As a general rule, neither you nor the tenant may unilaterally end the tenancy, unless the other party has violated the terms of the lease.

If you and the tenant both live up to your promises, however, the lease simply ends of its own accord at the end of the lease term. At this point, the tenant must either:

- move
- sign a new lease (with the same or different terms), or
- stay on as a month-to-month tenant with your approval.

As every landlord knows, however, life is not always so simple. Sooner or later, a tenant will stay beyond the end of the term or leave before it without any legal right to do so.

### 1. Giving Notice to the Tenant

Because a lease clearly states when it will expire, you may not think it's necessary to notify tenants before the expiration date. But doing so is a very good practice. And some states or cities (especially those with rent control) actually require reasonable notice before the lease expiration date if you want the tenant to leave.

We suggest giving the tenant at least 60 days' written notice that the lease is going to expire. This reminder has several advantages:

**Getting the tenant out on time.** Two months' notice allows plenty of time for the tenant to look for another place if he doesn't—or you don't—want to renew the lease.

**Giving you time to renegotiate the lease.** If you would like to continue renting to your present tenant but also change some lease terms or increase the rent, your notice reminds the tenant that the terms of the old lease will not automatically continue. Encourage the tenant to stay, but mention that you need to make some changes to the lease.

**Getting a new tenant in quickly.** If you know a tenant is going to move, you can show the unit to prospective tenants ahead of time, and minimize the time the space is vacant.

**Your options may be limited in a rent control area.** If your property is subject to rent control, you may be required to renew a tenant's lease unless there is a legally approved reason (just cause) not to. (See Chapter 3 for more on rent control.) Reasons such as your tenant's failure to pay rent or your desire to move in a close relative commonly justify non-renewal. If you do not have a reason for non-renewal that meets the city's test, you may be stuck with a perpetual month-to-month tenant. Check your city's rent control ordinance carefully.

### 2. If the Tenant Continues to Pay Rent After the Lease Expires

It's fairly common for landlords and tenants not to care, or not even to notice, that a lease has expired. The tenant keeps paying the rent, and the landlord keeps cashing the checks. Is everything just the same as it was before the lease expired? The answer depends on where you live.

**Creating a month-to-month tenancy.** In most states, you will have created a new, oral month-to-month tenancy on the terms that appeared in the old lease. In other words, you'll be stuck with the terms and rent in the old lease, at least for the first 30 days. If you want to change the terms in a new lease, you must abide by the law regarding giving notice for a month-to-month tenancy (see Section A, above). It will usually take you at least a month, while you go about giving notice to your now month-to-month tenant.

EXAMPLE 1: Zev had a one-year lease and paid rent on the first of every month. When the lease expired, Zev stayed on and his landlord, Maria, accepted another month's rent check from him. Under the laws of their state, this made Zev a month-to-month tenant, subject to the terms and conditions in his now-expired lease.

Maria wanted to institute a "no pets" rule and to raise the rent. But since Zev was now a month-to-month tenant, she had to give him 30 days' notice (as required by her state's law) to change the terms of the tenancy. She lost a full month of the higher rent while she complied with the 30-day requirement.

EXAMPLE 2: Learning from her experience with Zev, Maria gave her tenant Alice a 60-day notice before Alice's lease expired. In that notice, Maria also told Alice about the new "no pets" rule and the rent increase. Alice, who wanted to get a cat, decided to move when the lease expired. Meanwhile, Maria was able to show Alice's apartment to prospective tenants, and chose one who moved in—and started paying the higher rent—shortly after Alice's lease expired.

Of course, you can belatedly present the tenant with a new lease. If your tenant decides not to sign it, she can stay on as a month-to-month tenant, under the terms of the old lease, until you give her proper written notice to move on. As discussed above, this is usually 30 days.

**Automatically renewing the lease.** However, in a few states, including Pennsylvania, the rule is quite different. If your lease expires and you continue to accept rent, the two of you have created a new lease for the same length (such as one year) and terms (such as the amount of rent) as in the old lease. In other words, you have automatically renewed the lease. The effects are dramatic: You and the tenant are now legally obligated for a new lease with the same term as the old one.

To avoid problems of tenants staying longer than you want, be sure to notify the tenant well before the lease expiration date, and don't accept rent after this date. If a tenant just wants to stay an extra few days after a lease expires, and you agree, it is wise to put your understanding on this arrangement in a letter. See the sample letter extending the tenant's move-out date in Section B, above.

## 3. When a Lease Ends and You Want the Tenant Out

Once the lease expires, you don't have to keep renting to the tenant. If the tenant stays on after the lease ends and offers rent that you *do not accept,* the tenant is a "holdover" tenant. In some states, you must still give notice, telling the tenant to leave within a few days; if the tenant doesn't leave at the end of this period, you can start an eviction lawsuit. A few states allow landlords to file for eviction immediately, as soon as the lease expires.

**⚠ Avoid lease and rental agreement clauses that make holdover tenants pay a higher rent.** Some landlords attempt to discourage tenants from staying past the end of their tenancy by making the tenant agree, in advance, to pay as much as three times the rent if they do. Clauses like this may not be legal—they are a form of "liquidated damages" (damages that are set in advance, without regard to the actual harm suffered by the landlord), which are illegal in residential rentals in many states, including California. (However, they have been upheld in Texas.) The clause would probably not hold up in a rent control city; nor would it survive a challenge if the clause describes the rent hike as a "penalty."

---

### Retaliation and Other Illegal Tenancy Terminations

You can terminate a tenancy for a variety of reasons, such as nonpayment of rent, serious violations of the lease and illegal activity such as drug-dealing on the rental property. And unless state or local laws require a reason, you can, with proper notice, terminate a month-to-month rental agreement or decline to renew a lease without giving any reason at all. But you can't terminate a tenancy for the *wrong* reason—in retaliation against a tenant for exercising her legal rights or in a way that discriminates illegally.

Just as you can't engage in illegal discrimination when you rent a unit in the first place, you can't unlawfully discriminate when it comes to terminating a month-to-month tenancy or deciding not to renew a lease—for example, by deciding not to continue to rent to persons of a certain ethnicity because of your political beliefs. Discrimination is covered in detail in Chapter 5.

The second major landlord "no-no" when it comes to tenancy non-renewals is retaliation. In most states, you may not end a tenancy in retaliation for a tenant's legally protected activities, such as complaining to a building inspector that a rental unit is uninhabitable. If you do, and the tenant stays on despite your wishes, the tenant can defend herself against a lawsuit to evict her by proving retaliation. Chapter 16 discusses laws prohibiting retaliation.

---

## D. If the Tenant Breaks the Lease

A tenant who leaves (with or without notifying you beforehand) before a lease expires and refuses to pay the remainder of the rent due under the lease is said to have "broken the lease."

Once the tenant leaves for good, you have the legal right to retake possession of the premises, and re-rent to another tenant. A key question that arises is how much does a tenant with a lease owe if she walks out early? Let's start with the general legal rule. A tenant who signs a lease agrees at the outset to pay a fixed amount of rent: the monthly rent multiplied by the number of months of the lease. The tenant pays this amount in monthly installments over the term of the lease. In short, the tenant has obligated himself for the entire rent for the entire lease term. The fact that payments are made monthly doesn't change the tenant's responsibility to pay rent for the entire lease term. As discussed below, depending on the situation, you may use the tenant's security deposit to cover part of the shortfall, or sue the tenant for the rent owed.

### 1. Is the Tenant Really Gone?

Sometimes, it's hard to tell whether or not a tenant has left permanently. People do sometimes disappear for weeks at a time, for a vacation or family emergency. And even a tenant who doesn't intend to come back may leave behind enough discarded clothing or furniture to make it unclear.

Often your first hint that a tenant has abandoned the premises will be the fact that you haven't received the rent. Or you may simply walk by a window and notice the lack of furniture. Ordinarily, the mere appearance that the rental unit is no longer occupied doesn't give you the legal right to immediately retake possession. It does, however, often give you legal justification to inspect the place for signs of abandonment. (See Chapter 13, on tenants' privacy rights.)

Here are some tips for inspecting property you suspect has been abandoned:

- Is the refrigerator empty, or is most of the food spoiled?
- Have electricity and telephone service been canceled?

• Are closets and kitchen cupboards empty?

If you conclude, under your state's rules, that the property is abandoned, you have the right to retake possession of it. Each state has its own definition of abandonment and its own rules for regaining possession of rental property. In Colorado, for example, property is considered abandoned if the tenant fails to pay rent or otherwise contact the landlord for at least 30 days and the landlord has no evidence to indicate that the tenant has not abandoned the property.

Rather than trying to figure out if the situation satisfies your state's legal rules for abandonment, it may be easier to find the tenant and ask her whether or not she's coming back. (Also, if you try unsuccessfully to locate the tenant and then the original tenant shows up after you have re-rented the unit, evidence of your efforts will be some protection if the original tenant complains.) Start by phoning each personal and business reference on the tenant's rental application. If that doesn't work, ask neighbors and, finally, check with the police.

Another way to find a tenant who has left a forwarding address with the Post Office but not with you is to send the tenant a "return receipt requested" letter, and check the box on the form that asks the postal service to note the address where the letter was delivered. You'll get the tenant's new address when you receive the return receipt.

**Require tenants to notify you of extended absences.** Clause 16 of the form lease and rental agreements (Chapter 2) requires tenants to inform you when they will be gone for an extended time, such as two or more weeks.

By requiring tenants to notify you of long absences, you'll know whether property has been abandoned or the tenant is simply on vacation. In addition, if you have such a clause and, under its authority, enter an apparently abandoned unit only to be confronted later by an indignant tenant, you can defend yourself by pointing out that the tenant violated the lease.

## 2. When Breaking a Lease Is Justified

There are some important exceptions to the blanket rule that a tenant who breaks a lease owes the rent for the entire lease term. A tenant may be able to legally move out without providing the proper notice in the following situations:

• **You violated an important lease provision.** If you don't live up to your obligations under the lease—for example, if you fail to maintain the unit in accordance with health and safety codes—a court will conclude that you have "constructively evicted" the tenant. That releases the tenant from further obligations under the lease. (Section B6, above, discusses constructive evictions.)

• **State law allows the tenant to leave early.** A few states' laws list reasons that allow a tenant to break a lease. For example, in Delaware a tenant need only give 30 days' notice to end a long-term lease if he needs to move because his present employer relocated or because health problems (of the tenant or a family member) require a permanent move. In New Jersey, a tenant who has suffered a disabling illness or accident can break a lease and leave after 40 days' notice upon presenting proper proof of disability. Some states, such as Georgia, allow members of the military to break a lease because of a change in military orders. If your tenant has a good reason for a sudden move, you may want to research your state's law to see whether or not he's still on the hook for rent.

• **The rental unit is damaged or destroyed.** If the rental is significantly damaged—either by natural disaster or any other reason beyond the tenant's control—the tenant may consider the lease terminated and move out. (See Chapter 9 for more details on this subject.)

• **You seriously interfere with the tenant's ability to enjoy his or her tenancy**—for example, by sexually harassing the tenant (see Chapter 5) or violating the tenant's privacy rights. (See Chapter 13 for more on privacy.)

## 3. Your Duty to Mitigate Your Loss if the Tenant Leaves Early

If a tenant breaks the lease and moves out without legal justification, you normally can't just sit back and wait until the end of the term of the lease, and then sue the departed tenant for the total lost rent. In most states, you must try to re-rent the property reasonably quickly and keep your losses to a minimum—in legalese, to "mitigate damages." (Each state's rule is listed in "The Landlord's Duty to Re-Rent the Premises," below.)

Even if this isn't the legal rule in your state, trying to re-rent is obviously a sound business strategy. It's much better to have rent coming in every month than to wait, leaving a rental unit vacant for months, and then try to sue (and collect from) a tenant who's long gone.

If you don't make an attempt (or make an inadequate one) to re-rent, and instead sue the former tenant for the whole rent, you will collect only what the judge thinks is the difference between the fair rental value of the property and the original tenant's promised rent. This can depend on how easy it is to re-rent in your area. Also, a judge is sure to give you some time (probably at least 30 days) to find a new tenant.

EXAMPLE: Mark owns an apartment complex in a popular ski town, and typically rents units for the winter season, from November to April. One year when the snow was particularly sparse, he was dismayed to discover that Janice, his tenant, had apparently skipped out on the last four months of her lease. The law in his state obligated him to take reasonable steps to mitigate the loss—that is, to attempt to re-rent the unit and credit the proceeds against the four months' rent Janice owed. Mark advertised the unit and showed it to some interested people, but couldn't find an acceptable tenant.

Mark then sued Janice for the four months' rent, and showed the judge the advertisements, his activity log (substantiating the time he had spent trying to re-rent the place) and the credit reports of the proposed tenants whom he had rejected. Satisfied that Mark had made a reasonable effort to mitigate his damages, the judge entered a judgment against Janice amounting to four months' rent, plus Mark's expenses.

⚠️ **No double-dipping is allowed.** Even if your state doesn't strictly enforce the mitigation-of-damages rules, if you re-rent the property, you cannot also collect from the former tenant. Courts do not allow you to unjustly enrich yourself this way.

### a. How to Mitigate Your Damages

When you're sure that a tenant has left permanently, then you can turn your attention to re-renting the unit.

You do not need to relax your standards for acceptable tenants—for example, you are entitled to reject applicants with poor credit or rental histories. Also, you need not give the suddenly available property priority over other rental units that you would normally attend to first.

You are not required to rent the premises at a rate below its fair market value. Keep in mind, however, that refusing to rent at less than the original rate may be foolish. If you are unable to ultimately collect from the former tenant, you will get *no* income from the property instead of less. You will have ended up hurting no one but yourself.

EXAMPLE: When the mail began to pile up and the rent went unpaid, Jack suspected that Lorna, his tenant, had broken the lease and moved out. When his suspicions were confirmed, he added her apartment to the list of vacant units that needed his attention. In the same way that he prepared every unit, Jack cleaned the apartment and advertised it. Three months after Lorna left, Jack succeeded in re-renting the apartment.

Jack sued Lorna in small claims court and won a judgment that included the costs of advertising and cleaning and the three months' rent that he lost before the unit was re-rented.

## Consider a Buy-Out Agreement with a Tenant Who Wants to Leave Early

A tenant who wants to get out of a lease may offer to sweeten the deal by paying a little bit extra. In the world of big business, this is known as a "buy-out." For example, a tenant who wants to leave three months early might offer to pay half a month's extra rent and promise to be extra accommodating when you want to show the unit to prospective tenants. A sample Buy-Out Agreement is shown below.

---

### Sample Buy-Out Agreement Between Landlord and Tenant

This Agreement is entered into on January 3, 199X, between Colin Crest, Tenant, who leases the premises at 123 Shady Lane, Capitol City, California; and Marie Peterson, Landlord.

1. Under the attached lease, Tenant agreed to pay Landlord monthly rent of $600. Tenant has paid rent for the month of January, 199X.

2. Tenant's lease expires on June 30, 199X, but Tenant needs to break the lease and move out on January 15, 199X.

3. Landlord agrees to release Tenant on January 15, 199X, from any further obligation to pay rent in exchange for Tenant's promise to pay January's rent plus one and one-half month's rent ($900) by January 15, 199X.

4. Tenant agrees to allow Landlord to show his apartment to prospective new tenants on two hours' notice, seven days a week. If Tenant cannot be reached after Landlord has made a good-faith effort to do so, Landlord may enter and show the apartment.

5. If Tenant does not fulfill his promises as described in paragraphs 3 and 4 above, the attached lease, entered into on January 3, 199X, will remain in effect.

*Colin Crest*
Colin Crest, Tenant

*January 3, 199X*
Date

*Marie Peterson*
Marie Peterson, Landlord

*January 3, 199X*
Date

## The Landlord's Duty to Re-Rent the Premises

| State | Landlord must take reasonably prompt steps to re-rent | Landlord has no duty to look for and rent to another tenant | Law is unclear or courts have not addressed the issue | State | Landlord must take reasonably prompt steps to re-rent | Landlord has no duty to look for and rent to another tenant | Law is unclear or courts have not addressed the issue |
|---|---|---|---|---|---|---|---|
| Alabama | | X | | Nebraska | | | X |
| Alaska | X | | | Nevada | X | | |
| Arizona | X | | | New Hampshire | X | | |
| Arkansas | | | X | New Jersey | X | | |
| California | X | | | New Mexico | X | | |
| Colorado | | | X | New York | | | X |
| Connecticut | X | | | North Carolina | X | | |
| Delaware | X | | | North Dakota | X | | |
| Dist. of Columbia | X | | | Ohio | X | | |
| Florida | X | | | Oklahoma | X | | |
| Georgia | | | X | Oregon | X | | |
| Hawaii | X | | | Pennsylvania | | | X |
| Idaho | | | X | Rhode Island | X | | |
| Illinois | X | | | South Carolina | X | | |
| Indiana | X | | | South Dakota | | | X |
| Iowa | X | | | Tennessee | X | | |
| Kansas | X | | | Texas | X | | |
| Kentucky | X | | | Utah | X | | |
| Louisiana | X | | | Vermont | | | X |
| Maine | X | | | Virginia | X | | |
| Maryland | X | | | Washington | X | | |
| Massachusetts | | | X | West Virginia | | | X |
| Michigan | | | X | Wisconsin | X | | |
| Minnesota | | X | | Wyoming | | | X |
| Mississippi | | X | | | | | |
| Missouri | | | X | | | | |
| Montana | | | X | | | | |

If you need citations to a statute or court opinion, look in Footnotes 1, 2 and 3 of *Austin Hill Country Realty, Inc. v. Palisades Plaza, Inc.,* # 95-1273 (July 9, 1997) (Texas Supreme Court).

## Keep Good Records

If you end up suing a former tenant, you will want to be able to show the judge that you acted reasonably in your attempts to re-rent the property. Don't rely on your memory and powers of persuasion to convince the judge. Keep detailed records, including:

- the original lease
- receipts for cleaning and painting, with photos of the unit showing the need for repairs, if any
- your expenses for storing or properly disposing of any belongings the tenant left
- receipts for advertising the property and bills from credit reporting agencies investigating potential renters
- a log of the time you spent showing the property, and a value for that time
- a log of any people who offered to rent and, if you rejected them, documentation as to why, and
- if the current rent is less than the original tenant paid, a copy of the new lease.

### b.  The Tenant's Right to Find a Replacement Tenant

A tenant who wishes to leave before the lease expires may offer to find a suitable new tenant, so that the flow of rent will remain uninterrupted. Unless you have a new tenant waiting, you have nothing to lose by cooperating. Refusing to cooperate could even hurt you. If you refuse to accept an excellent new tenant and then withhold the lease-breaking tenant's deposit or sue for unpaid rent, you may wind up losing in court, because you turned down the chance to reduce your losses (mitigate your damages).

Of course, if the rental market is really tight in your area, you may be able to lease the unit easily at a higher rent or you may already have an even better prospective tenant on your waiting list. In that case, you won't care if a tenant breaks the lease, and you may not be interested in any new tenant he provides.

If you and the outgoing tenant agree on a replacement tenant, you and the new tenant should sign a new lease, and the outgoing tenant should sign a termination of lease form (discussed in Chapter 8). Since this is a new lease—not a sublease or assignment of the existing lease (also discussed in Chapter 8)—you can raise the rent if you wish, unless local rent control ordinances prohibit it.

## 4.  When You Can Sue

If a tenant leaves prematurely, you may need to go to court and sue for re-rental costs and the difference between the original and the replacement rent. Obviously, you should first use the tenant's security deposit to cover these costs. (See Chapter 15 discussion of using the deposit this way.)

Deciding *where* to sue is usually easy: Small claims court is usually the court of choice because it's fast, affordable and doesn't require a lawyer. If you're seeking an amount that's substantially above your state's limit, you may file in regular court—but if the excess is small, you may wisely decide to forego it and use the fast, cheap small claims court. If your lease contains an attorney fees clause (as does the form agreement in Chapter 2), you may be able to recover your attorney fees.

> EXAMPLE: Cree has a year's lease at $800 per month. She moves out with six months ($4,800 of rent) left on the lease. Cree's landlord, Robin, cannot find a new tenant for six weeks, and when she finally does, the new tenant will pay only $600 per month.
>
> Unless Cree can show Robin acted unreasonably, Cree would be liable for the $200 per month difference between what she paid and what the new tenant pays, multiplied by the number of months left in the lease at the time she moved out. Cree would also be responsible

for $1,200 for the time the unit was vacant, plus Robin's costs to find a new tenant. Cree would thus owe Robin $2,400 plus advertising and applicant screening costs. If Robin sues Cree for this money, and there is an attorney fee clause in her lease, Cree will also owe Robin these costs, which can be upwards of a few thousand dollars.

Knowing *when* to sue is trickier. You may be eager to start legal proceedings as soon as the original tenant leaves, but if you do, you won't know the extent of your losses, because you might find another tenant who will make up part of the lost rent. Must you wait until the end of the original tenant's lease? Or can you bring suit when you re-rent the property?

The standard approach, and one that all states allow, is to go to court after you re-rent the property. At this point, your losses—your expenses and the rent differential, if any—are known and final. The disadvantage is that you have had no income from that property since the original tenant left, and the original tenant may be long gone and not, practically speaking, worth chasing down.

Chapter 16 discusses how to file a small claims court suit. If you are suing in regular court and want legal advice, see Chapter 18, which covers how to find and work with a lawyer.

⚠️ **Give accurate and updated information to credit bureaus about former tenants.** The Fair Debt Collection Practices Act [FDCRA], (15 U.S.C. § 1692 and following) also applies when you give information to a credit reporting agency about a current or former tenant. The Act makes it illegal to give false information, and if the tenant disputes the debt, you must mention the fact that the sum is disputed when you report it. You must notify the credit bureau if the tenant pays all or part of the debt.

The FDCRA even makes it illegal to give falsely *positive* information which you know to be untrue. When a credit bureau calls to ask about your least-favorite tenant who's applied for a home loan, don't describe him in falsely glowing terms, no matter how much you'd like to see him leave!

## E. When a Tenant Dies

Occasionally, you may be faced with the death of a tenant who lives alone. Because lawyers and public agencies are bound to be involved, be sure to comply with the law, even though your first urge may be to clear out the property and rent it as quickly as possible.

Whenever you or someone else first suspects or learns of a death of a tenant, immediately call the police or fire department. Next, try to reach the tenant's emergency contact listed on the rental application.

### 1. Preserving the Deceased Tenant's Property

After the body is removed, you must take reasonable precautions to preserve the deceased tenant's property. You have no legal right to let relatives or friends take anything from the premises—and if you do allow this, you could be sued by the true heirs. The only possible exception is to allow the tenant's next of kin to remove personal effects needed for the funeral, such as the deceased's clothing.

Lock the door and keep everyone out of the premises. If you know or suspect that others have keys, you may even want to put a padlock on the door or change the locks. Open the rental unit only for a person with legal authority to dispose of the decedent's property (see subsection 2, below). This may involve you in some unpleasant confrontations with pushy relatives or friends, but you are far better off to refuse entry and endure some uncomfortable moments than to risk being sued as the one who allowed unauthorized persons to plunder the estate.

⚠ **Protect yourself from charges of appropriation.** It is not unusual for an appreciable amount of time to go by before someone shows up with the proper authority to claim the tenant's belongings and clear out the unit. Generally, you may store the belongings and re-rent the premises. Indeed, if the tenant had a fixed-term lease, you must take reasonably prompt steps to re-rent, in order to minimize your losses (discussed above). Be careful, however, to carefully inventory the possessions. As an added precaution, have a disinterested helper with you who can testify to your honesty and thoroughness.

## 2.  Releasing the Tenant's Property

You should and must release the decedent's personal belongings only to someone with legal authority. Depending on how the deceased left his affairs and the size of his estate, the authorized person will be:

- **The executor.** If the tenant left a will, it probably names an executor. This person is entitled to access to the property. If the tenant left enough valuable property, the executor will be supervised by the probate court and will have a court order showing his authority. Ask to see the original court order, which will have a file stamp from the court on the first page and the original signature of the judge.
- **The inheritors.** If there is no probate proceeding, there is no court-authorized executor. You may release property to the persons entitled (under the terms of a will or trust) to inherit it. Usually, the inheritors must give you a signed, sworn statement (affidavit or declaration signed under penalty of perjury) stating that they are entitled to the property; the particulars depend on state law. Also ask to see a certified copy of the death certificate.
- **The administrator.** If the tenant died without a will and left more than a certain amount of property (each state has its own rules), the probate court will appoint an administrator to

wind up his affairs. The tenant's close relatives will inherit the tenant's possessions.
- **The successor trustee.** If the tenant created a probate-avoiding living trust and transferred his personal property to it, the person in authority will be called the successor trustee. Ask to see the original trust document, signed and notarized, and a certified copy of the death certificate.

If someone shows up and claims to have the right to the tenant's belongings, how can you make sure that this person is, in fact, entitled to the items? Ask for a current, picture ID of the person claiming authority, and a legal document (one of those listed above) conferring authority. Make sure everyone who takes property signs a receipt for it.

⚠ **Don't get caught in the middle of a family fight.** If you are not sure of the authority of someone who wants to take the tenant's property, or if relatives are squabbling about who gets what, protect yourself. Insist that the claimants either show you convincing documents or show up with a probate court order.

Disputes are especially common between the surviving member of an unmarried couple and the relatives of the deceased member of the couple. Don't get caught in a nasty crossfire.

## 3.  Making a Claim on the Estate

After all the deceased tenant's property is removed, you may be left with losses not covered by the deposit:
- repair costs
- if the deceased rented month-to-month, unpaid rent from before and up to the tenant's death
- if the tenant died before the expiration of a fixed-term lease, unpaid rent for the balance of the lease term, less income you have as a consequence of re-renting, and
- storage costs.

To pay these bills, consider making a claim on the deceased tenant's estate (the assets he or she left). If a probate court proceeding has been initiated, you can submit a filled-out creditor's claim form (available from the court clerk) to the probate court. You will have a certain amount of time—a few months, in most states—in which to file your claim.

If the deceased tenant's assets were passed through a probate-avoiding trust, and there are no probate court proceedings, you will need to ask the successor trustee for payment. If there is neither a trust nor probate (because the tenant did not leave property of enough value to require probate), the best you can do is to bill the executor. If there is no will and no probate proceeding because the estate is too small, try billing the next of kin.

## F. Condominium Conversions

Converting a rental property into condominiums usually means the end of a tenant's tenancy. But condo conversions are not always simple.

Many states, such as California, Connecticut and New York, regulate the conversion of rental property into condominiums—that is, they limit the number of conversions and give existing tenants considerable rights, as explained below. Here are some of the basic issues that your state's condo conversion law may address:

**Government approval.** Converting rental property to condos usually requires plan approval (often called a "subdivision map approval") from a local planning agency. If the property is subject to rent control, there are probably additional requirements.

**Public input.** In most situations, the public—including current tenants—can speak out at planning agency hearings regarding the proposed condominium conversion and its impact on the rental housing market. You are usually required to give tenants notice of the time and place of these hearings.

**Tenants' right of first refusal.** Most condominium conversion laws demand that you offer the units for sale first to the existing tenants, at prices that are the same or lower than the intended public offering. To keep tenant opposition to a minimum, you may decide to voluntarily offer existing tenants a chance to buy at a significantly lower price.

**Tenancy terminations.** Month-to-month tenants who don't buy their units should receive notice to move at some point during the sales process. Tenants with leases usually have a right to remain through the end of the lease. The entire condo conversion approval process typically takes many months—time enough for current leases to expire before the final okay has been given.

**Renting after the conversion has been approved.** If you offer a lease or rental agreement *after* the condo conversion has been approved, many statutes require you to give the tenant plenty of clear written warnings (in large, bold-faced type) that the unit may be sold and the tenancy terminated on short notice. But if you continue to rent units after you've gotten subdivision approval, you'll usually do so on a month-to-month basis, so the short notice really won't be any different from what any month-to-month tenant would receive.

**Relocation assistance and special protections.** Some statutes require owners to pay current tenants a flat fee to help with relocation. Some also require owners to provide more notice or additional relocation assistance for elderly tenants or those with small children.

For advice on researching your state's statutes and court cases on condominium conversions, see the discussion of legal research in Chapter 18. ■

# Chapter 15

# Returning Security Deposits

As any small claims court judge will tell you, fights over security deposits account for a large percentage of the landlord-tenant disputes that wind up in court. A landlord's failure to return security deposits as legally required can result in substantial financial penalties if a tenant files suit.

Fortunately, you can take some simple steps to minimize the possibility that you'll spend hours haggling in court over back rent, cleaning costs and damage to your property. First, of course, you must follow the law scrupulously when you return security deposits. But it's also wise to send the tenant, before he or she moves out, a letter setting out your expectations for how the unit should be left.

This chapter shows you how to itemize deductions and refund security deposits as state laws require, and how to protect yourself both at the time of move-in and at termination. It describes the penalties you face for violating security deposit laws. This chapter also covers how to defend yourself against a tenant's lawsuit as well as the occasional necessity of taking a tenant to small claims court if the deposit doesn't cover unpaid rent, damage or cleaning bills.

We cover key aspects of state deposit law in this chapter and in Chapter 4. In addition, be sure to check local ordinances in all areas where you own property. Cities, particularly those with rent control, may add their own rules on security deposits.

Related topics covered in this book include:
- How to avoid deposit disputes by using clear lease and rental agreement provisions: Chapter 2
- How much you can charge for deposits; state requirements for keeping deposits in a separate account or paying interest: Chapter 4
- Highlighting security deposit rules in a move-in letter to new tenants; taking photographs and using a Landlord-Tenant Checklist to keep track of the condition of the premises before and after the tenant moves in: Chapter 7.

## A. Preparing a Move-Out Letter

Chapter 7 explains how a move-in letter can help get a tenancy off to a good start. Similarly, a move-out letter can also help reduce the possibility of disputes, especially over the return of security deposits.

Your move-out letter should tell the tenant how you expect the unit to be left, explain your inspection procedures, list the kinds of deposit deductions you may legally make and tell the tenant when and how you will send any refund that is due.

The Legal Forms Disk includes a copy of the Move-Out Letter. You'll also find a blank tear-out version in Appendix II at the back of this book.

A sample move-out letter is shown below. You may want to add or delete items depending on your own needs and how specific you wish to be.

Here are a few points you may want to include in a move-out letter:
- Specific cleaning requirements, such as bombing for fleas if the tenant has a dog, what to do about stained draperies that need special cleaning or how to fix holes left from picture hooks or clean dirty walls
- A reminder that fixtures (items that the tenant attaches more or less permanently to the wall, such as built-in bookshelves) must be left in place (see the discussion of fixtures in Chapter 9 and Clause 12 of the form agreements in Chapter 2)
- Details of how and when the final inspection will be conducted (see Section B, below)
- Information on state laws (if any) that allow a landlord to keep a tenant's security deposit if the tenant's forwarding address is not provided within a certain amount of time (see Section H, below).

## Move-Out Letter

July 5, 199X
Date

Jane Wasserman
Tenant

123 North Street, Apartment #23
Street address

Atlanta, Georgia 30360
City and State


Dear Jane ,
Tenant

We hope you have enjoyed living here. In order that we may mutually end our relationship on a positive note, this move-out letter describes how we expect your unit to be left and what our procedures are for returning your security deposit.

Basically, we expect you to leave your rental unit in the same condition it was when you moved in, except for normal wear and tear. To refresh your memory on the condition of the unit when you moved in, I've attached a copy of the Landlord-Tenant Checklist you signed at the beginning of your tenancy. I'll be using this same form to inspect your unit when you leave.

Specifically, here's a list of items you should thoroughly clean before vacating:

☐ Floors

    ☐ sweep wood floors

    ☐ vacuum carpets and rugs (shampoo if necessary)

    ☐ mop kitchen and bathroom floors

☐ Walls, baseboards, ceilings and built-in shelves

☐ Kitchen cabinets, countertops and sink, stove and oven—inside and out

☐ Refrigerator—clean inside and out, empty it of food, and turn it off, with the door left open

☐ Bathtubs, showers, toilets and plumbing fixtures

☐ Doors, windows and window coverings

☐ Other

_____

_____

_____

_____

_____

_____

_____

_____

_____

_____

_____

If you have any questions as to the type of cleaning we expect, please let me know.

Please don't leave anything behind—that includes bags of garbage, clothes, food, newspapers, furniture, appliances, dishes, plants, cleaning supplies or other items.

Please be sure you have disconnected phone and utility services, canceled all newspaper subscriptions and sent the post office a change of address form.

Once you have cleaned your unit and removed all your belongings, please call me at _____555-1234_____ to arrange for a walk-through inspection and to return all keys. Please be prepared to give me your forwarding address where we may mail your security deposit.

It's our policy to return all deposits either in person or at an address you provide within __one month_____ after you move out. If any deductions are made—for past due rent or because the unit is damaged or not sufficiently clean—they will be explained in writing.

If you have any questions, please contact me at _____555-1234_____.

Sincerely,

*Denise Parsons*
_____
Landlord/Manager

## B. Inspecting the Unit When a Tenant Leaves

After the tenant leaves, you will need to inspect the unit to assess what cleaning and damage repair is necessary. At the final inspection, check each item— for example, refrigerator or bathroom walls—on the Landlord-Tenant Checklist you and the tenant signed when the tenant moved in. (An excerpt is shown here. See Chapter 7 for a complete Checklist.) Note any item that needs cleaning, repair or replacement in the middle column, Condition on Departure. Where possible, note the estimated cost of repair or replacement in the third column; you can subtract those costs from the security deposit.

Many landlords do this final inspection on their own and simply send the tenant an itemized statement with any remaining balance of the deposit. If at all possible, we recommend that you make the inspection with the tenant who's moving out, rather than by yourself. A few states actually require this. Laws in Arizona, Maryland and Virginia, for example, specifically give tenants the right to be present when you conduct the final inspection. Doing the final inspection with the tenant present (in a conciliatory, non-threatening way) should alleviate any of the tenant's uncertainty concerning what deductions (if any) you propose to make from the deposit. It also gives the tenant a chance to present her point of view. But best of all, this approach avoids the risk that a tenant who feels unpleasantly surprised by the amount you withhold from the deposit will promptly take the matter to small claims court.

If you have any reason to expect a tenant to take you to court over deductions you plan to make from a security deposit, have the unit examined by another, more neutral person, such as another tenant in the same building. This person should be available to testify in court on your behalf, if necessary, should you end up in small claims court.

---

## Landlord-Tenant Checklist

### GENERAL CONDITION OF RENTAL UNIT AND PREMISES

572 Fourth St.

Street Address

Apt. 11    Washington, D.C.

Unit Number    City

|  | Condition on Arrival | Condition on Departure | Estimated Cost of Repair/Replacement |
|---|---|---|---|
| **LIVING ROOM** | | | |
| Floors & Floor Coverings | OK | OK | Ø |
| Drapes & Window Coverings | Mini-blinds discolored | Dirty | $10 |
| Walls & Ceilings | OK | Several holes in wall | $100 |
| Light Fixtures | OK | OK | Ø |
| Windows, Screens & Doors | Window rattles | OK | Ø |

**Photograph "before" and "after."** In Chapter 7, we recommend that you photograph or videotape the unit before the tenant moves in. You should do the same when the tenant leaves, so that you can make comparisons and have visual proof in case you are challenged later in court.

---

### Should You Let the Tenant Clean or Fix the Damage?

Many tenants, faced with losing a large chunk of their security deposit, may want the chance to do some more cleaning or repair any damage you've identified in the final inspection. A few states, including Montana, require you to offer the tenant a second chance at cleaning (if it's done within 24 hours) before you deduct cleaning charges from the security deposit. Even if your state does not require it, you may wish to offer a second chance anyway if the tenant seems sincere and capable of doing the work. This may help avoid arguments and maybe even a small claims action. But if you need to get the apartment ready quickly for another tenant or doubt the tenant's ability to do the work, just say no. And think twice if repairs are required, not just cleaning. If a tenant does a repair poorly—for example, improperly tacking down a carpet that later causes another tenant to trip and injure herself—you will be liable for the injury. (Chapter 10 discusses your liability for injuries on the premises.)

## C. Applying the Security Deposit to the Last Month's Rent

If no portion of the tenant's deposit was called last month's rent, you are not legally obliged to apply it in this way. When giving notice, a tenant may ask you to apply the security deposit towards the last month's rent. (Chapter 4 discusses last month's rent and deposits.)

Why should you object if a tenant asks to use a deposit you are already holding as payment for the last month's rent? The problem is that you can't know in advance what the property will look like when the tenant leaves. If the tenant leaves the property a mess, but the whole security deposit has gone to pay the last month's rent, obviously you will have nothing left to use to repair or clean the property. You will have to absorb the loss or sue the tenant.

You have two choices if you are faced with a tenant who wants to use a security deposit for last month's rent. The first alternative is to grant the tenant's request. Tell the tenant that you'll need to make a quick inspection first, and then, if you have good reason to believe that the tenant will leave the property clean and undamaged, don't worry about the last month's rent. (But don't forget to send the tenant a written statement setting out what happened to the deposit. You can prepare a brief letter, similar to the one we show in Section G, below, for returning the tenant's entire security deposit.)

Your second choice is to treat the tenant's non-payment (or partial payment) of the last month's rent as an ordinary case of rent nonpayment. This means preparing and serving the notice necessary to terminate the tenancy, and if the tenant doesn't pay, following up with an eviction lawsuit. But because it typically takes at least several weeks to evict a tenant, this probably won't get the tenant out much sooner than he would leave anyway. However, it will provide you with a court judgment for the unpaid last month's rent. This means that you may use the security deposit to pay for cleaning and repair costs, and apply any remainder to the judgment for nonpayment of rent. You then take your judgment and attempt to enforce it, as discussed in Section K, below.

EXAMPLE: Ari paid his landlord Jack a $600 deposit when he rented his $500 per month apartment on a month-to-month basis. The rental agreement required Ari to give 30 days' notice before terminating the tenancy.

Ari told Jack on November 1 that he would be leaving at the end of the month, but he did not pay his rent for November. When he left on December 1, he also left $500 worth of damages. Jack followed his state's procedures for itemizing and returning security deposits, and applied the $600 deposit to cover the damage. This left Jack with $100 for the $500 rent due, so he sued in small claims court for the $400 still owing. Jack was awarded a judgment for $400 plus the filing fee.

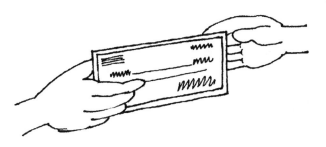

## D. Basic Rules for Returning Deposits

You are generally entitled to deduct from a tenant's security deposit whatever amount you need to fix damaged or dirty property (outside of "ordinary wear and tear") or to make up unpaid rent. (See Chapter 4, Section A.) But you must do it correctly, following your state's procedures. While the specific rules vary from state to state, you usually have between 14 and 30 days after the tenant leaves to return the tenant's deposit. See "Deadlines for Landlords to Itemize and Return Security Deposits," below.

State security deposit statutes typically require you to mail, within the time limit, the following to the tenant's last known address (or forwarding address if you have one):

1. The tenant's entire deposit, with interest if required (see Chapter 4 for state laws requiring interest), or

2. A written, itemized accounting as to how the deposit has been applied toward back rent and costs of cleaning and damage repair, together with payment for any deposit balance, including any interest that is required. (Section G, below, shows how to prepare an itemized statement, including how to handle situations when you're not sure of the exact deductions.)

Even if there is no specific time limit in your state or law requiring itemization, promptly presenting the tenant with a written itemization of all deductions and a clear reason why each was made is an essential part of a savvy landlord's overall plan to avoid disputes with tenants. In general, we recommend 30 days as a reasonable time to return deposits.

**Send an itemization even if you don't send money.** Quite a few landlords mistakenly believe that they don't have to account for the deposit to a tenant who's been evicted by court order or who breaks the lease. But a tenant's misconduct does not entitle a landlord to pocket the entire deposit without further formality. In general, even if the tenant leaves owing several months' rent—more than the amount of the deposit—you still must notify the tenant in writing, within the time limit, as to how the deposit has been applied toward cleaning or repair charges and unpaid rent. You may then need to sue the tenant if the deposit doesn't cover damage and unpaid rent.

The chart below shows the deadline each state sets for returning a tenant's security deposit after the tenancy is terminated. The term "No statutory deadline" means that the state either does not have a security deposit statute or has a statute but it does not specify a deadline for returning deposits.

## E. Deductions for Cleaning and Damage

As you can imagine, many disputes over security deposits revolve around whether or not it was

## Deadlines for Landlords to Itemize and Return Security Deposits

| State | Deadline for Returning Security Deposit | State | Deadline for Returning Security Deposit |
|---|---|---|---|
| Alabama | No statutory deadline | Michigan | 30 days |
| Alaska | 14 days if the tenant gives proper notice to terminate tenancy; 30 days if the tenant does not give proper notice | Minnesota | Three weeks after tenant leaves and landlord receives mailing address; five days if tenant must leave due to building condemnation |
| Arizona | 14 days | Mississippi | 45 days |
| Arkansas | 30 days | Missouri | 30 days |
| California | Three weeks | Montana | 30 days |
| Colorado | One month, unless lease agreement specifies longer period of time (which may be no more than 60 days); 72 hours if a hazardous condition involving gas equipment requires tenant to vacate | Nebraska | 14 days |
| | | Nevada | 30 days |
| | | New Hampshire | 30 days |
| | | New Jersey | 30 days; five days in case of fire, flood, condemnation or evacuation |
| Connecticut | 30 days, or within 15 days of receiving tenant's forwarding address, whichever is later | New Mexico | 30 days |
| | | New York | Reasonable time |
| Delaware | 15 days | North Carolina | 30 days |
| District of Columbia | 45 days | North Dakota | 30 days |
| | | Ohio | 30 days |
| Florida | 15 to 45 days depending on whether tenant disputes deductions | Oklahoma | 30 days |
| | | Oregon | 30 days |
| Georgia | One month | Pennsylvania | 30 days |
| Hawaii | 14 days | Rhode Island | 20 days |
| Idaho | 21 days or up to 30 days if landlord and tenant agree | South Carolina | 30 days |
| | | South Dakota | Two weeks |
| Illinois | 30-45 days depending on whether deductions were made | Tennessee | No statutory deadline |
| | | Texas | 30 days |
| Indiana | 45 days | Utah | 30 days, or within 15 days of receiving tenant's forwarding address, whichever is later |
| Iowa | 30 days | | |
| Kansas | 30 days | | |
| Kentucky | 30-60 days depending on whether tenant disputes deductions | Vermont | 14 days |
| | | Virginia | 30 days |
| Louisiana | No statutory deadline | Washington | 14 days |
| Maine | 21 days (tenancy at will) or 30 days (written rental agreement) | West Virginia | No statutory deadline |
| | | Wisconsin | No statutory deadline |
| Maryland | 30-45 days depending on whether tenant has been evicted or has abandoned the premises | Wyoming | No statutory deadline |
| Massachusetts | 30 days | | |

For details check, your statute. See "Citations for State Laws on Security Deposits" in Appendix I.

reasonable for the landlord to deduct the cost of cleaning or repairing the premises after the tenant moved. Unfortunately, standards in this area are often vague. Typically, you may charge for any cleaning or repairs necessary to restore the rental unit to its condition at the beginning at the tenancy, but not deduct for the cost of ordinary wear and tear.

## 1. Reasonable Deductions

In general, you may charge only for cleaning and repairs that are actually necessary. Items for which cleaning is often necessary—and costly—include replacing stained or ripped carpets or drapes (particularly smoke-contaminated ones), fixing damaged furniture and cleaning dirty stoves, refrigerators and kitchen and bathroom fixtures. You may also need to take care of such things as flea infestations left behind by the tenant's dog or mildew in the bathroom caused by the tenant's failure to clean properly. (That's why we recommend highlighting these types of trouble spots in a move-out letter. See Section A, above, for a sample move-out letter.)

That said, every move-out is different in its details, and there are simply no hard and fast rules on what is wear and tear and what is your tenant's responsibility. But here are some basic guidelines:

- You should not charge the tenant for filth or damage that was present when the tenant moved in.
- You should not charge the tenant for replacing an item when a repair would be sufficient. For example, a tenant who damaged the kitchen counter by placing a hot pan on it, shouldn't be charged for replacing the entire counter if an expertly done patch will do the job. Of course, you have to evaluate the overall condition of the unit—if it is a luxury property that looks like an ad in *Architectural Digest*, you don't need to make do with a patch.
- The longer a tenant has lived in a place, the more wear and tear can be expected. In practical terms, this means that you can't

always charge a tenant for cleaning carpets, drapes or walls or repainting.

- You should not charge for cleaning if the tenant paid a nonrefundable cleaning fee. Landlords in some states are allowed to charge a cleaning fee, which is separate from the security deposit and is specifically labeled as nonrefundable. (See Chapter 4.)
- You should charge a fair price for repairs and replacements.

You can deduct a reasonable hourly charge if you or your employees do any necessary cleaning. If you have cleaning done by an outside service, be sure to keep your canceled checks, and have the service itemize the work. It's wise to patronize only those cleaning services whose employees are willing to testify for you, or at least send a letter describing what they did in detail if the tenant sues you in small claims court, contesting your deposit deductions. (See Section J, below.)

**Don't overdo deductions from security deposits.** When you make deductions for cleaning or damage, it's often a mistake to be too aggressive. Tenants who believe they've been wronged (even if it isn't true) are likely to go to small claims court. The result will be that you or an employee will spend hours preparing your defense, waiting around the courthouse and presenting your side of the case. Even if you prevail (or, as is most likely, the judge makes a compromise ruling), the value of the time involved will have been considerable. In the long run, it may be wiser to withhold a smaller portion of the deposit in the first place.

See "What Can You Charge For?" for some examples of what a court will consider to be ordinary wear and tear, and what crosses the line and is considered damage that the tenant must pay for.

## 2. Common Disagreements

Common areas of disagreement between landlords and tenants concern repainting, carpets and fixtures.

| What Can You Charge For? | |
| --- | --- |
| **Ordinary Wear and Tear:** <br> **Landlord's Responsibility** | **Damage or Excessive Filth:** <br> **Tenant's Responsibility** |
| Curtains faded by the sun | Cigarette burns in curtains or carpets |
| Water-stained linoleum by shower | Broken tiles in bathroom |
| Minor marks on or nicks in wall | Large marks on or holes in wall |
| Dents in the wall where a door handle bumped it | Door off its hinges |
| Moderate dirt or spotting on carpet | Rips in carpet or urine stains from pets |
| A few small tack or nail holes in wall | Lots of picture holes or gouges in walls that require patching as well as repainting |
| A rug worn thin by normal use | Stains in rug caused by leaking fish tank |
| Worn gaskets on refrigerator doors | Broken refrigerator shelf |
| Faded paint on bedroom wall | Water damage on wall from hanging plants |
| Dark patches of ingrained soil on hardwood floors that have lost their finish and have been worn down to bare wood | Water stains on wood floors and windowsills caused by windows being left open during rainstorms |
| Warped cabinet doors that won't close | Sticky cabinets and interiors |
| Stains on old porcelain fixtures that have lost their protective coating | Grime-coated bathtub and toilet |
| Moderately dirty mini-blinds | Missing mini-blinds |
| Bathroom mirror beginning to "de-silver" (black spots) | Mirrors caked with lipstick and makeup |
| Clothes dryer that delivers cold air because the thermostat has given out | Dryer that won't turn at all because it's been over-loaded |
| Toilet flushes inadequately because mineral deposits have clogged the jets | Toilet won't flush properly because it's stopped up with a diaper |

### a. Painting

Although state laws provide no firm guidelines as to who is responsible for repainting when a rental unit needs it, courts usually rule that if a tenant has lived in your unit for many years, it should be done at your expense, not the tenant's. On the other hand, if a tenant has lived in a unit for less than a year, and the walls were freshly painted when she moved in but are now a mess, you are entitled to charge the tenant for all costs of cleaning the walls. If re-painting badly smudged walls is cheaper and more effective than cleaning, however, you can charge for repainting. See "When to Charge the Tenant for Repainting," below.

---

### When to Charge the Tenant for Repainting

One landlord we know uses the following approach, with excellent success, when a tenant moves out and repainting is necessary.

- If the tenant has occupied the premises for six months or less, the full cost of repainting (labor and materials) is subtracted from the deposit.
- If the tenant lived in the unit between six months and a year, and the walls are dirty, two-thirds of the painting cost is subtracted from the deposit.
- Tenants who occupy a unit for between one and two years and leave dirty walls are charged one-third of the repainting cost.
- No one who stays for two years or more is ever charged a painting fee. No matter how dirty the walls become, the landlord would always repaint as a matter of course if more than two years had passed since the previous painting. Obviously, this general rule must be modified occasionally to fit particular circumstances.

---

### b. Rugs and Carpets

If the living room rug was already threadbare when the tenant moved in a few months ago and looks even worse now, it's pretty obvious that the tenant's footsteps have simply contributed to the inevitable, and that this wear and tear is not the tenant's responsibility. On the other hand, a brand-new good quality rug that becomes stained and full of bare spots within months has probably been sub-jected to the type of abuse the tenant will have to pay for. In between, it's anyone's guess. But clearly the longer a tenant has lived in a unit, and the cheaper or older the carpet was when the tenant moved in, the less likely the tenant is to be held responsible for its deterioration.

> **EXAMPLE:** A tenant has ruined an eight-year old rug that had a life expectancy of ten years. If a replacement rug would cost $1,000, you would charge the tenant $200 for the two years of life that would have remained in the rug had their dog not ruined it.

### c. Fixtures

The law considers pieces of furniture or equipment that are physically attached to the rental property, such as bolted-on bookshelves, to be your property, even if the tenant (not you) paid for them. Disputes often arise when tenants, unaware of this rule, install a fixture and then attempt to remove it and take it with them when they leave. To avoid this kind of dispute, the lease and rental agreements in this book forbid tenants from altering the premises without your consent. That includes the installation of fixtures. (See Clause 12 of the form agreements in Chapter 2.)

If the tenant leaves behind a row of bookshelves, you can remove the shelves, restore the property to the same condition as before they were installed, and subtract the cost from the tenant's security deposit. Unless your lease or rental agreement says otherwise, you do not have to return the bookcases to the tenant. Legally, you've only removed something that has become part of the premises and hence your property. Chapter 9 offers suggestions on how to avoid disputes with tenants over fixtures.

## F.  Deductions for Unpaid Rent

In most states you can deduct any unpaid rent from a tenant's security deposit, including any unpaid utility charges or other financial obligations required under your lease or rental agreement.

⚠ **Even if the tenant's debt far exceeds the amount of the security deposit, do not ignore your statutory duties to itemize and notify the former tenant of your use of the security deposit.** It may seem like a waste of time, but some courts will penalize you for ignoring the statute, even if you later obtain a judgment that puts the stamp of approval on your use of the deposit.

### What to Do With Abandoned Belongings

State laws cover, often in some detail, how to handle belongings left behind by a tenant. Some states give the landlord an automatic lien (legal claim) against furniture and other personal items abandoned by a tenant. The landlord may sell these possessions if the security deposit or last month's rent does not cover the balance of the rent due under the lease or the damage to the premises. In other states, disposing of or selling property requires going to court.

For more information on how to deal with personal items a tenant has left behind, refer to your state statutes. Check your conclusions with a local expert, such as a rental property owners' association. If you have good reason to suspect that a tenant may cause problems later, you may want to consult a lawyer before you dispose of the tenant's possessions.

## 1.  Month-to-Month Tenancies

If you rent on a month-to-month basis, ideally your tenant will give the right amount of notice and pay for the last month's rent. Usually, the notice period is the same as the rental period, 30 days. Then, when the tenant leaves as planned, the only issue with respect to the security deposit is whether the tenant has caused any damage or left the place dirty. But there are three common variations on this ideal scenario, and they all allow you to deduct from the tenant's security deposit for unpaid rent:

- The tenant leaves as announced, but with unpaid rent behind.
- The tenant leaves later than planned, and hasn't paid for the extra days, or
- The tenant leaves as announced, but hasn't given you the right amount of notice.

Let's look at each situation.

### a.  The Tenant Leaves With Rent Unpaid

If the tenant has been behind on the rent for months, you are entitled to deduct what is owed from the security deposit—either during the tenancy or when the tenant leaves.

### b.  The Tenant Stays After the Announced Departure Date

A tenant who fails to leave when planned (or when requested, if you have terminated the rental agreement), obviously isn't entitled to stay on rent-free. When the tenant eventually does leave, you can figure the exact amount owed by prorating the monthly rent for the number of days the tenant has failed to pay.

EXAMPLE: Your tenant, Erin, gives notice on March 1 of her intent to move out. She pays you the rent of $600 for March. But because she can't get into her new place on time, Erin stays until April 5 without paying anything more for the extra five days. You are entitled to deduct $5/30$ (one-sixth) of the total month's rent, or $100, from Erin's security deposit.

### c. Giving Inadequate Notice

A tenant who gives less than the legally required amount of notice before leaving (typically 30 days) must pay rent for that entire period. If the tenant gave less than the legally required amount of notice and moved out, you are entitled to rent money for the balance of the notice period unless the place is re-rented within the 30 days. (Chapter 14 covers notice requirements for terminating a tenancy.)

EXAMPLE 1: Your tenant Tom moves out on the fifth day of the month, without giving you any notice or paying any rent for the month. The rental market is flooded and you are unable to re-rent the property for two months. You are entitled to deduct an entire month's rent (for the missing 30 days' notice) plus one-sixth of one month (for the five holdover days for which Tom failed to pay rent).

EXAMPLE 2: Sheila pays her $900 monthly rent on October 1. State law requires 30 day's notice to terminate a tenancy. On October 15th, Sheila informs you that she's leaving on the 25th. This gives you only ten days' notice, when you're entitled to 30. You're entitled to rent through the 30th day, counting from October 15, or November 14, unless you find a new tenant in the meantime. Because the rent is paid through October 31, Sheila owes you the prorated rent for 14 days in November. At $900 per month or $30 a day, this works out to $420, which you can deduct from Sheila's security deposit.

## 2. Fixed-Term Leases

If a tenant leaves before a fixed-term lease expires, you are usually entitled to the balance of the rent due under the lease, less any rent you receive from new tenants, or could have received if you had made a diligent effort to re-rent the property.

If a tenant leaves less than a month before the lease is scheduled to end, you can be almost positive that, if the case goes to court, a judge will conclude that the tenant owes rent for the entire lease term. It would be unreasonable to expect you to immediately find a new tenant to take over the few days left of the lease. But if the tenant leaves more than 30 days before the end of a lease, your duty to look for a new tenant will be taken more seriously by the courts. (See Chapter 14 for more on your duty to try to re-rent the property promptly.)

EXAMPLE: On January 1, Anthony rents a house from Will for $1,200 a month and signs a one-year lease. Anthony moves out on June 30, even though six months remain on the lease, making him responsible for a total rent of $7,200. Will re-rents the property on July 10, this time for $1,250 a month (the new tenants pay $833 for the last 20 days in July), which means that he'll receive a total rent of $7,083 through December 31. That's $117 less than the $7,200 he would have received from Anthony had he lived up to the lease, so Will may deduct $117 from Anthony's deposit. In addition, if Will spent a reasonable amount of money to find a new tenant (for newspaper ads, rental agency commissions and credit checks), he may also deduct this sum from the deposit.

## 3. Deducting Rent After You've Evicted a Tenant

In most states, if you successfully sue to evict a holdover tenant, you will obtain a court order telling the tenant to leave (which you give to a law enforcement agency to enforce) and a money judgment, ordering the tenant to pay you rent through the date of the judgment. Armed with these court orders, you can subtract from the security deposit:

- the amount of the judgment, and

- prorated rent for the period between the date of the judgment and the date the tenant actually leaves.

EXAMPLE: Marilyn sues to evict a tenant who fails to pay May's rent of $450. She gets an eviction judgment from the court on June 10 for rent prorated through that date. The tenant doesn't leave until the 17th, when the sheriff comes and puts him out. Marilyn can deduct the following items from the deposit:

- costs of necessary cleaning and repair, as allowed by state law
- the amount of the judgment (for rent through June 10)
- rent for the week between judgment and eviction (seven days at $15/day, or $105).

Before you subtract the amount of a court judgment for unpaid rent from a deposit, deduct any cleaning and repair costs and any unpaid rent not included in the judgment. The reason is simple. A judgment can be collected in all sorts of ways—for example, you can go after the former tenant's wages or bank account—if the security deposit is not large enough to cover everything owed you. However, you are much more limited when it comes to collecting money the tenant owes you for damage and cleaning if you don't have a judgment for the amount. If you don't subtract these items from the deposit, you'll have to file suit in small claims court. (See Section K, below.) But if you subtract the amount for cleaning, damage and any unpaid rent not covered in the judgment first, you will still have the judgment if the deposit isn't large enough to cover everything.

EXAMPLE 1: Amelia collected a security deposit of $1,200 from Timothy, whom she ultimately had to sue to evict for failure to pay rent. Amelia got a judgment for $160 court costs plus $1,000 unpaid rent through the date of the judgment. Timothy didn't leave until the sheriff came, about five days later, thus running up an additional prorated rent of $100. Timothy also left dirt and damage that cost $1,000 to clean and repair.

Amelia (who hadn't read this book) first applied the $1,200 security deposit to the $1,160 judgment, leaving only $40 to apply toward the rent of $100 which was not reflected in the judgment, as well as the cleaning and repair charges, all of which totaled $1,100. Amelia must now sue Timothy for the $1,060 he still owes her.

EXAMPLE 2: Now, assume that Monique was Timothy's landlord in the same situation. But Monique applied Timothy's $1,200 deposit first to the cleaning and damage charges of $1,000 and then to the $100 rent not reflected in the judgment. This left $100 to apply to the $1,160 judgment, the balance of which she can collect by garnishing Timothy's wages or bank account.

## G. Preparing an Itemized Statement of Deductions

Once you've inspected the premises and decided what you need to deduct for cleaning, repair, back rent or other purposes allowed by your state statute, you're ready to prepare a statement for the tenant. The statement should simply list each deduction and briefly explain what it's for.

This section includes samples of three security deposit itemization forms, which you can use for different types of deductions.

The Legal Forms Disk includes copies of all three itemization forms. You'll also find blank tear-out versions of these forms in Appendix II at the back of this book.

**If your city or state requires you to pay interest on a tenant's entire deposit, you must also refund this amount.** For details, see Chapter 4.

## 1. Returning the Entire Deposit

If you are returning a tenant's entire security deposit, (including interest, if required), simply send a brief letter like the one below.

## 2. Itemizing Deductions for Repairs, Cleaning and Related Losses

If you are making deductions from the tenant's security deposit only for cleaning and repair, or for Itemization (Deductions for Repairs, Cleaning and Unpaid Rent). A sample is shown below.

For each deduction, list the item and the dollar amount. If you've already had the work done, attach receipts to the itemization. If your receipts are not very detailed, add more information on labor and supplies, for example:

- "Carpet cleaning by ABC Carpet "Cleaners, $160, required by several large grease stains and candle wax imbedded in living room rug."
- "Plaster repair, $400, of several fist-sized holes in bedroom wall."
- "$250 to replace drapes in living room, damaged by cigarette smoke and holes."

Section E, above, will help you determine proper amounts to deduct for repairs and cleaning.

If you can't get necessary repairs made or cleaning done within the time required to return the security deposit, make a reasonable estimate of the cost. But keep in mind that if the tenant subsequently sues you, you will need to produce receipts for at least as much as the amount you deducted.

When you're trying to put a dollar amount on damages, the basic approach is to determine whether the tenant has damaged or substantially shortened the useful life of an item that does wear out. If the answer is yes, you may charge the tenant the prorated cost of the item, based on the age of the item, how long it might have lasted otherwise and the cost of replacement.

### Advance Notice of Deposit Deductions

Laws in the following five states give tenants the opportunity to inspect the rental unit to determine the accuracy of the landlord's list of damages before the final itemization is done. A tenant who disagrees with your proposed deductions has a specified amount of time to send you a written explanation as to this disagreement. Only then can the tenant sue you for deductions he or she considers improper.

| State | Rule |
|---|---|
| Florida | Landlord must send tenant a list of proposed deductions within 15 days after tenant vacates; tenant must send objections within 15 days of receiving landlord's list. (See the Attachment to Florida Leases and Rental Agreements in Appendix I.) |
| Georgia | Landlord must send tenant a list of proposed deductions within three days of the lease or rental agreement termination; tenant has a right to examine the premises within five days of lease termination. |
| Kentucky | Landlord must inspect and give tenant a list of deductions; tenant may inspect to ascertain the accuracy of the list. No time periods are specified for this process, but the landlord must still meet the state deadline for returning deposits. |
| Michigan | Landlord must send tenant an itemized list of proposed deductions within 30 days after the lease terminates; tenant must mail response within seven days of receiving landlord's list. |
| Tennessee | Landlord must mail a list of deductions to tenant; tenant may inspect to ascertain the accuracy of the list. No time periods are specified for this process, but the landlord must still meet the state deadline for returning deposits. |

Citations to these statutes are in "Citations for State Laws on Security Deposits" in Appendix I.

## Letter for Returning Entire Security Deposit

October 11, 199X
_____
Date

Gerry Fraser
_____
Tenant

976 Park Place
_____
Street address

Sacramento, CA 95840
_____
City and State

Dear _Gerry_____,
                        Tenant


Here is an itemization of your _____$1,500_____ security deposit on the property at

976 Park Place _____,

which you rented from me on a _____month-to-month_____ basis on

_____March 1_____,199_X_, and vacated on _____September 30_____, 199_X_.


As you left the rental property in satisfactory condition, I am returning the entire amount of the

security deposit of ____$1,500, plus $150 in interest, for a total of $1,650_____.


Sincerely,

Tom Stein
_____
Landlord/Manager

### 3. Itemizing Deductions for Repairs, Cleaning and Unpaid Rent

If you have to deduct for unpaid rent as well as cleaning and repairs, use the form Security Deposit Itemization (Deductions for Repairs, Cleaning and Unpaid Rent.) A sample is shown below.

⚠️ **Use "last month's rent" and "security deposit" correctly.** As explained in Chapter 4, some states do not allow you to use a deposit you have labeled "last month's rent" to cover damage or cleaning. If you live in a state that has adopted this approach, make sure that your security deposit itemization form complies with the law and that you use the available deposits correctly.

This Security Deposit Itemization (Deductions for Repairs, Cleaning and Unpaid Rent) form includes spaces for you to include unpaid rent not covered by a court judgment (line 6) and, if you have won an eviction lawsuit against the tenant, the amount of the court judgment you won (line 7). (Section F, above, shows you how to figure these amounts, and explains why it's better to deduct cleaning and damage costs from the security deposit before deducting any of a court judgment.) If the tenant has left without paying utility charges or another financial obligation required under your lease or rental agreement, provide details on line 6 (Defaults in Rent Not Covered by Any Court Judgment).

If there's a court judgment involved, explain how you applied the deposit in the Comments section at the bottom of the itemization form. This makes it clear that you are demanding the balance owed and that you can still collect any part of the judgment not covered by the security deposit.

### 4. Handling Deposits When a Tenant Files for Bankruptcy

Landlords often see a tenant's bankruptcy filing as the ultimate monkey-wrench in what may already be a less-than-perfect landlord-tenant relationship.

Indeed, once the tenant files, you can neither begin nor finish an eviction proceeding unless you get approval from the bankruptcy court to proceed (evictions and bankruptcy are explained in Chapter 17, Section I). Fortunately, the effect of the bankruptcy on your use of the security deposit is not so drastic.

Your course of action all depends on timing: When did the tenant file his petition, and when did you use the deposit to cover unpaid rent or damage? Here are three common scenarios and the rules for each:

- **Tenant hasn't paid the rent and/or has caused damage. You assess your total losses, deduct from (or use up) the deposit, and then tenant files for bankruptcy.** No problem here, since you used the money before the tenant filed. You're also on solid ground if you've gone to court and obtained a money judgment that can be satisfied fully, or at least partially, by the security deposit. The key is to use the funds, or get the judgment, before the tenant files. (See *In re Johnson,* 215 B.R. 381 (Bkrtcy.N.D.Ill. 1997).)

💡 **Take care of business quickly.** You probably won't know about your tenant's plans to file for bankruptcy. It's wise to asses your losses soon after the tenant vacates, and to leave a paper trail that will establish that the deposit was used before the filing date. If you keep deposits in a separate bank account and move these funds to another account as you use them, you'll have good proof.

- **Tenant causes damage that would normally be covered by the security deposit, or fails to pay the rent. Before you have the chance to use the money to pay for the damage or rent, you receive a notice from the bankruptcy court stating that the tenant has filed.** Once you receive this notice, you are prohibited from taking any action against the tenant, including using the security deposit, without an OK from the court (this is called a "Relief from Stay"). Instead of going to court, you

## Security Deposit Itemization
## (Deductions for Repairs and Cleaning)

Date: _____November 8, 199X_____

From: _____Rachel Tolan_____

_____123 Larchmont Lane_____

_____St. Louis, Missouri_____

To: _____Lena Coleman_____

_____456 Penny Lane, #101_____

_____St. Louis, Missouri_____

Property Address: _789 Cora Court, St. Louis, Missouri_____

Rental Period: _____January 1, 199X, to October 31, 199X_____

1. Security Deposit Received                          $ __600_____

2. Interest on Deposit (if required by lease or law):  $ __N/A_____

3. Total Credit (sum of lines 1 and 2)                              $ __600_____

4. Itemized Repairs and Related Losses:

   _Repainting of living room walls, required by crayon_

   _and chalk marks_____

   _____

   _____       Total Repair Cost: $ __260_____

5. Necessary Cleaning:

   _Sum paid to resident manager for 4 hours_

   _cleaning at $20/hour: debris-filled garage,_

   _dirty stove and refrigerator_____

   _____       Total Cleaning Cost: $ __80_____

6. Amount Owed (line 3 minus the sum of lines 4 and 5)

   ☐ a. Total Amount Tenant Owes Landlord:                  $ _____

   ☒ b. Total Amount Landlord Owes Tenant:                  $ __260_____

Comments: ___A check for $260 is enclosed._____

_____

_____

## Security Deposit Itemization
### (Deductions for Repairs, Cleaning and Unpaid Rent)

Date: _____December 19, 199X_____

From: _____Timothy Gottman_____

_____8910 Pine Avenue_____

_____Philadelphia, Pennsylvania_____

To: _____Monique Todd_____

_____999 Laurel Drive_____

_____Philadelphia, Pennsylvania_____

Property Address: _____456 Pine Avenue #7, Philadelphia, Pennsylvania_____

Rental Period: _____January 1, 199X, to October 31, 199X_____

1. Security Deposit Received                      $ _____1,200_____

2. Interest on Deposit (if required by lease or law):     $ _____N/A_____

3. Total Credit (sum of lines 1 and 2)                      $ _____1,200_____

4. Itemized Repairs and Related Losses:

   _____Carpet repair $160, drapery cleaning $140,_____

   _____plaster repair $400, painting of living room $100_____

   _____(receipts attached)_____

   _____        Total Repair Cost:   $ _____800_____

5. Necessary Cleaning:

   _____Sum paid to resident manager for 10 hours cleaning_____

   _____at $20/hour: debris-filled garage, dirty stove and_____

   _____refrigerator_____

   _____        Total Cleaning Cost: $ _____200_____

6. Defaults in Rent Not Covered by Any Court Judgment
   (list dates and rates):

   _____5 days at $20 day from November 6 to November 11_____

   _____(date of court judgment of date of physical eviction)_____

   _____$100_____

   _____        Total Rent Defaults: $ _____100_____

7. Amount of Court Judgment for Rent, Costs, Attorney Fees: $ _____1,160_____

8. Other Deductions:

    Specify: _____

    _____

    _____      $ _____

9. Amount Owed (line 3 minus the sum of lines 4, 5, 6, 7 and 8)

    ☒   a. Total Amount Tenant Owes Landlord:      $ ___1,060_____

    ☐   b. Total Amount Landlord Owes Tenant:      $ _____

Comments: _The security deposit has been applied as follows: $1,000 for damage and cleaning charges, $100 for defaults in rent (not covered by any court judgment) and the remaining $100 towards payment of the $1,160 court judgment. This leaves $1,060 still owed on the judgment. Please send that amount to me at once or I shall take appropriate legal action to collect it._

_____

_____

_____

_____

_____

_____

_____

_____

_____

_____

_____

_____

can just sit tight and wait until the bankruptcy proceeding is over. Then, you can use the money to cover the tenant's debt.

- **Tenant files for bankruptcy, then causes damage that would normally be covered by the security deposit.** Follow the same advice as above.

## H. Mailing the Security Deposit Itemization

Mail your security deposit itemization to the tenant's last known address or forwarding address as soon as is reasonably possible, along with payment for any balance you owe. Don't wait until the end of the legally specified period if you have all the information necessary to act sooner, as it almost guarantees that a large number of anxious tenants will contact you. And if you miss the deadline, you may be liable for hefty financial penalties, as discussed in Section J. Some states require landlords to use certified mail; check your state's statutes for any special mailing requirements. If the tenant hasn't left you a forwarding address, mail the itemization and any balance to the address of the rental property itself. That, after all, is the tenant's last address known to you. If your former tenant has left a forwarding address with the post office, it will forward the mail.

It will be useful for you to know the tenant's new address if the tenant's deposit doesn't cover all proper deductions and you want to sue in small claims court. (See Section K, below.) It will also help you collect any judgment you have against the tenant.

There are two ways that you can learn the new address:

- **Set up an account with the Postal Service.** You can pay the Post Office in advance to tell you whenever one of your letters is forwarded. Because of the cost involved, this procedure makes sense for landlords with many rental units.
- **Use "Return Receipt Requested."** For smaller landlords or people who rarely face this situation, it may not be worth your while to pre-pay. Instead, you can send the letter "Return Receipt Requested" and, on the Postal Service form, check the box that tells the carrier to note the address where the letter was delivered. This address will be on the receipt that is sent back to you.

If the tenant has left no forwarding address, the letter will come back to you. The postmarked envelope is your proof of your good-faith attempt to notify the tenant, in case the tenant ever accuses you of not returning the money properly. Some states, including Arkansas, Delaware, Iowa, Georgia and Kentucky, specifically allow the landlord to retain the deposit if he cannot locate the tenant after a reasonable effort or a certain amount of time has passed, such as 60 or 90 days. If your state laws do not specify what happens to the deposit if you cannot locate the tenant, you'll need to seek legal advice on what to do with the deposit.

## I. Security Deposits From Co-Tenants

When you rent to two or more co-tenants (they all sign the same written lease or rental agreement), you do not usually have to return or account for any of the deposit until they all leave. In other words, you're entitled to the benefit of the entire deposit until the entire tenancy ends. Legally, any question as to whether a departing co-tenant is entitled to any share of the deposit should be worked out among the co-tenants.

From a practical point of view, however, you may want to work out an agreement with a departing co-tenant who wants part of the deposit back. For instance, you may be willing to refund his share of the deposit if the new co-tenant gives you a check for that amount. The drawback of this approach is that the new co-tenant will not want to get stuck paying for damage that was caused by the departing tenant. If you accommodate this request, too, you may have to do an extra inspection in the middle of the lease term. (On the other hand, you may welcome an opportunity to discover and correct problems before they grow.)

> EXAMPLE: Bill and Mark were co-tenants who had each contributed $500 toward the $1,000 security deposit. Bill needed to move before the lease was up, and asked Len, their landlord, if he would accept Tom as a new co-tenant. Len agreed.
>
> Bill wanted his $500 back, and although Tom was willing to contribute his share of the deposit, he did not want to end up paying for damage that had been caused before he moved in. To take care of this, Len agreed to inspect if Tom would first give him a check for $500. When he got the check, Len inspected and found $200 worth of damage. He deducted this amount from Bill's share of the deposit, and wrote Bill a check for $300. Len left it up to Bill and Mark to fairly apportion the responsibility for the damage. With Tom's $500 check, the security deposit was once again topped-off.

## J. If a Tenant Sues You

No matter how meticulous you are about properly accounting to your tenants for their deposits, sooner or later you may be sued by a tenant who disagrees with your assessment of the cost of cleaning or repairs. Tenants may also sue if you fail to return the deposit when and how required, or violate other provisions of state or local law, such as a requirement that you pay interest on deposits.

Tenants usually sue in small claims court, where it's cheap to file, lawyers aren't necessary and disputes typically go before a judge (there are no juries) within 30 to 60 days, without formal rules of evidence. (We use the term small claims court here, but the exact name may vary depending upon the state. The courts are called "Justice of the Peace," "Conciliation," "District," "Justice," "City" or "County" in different places.)

The maximum amount for which someone can sue in small claims court varies among the states, but in most states it's about $3,000 to $7,500.

⚠️ **Penalties for violating security deposit statutes can turn a minor squabble into an expensive affair**. While it is rarely worth your while to go to court over a matter of $50 or even a couple of hundred dollars, the same is not true for the tenant. Why? Because many statutes allow a victorious tenant to collect not only actual damages (the amount improperly deducted from the deposit), but penalties as well. Small claims courts are empowered to award these penalties. (Section 4, below, covers landlord penalties for violating security deposit laws.)

This section suggests several strategies for dealing with small claims suits over security deposits, including how to prepare and present a case in small claims court.

📖 For more information on small claims court procedures, see Chapter 16 and *Everybody's Guide to Small Claims Court* (National Edition), by Ralph Warner (Nolo Press).

## 1. When a Tenant May Sue

Before going to court, the tenant will most likely express dissatisfaction by way of a letter or phone call demanding that you refund more than you did or fix some other problem involving the deposit. In some states, this sort of demand must be made before the tenant can begin a small claims suit. After making a demand, the tenant can bring suit immediately.

A tenant who is going to sue will probably do it fairly promptly, but may have up to a few years to do so, depending on the state. Don't throw out cleaning bills, receipts for repairs or photographs showing dirt and damages after only a few months, lest you be caught defenseless.

## 2. Settling a Potential Lawsuit

If you receive a demand letter or phone call from a tenant, your best bet is almost always to try to work out a reasonable compromise. Be open to the idea of returning more of the deposit to the tenant, even if you believe your original assessment of the cost of repairs and cleaning was more than fair and you feel you will surely win in court. For practical reasons, it usually doesn't make sense for you or an employee to prepare a small claims case and spend time in court to argue over $50, $100 or even $200. This is especially true because, fair or not, some judges are prone to split the difference between the landlord's and the tenant's claims.

If you and the tenant can't reach a reasonable compromise, you may wish to get help from a local landlord-tenant mediation service, described in Chapter 16.

If you arrive at a compromise settlement with your former tenant, you should insist that your payment be accepted as full and final satisfaction of your obligation to return the deposit. The best way to do this is to prepare and have the tenant sign a brief settlement agreement, like the sample shown below.

### Sample Settlement Agreement

Lionel Washington, "Landlord," and LaToya Jones, "Tenant," agree as follows:

1. Landlord rented the premises at 1234 State Avenue, Apartment 5, Santa Fe, New Mexico, to Tenant on July 1, 199X, pursuant to a written rental agreement for a tenancy from month-to-month.

2. Under the Agreement, Tenant paid Landlord $1,000 as a security deposit.

3. On October 31, 199X, Tenant vacated the premises.

4. Within 30 days (the time required by New Mexico law) after Tenant vacated the premises, Landlord itemized various deductions from the security deposit totaling $380 and refunded the balance of $620 to Tenant.

5. Tenant asserts that she is entitled to the additional sum of $300, only $80 of the deductions being proper. Landlord asserts that all the deductions were proper and that he owes Tenant nothing.

6. To settle the parties' entire dispute, and to compromise on Tenant's claim for return of her security deposit, Landlord pays to Tenant the sum of $150, receipt of which is hereby acknowledged by Tenant as full satisfaction of her claim.

| | |
|---|---|
| *12/1/9X* | *Lionel Washington* |
| Date | Lionel Washington, Landlord |
| *12/1/9X* | *LaToya Jones* |
| Date | LaToya Jones, Tenant |

## Splitting the Difference With Tenants

One landlord we know with thousands of units experiences about 250 move-outs each month. In about one-third, he receives a complaint from a tenant who claims too much of the deposit was withheld.

This landlord's general policy is to offer to settle for 70% of the disputed amount. Since the average amount withheld is $175, this means the landlord is willing to reduce this amount by $52.50. If a tenant refuses to accept this compromise, the landlord will often make a second offer of a 50% reduction.

He does this not because he thinks his original assessment was wrong, but because he finds that coming to a settlement with a tenant costs a lot less than fighting in court. However, if the settlement offer isn't accepted promptly by the tenant, he fights to win and almost always does.

## 3. Preparing for a Small Claims Court Hearing

If no compromise is possible and the tenant sues you, the court will officially notify you of the date, time and place of the small claims court hearing.

It's still not too late at this stage to try to work out a settlement by paying part of what the tenant's suing for. However, if you compromise at this stage, make sure the tenant has correctly dismissed the small courts court suit. Be sure your settlement is in writing.

## Who Goes to Court?

If your business is incorporated, you can send an employee such as a property manager, as long as the person is authorized to represent you in legal proceedings. If you are not incorporated, you'll probably have to go yourself, but a few states allow managers to go in your place. In most states you can be represented by a lawyer in small claims court, but it's rarely worth the cost. Procedures are simple and designed for non-lawyers.

Before your court hearing, gather tangible evidence showing the premises needed cleaning or were damaged when the tenant left. It is essential to take to court as many of the following items of evidence as you can:

- Copies of the lease or rental agreement, signed by both you and the tenant.
- Copies of move-in and move-out letters clarifying rules and policies on cleaning, damage repair and security deposits.
- A copy of the Landlord-Tenant Checklist that you should have filled out with the tenant

when the tenant moved in and when she moved out, signed by both you and the tenant. This is particularly important if the tenant admitted, on the Checklist, to damaged or dirty conditions when she moved out.

- Photos or a video of the premises before the tenant moved in which show how clean and undamaged the place was.

- Photos or a video after the tenant left which show a mess or damage.

- An itemization of hours spent by you or your repair or cleaning people on the unit, complete with the hourly costs for the work, plus copies of receipts for cleaning materials or credit card itemizations or canceled checks.

- Damaged items small enough to bring into the courtroom (a curtain with a cigarette hole would be effective).

- Receipts or a canceled check for professional cleaning (particularly of carpets and drapes) and repair.

- One, or preferably two, witnesses who were familiar with the property, saw it just after the tenant left and who will testify that the place was a mess or that certain items were damaged. People who helped in the cleaning or repair are particularly effective witnesses. There is no rule that says you can't have a close friend or relative testify for you, but given a choice, it's better to have a witness who's neither a friend nor kin.

- If it's difficult for a witness to come to court, a written statement (a signed letter) or a declaration under penalty of perjury can be used in most states. Documents, however, usually aren't as effective as live testimony. If you do present a written statement from a witness, make sure the statement includes the date of the event, exactly what the witness saw in terms of damage, any credentials that make the person qualified to testify on the subject and any other facts that have a bearing on the dispute. A sample statement is shown below.

## Sample Declaration of Paul Stallone, Cleaner

I, Paul Stallone, declare:

1. I am employed at A & B Maintenance Company, a contract cleaning and maintenance service located at 123 Abrego Street, Central City, Iowa. Gina Cabarga, the owner of an apartment complex at 456 Seventh Street, Central City, Iowa, is one of our accounts.

2. On May 1, 199x, I was requested to go to the premises at 456 Seventh Street, Apartment 8, Central City, Iowa, to shampoo the carpets. When I entered the premises, I noticed a strong odor, part of what seemed like stale cigarette smoke. An odor also seemed to come from the carpet.

3. When I began using a steam carpet cleaner on the living room carpet, I noticed a strong smell of urine. I stopped the steam cleaner, moved to a dry corner of the carpet, and pulled it from the floor. I then saw a yellow color on the normally-white foam-rubber pad beneath the carpet, as well as smelled a strong urine odor, apparently caused by a pet (probably a cat) having urinated on the carpet. On further examination of the parts of the carpet, I noticed similar stains and odors throughout the carpet and pad.

4. In my opinion, the living room carpet and foam-rubber pad underneath need to be removed and replaced and the floor should be sanded and sealed.

I declare under penalty of perjury under the laws of the State of Iowa that the foregoing is true and correct.

6/15/9X                 *Paul Stallone*
Date                        Paul Stallone, Cleaner

### Small Claims Suits Don't Affect Other Lawsuits

Nothing that happens in small claims court affects the validity of any judgment you already have—for example, from an earlier eviction suit—against the tenant. So, if you got a judgment against a tenant for $1,200 for unpaid rent as part of an eviction action, this judgment is still good, even though a tenant wins $200 against you in small claims court based on your failure to return the deposit.

## 4. Penalties for Violating Security Deposit Laws

If you don't follow state security deposit laws to the letter, you may pay a heavy price if a tenant sues you and wins. In addition to whatever amount you wrongfully withheld, you may have to pay the tenant extra or punitive damages (penalties imposed when the judge feels that the defendant has acted especially outrageously) and court costs. In many states if you "willfully" (deliberately and not through inadvertence) violate the security deposit statute, you may forfeit your right to retain any part of the deposit and may be liable for two or three times the amount wrongfully withheld, plus attorney's fees and costs.

## K. If the Deposit Doesn't Cover Damage and Unpaid Rent

Tenants aren't the only ones who can use small claims court. If the security deposit doesn't cover what a tenant owes you for back rent, cleaning or repairs (or if your state prohibits the use of the security deposit for unpaid rent), you may wish to file a small claims lawsuit against the former tenant.

Be sure your claim doesn't exceed your state's small claims court limit or, if it does, decide whether it make sense to scale it back to the limit. Given the costs of going to formal court, this can sometimes make sense.

For detailed advice, see *Everybody's Guide to Small Claims Court* (National Edition), by Ralph Warner (Nolo Press).

## 1. The Demand Letter

If you decide that it is worthwhile to go after your tenant for money owed, your first step is to write a letter asking for the amount of your claim. Although this may seem like an exercise in futility, the law in many states requires that you make a demand for the amount sued for before filing in small claims court. But even if there is no such requirement, it is almost essential that you send some sort of demand letter. It is not only useful in trying to settle your dispute, it's also an excellent opportunity to carefully organize the case you will present in court.

Your demand can consist of a brief cover letter along with a copy of your earlier written itemization of how you applied the tenant's security deposit to the charges (in which you also requested payment of the balance). (See Section G, above.)

## 2. Should You Sue?

If your demand letter does not produce results, think carefully before you rush off to your local small claims court. Ask yourself three questions:

- **Do I have a strong case?** Review the items of evidence listed in Section G, above. If you lack a substantial number of these pieces of ammunition you may end up losing, even if you are in the right. Small claims court is rarely about justice, but always about preparation and skill.
- **Can I locate the former tenant?**
- **Can I collect a judgment if I win?** Keep in mind that small claims judgments are usually good for ten years and, in many states, can be renewed. So if you have a spat with a

student or someone who may get a job soon, it might be worthwhile to get a judgment with the hope of collecting later.

If the answer to any of these questions is no, think twice about initiating a suit.

Pay particular attention to the third question, about how you will collect a judgment. The best way to collect any judgment against your ex-tenant is to garnish wages. If she's working, there is an excellent chance of collecting if payment is not made voluntarily. You can't, however, garnish a welfare, Social Security, unemployment, pension or disability check. So, if the person sued gets income from one of these sources, you may be wasting your time unless you can identify some other asset that you can efficiently get your hands on.

Bank accounts, motor vehicles and real estate are other common collection sources. But people who run out on their debts don't always have much in a bank account (or they may have moved the account to make it difficult to locate), and much of their personal property may be exempt under state debt protection laws.

In California, see *Collect Your Court Judgment*, by Gini Graham Scott, Stephen Elias and Lisa Goldoftas (Nolo Press).

**Don't poison the well.** If you are a landlord with many rental units and regularly use a local small claims court, make particularly sure that every case you bring is a good one. You do not want to lose your credibility with the court in future cases by ever appearing to be unfair or poorly prepared.

## Using Collection Agencies

If you don't want to sue in small claims court, consider hiring a licensed local collection agency to try to collect from the tenant. The agency will probably want to keep as its fee anywhere from one-third to one-half of what it collects for you. (The older the debt or the more difficult it is to locate the tenant, the more the agency will want.) If the agency can't collect, you can authorize it to hire a lawyer to sue the ex-tenant, usually in a formal (non-small claims) court. Many collection agencies pay all court costs, hoping to recover them if and when they collect the resulting judgment. In exchange for taking the risk of paying costs and losing the case, however, collection agency commissions often rise an additional 15%–20% when they hire a lawyer to sue.

Of course, turning a matter over to a collection agency doesn't necessarily mean you wash your hands of the matter. The collection agency still takes direction from you. If the tenant defends against a lawsuit filed by a collection agency's lawyer, you must be involved in the litigation. The only way to walk away from it completely is to sell the debt to the collection agency, which may pay you only a fraction of the amount owed.

# Chapter 16

# Problems With Tenants: How to Resolve Disputes Without a Lawyer

*"May you have a lawsuit in which you know you are right."*

**— Old Mexican curse**

Legal disputes—actual and potential—come in all shapes and sizes when you're a landlord. Here are some of the more common ones:

- **Rent.** You and your tenant disagree about the validity, timing or methods of a rent increase.
- **Habitability.** Your tenant threatens to withhold rent because he claims a leaky roof or some other defect has made the living room unusable.
- **Access to the premises.** Your tenant won't let you show her apartment to prospective new tenants or enter for some other good reason. You feel it's your legal right to do so, and your tenant claims that your legal reason for invading her privacy is bogus.
- **Security deposits.** You and a departing tenant disagree about how much security deposit you owe the tenant based on your claim that the unit is dirty or damaged or both.
- **Lease or rental agreement violation.** Your tenant (or former tenant) has failed to pay rent, moved in a new roommate (or a pet) without your permission, hosted a series of loud parties or in some other way violated your lease or rental agreement.

How you handle such disputes can have a profound effect on your bottom line, not to mention your mental health. In some cases, such as a tenant's nonpayment of rent, your only option may be to terminate the tenancy. Rarely should lawyers and litigation be your first choice. Instead, you will usually want to consider alternatives that can give you better control over the time, energy and money you spend.

This chapter discusses four commonly available options to resolve a legal dispute without a lawyer:

- negotiation
- mediation
- arbitration, and
- small claims court.

While we focus here on disputes with tenants, you should also find much of the advice useful for resolving all types of business disputes—for example, with your manager, insurance company or repairperson.

This chapter also explains how to avoid charges of retaliation in your dealings with tenants.

How to terminate a tenancy based on nonpayment of rent and other illegal acts is discussed in Chapter 17.

---

### Put It in Writing

To help avoid legal problems in the first place, and minimize those that can't be avoided, it makes sense to adopt efficient, easy-to-follow systems to document important facts of your relationship with your tenants. Throughout this book, we recommend many forms and recordkeeping systems that will help you do this, including move-in and move-out letters, a landlord-tenant checklist and a maintenance/repair request form. The key is to establish a good paper trail for each tenancy, beginning with the rental application and lease or rental agreement through a termination notice and security deposit itemization. Such documentation will be extremely valuable if attempts at resolving your dispute fail and you end up evicting or suing a tenant, or being sued by a tenant. Also, you'll obviously want to keep copies of any correspondence and notes of your conversations with tenants. Chapter 7 recommends a system for organizing tenant information, including records of repair requests.

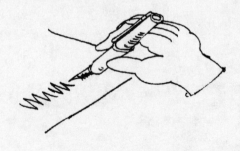

## A. Negotiating a Settlement

If you have a conflict with your tenant over rent, repairs, your access to the rental unit, noise or some other issue that doesn't immediately warrant an eviction, a sensible first step is to meet with the tenant—even one you consider to be a hopeless troublemaker—to see if the problem can be resolved. This advice is based on the simple premise that unless you have the legal grounds (and the determination) to evict a tenant, it's almost always best to try and negotiate a settlement rather than let the dispute escalate into a court fight. This is doubly true if you are convinced your case is just. Given the cost and delays built into the arthritic American legal system, the more you rely on it, the more you are likely to regret going to court.

So forget about suing, except possibly in small claims court (see Section D, below), and try to evaluate the legal and financial realities objectively. Your goal should be to achieve the best result at the lowest cost. If instead you act on the conviction (whether it's right or wrong makes no difference) that your rights are being trampled by the other side, chances are you'll end up spending far too much time and money fighting for "the principle" involved. Over time, a landlord who allows himself to be controlled by this sort of emotional reaction is almost sure to fare emotionally and financially poorer than a person who keeps an eye on the overall objective—to make a good living and enjoy doing it.

Your first step in working towards a compromise with an unhappy or problem tenant is to call the tenant and arrange a time to meet. Dropping over unannounced to talk may work in some circumstances, but is generally not a good idea, since it may emotionally threaten the tenant and put him in a defensive position. It may be appropriate to write a letter first, offering to meet with the tenant to work something out. (See, for example, the sample letter in Chapter 9 in which the landlord suggests a compromise with a tenant who withholds rent because of defective conditions in his apartment.)

### Use Warning Notices Appropriately

In some situations, it may be appropriate to give a tenant a written notice to cease the problem or disruptive activity, particularly if the tenant has not created other problems and you feel that he's apt to respond to your polite but firm reprove.

What happens if the tenant does not reform, despite your reminder? If the misbehavior is grounds for terminating the tenancy and you want him out, in a sense you'll have to start over—you'll have to give him a formal termination notice that meets your state's requirements. (Termination notices are explained in Chapter 17.) Your warning note will not quality as a termination notice. For example, if your tenant has kept a dog in violation of the lease, and he keeps the pet despite your polite note asking him to remove the dog, in most states you'll have to give him a formal notice telling him to get rid of the dog within a certain number of days or move. (If he does neither, you can file for eviction.) In short, an informal warning may simply allow an obdurate tenant to delay the inevitable.

A sample warning letter is shown below. You can use this warning letter for many purposes, such as warning the tenant to stop having loud parties, repair damage to your property or get rid of a long-term guest. But don't waste your time with someone unlikely to respond, and always be prepared with a formal termination notice if the situation doesn't improve.

You will find a Warning Letter for Lease or Rental Agreement Violation on the Legal Forms Disk as well as a blank tear-out form in Appendix II.

## Warning Letter for Lease or Rental Agreement Violation

_November 4, 199X_
Date

_Jerry Brooks_
Tenant

_179 Lynwood Drive_
Street address

_Tampa, Florida 33611_
City and State

Dear _Jerry_,
       Tenant

This is a reminder that your lease prohibits _annoying, disturbing or interfering with the quiet_ _enjoyment and peace and quiet of any other tenant or nearby resident (Clause 13)_

(violation) It has come to my attention that, starting _(on November 2_ , 199 _X_ ,

(date of violation) ~~and continuing to the present,~~ you have broken this condition of your tenancy by _holding a noisy party that lasted until 3 a.m. disturbing other tenants_

It is our desire that you and all other tenants enjoy living in your rental unit. To make sure this occurs, we enforce all terms and conditions of our leases. So please immediately _keep noise within reasonable limits and no loud parties after midnight on weekends or 10 p.m. on_ _weekdays_

If it proves impossible to promptly resolve this matter, we will exercise our legal right to begin eviction proceedings.

Please contact me if you would like to discuss this matter further and clear up any possible misunderstandings.

Yours truly,

_Clark Johnson_
Landlord/Manager

_Belle Epoque, 387 Golf Road_
Street address

_Tampa, Florida 33611_
City and State

_813-555-1234_
Phone

Here are some helpful pointers for negotiating with tenants:

- **Solicit the tenant's point of view.** Once the tenant starts talking, listen closely and don't interrupt, even if some of his points are not true or some of his opinions are inflammatory.

- **When the tenant has wound down, acknowledge that you have heard his key points, even if you disagree with them.** Sometimes it's even a good idea to repeat the tenant's concerns so he will realize you know what they are and will stop repeating them.

- **Avoid personal attacks.** This only raises the level of hostility and makes settlement more difficult. Equally important, don't react impulsively to the emotional outbursts of the tenant.

- **Be courteous, but don't be weak.** If you have a good case, let the tenant know you have the resources and evidence to fight and win if you can't reach a reasonable settlement.

- **Before the negotiation goes too far, try and determine if the tenant is a truly an unbearable jerk who you really want to be rid of or just another slightly annoying person.** If a tenant falls into the first category, your strategy should be to terminate the tenancy as soon as legally and practically possible.

- **If possible, try to structure the negotiation as a mutual attempt to solve a problem.** For example, if a tenant's guests have been disturbing the neighbors, jointly seek solutions that recognize the interests of both parties.

- **Try to figure out the tenant's priorities.** Maybe dollars are less important than pride, in which case a formula for future relations that meets the needs of a thin-skinned tenant to be treated with respect might solve the problem.

- **Put yourself in the tenant's shoes.** What would you want to settle? Sometimes your answer may be something like "a sense that I've won." Fine—the best settlements are often those in which both sides feel they've won (or at least not given up anything fundamental). So your job is to let the tenant have at least a partial sense of victory on one or more of the issues in dispute.

- **When you propose a specific settlement, make it clear that you're attempting to compromise.** Offers of settlement (clearly labeled as such) can't be introduced against you if you ever end up in court.

- **Money is a powerful incentive to settlement.** If you are going to have to pay something eventually, or spend a lot of time and money on a costly eviction lawsuit or preparing a small claims case, it makes overall financial sense to come to the negotiating table willing to pay—perhaps by reducing rent for a short period of time, cutting in half the money owed for damages to the premises, or offering an outright cash settlement for the tenant to leave (with payment made only as the tenant leaves and hands you the keys). Savvy landlords know that many financially strapped tenants may settle at a surprisingly low figure if they can walk away from the bargaining table with payment in hand. If this saves the costs and delays inherent in a long eviction battle, and allows you to re-rent the unit to a paying tenant, it can be well worth the money.

- **If you reach an understanding with your tenant, promptly write it down and have all parties sign it.** You or your lawyer should volunteer to prepare the first draft. If you're paying the tenant some money as part of your agreement, make sure the tenant acknowledges in writing that your payment fully satisfies her claim. Chapter 15 includes an example of a settlement agreement for a security deposit dispute that you can use as a model for settling disputes.

- **If the negotiation process indicates a larger problem with tenant dissatisfaction, think carefully how to avoid similar disputes in the future**—for example, you may need to revise your systems for handling repair complaints or returning security deposits.

## Talking With Your Tenant Pays Off

Lorene, a single mother who had rented one of Ben's apartments for two years with little trouble, suddenly stopped paying rent. She claimed that a long list of minor problems—including peeling paint, mold and leaky faucets—justified nonpayment.

Ben, the landlord, considered Lorene's rent withholding to be ridiculous, and his first reaction was to evict her. But after careful thought, Ben called and asked Lorene to meet with him instead.

After listening to all of Lorene's complaints and conceding that several were valid, Ben steered the conversation around to the amount of the rent. It turned out that Lorene hadn't received her child support payments for three months because her ex-husband was out of work and she didn't know when he would be able to resume payments. Lorene's own salary was not enough to pay the rent.

Ben suggested that Lorene move to a smaller, less expensive unit in one of his buildings. He even offered to provide a truck and have his manager kick in a few hours of labor to help her move. Ben also suggested that the current month's rent be charged at the new unit's lower rate, even though it would take a week for Lorene to move.

The result was that Ben converted Lorene back into a paying tenant, at the same time he was able to re-rent the original unit—with the mold, peeling paint and leaky faucet problems solved—almost immediately. True, Ben lost a few dollars of rent and paid his manager to do some moving work, but compared to the attorney fees, court costs and loss of rent that would have resulted from an eviction fight, he was far, far ahead.

**Recommended Reading on Negotiation.**
*Getting to Yes: Negotiating Agreement Without Giving In*, by Roger Fisher and William Ury (Penguin Books). This classic offers a strategy for coming to mutually acceptable agreements in all kinds of situations, including landlord-tenant disputes.

*Getting Past No: Negotiating Your Way From Confrontation to Cooperation*, by William Ury (Bantam Books). This sequel to *Getting to Yes* discusses techniques for negotiating with obnoxious, stubborn and otherwise difficult people.

## B. Understanding Mediation

If you're unsuccessful negotiating a settlement, but still want to work something out with the tenant, you may wish to try mediation by a neutral third party, often available at little or no cost from a publicly funded program. (See "How to Find a Mediation Group," below.)

Mediation can make good sense, especially if:
- you are dealing with someone who has proven to be a good tenant in the past and you think the tenant is worth dealing with in the future
- the tenant is as receptive as you are to some method of avoiding the expense and delay of litigation, or the possibility of being evicted
- the tenant is up-to-date on rent (or the rent money is put in some type of escrow account), or
- you are trying to avoid the risk of one influential tenant poisoning your relationship with others.

If mediation doesn't make sense, make clear your intention (and legal right) to sue or evict the tenant. (See Section D and Chapter 17.)

Many people confuse mediation with arbitration (discussed in Section C). While both are nonjudicial ways to resolve disputes, there's a huge difference: Arbitration results in a binding decision, while

mediation doesn't, since the mediator has no power to impose a decision but is there simply to help the parties work out a mutually acceptable solution to their dispute.

Mediation in landlord-tenant disputes is usually fairly informal. More likely than not, the mediator will have everyone sit down together from the very beginning and allow both parties to express all their issues—even emotional ones. This often cools people off considerably and frequently results in a fairly quick compromise. If the dispute is not resolved easily, however, the mediator may suggest ways to resolve the problem, or may even keep everyone talking long enough to realize that the real problem goes deeper than the one being mediated. Typically this is done through a caucus process—each side is put in a separate room. The mediator talks to each person sequentially to try and determine his or her bottom line. Then, shuttling back and forth, the mediator helps the parties structure an acceptable solution. At some point, everyone has to get back together to sign off.

For example, if a tenant has threatened rent withholding because of a defect in the premises, the mediator may discover that the tenant's real grievance is that your manager is slow to make repairs. This may lead to the further finding that the manager is angry at the tenant for letting her kids pull up his tulips. So the final solution may fall into place only when the tenant agrees to provide better supervision for the kids in exchange for the manager getting the repairs done pronto.

Does mediation really work? Surprisingly, yes, given the fact that there's no one to impose a solution. One reason is the basic cooperative spirit that goes into mediation. By agreeing to mediate a dispute in the first place, you and the tenant must jointly establish the rules which, in turn, sets the stage for cooperating to solve your dispute. Also, the fact that no judge or arbitrator has the power to impose what may be an unacceptable solution reduces the fear factor on both sides. This, in turn, often means both landlord and tenant take less extreme—and more conciliatory—positions.

*How to Mediate Your Dispute*, by Peter Lovenheim (Nolo Press). This book explains the mediation process from start to finish, including how to prepare for mediation and draft a legally enforceable agreement.

---

### How to Find a Mediation Group

For information on local mediation programs, call your mayor's or city manager's office, and ask for the staff member who handles "landlord-tenant mediation matters" or "housing disputes." That person should refer you to the public office or business or community group that attempts to informally —and at little or no cost—resolve landlord-tenant disputes before they reach the court stage. You can also contact the American Arbitration Association (see "How to Find an Arbitrator," below), or a neighborhood dispute resolution center, and arrange for mediation. If possible, split the mediation cost (if any) with your tenant.

---

## C. Using Arbitration

Many organizations that offer mediation also conduct arbitration if the parties can't reach an agreement. Almost any dispute with a tenant or other party that can be litigated can be arbitrated. With arbitration, you get a relatively quick, relatively inexpensive solution to a dispute without going to court. Like a judge, the arbitrator—a neutral third party—has power to hear the dispute and make a final, binding decision. Where does this power come from? From you and the other party. In binding arbitration, you agree in advance in writing to submit to arbitration and to be bound by the arbitrator's decision.

You can include a clause in your lease or rental agreement that requires that arbitration be used for any contractual dispute, although this usually makes sense more for longer term leases of expensive properties. Otherwise, you and the tenant can also decide to use arbitration after a dispute arises. If you and the tenant agree to binding arbitration, an informal hearing is held. Each person tells his or her side of the story, and an arbitrator reaches a decision, which is enforceable in court.

If the losing party doesn't pay the money required by an arbitration award, the winner can easily convert the award to a court judgment, which can be enforced like any other court judgment. Unlike a judgment based on litigation, however, you generally can't take an appeal from an arbitration-based judgment. (An exception is when there was some element of fraud in the procedures leading to the arbitration award.)

---

### How to Find an Arbitrator

To find an arbitrator or learn more about arbitration, contact the American Arbitration Association, the oldest and largest organization of its kind, with regional offices in 36 U.S. cities. You can reach the main office in New York City by calling 212-484-4000.

Keep in mind that you are not required to use an organization for arbitration. You and the other party are free to choose your own arbitrator or arbitration panel, and to set your own procedural rules. Just remember that for arbitration to be binding and legally enforceable, you need to follow the simple guidelines set down in your state's arbitration statute. You can usually find the statute by looking in the statutory index under "Arbitration" or checking the table of contents for the civil procedure sections. (See Chapter 18 for advice on doing this kind of legal research.)

## D. Representing Yourself in Small Claims Court

If your attempts at settling a dispute involving money fail, you may end up in a lawsuit. Fortunately, there are many instances when you can competently and cost-efficiently represent yourself in court. This is almost always true when your case is at the small claims level.

A few states use names other than small claims court, but traditionally the purpose has been the same: to provide a speedy, inexpensive resolution of disputes that involve relatively small amounts of money (generally less than $3,500). (The chart below lists each state's small claims court limit.)

Most people who go to small claims court handle their own cases. In fact, in some states, including California, Michigan and New York, lawyers aren't allowed to represent clients in small claims court. In any event, representing yourself is almost always the best choice—after all, the main reason to use the small claims court is because the size of the case doesn't justify the cost of hiring a lawyer.

A landlord can use small claims court for many purposes—for example, to collect unpaid rent or to seek money for property damage after a tenant

moves out and her deposit is exhausted. In short, in a variety of circumstances, small claims court offers a great opportunity to collect money that would otherwise be lost because it would be too expensive to sue in regular court. And in a few states eviction suits can be filed in small claims court. (Chapter 17 includes a list of states that allow evictions in small claims court.)

Landlords can also be sued in small claims court—for example, by a tenant who claims that you failed to return a security deposit. Chapter 15 discusses small claims suits over security deposits.

**Don't waste your time suing total deadbeats.** As a general rule, if you suspect you cannot collect the money—from a paycheck, bank account or other financial resource—don't waste your time in small claims court. A judgment you can't collect is worthless.

**Recommended Reading on Small Claims Court.** *Everybody's Guide to Small Claims Court* (National Edition), by Ralph Warner (Nolo Press), provides detailed advice on bringing or defending a small claims court case, preparing evidence and witnesses for court and collecting your money judgment when you win. *Everybody's Guide to Small Claims Court* will also be useful in defending yourself against a tenant who sues you in small claims court—for example, claiming that you failed to return a cleaning or security deposit.

## 1. Learning the Rules

Small claims court procedures are relatively simple and easy to master. Basically, you pay a small fee, file your lawsuit with the court clerk, see to it that the papers are served on your opponent, show up on the appointed day, tell the judge your story and present any witnesses and other evidence. The key to winning is usually to present evidence to back up your story. For example, a photograph of a dirty or damaged apartment and the convincing testimony of someone who helped you clean up are usually all you need to prevail if you are trying to recover money over and above the tenant's deposit or defending against a tenant's suit for the return of a deposit.

Court rules—dealing with such things as where you file your lawsuit, how papers can be served on your opponent (service of process), the deadline (statute of limitations) for filing a small claims suit—are usually published in a free booklet or information sheet provided by the small claims clerk. In addition, clerks in small claims court are expected to explain procedures to you. In some states, they may even help you fill out the necessary forms, which are quite simple anyhow. If necessary, be persistent. If you ask enough questions, you'll get the answers you need to handle your own case comfortably. Also, in some states such as California, you can consult a small claims court advisor for free.

## 2. Meeting the Jurisdictional Limits

How much can you sue for in small claims court? The maximum amount varies from state to state. Generally, the limit is $2,000 to $3,500. But more recently, recognizing that formal courts have become prohibitively expensive for all but large disputes, many states have begun to increase the monetary size of the cases their small claims courts can consider. For example, in California, landlords can sue for $5,000. In Minnesota, the small claims limit is $7,500 and in Tennessee's Court of Simplified Procedure it is $10,000. Check your state's small claims court limit on the chart below, but also ask the court clerk for the most current limit; state legislatures regularly increase these limits.

**You can scale your case down to fit small claims court limits.** Don't assume that your case can't be brought in small claims court if it's for slightly more than the limit. Rather than hiring a lawyer or trying to go it alone in formal court, your most cost-effective option may be to sue for the small claims maximum and forget the rest.

## E. How to Avoid Charges of Retaliation

As we've discussed throughout this book, residential tenants have a number of legal rights and remedies. While the specifics vary by state, here are a few rights tenants typically have:

- the right to complain to governmental authorities about health or safety problems, and, in many states, the right to withhold rent, or even to file a lawsuit against a landlord who fails to keep the premises in proper repair (see Chapter 9)
- the right to be free from discriminatory conduct based on factors such as race, religion, children, sex and disability, and to complain to administrative agencies, or even courts, when she (the tenant) feels her rights are being violated (see Chapter 5)
- privacy rights limiting landlord's access (see Chapter 13)
- the right to engage in political activity. For example, a tenant who actively campaigns for local candidates whom you find obnoxious, organizes a tenant union or campaigns for a rent control ordinance, has an absolute right to do so without fear of intimidation.

Because tenant protection laws would be meaningless if you could legally retaliate against a tenant who asserts his legal rights, the laws or court decisions in most states forbid such retaliation. For example, the right of a tenant to complain to the local fire department about a defective heater would be worth little if you, angry about the complaint, could retaliate against her with an immediate termination notice, or by doing anything else that works to the tenant's disadvantage such as increasing rent. The general idea is that tenants should not be punished by landlords just because they are invoking their legal rights or remedies.

Unfortunately, tenants sometimes unfairly accuse landlords of retaliatory misconduct—for example, a tenant who can't or won't pay a legitimate rent increase may claim you are guilty of retaliation. The same sort of unreasonable reliance on tenant

## Small Claims Court Limits

| State | Amount | State | Amount |
|---|---|---|---|
| Alabama | $3,000 | Nevada | $3,500 |
| Alaska | $7,500 | New Hampshire | $2,500 |
| Arizona | $2,500 (Small Claims Court) $5,000 (Regular Justice Court) | New Jersey | $2,000 (Small Claims Court) $10,000 (Special Civil Court) |
| Arkansas | $3,000 | New Mexico | $5,000 |
| California | $5,000 | New York | $3,000 |
| Colorado | $5,000 | North Carolina | $3,000 |
| Connecticut | $2,500 | North Dakota | $5,000 |
| Delaware | $15,000 | Ohio | $3,000 |
| District of Columbia | $5,000 | Oklahoma | $4,500 |
| Florida | $5,000 (Small Claims Court) $15,000 (County Court) | Oregon | $3,500 |
| | | Pennsylvania | $5,000 |
| Georgia | $5,000 | Rhode Island | $1,500 |
| Hawaii | $3,500[1] | South Carolina | $5,000 |
| Idaho | $3,000 | South Dakota | $4,000 |
| Illinois | $5,000 | Tennessee | $15,000[3] |
| Indiana | $6,000[2] | Texas | $5,000 |
| Iowa | $4,000 | Utah | $5,000 |
| Kansas | $1,800 | Vermont | $3,500 |
| Kentucky | $1,500 | Virginia | $15,000[4] |
| Louisiana | $2,000 | Washington | $2,500 |
| Maine | $4,500 | West Virginia | $5,000 |
| Maryland | $2,500 | Wisconsin | $5,000[5] |
| Massachusetts | $2,000 | Wyoming | $4,000; County Court, $7,000 |
| Michigan | $1,750 | | |
| Minnesota | $7,500 | [1] No limit in deposit cases. | |
| Mississippi | $2,500 | [2] $6,000 in Marion and Lake Counties; $3,000 in others. | |
| Missouri | $3,000 | [3] $25,000 if county population over 700,000. | |
| Montana | $3,000 | [4] Depends on jurisdiction. $15,000 is maximum. | |
| Nebraska | $2,100 | [5] No limit on eviction suits | |

protection laws can occur when you seek to terminate the tenancy for a perfectly legitimate reason and the tenant doesn't want to move. How do you cope with this sort of cynical misuse of the law? As with most things legal, there is no single answer. However, if you plan ahead and consider how one tenant might misuse the law and how you can counter this misuse, you should be able to minimize any legal problems.

You start with one great advantage when faced with a tenant who attempts to defeat your legitimate rent increase or tenancy termination with phony retaliation claims. As a business person, you have the organizational ability and mind-set to plan ahead—anticipate that some tenants will adopt these tactics and prepare to meet them. The tenant, on the other hand, will probably be dealing with the situation on a first-time, ad hoc basis, and often will have a superficial, or just plain wrong, knowledge of the law.

Here are some tips on how to anticipate what tenants might do, so you're prepared to avoid or counter false retaliation claims.

**Establish a good paper trail to document important facts of your relationship with your tenants.** For example, set up clear, easy-to-follow procedures for tenants to ask for repairs and respond quickly when complaints are made, coupled with annual safety inspections. (We show you how in Chapter 9.) This sort of policy will go a long way toward demonstrating that a complaint is phony—for example, if a tenant faced with a rent increase or tenancy termination suddenly complains to an outside agency about some defect in the premises they rent, without talking to you first. Also, if your periodic inquiries result in complaints from several tenants, but you only end one tenancy, you can show you don't have a policy of retaliating against tenants who do complain.

**Be prepared to demonstrate that you have a good reason to end the tenancy—even though the law in your area may say that a landlord doesn't need a reason to terminate a tenancy.** In other words, in anticipation of the possibility that a tenant

may claim that you are terminating her tenancy for retaliatory reasons, you should be prepared to prove that your reasons were valid and not retaliatory. When you think of it, this burden isn't as onerous as it might first appear. From a business point of view, few landlords will ever want to evict an excellent tenant. And assuming there is a good reason why you want the tenant out—for example, the tenant repeatedly pays his rent late in violation of the rental agreement—you only need document it.

**Have legitimate business reasons for any rent increase or other change in the conditions of the tenancy, and make the changes reasonable.** The best answer to a charge of retaliation is proof that your act was based on legitimate business reasons and was wholly independent of any exercise by tenants of their rights. (See Chapter 3 for advice.)

**If a tenant makes a complaint for even an arguably legitimate reason at about the time you were going to raise the rent or give the month-to-month tenant a termination notice anyway, wait.** First take care of the complaint. Next, let some time pass. Then, do what you planned to do anyway (assuming you can document a legitimate reason for your action). Be sure to check State Laws Prohibiting Landlord Retaliation in Appendix I to see whether your state has any law as to the time period when retaliation is presumed. For example, the laws of Iowa and Kentucky presume retaliation if the landlord's action—such as ending the tenancy—occurred within one year of the tenant's exercise of a legal right such as a complaint about defective conditions. In other states, this time period is shorter: Delaware (90 days); Arizona, California and the District of Columbia (six months). In these circumstances, the landlord must prove that retaliation has not occurred.

The delay may cost you a few bucks, or result in some inconvenience, or even cause you to lose some sleep while you gnash your teeth, but all of these are preferable to being involved in litigation over whether or not your conduct was in retaliation for the tenant's complaint.

EXAMPLE: A tenant, Fanny, makes a legitimate complaint to the health department about a defective heater in an apartment she rents from Abe. Even though Fanny does so without having had the courtesy to tell Abe or his manager first, Fanny is still within her legal rights to make the complaint. About the same time Fanny files the complaint, neighboring tenants complain to Abe, not for the first time, about Fanny's loud parties that last into the wee hours of the morning. Other tenants threaten to move out if Fanny doesn't. In response to the neighboring tenants complaints, Abe gives Fanny a 30-day notice. She refuses to move and Abe must file an eviction lawsuit. Fanny responds that the eviction was in retaliation for her complaint to the health department. A contested trial results. Perhaps Abe will win in court, but in this situation, there is a good chance he won't.

Now, let's look at how you might better handle this problem:

**Step 1.** Fix the heater.

**Step 2.** Write the tenant, reminding her of your established complaint procedures. Tell her very politely that you consider this sort of repair a routine matter which, in the future, can be handled more quickly and easily by telling you instead of the public agency. A sample letter is shown below.

**Step 3**. Carefully document the noise complaints of the neighbors. If possible, get them in writing. Feel out the neighbors about whether they would testify in court if necessary. Also, consider whether an informal meeting between all affected parties or a formal mediation procedure might solve the problem.

**Step 4.** Write the tenant about the neighbors' complaints. The first letter should be conciliatory. Offer to meet with the tenant to resolve the problem, but also remind the tenant of the rental agreement (or lease) provision banning illegal conduct, and that excessive noise after a certain hour is a violation of city or county ordinances. If the first letter doesn't work, follow up with another letter, even if you

## Sample Letter Reminding Tenant of Complaint Procedure

February 1, 199X

Fanny Hayes
Sunny Dell Apartments
123 State Street, Apt. 15
Newark, NJ 07114

Dear Ms. Hayes:

As you know, Ms. Sharon Donovan, my resident manager at Sunny Dell Apartments, repaired the heater in your unit yesterday, on January 31.

Ms. Donovan informs me that you never complained about the heater or requested its repair. In fact, she learned about the problem for the first time when she received a telephone call to that effect from Cal Mifune of the County Health Department. Apparently, you notified the Health Department of the problem without first attempting to resolve it with Ms. Donovan.

While you certainly do have a legal right to complain to a governmental agency about any problem, you should be aware that the management of Sunny Dell Apartments takes pride in its quick and efficient response to residents' complaints and requests for repairs.

In the future, we hope that you'll follow our complaint procedure and contact the manager if you have a problem with any aspect of your apartment.

Sincerely,

*Abe Horowitz*

Abe Horowitz, Owner

don't think this will do any good either. These letters will help you greatly should a court fight develop later.

**Step 5.** If possible, wait a few months, during which you should carefully document any more complaints before giving the tenant a 30-day notice. As a general rule, the longer you can reasonably delay court action, the less likely a claim of retaliation by the tenant will stick.

This sort of preparatory work may influence the tenant not to claim you are guilty of retaliatory conduct. However, even if it does not, and you do end up in court, you should win easily.

Defending yourself against charges of retaliation is well beyond the scope of this book, and a lawyer is strongly advisable. A good insurance policy which protects you from so-called "illegal acts" may cover you if your act is not deliberate and intentional and you can turn your legal defense over to the insurance company. Chapter 10 covers insurance in more detail. ■

Chapter **17**

# Terminations and Evictions

Unfortunately, even the most sincere and professional attempts at conscientious landlording sometimes fail, and you need to get rid of a troublesome tenant—someone who pays the rent late, keeps a dog in violation of a no-pets clause in the lease, repeatedly disturbs other tenants and neighbors by throwing loud parties or selling drugs, or otherwise violates your agreement or the law.

Termination is the first step toward an eventual eviction. You'll need to send the tenant a notice announcing that the tenancy is over, and that if he doesn't leave, you'll file an eviction lawsuit. Or the notice may give the tenant a few days to clean up his act (pay the rent, find a new home for the dog). If the tenant leaves (or reforms) as directed, no one goes to court.

Eviction itself—that is, physically removing the tenant and his possessions from your property— generally can't be done until you have gone to court and proved that the tenant did something wrong that justifies ending the tenancy. If you win the eviction lawsuit, you can't just move the tenant and his things out onto the sidewalk. In most states, you must hire the sheriff or marshal to perform that task.

This chapter explains when and how you can terminate a tenancy based on nonpayment of rent and other illegal acts. It also provides an overview of the eviction procedure that follows a termination notice, and tells you what you can—and cannot— do under the law.

Related topics covered in this book include:
- Rent control laws that require a legally recognized reason, or "just cause," to evict: Chapter 3
- Evicting a resident manager: Chapter 6
- Substantially failing to maintain rental property so that tenants cannot use it (constructive eviction): Chapter 9
- Ending a month-to-month tenancy with a 30-day notice: Chapter 14

- Using a security deposit to cover unpaid rent after you've evicted a tenant: Chapter 15
- How to use a warning letter, negotiation or mediation to resolve a dispute with a tenant: Chapter 16
- How to get legal help for an eviction lawsuit: Chapter 18.

**Watch out for charges of retaliation.** Landlords in most states may not end a tenancy in response to a tenant's legitimate exercise of a legal right, such as rent withholding, or in response to a complaint to a housing inspector or after a tenant has organized other tenants. What if your tenant has exercised a legal right (such as using a repair and deduct option) but is also late with the rent? Naturally, the tenant will claim that the real motive behind your eviction is retaliation.

In some states, the burden will be on you to prove that your motive is legitimate if you evict within a certain time (typically six months) of a tenant's use of a legal remedy or right. In others, it's up to the tenant to prove your motive. Chapter 16 includes advice on how to avoid charges of retaliation, and Appendix I gives details on state laws prohibiting landlord retaliation.

## A. The Landlord's Role in Evictions

The linchpin of an eviction lawsuit (sometimes called an unlawful detainer, or UD lawsuit) is properly terminating the tenancy before you go to court. You can't proceed with your lawsuit, let alone get a judgment for possession of your property or for unpaid rent, without terminating the tenancy first. This usually means giving your tenant adequate written notice, in a specified way and form. If the tenant doesn't move (or reform), you can file a lawsuit to evict.

State laws set out very detailed requirements for landlords who want to end a tenancy. Each state has its own procedures as to how termination notices and eviction papers must be written and delivered ("served"). Different types of notices are often required for different types of situations. You must follow state rules and procedures exactly. Otherwise, you will experience delays in evicting a tenant—and maybe even lose your lawsuit—even if your tenant has bounced rent checks from here to Mandalay.

Because an eviction judgment means the tenant won't have a roof over his head (and his children's heads), state laws are usually very demanding of landlords. In addition, many rent control cities go beyond state laws (which typically allow the termination of a month-to-month tenant at the will of the landlord) and require the landlord to prove a legally recognized reason, or just cause, for eviction.

Even if you properly bring and conduct an eviction lawsuit for a valid reason, you are not assured of winning and having the tenant evicted if the tenant decides to mount a defense. You always run the risk of encountering a judge who, despite the merits of your position, will hold you to every technicality and bend over backwards to sustain the tenant's position. The way that you have conducted business with the tenant may also affect the outcome: A tenant can point to behavior on your part, such as retaliation, that will shift attention away from the tenant's wrongdoing and sour your chances of victory. Simply put, unless you thoroughly know your legal rights and duties as a landlord before you go to court, and unless you dot every "i" and cross every "t," you may end up on the losing side. Our advice, especially if your action is contested, is to be meticulous in your business practices and lawsuit preparation.

It is beyond the scope of this book to provide all the step-by-step instructions and forms necessary to terminate a tenancy or evict a tenant. This chapter will get you started, and Chapter 18 shows how to research termination and eviction rules and procedures in your state. Your state or local apartment association may also publish useful guides on the subject.

## Alternatives to Eviction

Before you proceed with an eviction lawsuit, consider whether it might be cheaper in the long run to pay the tenant a few hundred dollars to leave right away. A potentially lengthy lawsuit—during which you can't accept rent that you may be unable to collect even after winning a judgment—may be more expensive and frustrating than buying out the tenant and quickly starting over with a better one. Especially if there's a possibility that your tenant might win the lawsuit (as well as a judgment against you for court costs and attorney fees), you may well be better off compromising—perhaps letting the tenant stay a few more weeks at reduced or no rent.

Chapter 16 provides tips on avoiding an eviction lawsuit by negotiating a settlement with a tenant.

## B. Termination Notices

You may terminate a month-to-month tenancy simply by giving the proper amount of notice (30 days in most states). Reasons are usually not required. (Chapter 14 discusses ending a month-to-month tenancy.) Leases expire on their own at the end of their term, and you generally aren't required to renew them.

If your tenant has done something wrong, you'll usually want him out sooner. State laws allow you to do this by serving the tenant with one of three different types of termination notices, depending on the reason why you want the tenant to leave. Although terminology varies somewhat from state to state, the substance of the three types of notices is remarkably the same.

- **Pay Rent or Quit** notices are typically used when the tenant has not paid the rent. They give the tenant a few days (three to five in most states) to pay or move out ("quit").

- **Cure or Quit** notices are typically given after a violation of a term or condition of the lease or rental agreement, such as a no pets clause or the promise to refrain from making excessive noise. Typically, the tenant has a set amount of time in which to correct, or "cure," the violation; a tenant who fails to do so must move or face an eviction lawsuit.
- **Unconditional Quit** notices are the harshest of all. They order the tenant to vacate the premises with no chance to pay the rent or correct the lease or rental agreement violation. In most states, unconditional quit notices are allowed only when the tenant has repeatedly:
  - violated a lease or rental agreement clause
  - been late with the rent
  - seriously damaged the premises, or
  - engaged in illegal activity.

Many states have all three types of notices on the books. But in some states, Unconditional Quit notices are the *only* notice statutes, as noted in "No Second Chances," below. Landlords in these states may extend second chances if they wish, but no law requires them to do so.

⚠️ **A pay or quit notice signed by your manager or lawyer may trigger the Fair Debt Collection Practices Act.** This Act (15 U.S.C. § 1692 and following) governs debt collectors and requires, among other things, that debtors be given 30 days in which to respond to a demand for payment. A federal trial court in New York has ruled that when an attorney or property manager signs a pay or quit notice, they are acting as a debt collector. Consequently, the tenant must have 30 days to pay or quit, regardless of a state's three- or five-day provision.

The trial court's ruling has been appealed to the Second Circuit Court of Appeals, which will decide whether the Act should apply to pay or quit notices signed by someone other than the property owner. (*Romea v. Heiberger*, No. 98-7259). A decision in favor of tenants will have an enormous impact on the ability of landlords in Connecticut, New York

and Vermont (states covered by the Second Circuit Court of Appeals) to use managers and lawyers to terminate and evict for nonpayment of rent. (Whether other states would choose to follow such a decision is impossible to predict.) To find out how the issue has been resolved, contact your state's consumer protection agency (there's a list in Appendix I). In the meantime, consider signing all pay or quit notices yourself.

---

### No Second Chances

Landlords in these states may use Unconditional Quit notices and demand that tenants leave without giving them a chance to pay the rent, correct the lease violation or reform their behavior.

| | | |
|---|---|---|
| Arkansas | Ohio | Texas |
| Louisiana | Pennsylvania | West Virginia |
| Missouri | South Dakota | Wyoming |
| North Dakota | | |

---

You may have a choice among these three notices, depending on the situation. For example, a Wisconsin landlord may give month-to-month tenants an Unconditional Quit *or* a Pay Rent or Quit notice for late payment of rent. The tenant cannot insist on the more lenient notice.

For the details and citations to your state's statutes on termination notices, see the following tables in Appendix I:

- Notice Required to Change or Terminate a Month-to-Month Tenancy
- State Laws on Termination for Nonpayment of Rent
- State Laws on Termination for Violation of Lease, and
- State Laws on Unconditional Quit Terminations.

Speech bubble: SO, SOMEHOW I SPENT MY RENT MONEY... BY ACCIDENT.

## C. Late Rent

Not surprisingly the number one reason landlords terminate a tenancy is nonpayment of rent. If a tenant is late with the rent, in most states you can immediately send a termination notice, giving the tenant a few days—usually three to five—in which to pay up. The exact number of days varies from state to state. But not every state requires you to give a tenant a second chance to pay the rent; as noted in "No Second Chances," in a few states if the tenant fails to pay rent on time, you can simply demand that he leave by sending an Unconditional Quit notice.

### 1. Legal Late Periods

In most states, you can send a Pay Rent or Quit notice as soon as the tenant is even one day late with the rent. A handful of states (Connecticut, Delaware, Maine, Oregon and Rhode Island) will not let you send a termination notice (either a Pay Rent or Quit notice or an Unconditional Quit notice) until the rent is a certain number of days late. In these states, tenants enjoy a statutory "grace period," plus the time specified in the Pay Rent or Quit notice, in which to come up with the rent.

> **EXAMPLE:** Lara, a Maine tenant, couldn't pay her rent on time. State law required her landlord Luke to wait until the rent was seven days late before he could send a termination notice. Luke did so on the eighth, giving Lara notice that she must pay or move within seven days. In all, Lara had fourteen days in which to pay the rent before Luke could file for eviction.

**Late rent fees are unaffected by Pay Rent or Quit time periods or legal late periods.** If your lease or rental agreement specifies late fees, they'll kick in as soon as your lease or rental agreement (or in some states, state law) says they can. The number of days specified in your Pay Rent or Quit notice will not affect them, nor will a legally required grace period. (Chapter 3 discusses late rent fees.)

### 2. Accepting Rent After You Deliver a Termination Notice

If the tenant is late with the rent and you deliver a termination notice—whether or not it gives the tenant a few days to pay the rent—you can expect a phone call or a visit from your tenant, hoping to work something out. Chapter 16 offers some pointers on negotiating and dealing with these requests. Here are the legal rules.

#### a. If the Tenant Pays the Whole Rent

If you have sent a Pay Rent or Quit notice but then accept rent for the entire rental term, you have canceled the termination notice for that period. In most states, it's as if the tenant had paid on time in the first place.

EXAMPLE: Zoe's rent was due on the first of the month. She didn't pay on time, and her landlord sent her a Three-Day Pay Rent or Quit notice. Zoe borrowed money from her parents and paid on the third day, saving her tenancy and avoiding an eviction lawsuit.

## b. If the Tenant Is Chronically Late Paying Rent

In several states, you don't have to give tenants a second chance to pay the rent if they are habitually late. Typically, you're legally required to give the tenant a chance to pay and stay only once or twice within a certain period. In Connecticut, for example, if your tenant has been late with the rent more than once in the past six months, the next time he doesn't pay on time you don't have to give him the option of paying the rent or leaving. Instead, you can send him an Unconditional Quit notice that simply tells him to leave within five days.

Some states insist that you give the tenant a *written* Pay Rent or Quit notice for the first late payment, so that there is proof that rent was late. Other statutes allow you to use the Unconditional Quit notice merely for "repeated lateness." In that case, you need not have given the tenant a notice to pay or quit for the first tardiness, but it's good business practice to do so anyway. If your tenant claims that he has always paid the rent on time, you'll have prior Pay Rent or Quit notices to show otherwise.

| States That Limit Number of Times a Tenant Can Pay and Stay | | |
| --- | --- | --- |
| **State** | **Number of late rent payments required before landlord can send Unconditional Quit notice** | **Notice to Pay or Quit required for all prior late payments?** |
| **Georgia** | Two within 12 months | yes |
| **Maryland** | Three within 12 months, but Landlord must have won an eviction lawsuit for each prior nonpayment of rent episode* | yes |
| **Massachusetts** | Two within 12 months | yes |
| **New Hampshire** | Three within 12 months | yes |
| **New Jersey** | Habitual failure to pay rent on time | no |
| **South Carolina** | Repeated nonpayment of rent | no |
| **Vermont** | Three within 12 months | yes |
| **Virginia** | Two within 12 months | yes |

* Tenants in Maryland can reinstate their tenancy by paying rent and court costs after the landlord has won the eviction lawsuit, but before physical eviction.

Citations to the code sections are found in "State Laws on Unconditional Quit Terminations" in Appendix I.

**You can always use a 30-day notice for month-to-month tenants who are chronically late.** You need not worry about the complexities of your state's unconditional quit procedure for month-to-month tenants who repeatedly pay late. Simply terminate the tenancy with a 30-day notice, which may be quicker, in the long run, if the tenant challenges your use of the unconditional quit notice. Even if you live in a rent control area that requires landlords to have good reason to evict, repeatedly paying late is ample legal reason to end a tenancy.

### c. If You Accept a Partial Rent Payment

By accepting even a partial amount of rent a tenant owes—whether for past months or even just the current month—you will, in most states, cancel the effect of a Pay Rent or Quit notice. But you can still go ahead with your attempts to get the tenant out—just pocket your tenant's payment with one hand and simultaneously hand him a new termination notice with the other, demanding that he pay the new balance or leave.

EXAMPLE: Danny's rent of $600 was due on the first of the month. Danny didn't pay January's rent and didn't have enough for February, either. On February 2, Danny's landlord, Ali, sent him a three-day notice to pay $1,200 or leave. Danny paid $600 on February 3 and thought that he'd saved his tenancy. He was amazed when, later that day, Ali handed him a new notice to pay $600 or leave. Ali properly filed for eviction on February 7 when Danny failed to pay.

**If you sign a written agreement with the tenant setting up a payment schedule for delayed or partial rent (discussed in Chapter 3), you must comply with this agreement.** If the tenant does not end up honoring this agreement, you may then take steps to terminate the tenancy.

## D. Other Tenant Violations of the Lease or Rental Agreement

In addition to nonpayment of rent, you may terminate a tenancy if a tenant violates other terms of the lease or rental agreement, such as:

- keeping a pet in violation of a no-pets rule
- bringing in an unauthorized tenant
- subleasing or assigning without your permission
- repeatedly violating "house rules" that are part of the lease or rental agreement, such as using common areas improperly, making too much noise, having unruly guests or abusing recreation facilities, or
- giving false information concerning an important matter on the rental application or lease.

### a. Giving Tenants Another Chance

The laws in most states insist that you give the tenant a few days (anywhere from five to 30 days, depending on the state) to correct, or "cure," the violation before the tenancy can end. However, there are two important "but ifs" that allow you to use an Unconditional Quit notice instead of the more generous Cure or Quit notice:

**Repeated violations.** If the tenant has violated the same lease clause two or more times within a certain period of time, he may lose the right to a second chance. You may give him an Unconditional Quit notice instead.

**The violation cannot be corrected.** Some lease violations cannot be corrected because the effect of the violation is permanent. For instance, suppose your lease prohibits tenant alterations or improvements without your consent. (See Clause 12 of the form agreements in Chapter 2.) If, without asking, your tenant removes and discards the living room wallpaper, you can hardly demand that the tenant cease violating the lease clause because it is simply too late to save the wallpaper. If a lease violation cannot be cured, you may use an Unconditional Quit notice.

### b. Criminal Convictions

As discussed in Chapter 1, you are generally free to reject prospective tenants with criminal records. Sometimes, however, you won't know about these convictions until you have already rented the unit. Maybe you never checked the applicant's background or you didn't have access to reliable information. Regardless of why you didn't know beforehand, if you learn that a tenant has a record—and particularly if he is a convicted sex offender—your first impulse will probably be to look for a way to get him out of your building. Here's what to do.

**Month-to-month tenants.** You may terminate any month-to-month tenancy with a 30-day notice, and you need not give a reason, as long as you do not have discriminatory or retaliatory motives. Note, however, that tenants in rent control cities with "just cause" eviction protection, and all tenants in New Hampshire and New Jersey (where there are state-wide just cause protections) may be able to resist a termination on this basis.

**Tenants with leases.** You will not be able to terminate an otherwise law- and rule-abiding tenant purely because you now know that he has a criminal past, no matter how unsavory or alarming. However, if your lease or rental agreement states that false and material information on the rental application will be grounds for termination (as does the one at the back of this book), you can terminate and evict on this basis.

## E. Violations of a Tenant's Legal Responsibilities

Virtually every state allows you to terminate the tenancy of a tenant who has violated basic responsibilities imposed by law, including:

- grossly deficient housekeeping practices that cause an unhealthy situation, such as allowing garbage to pile up
- seriously misusing appliances, like damaging the freezer while attempting to defrost it with an icepick

- repeatedly interfering with other tenants' ability to peacefully enjoy their homes, such as hosting late parties, playing incessant, loud music or running a noisy small business (repairing cars in the driveway of a rental duplex, for example)
- substantially damaging the property—for instance, knocking holes in the walls or doors, and
- allowing or participating in illegal activities on or near the premises, such as drug dealing or gambling.

Many careful landlords incorporate these obligations into their leases or rental agreements—something we recommend in Chapter 2, Clause 13, "Violating Laws and Causing Disturbances." But even if these obligations are not mentioned in your rental documents, tenants are still legally bound to observe them.

If a tenant or guest substantially damages the premises, you'll be within your rights to use an Unconditional Quit notice. The law does not require you to give tenants accused of serious misbehavior a second chance. Tenants who have earned this type of termination notice generally get only five to ten days to move out.

## F. Tenant's Illegal Activity on the Premises

In recent years, many states have responded aggressively to widespread drug dealing in residential neighborhoods by making it easier for landlords to evict based on these activities. Indeed, in some states you must evict known drug dealers or risk having authorities close down or even confiscate your entire property. (Chapter 12 discusses the problems faced by landlords who rent to drug dealing tenants.) To say the least, the threat of losing rental property is strong motivation to quickly evict tenants suspected of engaging in illegal acts.

You don't always have to wait until the tenant is convicted of a crime or even arrested. In Texas and North Carolina, you may evict as long as you have a "reasonable suspicion" that illegal activity is afoot and the tenant or the tenant's guests are involved. By contrast, in New Jersey you may not begin an eviction for illegal activity unless there's been a criminal conviction for criminal acts on the rented premises.

Evictions based on criminal activity are often called "expedited evictions" because they take less time than a normal eviction. Expedited evictions are preceded by an Unconditional Quit notice that tells the tenant to move out (and do it quickly). If the tenant stays, you can go to court and file for eviction. The court hearing on the eviction is typically held within a few days, and if you win, the tenant is given very little time to move. For example, in Oregon the tenant has 24 hours to vacate after a landlord wins in court.

---

### Tips on Dealing With a Tenant During an Eviction

- Avoid all unnecessary one-on-one personal contact with the tenant during the eviction process unless it occurs in a structured setting —for example, at a neighborhood dispute resolution center or in the presence of a neutral third party.

- Keep your written communications to the point and as neutral as you can, even if you are boiling inside. Remember, any manifestations of anger on your part can come back to legally haunt you somewhere down the line.

- Treat the tenant like she has a right to remain on the premises, even though it is your position that she doesn't. Until the day the sheriff or marshal shows up to evict the tenant, the tenant's home is legally her castle, and you may come to regret any actions on your part that don't recognize that fact.

---

# G. How Eviction Lawsuits Work

When the deadline in the termination notice passes, your tenant will not be automatically evicted. In almost every state, you must file and win an eviction lawsuit before the sheriff or marshal can physically evict a tenant who refuses to leave after receiving the termination notice. The whole process may take weeks—or months—depending on whether or not the tenant contests the eviction in court.

California landlords should consult *The Landlord's Law Book, Volume II, Evictions,* by David Brown (Nolo Press). It contains eviction information and tear-out court forms.

## 1. What Court Hears Evictions?

Eviction lawsuits are filed in a formal trial court (called "municipal," "county" or "justice") or in small claims court. A few states, including Illinois, New York and Massachusetts, have separate landlord-tenant courts in larger cities, similar to a small claims courts, specifically set up to handle evictions. Some states give landlords the choice; others confine eviction lawsuits to one court or the other. If you have a choice, you'll want to consider:

- **Amount of unpaid rent.** If you're also suing for unpaid rent which is higher than the small claims court's jurisdictional amount, you must use a higher court. (States' small claims court limits are listed in Chapter 16.)

- **Attorney fees clause.** If your lease or rental agreement contains an attorney fees clause, you have a strong case and a reasonable chance of collecting from your tenant, you may want to hire an attorney and go to formal court, figuring that the fee will come from the tenant's pocket when you win. On the other hand, if the tenant has little or no funds, your chances of collection are dim and you may realistically choose small claims instead.

There are important differences between regular trial courts and small claims (or landlord-tenant) court.

- In small claims court, the regular rules of evidence are greatly relaxed, and you can show or tell the court your side of the story without adhering to the "foundation" requirements that apply in higher courts. ("Laying a foundation" is explained in "Rules of Evidence in Formal Court," below.)

- In regular court, you and the tenant may engage in a pre-trial process called "discovery," in which you ask each other about the evidence that supports your positions. Information gathered during discovery can be used at trial. Discovery includes depositions (where witnesses are questioned under oath), interrogatories (sets of pre-printed questions that cover information normally involved in a landlord-tenant dispute) and "requests for admissions," (specific statements of fact that the other side is asked, under oath, to admit or deny). The discovery process is normally available in formal court, but not in small claims or landlord-tenant courts.

- In regular court, you and the tenant may each attempt to wash the case out of court quickly by filing pretrial requests to the court to dismiss or limit the case. In small claims and

landlord-tenant court, the idea is to decide the entire case after one efficient court hearing, and these motions are not used.

## Evictions in Small Claims Court

Landlords in these states may file evictions in small claims court.

| | |
|---|---|
| Arizona (Justice Court) | New Mexico |
| Delaware | North Carolina |
| Florida | Pennsylvania |
| Georgia | South Carolina |
| Indiana | Tennessee |
| Iowa | Virginia |
| Kentucky | West Virginia |
| Louisiana | Wisconsin |
| Maine | Wyoming |
| Maryland | |

*Everybody's Guide to Small Claims Court,* by Ralph Warner (Nolo Press), describes the workings of your small claims court in detail.

*Represent Yourself in Court,* by Paul Bergman and Sara Barrett-Berman (Nolo Press), explains how to present evidence and arguments in formal court.

## Rules of Evidence in Formal Court

It's important to back up your eviction lawsuit with as much hard evidence as possible. For example, if the basis of the termination is that the tenant has violated a rental rule (by keeping a pet), be sure that you have a copy of the lease and rules that your tenant signed when he moved in.

In small claims court, you can present practically any evidence you want to the judge. (Chapters 15 and 16 provide information useful for small claims cases.) But if you are in a formal court, the judge will not examine documentary evidence until you have established that it is likely to be trustworthy. Presenting the legal background of evidence is called "laying a foundation." Here are a few hints on how to prepare evidence for formal court.

- **Photographs**. If your termination notice is based on your tenant knocking a hole in the kitchen wall, you'll want to show the judge a photograph of the gaping hole. But before the picture can be admitted into evidence, someone will have to testify that the picture is a fair and accurate depiction of the way the wall looked. It's best to ask a neutral witness look at the wall and come to court prepared to testify that, yes, the photo is an accurate portrayal. Your witness need not have taken the photo.

- **Letters.** You may have sent a termination notice for nonpayment of rent because your tenant improperly used the repair and deduct remedy by failing to give you a reasonable amount of time to fix the problem yourself. You'll want to show the judge a copy of the letter you sent to the tenant, promising to fix the defect within the week (the tenant didn't wait). In court, this means you'll need to introduce your letter into evidence. To do this, you can simply testify that the letter is a true copy, that the signature is your own and that you mailed or handed it to your tenant.

- **Government documents.** If your tenant has withheld rent because of what she claims are uninhabitable conditions, you may decide to evict for nonpayment of rent. If the tenant filed a complaint with a local health department and they issued a report giving your property a clean bill of health, you'll want the report considered by the court (admitted into evidence). Ask the health department inspector to testify that he wrote the report as part of his normal duties when investigating possible health violations. To get the inspector to court, you'll need to ask the judge for an order, called a "subpoena," that you can serve on the inspector.

## Attorneys and Eviction Services

Depending on your location, particular situation and the availability of self-help eviction guides, you may be able to handle all, or most of, an eviction lawsuit yourself. Many landlords hire "legal typing services" or "independent paralegals" (discussed in Chapter 18) to help with evictions. But there are some circumstances when you should definitely consult an attorney who specializes in landlord-tenant law:

- Your tenant is already represented by a lawyer, even before you proceed with an eviction.
- Your property is subject to rent control rules governing eviction.
- The tenant you are evicting is an ex-manager whom you have fired.
- Your tenant contests the eviction in court.
- Your tenant files for bankruptcy.
- The property you own is too far from where you live. Since you must file an eviction lawsuit where the property is located, the time and travel involved in representing yourself may be too great.

## 2. First Steps: The Complaint and Summons

An eviction lawsuit begins when you file a legal document called a "Complaint." The Complaint lists the facts that you think justify the eviction. It also asks the court to order the tenant to leave, pay back rent, damages directly caused by his unlawfully remaining on the property, court costs and sometimes attorney fees.

Fortunately, your Complaint need not be a lengthy or complicated legal document. In some states, landlords use a pre-printed Complaint form, prepared by the court, that allows you to simply check an appropriate box, depending on what you intend to argue. And even in states which still follow an old-fashioned approach of requiring that documents be typed-up on numbered legal paper, you can find the information you need from legal form books available at law libraries. These books contain "canned" forms that fit many different situations. When you sign your Complaint, be sure to note under your typed name that you are appearing "Pro per" or "Pro se," if you have not hired a lawyer.

Normally, you cannot sue a tenant for anything but back rent and damages. Because an eviction procedure is so quick, most states do not allow you to add other legal beefs to an eviction Complaint. For example, if you claim that the tenants have damaged the sofa and their security deposit won't cover the cost of replacement, you must sue the tenants in small claims court in a separate lawsuit.

When you file a Complaint, the clerk will assign a date on which the case will be heard by the court. That date is entered on the Summons, a piece of paper that tells the tenant he's been sued and must answer your charges in writing and appear in court within a specified number of days or lose the lawsuit. You must then arrange for the tenant to be given the Complaint and the Summons. In legal jargon, this is called "service of process."

State laws are quite detailed as to the proper way to deliver, or "serve," court papers. Most critically, neither you (including anyone who has an ownership interest in your business) nor your employees can serve these papers. (In some states, any adult not involved in the lawsuit can serve papers.) The method of delivery is specified, as well: Typically, the preferred way is "personal" service, which means that a law enforcement officer or professional process server personally hands the tenant the papers.

If, despite repeated attempts, the process server cannot locate the tenant, most states allow something called "substituted service." This means the process server leaves a copy of the papers with a competent adult at the tenant's home, or mails the papers first-class and also leaves a copy in a place where the tenant will likely see it, such as posted on his front door.

Failure to properly serve the tenant is one of the most common errors landlords make, and may result in court dismissal of your lawsuit even before trial. Even a seemingly minor mistake—such as forgetting to check a box, checking one you shouldn't or filling in contradictory information—will increase the chances that your tenant can successfully contest the lawsuit. Again, it is vital that you pay close attention to your state rules and procedures on evictions.

## 3. The Tenant's Answer to the Complaint

The next step in a typical eviction lawsuit involves the tenant's response to your claims that something he's done (or not done) justifies his eviction. At this point, the lawsuit has gone beyond the technicalities of the way you filed the lawsuit, and you and the tenant are meeting the reasons for the eviction head-on.

The tenant must file a document called an Answer on or before the date printed on the Summons. Like your Complaint, it need not be a complex document. Your tenant will probably consult the same set of legal form books that you used in writing your Complaint.

In general, the Answer may contain two kinds of responses:

- **Denials**. The tenant may dispute that what you say is true. For example, if you are evicting for nonpayment of rent and your tenant claims that he paid his rent to the manager, he will simply deny that the rent is unpaid. Or, if you've filed an eviction lawsuit because the tenant has a dog, but the tenant claims that the animal actually belongs to the tenants in the next unit, he'll also simply check the "denials" box. If there is no Answer form, you'll see a typed paragraph that looks something like this: "Defendant denies the allegations in Paragraph X of Plaintiff's Complaint." (You are the plaintiff in the lawsuit; the tenant is the defendant.)

- **Affirmative Defenses.** The Answer is also the place where your tenant can state what the law calls "affirmative defenses"—good legal reasons (such as discrimination or retaliation) that he hopes will excuse what would otherwise be grounds for eviction. For example, a tenant who's being evicted for not paying the rent might use a habitability defense to justify his actions—in this case, the tenant would claim that he used some of the rent money to pay for repairing a serious problem you had ignored.

### When Tenants Ignore the Summons and Complaint

If you properly terminate a tenancy and the tenant doesn't respond to the Summons and Complaint—he doesn't file an Answer or show up in court—you will usually automatically win the lawsuit. The court will grant what's called a "default judgment" against the tenant, ordering him to pay unpaid rent and, if your lease or rental agreement has an attorney fees and costs clause, those expenses as well. Of course, you will still have to hire the local law enforcement personnel to carry out the actual eviction, and you'll have to look to your security deposit to cover the monetary judgment. (This is discussed in Chapter 15.) If the deposit is insufficient, you can always sue for the balance in small claims court.

### Complete Your Lawsuit, Even If You Think You've Won Already

It's very common for tenants to move out after receiving a Summons and Complaint. Especially if the security deposit will cover your losses, or you know that attempting to collect any excess won't be worth your time and trouble, you might be tempted to forget about the lawsuit and turn your attentions to re-renting quickly.

Never walk away from a lawsuit without formally ending it. Usually, this will involve appearing in court and asking the judge to dismiss the case. Doing so preserves your reputation as someone who uses the courts with respect—if you are simply a no-show, expect a chilly reception the next time you appear in court. In addition, if you don't appear for trial but the tenant does, *the tenant* may win and be entitled to move back in and collect court costs and attorney fees.

If you and the tenant have reached a settlement that involves the tenant paying you money but the tenant hasn't paid you yet, it's a good idea to take that written settlement with you to court and ask the judge to make it part of his ruling while dismissing the case. Depending on the rules in your state, you will then have a court order (sometimes called a "stipulated settlement") that you can immediately use if the tenant fails to pay voluntarily. (You can take it to a collection agency or use it to garnish wages.) Otherwise, you'll have to take the written agreement to small claims court to get a judgment.

Finally, don't overlook the possibility that the tenant may not have actually moved out (or may move back in). You'll be on safe ground if you get a judgment before retaking possession.

## 4. The Trial

Many eviction cases never end up in trial—for example, because the tenant moves out or negotiates a settlement with the landlord. But each case that does go to trial will have its own unpredictable twists and turns that can greatly affect trial preparation and tactics. For this reason, you will probably need to hire a lawyer, if you haven't done so already, to assist you prepare for and conduct the trial.

What you must prove at trial obviously depends on the issues raised in your Complaint and the tenant's Answer. For example, the testimony in a case based on nonpayment of rent where the tenant's defense is that you failed to keep the premises habitable will be very different from that in a case based on termination of a month-to-month tenancy by 30-day notice where the tenant denies receiving the notice.

All contested evictions are similar, however, in that you have to establish the basic elements of your case through solid evidence that proves your case (and refutes your tenant's defense). In formal court, you'll have to abide by your state's rules of evidence. But in an informal court, you may be able to introduce letters and secondhand testimony ("I heard her say that..."). Also, you can introduce evidence without elaborate "foundations." (See "Rules of Evidence in Formal Court," above.)

## 5. The Judgment

Eviction lawsuits are typically decided on the spot or very soon thereafter, after the judge has heard the witnesses and consulted any relevant statutes, ordinances and higher court opinions.

### a. If You Win

If you win the eviction case, you get an order from the judge declaring that you are entitled to possession of the property (you may get a money judgment for back rent and court costs and attorney fees, too). You'll need to take the order, called a judgment, to the local law enforcement official who will carry out the eviction.

Unfortunately, having a judgment for the payment of money is not the same as having the money itself. Your tenant may be unable (or unwilling) to pay you—despite the fact that you have converted your legal right to be paid into a formal court order. Unless the tenant voluntarily pays up, you will have to collect the debt—for example, by using the tenant's security deposit or hiring a collection agency. (See Chapter 15 for more on these topics.)

### b. If You Lose

If you lose the eviction case, your tenant can stay and you'll likely end up paying for your tenant's court costs and fees. You may also be hit with money damages if the judge decides you acted illegally, as in the case of discrimination or retaliation.

If your tenant wins by asserting a habitability defense, the court may hold onto the case even after the trial is over. That's because the court doesn't want to simply return the tenant to an unfit dwelling. In some states, a judge may order you to make repairs while the rent is paid into a court account; when an inspector certifies that the dwelling is habitable, the judge will release the funds.

### 6. How Tenants May Stop or Postpone an Eviction

If you win the eviction lawsuit, you'll want to move quickly to physically remove the tenant from the property. In rare instances, a tenant may be able to get the trial judge to stop the eviction, but only if he can convince the court of two things:

- Eviction would cause a severe hardship for the tenant or his family. For example, the tenant may be able to persuade the judge that alternate housing is unavailable and his job will be in jeopardy if he is forced to move, and

- The tenant is willing and able to pay any back rent owed (and your costs to bring the lawsuit) and future rent, as well.

It's very unusual for a judge to stop an eviction, for the simple reason that if the tenant's sympathetic predicament (and sufficient monetary reserves) weren't persuasive enough to win the case for him in the first place, it's unlikely that these arguments can prevail after the trial.

The tenant may, however, ask for a postponement of the eviction. Typically, evictions are postponed in three situations:

- **Pending an appeal**. If the tenant files an appeal, he may ask the trial judge to postpone ("stay") the eviction until a higher court decides the case. A tenant who has been evicted in small claims court may, in a few states, enjoy an automatic postponement during the appeal. Of course, this is one reason why smart landlords in these states never use small claims court.
- **Until the tenant's circumstances improve.** A tenant may be able to persuade a judge to give him a little more time to find a new home.
- **Until the weather improves.** Contrary to popular belief, judges in many cold-climate states (including Alaska, Minnesota and North Dakota) are not required to postpone an eviction on frigid days. But there's nothing to stop tenants from asking the judge anyway. In the District of Columbia, however, a landlord may not evict on a day when the National Weather Service predicts at 8:00 a.m. that the temperature at the National Airport will fall below freezing within the next 24 hours. (D.C. Code § 45-2551(k).)

### 7. Eviction

In most states, you cannot move a tenant's belongings out on the street, even after winning an eviction lawsuit. Typically, you must give the judgment to a local law enforcement officer, along with a fee which the tenant has been charged for as part of your costs. The sheriff or marshal gives the tenant a notice telling him that he'll be back, sometimes within just a few days, to physically remove him if the tenant isn't gone.

## H. Illegal "Self-Help" Evictions

As any experienced landlord will attest, there are occasional tenants who do things so outrageous that the landlord is tempted to bypass normal legal protections and take direct and immediate action to protect his property. For example, after a tenant's numerous promises to pay rent, a landlord may consider changing the locks and putting the tenant's property out in the street. Or, a landlord who is responsible for paying the utility charges may be tempted to simply not pay the bill in the hopes that the resulting lack of water, gas or electricity will hasten a particularly outrageous tenant's departure. When you realize how long a legal eviction can sometimes take, these actions can almost seem sensible.

If you are tempted to take the law into your own hands to force or scare a troublesome tenant out of your property, heed the following advice: *Don't do it!* Shortcuts such as threats, intimidation, utility shutoffs or attempts to physically remove a tenant are illegal and dangerous, and if you resort to them you may well find yourself on the wrong end of a lawsuit for trespass, assault, battery, slander and libel, intentional infliction of emotional distress and wrongful eviction. So, although the eviction process can often entail some trouble, expense and delay, it's important to understand that it is the only game in town.

If you are sued by a tenant whom you forcibly evicted or tried to evict, the fact that the tenant didn't pay rent, left your property a mess, verbally abused you or otherwise acted outrageously will not be a valid defense. You will very likely lose the lawsuit, and it will cost you far more than evicting the tenant using normal court procedures.

Today virtually every state forbids "self-help" evictions—their eviction statutes warn landlords that their procedures are the *only* way to retake possession of rental property. And in many states the penalties for violating these laws are steep. Tenants who have been locked out, frozen out by having the heat cut off or denied electricity or water can sue not only for their actual money losses (such as the need for temporary housing, the value of food that spoiled when the refrigerator stopped running or the cost of an electric heater when the gas was shut off), but also for penalties as well. For example, in Arizona a landlord can be forced to pay the tenant up to two months' rent or the tenant's actual damages, whatever is higher. And in Connecticut, the landlord may even be prosecuted for a misdemeanor. In some states, the tenant can collect and still remain in the premises; in others, he is entitled to monetary compensation only. (See "Consequences of Self-Help Evictions," below.)

Even if your state has not legislated against self-help evictions, throwing your tenant out on your own is highly risky and likely to land you in more legal entanglements than had you gone to court for an eviction judgment in the first place. The potential

## Consequences of Self-Help Evictions

Virtually every state outlaws self-help evictions, and those listed below have legislated specific penalties for violations. If your state is not listed, don't assume that you can violate the law with impunity. A judge can always devise a penalty to fit your case.

| State | Amount Tenant Can Sue You For | Tenant's Court Costs & Attorney Fees Covered? | Can Tenant Choose to Stay? | Statute or Legal Authority |
|---|---|---|---|---|
| Alaska | One and one-half times the actual damages. | No | Yes | Alaska Stat. § 34.03.210 |
| Arizona | Two months' rent or twice the actual damages, whichever is greater. | No | Yes | Ariz. Rev. Stat. § 33-1367 |
| California | Actual damages plus $100 per day of violation ($250 minimum). Tenant may ask for an injunction prohibiting any further violation during the court action. | Yes | Yes | Cal. Civil Code § 789.3 |
| Connecticut | You may be prosecuted for a misdemeanor. Tenant may collect up to double actual damages. | Yes | Yes | Conn. Gen. Stat. Ann. §§ 47a-43, 47a-46, and 53a-214 |
| District of Columbia | Actual and punitive damages. | No | No | *Mendes v. Johnson*, 389 A.2d 781 (DC 1978) |
| Hawaii | Two months' rent or free occupancy for two months (tenant must have been excluded "overnight"). Court may order you to stop illegal conduct. | Yes | Yes | Hawaii Rev. Stat. § 521-63(c) |
| Iowa | Actual damages. If tenant elects to terminate, you must return entire security deposit. | Yes | Yes | Iowa Code § 562A.26 |
| Kansas | Actual damages or one and one-half months' rent, whichever is greater. | No | Yes | Kan. Stat. Ann. § 58-2563 |
| Kentucky | Three months' rent. | Yes | Yes | Ky. Rev. Stat. Ann. § 383.655 |
| Maine | Actual damages or $250, whichever is greater. The court may award costs and fees to you if it finds that the tenant brought a frivolous court lawsuit or one intended to harass you. | Yes | No | Me. Rev. Stat. Ann. tit. 14, § 6014 |
| Massachusetts | Three months' rent or three times the actual damages. | Yes | Yes | Mass. Gen. Comp. Laws 186 § 15F |
| Michigan | Actual damages or $200, whichever is greater. | No | Yes | Mich. Comp. Laws Ann § 600.2918 |
| Minnesota | $500 or three times the actual damages, whichever is greater. | Yes | Yes | Minn. Stat. § 504A.521 |
| Montana | Three months' rent or three times the actual damages, whichever is greater. | Yes | Yes | Mont. Code Ann. § 70-24-411 |
| Nebraska | Up to three months' rent. | Yes | Yes | Neb. Rev. Stat. § 76-1430 |
| Nevada | Up to $1,000 or actual damages, whichever is greater, or both. | No | Yes | Nev. Rev. Stat. Ann. § 118A.390 |

## Consequences of Self-Help Evictions (continued)

| State | Amount Tenant Can Sue You For | Tenant's Court Costs & Attorney Fees Covered? | Can Tenant Choose to Stay? | Statute or Legal Authority |
|---|---|---|---|---|
| New Hampshire | Actual damages or $1,000, whichever is greater; if court finds that you knowingly or willingly broke the law, two to three times this amount. Each day that a violation continues is a separate violation. If the court finds tenant brought a frivolous suit or one intened to harass, it may order tenant to pay landlord's costs and fees. | Yes | Yes | N.H. Rev. Stat. Ann. §§ 540-A:3, A:4, 358-A:10 |
| New Mexico | A prorated share of the rent for each day of violation, actual damages and civil penalties. | Yes | Yes | N.M. Stat. Ann. § 47-8-36 |
| North Carolina | Actual damages. | No | Yes | N.C. Gen. Stat. § 42-25.9 |
| Ohio | Actual damages. | Yes | No | Oh. Rev. Code Ann. § 5321.15 |
| Oklahoma | Twice the average monthly rental or twice the actual damages, whichever is greater. | No | Yes | Okla. Stat. tit. 41, § 123 |
| Oregon | Two months' rent or twice the actual damages, whichever is greater. | No | Yes | Ore. Rev. Stat. § 90.375 |
| Pennsylvania | Self-help evictions are not allowed. | Judge decides | Judge decides | *Wofford v. Vavreck*, 22 D. & C 3d 444 (1981); and *Kuriger v. Cramer*. 1985. PA. 1209 |
| Rhode Island | Three months' rent or three times the actual damages, whichever is greater. | Yes | Yes | R.I. Gen. Laws § 34-18-34 |
| South Carolina | Three months' rent or twice the actual damages, whichever is greater. | Yes | Yes | S.C. Code Ann. § 27-40-660 |
| South Dakota | Two months' rent. A tenant who elects to terminate the lease is entitled to the return of the full security deposit. | No | Yes | S.D. Codified Laws Ann. § 43-32-6 |
| Tennessee | Actual and punitive damages. A tenant who elects to terminate the lease is entitled to the return of the full security deposit. | Yes | Yes | Tenn. Code Ann. § 66-28-504 |
| Texas | Actual damages, one month's rent or $500, whichever is greater. Tenant who files a lawsuit in bad faith is liable for your actual damages, one month'srent or $500, whichever is greater. NOTE: If tenant has not paid the rent, landlord may follow specified steps to cut utilities or change locks. | Yes | Yes | Texas Prop. Code §§ 92.008, 92.0081, 92.009 |
| Vermont | Actual damages. Court may award costs and fees to you if the court finds that the tenant brought a frivolous lawsuit or one intended to harass you. | Yes | Yes | Vt. Stat. Ann. tit. 9, § 4464 |
| Virginia | Actual damages. | Yes | Yes | Va. Code Ann. §§ 55-248.26, 55-225.2 |
| Washington | Actual damages. For utility shut-offs only, actual damages and up to $100 per day of no service. Court may award costs and fees to the prevailing party. | Yes (includes costs of arbitration) | Yes | Wash. Rev. Code Ann. §§ 59.18.290, 59.18.300 |

for nastiness and violence is great; the last thing you want is a patrol car at the curb while you and your tenant wrestle over the sofa on the lawn. And you can almost count on a lawsuit over the "disappearance" of your tenant's valuable possessions, which she'll claim were lost or taken when you removed her belongings. Using a neutral law enforcement officer to enforce a judge's eviction order will avoid these unpleasantries.

⚠️ **Don't seize tenants' property under the guise of handling "abandoned" property.** A few states allow you to freely dispose of a tenant's leftover property when he has moved out. Do so only if it is quite clear that the tenant has left permanently, intending to turn the place over to you. Seizing property under a bogus claim that the tenant had abandoned it will expose you to significant monetary penalties.

## I. Stopping Eviction by Filing for Bankruptcy

Tenants with significant financial burdens may decide to declare bankruptcy. There are several kinds of bankruptcy; the most common are "Chapter 7," in which most debts are wiped out after as many creditors as possible have been paid; or "Chapter 13," in which the debts remain but are paid off over time according to a court-approved plan.

As soon as a tenant files a bankruptcy petition—and whether or not you know about it—an automatic "stay" (court order) takes effect. It bars you from terminating a tenancy or starting or continuing an eviction proceeding. This is true even if your lease or rental agreement says you can immediately terminate a tenancy if the tenant files for bankruptcy. (11 U.S. Code § 365(e).)

(We suggest that you watch for news of bankruptcy law changes. As this book goes to press, Congress is considering landlord-friendly bankruptcy reform that would remove evictions from the automatic stay explained above.)

This means that if your tenant has filed for either Chapter 7 or 13 bankruptcy and is behind in the rent, becomes unable to pay the rent or violates another term of his tenancy (such as keeping a pet in violation of a no-pets clause), you can't deliver a termination notice or proceed with an eviction. Even if you have already gone to court and obtained an eviction order, the eviction process must stop if the tenant files for bankruptcy.

Don't jump to the conclusion, however, that tenants who file for bankruptcy can violate their lease or not pay the rent with impunity. At most, filing for bankruptcy buys them a little time. You can simply go to the federal bankruptcy court and ask the judge to remove the automatic stay. (11 U.S. Code §§ 362(a)(1), (2) & (3).) In most cases, you'll get the stay lifted within a matter of days and can continue with the termination and eviction.

### A Tenant's Lease After Bankruptcy

Filing for bankruptcy affects a tenancy even if the tenant is not behind in the rent or otherwise in violation of his lease. After he files, the "bankruptcy trustee" (a person appointed by the bankruptcy court to oversee the case) must decide whether to carry on with or terminate the lease or rental agreement. In most situations, the trustee will let the tenant keep the lease, since it wouldn't be of any benefit to his creditors to force him to incur the expense of finding a new home and moving. First, however, he must pay any unpaid back rent.

If the trustee keeps the lease, you have the right to ask the bankruptcy court to demand that the tenant show proof of his ability to pay future rent. (11 U.S. Code §§365(b)(1)(A), (B) & (C).) Of course, if he becomes unable to pay the rent after the lease is assumed, you can ask the bankruptcy court to lift the stay so that you can terminate and, if necessary, evict.

Chapter **18**

# Lawyers and Legal Research

Landlords should be prepared to deal with most routine legal questions and problems without a lawyer. If you bought all the needed information at the rates lawyers charge—$150 to $250 an hour—it should go without saying that you'd quickly empty your bank account. Just the same, there are times when good advice from a specialist in landlord-tenant law will be helpful, if not essential—for example, in lawsuits by tenants alleging housing discrimination or claiming that dangerous conditions or wrongful acts caused injury or in complicated eviction lawsuits. Throughout this book, we point out specific instances when an attorney's advice or services may be useful.

Fortunately, for an intelligent landlord there are a number of other ways to acquire a good working knowledge of the legal principles and procedures necessary to handle problems with tenants and managers. Of course, that's the main purpose of this book. But in addition to the information we provide, this chapter specifically recommends a strategy to most efficiently and effectively use legal services and keep up to date on landlord-tenant law, so that you can anticipate and avoid many legal problems.

As a sensible landlord, it doesn't make sense to try and run your business without ever consulting a lawyer. When legal problems are potentially serious and expensive, it makes sense to get expert help. But since you almost surely can't afford all the services a lawyer might offer, you obviously need to set priorities. When thinking about a legal problem, ask yourself: "Can I do this myself?" "Can I do this myself with some help from a lawyer?" "Should I simply put this in my lawyer's hands?"

Or, put another way, your challenge isn't to avoid lawyers altogether but rather to use them on a cost-effective basis. Ideally, this means finding a lawyer who's willing to serve as a kind of self-help law coach, to help you educate yourself. Then, you can often do routine or preliminary legal work on your own, turning to your lawyer only occasionally for advice and fine-tuning.

## How Lawyers Can Help Landlords

Here are some important ways lawyers can help landlords:

- to review key documents you have drafted, such as your lease or manager agreement
- to confirm that you have a good claim or defense vis-a-vis an individual tenant—whether it's a dispute over how much security deposit you must return or your right to raise the rent
- to make a quick phone call or write a letter to the tenant and get a problem resolved quickly
- to point you to the law that applies in a given situation
- to provide any needed assistance with evictions, including preparing notices and forms
- to answer questions along the way if you're representing yourself in court or in a mediation proceeding, and
- to handle legal problems that are—or are threatening to become—serious, such as a tenant's personal injury lawsuit or discrimination charge.

## A. Finding a Lawyer

How frequently you'll need a lawyer's help will depend on many factors, including the type, number and location of rental units you own, the kinds of problems you run into with tenants, the number of property managers and other employees you hire, and your willingness to do some of the legal work yourself.

In looking for a lawyer you can work with, and to manage your subsequent relationship with that person, always remember one key thing—you're the boss. Just because your lawyer has specialized training, knowledge, skills and experience in dealing with legal matters is no reason for you to abdicate control over legal decision-making and how much time and money should be spent on a particular legal problem. We say this because despite the fact that you have an intimate knowledge of your business and are in the best position to call the shots, some lawyers will be willing or even eager to try and run your business for you while overcharging you for the privilege. The key is to find a lawyer who can provide the amount and type of legal services you need.

## How Not to Find a Lawyer

The worst lawyer referral sources are:
- Heavily advertised legal clinics, which are less likely to offer competitive rates for competent representation in this specialized area. While they may offer low flat rates for routine services such as drafting a will, it's less common to see legal clinics charge reasonable flat fees for other specific services.
- Referral panels set up by local bar associations or others. While bar association panels sometimes do minimal screening before qualifying the expertise of lawyers in landlord-tenant law, usually the emphasis is on the word "minimal." You may get a good referral from these panels, but they often refer people to inexperienced practitioners who don't have enough clients and who use the panel as a way of generating needed business. And when it comes to private referral services, which are legal in some states, forget it. These groups typically make little attempt to evaluate a lawyer's skill and experience. They simply supply the names of lawyers who have paid to list with the service (or have agreed to give the service a kickback based on fees you pay).

## 1. Compile a List of Prospects

Finding a good, reasonably priced lawyer expert in landlord-tenant legal issues is not always an easy task. If you just pick a name out of the telephone book—even someone who advertises as a landlord law expert—you may get an unsympathetic lawyer, or one who will charge too much, or one who's not qualified to deal with your particular problem. If you use an attorney you or a friend or relative has relied on for other legal needs, you will very likely end up with someone who doesn't know enough about landlord-tenant law.

This sorry result is not inevitable—there are competent landlords' lawyers who charge fairly for their services. As a general rule, deep experience in landlord-tenant law is most important. As with so many other areas of the law, the information needed to practice effectively in this field has become increasingly specialized in the past two decades—so much so that a general practitioner simply won't do.

The best way to find a suitable attorney is through some trusted person who has had a satisfactory experience with one. Your best referral sources are other landlords in your area. Ask the names of their lawyers and a little bit about their experiences. Also ask rental property owners about other lawyers they've worked with, and what led them to make a change. If you talk to a few landlords, chances are you'll come away with several leads on good lawyers experienced in landlord-tenant law.

There are several other sources for possible candidates in your search for a lawyer:
- Your local landlords' association will likely know of lawyers who have experience in landlord-tenant law.
- Articles about landlord-tenant law in trade magazines and newspapers are often written by lawyers. Even if these people live in other parts of the country, it can make sense to track down the authors, since experts in this increasingly complex field meet and share information at national conferences or online.

They may be able to provide top-notch referrals in your area.

- Your state's continuing legal education (CLE) program—usually run by a bar association, a law school or both—can identify lawyers who have lectured or written on landlord-tenant law for other lawyers. Someone who's a "lawyer's lawyer" presumably has the extra depth of knowledge and experience to do a superior job for you—but may charge more, unfortunately.

## 2. Shop Around

After several reliable people give you the names of hopefully top-notch prospects, your job has just begun. You need to meet with each attorney and make your own evaluation. If you explain that, as a local landlord, you have a continuing need for legal help, many lawyers will be willing to speak to you for a half hour or so at no charge or at a reduced rate so that you can size them up and make an informed selection. Briefly explain your business and legal needs and how much work you plan to do yourself.

Look for experience, personal rapport and accessibility. Some of these traits will be apparent almost immediately. Others may take longer to discover. In addition to the person making the original recommendation, you may want to talk with some of the lawyer's other landlord clients about their satisfaction with the lawyer's work. A lawyer should be able to provide you with such a list.

Here are some things to look for in your first meeting:

**Will the lawyer answer all your questions about fees, his experience in landlord-tenant matters and your specific legal problems?** Stay away from lawyers who make you feel uncomfortable asking questions. Pay particular attention to the rapport between you and your lawyer. No matter how experienced and well-recommended a lawyer is, if you feel uncomfortable with that person during your first meeting or two, you may never achieve an ideal lawyer-client relationship. Trust your instincts and seek a lawyer whose personality is compatible with your own. Be sure you understand how the lawyer charges for services. (Section B discusses various fee arrangements with lawyers.)

**Will the lawyer provide the kind of legal help you want?** If you plan to be actively involved in dealing with your legal business, look for a lawyer who doesn't resent your participation and control. By reading this book all the way through and consulting other resources, such as those available at a nearby law library (Section F discusses how to do legal research), you can answer many of your questions on your own. For example, you might do the initial legal work in evictions and similar procedures yourself, but turn over to a lawyer cases which become hotly contested or complicated.

Unfortunately, some lawyers are uncomfortable with the very idea of helping people help themselves. They see themselves as all-knowing experts and expect their clients to accept and follow their advice without question. Obviously, this is not the type of lawyer a self-helper will want.

**Is the lawyer willing to assist you when you have specific questions, billing you on an hourly basis when you handle your own legal work—such as evictions?** One key to figuring out if a lawyer is really willing to help you help yourself is to ask: Is he willing to answer your questions over the phone and charge only for the brief amount of time the conversation lasted? If instead he indicates that he prefers to provide advice in more time-consuming (and therefore profitable) office appointments, you'll want to keep looking. There are plenty of lawyers who will be very happy to bill you hourly to help you help yourself. By providing helpful consultations on problems that are routine or involve small dollar amounts, a lawyer can generate referrals for full-service representation on bigger, more complex matters that you (or your friends or family) face in the future. And if despite his initial assurances, the lawyer later tries to dissuade you from representing yourself, or won't give any advice over the phone despite your invitation to bill you for it, find someone else.

**Will the lawyer clearly lay out all your options for handling a particular legal problem, including alternate dispute resolution methods such as mediation?**

**Will the lawyer be accessible when you need legal services?** Unfortunately, the complaint logs of all law regulatory groups indicate that many lawyers are not reasonably available to their clients in times of need. If every time you have a problem there's a delay of several days before you can talk to your lawyer on the phone or get an appointment, you'll lose precious time, not to mention sleep. And almost nothing is more aggravating than to leave a legal question or project in a lawyer's hands and then have weeks or even months go by without anything happening. So be sure to discuss with any lawyer whether she will really commit herself to returning your phone calls promptly, work hard on your behalf and follow through on all assignments.

**If your property is in a rent-controlled city, does the lawyer practice in or near that city and know its rent control laws and practices?**

**Does the lawyer represent tenants, too?** Chances are that a lawyer who represents both landlords and tenants can advise you well on how to avoid many legal pitfalls of being a landlord. On the other hand, you'll want to steer clear of lawyers who represent mostly tenants, since their sympathies (world view) are likely to be different from yours.

## Researching Lawyers

A good source for background information about individual lawyers is the Martindale-Hubbell Law Directory, available at most law libraries and some local public libraries. This resource contains biographical sketches of most practicing lawyers and information about their experience, specialties, education and the professional organizations to which they belong. Many firms also list their major clients in the directory—an excellent indication of the types of problems with which they've had experience. Be aware, however, that lawyers purchase the space for their biographical sketches, so don't be overly impressed by long biographies.

In addition, almost every lawyer listed in the directory, whether or not he or she has purchased space for a biographical sketch, is rated AV, BV or CV. These ratings come from confidential opinions that Martindale-Hubbell solicits from lawyers and judges.

The first letter is for Legal Ability, which is rated as follows:

A—Very High to Preeminent

B—High to Very High

C—Fair to High

The V part of the rating is supposed to stand for Very High General Recommendation—meaning that the rated lawyer adheres to professional standards of conduct and ethics. In truth, the fact that a lawyer has a "V" is practically meaningless, because lawyers who don't qualify for it aren't rated at all. *Martindale-Hubbell* prudently cautions that such absence shouldn't be construed as a reflection on the lawyer, since there many reasons for the absence of a rating. Some lawyers, for example, ask that their rating not be published and others are too new to a community to be known among the local lawyers and judges who are the sources for ratings.

So don't make the rating system your sole criterion for deciding on a potential lawyer for your business. On the other hand, it is reasonable to put some confidence in the fact that a lawyer who gets high marks from other business clients and an "AV" rating from *Martindale-Hubbell* will have experience and expertise.

## B. Types of Fee Arrangements With Lawyers

How you pay your lawyer depends on the type of legal services you need and the amount of legal work you have. Once an agreement is reached, it's a good idea to ask for a written fee agreement—basically an explanation of how the fees and costs will be billed and paid. As part of this, negotiate an overall cap on what you can be billed absent your specific agreement.

If a lawyer will be delegating some of the work on your case to a less experienced associate, paralegal or secretary, that work should be billed at a lower hourly rate. Be sure to get this information recorded in your initial written fee agreement.

There are four basic ways that lawyers charge for their services.

**Hourly fees.** In most parts of the United States, you can get competent services for your rental business for $125 to $225 an hour, with most lawyers billing in ten- or 15-minute increments. Comparison shopping among lawyers will help you avoid overpaying. But the cheapest hourly rate isn't necessarily the best. You can often benefit by hiring a more experienced landlord's attorney, even if her hourly rates are high, since she will be further along the learning curve than a general practitioner, and should take less time to review and advise you on the particulars of your job.

**Flat fees.** Sometimes, a lawyer will quote you a flat fee for a specific job. For example, a lawyer may offer to represent you in court for routine eviction cases (such as for nonpayment of rent) that present little trouble, even when they are contested by the tenant (which is actually fairly rare). In a flat fee agreement, you pay the same amount regardless of how much time the lawyer spends on a particular job. If you own many rental units and anticipate providing a fair amount of business over the years, you have a golden opportunity to negotiate flat fees that are substantially below the lawyer's normal hourly rate. After all, the lawyer will see you as a very desirable client, since you'll generate continuing business for many years to come.

**Retainer fees.** In some circumstances, it can also make sense to hire a lawyer for a flat annual fee, or retainer, to handle all of your routine legal questions and business, such as noncontested eviction cases. You'll usually pay in equal monthly installments and, normally, the lawyer will bill you an additional amount for extraordinary services—such as representing you in a complicated eviction lawsuit. Since the lawyer can count on a reliable source of income, you can expect lower overall fees. Obviously, the key to making a retainer fee arrangement work is to have a written agreement clearly defining what's routine and what's extraordinary. This type of fee arrangement is more economically feasible for larger landlords (a dozen or more rental units) with regular legal needs. Also, retainer fee agreements are usually best negotiated after you and your lawyer have worked together long enough to have established a pattern—you know and trust each other well enough to work out a mutually beneficial arrangement.

**Contingency fees.** This is a percentage (such as one-third) of the amount the lawyer obtains for you in a negotiated settlement or through a trial. If the lawyer recovers nothing for you, there's no fee. Contingency fees are common in personal injury cases, but relatively unusual for the kinds of legal advice and representation landlords need.

## C. Saving on Legal Fees

There are many ways to hold down the cost of legal services. Here is a short list of some of the key ways to save on legal fees.

**Be organized.** Especially when you are paying by the hour, it's important to gather important documents, write a short chronology of events and concisely explain a problem to your lawyer. Since papers can get lost in a lawyer's office, keep a copy of everything that's important, such as your lease or rental agreement, move-in letter to new tenants, correspondence with tenants, repair logs and other records. (See the Chapter 7 discussion on organizing tenant records.)

**Be prepared before you meet.** Whenever possible, put your questions in writing and mail, fax or deliver them to your lawyer before meetings, even phone meetings. That way the lawyer can find answers if he doesn't know them off the top of his head without having to call you back and charge for a separate phone conference. Early preparation also helps focus the meeting so there is less of a chance of digressing into (and having to pay to discuss) unrelated topics.

**Read trade journals in your field, such as publications of your local or state apartment association.** Law changes continuously, so you'll want to keep up with specific legal developments affecting your business. Send pertinent clippings to your lawyer—and encourage your lawyer to do the same for you. This can dramatically reduce legal research time.

**Show that you're an important client.** Mutual respect is key in an attorney-client relationship. The single most important way to show your lawyer how much you value the relationship is to pay your bills on time. Beyond that, let your lawyer know about plans for expansion and your business's possible future legal needs. And drop your lawyer a line when you've recommended him or her to your landlord colleagues.

**Bundle your legal matters.** You'll save money if you consult with your lawyer on several matters at one time. For example, in a one-hour conference, you may be able to review with your lawyer several items—such as a new lease or rental agreement clause, anti-age discrimination policy or advertisement for your apartment complex. Significant

savings are possible because lawyers commonly divide their billable hours into parts of an hour. For example, if your lawyer bills in 15-minute intervals and you only talk for five minutes, you are likely to be charged for the whole 15. So it usually pays to gather your questions and ask them all at once, rather than calling every time you have a question.

---

### Costs Can Mount Up

In addition to the fees they charge for their time, lawyers often bill for some costs as well—and these costs can add up quickly. When you receive a lawyer's bill, you may be surprised at both the amount of the costs and the variety of the services for which the lawyer expects reimbursement. These can include charges for:

- photocopying
- faxes
- overnight mail
- messenger service
- expert witness fees
- court filing fees
- long distance phone calls
- process servers
- work by investigators
- work by legal assistants or paralegals
- deposition transcripts
- online legal research, and
- travel.

Many sensible lawyers absorb the cost of photocopying, faxes, local phone calls and the like as normal office overhead—part of the cost of doing business—but that's not always the case. So in working out the fee arrangements, discuss the costs you'll be expected to pay. If a lawyer is intent on nickel-and-diming you to death, look elsewhere. For example, if you learn the law office charges $3 or more for each page it faxes, red flags should go up. On the other hand, it is reasonable for a lawyer to pass along costs of things like court costs, process server fees and any work by investigators.

**Carefully review lawyer bills.** Always read your bill. Like everyone else, lawyers make mistakes, and your charges may be wrong. For example, a ".1" of an hour (six minutes) may be transposed into a "1." (one hour) when the data are entered into the billing system. That's $200 instead of $20 if your lawyer charges $200 per hour. If you have any questions about your bill, feel free to ask your lawyer. You hired him to provide a service and you have the right to expect a clear explanation of your bill.

**Use non-lawyer professionals for evictions.** Look to "legal typing services" or "independent paralegals" for help with evictions in large metropolitan areas. For a flat fee that is usually much lower than what lawyers charge, and often at a faster pace, non-lawyer eviction services take the basic information from you, provide the appropriate eviction forms and fill them out according to your instructions. This normally involves typing your eviction papers so they'll be accepted by the court, arranging for filing and then serving the papers on the tenant.

Typing services and paralegals aren't lawyers, and most handle only routine cases. They can't give legal advice about the requirements of your specific case and can't represent you in court if the tenant contests the eviction suit. You must decide what steps to take in your case, and the information to put in the needed forms.

To find a non-lawyer eviction service, check with a landlords' association or look in the telephone book under "Eviction Services" or "Paralegals." Be sure the eviction service or typing service is reputable and experienced, as well as reasonably priced. (The cost should not exceed a few hundred dollars for the service and fees.) Ask for references and check them. As a general matter, the longer a typing service has been in business, the better.

**Recommended Reading on Lawsuits.** California landlords can handle eviction lawsuits themselves by using *The Landlord's Law Book: Evictions,* by Attorney David Brown (Nolo Press). Contact your state or local apartment association for information on any step-by-step guides to evictions in your state.

*Represent Yourself in Court,* by Paul Bergman and Sara Berman-Barrett (Nolo Press), offers more general advice on handling any civil lawsuit on your own or with a lawyer-coach's help.

**Lawyer fees are a tax-deductible business expense.** If you visit your lawyer on a personal legal matter (such as reviewing a contract for the purchase of a house) and you also discuss a business problem (such as a new policy for hiring managers), ask your lawyer to allocate the time spent and send you separate bills. At tax time, you can easily list the business portion as a tax-deductible business expense.

## D. Resolving Problems With Your Lawyer

If you see a problem emerging with your lawyer, nip it in the bud. Don't just sit back and fume; call or write your lawyer. Whatever it is that rankles, have an honest discussion about your feelings. Maybe you're upset because your lawyer hasn't kept you informed about what's going on in your lawsuit against your tenant for property damage or maybe your lawyer has missed a promised deadline for reviewing your new system for handling maintenance and repair problems. Or maybe last month's bill was shockingly high or you question the breakdown of how your lawyer's time was spent.

Here's one way to test whether a lawyer-client relationship is a good one—ask yourself if you feel able to talk freely with your lawyer about your degree of participation in any legal matter and your control over how the lawyer carries out a legal assignment. If you can't frankly discuss these sometimes sensitive matters with your lawyer, fire that lawyer and hire another one. If you don't, you'll surely waste money on unnecessary legal fees and risk having legal matters turn out badly.

Remember that you're always free to change lawyers. If you do, be sure to fire your old lawyer before you hire a new one. Otherwise, you could find yourself being billed by both lawyers at the same time. Also, be sure to get all important legal documents back from a lawyer you no longer employ. Tell your new lawyer what your old one has done to date and pass on the file.

But firing a lawyer may not be enough. Here are some tips on resolving specific problems:

- If you have a dispute over fees, the local bar association may be able to mediate it for you.
- If a lawyer has violated legal ethics—for example, conflict of interest, overbilling or not representing you zealously—the state agency that licenses lawyers may discipline or even disbar the lawyer. Although lawyer oversight groups are typically biased in favor of the legal profession, they will often take action if your lawyer has done something seriously wrong.
- Where a major mistake has been made—for example, a lawyer has missed the deadline for filing a case—you can sue for malpractice. Many lawyers carry malpractice insurance, and your dispute may be settled out of court.

---

### Your Rights as a Client

As a client, you have the following rights:

- courteous treatment by your lawyer and staff members
- an itemized statement of services rendered and a full advance explanation of billing practices
- charges for agreed-upon fees and no more
- prompt responses to phone calls and letters
- confidential legal conferences, free from unwarranted interruptions
- up-to-date information on the status of your case
- diligent and competent legal representation, and
- clear answers to all questions.

---

*Mad at Your Lawyer*, by Tanya Starnes (Nolo Press), shows you in detail how to successfully handle almost every imaginable problem with your lawyer.

## E. Attorney Fees in a Lawsuit

If your lease or written rental agreement has an attorney fees provision (see Clause 19 of the form agreements in Chapter 2), you are entitled to recover your attorney fees if you win a lawsuit based on the terms of that agreement. There's no guarantee, however, that a judge will award attorney fees equal to your attorney's actual bill, or that you will ultimately be able to collect the money from the tenant or former tenant. Also, as discussed in Chapter 2, an attorney fees clause in your lease or rental agreement usually works both ways. Even if the clause doesn't say so, you're liable for the tenant's attorney fees if you lose. (Landlord's insurance does not cover such liability where the lawsuit is unrelated to items covered by the policy, such as eviction lawsuits by the landlord and security deposit refund suits by the tenant. Chapter 10 discusses insurance.)

## F. Doing Your Own Legal Research

Using this book is a good way to educate yourself about the laws that affect your business—but one book is not enough by itself. While we recommend that you get copies of state, local and federal laws that affect your landlording business (see Section 1, just below), at one time or another you'll probably need to do some further research. For example, you may want to read a specific court case or research a more open-ended question about landlord-tenant law—for instance, your liability for an assault that took place on your rental property.

Lawyers aren't the only source for legal help. There's a lot you can do on your own. Law libraries are full of valuable information, such as state statutes that regulate the landlord-tenant relationship. Your first step is to find a law library that's open to the public. You may find such a library in your county courthouse or at your state capitol. Publicly funded law schools generally permit the public to use their libraries, and some private law schools grant access to their libraries—sometimes for a modest fee.

Don't overlook the reference department of the public library if you're in a large city. Many large public libraries have a fairly decent legal research collection. Also, ask about using the law library in your own lawyer's office. Some lawyers, on request, will share their books with their clients.

**Recommended Reading on Legal Research.** We don't have space here to show you how to do your own legal research in anything approaching a comprehensive fashion. To go further, we recommend two excellent resources.

The first is *Legal Research: How to Find and Understand the Law*, by Stephen Elias and Susan Levinkind. This nontechnical book gives easy-to-use, step-by-step instructions on how to find legal information. The other is *Legal Research Made Easy: A Roadmap Through the Law Library Maze*, by Robert C. Berring, a videotape presentation on the subject. Both are published by Nolo Press.

## 1. State, Local and Federal Law

Every landlord is governed by state, local and federal law. In some areas, like antidiscrimination standards, laws overlap. When they do overlap, the stricter laws will apply. In practical terms, this usually means that the laws that give tenants the most protection (rights and remedies) will prevail over less protective laws.

### a. State Statutes

If you're a typical landlord, you'll be primarily concerned with state law. State statutes regulate many aspects of the landlord-tenant relationship, including deposits, landlord's right of entry, discrimination, housing standards, rent rules, repair and maintenance responsibilities and eviction procedures.

Your state consumer protection agency or attorney general's office may provide publications at little or no cost explaining state laws that affect landlords, or copies of the state statutes themselves. Also, representatives of state agencies can often help explain how the landlord-tenant laws they administer are interpreted. (Appendix I includes a list of State Consumer Protection Offices.)

We refer to many of the state laws affecting landlords throughout this book and include citations so that you can do additional research. State laws or codes are collected in volumes and are available in many public libraries and in most law libraries. Depending on the state, statutes may be organized by subject matter or by title number ("chapter"), with each title covering a particular subject matter, or simply numbered sequentially, without regard to subject matter.

"Annotated codes" contain not only all the text of the laws (as do the regular codes), but also a brief summary of some of the court decisions (discussed in Section 2) interpreting each law and often references to treatises and articles that discuss the law. Annotated codes have comprehensive indexes by topic, and are kept up-to-date with paperback supplements ("pocket parts") stuck in a pocket inside the back cover of each volume.

Because it's so important that you have immediate access to the laws that affect your business, we recommend that you buy copies of the state codes that affect your business. In major population states, such as California, this is easy, since paperback codes are available. They are sold in a number of different editions and are available at any law bookstore. If buying the code is too expensive, you can simply copy the relevant sections from the codes at the law library each year. Remember that you'll need a new volume every year or two—depending on how often your state legislature meets. Never rely on an old set of statutes, because statutes are frequently amended.

## b. Local Ordinances

Local ordinances, such as rent control rules, health and safety standards and requirements that you pay interest on tenants' security deposits, will also affect your business. Contact your city manager's or mayor's office for information on local ordinances that affect landlords. If you own rental property in a city with rent control, be sure to get a copy of the ordinance, as well as all rules issued by the rent board covering rent increases and hearings.

## c. Federal Statutes and Regulations

Congress has enacted laws, and federal agencies such as the U.S. Department of Housing and Urban Development (HUD) have adopted regulations, covering discrimination, wage and hour laws affecting employment of managers and landlord responsibilities to disclose environmental health hazards. We refer to relevant federal agencies throughout this book and suggest you contact them for publications that explain federal laws affecting landlords, or copies of the federal statutes and regulations themselves.

We include citations for many of the federal laws affecting landlords throughout this book. The U.S. Code is the starting place for most federal statutory research. It consists of 50 separate numbered titles. Each title covers a specific subject matter. Two versions of the U.S. Code are published in annotated form: *The United States Code Annotated, (U.S.C.A.),* (West Publishing Co.) and the *United States Code Service (U.S.C.S.),* (Bancroft-Whitney/Lawyer's Co-op). Most law libraries carry both.

Most federal regulations are published in the Code of Federal Regulations (C.F.R.), organized by subject into 50 separate titles.

## 2. Court Decisions

Sometimes the answer to a legal question cannot be found in a statute. This happens when:

- court cases and opinions have greatly expanded or explained the statute, taking it beyond its obvious or literal meaning; or
- the law that applies to your question has been made by judges, not legislators.

## a. Court Decisions That Explain Statutes

Statutes and ordinances do not explain themselves. For example, a state law may require you to offer housing that is weatherproofed, but that statute alone may not tell you whether that means you must provide both storm windows and window screens. Chances are, however, that others before you have had the same questions, and they may have come up in the context of a lawsuit. If a judge interpreted the statute and wrote an opinion on the matter, that written opinion, once published, will become "the law" as much as the statute itself. If a higher court (an appellate court) has also examined the question, then its opinion will rule.

To find out if there are written court decisions that interpret a particular statute or ordinance, look in an "annotated code" (discussed in Section 1, above). If you find a case that seems to answer your question, it's crucial to make sure that the decision you're reading is still "good law"—that a more recent opinion from a higher court has not reached a different conclusion. To make sure that you are relying on the latest and highest judicial pronouncement, you must use the library research tool known as *Shepard's. Legal Research: How to Find and Understand the Law,* by Stephen Elias and Susan Levinkind (Nolo Press), has a good, easy-to-follow explanation of how to use the *Shepard's* system to expand and update your research.

## b. Court Decisions That Make Law

Many laws that govern the way you must conduct your business do not even have an initial starting point in a statute or ordinance. These laws are entirely court-made, and are known as "common" law (see the explanation of common law in Chapter 9, Section A). An example is the implied warranty of habitability, which is court-made in many states.

Researching common law is more difficult than statutory law, because you do not have the launching pad of a statute or ordinance. With a little perseverance, however, you can certainly find your way to the cases that have developed and explained the legal concept you wish to understand. A good beginning is to ask the librarian for any "practice guides" written in the field of landlord-tenant law. These are outlines of the law, written for lawyers, that are kept up-to-date and are designed to get you quickly to key information. Because they are so popular and easy to use, they are usually kept behind the reference counter and cannot be checked out. More sophisticated research techniques, such as using a set of books called "Words and Phrases," (which sends you to cases based on key words) are explained in the book *Legal Research,* mentioned above.

If a case you have found in an annotated code (or through a practice guide or key word search) looks important, you may want to read the opinion. You'll need the title of the case and its "citation," which is like an address for the set of books, volume and page where the case can be found. Ask the law librarian for help.

### c.   How to Read a Case Citation

If you find a citation to a case that looks important, you may want to read the opinion. You'll need the title of the case and its citation, which is like an address for the set of books, volume and page where the case can be found. Ask the law librarian for help.

Although it may look about as decipherable as hieroglyphics, once understood, a case citation gives lots of useful information in a small space. It tells you the names of the people or companies involved, the volume of the reporter (series of books) in which the case is published, the page

number on which it begins and the year in which the case was decided.

> EXAMPLE: *Smith v. Jones Int'l,* 123 N.Y.S.2d 456 (1994). Smith and Jones are the names of the parties having the legal dispute. The case is reported in volume 123 of the New York Supplement, Second Series, beginning on page 456; the court issued the decision in 1994.

Most states publish their own official state reports. All published state court decisions are also included in seven regional reporters. There are also special reports for U.S. Supreme Court and other federal court decisions. (See "Common Abbreviations in Case Citations," below.)

### Law Review Articles

Law schools and other state and local bar associations publish periodicals that may contain timely articles on legal issues that affect tenants. But academic journals rarely contain useful, practical information. Local bar association journals and other publications aimed at practicing lawyers are likely to be much more helpful.

### 3.   Online Legal Research

If you have access to the Internet, there is a limited amount of legal research that you can accomplish using your computer. We say "limited" because not every statute, ordinance or court decision is available online; and, unless you know the name of what you're looking for (its code section number, for example), it can be difficult to find.

That said, here are some useful sites:

- State statutes online: Many states, listed below, have posted their statutes online.
- TenantNet [tenant.net/main.html]. This site provides information about landlord-tenant

law, with a focus on tenants' rights. TenantNet is designed primarily for tenants in New York City, but offers information about the law in many other states as well as the text of the Federal Fair Housing Acts.

- The U.S. House of Representatives Internet Law Library [law.house.gov/92.html]. This site provides the entire federal Code of Regulations, plus federal consumer protection laws, including the federal bankruptcy code and bankruptcy rules, and selected state consumer protection laws.

- Cornell University [www.law.cornell.edu/states/index.html]. In addition to state statutes, this site provides links to other Internet sites with state law, including state court sites and, in some cases, local sites that post municipal ordinances.

- piperInfo [www.piperinfo.com/state/states.html]. Local governments are beginning to stake out turf on the Internet. Sometimes this presence is nothing more than a not-so-slick public relations page, but sometimes it includes a large body of information, including local ordinances available for searching and downloading. This site is the best source for finding local governments online.

*Law on the Net* and *Government on the Net*, by James Evans (Nolo Press), are both comprehensive guides to thousands of online legal resources, including court opinions, legislation, codes and govenment sites.

## Computerized Research Services: Helpful but Costly

Several companies now offer full-scale legal research services, which make it relatively easy to search a huge database of statutes, court decisions, regulations and legal articles.

If you are not connected with a large law office or law school, you will likely find it difficult to get access to either of the two main legal research systems, Westlaw and Lexis. A small but growing number of law libraries or public libraries, however, offer these services.

Once found, there are two other major barriers to using these systems. One is cost. Be prepared for sticker shock—you can end up paying as much as $300 per hour. Second, it takes time and training to learn how to navigate these legal research systems efficiently. However, if you are already savvy on how to use computerized information retrieval services and are involved in a dispute worth a considerable sum, you may want to give it a try.

If you wish to use one of these systems, either ask a law librarian where the nearest terminal available to the public is located, or write to the companies directly.

For more information about Westlaw, contact West Publishing Co., 50 West Kellogg Boulevard, P.O. Box 3526, St. Paul, MN 55165, 800-WESTLAW or 800-937-8529.

For Lexis, contact Lexis Mead Data Central, 200 Park Ave., New York, NY 10017, 800-45LEXIS or 800-455-3947.

## 4. How to Find Your State Statutes Online

Many states have made their statutes available online. If your state has done so, you can use your computer and browser to read any of the statutes cited in this book.

To show you how to find landlord-tenant statutes online, we're going to assume that you have a basic familiarity with your computer, your browser and the Internet. For more detailed descriptions of how to do legal research online, see *Legal Research: Online and in the Library*, by Elias and Levinkind (Nolo Press).

Let's suppose that you are a landlord in Missouri and would like to read your state's statute on security deposits. After consulting "Citations for State Laws on Security Deposits" in Appendix I, you know that the statute's number is Section 535.300. The following steps show you how to find that statute.

**Step 1: Go to Findlaw.** We suggest that you use the Internet search engine known as Findlaw (www.findlaw.com). When you enter Findlaw's URL in your browser, you'll see their Homepage, as shown in Figure 1.

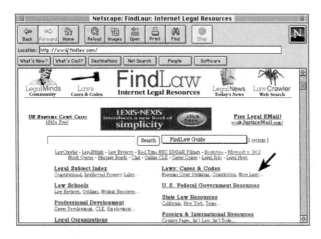

Figure 1

**Step 2: Choose the link that will take you to state statutes**. In Figure 1, you see a number of links. Since you're looking for state statutes, you'll

want to click on the State Laws link, under the Laws: Cases & Codes main link. The resulting page is shown in Figure 2.

Figure 2

**Step 3: Choose your state.** As you look at the page shown in Figure 2 (you may have to scroll down a bit), you'll see the 50 states listed under State Resources Indexes. When you click on the state you're interested in—for this example, Missouri—you'll see the page shown in Figure 3.

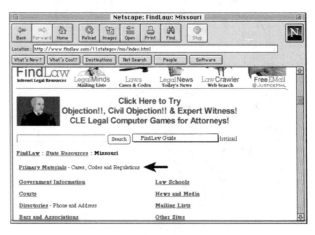

Figure 3

**Step 4: Choose the link that will take you to the state statutes.** In Figure 3, you'll see that Findlaw has put Missouri cases, codes and regulations under its Primary Materials link. (Remember, "codes" is another word for statutes.) When you choose that link, you'll get the screen shown in Figure 4.

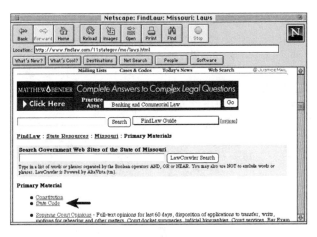

Figure 4

**Step 5: Choose the State Code.** Under the Primary Materials link, you could choose to go to the Constitution or the Code. When you click on the State Code link, you'll get the page shown in Figure 5.

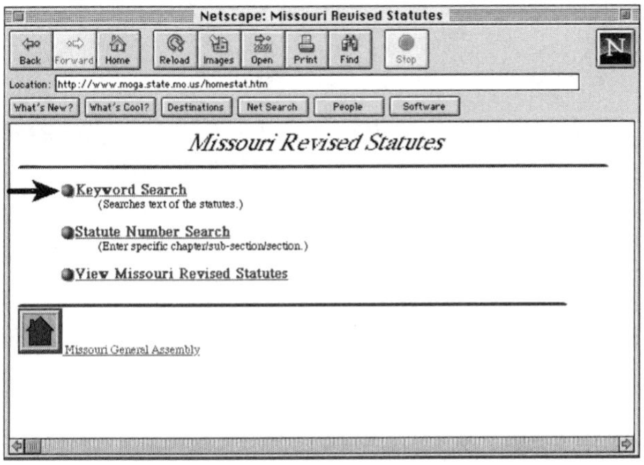

**Step 6: Search for your statute.** You'll see that the Missouri site gives you three ways to read the statutes:

1. If you don't know the statute's number, you can enter a "keyword" that is likely to be in it. For example, you could ask Findlaw to look for statutes containing the words "security" and "deposit."
2. If you know the statute number, you could ask Findlaw to take you directly there.
3. If you just want to browse through the statutes, you could ask Findlaw to give you the code's table of contents, which is linked to the codes.

For our example, we'll ask Findlaw to do the Number search described in 2, above. Clicking on the Statute Number Search link brings us to a page with a query box, shown in Figure 6.

When you do a search like this for your state, you may find that your state's statute page is designed differently than the one shown in Figure 5. But the basic choice of initial "clicks" in Findlaw is the same for every state. Usually, you can figure out how to get to the codes with a little trial and error.

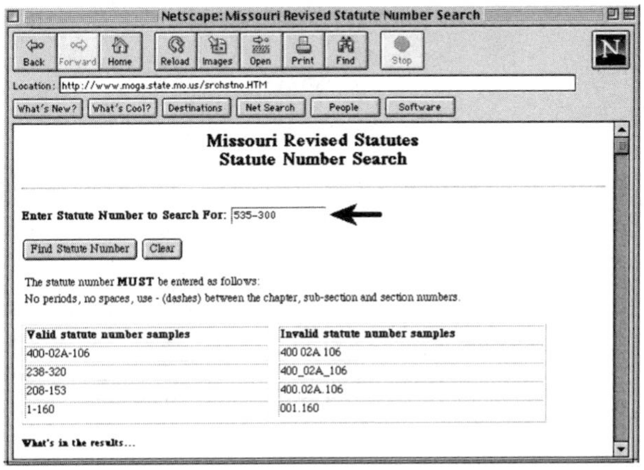

![Netscape: Missouri Revised Statutes window showing Missouri Revised Statutes page with Keyword Search, Statute Number Search, and View Missouri Revised Statutes options]

Figure 5

![Netscape: Missouri Revised Statute Number Search window showing Statute Number Search form with Enter Statute Number to Search For: 535-300]

Figure 6

**Step 7: Type in the statute number.** When you enter the statute number, as directed in the page's instructions, you'll be taken to another page with a link to the statute, shown in Figure 7.

**Step 8: Ask for the statute.** Finally, you're close to the statute itself. Clicking on the Section 535-300 link brings you to the page shown in Figure 8.

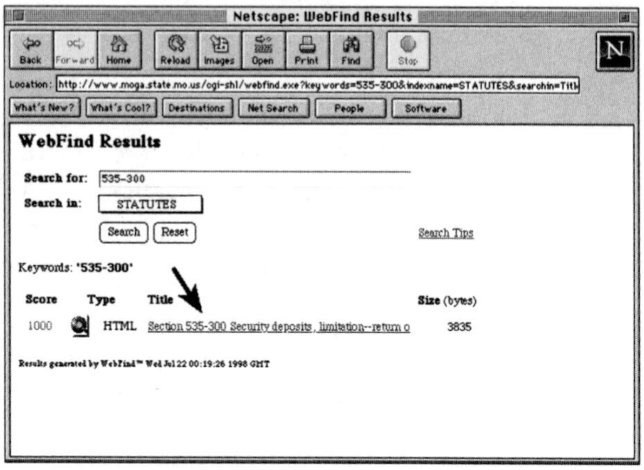

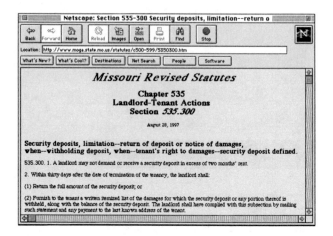

Figure 7

Figure 8

# Appendix I

# State Laws and Agencies

## Attachment to Florida Leases and Rental Agreements

Fla. Stat. Ann. § 83.49(3)(a). Upon the vacating of the premises for termination of the lease, the landlord shall have 15 days to return the security deposit together with interest if otherwise required in which to give the tenant written notice by certified mail to the tenant's last known mailing address of his intention to impose a claim on the deposit and the reason for imposing the claim. The notice shall contain a statement in substantially the following form:

This is a notice of my intention to impose a claim for damages in the amount of _____ upon your security deposit, due to _____.
It is sent to you as required by s. 83.49(3), Florida Statutes. You are hereby notified that you must object in writing to this deduction from your security deposit within 15 days from the time you receive this notice or I will be authorized to deduct my claim from your security deposit. Your objection must be sent to _____
_____ (landlord's address).

If the landlord fails to give the required notice within the fifteen-day period, he forfeits his right to impose a claim upon the security deposit.

(b)   Unless the tenant objects to the imposition of the landlord's claim of the amount thereof within 15 days after receipt of the landlord's notice of intention to impose a claim the landlord may then deduct the amount of his claim and shall remit the balance of the deposit to the tenant within 30 days after the date of the notice of intention to impose a claim for damages.

(c)   If either party institutes an action in a court of competent jurisdiction to adjudicate his right to the security deposit, the prevailing party is entitled to receive his court costs plus a reasonable fee for his attorney. The court shall advance the cause on the calendar.

# Landlord-Tenant Statutes

Here are some of the key statutes pertaining to landlord-tenant law in each state.

| | | | |
|---|---|---|---|
| **Alabama** | Ala. Code §§ 35-9-1 to -100 | **Missouri** | Mo. Ann. Stat. §§ 441.010-.650; and §§ 535.150-.300 |
| **Alaska** | Alaska Stat. §§ 34.03.010 to .380 | **Montana** | Mont. Code Ann. §§ 70-24-101 to -25-206 |
| **Arizona** | Ariz. Rev. Stat. Ann. §§ 12-1171 to -1183; §§ 33-1301 to -1381 | **Nebraska** | Neb. Rev. Stat. §§ 76-1401 to -1449 |
| **Arkansas** | Ark. Code Ann. §§ 18-16-101 to -306 | **Nevada** | Nev. Rev. Stat. Ann. §§ 118A.010-.520 |
| **California** | Cal. [Civ.] Code §§ 1925-1954, 1961-1962.7, 1995.010-1997.270 | **New Hampshire** | N.H. Rev. Stat. Ann. §§ 540:1-540-A:8 |
| | | **New Jersey** | N.J. Stat. Ann. §§ 46:8-1 to -49 |
| **Colorado** | Colo. Rev. Stat. §§ 38-12-101 to -104, -301 to -302 | **New Mexico** | N.M. Stat. Ann. §§ 47-8-1 to -51 |
| **Connecticut** | Conn. Gen. Stat. Ann. §§ 47a-1 to 50a | **New York** | N.Y. [Gen. Oblig.] Law §§ 7-101 to -109; N.Y. [Real Prop.] Law §§ 220-238; N.Y. [Mult. Dwell.] Law §§ 1-11; N.Y. [Mult. Resid.] Law §§ 305 |
| **Delaware** | Del. Code Ann. tit. 25, §§ 5101-7013 | | |
| **Dist. of Columbia** | D.C. Code Ann. §§ 45-1401 to -1597, -2501 to -2593 | **North Carolina** | N.C. Gen. Stat. §§ 42-1 to -56 |
| **Florida** | Fla. Stat. Ann. §§ 83.40-.66 | **North Dakota** | N.D. Cent. Code §§ 47-16-01 to -41 |
| **Georgia** | Ga. Code Ann. §§ 44-7-1 to -81 | **Ohio** | Ohio Rev. Code Ann. §§ 5321.01-.19 |
| **Hawaii** | Haw. Rev. Stat. §§ 521-1 to -78 | **Oklahoma** | Okla. Stat. tit. 41, §§ 1-136 |
| **Idaho** | Idaho Code §§ 6-301 to -324 and §§ 55-201 to -313 | **Oregon** | Or. Rev. Stat. §§ 90.100-.435 |
| | | **Pennsylvania** | Pa. Stat. Ann. tit. 68, §§ 250.101-.342 |
| **Illinois** | Ill. Rev. Stat. ch. 765 para. 705/0.01-740/5 | **Rhode Island** | R.I. Gen. Laws §§ 34-18-1 to -19 |
| | | **South Carolina** | S.C. Code Ann. §§ 27-40-10 to -910 |
| **Indiana** | Ind. Code Ann. §§ 32-7-1-1 to 37-7-19 | **South Dakota** | S.D. Codified Laws Ann. §§ 43-32-1 to -26 |
| **Iowa** | Iowa Code Ann. §§ 562A.1-.36 | **Tennessee** | Tenn. Code Ann. §§ 66-28-101 to -517 |
| **Kansas** | Kan. Stat. Ann. §§ 58-2501 to -2573 | **Texas** | Tex. [Prop.] Code Ann. §§ 91.001-92.301 |
| **Kentucky** | Ky. Rev. Stat. Ann. §§ 383.010-.715 | | |
| **Louisiana** | La. Rev. Stat. Ann. §§ 9:3201-:3259; La. Civ. Code Ann. art. 2669-2742 | **Utah** | Utah Code Ann. §§ 57-17-1 to -5, -22-1 to -6 |
| **Maine** | Me. Rev. Stat. Ann. tit. 14, §§ 6001-6045 | **Vermont** | Vt. Stat. Ann. tit. 9, §§ 4451-4468 |
| **Maryland** | Md. Code Ann., [Real Prop.] §§ 8-101 to -501 | **Virginia** | Va. Code Ann. §§ 55-218.1 to -248.40 |
| | | **Washington** | Wash. Rev. Code Ann. §§ 59.04.010-.900, .18.010-.910 |
| **Massachusetts** | Mass. Gen. Laws Ann. ch. 186 §§ 1-21 | | |
| **Michigan** | Mich. Comp. Laws Ann. § 554.601-.640 | **West Virginia** | W. Va. Code §§ 37-6-1 to -30 |
| **Minnesota** | Minn. Stat. Ann. §§ 504.01-.35 | **Wisconsin** | Wis. Stat. Ann. §§ 704.01-.40 |
| **Mississippi** | Miss. Code Ann. §§ 89-8-1 to -27 | **Wyoming** | Wyo. Stat. §§ 34-2-125 to -130 |

## State Rent Rules

Here are citations for statutes that set out rent rules in each state. When a state has no statute, the space is left blank.
See the "Notice Required to Change or Terminate a Month-to-Month Tenancy" Chart in this Appendix for citations to statutes for raising rent.

| State | When Rent is Due | Grace Period | Where Rent is Due |
|---|---|---|---|
| Alabama | | | |
| Alaska | Alaska Stat. § 34.03.020(c) | | Alaska Stat. § 34.03.020(c) |
| Arizona | Ariz. Rev. Stat. Ann. § 33-1314(C) | | Ariz. Rev. Stat. Ann. § 33-1314(C) |
| Arkansas | | | |
| California | Cal. [Civ.] Code § 1947 | | |
| Colorado | | | |
| Connecticut | Conn. Gen. Stat. Ann. § 47a-3a | Conn. Gen. Stat. Ann. § 47a-15a | Conn. Gen. Stat. Ann. § 47a-3a |
| Delaware | Del. Code Ann. tit. 25, § 5501(b) | Del. Code Ann. tit. 25, § 5501(d) | Del. Code Ann. title 25, § 5501(b) |
| D.C. | | | |
| Florida | Fla. Stat. Ann. § 83.46 | | |
| Georgia | | | |
| Hawaii | Haw. Rev. Stat. § 521-21(b) | | Haw. Rev. Stat. § 521-21(b) |
| Idaho | Idaho Code §§ 55-201 to -313 | | |
| Illinois | | | |
| Indiana | *Watson v. Penn*, 108 Ind. 21 (1886), 8 N.E. 636 (1886) | | |
| Iowa | Iowa Code Ann. § 562A.9(3) | | Iowa Code Ann. § 562A.9(3) |
| Kansas | Kan. Stat. Ann. § 58-2545 | | Kan. Stat. Ann. § 58-2545 |
| Kentucky | Ky. Rev. Stat. Ann. § 383.565(2) | | Ky. Rev. Stat. Ann. § 383.565(2) |
| Louisiana | | | |
| Maine | | Me. Rev. Stat. Ann. tit. 14, § 6028 | |
| Maryland | | | |
| Massachusetts | | Mass. Gen. Laws Ann. ch. 186 § 15B(1)(c) | Mass. Gen. Laws Ann. ch. 186 § 15B(1)(c) |
| Michigan | Hilsendegen v. Scheich, 55 Mich. 468 (1885), 21 N.W. 2d 894 (1885) | | |
| Minnesota | | | |

## State Rent Rules (continued)

| State | Returned Late Charges | Check Charges |
|---|---|---|
| Alabama | | |
| Alaska | | |
| Arizona | Ariz. Rev. Stat. Ann. § 33-1368(B) | |
| Arkansas | | |
| California | *Jack v. Sinsheimer*, 125 C563 (1899); *Ricker v. Rombough*, 120 Cal App 2d Supp 912 (1953), but see *Canal-Randolph Anaheim, Inc. v. Wilcowski*, 78 Cal.App. 3d 477 (1978) | |
| Colorado | | |
| Connecticut | Conn. Gen. Stat. Ann. §§ 47a-4(a)(8), 47a-15a | |
| Delaware | Del. Code Ann. tit. 25, § 5501(d) | |
| D.C. | | |
| Florida | | |
| Georgia | | |
| Hawaii | | |
| Idaho | | |
| Illinois | | |
| Indiana | | |
| Iowa | | |
| Kansas | | |
| Kentucky | | |
| Louisiana | | |
| Maine | Me. Rev. Stat. Ann. tit. 14, § 6028 | |
| Maryland | Md. Code Ann., [Real Prop.] § 8-208(3) | |
| Massachusetts | Mass. Gen. Laws Ann. ch. 186 §11; Mass. Gen. Laws Ann. ch. 186 §15B(1)(c) | |
| Michigan | | |
| Minnesota | | |

## State Rent Rules

| State | When Rent is Due | Grace Period | Where Rent is Due |
|---|---|---|---|
| Mississippi | | | |
| Missouri | | | |
| Montana | Mont. Code Ann. § 70-24-201(2)(c) | | Mont. Code Ann. § 70-24-201(2)(b) |
| Nebraska | Neb. Rev. Stat. § 76-1414(3) | | Neb. Rev. Stat. § 76-1414(3) |
| Nevada | Nev. Rev. Stat. Ann. §§ 118A.210-.250 | | |
| New Hampshire | | | |
| New Jersey | | | |
| New Mexico | N.M. Stat. Ann. § 47-8-15(B) | | N.M. Stat. Ann. § 47-8-15(B) |
| New York | | | |
| North Carolina | | N.C. Gen Stat. § 42-46 | |
| North Dakota | N.D. Cent. Code § 47-16-07 | | |
| Ohio | | | |
| Oklahoma | Okla. Stat. tit. 41, § 109 | | Okla. Stat. tit. 41, § 109 |
| Oregon | Or. Rev. Stat. § 90.240(5)(a) | Or. Rev. Stat. § 90.260 | Or. Rev. Stat. § 90.240(4)(a) |
| Pennsylvania | | | |
| Rhode Island | R.I. Gen. Laws § 34-18-15(c) | R.I. Gen. Laws § 34-18-35 | R.I. Gen. Laws § 34-18-15(c) |
| South Carolina | S.C. Code Ann. § 27-40-310 | | S.C. Code Ann. § 27-40-310 |
| South Dakota | S.D. Codified Laws Ann. § 43-32-12 | | |
| Tennessee | Tenn. Code Ann. § 66-28-201(c) | | Tenn. Code Ann. § 66-28-201(c) |
| Texas | | | |
| Utah | | | |
| Vermont | | | |
| Virginia | Va. Code Ann. § 55-248.7(C) | | |
| Washington | | | |
| West Virginia | | | |
| Wisconsin | | | |
| Wyoming | | | |

## State Rent Rules (continued)

| State | Late Charges | Returned Check Charges |
|-------|--------------|------------------------|
| Mississippi | | |
| Missouri | | |
| Montana | | |
| Nebraska | | |
| Nevada | | Nev. Rev. Stat. Ann. § 118A.200(3)(c) |
| New Hampshire | | |
| New Jersey | N.J. Stat.Ann. § 2A-42-6.1 | |
| New Mexico | N.M. Stat. Ann § 47-8-15(D) | |
| New York | | |
| North Carolina | N.C. Gen. Stat. § 42-46 | |
| North Dakota | | |
| Ohio | | |
| Oklahoma | *Sun Ridge Investors, Ltd. v. Parker* 956 P.2d 876 (1998) | |
| Oregon | Or. Rev. Stat. § 90.260 | Or. Rev Sat. § 90.302(3)(b) |
| Pennsylvania | | |
| Rhode Island | | |
| South Carolina | | |
| South Dakota | | |
| Tennessee | Tenn. Code Ann. § 66-28-201(d) | |
| Texas | | |
| Utah | | |
| Vermont | | |
| Virginia | | |
| Washington | | |
| West Virginia | | |
| Wisconsin | | |
| Wyoming | | |

## Selected Rent Control Ordinances

### CALIFORNIA

### Los Angeles

**Ordinance Adoption Date**

4/21/79; (Los Angeles Municipal Code, Chapter XV), latest amendment 2/19/91.

**Exceptions**

Units constructed (or substantially renovated with at least $10,000 in improvements) after 10/1/78, "luxury" units (defined as 0,1,2,3, or 4+ bedroom units renting for at least $302, $420, $588, $756, or $823, respectively, as of 5/31/78), single-family residences, except where three or more houses are located on the same lot. [Sec. 151.02.G,M.]

**Administration**

Appointed seven-member Rent Adjustment Commission, 111 N. Hope St., Los Angeles, CA 90012. For information regarding ordinance, call 213-367-9099 or 800-994-4444.

**Registration**

Required. [Sec. 151.11.B.] Tenant may defend any unlawful detainer action on the basis of the landlord's failure to register the property [Sec. 151.09.F].

**Rent Formula**

Except with permission of Commission or Community Development Department, rents may not be increased by more than a 3% to 8%, percentage based on the "Urban All Items Consumer Price Index" for the Los Angeles/Long Beach/Anaheim/Santa Monica/Santa Ana areas. The figure is published each year by the Community Development Department on or before May 30th, and applies to rent increases to be effective the following July 1st through June 30th of the next year. The actual percentage is calculated by averaging the CPI over the previous 12-month period beginning the September 30th before that, but in any event cannot fall below 3% or exceed 8%. In addition, if the landlord pays for gas or electricity for the unit, she may raise the rent an additional 1% for each such type of utility service. [Sections 151.06.D, 151.07.A.6.]

**Individual Adjustments**

Landlord may apply to the Rent Adjustment Commission for higher increase to obtain "just and reasonable return." (This does not include "negative cash flow" based on recent purchase, but does include negative "operating expense," not counting landlord's mortgage payment.)

[Sec. 151.07.B.] Also, landlord may apply to Community Development Department for permission to pass on to the tenant 50% of the cost of capital improvements not directly benefiting the landlord—for example, new roof costs would be considered, but not costs of renovations to manager's units or advertising signs—spread out over five or more years. [Sec. 151.07.A.]

**Rent-Increase Notice Requirements**

Landlord must post conspicuously or give tenant a copy of current registration statement showing that the property is registered with Board. [Sec. 151.05.A.] Landlord who applies to Board for a rent higher than maximum is required to provide written justification for the difference. [Sec. 151.05.C.]

**Vacancy Decontrol**

Landlord may charge any rent after a tenant either vacates voluntarily or is evicted for nonpayment of rent, breach of a rental agreement provision, or to substantially remodel. Controls remain if landlord evicts for any other reason, fails to remodel after evicting for that purpose, or terminates or fails to renew a subsidized-housing lease with the city housing authority. Once a vacated unit is re-rented, it is subject to rent control based on the higher rent. [Sec. 151.06.C.]

**Eviction**

Landlord must show just cause to evict.

**Penalties**

Violation of ordinance, including failing to include proper information in eviction notices, is a misdemeanor punishable by maximums of $500 fine and six months imprisonment. [Sec. 151.10.B.] Tenant may sue in court for three times any rent in excess of legal rent collected, plus attorney fees. [Sec. 151.10.A.]

**Other Features**

Landlord must pay 5% annual interest rate on deposits held over a year. Interest payments need only be made every five years, and when deposit refunded at end of tenancy. (This part of the ordinance, however, is not being enforced at this time, while a legal challenge proceeds through the appeals courts.)

Los Angeles also has a Rent Escrow Adjustment Program (REAP) ordinance that applies to all rent-controlled units. Under this ordinance, a tenant whose landlord has received a 30-day notice from local health or building inspectors to correct serious housing code violations may withhold rent and pay it to a city escrow fund, if the landlord has failed to correct the violation within the 30-day period.

## Oakland

### Ordinance Adoption Date

10/7/80; latest amendment 11/97.

### Exceptions

Units constructed after 1/1/83, buildings "substantially rehabilitated" at cost of 50% of that of new construction (as determined by Chief Building Inspector) properties with HUD-insured mortgages. Landlord may not charge the new tenant more than twice the annual allowable increase. [Sec. 8.22.030.]

### Administration

Appointed seven-member Residential Rent Arbitration Board, 300 Lakeside Drive, Oakland, CA 94612, 510-238-3721 (to leave message) or call Sentinel Fair Housing, 510-836-2687.

### Registration

Not required.

### Rent Formula

Rents may not be increased more than 3% in any 12-month period for occupied units, and 6% in any 12-month period for units vacated after the landlord terminated the tenancy. The 6% increase is one-time only. [Sec. 8.22.060.]

### Individual Adjustments

Tenant can contest an increase in excess of that allowed (but only if his rent is current) by filing a petition with the Board. The petition must be filed within 30 days. Hearing officer may consider costs of capital improvements, repairs, maintenance, and debt service, and past history of rent increases. [Sec. 8.22.080, 8.22.060.]

### Rent-Increase Notice Requirements

Landlords are required to notify tenants of the Residential Rent Arbitration Board at outset of the tenancy, in an addendum to the lease or rental agreement. [Sec. 5.d.]

### Vacancy Decontrol

Landlord may charge any rent after a tenant vacates voluntarily. If tenant vacates "involuntarily," landlord may not charage the new tenant more than twice the annual allowable increase. Once the property is re-rented, it is subject to rent control based on the higher rent. [Sec. 8.22.060.]

### Eviction

Ordinance does not require just cause to evict, but there are other requirements.

### Penalties

Violation of ordinance is infraction (petty offense) punishable on first, second, and third offenses within 12-month period by fines of up to $100, $200 and $500 respectively. A fourth offense within 12 months is a misdemeanor punishable by maximums of a $1,000 fine and/or six months' imprisonment. [Sec. 9.1.]

## San Francisco

### Ordinance Adoption Date

6/79; (San Francisco Administrative Code, Chapter 37), latest amendment 11/98.

### Exceptions

Units constructed after 6/79, buildings over 50 years old and "substantially rehabilitated" since 6/79. [Sec. 37.2(p).]

### Administration

Appointed five-member Residential Rent Stabilization and Arbitration Board, [Sec. 37.4], 25 Van Ness Avenue, Suite 320, San Francisco, CA 94102, 415-554-9550 (automated information system) and 415-554-9551 (counselor).

### Registration

Not required.

### Rent Formula

Rents may not be increased by more than 7% in any 12-month period. (Increase allowed each year is 60% of the "Urban All Items Consumer Price Index" for the San Francisco-Oakland Metropolitan Area, but not more than 7%.) The figure is published each year by the Board. [Sec. 37.3.] A landlord who has not increased the rent during a previous 12-month period may accumulate his/her rights to increases and impose them in later years. Landlord may apply to Board for certification of capital improvements the amortized cost of which may also be passed through to the tenant, but such increases are limited to 10% of the base rent each year. [Sec. 37.7.]

### Individual Adjustments

Landlord may apply to Board for higher increase based on increased costs, including utility and capital-improvement costs. Hearing officer decides case based on various factors, including operating and maintenance expenses, but not "negative cash flow" based on recent purchase. Hearing officer may also consider rent-increase history and failure to make repairs. Tenant may contest any claimed pass-through of utility costs, or request rent reduction based on decrease of services or poor maintenance. Either party may request an "expedited hearing." [Sections. 37.8.]

### Rent-Increase Notice Requirements

Landlord must give tenant written itemized breakdown of rent increases—for example, what portion reflects costs of capital improvements—on or before the date of service of the rent-increase notice. [Sec. 37.6(b).]

### Vacancy Decontrol

Landlord may charge any rent after a tenant vacates voluntarily or is evicted for good cause. Once the property is re-rented, it is subject to rent control based on the higher rent. [Sec. 37.3(a).]

### Eviction

Landlord must show just cause to evict. [Sec. 37.9.] There is a perment moratorium on owner move-in evictions, protecting tenants who are 1) 60 years old or older and have lived in the rental for at least ten years; 2) disabled or blind and have lived in the rental for at least ten years; or 3) disabled and have a "catastrophic illness" and have lived in the rental for at least five years. The moratorium does not apply in certain situations.

### Penalties

Violation of ordinance, including wrongful eviction or eviction attempts, is a misdemeanor punishable by maximums of a $2,000 fine and six months imprisonment. [Sec. 37.10.]

### Other Features

Landlord must pay 5% annual interest on deposits held over a year, with payments made on tenant's move-in anniversary date each year and when the deposit is refunded at the end of the tenancy. [Administrative Code, Chapter 49.]

## San Jose

### Ordinance Adoption Date

7/7/79; (San Jose Municipal Code, Title 17, Chapter 17.23), latest amendment 7/19/91.

### Exceptions

Units constructed after 9/7/79, single-family residences, duplexes, and condominium units. [Sec. 17.23.150.]

### Administration

Appointed seven-member Advisory Commission on Rents, 4 N. Second St., Suite 600, San Jose, CA 95113-1305, 408-277-5431.

### Registration

Required.

### Rent Formula

Rents may not be increased more than 8% in any 12-month period, and may not be increased more than once within the 12 months. However, a landlord who has not raised the rent for over 24 months is entitled to a 21% increase. [Sections. 17.23.180, 17.23.210.]

### Individual Adjustments

Tenant can contest an increase in excess of that allowed by filing a petition before rent increase takes effect (30 days), or lose the right to object. Disputes initiated by tenant petition are heard by a mediation hearing officer, who may consider costs of capital improvements, repairs, maintenance, and debt service, and past history of rent increases. Either party may appeal mediator's decision and invoke binding arbitration. Tenant can also petition to contest rent based on housing-code violations or decrease in services. [Sections. 17.23.220-17.23.440.]

### Rent-Increase Notice Requirements

Where rent increase exceeds 8%, rent-increase notice must advise tenant of her right to utilize the Rental Dispute Mediation and Arbitration Hearing Process, giving the address and telephone number of the city's rent office. The notice must also indicate the time limit within which the tenant may do this. [Sec. 17.23.270.]

### Vacancy Decontrol

Landlord may charge any rent after a tenant vacates voluntarily or is evicted following three-day notice for nonpayment of rent or other breach of the rental agreement. Once the property is re-rented, it is subject to rent control based on the higher rent. [Sec. 17.23.190.]

### Eviction

Ordinance does not require showing of just cause to evict.

### Penalties

Violation of ordinance by charging rent in excess of that allowed following mediation/arbitration, by retaliation against the tenant for asserting his rights, or by attempting to have tenant waive rights under ordinance is a misdemeanor punishable by maximums of a $500 fine and six months imprisonment. [Sections 17.23.515-17.23.530.]

Tenant may sue landlord in court for excess rents charged, plus treble damages or $500 (whichever is greater). [Sec. 17.23.540.]

## OTHER STATES

### District of Columbia

#### Ordinance Adoption Date

7/17/85; (Rental Housing Act of 1985, District of Columbia Code §45-2501 et seq.); latest amendment in §18, Omnibus Budget Support Congressional Review Emergency Act of 1995 (D.C. Act 11-124, July 27, 1995; 42 DCR 4160).

#### Exceptions

Any rental unit in any federally or District-owned housing accommodation, buildings constructed after 12/75, rental additions after 1/80, buildings with four or less rental units, cooperative housing, housing which receives rehabilitation assistance. [D.C. Code §42-2515.]

#### Administration

Appointed three-member Rental Housing Commission, [D.C. Code §45-2511], North Potomac Building, 614 H Street, NW, Room 1105, Washington, DC 20001, 202-727-7315.

#### Registration

Required, and landlord cannot increase the rent if the building is not registered. [D.C. Code §45-2518, §45-2515.]

#### Rent Formula

Rents may not be increased by more than 10% in any 12-month period. (Increase allowed each year equal to the change during the previous year in the DC Standard Metropolitan Statistical Area Consumer Price Index for Urban Wage Earners and Clerical Workers for all items during the preceding calendar year.) [D.C. Code §45-2516(b).]

#### Rent-Increase Notice Requirements

Landlord must give tenant 30 days written notice of any rent adjustment with a statement of the current rent, the increased rent, and the utilities covered by the rent which justify the adjustment. [D.C. Code §45-2518(a)(1)(E) and (f).] In addition, any notice must include a summary of tenants' rights and a list of sources of technical assistance.

#### Vacancy Decontrol

If tenant vacates voluntarily or is evicted for not paying rent or using the rental unit for illegal purposes, the landlord may increase the rent 12% above the rent ceiling. Landlord may do this only once per 12-month period. [D.C. Code § 45-2523.]

#### Eviction

Landlord must show just cause to evict. [D.C. Code § 45-2551.]

#### Penalties

A landlord who demands or receives any rent in excess of the maximum allowable rent or substantially reduces or eliminates related services previously provided for a rental unit, will be liable for the amount by which the rent exceeds the applicable rent ceiling or for three times that amount (in the event of bad faith) and/or for a rollback of the rent to the amount the Rental Housing Commission allows. A landlord who violates the chapter in any way will be subject to a civil fine of not more than $5,000 for each violation. [D.C. Code § 45-2591.]

Tenant may challenge a rent increase by filing a petition with the Rent Administrator within three years of the increase. [D.C. Code §45-2516(e).]

### Newark, New Jersey

#### Ordinance Adoption Date

November 20, 1973 (Title 15, Housing Chapters 9A and 9B). Last amended in 12/96.

#### Exceptions

Owner-occupied one-, two-, three- and four-unit dwellings and public housing. Units that have been rehabilitated by federal or state programs and that receive Section 8 rent subsidies or federal housing vouchers may raise rents only up to fair market value, as determined by the federal Department of Housing and Urban Development. These units lose their exemption if they are withdrawn from Section 8 or the Rental Rehabilitation Program. [15:9B2.] New construction, previously vacant properties and substantially rehabilitated vacant units are all exempt from rent control for five years. [15:9B-17.]

#### Administration

Appointed five-member Rent Control Board. [15:9B-9.] Office of Boards, City of Newark, Room 112, 920 Broad Street, Newark, New Jersey 07102. For information regarding ordinance, call 973-733-3675.

#### Registration

Required. [15:9A-10.]

### Rent Formula

Rents may not be increased by more than 5% for dwellings of 49 units or less, or 4% for dwellings of 50 units or more. [15:9B-3.]

### Individual Adjustments

Landlord may increase the rent for hardship, for a capital improvement surcharge, a substantial rehabilitation exemption, a utilities surcharge and after a unit is vacated. [15:9B-7, 15:9B-8, 15:9B-17(c), 15:9B-16.]

### Rent-Increase Notice Requirements

Landlord must notify the Board and tenant at least 60 days before the effective date of the increase.

The Board or the tenant may request a hearing within 30 days of receipt of notice from the landlord. [15:9B-7 and 8.] For a utilities surcharge, the landlord must send notice to the tenant within 14 days after the landlord applies to the Board. [15:9B-16.]

### Vacancy Decontrol

Vacant units which remain vacant for a minimum of 18 months remain outside of the rent control ordinance for a period of five years. [15:9B-17(b).] Apartments which become vacant and in which the landlord spent more than $100 times the number of rooms in the unit for the purpose of rehabilitating the apartment may have their rent increased a maximum of 25% of the prior rent. Landlord must post his application to the Board for this rent increase in a conspicuous place in the apartment building on the date of the application. [15:9B-17(d).]

### Eviction

Landlord must show just cause to evict.

### Penalties

Violation of ordinance is punishable by a maximum of $500 fine and/or 90 days imprisonment. [15:9A- 14 and 15:9B-18.]

### Other Features

Landlord may seek a tax surcharge from a tenant because of an increase in municipal property taxes after giving the tenant one month's notice. [15:9B-5.] If there is a tax decrease, the tenant is also entitled to a rent reduction. [15:9B-6.]

## New York

New York's rent regulation programs, which affect mainly New York City tenants, are divided into those apartments that are under rent control and those that are under rent stabilization.

**Rent Control** The rent control program applies only to residential buildings constructed before February 1, 1947, and containing three or more units (there are only about 100,000 rent control units). In order for an apartment that meets these specifications to be under rent control, the tenant must have lived there continuously since July 1, 1971. In addition, rent control covers one-family dwellings and apartments in two-family dwellings built before February 1, 1947, if the same tenant has lived there continuously since May 1, 1953. When a rent controlled apartment is vacated, it either becomes rent stabilized or completely removed from regulation.

Since there are no new rent control tenants, the program is dying out.

*Rent Stabilization:* Apartments are under rent stabilization if they are in buildings of more than six units, built between February 1, 1947, and January 1, 1974. There are over 1,100,000 rent stabilized units. Tenants in buildings built before February 1, 1947, who moved in after June 30, 1971, are also covered by rent stabilization. In addition, buildings of three or more apartments constructed or extensively renovated since 1974 with special tax benefits are also covered by rent stabilization.

### Ordinance Adoption Date

Emergency Housing Rent Control Law of 1946, Emergency Tenant Protection Act of 1974, and New York City Administrative Code Sections 26-501 to 26-520, adopted 1969, all amended by the Rent Regulation Reform Act of 1993. Further amendments were made in June 1997.

### Exceptions, Rent Control and Rent Stabilization

Buildings with more than six units or built after 1974. Tenants who are 62 years or older may qualify for a full or partial exemption from rent increases. Seniors are eligible if their incomes are below a maximum limit set by local law, they are paying at least 1/3 of their income for rent and their leases are for one- or two-year terms. [Senior Citizen Rent Increase Exemption-SCRIE, NYC Admin. Code Sections 26-601 to 26-615.]

Vacated apartments that rent for more than $2,000, including any rent increases that are the result of passed-on renovation costs, are deregulated immediately.

### Administration

New York State Division of Housing and Community Renewal (DHCR) administers rent regulations both in and outside NYC. DHCR has a Central Rent Information Hotline, 718-739-6400; 163 W. 125th Street, 5th Floor,

New York, NY 10027, or 156 William Street, 9th Floor, New York, NY 10038. In addition, NYC has an appointed nine-member Rent Guidelines Board (RGB) which establishes the guidelines for annual rent adjustments. [NYC Admin. Code Sec. 26-510.] Rent Guidelines Board, 51 Chambers Street, Room 202, New York, NY 10007 212-349-2262.

### Registration

Owners had to register with the DHCR, no later than 6/30/84. For apartments which became subject to rent stabilization after 1984, an owner is required to file an initial registration within 90 days after the property becomes subject to rent stabilization. After the initial registration, owners must file an annual registration statement giving the April 1st rent for each unit and provide tenants with a copy of their statement. Owners who don't comply can't increase the rent and are subject to additional penalties. [NYC Admin. Code Sec. 26-517.]

### Rent Formula

*Rent Control:* A Maximum Base Rent (MBR) system is established for each apartment and adjusted every two years to reflect changes in operating costs. The rent that rent-controlled tenants pay is called the Maximum Collectible Rent (MCR), which is usually less than the MBR. Owners who certify that they are providing "essential" services are entitled to raise rents up to 7.5% each year until they reach the MBR. Tenants can challenge the proposed increase on the grounds that the building has safety or health code violations or that the owner's expenses do not warrant an increase.

*Rent Stabilization:* Landlord can increase the rent when an apartment is vacated based on city guidelines plus an adjustment called the "vacancy allowance." The rent may be increased at least 20% if the lease is for two or more years and the previous tenant has either moved or died. When a landlord renovates a vacant unit, the rent may be increased by $1 for every $40 spent.

### Rent-Increase Notice Requirements

Owner can increase the rent for increase in services, capital investments or hardship, but must first file an application with the DHCR, which then serves the tenants notice of the increase in rent. The increase in the monthly stabilization rent can only be 1/40th of the total cost of the improvements. [NYC Rent Stabilization Code Part 2522.4.] Landlords can also include the price of fuel in a rent increase in rent controlled apartments only. This is known as a "pass-along."

### Vacancy Decontrol

When a rent-controlled apartment becomes vacated, it falls under rent stabilization if it is in a building with six or more units; otherwise it becomes deregulated. [NYC Rent Stabilization Law Sec. 26-504.]

Luxury Decontrol: Units rented by tenants whose combined yearly income exceeds $175,000 for two consecutive years and who pay $2,000 or more in rent will be deregulated.

### Eviction

Landlord must show just cause to evict. [NYC Rent Stabilization Code Part 2524.1, .3.] In addition, a landlord can't refuse to renew a lease of a tenant who is over 62 or disabled because the landlord wants the apartment for personal use. [Rent Stabilization Code 2524.4(a).] A landlord may demolish a building with few units if the tenants are relocated to comparable housing.

### Penalties

If a tenant's rights are violated, DHCR can reduce rents and levy civil penalties against the owner ranging from $100 to a maximum of $2,500 for subsequent offense, depending on the violation. If the landlord overcharged the rent, the DHCR can assess treble damages. There is a retroactive four-year maximum on rent overcharge refunds for complaints filed after April 1, 1984, and a two-year maximum on treble damages. Landlords who harass tenants in an effort to get them to vacate their apartments may be charged with a class B felony, punishable by up to four years in state prison. [NYC Admin. Code Sec. 26-516.]

### Other Features

An owner must include a copy of the Rent Stabilization Rider with a tenant's lease, which describes the rights and obligations of tenants and owners under the Rent Stabilization Law. The Rider informs a rent-stabilized tenant signing a vacancy lease of the legal regulated rent in effect immediately prior to the vacancy and explains how the present rent was computed.

In most cases, tenants must place rent into escrow accounts during disputes with landlords.

Tenants' succession rights extend to spouses and unmarried domestic partners only, and are limited to one generation.

## Notice Required to Change or Terminate a Month-to-Month Tenancy

Except where noted, the amount of notice a landlord must give to increase rent or change another term of the rental agreement in month-to-month tenancy is the same as that required to end a month-to-month tenancy. Be sure to check state and local rent control laws, which may have different notice requirements.

| State | Tenant | Landlord | Statute | Comments |
|---|---|---|---|---|
| Alabama | 10 days | 10 days | Ala. Code § 35-9-3 | No state statute on the amount of notice required to change rent or other terms. |
| Alaska | One month | One month | Alaska Stat. § 34.03.290(b) | |
| Arizona | 30 days | 30 days | Ariz. Rev. Stat. Ann. § 33.1375 | |
| Arkansas | 30 days | 30 days | Ark. Code Ann. § 18-16-101 | |
| California | 30 days | 30 days | Cal. Civ. Code § 1946 | Landlord and tenant may agree to a shorter termination period, but not less than seven days. |
| Colorado | | | No statute | |
| Connecticut | 3 days | 3 days | Conn. Gen. Stat. § 47a-23 | Three days do not include the day the notice is served or the day the termination or change is to take effect. |
| Delaware | 60 days | 60 days | Del. Code Ann. tit. 25, § 5106 and 5107 | After receiving notice of landlord's proposed change terms, Tenant has 15 days to terminate tenancy. Otherwise, changes will take effect as announced. |
| District of Columbia | 30 days | 30 days | D.C. Code Ann. § 45-1402 | No state statute on the amount of notice required to change rent or other terms. |
| Florida | 15 days | 15 days | Fla. Stat. Ann. § 83.57 | No state statute on the amount of notice required to change rent or other terms. Tenant can terminate with seven days notice if landlord doesn't comply with a material provision of the lease. |
| Georgia | 30 days | 60 days | Ga. Code Ann. § 44-7-7 | No state statute on the amount of notice required to change rent or other terms. |
| Hawaii | 28 days | 45 days | Haw. Rev. Stat. §§ 521-71 and 521-21(d) | |
| Idaho | 30 days | 30 days | Idaho Code § 55-208 and 55-307 | Landlords must provide 15 days' notice to increase rent or change tenancy. |
| Illinois | 30 days | 30 days | Ill. Rev.stat.ch. 735 ¶ 5/9-207 | |
| Indiana | 30 days | 30 days | Ind. Code Ann. § 32-7-1-3 | |
| Iowa | 30 days | 30 days | Iowa Code Ann. §§ 562A.34, 562A.13.5 | |
| Kansas | 30 days | 30 days | Kan. Stat. Ann. § 58-2570 | No state statute on the amount of notice required to change rent or other terms. |
| Kentucky | 30 days | 30 days | Ky. Rev. Stat. Ann. § 383.695 | |
| Louisiana | 10 days | 10 days | La. Civ. Code Ann. art. 2686 | No state statute on the amount of notice required to change rent or other terms. |
| Maine | 30 days | 30 days | Me. Rev. Stat. Ann. tit. 14 § 6002 | |
| Maryland | 30 days | 30 days | Md. Code Ann. [Real Prop.] § 8-402 | |
| Massachusetts | 30 days | 30 days | Mass. Gen. Laws Ann. ch. 186 § 12 | |
| Michigan | 30 days | 30 days | Mich. Comp. Laws Ann. § 554.134 | No state statute on the amount of notice required to change rent or other terms. |
| Minnesota | 30 days | 30 days | Minn. Stat. Ann. § 504A.225 | No state statute on the amount of notice required to change rent or other terms. |
| Mississippi | 30 days | 30 days | Miss. Code. Ann. § 89-8-19 | No state statute on the amount of notice required to change rent or other terms. |
| Missouri | 30 days | 30 days | Mo. Ann. Stat. § 441.060 | No state statute on the amount of notice required to change rent or other terms. |

## Notice Required to Change or Terminate a Month-to-Month Tenancy (continued)

| State | Tenant | Landlord | Statute | Comments |
|---|---|---|---|---|
| Montana | 30 days | 30 days | Mont. Code Ann. § 70-24-441 | No state statute on the amount of notice required to change rent or other terms. |
| Nebraska | 30 days | 30 days | Neb. Rev. Stat. § 76-1437 | No state statute on the amount of notice required to change rent or other terms. |
| Nevada | 30 days | 30 days 118A.300 | Nev. Rev. Stat. Ann. §§ 40.251, to increase rent. | Landlords must provide 45 days' notice |
| New Hampshire | 30 days | 30 or 7 days | N.H. Rev. Stat. Ann. §§ 540:2 and 540:3 | Landlord may terminate only for just cause. |
| New Jersey | No statute | No statute | No statute cause. | Landlord may terminate only for just |
| New Mexico | 30 days | 30 days | N.M. Stat. Ann. § 47-8-37 | Landlord most deliver rent increase notice at least 30 days before rent due date. |
| New York | one month | one month | N.Y. Cons. Laws Real Property § 232-b | No state statute on the amount of notice required to change rent or other terms. |
| North Carolina | 7 days | 7 days | N.C. Gen. Stat. § 42-14 | No state statute on the amount of notice required to change rent or other terms. |
| North Dakota | 30 days | 30 days | N.D. Cent. Code § 47-16-15 | Tenant may terminate with 25 day's notice if landlord has changed the terms of the lease. |
| Ohio | 30 days | 30 days | Ohio Rev. Code Ann. § 5321.17 | No state statute on the amount of notice required to change rent or other terms. |
| Oklahoma | 30 days | 30 days | Okla. Stat. tit. 41 § 111 | No state statute on the amount of notice required to change rent or other terms. |
| Oregon | 30 days | 30 days | Or. Rev. Stat. § 91.060 | |
| Pennsylvania | No statute | No statute | No statute | |
| Rhode Island | 30 days | 30 days | R.I. Gen. Laws §§ 34-18-16.1 and 34-18-37 | |
| South Carolina | 30 days | 30 days | S.C. Code Ann. § 27-40-770 | No state statute on the amount of notice required to change rent or other terms. |
| South Dakota | 30 days | 30 days | S.D. Codified Laws Ann. §§ 43-32-13and 43-32-22 | Tenant can terminate within 15 days of receiving landlord's modification notice |
| Tennessee | 30 days | 30 days | Tenn. Code Ann. § 66-28-512 | No state statute on the amount of notice required to change rent or other terms. |
| Texas | 30 days | 30 days | Tex. [Prop.] Code Ann. § 91.001 (but only if property is sold) | No state statute on the amount of notice required to change rent or other terms. |
| Utah | No statute | No statute | No statute | |
| Vermont | 30 days | 30 days | Vt. Code Ann. tit. 9 § 4467, 4456 | If there is no written rental agreement, the landlord must provide 60 days' notice to notice to terminate (but only 30 days if property is sold). Landlord must give 60 days' notice to incease rent. |
| Virginia | 30 days | 30 days | Va. Code Ann. § 55-248-37 | No state statute on the amount of notice required to change rent or other terms. |
| Washington | 30 days | 20 days | Wash. Rev. Code Ann. §§ 555.248.37, 59.18.200, 59.18.140, 59.18.352 | Tenant may terminate without notice if threatened with a weapon by another tenant and landlord fails to begin an eviction proceeding within seven days of the arrest of that tenant. |
| West Virginia | 30 days | 30 days | W. Va. Code § 37-6-5 | No state statute on the amount of notice required to change rent or other terms. |
| Wisconsin | 28 days | 28 days | Wis. Stat. Ann. § 704.19 | No state statute on the amount of notice required to change rent or other terms. |
| Wyoming | No statute | No statute | No statute | |

# Citations for State Laws on Security Deposits

Here are citations for statutes pertaining to security deposits in each state. Details on various aspects of security deposits are provided in Chapters 4 and 15.

This table is limited to security deposit statutes. Some states—Alabama, Idaho, West Virginia and Wyoming—do not have statutes on security deposits. That doesn't mean that there is no law on the subject. Court decisions (what lawyers call "case law") in your state may set out quite specific requirements for refundability of deposits, whether they should be held in interest-bearing accounts and the like. This book doesn't cover all this case law; you may need to check it out yourself. To find out whether courts in your state have made decisions you need to be aware of, you may need to do some legal research on your own (see Chapter 18).

| State | Citation |
|---|---|
| Alabama | No statute |
| Alaska[1] | Alaska Stat. § 34.03.070 |
| Arizona | Ariz. Rev. Stat. Ann. §§ 33-1321 |
| Arkansas[2] | Ark. Code Ann. §§16-303 to -306 |
| California | Cal. [Civ.] Code § 1950.5 |
| Colorado | Colo. Rev. Stat. §§ 38-12-102 to -104 |
| Connecticut | Conn. Gen. Stat. Ann. § 47a-21 |
| Delaware | Del. Code Ann. tit. 25, § 5514 |
| District of Columbia | D.C. Code Ann. § 45-2527 and D.C. Mun. Regs. tit. 14, §§ 308-311 |
| Florida | Fla. Stat. Ann. § 83.49 |
| Georgia[3] | Ga. Code Ann. §§ 44-7-30 to -36 |
| Hawaii | Haw. Rev. Stat. § 521-44 |
| Idaho | Id. Code § 6-321 |
| Illinois[4] | Ill. Rev. Stat. ch. 765 para. 710, 715 |
| Indiana | Ind. Code Ann. §§ 32-7-5-1 to -19 |
| Iowa | Iowa Code Ann. § 562A.12 |
| Kansas | Kan. Stat. Ann. § 58-2550 |
| Kentucky | Ky. Rev. Stat. Ann. § 383.580 |
| Louisiana | La. Rev. Stat. §9.3251 |
| Maine[5] | Me. Rev. Stat. Ann. tit. 14, §§ 6031-6038 |
| Maryland | Md. Code Ann. [Real Prop.] § 8-203 |
| Massachusetts | Mass. Gen. Laws Ann. ch. 186 § 15B |
| Michigan | Mich. Comp. Laws Ann. §§ 554.602-.613 |
| Minnesota | Minn. Stat. Ann. § 504A.221 |
| Mississippi | Miss. Code Ann. § 89-8-21 |
| Missouri | Mo. Ann. Stat. § 535.300 |
| Montana | Mont. Code Ann. §§ 70-25-101 to -206 |
| Nebraska | Neb. Rev. Stat. § 76-1416 |
| Nevada | Nev. Rev. Stat. Ann. §§ 118A.240-.250 |
| New Hampshire[6] | N.H. Rev. Stat. Ann. §§ 540-A:5 to :8 |
| New Jersey[7] | N.J. Stat. Ann. §§ 46:8-19 to -26 |
| New Mexico | N.M. Stat. Ann. § 47-8-18 |
| New York[8] | N.Y. Gen. Oblig. Law §§ 7-101 to -109 |
| North Carolina | N.C. Gen. Stat. §§ 42-50 to -56 |
| North Dakota | N.D. Cent. Code § 47-16-07.1 |
| Ohio | Ohio Rev. Code Ann. § 5321.16 |
| Oklahoma | Okla. Stat. tit. 41 § 115 |
| Oregon | Or. Rev. Stat. § 90.300 |
| Pennsylvania | Pa. Stat. Ann. tit. 68, §§ 250.511a-.512 |
| Rhode Island | R.I. Gen. Laws § 34-18-19 |
| South Carolina | S.C. Code Ann. § 27-40-410 |
| South Dakota | S.D. Codified Laws Ann. §§ 43-32-6.1, -24 |
| Tennessee[9] | Tenn. Code Ann. § 66-28-301 |
| Texas | Tex. Prop. Code Ann. §§ 92.101-.109 |
| Utah | Utah Code Ann. §§ 57-17-1 to -5 |
| Vermont | Vt. Stat. Ann. tit. 9, § 4461 |
| Virginia | Va. Code Ann. § 55-248.11 |
| Washington | Wash. Rev. Code Ann. §§ 59.18.260 -.285 |
| West Virginia | No statute |
| Wisconsin | Wisc. Admin. Code ATCP § 134.06 |
| Wyoming | No statute |

**Exemptions from State Security Deposit Laws**

[1] Any rental unit where the rent exceeds $2,000 per month (Alaska)

[2] Landlord who owns five or fewer rental units, unless these units are managed by a third party for a fee (Arkansas)

[3] Landlord who owns ten or fewer rental units, unless these units are managed by an outside party (Georgia)

[4] Landlord who owns four or fewer dwelling units (Illinois)

[5] Rental unit which is part of a structure with five or fewer units, one of which is occupied by landlord (Maine)

[6] Landlord who leases a single-family residence and owns no other rental property or landlord who leases rental units in an owner-occupied building of five units or less. (Exemption does not apply to any individual unit in owner-occupied building that is occupied by a person 60 years of age or older.) (New Hampshire)

[7] Owner-occupied building with two or less units where tenant fails to provide 30 days' written notice to landlord invoking provisions of act (New Jersey)

[8] Landlord who rents out fewer than six rental units (New York)

[9] Rental properties outside of Davidson, Knox, Hamilton and Shelby Counties (Tennessee)

## States That Require Landlords to Pay Interest on Deposits

| | |
|---|---|
| **Connecticut** | Interest payments must be made annually and at termination of tenancy. The interest rate must be equal to the average rate paid on savings deposits by insured commercial banks, as published by the Federal Reserve Board Bulletin in November of the prior year, but not less than 1.5%. |
| **Dist. of Columbia** | Interest payments at the prevailing passbook rate must be made at termination of tenancy. |
| **Florida** | Interest payments (if any—account need not be interest-bearing) must be made annually and at termination of tenancy. However, no interest is due a tenant who wrongfully terminates the tenancy before the end of the rental term. If landlord is paying interest, details on interest rate and time of payment must be provided in lease or rental agreement. |
| **Illinois** | Landlords who rent 25 or more units in either a single building or a complex of buildings located on contiguous properties must pay interest on deposits held for more than six months. Interest must be paid annually and at termination of tenancy. |
| **Iowa** | Interest payment (if any—account need not be interest-bearing) must be made at termination of tenancy. Interest earned during first five years of tenancy belongs to landlord. |
| **Maryland** | Interest must be paid (at an annual rate of 4%) only on security deposits of $50 or more, at six-month intervals, not compounded. |
| **Massachusetts** | Landlord must pay tenant 5% interest per year or the amount received from the bank where the deposit has been held. Interest should be paid to the tenant yearly, and within 30 days of termination date. Interest will not accrue for the last month for which rent was paid in advance. |
| **Minnesota** | Landlord must pay 3% (simple, noncompounded) annual interest until 5/1/00. After that, 4% per year. Any interest amount less than $1 is excluded. |
| **New Hampshire** | A landlord who holds a security deposit for a year or longer must pay interest at a rate equal to the interest rate paid on regular savings accounts in the New Hampshire bank, savings and loan association or credit union where it is deposited. If a landlord mingles security deposits in a single account, the landlord must pay the actual interest earned proportionately to each tenant. Upon request, a landlord must give the tenant the name of any institution where the security deposit is held, the account number, the amount on deposit and the interest rate on the deposit, and must allow the tenant to examine his security deposit records. A tenant may request the interest accrued every three years, 30 days before that year's tenancy expires. The landlord must comply with the request within 15 days of the expiration of that year's tenancy. |
| **New Jersey** | Landlord must place the deposit in an insured money market account or other account where the fund matures in one year or less. Landlord must pay tenant interest on account, minus an amount not to exceed 1% per annum of the amount invested, or 12.5% of the aggregate interest, whichever is higher, less the amount of any service fee charged by the financial institution holding the deposit. |
| **New Mexico** | Landlord who receives more than one month's rent deposit on a year lease must pay the tenant, annually, interest equal to the passbook interest. |
| **New York** | Landlord must hold money in interest-bearing bank account and pay the tenant interest (less I% for expenses) on it. |
| **North Dakota** | Landlord must pay interest if the period of occupancy is at least nine months. Money must be held in a federally insured interest-bearing savings or passbook account. |
| **Ohio** | Any security deposit in excess of $50 or one month's rent, whichever is greater, must bear interest on the excess at the rate of 5% per annum if the tenant stays for six months or more. Interest must be paid annually and upon termination of tenancy. |
| **Pennsylvania** | Tenant who occupies rental unit for two or more years is entitled to interest beginning with the 25th month of occupancy. Landlord must pay tenant interest (minus fee of 1%) at the end of the third and subsequent years of the tenancy. |
| **Virginia** | Landlord must accrue interest in six-month increments, at a rate equal to the Federal Reserve Board discount rate as of January 1 of each year, on all money held as security. No interest is payable unless the landlord holds the deposit for over 13 months after the date of the rental agreement for continuous occupancy of the same unit. Interest begins accruing from the effective date of the rental agreement and must be paid only upon termination of tenancy. |

# State Fair Housing Agencies

The name, address and phone number of the state organization responsible for administering and enforcing state fair housing laws or handling discrimination complaints is listed here. In states where there is no state agency, contact the U.S. Department of Housing and Urban Development (HUD) for information.

## Alabama
No state agency. Contact HUD.

## Alaska
Commission on Human Rights
800 A Street, Suite 204
Anchorage, AK 99501
907-276-7474

## Arizona
Office of the Attorney General,
   Civil Rights Section
1275 W. Washington Street
Phoenix, AZ 85007
602-542-5263 Phoenix
520-628-6500 Tucson

## Arkansas
Department of Housing & Urban
   Development
TCBY Tower
425 West Capitol Avenue, Suite 900
Little Rock, AR 72201
501-324-6296

## California
Department of Fair Employment &
   Housing
1330 Broadway, Suite 1530
Oakland, CA 94612-2512
800-233-3212
510-286-6291

## Colorado
Civil Rights Division
1560 Broadway, Suite 1050
Denver, CO 80202
303-894-2997

## Connecticut
Commission on Human Rights &
   Opportunities
21 Grand Street
Hartford, CT 06106
860-541-3400

## Delaware
Division of Human Relations
Carvel State Office Building
820 North French Street
Wilmington, DE 19801
302-577-5050

## District of Columbia
Commission on Human Rights
2000 14th Street NW
Washington, DC 20009
202-939-8740

## Florida
Commission on Human Relations
325 John Knox Road
Building F, Suite 240
Tallahassee, FL 32399
850-488-7082

## Georgia
Fair Housing and Equal Opportunity
   Commission
710 Cain Tower
229 Peachtree St., N.E.
Atlanta, GA 30303-1650
404-656-1736

## Hawaii
Civil Rights Commission
830 Punchbowl St.
Honolulu, HI 96813
808-586-8636

## Idaho
Commission on Human Rights
450 West State Street
Boise, ID 83720
208-814-2873

## Illinois
Department of Human Rights
100 West Randolph Street, Suite 10-100
Chicago, IL 60601
312-917-6200

## Indiana
Civil Rights Commission
100 North Senate Avenue, Room N103
Indianapolis, IN 46204
317-232-2600

## Iowa
Civil Rights Commission
211 East Maple
Des Moines, IA 50319
515-281-4121

## Kansas
No state agency. Contact HUD.

## Kentucky
Commission on Human Rights
Heyburn Building
332 W. Broadway, 7th Floor
Louisville, KY 40202
502-574-3190

## Louisiana
Department of Justice, Equal Opportunity
   Section
P.O. Box 94095
Baton Rouge, LA 70804-9095
504-342-7900

## Maine
Human Rights Commission
State House
Augusta, ME 04333
207-624-6050

## Maryland
Commission on Human Relations
6 St. Paul St., 9th Floor
Baltimore, MD 21202
410-767-8600

## Massachusetts
Commission Against Discrimination
One Ashburton Place
Boston, MA 02108
617-727-3990

## Michigan
Department of Civil Rights
303 West Kalamazoo
Lansing, MI 48913
517-335-3165

## State Fair Housing Agencies (continued)

**Minnesota**
Department of Human Rights
190 E. Fifth St.
Suite 700
St. Paul, MN 55101
612-296-5663

**Mississippi**
No state agency. Contact HUD.

**Missouri**
Commission for Human Rights
3315 West Truman
Jefferson City, MO 65102
314-751-3325

**Montana**
Human Rights Commission
616 Helena Avenue
Helena, MT 59624
406-444-2884

**Nebraska**
Equal Opportunity Commission
P.O. Box 94934
Lincoln, NE 68509
402-471-2024

**Nevada**
No state agency. Contact HUD.

**New Hampshire**
Commission for Human Rights
2 Chenell Dr.
Concord, NH 03301
603-271-2767

**New Jersey**
Division on Civil Rights
383 West State Street
Trenton, NJ 08618
609-292-4605

**New Mexico**
Human Rights Commission
Aspen Plaza
1596 Pacheco Street
Santa Fe, NM 87501
505-827-6812

**New York**
Division of Human Rights
55 West 125th Street, 13th Floor
New York, NY 10027
212-961-8400

**North Carolina**
Human Relations Commission
121 West Jones Street
Raleigh, NC 27603
919-733-7996

**North Dakota**
No state agency. Contact HUD.

**Ohio**
Civil Rights Commission
220 Parsons Avenue
Columbus, OH 43215
614-466-2785

**Oklahoma**
Human Rights Commission
2101 North Lincoln Boulevard, Room 480
Oklahoma City, OK 73105
405-521-3441

**Oregon**
Bureau of Labor and Industry,
   Civil Rights Division
800 NE Oregon Street
Portland, OR 97232
503-731-4075

**Pennsylvania**
Human Relations Commission
101 South Second Street, Suite 300
Harrisburg, PA 17105
717-787-4410

**Rhode Island**
Commission for Human Rights
10 Abbott Park Place
Providence, RI 02903
401-277-2661

**South Carolina**
Human Affairs Commission,
   Fair Housing Division
2611 Forest Drive
Columbia, SC 29204
803-253-6336

**South Dakota**
Division of Human Rights
222 East Capitol Street
Pierre, SD 57501
605-773-4493

**Tennessee**
Human Rights Commission
530 Church Street
Nashville, TN 37243
615-741-5825

**Texas**
Commission on Human Rights
6330 Hwy. 290
Austin, TX 78723
512-437-3450

**Utah**
Industrial Commission,
   Anti-Discrimination Division
160 East 300 South
Salt Lake City, UT 84114
801-530-6435

**Vermont**
Human Rights Commission
135 State Street, 2nd Floor
Montpelier, VT 05633-6301
802-828-2480
800-416-2010

**Virginia**
Office of Fair Housing
3600 West Broad Street
Richmond, VA 23230
804-367-8530
888-551-FAIR

**Washington**
Human Rights Commission
402 Evergreen Plaza Building
711 South Capitol Way
Olympia, WA 98504
360-753-6770

**West Virginia**
Human Rights Commission
1321 Plaza East
Charleston, WV 25301
304-558-2616

**Wisconsin**
Department of Industry, Labor and Human
   Relations, Equal Rights Division
P.O. Box 8928
201 East Washington Avenue
Madison, WI 53708
608-266-7552

**Wyoming**
No state agency. Contact HUD.

## State Consumer Protection Offices

Your state consumer protection agency can provide general information and referrals on your state law. Many also provide free written brochures on landlord-tenant law.

| State | State Consumer Protection Offices (Source for Information Publications, if different) | Phone Number | FAX |
|---|---|---|---|
| Alabama | Office of the Attorney General, Consumer Assistance, 11 South Union Street, Montgomery, AL 36130 | 334-242-7334 800-392-5658 | 334-242-2433 |
| Alaska | The Consumer Protection section in the office of the Attorney General has been closed. | | |
| Arizona | Office of the Attorney General, Consumer Information and Complaints, 1275 West Washington Street, Phoenix, AZ 85007 | 602-542-5673 800-352-8431 602-542-5002 (TTY) | 602-542-1275 |
| Arkansas | Office of the Attorney General, Advocacy Division, 200 Tower Building, 323 Center Street, Little Rock, AR 72201 | 501-682-2341 800-482-8982 501-652-6073 (TTY) | 501-682-8084 |
| | (Office of the Attorney General, Consumer Protection Division, 200 Catkett-Prien Building, 323 Center Street/Little Rock, AR 72201) | 800-482-8982 | 501-682-8084 |
| California | Department of Consumer Affairs, Consumer Assistance Office, 400 R Street, Room 1040, Sacramento, CA 95814 | 916-445-1254 800-344-9940 | |
| Colorado | Office of the Attorney General, Consumer Protection Unit, 1525 Sherman Street, 5th Floor, Denver, CO 80203 | 303-866-5189 800-332-2071 | 303-866-5691 |
| | (Housing Information & Referral Services, 1905 Sherman Street, Suite 920, Denver, CO 80203) | 303-831-1935 | |
| Connecticut | Department of Consumer Protection, 165 Capitol Avenue, Hartford, CT 06106 | 800-842-2649 203-566-2534 | 203-566-1531 |
| | (Department of Banking, 260 Constitution Plaza, Hartford, CT 06103) | 203-240-8200 | 203-240-8178 |
| Delaware | Department of Justice, Consumer Protection Unit, 820 North French Street, 4th Fl., Wilmington, DE 19801 | 302-577-3250 | 302-577-6499 |
| District of Columbia | Department of Consumer and Regulatory Affairs, 614 H Street NW, Room 1120, Washington, DC 20001 | 202-727-7120 | 202-727-8073 |
| Florida | Division of Consumer Services, Department of Agriculture and Consumer Services, 407 S. Calhoun St., Room 235, Tallahassee, FL 32399 | 800-435-7352 904-488-2221 | 904-487-4177 |

## State Consumer Protection Offices (continued)

| State | State Consumer Protection Offices (Source for Information Publications, if different) | Phone Number | FAX |
|---|---|---|---|
| Georgia | Governor's Office of Consumer Affairs, 2 Martin Luther King Jr. Drive, S.E., Plaza Level-East Tower, Atlanta, GA 30344 | 404-651-8600 404-656-3790 | 404-651-9018 |
| | (Georgia Housing & Finance Authority, Tenant/Landlord Authority, 60 Executive Park South, NE, Suite 250, Atlanta, GA 30329-2231) | 404-679-4840 | 404-679-4837 |
| Hawaii | Department of Commerce and Consumer Affairs, Office of Consumer Protection, 828 Fort St. Mall, Suite 600 B, P.O. Box 3767, Honolulu, HI 96813 | 808-586-2636 | 808-586-2640 |
| Idaho | Office of the Attorney General, Consumer Protection Division, 210 State House, P.O. Box 83720, Boise, ID 83720-1000 | 208-334-2424 800-432-3545 | 208-334-2840 |
| Illinois | Office of the Attorney General, Consumer Protection Division, 100 West Randolph, 12th Floor, Chicago, IL 60601 | 312-814-3000 800-252-8666 | |
| Indiana | Office of the Attorney General, Consumer Protection Division, Indiana Gov't Center South, 5th Floor, 402 West Washington, Indianapolis, IN 46204-2270 | 317-232-6330 800-382-5516 | 317-232-7979 |
| Iowa | Office of the Attorney General, Consumer Protection Division, Hoover State Office Building, Des Moines, IA 50319 | 515-281-5926 | 515-281-6771 |
| Kansas | Office of the Attorney General, Consumer Protection Division, Kansas Judicial Center, 2nd Floor, Topeka, KS 66612 | 913-296-3751 800-432-2310 | 913-291-3699 |
| Kentucky | Consumer Protection Division, Office of Attorney General, P.O. Box 2000, Frankfort, KY 40602-2000 | 502-564-2200 800-432-9257 | |
| Louisiana | Office of the Attorney General, Consumer Protection Section, P.O. Box 94095, Baton Rouge, LA 70804-9095 | 504-342-9638 | 504-342-9637 |
| Maine | Department of the Attorney General, Public Protection Unit, 6 State House Station, Augusta, ME 04333-0006 | 800-332-8529 207-624-8527 | 207-582-7699 |
| Maryland | Office of the Attorney General, Consumer Protection Division, 200 St. Paul Place, Baltimore, MD 21202-2022 | 410-528-8662 | 410-576-6566 |
| Massachusetts | Office of the Attorney General, Consumer Complaint & Information Section, 1 Ashburton Place, Boston, MA 02108 | 617-727-5765 | 617-227-5765 |
| Michigan | Office of the Attorney General, Consumer Protection Division, P.O. Box 30213, Lansing, MI 48909 | 517-373-1140 | 517-241-1850 |
| Minnesota | Office of the Attorney General, Consumer Services Division, 1400 NCL Tower, 445 Minnesota Street, St. Paul, MN 55101-2130 | 612-296-3353 800-657-3787 | 612-297-4193 |

## State Consumer Protection Offices (continued)

| State | State Consumer Protection Offices (Source for Information Publications, if different) | Phone Number | FAX |
|---|---|---|---|
| Mississippi | Office of the Attorney General, Consumer Protection Division, P.O. Box 22947, Jackson, MS 39225-2947 | 601-359-4230<br>800-281-4418 | 601-359-4198 |
| Missouri | Office of the Attorney General, Consumer Protection Division, P.O. Box 899, Jefferson City, MO 65102 | 314-751-3321<br>800-392-8222 | 314-751-7948 |
| Montana | Department of Commerce, Consumer Affairs Unit, 1424 Ninth Avenue, Helena, MT 59620 | 406-444-3553 | 406-444-2903 |
| Nebraska | Office of the Attorney General, Consumer Protection Division, 2115 State Capitol Building, P.O. Box 98920, Lincoln, NB 68509-8920 | 402-471-2682 | 402-471-3297 |
| Nevada | Commissioner of Consumer Affairs, Department of Business and Industry, State Mail Room Complex, Las Vegas, NV 89158 | 702-486-7355 | 702-486-7901 |
| New Hampshire | Department of Justice, Consumer Protection Bureau, 33 Capitol Street, Concord, NH 03301 | 603-271-3641 | 603-271-2110 |
| | (New Hampshire Legal Assistance, 15 Green Street, Concord, NH 03301) | 603-224-3333 | 603-224-6067 |
| New Jersey | Consumer Protection Office, 124 Halsey St., Newark, NJ 07101 | 201-504-6534 | 201-648-3538 |
| | (Administrative Division of the Courts, Civil Practice Division, R.J.H. Justice Complex, Courts Building, 7th Floor CN 037, Trenton, NJ 08625) | 609-984-0275 | 609-292-3320 |
| New Mexico | Office of the Attorney General, Consumer Protection Division, P.O. Drawer 1508, Santa Fe, NM 87504 | 505-827-6060<br>800-678-1508 | 505-827-5826 |
| New York | Assistant Attorney General, Bureau of Consumer Fraud and Protection, Office of Attorney General, State Capital, Albany, NY 12223-12224 | 518-474-5481 | |
| North Carolina | Office of the Attorney General, Consumer Protection Section, Department of Justice, P.O. Box 629, Raleigh, NC 27602 | 919-733-7741 | 919-715-0577 |
| North Dakota | Office of the Attorney General, Consumer Protection Division, 600 East Boulevard, Bismarck, ND 58505-0400 | 701-224-3404<br>800-472-2600 | |
| Ohio | Office of the Attorney General, Consumer Protection Division, State Office Tower, 30 East Broad Street, 25th Floor, Columbus, OH 43215-3428 | 614-466-4986<br>800-282-0515 | |
| | (Ohio Legal Services Association, 861 North High Street, Columbus, OH 43215) | 614-299-2114<br>800-589-5888 | |
| Oklahoma | Office of the Attorney General, Consumer Affairs Division, 2300 N. Lincoln Blvd., Oklahoma City, OK 73105-3498 | 405-521-4274 | 405-528-1867 |

## State Consumer Protection Offices (continued)

| State | State Consumer Protection Offices (Source for Information Publications, if different) | Phone Number | FAX |
|---|---|---|---|
| **Oregon** | Department of Justice, Financial Fraud Division, 1162 Court Street, NE, Salem, OR 97310 | 503-378-4732 | 503-373-7067 |
| **Pennsylvania** | Office of the Attorney General, Bureau of Consumer Protection, Strawberry Square, 14th Floor, Harrisburg, PA 17120 | 717-787-9707 800-441-2555 | 717-787-8242 |
| **Rhode Island** | Department of the Attorney General, Consumer Protection Division, 72 Pine St., Providence, RI 02903 | 401-277-4400 | 401-277-1331 |
| **South Carolina** | Department of Consumer Affairs, 1101 Williams Street, Columbia, SC 29211 | 803-734-3970 800-922-1594 | 803-734-9365 |
| **South Dakota** | Office of the Attorney General, Division of Consumer Affairs, State Capitol Building, 500 East Capitol, Pierre, SD 57501 | 605-773-4400 800-300-1986 | 605-773-4106 |
| **Tennessee** | Department of Commerce and Insurance, Division of Consumer Affairs, 500 James Robertson Parkway, 5th Floor, Nashville, TN 37243-0600 | 615-741-3491 800-342-8385 | 615-741-4747 |
| **Texas** | Office of the Attorney General, Consumer Protection Division, P.O. Box 12548, Austin, TX 78711 | 512-463-2070 | 512-463-2063 |
| **Utah** | Division of Consumer Protection, Dept. of Commerce, 160 East 300 South, P.O. Box 45804, Salt Lake City, UT 84145-0804 | 801-530-6001 | 801-530-6601 |
| **Vermont** | Office of the Attorney General, Consumer Assistance, 109 State Street, Montpelier, VT 05609-1001 | 802-828-3171 800-649-2424 | 802-828-2154 |
| **Virginia** | Department of Agriculture and Consumer Services, Office of Consumer Affairs, 1100 Bank St., Richmond, VA 23219 | 804-786-2042 800-552-9963 | 804-371-7479 |
| **Washington** | Office of the Attorney General, Consumer Resource Center, 1125 Washington Street SE, P.O. Box 40100, Olympia, WA 98504-0100 | 360-753-6210 800-551-4636 | 360-586-8474 |
| **West Virginia** | Office of the Attorney General, Consumer Protection Division, 812 Quarrier St., Charleston, WV 25301 | 304-558-8986 800-368-8808 | 304-558-0140 |
|  | (West Virginia Legal Services Plan, Inc., 922 Quarrier Street, Charleston, WV 25301) | 800-642-8279 304-342-6814 | 304-342-3011 |
| **Wisconsin** | Department of Agriculture, Trade and Consumer Protection, Consumer Protection Bureau, P.O. Box 8911, Madison, WI 53707 | 608-224-4939 | 608-224-5045 |
| **Wyoming** | Office of the Attorney General, Consumer Affairs Division, 123 State Capitol Building, Cheyenne, WY 82002 | 307-777-7874 | 307-777-7841 |

## State Laws on Rent Withholding and Repair and Deduct Remedies

Here are citations for state laws that allow tenants to withhold rent or use the repair and deduct remedy for landlord's failure to provide habitable premises.

| State | Statute on rent withholding | Statute on repair and deduct |
|---|---|---|
| Alabama | No statute | No statute |
| Alaska | Alaska Stat. § 34.03.190 | Alaska Stat. § 34.03.180 |
| Arizona | Ariz. Rev. Stat. Ann. § 33-1365 | Ariz. Rev. Stat. Ann. §§ 33-1363, -1364 |
| Arkansas | No statute | No statute |
| California | *Green v. Superior Court*, 10 Cal. 3d 616 (1974) | Cal. [Civ.] Code § 1942 |
| Colorado | No statute | No statute |
| Connecticut | Conn. Gen. Stat. Ann. §§ 47a-14a to -14h | Conn. Gen. Stat. Ann. § 47a-13 |
| Delaware | Del. Code Ann. tit. 25 §§ 5306(b), 5308(b)(3) | Del. Code Ann. tit. 25, §§ 5307, 5308 |
| District of Columbia | *Javins v. First Nat'l Realty Corp.*, 428 F.2d 1071 (D.C. Cir. 1970) | No statute |
| Florida | Fla. Stat. Ann. § 83.60 | No statute |
| Georgia | No statute | No statute |
| Hawaii | Haw. Rev. Stat. § 521-78 | Haw. Rev. Stat. § 521-64 |
| Idaho | No statute | No statute |
| Illinois | Ill. Rev. Stat. ch. 765 para. 735/2-/2.1 | No statute |
| Indiana | No statute | No statute |
| Iowa | Iowa Code Ann. § 562A.24 | Iowa Code Ann. § 562A.23 |
| Kansas | Kan. Stat. Ann. § 58-2561 | No statute |
| Kentucky | Ky. Rev. Stat. Ann. § 383.645 | Ky. Rev. Stat. Ann. §§ 383.635, 383.640 |
| Louisiana | No statute | La. Civ. Code Ann. art. 2694 |
| Maine | Me. Rev. Stat. Ann. tit. 14, § 6021 | Me. Rev. Stat. Ann. tit. 14, § 6026 |
| Maryland | Md. Code Ann., [Real Prop.] §§ 8-118, -211, -211.1 | No statute |
| Massachusetts | Mass. Gen. Laws Ann. ch. 239, § 8A | Mass. Gen. Laws Ann. ch. 186 § 14 |
| Michigan | Mich. Comp. Laws § 125.530 | No statute |
| Minnesota | Minn. Stat. Ann. §§ 504.26, 504A.135S, 504A.171, 504A.585 | No statute |
| Mississippi | No statute | Miss. Code Ann. § 89-8-15 |
| Missouri | Mo. Ann. Stat. §§ 441.580, 441.570 | No statute |
| Montana | Mont. Code Ann. § 70-24-421 | Mont. Code Ann. §§ 70-24-406, -407, -408 |
| Nebraska | Neb. Rev. Stat. §§ 76-1425, -1428 | Neb. Rev. Stat. § 76-1427 |
| Nevada | Nev. Rev. Stat. Ann. § 118A.490 | Nev. Rev. Stat. Ann. §§ 118A.360, -.380 |
| New Hampshire | N.H. Rev. Stat. Ann. § 540:13d | No statute |
| New Jersey | N.J. Stat. Ann. §§ 2A: 42-85 to -96 | No statute |
| New Mexico | N.M. Stat. Ann. § 47-8-27.2 | No statute |
| New York | N.Y. [Mult. Resid.] Law § 305-a | N.Y. [Mult. Resid.] Law § 305-c and N.Y. [Real Prop.] Law § 235-a |
| North Carolina | No statute | No statute |
| North Dakota | No statute | N.D. Cent. Code § 47-16-13 |
| Ohio | Ohio Rev. Code Ann. § 5321.07 | No statute |
| Oklahoma | Okla. Stat. tit. 41, § 121 | Okla. Stat. tit. 41, § 121 |
| Oregon | Or. Rev. Stat. § 90.370 | Or. Rev. Stat. § 90.365 |
| Pennsylvania | Pa. Stat. Ann. tit. 68, § 250.206 | Pa. Stat. Ann. tit. 68, § 339.6 |
| Rhode Island | R.I. Gen. Laws § 34-18-32 | R.I. Gen. Laws §§ 34-18-30, -31 |
| South Carolina | S.C. Code Ann. §§ 27-40-640, -790 | S.C. Code Ann. § 27-40-630 |
| South Dakota | S.D. Codified Laws Ann. § 43-32-9 | S.D. Codified Laws Ann. § 43-32-9 |
| Tennessee | Tenn. Code Ann. § 68-111-104 | Tenn. Code Ann. § 66-28-502 |
| Texas | No statute | Tex. [Prop.] Code Ann. §§ 92.0561, 92.056 |
| Utah | No statute | No statute |
| Vermont | Vt. Stat. Ann. tit. 9, § 4458 | Vt. Stat. Ann. tit. 9, § 4459 |
| Virginia | Va. Code Ann. §§ 55-248.25 to .30 | Va. Code Ann. § 55-248.23 |
| Washington | Wash. Rev. Code Ann. § 59.18.115 | Wash. Rev. Code Ann. § 59.18.100 |
| West Virginia | No statute | No statute |
| Wisconsin | Wisc. Stat. Ann. § 704.07(4) | No statute |
| Wyoming | No statute | No statute |
| Washington | Wash. Rev. Code Ann. § 59.18.115 | Wash. Rev. Code Ann. § 59.18.100 |
| West Virginia | No statute | No statute |
| Wisconsin | Wisc. Stat. Ann. § 704.07(4) | No statute |
| Wyoming | No statute | No statute |

## State Lead Hazard Reduction Laws

| State | Statute | Summary |
| --- | --- | --- |
| Alabama | Ala. Code § 22-37-3 | Requires plumbing components to be lead-free at time of installation or repair. |
| | Ala. Code §§ 22-37A-1 and following | Allows state health officer to investigate lead contamination generally or at request of owner or occupant. |
| | | Requires certification of lead hazard reduction professionals. |
| Arizona | Ariz. Rev. Stat. Ann. §§ 36-1671 and following | Ariz. Rev. Stat. Ann. §§36-1671 and following |
| | | Forbids the use of lead-based paint on any interior surface of a dwelling that may be within reach of a child under seven years. |
| | | Authorizes Department of Health to develop local programs to detect and prevent lead-based paint poisoning in interior and exterior of buildings built before 1978 that are accessible to children under age seven. |
| | | Provides for promulgation of regulations concerning certification of lead abatement professionals. |
| Arkansas | Ark. Stat. §§ 20-27-601 to 20-27-608 | Permits the state to investigate the sources of lead hazards when a child is diagnosed with an elevated blood-lead level. |
| | | Requires the state to notify the owner/occupier of a dwelling of detected lead hazards and requires abatement. |
| | | Prohibits evicting the occupants of an affected residence. |
| | | Mandates licensing for lead abatement workers as well as standards for removal of lead hazards. |
| California | Cal. Health and Safety Code §§ 105185 and following | Establishes training, certification and accreditation for lead abatement professionals. |
| | Cal. Civ. Code §§ 1102 to 1102.6 | Requires an owner of a property to disclose lead-based paint hazards to prospective buyers. |
| | Cal. Labor Code §§ 6716-6717 | Establishes standards for lead abatement workers. |
| | Cal. Health & Safety Code §§ 124160 and 124165 | Directs Department of Health to take steps necessary to reduce children's excessive exposure to lead. |
| Colorado | Co. Rev. Stat. § 25-5-1104 | Requires the Department of Public Health to establish a plan to reduce children's lead levels and control exposure to lead paint hazards in residences and child-occupied facilities. |
| Connecticut | Conn. Gen. Stat. § 8-219e | Provides government loans to persons seeking to remove lead-based paint. |
| | Conn. Gen. Stat. §§ 19a-111 to 19a-111d | Owners of dwellings with reported high blood-lead levels in occupants under six years old are required to abate the lead hazard. An owner may be responsible for relocating residents. |
| | Conn. Gen. Stat. § 21a-82 | Forbids the use of lead-based paint in tenements or municipally owned buildings unless it adheres to state and federal regulations. |
| | Conn. Gen. Stat. § 47a to 54f | Prohibits paint in tenement houses that is cracked, chipped, blistered, flaking, loose or peeling so as to constitute a health hazard. |
| Delaware | Del. Code Title 31 § 4114(d) | Bans the use of lead-based paint on any dwelling unit surface, including fences and outbuildings. |
| District of Columbia | D.C. Code Ann. §§ 6-997.1 and following | Establishes lead-based paint abatement program under Mayor's office. |
| | | Provides for certification and permits for lead abatement activities. |
| | | Requires owners to keep records of lead-based paint abatement activities |

## State Lead Hazard Reduction Laws (continued)

| State | Statute | Summary |
|---|---|---|
| **District of Columbia (continued)** | | Provides for random inspections of lead-based paint abatement activities. |
| | | Prohibits use of lead-based paint in any structure, fixture, appliance or furniture. |
| | | Law does not apply to efficiencies or housing built after 1978. |
| **Georgia** | Ga. Code § 31-41-2 | Requires the enactment of regulations to train, license and certify lead hazard abatement professionals. |
| **Hawaii** | Hi. Rev. Stat. § 321-11(27) | Places lead abatement practices and training programs within the Department of Health. |
| **Illinois** | 410 Ill. Comp. Stat. 45/2 and following | An owner of a dwelling has between 30 and 90 days to mitigate the lead hazard. Abatement must be conducted by a licensed contractor. If abatement requirements are not met, the department may withhold rent from the owner or relocate the occupants until the procedures are complied with. |
| | | Requires an owner to give written notice to prospective residents that a lead hazard has been identified in the dwelling unit. All owners of pre-1978 residential buildings must give prospective lessees a brochure on the potential hazards posed by lead in dwelling units. |
| **Indiana** | In. Code Ann. §§ 13-17-14-1 and following | Regulates abatement when children six years old and younger will be affected; requires lead-based paint workers to be licensed. Establishes trust fund to provide money for programs in target housing. |
| **Iowa** | Iowa Code § 135.100 to 135.105 | Department of Public Health must design programs to eliminate or reduce dangerous levels of lead in children by implementing an abatement grant program to assess homes and assist in abatement. |
| **Kentucky** | Ky. Rev. Stat. §§ 211.900 to 201-905 and 211-.994 | Permits the Human Resources Department to inspect a dwelling if an occupant is reported to have an elevated blood-lead level. |
| | | Gives the owner of a residential unit 30 days to remove, replace or cover any lead hazard surfaces that are accessible to children under the age of six. |
| | | If the Department determines that a child under six is in immediate danger from the presence of a lead hazard, the occupant may terminate the rental agreement without reprisal. |
| **Louisiana** | La. Rev. Stat. 40:1299.26-29 | Mandates that an owner of residential property must remove or cover any lead-bearing materials within 30 days of a violation, if a child under six or a mentally retarded person resides at the premises. |
| | La. Rev. Stat. 30:2351-2351.59 | Requires licenses for lead contractors, reduction planners and inspectors. The statute also includes a whistle blower provision to facilitate reporting the improper handling of lead-containing substances. |
| **Maine** | Me. Rev. Stat. Title 22 §§ 1314 to 1326 | Restricts the use of any lead-based paint on any fixtures or exposed surface of a dwelling. |
| | | Permits the Department of Human Services to inspect residences, provide notice to owners and occupants of any lead hazards and order abatement of exposed surfaces containing a lead hazard. |
| **Maryland** | Md. Ann. Code 83B §§ 2-307 and 1402 and following | Establishes lead hazard reduction grant and load programs for owners of residential property to fund lead hazard reduction activities with the emphasis on replacement of windows containing lead-based paint on friction surfaces and concentrating on residential properties constructed prior to 1950; with children who have been diagnosed with elevated blood-lead; families of limited income; or to test innovative methods of lead hazard reduction. |
| | Md. Env. Code § 6-301 | Prohibits the use of lead-based paint on any interior or exterior surface commonly within the reach of children. |
| | | Requires the training and licensure of lead abatement professionals. |
| | Md. Env. Code §§ 6-801 to 6-852 | Requires owners to register their properties containing lead hazards and abate. Provides immunity from liability under certain circumstances. Requires owners to give tenants a lead poisoning information packet. |
| | Md. Real Prop. Code § 8-211.1 | Allows lessee to ask the District Court to hold rent in escrow without reprisal where an owner has failed to comply with lead abatement laws. |

## State Lead Hazard Reduction Laws (continued)

| State | Statute | Summary |
|-------|---------|---------|
| **Massachusetts** | Mass. Gen. Laws Chapter 111, §§ 127b1/2, 189A-199 | Requires training and licensing of lead abatement professionals. |
| | | Permits inspection of the premises for lead hazards. |
| | | Owners of residential dwellings must remove or cover lead hazards. |
| | | Owners must disclose lead hazards to prospective buyers of the property. |
| | Mass. Gen. Laws Chapter 23B | Provides for a grant and load program for abatement of lead-based materials in dwellings. |
| **Michigan** | Mich. Comp. Laws Ann. § 565.957 | Provides for Department of Public Health to make recommendations to governor for lead-based paint poisoning program. |
| | Mich. Comp. Laws. Ann. § 333.12101 | Requires disclosure of lead-based paint to prospective buyers. |
| **Minnesota** | Minn. Stat. §§ 144.9501 to 144.9509 | Requires lead abatement contractors to be registered with the state. |
| | | Provides for the development of residential lead abatement procedures. |
| | | Requires owners to abate lead hazards if residents are children under six or pregnant women. |
| **Mississippi** | Ms. Code §§ 49-17-501 and following | Authorizes the Department of Environmental Quality to establish certification programs for lead abatement workers. Requires licensing and certification of lead-based paint abatement professionals. |
| **Missouri** | Mo. Stat. §§ 701.300 and following | Requires residential lead hazard abatement. |
| | | Provides for the licensure of abatement professionals. |
| **Nebraska** | Neb. Rev. Stat. § 71-6319 to § 71-6333 | Lead abatement workers must be licensed; law establishes a training and certification program. |
| **New Hampshire** | N.H. Rev. Stat. § 130-A | Permits the Health Department to inspect residential dwellings. |
| | | Requires an owner to abate lead hazards within 90 days of notice. Owners are prohibited from evicting occupants with children under six upon finding the presence of a lead hazard. |
| | | Owners must disclose lead hazard violations to prospective buyers. |
| | | Prohibits knowingly leasing a property with a lead hazard to occupants with children under six. |
| | | Prohibits use of paint with more than .06% lead in any dwelling unit. |
| **New Jersey** | N.J. Rev. Stat. §§ 26:2-130 to 26:2-137 | Provides screening for every child five years old and younger; results must be given to parents or guardians. |
| | | Requires certification for lead abatement professionals. |
| | | Establishes a grant program for local health boards to abate lead hazards. |
| | N.J. Rev. Stat. §§ 24:14A-1 to 24:14A-11 | Forbids the use of lead-based paint on residential surfaces reachable by children. |
| | | Mandates the removal and disposal of lead paint within ten days of a violation. |
| | | Prohibits retaliatory eviction for the purpose of avoiding abatement. |
| **New York** | N.Y. Stat. Public Health Code §§ 1370 to 1375 | Forbids the use of lead-based paint on any residential porches or interior surfaces. |
| | | Notification of owner/occupant about the lead hazard and suggested abatement procedures. |
| | | Mandatory screening of children in pre-school or day care. |
| **North Carolina** | N.C. Gen. Stat. § 130A-131.5 | Establishes lead poisoning prevention program and authorizes commission to adopt rules for prevention of lead poisoning in children. |
| | N.C. Gen. Stat. § 130A-131.7(9) | Requires certain cleaning and maintenance procedures to prevent lead hazards. |
| | N.C. Gen. Stat. §§ 130A-453.02, .03 | Requires certification of lead abatement professionals. |

## State Lead Hazard Reduction Laws (continued)

| State | Statute | Summary |
|---|---|---|
| Ohio | Ohio Rev. Code §§ 3742 and following | Requires licensure for lead abatement professionals. |
| | | Permits the Health Department to inspect dwellings for lead hazards. |
| Oklahoma | Ok. Rev. Stat. Title 27A §§ 2-12-101 to 2-12-501 | Establishes certification requirements for workers in federally assisted housing (private property owners may use certified workers, but are not required to do so). |
| Oregon | Or. Stat. §§ 431.920, 701.500 to 701.515 | Establishes training and licensing programs for lead-based paint workers; authorizes education and screening programs. |
| Pennsylvania | Pa. Stat. Ann. tit. 35, §§ 5901 to 5916 | Establishes guidelines for the certification of lead hazard reduction contractors. |
| Rhode Island | R.I. Gen. Laws Title 23 § 24.6 | Requires lead inspectors and abatement professionals to be licensed. |
| | | Prohibits the use of lead-based paint in residential property accessible to children under six. Permits inspections of dwellings by the Health Department. Provides for emergency abatement if occupants have lead poisoning. |
| | | Owners must disclose lead hazards to potential buyers or lessees. |
| South Carolina | S.C. Code § 44-53-1310 and following | Provides for state inspections and requires owner to remove or cover lead hazards within 30 days of a violation. |
| | | Prohibits use of lead-based paint on interior or exterior of dwelling or on fixtures or furniture. |
| Tennessee | Tn. Code Ann. § 68-131-401 | Department of Environment and Conservation to establish a certificaiton program for lead-based paint workers. |
| Texas | Tx. Civil Stat. Art. 9029 | Department of Health to establish a training, certification and accreditation program for lead-based paint workers who work in child-occupied facilities. |
| Vermont | Vt. Stat. tit. 18 §§ 1751 to 1765 | Establishes training and certification for lead abatement professionals. Requires owners to disclose lead hazards to prospective buyers or lessees. |
| | | Allows the commissioner of the department of health to inspect other dwelling units in a building upon receiving a report that a child who lives in one unit has been severely lead poisoned. Establishes essential maintenance practices. |
| | | Requires insurers to provide liability coverage of lead-based paint hazards. |
| Virginia | Va. Uniform Statewide Building Code, Vol. 11, §§ 1701, R224, PM 305.4 | Prohibits application of lead-based paint on any interior or exterior surface of a dwelling. Requires lead hazards to be removed or covered. |
| | Va. Code Ann. § 54.1-503 | Requires license for lead abatement activities. |
| | Va. Code Ann. § 55-519 | Requires owner to disclose lead-based paint to prospective buyers. |
| West Virginia | W. Va. Code §§ 16-35-1 and following | Requires licensure of lead risk assessment, inspection and abatement professionals. |
| | | Requires owner of building to notify health department before undertaking a lead abatement project. |
| | | Directs the health department to establish a lead abatement and education program. |
| Wisconsin | Wisc. Stat. §§ 254.11 to 254.178 | Prohibits the use of lead-bearing paint; requires doctors to report lead poisoning or exposure; establishes guidelines for screening children under six years of age. When notified that a child under six years of age has been lead poisoned, department of health shall inspect the dwelling and may order the owner to abate the hazard within 30 days. Requires insurance coverage in certain circumstances. |

In order to completely understand your compliance duties, read the entire statute or regulation. Tips on using the law library are in Chapter 18. Some cities may have additional requirements.

Summaries courtesy of Barbara Ann Vassallo, Esq., coordinator of state and local government affairs for the National Apartment Association, Washington, D.C., and Doug Farquhar, National Conference of State Legislatures, Denver, Colorado.

## State Laws on Landlord's Access to Rental Property

This is a synopsis of state laws that specify circumstances when a landlord may enter rental premises and the amount of notice required for such entry.

| State | State law citation | Amount of notice required for landlord to enter | To deal with an emergency | To inspect the premises | To make repairs, alterations, or improvements | To show property to prospective tenants or purchasers | During tenant's extended absence |
|---|---|---|---|---|---|---|---|
| Alabama | No statute | | | | | | |
| Alaska | Alaska Stat. § 34.03.140 | 24 Hours | ✔ | ✔ | ✔ | ✔ | ✔ |
| Arizona | Ariz. Rev. Stat. Ann. § 33-1343 | Two Days | ✔ | ✔ | ✔ | ✔ | |
| Arkansas | No statute | | | | | | |
| California | Cal. Civ. Code § 1954 | 24 Hours | ✔ | | ✔ | ✔ | |
| Colorado | No statute | | | | | | |
| Connecticut | Conn. Gen. Stat. Ann. §§ 47a-16 to -16a | Reasonable notice | ✔ | ✔ | ✔ | ✔ | ✔ |
| Delaware | Del. Code Ann. Tit. 25 §§ 5509, 5510 | Two Days | ✔ | ✔ | ✔ | ✔ | ✔ |
| District of Columbia | No statute | | | | | | |
| Florida | Fla. Stat. Ann. § 83.53 | 12 Hours | ✔ | ✔ | ✔ | ✔ | ✔ |
| Georgia | No statute | | | | | | |
| Hawaii | Haw. Rev. Stat. § 521-53, -70(b) | Two Days | ✔ | ✔ | ✔ | ✔ | ✔ |
| Idaho | No statute | | | | | | |
| Illinois | No statute | | | | | | |
| Indiana | No statute | | | | | | |
| Iowa | Iowa Code Ann. §§ 562A.19, .28, .29 | 24 Hours | ✔ | ✔ | ✔ | ✔ | ✔ |
| Kansas | Kan. Stat. Ann. §§ 58-2557, -2565 | Reasonable notice | ✔ | ✔ | ✔ | ✔ | ✔ |
| Kentucky | Ky. Rev. Stat. Ann. §§ 383.615 | Two Days | ✔ | ✔ | ✔ | ✔ | ✔ |
| Louisiana | No statute | | | | | | |
| Maine | Me. Rev. Stat. Ann. Tit. 14 § 6025 | 24 Hours | ✔ | ✔ | ✔ | ✔ | |
| Maryland | No statute | | | | | | |
| Massachusetts | Mass. Gen. Laws Ann. ch. 186 § 15B1(a) | | | ✔ | ✔ | ✔ | |
| Michigan | No statute | | | | | | |
| Minnesota | Minn. Stat. Ann. § 504.183 | Reasonable notice | ✔ | ✔ | ✔ | ✔ | |

## State Laws on Landlord's Access to Rental Property (continued)

| State | State law citation | Amount of notice required for landlord to enter | To deal with an emergency | To inspect the premises | To make repairs, alterations, or improvements | To show property to prospective tenants or purchasers | During tenant's extended absence |
|-------|--------------------|-----------------------------------|:---:|:---:|:---:|:---:|:---:|
| Mississippi | No statute | | | | | | |
| Missouri | No statute | | | | | | |
| Montana | Mont. Code Ann. § 70-24-312 | 24 Hours | ✔ | ✔ | ✔ | ✔ | ✔ |
| Nebraska | Neb. Rev. Stat. § 76-1423 | One Day | ✔ | ✔ | ✔ | ✔ | ✔ |
| Nevada | Nev. Rev. Stat. Ann. § 118A.330 | 24 Hours | ✔ | ✔ | ✔ | ✔ | |
| New Hampshire | N.H. Rev. Stat. Ann. § 540-A:3 | Notice which is adequate under the circumstances | ✔ | Tenant's prior consent is necessary. | | | |
| New Jersey | No statute | | | | | | |
| New Mexico | N.M. Stat. Ann. § 47-8-24 | 24 hours | ✔ | ✔ | ✔ | ✔ | ✔ |
| New York | No statute | | | | | | |
| North Carolina | No statute | | | | | | |
| North Dakota | N.D. Cent. Code § 47-16-07.3 | Reasonable notice | ✔ | ✔ | ✔ | ✔ | |
| Ohio | Ohio Rev. Code Ann. § 5321.04(B), .05(B) | 24 Hours | ✔ | ✔ | ✔ | ✔ | |
| Oklahoma | Okla. Stat. Tit. 41, § 128 | One Day | ✔ | ✔ | ✔ | ✔ | |
| Oregon | Or. Rev. Stat. § 90.322 | 24 Hours | ✔ | ✔ | ✔ | ✔ | |
| Pennsylvania | No statute | | | | | | |
| Rhode Island | R.I. Gen. Laws § 34-18-26 | Two Days | ✔ | ✔ | ✔ | ✔ | ✔ |
| South Carolina | S.C. Code Ann. § 27-40-530 | 24 Hours | ✔ | ✔ | ✔ | ✔ | ✔ |
| South Dakota | No statute | | | | | | |
| Tennessee | Tenn. Code Ann. § 66-28-403 | | ✔ | ✔ | ✔ | ✔ | ✔ |
| Texas | No statute | | | | | | |
| Utah | Utah Code Ann. § 57-22-5(c) | | ✔ | | ✔ | | |
| Vermont | Vt. Stat. Ann. Tit. 9 § 4460 | 48 Hours | ✔ | ✔ | ✔ | ✔ | |
| Virginia | 1 Va. Code Ann. § 55-248.18 | Reasonable notice | ✔ | ✔ | ✔ | ✔ | ✔ |
| Washington | Wash. Rev. Code Ann. § 59.18.150 | Two Days | ✔ | ✔ | ✔ | ✔ | |
| West Virginia | No statute | | | | | | |
| Wisconsin | Wis. Stat. Ann. § 704.052 | Reasonable notice | ✔ | ✔ | ✔ | ✔ | |
| Wyoming | No statute | | | | | | |

# State Laws Prohibiting Landlord Retaliation

This chart lists states that do not allow landlords to retaliate—by eviction, rent hikes or other negative treatment—when tenants complain about living conditions, exercise legal rights such as the use of repair and deduct statutes and rent withholding and organize other tenants.

| State | Tenant's Complaint to Landlord or Government Agency | Tenant's Involvement in Tenants' Organization | Tenant's Exercise of a Legal Right | Retaliation Is Presumed If Negative Reaction by Landlord Within Specified Time of Tenant's Act | Statute |
|---|---|---|---|---|---|
| Alabama | | | | | No statute |
| Alaska | ✔ | ✔ | ✔ | | Alaska Stat. § 34.03.310 |
| Arizona | ✔ | ✔ | | 6 months | Ariz. Rev. Stat. § 33-1381 |
| Arkansas | ✔ | | | | Ark. Stat. Ann. § 20-27-608 |
| California | ✔ | ✔ | ✔ | 6 months | Cal. Civ. Code § 1942.5 |
| Colorado | | | | | No statute |
| Connecticut | ✔ | ✔ | ✔ | 6 months | Conn. Gen. Stat. §§ 47a-20, 47a-33 |
| Delaware | ✔ | ✔ | ✔ | 90 days | Del. Code Ann. tit. 25 § 5516 |
| D.C. | ✔ | ✔ | ✔ | 6 months | D.C. Code § 45-2552 |
| Florida | ✔ | ✔ | | | Fla. Stat. § 83.64 |
| Georgia | | | | | No statute |
| Hawaii | ✔ | | | | Hw. Rev. Stat. § 521-74 |
| Idaho | ✔ | ✔ | ✔ | | Wright v. Brady, 126 Idaho 671, 889 P.2d 105. (Ct. App. 1995). |
| Illinois | ✔ | | | | 765 Ill. Comp. Stat. 720/1 |
| Indiana | | | | | No statute |
| Iowa | ✔ | ✔ | | 1 year | Iowa Code § 562A.36 |
| Kansas | ✔ | ✔ | | | Kan. Stat. Ann. § 58-2572 |
| Kentucky | ✔ | ✔ | | 1 year | Ky. Rev. Stat. § 383.705 |
| Louisiana | | | | | No statute |
| Maine | ✔ | | ✔ | 6 months | 14 Me. Rev. Stat. § 6001 |
| Maryland | ✔ | ✔ | ✔ | | Md. Real Property Code Ann. § 8-208.1 |
| Massachusetts | ✔ | ✔ | ✔ | 6 months | Mass. Ann. Laws ch. 239 § 2A; ch. 186 § 18 |
| Michigan | ✔ | ✔ | ✔ | 90 days | Mich. Stat. Ann. § 27A.5720 |
| Minnesota | ✔ | | ✔ | 90 days | Minn. Stat. § 504A.551 |
| Mississippi | | | | | Miss. Code Ann. § 89-8-17 |

## State Laws Prohibiting Landlord Retaliation (continued)

| State | Tenant's Complaint to Landlord or Government Agency | Tenant's Involvement in Tenants' Organization | Tenant's Exercise of a Legal Right | Retaliation Is Presumed If Negative Reaction by Landlord Within Specified Time of Tenant's Act | Statute |
|---|---|---|---|---|---|
| Missouri | ✔ | | ✔ | 1 year | Mo. Rev. Stat. § 441.620 |
| Montana | ✔ | ✔ | | 6 months | Mont. Code Ann. § 70-24-431 |
| Nebraska | ✔ | ✔ | | | Neb. Rev. Stat. § 76-1439 |
| Nevada | ✔ | ✔ | ✔ | | Nev. Rev. Stat. Ann. § 118A.510 |
| New Hampshire | ✔ | ✔ | ✔ | 6 months | N.H. Rev. Stat. Ann. §§ 540:13-a & 540:13-b |
| New Jersey | ✔ | ✔ | ✔ | | N.J. Stat. § 2A:42-10.10 & 2A:42-10.12 |
| New Mexico | ✔ | ✔ | ✔ | | N.M. Stat. Ann. § 47-8-39 |
| New York | ✔ | ✔ | ✔ | | N.Y. Consolidated Laws Real Prop. §§ 223-b & 230 |
| North Carolina | ✔ | ✔ | ✔ | | N.C. Gen. Stat. § 42-37.1 |
| North Dakota | | | | | No statute |
| Ohio | ✔ | ✔ | | | Ohio Rev. Code Ann. 5321.02 |
| Oklahoma | | | | | No statute |
| Oregon | ✔ | ✔ | ✔ | | Or. Rev. Stat. § 90.385 |
| Pennsylvania | | | ✔ | | Pa. Stat. Ann. tit. 68 §§ 250.205, 399.11 |
| Rhode Island | ✔ | | ✔ | | R.I. Gen. Laws Ann. §§ 34-20-10 & -11 |
| South Carolina | ✔ | | | | S.C. Code Ann. § 27-40-910 |
| South Dakota | ✔ | ✔ | ✔ | 6 months | S.D. Cod. Laws Ann. § 43-32-27, -28 |
| Tennessee | ✔ | | ✔ | | Tenn. Code Ann. § 66-28-514 & § 68-111-105 |
| Texas | ✔ | | ✔ | 6 months | Tex. Prop. Code § 92.331 |
| Utah | ✔ | | | | Building Monitoring Sys. v. Paxton, 905 P.2d 1215 (Utah 1995). |
| Vermont | ✔ | ✔ | | | 9 Vt. Stat. Ann. § 4465 |
| Virginia | ✔ | ✔ | ✔ | | Va. Code Ann. § 55-248.39 |
| Washington | ✔ | | ✔ | 90 days | Wash. Rev. Code §§ 59.18.240 & 59.18.250 |
| West Virginia | ✔ | | | | W. Va. Code § 55-3A-1, -3; Imperial Colliery Co. v. Fout, 179 W. Va. 776, 373 S.E.2d 489 (1988). |
| Wisconsin | ✔ | | ✔ | | Wis. Stat. § 704.45 |
| Wyoming | | | | | No statute |

## State Laws on Termination for Nonpayment of Rent

If the tenant is late with the rent, in most states you cannot immediately file for eviction. Instead, you must give written notice that the tenant has a specified number of days in which to pay up or move. If the tenant does neither, you can file. In a few states, you must wait a few days before giving the tenant the notice. And some states, as noted, allow the landlord to file for eviction immediately.

| State | Statute | Time Tenant Has to Pay Rent or Move Before You Can File for Eviction | Legal Late Period: How Long You Must Wait Before Giving Notice to Pay or Quit |
|---|---|---|---|
| Alabama | | You can file for eviction immediately. | |
| Alaska | Alaska Stat. §§ 09.45.090, 34.03.220 | 7 days | |
| Arizona | Ariz. Rev. Stat. § 33-1368 | 5 days | |
| Arkansas | Ark. Stat. §§ 18-16-304 and 18-16-01 | Tenant may be prosecuted for a misdemeanor if the rent is not paid after 10 days' notice. | |
| California | Cal. Code of Civil Procedure § 1161 | 3 days | |
| Colorado | Colo. Rev. Stat. § 13-40-104 | 3 days | |
| Connecticut | Conn. Gen. Stat. §§ 47a-23, 47a-15a | 1. 15 days<br>2. If tenant is late more than once in a six-month period, you can use an Unconditional Quit notice. Tenant has 3 days to leave before you can file. | 1. No grace period.<br>2. Unconditional Quit notice cannot be delivered until the rent is 9 days late |
| Delaware | 25 Del. Code §§ 5501(d), 5502 | 5 days | If rental agreement provides for a late charge, but you do not maintain an office in the county in which the rental unit is located, due date for the rent is extended 3 days; thereafter, you may serve a 5-day notice. |
| District of Columbia | D.C. Code § 45-2551 | 30 days | |
| Florida | Fla. Stat. §§ 83.20, 83.56(3) | 3 days | |
| Georgia | Ga. Code Ann. §§ 44-7-50, 44-7-52 | You may demand the rent as soon as it is due and, if not paid, can file eviction lawsuit. Tenant then has 7 days to pay to avoid eviction. | |
| Hawaii | Hawaii Rev. Stat. § 521-68(a) | 5 days | |
| Idaho | Idaho Code § 6-303 | 3 days | |
| Illinois | Ill. Comp. Stat. chap. 735 para. 5/9-209 | 5 days | |
| Indiana | Ind. Code Ann. § 32-7-1-5 | 10 days | |
| Iowa | Iowa Code § 562A.27 | 3 days | |
| Kansas | Kan. Rev. Stat. §§ 58-2507, 58-2508, 58-2564 | 3 days or, at your option, 10 days for tenancies over 3 months. | |

## State Laws on Termination for Nonpayment of Rent (continued)

| State | Statute | Time Tenant Has to Pay Rent or Move Before You Can File for Eviction | Legal Late Period: How Long You Must Wait Before Giving Notice to Pay or Quit |
|---|---|---|---|
| Kentucky | Ky. Stat. Ann. § 383.660 | 7 days | |
| Louisiana | La. Civil Code Art. 2712 | Landlord can file for eviction immediately; tenant has 5 days to vacate. | |
| Maine | Me. Rev. Stat. tit. 14, § 6002 | 7 days | Notice cannot be delivered until the rent is 7 days late. |
| Maryland | Md. Real Property Code § 8-401 | 5 days' notice to appear in court; if tenant doesn't pay and you win, tenant has 4 days to vacate. If tenant pays all back rent and court costs before execution of evictions, tenant can stay. | |
| Massachusetts | Mass. Ann. Laws ch. 186 § 11 & §12 | 10 days; additional 4 days to quit if tenant doesn't pay. | |
| Michigan | Mich. Comp. Laws § 554.134 | 7 days | |
| Minnesota | Minn. Stat. § 504B.135 | 14 days | |
| Mississippi | Miss. Code §§ 89-7-27, 89-7-45 | 3 days, but tenant may stay if rent and costs are paid prior to removal. | |
| Missouri | | You can file for eviction immediately. | |
| Montana | Mont. Code Ann. § 70-24-422(2)(a) | 3 days | |
| Nebraska | Neb. Rev. Stat. § 76-1431 | 3 days | |
| Nevada | Nev. Rev. Stat. Ann. §§ 40.251, 40.253, 40.2512 | 5 days | |
| New Hampshire | N.H. Rev. Stat. Ann. §§ 540:2, 540:3, 540:9 | 7 days, but tenant must also pay you $15. | |
| New Jersey | N.J. Stat. §§ 2A:18-61.2, 2A:42-9 | 30 days, and you must accept rent any time up to the day of trial. | |
| New Mexico | N.M. Stat. Ann. § 47-8-33 | 3 days | |
| New York | N.Y. Real Prop. Actions Law § 711 | 3 days | |
| North Carolina | N.C. Gen. Stat. § 42-3 | 10 days | |
| North Dakota | N.D. Cent. Code §33-06-01 | Landlord can file for eviction when rent is 3 days overdue. No notice or option to pay required. | |
| Ohio | | You can terminate with an Unconditional Quit notice. | |
| Oklahoma | 41 Okla. Stat. §131 | 5 days | |
| Oregon | Ore. Rev. Stat. § 90.400(2)(b) | 72 hours (3 days) or | Notice cannot be delivered until the rent is 8 days late. |
| | | 144 hours (6 days), but only if lease or rental agreement so provides. | Notice cannot be delivered until the rent is 5 days late. |

| | | **State Laws on Termination for Nonpayment of Rent (continued)** | |
|---|---|---|---|
| **State** | **Statute** | **Time Tenant Has to Pay Rent or Move Before You Can File for Eviction** | **Legal Late Period: How Long You Must Wait Before Giving Notice to Pay or Quit** |
| Pennsylvania | Pa. Stat. Ann. § 250.501(b) | 10 days | |
| Rhode Island | R.I. Gen. Laws § 34-18-35 | 5 days, but tenant can stay if he pays back rent prior to commencement of suit. If tenant has not received a pay or quit notice within past 6 months, tenant can stay if he pays back rent and costs prior to hearing on eviction. | Notice cannot be delivered until rent is 15 days late. |
| South Carolina | S.C. Code Ann. § 27-40-710 | 5 days | |
| South Dakota | S.D. Codified Laws Ann. § 21-16-1 | You can file for eviction after giving tenant 3 days' notice to move. | |
| Tennessee | Tenn. Code Ann. § 66-28-505 | 14 days to pay; tenant has an additional 16 days to vacate if he fails to pay. | |
| Texas | Tx. Prop. Code Ann § 24.005 | No statute: You can file for eviction after giving 3 days' notice to move (lease may specify a shorter time). | |
| Utah | Utah Code Ann. § 78-36-3 | 3 days | |
| Vermont | Vt. Stat. Ann. tit. 9, § 4467 | Tenant gets 14 days' notice, but the 14 days cannot begin until the 16th day of the rental period. | |
| Virginia | Va. Code Ann. §§ 55-225, §55-243 | 5 days. Tenant who pays rent, costs and reasonable attorney fees before the first court day can stay. | |
| Washington | Wash. Rev. Code § 59.12.030 | 3 days | |
| West Virginia | W. Va. Code § 55-3A-1 | You can file for eviction immediately. | |
| Wisconsin | Wis. Stat. Ann. § 704.17 | Month-to-month tenants: 5 days, but you may also use an Unconditional Quit notice. Tenants with a lease less than one year, and year-to-year tenants: 5 days (you may not use an Unconditional Quit notice). Tenants with a lease longer than one year: 30 days (you may not use an Unconditional Quit notice). | |
| Wyoming | | You can file for eviction when rent is 3 days or more late and you have given at least 3 days' notice. No option to pay required. | |

## State Laws on Termination for Violation of Lease

Many states give the tenant a specified amount of time to cease the lease or rental agreement violation or move before the landlord can file for eviction. In some states, if the tenant has not ceased or cured the violation at the end of that period, he gets additional time to move before the landlord files; in others, the tenant must move as soon as the cure period expires. And some states allow the landlord to terminate with an Unconditional Quit notice, without giving the tenant a chance to cure or cease the violation.

| State | Legal Authority | Time Tenant Has to Cure the Violation or Move Before Landlord Can File for Eviction |
|---|---|---|
| Alabama | | Landlord can terminate with an Unconditional Quit notice. |
| Alaska | Alaska Stat. §§ 09.45.090, 34.03.220 | 10 days, except for failing to pay utility bills, resulting in shut-off—then, 3 days to cure (additional 2 to vacate) |
| Arizona | Ariz. Rev. Stat. § 33-1368 | 5 days for violations materially affecting health and safety; 10 days for other violations of the lease terms |
| Arkansas | | Landlord can terminate with an Unconditional Quit notice. |
| California | Cal. Code of Civil Procedure § 1161 | 3 days |
| Colorado | Colo. Rev. Stat. § 13-40-104(1)(e) | 3 days |
| Connecticut | Conn. Gen. Stat. § 47a-15 | 15 days, but no right to cure for nonpayment of rent or serious nuisance. |
| Delaware | 25 Del. Code § 5513 | 7 days |
| District of Columbia | D.C. Code § 45-2551 | 30 days |
| Florida | Fla. Stat. §83.56 | 7 days |
| Georgia | | Landlord can terminate with an Unconditional Quit notice. |
| Hawaii | Hawaii Rev. Stat. §§ 521-69, 666-3 | 10 days, except 24 hours to cease a nuisance |
| Idaho | Idaho Code § 6-303 | 3 days |
| Illinois | | Landlord can terminate with an Unconditional Quit notice. |
| Indiana | | Landlord can terminate with an Unconditional Quit notice. |
| Iowa | Iowa Code § 562A.27 | 14 days to cure and an additional 16 to vacate |
| Kansas | Kan. Stat. Ann. § 58-2564 | 14 days to cure and an additional 16 to vacate |
| Kentucky | Ky. Rev. Stat. § 383.660 | 15 days |
| Louisiana | | Landlord can terminate with an Unconditional Quit notice. |
| Maine | | Landlord can terminate with an Unconditional Quit notice. |
| Maryland | Md. Real Property Code § 8-402.1 | 30 days |
| Massachusetts | | Landlord can terminate with an Unconditional Quit notice. |
| Michigan | Mich. Stat. Ann. § 27A.5714 | 7 days |
| Minnesota | | Landlord can terminate with an Unconditional Quit notice. |
| Mississippi | Miss. Code § 89-8-13 | 30 days |

## State Laws on Termination for Violation of Lease (continued)

| State | Legal Authority | Time Tenant Has to Cure the Violation or Move Before Landlord Can File for Eviction |
|-------|-----------------|-----------------------------------------------------------------------------------|
| Missouri | | Landlord can terminate with an Unconditional Quit notice. |
| Montana | Mont. Code Ann. § 70-24-422 | 14 days, except 3 days if unauthorized pet or person on premises |
| Nebraska | Neb. Rev. Stat. § 76-1431 | For all violations: 14 days to cure, 16 additional days to vacate |
| Nevada | Nev. Rev. Stat. Ann. § 40.2516 | For all violations: 3 days to cure, 2 additional days to vacate |
| New Hampshire | | Landlord can terminate with an Unconditional Quit notice. |
| New Jersey | Vijon v. Custodio, 598 A2.d. 251 (N.J. Supr. L. 1991) | No statute, but case law requires that the tenant be given an opportunity to cure the violation or condition up to the entry of judgment in favor of the landlord |
| New Mexico | N.M. Stat. Ann. § 47-8-33 | 7 days |
| New York | N.Y. Cons. Laws Real Prop. § 711(6) & §711(3) | 30 days (in cities with a population of 1 million or more) for twice removing the batteries from or disassembling a smoke or fire detector; and if specified in the lease, for failure to pay taxes or assessments |
| North Carolina | | Landlord can terminate with an Unconditional Quit notice. |
| North Dakota | | Landlord can terminate with an Unconditional Quit notice. |
| Ohio | Ohio Rev. Code Ann. § 5321.11 | 30 days; landlord can use Unconditional Quit notice for illegal activites |
| Oklahoma | Okla. Stat. tit. 41, § 132 | 10 days to cure, additional 5 days to vacate |
| Oregon | Ore. Rev. Stat. §§ 90.400, 90.405 | 14 days to cure, additional 16 days to vacate; for an illegal pet: 10 days to remove pet |
| Pennsylvania | | Landlord can terminate with an Unconditional Quit notice. |
| Rhode Island | R.I. Gen. Laws § 34-18-36 | 20 days |
| South Carolina | S.C. Code Ann. § 27-40-710 | 14 days |
| South Dakota | | Landlord can terminate with an Unconditional Quit notice. |
| Tennessee | Tenn. Code Ann. § 66-28-505 | 14 days to cure; tenant has an additional 16 to vacate |
| Texas | | Landlord can terminate with an Unconditional Quit notice. |
| Utah | Utah Code Ann. § 78-36-3 | 3 days |
| Vermont | | Landlord can terminate with an Unconditional Quit notice. |
| Virginia | Va. Code. Ann. § 55-248.31 | 21 days to cure, additional 9 to quit |
| Washington | Wash. Rev. Code Ann. § 59.12.030 | 10 days |
| West Virginia | W. Va. Code §55-3A-1 | Landlord can terminate with an Unconditional Quit notice. |
| Wisconsin | Wis. Stat. § 704.17(3) | If you have a lease of more than one year: 30 days. Otherwise landlord can terminate with an Unconditional Quit notice |
| Wyoming | | Landlord can terminate with an Unconditional Quit notice. |

# State Laws on Unconditional Quit Terminations

Every state allows landlords to terminate a tenancy for specified reasons, without giving a second chance. Some states allow landlords to deliver Unconditional Quit notices for late rent or any lease violation; others reserve this harsh measure only for repeated violations or serious misbehavior, such as illegal activity.

| State | Statute | Time To Move Out Before Landlord Can File For Eviction | When Unconditional Quit Notice Can Be Used |
|---|---|---|---|
| Alabama | Ala. Code § 35-9-6 | 10 days | Violation of any lease term |
| Alaska | Alaska Stat. §§ 34.03.220 (a)(1); 09.45.090)a)(2)(G), 34.03.220(e), 34.03.300(a) | 24 hours | Tenant or guest intentionally causing more than $400 of damage to landlord's property |
| | | 5 days | Illegal activity on the premises |
| | | 3 days | Failure to pay utility bills twice within six months |
| | | 10 days | Refusal to allow the landlord to enter |
| Arizona | Ariz. Rev. Stat. §§ 33-1368(A)(2), 33-1368, §33-1377 | 5 days | Material misrepresentation of criminal record or current criminal activity, or prior eviction record |
| | | Immediately | Discharging a weapon, prostitution, use or sale of illegal drugs, assaults or breach of the rental agreement that threaten harm to others |
| Arkansas | Ark. Stat. Ann. §§ 18-60-304, 18-16-107, 18-16-101 | 3 days | Nonpayment of rent |
| | | 10 days | Failure to vacate after giving notice (tenant is liable for twice the rent, and can be prosecuted for a misdemeanor) |
| California | Cal. Code of Civil Procedure § 1161 | 3 days | Assigning or subletting without permission, committing waste or a nuisance, illegal activity on the premises |
| Colorado | Colo. Rev. Stat. § 13-40-104(1)(e.5) | Immediately | Any repeated violation of a lease clause |
| Connecticut | Conn. Gen. Stat. §§ 47a-23, 47a-31, 47a-15 | 3 days | Nonpayment of rent, nuisance, violation of the rental agreement |
| | | Immediately | Conviction for prostitution or gambling |
| Delaware | 25 Del. Code §§ 5513(b) | 7 days | Material violation of lease rule other than nonpayment of rent or same violation repeated within 12 months |
| | | Immediately | Violation of law or breach of the rental agreement that causes or threatens to cause irreparable harm to the landlord's property or other tenants |
| District of Columbia | D.C. Code § 45-2551(c) | 30 days | Performing an illegal act within the rental unit |
| Florida | Fla. Stat. §83.56 | 7 days | Intentional destruction of your or other tenants' property or unreasonable disturbances |
| Georgia | Ga. Code Ann. §§4407-50 to 52 | Immediately | Nonpayment of rent twice within 12 months, committing waste, holding over |
| Hawaii | Hawaii Rev. Stat. §§ 521-70(c), 666-3 | Immediately | Using the dwelling for any purpose other than as a home |
| | | 5 days | Second failure to abate a nuisance within 24 hours of receiving notice |

## State Laws on Unconditional Quit Terminations (continued)

| State | Statute | Time to Move Out Before Landlord Can File for Eviction | When Unconditional Quit Notice Can Be Used |
|-------|---------|--------------------------------------------------------|--------------------------------------------|
| Idaho | Idaho Code § 6-303 | 3 days | Assigning or subletting without the consent of the landlord or causing serious damage to the property |
| Illinois | Ill. Rev. Stat. chap. 735 para. 5/9-210 | 10 days | Failure to abide by any term of the lease |
| | | 5 days | Unlawful use or sale of any controlled substance |
| Indiana | Ind. Code Ann. § 32-7-1-7 | Immediately | Nonpayment of rent, holdover tenants and (periodic tenants only) committing waste |
| Iowa | Iowa Code Ann. § 562A.27A | 3 days | Creating a clear and present danger to the health or safety of the landlord, tenants or neighbors within 1,000 feet of the property boundaries |
| Kansas | Kan. Stat. Ann. § 58-2564 | 30 days | Failure to correct a material violation of the lease within 14 days of being notified |
| Kentucky | Ky. Rev. Stat. § 383.660 | 14 days | Repeating the same material violation of the lease within 6 months of being given a first cure or quit notice |
| Louisiana | La. Civil Code Arts. 2712, 2729 | Immediately | Failure to pay rent or fulfill legal obligations |
| Maine | Me. Rev. Stat. Ann. tit. 14, § 6002 | 7 days | Violations of law, damage to the premises or maintaining a nuisance |
| Maryland | Md. Real Prop. Code Ann. § 8-401(e) | Immediately | Third court judgment within 12 months for nonpayment of rent |
| Massachusetts | Mass. Ann. Laws Ch. 186 § 11 | 14 days | Receiving a second notice to pay rent or quit within one year |
| Michigan | Mich. Stat. Ann. § 27A.5714 | 7 days | Willfully or negligently causing a serious and continuing health hazard or damage to the premises or possession of illegal drugs (but landlord must first file a police report) |
| Minnesota | Minn. Stat. § 566.03 | Immediately | Violation of a condition of the lease, nonpayment of rent |
| Mississippi | Miss. Code Ann. § 89-13-(3)(b) | 14 days | Repeating the same act—which a court has found constituted a lease violation—within 6 months |
| Missouri | Mo. Ann. Stat. § 441.020 | Immediately | Using the premises for gambling or prostitution |
| | Mo. Ann. Stat. §§ 441.030, 441.040 | 10 days | Assigning or subletting without consent, seriously damaging the premises or violating the lease |
| Montana | Mont. Code Ann. § 70-24-422 | 5 days | Repeating the same act—which constituted a lease violation and for which notice was given—within 6 months; or destroying or removing any part of the premises |
| Nebraska | Neb. Rev. Stat. § 76-1431(1) | 14 days | Repeating the same act—which constituted a lease violation and for which notice was given—within 6 months |
| Nevada | Nev. Rev. Stat. Ann. §§ 40.2514, 40.2516 | 3 days | Assigning or subletting in violation of the lease, substantial damage to the property, conducting an unlawful business, permitting or creating a nuisance or unlawful possession for sale, manufacture or distribution of illegal drugs |
| | | Immediately | Violation of a lease term where the consequences cannot be undone |

## State Laws on Unconditional Quit Terminations (continued)

| State | Statute | Time to Move Out Before Landlord Can File for Eviction | When Unconditional Quit Notice Can Be Used |
|-------|---------|---------------------------------------------------------|---------------------------------------------|
| New Hampshire | N.H. Rev. Stat. Ann. §§ 540:2, 540:3 | 7 days | Causing substantial damage to premises, behavior that adversely affects the health and safety of other tenants, third notice for nonpayment of rent within 12 months |
| | | 30 days | Failure to comply with a material term of lease |
| New Jersey | N.J .Stat. §§ 2A:18-53, 2A:18-61.2, 2A:18-53, 2A:18-61.2 | 3 days | Disorderly conduct; willful or grossly negligent destruction of landlord' s property; assaults upon or threats against the landlord; termination of tenant' s employment as a building manager, janitor or other employee of the landlord; conviction for use, possession or manufacture of an illegal drug either on the property or adjacent to it within the last two years *unless* the tenant has entered a rehabilitation program (includes harboring anyone so convicted) |
| | | 30 days | Habitual failure to pay rent; continued violations, despite repeated warnings, of the landlord' s reasonable rules and regulations |
| New Mexico | N.M. Stat. Ann §§ 47-8-33, 47-8-33(B) | 3 days | Substantial violation of the lease |
| | | 7 days | Repeated violation of a term of the rental agreement within 6 months |
| New York | N.Y. Cons. Laws Real Prop. §711 | Immediately | Using the premises for illegal purposes; being adjudicated a bankrupt by a court (questionable validity) |
| North Carolina | N.C. Gen. Stat. §42-26 | Immediately | Violation of a lease term that specifies that eviction will result from non-compliance. |
| | N.C. Gen. Stat. §42-59 to -76 | Immediately | Tenant or guest engaging in criminal activity on or near the property, failure of tenant to immediately notify landlord or law enforcement about the re-entry into the tenant' s dwelling of someone who has been previously banned from the property pursuant to this law (no criminal conviction or arrest necessary for banned trespasser) |
| North Dakota | N.D. Cent. Code §§ 33-06-01, 33-06-02 | 3 days | Violation of a material term of the lease, failure to pay rent or unreasonably disturbing other tenants |
| Ohio | Ohio Rev. Code Ann. §§ 1923.02 to 1923.04, 5321.17 | 3 days | Nonpayment of rent; violation of a written lease or rental agreement; when the landlord has "reasonable cause to believe" that the tenant has used, sold or manufactured an illegal drug on the premises (conviction or arrest not required) |
| Oklahoma | Okla. Stat. tit. 41, § 32 | Immediately | When the tenant has threatened or caused immediate and irremediable harm to the premises or any person and has not remedied the problem "as promptly as conditions require" upon being made aware of it |

## State Laws on Unconditional Quit Terminations (continued)

| State | Statute | Time to Move Out Before Landlord Can File for Eviction | When Unconditional Quit Notice Can Be Used |
|---|---|---|---|
| **Oregon** | Ore. Rev. Stat. §§ 900.400(3), 166.165, 90.405 | 24 hours | Tenant or his guest inflicting (or threatening to inflict) immediate, substantial personal injury to landlord, other tenants, neighbors or guests; intentionally causing substantial property damage; subletting without permission; committing any act "outrageous in the extreme," including prostitution or manufacture or sale of illegal drugs; intentionally or recklessly injuring someone (or placing that person in fear of imminent danger) because of the tenant's perception of that person's race, color, religion, national origin or sexual orientation |
| | | 10 days | Second failure to remove an illegal pet within 6 months |
| **Pennsylvania** | Pa. Stat. Ann. tit. 68, §§ 250.501, 250.505-A | 15 days (for lease 1 yr or less, but lease may specify a shorter time) | Violations of the terms of the lease |
| | | 30 days (for lease more than 1 yr, but lease may specify a shorter time) | Nonpayment of rent only |
| | | 10 days (any tenancy) | First conviction for illegal sale, manufacture or distribution of an illegal drug; or a repeated use of an illegal drug; or the seizure by law enforcement of an illegal drug within the leased premises |
| **Rhode Island** | R.I. Gen. Laws §§ 34-18-36, 11-34-18-36(3)(f), 34-18-36, 34-18-24 | 20 days | Committing an act which violates the lease or rental agreement or affects health or safety twice within 6 months (notice must have been given for the first violation) |
| | | Immediately | "Seasonal tenant" whose lease begins no earlier than May 1 and expires no later than October 15, with no right of extension or renewal, who has been charged with violating a local occupancy ordinance, making excessive noise or disturbing the peace; any tenant who uses the premises to use or sell illegal drugs or commits or attempts to commit any crime of violence on or in any public space adjacent to the premises |
| **South Carolina** | S.C. Code Ann. § 27-40-710 | Immediately | Repeated nonpayment of rent, allowing illegal activities on the property or failing to maintain dwelling as required by law. |
| **South Dakota** | S.D. Cod. Laws §§ 21-16-1, 21-16-12 | 3 days | Any lease violation, including nonpayment of rent and substantial damage to the property |

## State Laws on Unconditional Quit Terminations (continued)

| State | Statute | Time to Move Out Before Landlord Can File for Eviction | When Unconditional Quit Notice Can Be Used |
|-------|---------|------------------------|------------------------------------------|
| **Tennessee** | Tenn. Code Ann. § 66-28-505 | 14 days | Repeating an act which violates the lease or rental agreement or affects health or safety twice within 6 months (notice must have been given for the first violation) |
| **Texas** | Tex. Prop. Code § 24.005 | 3 days (lease may specify a shorter time) | Any violation of the lease, including nonpayment of rent |
| **Utah** | Utah Code Ann. § 78-36-3 | 3 days | Assigning or subletting without permission, carrying on an unlawful business on the premises or maintaining a nuisance |
| **Vermont** | Vt. Stat. Ann. tit. 9, §§ 4467(a), 4467(b) | 30 days | Third time tenant is late with the rent (and has received proper notice) within a 12-month period, any violation of the lease or landlord/tenant law |
| **Virginia** | Va. Stat. Ann. tit. 9, §§ 55-225, 55-243, 55-248.31, 55-248.31 | 5 days | Second time tenant is late with the rent (for which he received proper notice) within a 12-month period |
| | | 30 days | Material, unremediable breach of the lease or rental agreement or acts which materially and permanently affect others' health and safety |
| | | Immediately | A breach of the lease or rental agreement that is willful or a criminal act, is not remediable and is a threat to the health or safety of others |
| **Washington** | Wash. Rev. Code § 59.12.030 | 3 days | Serious damage, carrying on an unlawful business, maintaining a nuisance |
| **West Virginia** | W. Va. Code §55-3A-1 | Immediately | Nonpayment of rent, violation of lease clause, deliberate or negligent damage to the property |
| **Wisconsin** | Wis. Stat. Ann. §§ 704.17, 704.17(2), §704.17 | 14 days (month-to-month tenants) | Failure to pay rent, violation of the rental agreement or substantial damage to the property |
| | | 14 days (tenants with a lease of less than one year, or year-to-year tenants) | Failing to pay the rent on time twice within one year (must have received proper notice for the first violation) |
| | | 5 days (all tenants) | Causing a nuisance on the property (landlord must have written notice from a law enforcement agency regarding the nuisance) |
| **Wyoming** | Wyo. Stat. § 1-21-1002 | 3 days | Nonpayment of rent, hold-over tenants |

# Appendix **II**

# Tear-Out Forms

| Chapter | Form Name | File Name |
|---|---|---|
| 1 | Rental Application | RENTAPP |
| 1 | Consent to Background and Reference Check | CONCHECK |
| 1 | Tenant References | SCREEN |
| 1 | Receipt and Holding Deposit Agreement | RECEIPT |
| 2 | Month-to-Month Residential Rental Agreement | RENTALAG |
| 2 | Month-to-Month Residential Rental Agreement (Spanish Version) | |
| 2 | Fixed-Term Residential Lease | FIXLEASE |
| 2 | Fixed-Term Residential Lease (Spanish Version) | |
| 2 | Cosigner Agreement | COSIGNER |
| 3 | Agreement for Delayed or Partial Rent Payments | DELAY |
| 6 | Property Manager Agreement | MANAGER |
| 7 | Landlord-Tenant Checklist | CHKLIST |
| 7 | Move-In Letter | MOVEIN |
| 8 | Termination of Lease | TERMIN |
| 8 | Consent to Assignment of Lease | CONLEASE |
| 8 | Letter to Original Tenant and New Co-Tenant | TENLET |
| 9 | Resident's Maintenance/Repair Request | MAINREQ |
| 9 | Time Estimate for Repair | REPAIR |

# Rental Application

*Separate application required from each applicant age 18 or older.*

---

**THIS SECTION TO BE COMPLETED BY LANDLORD**

Address of Property to Be Rented: _____

_____

Rental Term: ☐ month-to-month  ☐ lease from _____ to _____

**Amounts Due Prior to Occupancy**

First month's rent ............................................................... $_____

Security deposit ................................................................. $_____

Credit check fee ................................................................ $_____

Other (specify): _____ $_____

TOTAL ...................................... $_____

---

## Applicant

Full Name—include all names you use(d): _____

Home Phone: (_____)                    Work Phone: (_____) _____

Social Security Number: _____    Driver's License Number/State: _____

Vehicle Make: _____    Model: _____    Color: _____    Year: _____

License Plate Number/State: _____

## Additional Occupants

List everyone, including children, who will live with you:

| Full Name | Relationship to Applicant |
|---|---|
|  |  |
|  |  |
|  |  |
|  |  |

## Rental History

Current Address: _____

Dates Lived at Address: _____    Reason for Leaving: _____

Landlord/Manager: _____    Landlord/Manager's Phone: (_____) _____

Previous Address: _____

Dates Lived at Address: _____    Reason for Leaving: _____

Landlord/Manager: _____    Landlord/Manager's Phone: (_____) _____

Previous Address: _____

Dates Lived at Address: _____ Reason for Leaving: _____

Landlord/Manager: _____ Landlord/Manager's Phone: ( )_____

## Employment History

Name and Address of Current Employer: _____

_____ Phone: ( )_____

Name of Supervisor: _____ Supervisor's Phone: ( )_____

Dates Employed at This Job: _____ Position or Title: _____

Name and Address of Previous Employer: _____

_____ Phone: ( )_____

Name of Supervisor: _____ Supervisor's Phone: ( )_____

Dates Employed at This Job: _____ Position or Title: _____

## Income

1. Your gross monthly employment income (before deductions): _____ $_____

2. Average monthly amounts of other income (specify sources): _____ $_____

_____

_____

TOTAL: _____ $_____

## Credit and Financial Information

| Bank/Financial Accounts | Account Number | Bank/Institution | Branch |
|---|---|---|---|
| Savings Account: | | | |
| Checking Account: | | | |
| Money Market or Similar Account: | | | |

| Credit Accounts & Loans | Type of Account (Auto loan, Visa, etc.) | Account Number | Name of Creditor | Amount Owed | Monthly Payment |
|---|---|---|---|---|---|
| Major Credit Card: | | | | | |
| Major Credit Card: | | | | | |
| Loan (mortgage, car, student loan, etc.): | | | | | |
| Other Major Obligation: | | | | | |

## Miscellaneous

Describe the number and type of pets you want to have in the rental property: _____

_____

Describe water-filled furniture you want to have in the rental property: _____

_____

Do you smoke?   ☐ yes  ☐ no

Have you ever:   Filed for bankruptcy? ☐ yes  ☐ no      Been sued? ☐ yes  ☐ no

Been evicted? ☐ yes  ☐ no      Been convicted of a crime? ☐ yes  ☐ no

Explain any "yes" listed above: _____

_____

## References and Emergency Contact

Personal Reference: _____      Relationship: _____

Address: _____

_____      Phone: (        )_____

Personal Reference: _____      Relationship: _____

Address: _____

_____      Phone: (        )_____

Contact in Emergency: _____      Relationship: _____

Address: _____

_____      Phone: (        )_____

I certify that all the information given above is true and correct and understand that my lease or rental agreement may be terminated if I have made any false or incomplete statement in this application. I authorize verification of the information provided in this application from my credit sources, credit bureaus, current and previous landlords and employers, and personal references.

_____

Date                     Applicant

Notes (Landlord/Manager): _____

_____

_____

_____

_____

# Consent to Background and Reference Check

I authorize _____

to obtain information about me from my credit sources, current and previous landlords and employers

and personal references. I authorize my credit sources, credit bureaus, current and previous landlords

and employers, and personal references to disclose to _____

_____ such information about me as

_____ may request.

_____

Name

_____

Address

_____

Phone Number

_____          _____

Date                                      Applicant

# Tenant References

Name of Applicant:_____

Address of Rental Unit:_____

## Previous Landlord or Manager

Contact (name, property owner or manager, address of rental unit): _____

_____

Date: _____

## Questions

When did tenant rent from you (move-in and move-out dates)? _____

What was the monthly rent? _____

Did tenant pay rent on time? _____

Was tenant considerate of neighbors—that is, no loud parties and fair, careful use of common areas? _____

_____

Did tenant have any pets? If so, were there any problems? _____

_____

Did tenant make any unreasonable demands or complaints? _____

_____

Why did tenant leave? _____

_____

Did tenant give the proper amount of notice before leaving? _____

Did tenant leave the place in good condition? Did you need to use the security deposit to cover damage?

_____

Any particular problems you'd like to mention? _____

_____

_____

Would you rent to this person again? _____

_____

Other Comments: _____

_____

_____

_____

_____

_____

**Employment Verification**

Contact (name, company, position): _____

Date: _____

Salary: _____ Dates of Employment: _____

Comments: _____

_____

_____

_____

_____

_____

_____

_____


**Personal Reference**

Contact (name and relationship to applicant): _____

Date: _____ How long have you known the applicant? _____

Would you recommend this person as a prospective tenant? _____

Comments: _____

_____

_____

_____

_____

_____

_____

_____


**Credit and Financial Information**

_____

_____

_____

_____

_____


**Notes, Including Reason for Rejecting Applicant**

_____

_____

_____

_____

# Receipt and Holding Deposit Agreement

This will acknowledge receipt of the sum of $_____ by _____

_____ ("Landlord") from _____

_____ ("Applicant") as a holding deposit to

hold vacant the rental property at _____

_____,

until _____ at _____. The property will be rented to Applicant

on a _____ basis at a rent of $_____ per month, if Applicant

signs Landlord's written _____ and pays Landlord the

first month's rent and a $_____ security deposit on or before that date, in which

event the holding deposit will be applied to the first month's rent.

This Agreement depends upon Landlord receiving a satisfactory report of Applicant's

references and credit history. Landlord and Applicant agree that if Applicant fails to sign

the Agreement and pay the remaining rent and security deposit, Landlord may retain of

this holding deposit a sum equal to the prorated daily rent of $_____ per day

plus a $_____ charge to compensate Landlord for the inconvenience.


_____     _____

Date                        Applicant


_____     _____

Date                        Landlord

# Month-to-Month Residential Rental Agreement

### Clause 1. Identification of Landlord and Tenant

This Agreement is entered into between _____

_____ ("Tenant") and

_____ ("Landlord"). Each

Tenant is jointly and severally liable for the payment of rent and performance of all other terms of

this Agreement.

### Clause 2. Identification of Premises

Subject to the terms and conditions in this Agreement, Landlord rents to Tenant, and Tenant rents

from Landlord, for residential purposes only, the premises located at _____

_____ ("the premises"),

together with the following furnishings and appliances: _____

_____.

Rental of the premises also includes _____

_____.

### Clause 3. Limits on Use and Occupancy

The premises are to be used only as a private residence for Tenant(s) listed in Clause 1 of this

Agreement, and their minor children. Occupancy by guests for more than _____

is prohibited without Landlord's written consent and will be considered a breach of this Agreement.

### Clause 4. Term of the Tenancy

The rental will begin on _____, 199____, and continue on a month-to-month

basis. Landlord may terminate the tenancy or modify the terms of this Agreement by giving the

Tenant _____ days written notice. Tenant may terminate the tenancy by giving the

Landlord _____ days written notice.

### Clause 5. Payment of Rent

*Regular monthly rent.*

Tenant will pay to Landlord a monthly rent of $_____ , payable in advance on the first

day of each month, except when that day falls on a weekend or legal holiday, in which case rent is

due on the next business day. Rent will be paid in the following manner unless Landlord designates

otherwise:

*Delivery of payment.*

Rent will be paid:

☐ by mail, to _____

☐ in person, at _____

*Form of payment.*

Landlord will accept payment in these forms:

☐ personal check made payable to _____

☐ cashier's check made payable to _____

☐ credit card

☐ money order

☐ cash

*Prorated first month's rent.*

For the period from Tenant's move-in date, _____, 199_____, through the end of the month, Tenant will pay to Landlord the prorated monthly rent of $_____.

This amount will be paid on or before the date the Tenant moves in.

## Clause 6. Late Charges

If Tenant fails to pay the rent in full before the end of the _____ day after it's due, Tenant will pay Landlord a late charge as follows: _____

_____ .

Landlord does not waive the right to insist on payment of the rent in full on the date it is due.

## Clause 7. Returned Check and Other Bank Charges

If any check offered by Tenant to Landlord in payment of rent or any other amount due under this Agreement is returned for lack of sufficient funds, a "stop payment" or any other reason, Tenant will pay Landlord a returned check charge of $_____.

## Clause 8. Security Deposit

On signing this Agreement, Tenant will pay to Landlord the sum of $_____ as a security deposit. Tenant may not, without Landlord's prior written consent, apply this security deposit to the last month's rent or to any other sum due under this Agreement. Within _____ after Tenant has vacated the premises, returned keys and provided Landlord with a forwarding address, Landlord will return the deposit in full or give Tenant an itemized written statement of the reasons for, and the dollar amount of, any of the security deposit retained by Landlord, along with a check for any deposit balance.

### Clause 9. Utilities

Tenant will pay all utility charges, except for the following, which will be paid by Landlord:

_____

_____ .

### Clause 10. Assignment and Subletting

Tenant will not sublet any part of the premises or assign this Agreement without the prior written consent of Landlord.

### Clause 11. Tenant's Maintenance Responsibilities

Tenant will: (1) keep the premises clean, sanitary and in good condition and, upon termination of the tenancy, return the premises to Landlord in a condition identical to that which existed when Tenant took occupancy, except for ordinary wear and tear; (2) immediately notify Landlord of any defects or dangerous conditions in and about the premises of which Tenant becomes aware; and (3) reimburse Landlord, on demand by Landlord, for the cost of any repairs to the premises damaged by Tenant or Tenant's guests or business invitees through misuse or neglect.

Tenant has examined the premises, including appliances, fixtures, carpets, drapes and paint, and has found them to be in good, safe and clean condition and repair, except as noted in the Landlord-Tenant Checklist.

## Clause 12. Repairs and Alterations by Tenant

a. Except as provided by law, or as authorized by the prior written consent of Landlord, Tenant will not make any repairs or alterations to the premises, including nailing holes in the walls or painting the rental unit.

b. Tenant will not, without Landlord's prior written consent, alter, re-key or install any locks to the premises or install or alter any burglar alarm system. Tenant will provide Landlord with a key or keys capable of unlocking all such re-keyed or new locks as well as instructions on how to disarm any altered or new burglar alarm system.

## Clause 13. Violating Laws and Causing Disturbances

Tenant is entitled to quiet enjoyment of the premises. Tenant and guests or invitees will not use the premises or adjacent areas in such a way as to: (1) violate any law or ordinance, including laws prohibiting the use, possession or sale of illegal drugs; (2) commit waste (severe property damage); or (3) create a nuisance by annoying, disturbing, inconveniencing or interfering with the quiet enjoyment and peace and quiet of any other tenant or nearby resident.

## Clause 14. Pets

No animal, bird or other pet will be kept on the premises, even temporarily, except properly trained dogs needed by blind, deaf or disabled persons and _____ under the following conditions: _____

_____ .

## Clause 15. Landlord's Right to Access

Landlord or Landlord's agents may enter the premises in the event of an emergency, to make repairs or improvements or to show the premises to prospective buyers or tenants. Landlord may also enter the premises to conduct an annual inspection to check for safety or maintenance problems. Except in cases of emergency, Tenant's abandonment of the premises, court order, or where it is impractical to do so, Landlord shall give Tenant _____ notice before entering.

## Clause 16. Extended Absences by Tenant

Tenant will notify Landlord in advance if Tenant will be away from the premises for _____ or more consecutive days. During such absence, Landlord may enter the premises at times reasonably necessary to maintain the property and inspect for needed repairs.

### Clause 17. Possession of the Premises

*a. Tenant's failure to take possession.*

If, after signing this Agreement, Tenant fails to take possession of the premises, Tenant will still be responsible for paying rent and complying with all other terms of this Agreement.

*b. Landlord's failure to deliver possession.*

If Landlord is unable to deliver possession of the premises to Tenant for any reason not within Landlord's control, including, but not limited to, partial or complete destruction of the premises, Tenant will have the right to terminate this Agreement upon proper notice as required by law. In such event, Landlord's liability to Tenant will be limited to the return of all sums previously paid by Tenant to Landlord.

### Clause 18. Tenant Rules and Regulations

☐ Tenant acknowledges receipt of, and has read a copy of, tenant rules and regulations, which are attached to and incorporated into this Agreement by this reference.

### Clause 19. Payment of Court Costs and Attorney Fees in a Lawsuit

In any action or legal proceeding to enforce any part of this Agreement, the prevailing party

☐ shall not / ☐ shall recover reasonable attorney fees and court costs.

### Clause 20. Disclosures

Tenant acknowledges that Landlord has made the following disclosures regarding the premises:

☐ Disclosure of Information on Lead-Based Paint and/or Lead-Based Paint Hazards

☐ Other disclosures:

_____

_____

_____

### Clause 21. Authority to Receive Legal Papers

The Landlord, any person managing the premises and anyone designated by the Landlord are authorized to accept service of process and receive other notices and demands, which may be delivered to:

☐ The Landlord, at the following address: _____

_____

☐ The manager, at the following address: _____

_____

☐ The following person, at the following address: _____

_____

## Clause 22. Additional Provisions

Additional provisions are as follows: _____

_____

_____

_____

_____

_____

_____

_____

## Clause 23. Validity of Each Part

If any portion of this Agreement is held to be invalid, its invalidity will not affect the validity or enforceability of any other provision of this Agreement.

## Clause 24. Grounds for Termination of Tenancy

The failure of Tenant or Tenant's guests or invitees to comply with any term of this Agreement, or the misrepresentation of any material fact on Tenant's Rental Application, is grounds for termination of the tenancy, with appropriate notice to Tenant and procedures as required by law.

## Clause 25. Entire Agreement

This document constitutes the entire Agreement between the parties, and no promises or representations, other than those contained here and those implied by law, have been made by Landlord or Tenant. Any modifications to this Agreement must be in writing signed by Landlord and Tenant.

_____  _____  _____
Date                       Landlord or Landlord's Agent     Title

_____
Street Address

_____  _____
City, State & Zip                                     Phone

_____  _____  _____
Date                       Tenant                           Phone

_____  _____  _____
Date                       Tenant                           Phone

_____  _____  _____
Date                       Tenant                           Phone

# Contrato Mensual de Arrendamiento

## Cláusula 1. Identificación del Arrendador y de los Inquilinos.

Este Contrato es preparado y efectivo a partir de _____, entre

_____ ("Inquilinos")

y _____ ("Arrendador").

Cada Inquilino es conjunta y seriamente responsable del pago de renta y del cumplimiento de todos los demás términos de este Contrato.

## Cláusula 2. Identificación de la Propiedad.

De acuerdo con los términos y condiciones referidas en este Contrato, el Arrendador renta al Inquilino, y éste renta del Arrendador, sólamente para residir, la propiedad ubicada en _____

_____ , ("la propiedad"),

junto con el mobiliario y los aparatos electrodomésticos siguientes: _____

_____

La renta de la propiedad también incluye _____

_____ .

## Cláusula 3. Límitaciones en el Uso y Ocupación.

La propiedad se utilizará sólo como residencia privada por el Inquilino designado en la Cláusula 1 de este Contrato y sus hijos menores. Está prohibido que invitados habiten la propiedad por más de _____, excepto con previo consentimiento por escrito del Arrendador. De lo contrario, será considerado como una violación a este Contrato.

## Cláusula 4. Período de Arrendamiento.

La renta comenzará el día _____ de _____ de _____, y podrá continuarse el arrendamiento, mediante la renovación por cada mes. El Arrendador puede dar por terminado este Contrato o modificar sus términos, siempre que notifique por escrito, al Inquilino, con _____ días de anticipación. El Inquilino puede terminar este Contrato, notificándoselo al Arrendador por escrito y con _____ días de anticipación.

## Cláusula 5. Renta y Fechas de Pago.

*Renta Regular Mensual.*

El Inquilino pagará por adelantado, una renta mensual de $ _____ , el primer día del mes; excepto cuando éste sea en un fin de semana o en un día feriado oficial, en cuyo caso deberá ser pagada el próximo día laboral. Si no existe otra decisión por parte del Arrendador, la renta deberá ser pagada de la manera siguiente:

*Entrega de pago.*

El arriendo será pagado:

☐ Por correo, dirigido a _____

☐ Personalmente, en _____

*Forma de Pago.*

El Arrendador recibirá los pagos en:

☐ Cheque Personal escrito en favor de _____

☐ Cheque de Caja escrito en favor de _____

☐ Tarjeta de Crédito

☐ Giro Postal

☐ Efectivo

*Prorrateo del Primer mes de renta.*

Para el período comenzando con la fecha en que se mudará el Inquilino, el día _____

de _____ de _____ , hasta el fin del mes en curso, el Inquilino pagará

al arrendador la renta mensual prorratada de $ _____. Esta suma se pagará antes o en la

fecha en que se mude el Inquilino a la propiedad.

## Cláusula 6. Cobros por Mora.

Si el Inquilino falla en el pago total de la renta, antes del final del día siguiente a la fecha de pago,

tendrá que pagar costos por atrasos como se explica a continuación: _____

_____ .

El Arrendador no descartará el derecho de insistir en el pago total de la renta en la fecha debida.

## Cláusula 7. Pagos por Cheques Sin Fondo y Recargos Bancarios.

En el caso de cualquier cheque, ofrecido por el Inquilino al Arrendador como pago de renta o

cualquier otra suma debida bajo este Contrato, sea regresado por insuficiencia de fondos, un "paro

de pago" o cualquier otra razón, el Inquilino deberá pagar un recargo por la cantidad de

$_____.

## Cláusula 8. Depósito de Garantía.

Al firmar el presente Contrato, el Inquilino pagará al Arrendador, la cantidad de $_____

como depósito de seguridad. Este depósito no puede aplicarse al último mes de renta o a cualquier

cantidad debida bajo este Contrato; excepto con previo consentimiento por escrito del Arrendador.

Dentro de _____ , después de que el Inquilino haya desocupado la

propiedad, haya entregado las llaves y proporcionado la dirección donde contactarse, el Arrendador

le entregará el depósito en su totalidad o le detallará de manera escrita, las razones y la cantidad

que es retenida por él, junto con un cheque por la cantidad de su diferencia.

**Cláusula 9. Servicios Publicos.**

El Inquilino pagará todos los servicios publicos, exceptuando los siguientes, los cuales serán pagados por el Arrendador: _____

_____

**Cláusula 10. Prohibición de Traspaso o Sub-arrendamiento.**

El Inquilino no puede sub-arrendar cualquier parte de la propiedad o traspasar este Contrato, sin previo consentimiento por escrito del Arrendador.

**Cláusula 11. Responsabilidad del Inquilino de Mantenimiento de la propiedad.**

El Inquilino acepta: (1) mantener la propiedad limpia e higiénica, en buena condición, y cuando el arrendamiento termine, regresar la propiedad al Arrendador en idéntica condición a la que existía cuando la habitaron, exceptuando el deterioro causado por el uso; (2) Notificar de inmediato al Arrendador, sobre cualquier defecto o condición peligrosa que note en o alrededor de la propiedad; y (3) reembolsar al Arrendador, bajo demanda de éste, los costos de cualquier reparación de daños a la propiedad, ocasionados por uso indebido o negligencia del Inquilino o sus invitados.

El Inquilino ha revisado la propiedad, incluyendo los aparatos electro-domésticos, accesorios, alfombras, cortinas y pintura, y los ha encontrado en buenas condiciones, seguras, y limpias, exceptuando las que están en la Lista Arrendador-Inquilino.

## Cláusula 12. Reparaciones y Modificaciones hechas por el Inquilino.

a. Exceptuando lo provisto por la ley o con la autorización previa y por escrito del Arrendador, el Inquilino no debe hacer modificaciones o reparaciones en la propiedad, incluído el hacer hoyos en las paredes o pintar el lugar.

b. El Inquilino no debe alterar las cerraduras, ni cambiarlas, ni instalar o modificar el sistema de alarma; excepto que haya recibido del Arrendador, una autorización previa y por escrito. El Inquilino deberá proveer al Arrendador una copia de llave o llaves para abrir cada cerradura modificada o nueva, así como instrucciones de cómo desarmar un sistema de alarma modificado o nuevo.

## Cláusula 13. Causar Disturbios y Violaciones a la Ley.

El Inquilino tiene derecho al goce pacífico de la propiedad. Este y sus invitados no deben usar la propiedad o áreas aledañas, de manera que: (1) Viole cualquier ley o reglamento, incluyendo leyes que prohiben el uso, posesión o venta ilegal de drogas; (2) Permite el uso abusivo de la propiedad (daño serio a la propiedad); o (3) Cree un estorbo al molestar, provocar disturbios, provocar inconvenientes o interferir en el disfrute de paz y tranquilidad de otros inquilinos o vecinos.

## Cláusula 14. Mascotas.

No se permite, ni siquiera temporalmente, tener ningún animal, pájaro u otros animales en la propiedad, excepto perros entrenados para auxiliar a ciegos, sordos o personas con incapacidades físicas, y _____

bajo las condiciones siguientes: _____

_____

_____.

## Cláusula 15. Derecho del Arrendador al Acceso a la Propiedad.

El Arrendador o agentes de éste pueden entrar a la propiedad, en caso de emergencia, para hacer reparaciones o mejoras, o para mostrar la propiedad a potenciales nuevos inquilinos o compradores en perspectiva. También podrá entrar para la inspección anual para revisar la seguridad o chequear problemas de mantenimiento. Excepto en caso de emergencia, por el abandono de la propiedad por parte del Inquilino, orden de la corte, o cuando no sea práctico, el Arrendador deberá notificarle al Inqui ino de su intención de entrar a la propiedad con _____ de anticipación.

## Cláusula 16. Ausencias Prolongadas del Inquilino.

El Inquilino deberá previamente notificar al Arrendador, si estará ausente de la propiedad por _____ días consecutivos o más. Durante este tiempo, el Arrendador podrá entrar, cuando sea necesario, a la propiedad para inspeccionarla, para mantenimiento o para reparaciones necesarias.

### Cláusula 17. Tomar Posesión de la propiedad.

*a. Falla del Inquilino en tomar posesión de la propiedad.*

Si después de haber firmado este Contrato, el Inquilino no toma posesión de la propiedad, aún será responsable por pago de la renta y cumplimiento de todos los demás términos de este Contrato.

*b. Falla del Arrendador en entregar la propiedad.*

Si el Arrendador no puede entregar la posesión de la propiedad al Inquilino, por cualquier razón fuera de su control, incluyendo, pero no limitado a, destrucción parcial o completa de la propiedad, el Inquilino tendrá el derecho de terminar este Contrato, mediante aviso previo y apropiado como lo señala la ley. En tal situación, la responsabilidad del Arrendador hacia el Inquilino, estará limitada a la devolución de todas las cantidades previamente pagadas por el Inquilino al Arrendador.

### Cláusula 18. Normas y Regulaciones del Inquilino.

☐ El Inquilino reconoce lo recibido y que ha leído una copia de las Normas y Regulaciones del Inquilino; las cuales como referencia, están adjuntas e incorporadas al presente Contrato.

### Cláusula 19. Pago del Abogado y Costos de la Corte en Caso de un Juicio.

En cualquier acción jurídico-legal para hacer cumplir total o parcialmente este Contrato, la parte prevaleciente ☐ No deberá / ☐ Deberá recuperar honorarios justos del abogado y costos de la corte.

### Cláusula 20. Divulgaciones.

El Inquilino reconoce que el Arrendador le ha hecho las siguientes divulgaciones con respecto a la propiedad:

☐ Distribución de información sobre pintura a base de plomo y/o los peligros de este tipo de pintura.

☐ Otras divulgaciones:

_____

_____

_____.

### Cláusula 21. Personal Autorizado para Recibir Documentos Legales.

El Arrendador, la persona que administre la propiedad, o a quien haya designado el Arrendador, están autorizados para aceptar servicio de proceso, y recibir otras noticias y demandas, las cuales pueden ser entregadas a:

☐ El Arrendador, a la siguiente dirección: _____

_____

☐ El Administrador, a la siguiente dirección:_____

_____.

☐ A la persona designada, a la siguiente dirección:_____

_____.

### Cláusula 22. Disposiciones Adicionales.

Disposiciones adicionales son las siguientes: _____

_____

_____

_____

_____

_____

_____

_____ .

### Cláusula 23. Validez de las Cláusulas de este Contrato.

Si cualquier clausula de este Contrato es invalidado, ésto no afectará la validez o cumplimiento de las partes restantes de este Contrato.

### Cláusula 24. Razones para Cancelar el Contrato de Arrendamiento.

El incumplimiento de cualesquiera de los términos de este Contrato, por parte del Inquilino o sus invitados o la relación Falsa de un hecho esencial en la solicitud del Inquilino, será razón para dar por cancelado el Contrato de arrendamiento, seguido con la debida notificación al Inquilino, de acuerdo con lo requerido por la ley.

### Cláusula 25. Contrato Completo.

Este documento constituye el Contrato completo entre las partes, y el Arrendador y el Inquilino no han hecho otro compromiso, a no ser los contenidos en este Contrato o los señalados por la ley. Cualquier modificación al presente documento, debe ser por escrito y firmado por ambas partes.

_____    _____    _____
Fecha                      Arrendador o su representant        Título

_____
Número y Nombre de la Calle

_____    _____    _____    _____
Ciudad                     Estado             Código Postal      Teléfono

_____    _____    _____
Fecha                      Nombre del Inquilino                Teléfono

_____    _____    _____
Fecha                      Nombre del Inquilino                Teléfono

_____    _____    _____
Fecha                      Nombre del Inquilino                Teléfono

# Fixed-Term Residential Lease

## Clause 1. Identification of Landlord and Tenant

This Agreement is entered into between _____

_____ ("Tenant") and

_____ ("Landlord"). Each

Tenant is jointly and severally liable for the payment of rent and performance of all other terms of

this Agreement.

## Clause 2. Identification of Premises

Subject to the terms and conditions in this Agreement, Landlord rents to Tenant, and Tenant rents

from Landlord, for residential purposes only, the premises located at _____

_____ ("the premises"),

together with the following furnishings and appliances: _____

_____ .

Rental of the premises also includes _____

_____ .

## Clause 3. Limits on Use and Occupancy

The premises are to be used only as a private residence for Tenant(s) listed in Clause 1 of this

Agreement, and their minor children. Occupancy by guests for more than _____

is prohibited without Landlord's written consent and will be considered a breach of this Agreement.

## Clause 4. Term of the Tenancy

The term of the rental will begin on _____, 199____, and end on

_____, 199____. If Tenant vacates before the term ends, Tenant will be

liable for the balance of the rent for the remainder of the term.

## Clause 5. Payment of Rent

*Regular monthly rent.*

Tenant will pay to Landlord a monthly rent of $_____ , payable in advance on the first

day of each month, except when that day falls on a weekend or legal holiday, in which case rent is

due on the next business day. Rent will be paid in the following manner unless Landlord designates

otherwise:

*Delivery of payment.*

Rent will be paid:

☐ by mail, to _____

☐ in person, at _____

*Form of payment.*

Landlord will accept payment in these forms:

☐ personal check made payable to _____

☐ cashier's check made payable to _____

☐ credit card

☐ money order

☐ cash

*Prorated first month's rent.*

For the period from Tenant's move-in date, _____, 199____, through the end of the month, Tenant will pay to Landlord the prorated monthly rent of $_____. This amount will be paid on or before the date the Tenant moves in.

## Clause 6. Late Charges

If Tenant fails to pay the rent in full before the end of the _____ day after it's due, Tenant will pay Landlord a late charge as follows: _____

_____ .

Landlord does not waive the right to insist on payment of the rent in full on the date it is due.

## Clause 7. Returned Check and Other Bank Charges

If any check offered by Tenant to Landlord in payment of rent or any other amount due under this Agreement is returned for lack of sufficient funds, a "stop payment" or any other reason, Tenant will pay Landlord a returned check charge of $_____.

## Clause 8. Security Deposit

On signing this Agreement, Tenant will pay to Landlord the sum of $_____ as a security deposit. Tenant may not, without Landlord's prior written consent, apply this security deposit to the last month's rent or to any other sum due under this Agreement. Within _____ after Tenant has vacated the premises, returned keys and provided Landlord with a forwarding address, Landlord will return the deposit in full or give Tenant an itemized written statement of the reasons for, and the dollar amount of, any of the security deposit retained by Landlord, along with a check for any deposit balance.

**Clause 9. Utilities**

Tenant will pay all utility charges, except for the following, which will be paid by Landlord:

_____

_____ .

**Clause 10. Assignment and Subletting**

Tenant will not sublet any part of the premises or assign this Agreement without the prior written consent of Landlord.

**Clause 11. Tenant's Maintenance Responsibilities**

Tenant will: (1) keep the premises clean, sanitary and in good condition and, upon termination of the tenancy, return the premises to Landlord in a condition identical to that which existed when Tenant took occupancy, except for ordinary wear and tear; (2) immediately notify Landlord of any defects or dangerous conditions in and about the premises of which Tenant becomes aware; and (3) reimburse Landlord, on demand by Landlord, for the cost of any repairs to the premises damaged by Tenant or Tenant's guests or business invitees through misuse or neglect.

Tenant has examined the premises, including appliances, fixtures, carpets, drapes and paint, and has found them to be in good, safe and clean condition and repair, except as noted in the Landlord-Tenant Checklist.

## Clause 12. Repairs and Alterations by Tenant

a. Except as provided by law, or as authorized by the prior written consent of Landlord, Tenant will not make any repairs or alterations to the premises, including nailing holes in the walls or painting the rental unit.

b. Tenant will not, without Landlord's prior written consent, alter, re-key or install any locks to the premises or install or alter any burglar alarm system. Tenant will provide Landlord with a key or keys capable of unlocking all such re-keyed or new locks as well as instructions on how to disarm any altered or new burglar alarm system.

## Clause 13. Violating Laws and Causing Disturbances

Tenant is entitled to quiet enjoyment of the premises. Tenant and guests or invitees will not use the premises or adjacent areas in such a way as to: (1) violate any law or ordinance, including laws prohibiting the use, possession or sale of illegal drugs; (2) commit waste (severe property damage); or (3) create a nuisance by annoying, disturbing, inconveniencing or interfering with the quiet enjoyment and peace and quiet of any other tenant or nearby resident.

## Clause 14. Pets

No animal, bird or other pet will be kept on the premises, even temporarily, except properly trained dogs needed by blind, deaf or disabled persons and _____ under the following conditions: _____

_____ .

## Clause 15. Landlord's Right to Access

Landlord or Landlord's agents may enter the premises in the event of an emergency, to make repairs or improvements or to show the premises to prospective buyers or tenants. Landlord may also enter the premises to conduct an annual inspection to check for safety or maintenance problems. Except in cases of emergency, Tenant's abandonment of the premises, court order, or where it is impractical to do so, Landlord shall give Tenant _____ notice before entering.

## Clause 16. Extended Absences by Tenant

Tenant will notify Landlord in advance if Tenant will be away from the premises for _____ or more consecutive days. During such absence, Landlord may enter the premises at times reasonably necessary to maintain the property and inspect for needed repairs.

## Clause 17. Possession of the Premises

*a. Tenant's failure to take possession.*

If, after signing this Agreement, Tenant fails to take possession of the premises, Tenant will still be responsible for paying rent and complying with all other terms of this Agreement.

*b. Landlord's failure to deliver possession.*

If Landlord is unable to deliver possession of the premises to Tenant for any reason not within Landlord's control, including, but not limited to, partial or complete destruction of the premises, Tenant will have the right to terminate this Agreement upon proper notice as required by law. In such event, Landlord's liability to Tenant will be limited to the return of all sums previously paid by Tenant to Landlord.

## Clause 18. Tenant Rules and Regulations

☐ Tenant acknowledges receipt of, and has read a copy of, tenant rules and regulations, which are attached to and incorporated into this Agreement by this reference.

## Clause 19. Payment of Court Costs and Attorney Fees in a Lawsuit

In any action or legal proceeding to enforce any part of this Agreement, the prevailing party

☐ shall not / ☐ shall recover reasonable attorney fees and court costs.

## Clause 20. Disclosures

Tenant acknowledges that Landlord has made the following disclosures regarding the premises:

☐ Disclosure of Information on Lead-Based Paint and/or Lead-Based Paint Hazards

☐ Other disclosures:

_____

_____

_____

## Clause 21. Authority to Receive Legal Papers

The Landlord, any person managing the premises and anyone designated by the Landlord are authorized to accept service of process and receive other notices and demands, which may be delivered to:

☐ The Landlord, at the following address: _____

_____

☐ The manager, at the following address: _____

_____

☐ The following person, at the following address: _____

_____

## Clause 22. Additional Provisions

Additional provisions are as follows: _____

_____

_____

_____

_____

_____

_____

_____

## Clause 23. Validity of Each Part

If any portion of this Agreement is held to be invalid, its invalidity will not affect the validity or enforceability of any other provision of this Agreement.

## Clause 24. Grounds for Termination of Tenancy

The failure of Tenant or Tenant's guests or invitees to comply with any term of this Agreement, or the misrepresentation of any material fact on Tenant's Rental Application, is grounds for termination of the tenancy, with appropriate notice to Tenant and procedures as required by law.

## Clause 25. Entire Agreement

This document constitutes the entire Agreement between the parties, and no promises or representations, other than those contained here and those implied by law, have been made by Landlord or Tenant. Any modifications to this Agreement must be in writing signed by Landlord and Tenant.

_____    _____    _____
Date               Landlord or Landlord's Agent         Title

_____
Street Address

_____    _____
City, State & Zip                                     Phone

_____    _____    _____
Date               Tenant                               Phone

_____    _____    _____
Date               Tenant                               Phone

_____    _____    _____
Date               Tenant                               Phone

# Contrato de Arrendamiento Residencial a Plazo Fijo

**Cláusula 1. Identificación del Arrendador y de los Inquilinos.**

Este Contrato es preparado y efectivo a partir de _____, entre

_____ ("Inquilinos")

y _____ ("Arrendador").

Cada Inquilino es conjunta y seriamente responsable del pago de renta y del cumplimiento de todos

los demás términos de este Contrato.

**Cláusula 2. Identificación de la Propiedad.**

De acuerdo con los términos y condiciones referidas en este Contrato, el Arrendador renta al

Inquilino, y éste renta del Arrendador, sólamente para residir, la propiedad ubicada en _____

_____ , ("la propiedad"),

junto con el mobiliario y los aparatos electrodomésticos siguientes: _____

_____

La renta de la propiedad también incluye _____

_____.

**Cláusula 3. Límitaciones en el Uso y Ocupación.**

La propiedad se utilizará sólo como residencia privada por el Inquilino designado en la Cláusula 1

de este Contrato y sus hijos menores. Está prohibido que invitados habiten la propiedad por más de

_____, excepto con previo consentimiento por escrito del Arrendador. De lo

contrario, será considerado como una violación a este Contrato.

**Cláusula 4. Período de Arrendamiento.**

La renta comenzará el día _____ de _____ de _____, y podrá continuarse el

arrendamiento, mediante la renovación por cada mes. El Arrendador puede dar por terminado este

Contrato o modificar sus términos, siempre que notifique por escrito, al Inquilino, con _____

días de anticipación. El Inquilino puede terminar este Contrato, notificándoselo al Arrendador por

escrito y con _____ días de anticipación.

**Cláusula 5. Renta y Fechas de Pago.**

*Renta Regular Mensual.*

El Inquilino pagará por adelantado, una renta mensual de $ _____ , el primer día del mes;

excepto cuando éste sea en un fin de semana o en un día feriado oficial, en cuyo caso deberá ser

pagada el próximo día laboral. Si no existe otra decisión por parte del Arrendador, la renta deberá

ser pagada de la manera siguiente:

*Entrega de pago.*

El arriendo será pagado:

☐ Por correo, dirigido a _____

☐ Personalmente, en _____

*Forma de Pago.*

El Arrendador recibirá los pagos en:

☐ Cheque Personal escrito en favor de _____

☐ Cheque de Caja escrito en favor de _____

☐ Tarjeta de Crédito

☐ Giro Postal

☐ Efectivo

*Prorrateo del Primer mes de renta.*

Para el período comenzando con la fecha en que se mudará el Inquilino, el día _____ de _____ de _____ , hasta el fin del mes en curso, el Inquilino pagará al arrendador la renta mensual prorratada de $ _____. Esta suma se pagará antes o en la fecha en que se mude el Inquilino a la propiedad.

## Cláusula 6. Cobros por Mora.

Si el Inquilino falla en el pago total de la renta, antes del final del día siguiente a la fecha de pago, tendrá que pagar costos por atrasos como se explica a continuación: _____ _____.

El Arrendador no descartará el derecho de insistir en el pago total de la renta en la fecha debida.

## Cláusula 7. Pagos por Cheques Sin Fondo y Recargos Bancarios.

En el caso de cualquier cheque, ofrecido por el Inquilino al Arrendador como pago de renta o cualquier otra suma debida bajo este Contrato, sea regresado por insuficiencia de fondos, un "paro de pago" o cualquier otra razón, el Inquilino deberá pagar un recargo por la cantidad de $_____.

## Cláusula 8. Depósito de Garantía.

Al firmar el presente Contrato, el Inquilino pagará al Arrendador, la cantidad de $_____ como depósito de seguridad. Este depósito no puede aplicarse al último mes de renta o a cualquier cantidad debida bajo este Contrato; excepto con previo consentimiento por escrito del Arrendador. Dentro de _____ , después de que el Inquilino haya desocupado la propiedad, haya entregado las llaves y proporcionado la dirección donde contactarse, el Arrendador le entregará el depósito en su totalidad o le detallará de manera escrita, las razones y la cantidad que es retenida por él, junto con un cheque por la cantidad de su diferencia.

**Cláusula 9. Servicios Publicos.**

El Inquilino pagará todos los servicios publicos, exceptuando los siguientes, los cuales serán

pagados por el Arrendador: _____

_____

**Cláusula 10. Prohibición de Traspaso o Sub-arrendamiento.**

El Inquilino no puede sub-arrendar cualquier parte de la propiedad o traspasar este Contrato, sin

previo consentimiento por escrito del Arrendador.

**Cláusula 11. Responsabilidad del Inquilino de Mantenimiento de la propiedad.**

El Inquilino acepta: (1) mantener la propiedad limpia e higiénica, en buena condición, y cuando el

arrendamiento termine, regresar la propiedad al Arrendador en idéntica condición a la que existía

cuando la habitaron, exceptuando el deterioro causado por el uso; (2) Notificar de inmediato al

Arrendador, sobre cualquier defecto o condición peligrosa que note en o alrededor de la propiedad;

y (3) reembolsar al Arrendador, bajo demanda de éste, los costos de cualquier reparación de daños a

la propiedad, ocasionados por uso indebido o negligencia del Inquilino o sus invitados.

El Inquilino ha revisado la propiedad, incluyendo los aparatos electro-domésticos, accesorios,

alfombras, cortinas y pintura, y los ha encontrado en buenas condiciones, seguras, y limpias,

exceptuando las que están en la Lista Arrendador-Inquilino.

**Cláusula 12. Reparaciones y Modificaciones hechas por el Inquilino.**

    a. Exceptuando lo provisto por la ley o con la autorización previa y por escrito del Arrendador, el Inquilino no debe hacer modificaciones o reparaciones en la propiedad, incluído el hacer hoyos en las paredes o pintar el lugar.

    b. El Inquilino no debe alterar las cerraduras, ni cambiarlas, ni instalar o modificar el sistema de alarma; excepto que haya recibido del Arrendador, una autorización previa y por escrito. El Inquilino deberá proveer al Arrendador una copia de llave o llaves para abrir cada cerradura modificada o nueva, así como instrucciones de cómo desarmar un sistema de alarma modificado o nuevo.

**Cláusula 13. Causar Disturbios y Violaciones a la Ley.**

El Inquilino tiene derecho al goce pacífico de la propiedad. Este y sus invitados no deben usar la propiedad o áreas aledañas, de manera que: (1) Viole cualquier ley o reglamento, incluyendo leyes que prohiben el uso, posesión o venta ilegal de drogas; (2) Permite el uso abusivo de la propiedad (daño serio a la propiedad); o (3) Cree un estorbo al molestar, provocar disturbios, provocar inconvenientes o interferir en el disfrute de paz y tranquilidad de otros inquilinos o vecinos.

**Cláusula 14. Mascotas.**

No se permite, ni siquiera temporalmente, tener ningún animal, pájaro u otros animales en la propiedad, excepto perros entrenados para auxiliar a ciegos, sordos o personas con incapacidades físicas, y _____

bajo las condiciones siguientes: _____

_____

_____

**Cláusula 15. Derecho del Arrendador al Acceso a la Propiedad.**

El Arrendador o agentes de éste pueden entrar a la propiedad, en caso de emergencia, para hacer reparaciones o mejoras, o para mostrar la propiedad a potenciales nuevos inquilinos o compradores en perspectiva. También podrá entrar para la inspección anual para revisar la seguridad o chequear problemas de mantenimiento. Excepto en caso de emergencia, por el abandono de la propiedad por parte del Inquilino, orden de la corte, o cuando no sea práctico, el Arrendador deberá notificarle al Inqui ino de su intención de entrar a la propiedad con _____ de anticipación.

**Cláusula 16. Ausencias Prolongadas del Inquilino.**

El Inquilino deberá previamente notificar al Arrendador, si estará ausente de la propiedad por _____ días consecutivos o más. Durante este tiempo, el Arrendador podrá entrar, cuando sea necesario, a la propiedad para inspeccionarla, para mantenimiento o para reparaciones necesarias.

## Cláusula 17. Tomar Posesión de la propiedad.

a. *Falla del Inquilino en tomar posesión de la propiedad.*

Si después de haber firmado este Contrato, el Inquilino no toma posesión de la propiedad, aún será responsable por pago de la renta y cumplimiento de todos los demás términos de este Contrato.

b. *Falla del Arrendador en entregar la propiedad.*

Si el Arrendador no puede entregar la posesión de la propiedad al Inquilino, por cualquier razón fuera de su control, incluyendo, pero no limitado a, destrucción parcial o completa de la propiedad, el Inquilino tendrá el derecho de terminar este Contrato, mediante aviso previo y apropiado como lo señala la ley. En tal situación, la responsabilidad del Arrendador hacia el Inquilino, estará limitada a la devolución de todas las cantidades previamente pagadas por el Inquilino al Arrendador.

## Cláusula 18. Normas y Regulaciones del Inquilino.

☐ El Inquilino reconoce lo recibido y que ha leído una copia de las Normas y Regulaciones del Inquilino; las cuales como referencia, están adjuntas e incorporadas al presente Contrato.

## Cláusula 19. Pago del Abogado y Costos de la Corte en Caso de un Juicio.

En cualquier acción jurídico-legal para hacer cumplir total o parcialmente este Contrato, la parte prevaleciente ☐ No deberá / ☐ Deberá recuperar honorarios justos del abogado y costos de la corte.

## Cláusula 20. Divulgaciones.

El Inquilino reconoce que el Arrendador le ha hecho las siguientes divulgaciones con respecto a la propiedad:

☐ Distribución de información sobre pintura a base de plomo y/o los peligros de este tipo de pintura.

☐ Otras divulgaciones:

_____

_____

_____.

## Cláusula 21. Personal Autorizado para Recibir Documentos Legales.

El Arrendador, la persona que administre la propiedad, o a quien haya designado el Arrendador, están autorizados para aceptar servicio de proceso, y recibir otras noticias y demandas, las cuales pueden ser entregadas a:

☐ El Arrendador, a la siguiente dirección: _____

_____

☐ El Administrador, a la siguiente dirección:_____

_____.

☐ A la persona designada, a la siguiente dirección:_____

_____.

**Cláusula 22. Disposiciones Adicionales.**

Disposiciones adicionales son las siguientes: _____

_____

_____

_____

_____

_____

_____

_____ .

**Cláusula 23. Validez de las Cláusulas de este Contrato.**

Si cualquier clausula de este Contrato es invalidado, ésto no afectará la validez o cumplimiento de las partes restantes de este Contrato.

**Cláusula 24. Razones para Cancelar el Contrato de Arrendamiento.**

El incumplimiento de cualesquiera de los términos de este Contrato, por parte del Inquilino o sus invitados o la relación Falsa de un hecho esencial en la solicitud del Inquilino, será razón para dar por cancelado el Contrato de arrendamiento, seguido con la debida notificación al Inquilino, de acuerdo con lo requerido por la ley.

**Cláusula 25. Contrato Completo.**

Este documento constituye el Contrato completo entre las partes, y el Arrendador y el Inquilino no han hecho otro compromiso, a no ser los contenidos en este Contrato o los señalados por la ley. Cualquier modificación al presente documento, debe ser por escrito y firmado por ambas partes.

| _____ | _____ | _____ |
| Fecha | Arrendador o su representant | Título |

_____
Número y Nombre de la Calle

| _____ | _____ | _____ | _____ |
| Ciudad | Estado | Código Postal | Teléfono |

| _____ | _____ | _____ |
| Fecha | Nombre del Inquilino | Teléfono |

| _____ | _____ | _____ |
| Fecha | Nombre del Inquilino | Teléfono |

| _____ | _____ | _____ |
| Fecha | Nombre del Inquilino | Teléfono |

# Cosigner Agreement

1. This Agreement is entered into on _____, 199____, between

   _____ ("Tenant"),

   _____ ("Landlord") and

   _____ ("Cosigner").

2. Tenant has leased from Landlord the premises located at _____

   _____ ("Premises").

   Landlord and Tenant signed a lease or rental agreement specifying the terms and conditions of

   this rental on _____, 199____. A copy of the lease or rental

   agreement is attached to this Agreement.

3. Cosigner agrees to be jointly and severally liable with Tenant for Tenant's obligations arising out

   of the lease or rental agreement described in Paragraph 2, including but not limited to unpaid

   rent, property damage and cleaning and repair costs that exceed Tenant's security deposit.

   Cosigner further agrees that Landlord will have no obligation to report to Cosigner should Tenant

   fail to abide by the terms of the lease or rental agreement. (For example, if Tenant fails to pay the

   rent on time or damages the premises, Landlord has no duty to warn or inform Cosigner, and may

   demand that Cosigner pay for these obligations immediately.)

4. If Tenant assigns or subleases the Premises, Cosigner shall remain liable under the terms of this

   Agreement for the performance of the assignee or sublessee, unless Landlord relieves Cosigner by

   express written termination of this Agreement.

5. If Landlord and Cosigner are involved in any legal proceeding arising out of this Agreement, the

   prevailing party shall recover reasonable attorney fees, court costs and any costs reasonably

   necessary to collect a judgment.

_____        _____

Date                           Landlord/Manager

_____        _____

Date                           Tenant

_____        _____

Date                           Cosigner

# Agreement for Delayed or Partial Rent Payments

This Agreement is made between _____ "Tenant(s),"

and _____ "Landlord/Manager."

1. _____ "Tenant(s)" has/have paid

_____

_____

on _____, 199____, which was due _____, 199____.

2. _____ (Landlord/Manager)

agrees to accept all the remainder of the rent on or before _____, 199____,

and to hold off on any legal proceeding to evict _____

_____ (Tenant(s)) until that date.

| | |
|---|---|
| _____ | _____ |
| Date | Landlord/Manager |
| _____ | _____ |
| Date | Tenant |
| _____ | _____ |
| Date | Tenant |
| _____ | _____ |
| Date | Tenant |

# Property Manager Agreement

## 1. Parties

This Agreement is between _____,

Owner of residential real property at _____,

_____, and

_____,

Manager of the property. Manager will be renting unit _____ of the property under

a separate written rental agreement that is in no way contingent upon or related to this agreement.

## 2. Beginning Date

Manager will begin work on _____.

## 3. Responsibilities

Manager's duties are set forth below:

### Renting Units

☐ answer phone inquiries about vacancies

☐ show vacant units

☐ accept rental applications

☐ select tenants

☐ accept initial rents and deposits

☐ other (specify) _____

☐ _____

### Vacant Apartments

☐ inspect unit when tenant moves in

☐ inspect unit when tenant moves out

☐ clean unit after tenant moves out, including:

    ☐ floors, carpets and rugs

    ☐ walls, baseboards, ceilings, lights and built-in shelves

    ☐ kitchen cabinets, countertops, sinks, stove, oven and refrigerator

    ☐ bathtubs, showers, toilets and plumbing fixtures

    ☐ doors, windows, window coverings and mini-blinds

    ☐ other (specify) _____

    ☐ _____

**Rent Collection**

☐ collect rents when due

☐ sign rent receipts

☐ maintain rent-collection records

☐ collect late rents and charges

☐ inform Owner of late rents

☐ prepare late rent notices

☐ serve late rent notices on tenants

☐ serve rent increase and tenancy termination notices

☐ deposit rent collections in bank

☐ other (specify) _____

☐ _____

**Maintenance**

☐ vacuum and clean hallways and entryways

☐ replace lightbulbs in common areas

☐ drain water heaters

☐ clean stairs, decks, patios, facade and sidewalks

☐ clean garage oils on pavement

☐ mow lawns

☐ rake leaves

☐ trim bushes

☐ clean up garbage and debris on grounds

☐ shovel snow from sidewalks and driveways or arrange for snow removal

☐ other (specify) _____

☐ _____

**Repairs**

☐ accept tenant complaints and repair requests

☐ inform Owner of maintenance and repair needs

☐ maintain written log of tenant complaints

☐ handle routine maintenance and repairs, including:

    ☐ plumbing stoppages

    ☐ garbage disposal stoppages/repairs

    ☐ faucet leaks/washer replacement

    ☐ toilet tank repairs

    ☐ toilet seat replacement

☐ stove burner repair/replacement

☐ stove hinges/knobs replacement

☐ dishwasher repair

☐ light switch and outlet repair/replacement

☐ heater thermostat repair

☐ window repair/replacement

☐ painting (interior)

☐ painting (exterior)

☐ replacement of keys

☐ other (specify)

☐ _____

## Other Responsibilities

_____

_____

_____

_____

### 4. Hours and Schedule

Manager will be available to tenants during the following days and times: _____

_____. If the hours required to carry out

any duties may reasonably be expected to exceed _____ hours in any week, Manager shall

notify Owner and obtain Owner's consent before working such extra hours, except in the event of an

emergency. Extra hours worked due to an emergency must be reported to Owner within 24 hours.

### 5. Payment Terms

a. Manager will be paid:

☐ $ _____ per hour

☐ $ _____ per week

☐ $ _____ per month

☐ Other: _____

b. Manager will be paid on the specified intervals and dates:

☐ Once a week on every _____

☐ Twice a month on _____

☐ Once a month on _____

☐ Other: _____

## 6. Ending the Manager's Employment

Owner may terminate Manager's employment at any time, and Manager may quit at any time.

## 7. Additional Agreements and Amendments

a. Owner and Manager additionally agree that: _____

_____

_____

_____

_____

_____

_____

_____

_____

_____

_____

_____.

b. All agreements between Owner and Manager relating to the work specified in this Agreement are incorporated in this Agreement. Any modification to the Agreement must be in writing and signed by both parties.

## 8. Place of Execution

Signed at _____, _____
          City                                   State

_____   _____

Date                      Owner

_____   _____

Date                      Manager

# Landlord-Tenant Checklist

## GENERAL CONDITION OF RENTAL UNIT AND PREMISES

| Street Address | | Unit Number    City | |

| | Condition on Arrival | Condition on Departure | Estimated Cost of Repair/Replacement |
|---|---|---|---|
| **LIVING ROOM** | | | |
| Floors & Floor Coverings | | | |
| Drapes & Window Coverings | | | |
| Walls & Ceilings | | | |
| Light Fixtures | | | |
| Windows, Screens & Doors | | | |
| Front Door & Locks | | | |
| Fireplace | | | |
| Other | | | |
| Other | | | |
| **KITCHEN** | | | |
| Floors & Floor Coverings | | | |
| Walls & Ceilings | | | |
| Light Fixtures | | | |
| Cabinets | | | |
| Counters | | | |
| Stove/Oven | | | |
| Refrigerator | | | |
| Dishwasher | | | |
| Garbage Disposal | | | |
| Sink & Plumbing | | | |
| Windows, Screens & Doors | | | |
| Other | | | |
| Other | | | |
| **DINING ROOM** | | | |
| Floors & Floor Covering | | | |
| Walls & Ceilings | | | |
| Light Fixtures | | | |
| Windows, Screens & Doors | | | |
| Other | | | |

|  | Condition on Arrival | | | Condition on Departure | | | Estimated Cost of Repair/Replacement |
|---|---|---|---|---|---|---|---|
| **BATHROOM(S)** | **Bath 1** | **Bath 2** | | **Bath 1** | **Bath 2** | | |
| Floors & Floor Coverings | | | | | | | |
| Walls & Ceilings | | | | | | | |
| Windows, Screens & Doors | | | | | | | |
| Light Fixtures | | | | | | | |
| Bathtub/Shower | | | | | | | |
| Sink & Counters | | | | | | | |
| Toilet | | | | | | | |
| Other | | | | | | | |
| Other | | | | | | | |
| **BEDROOM(S)** | **Bdrm 1** | **Bdrm 2** | **Bdrm 3** | **Bdrm 1** | **Bdrm 2** | **Bdrm 3** | |
| Floors & Floor Coverings | | | | | | | |
| Windows, Screens & Doors | | | | | | | |
| Walls & Ceilings | | | | | | | |
| Light Fixtures | | | | | | | |
| Other | | | | | | | |
| Other | | | | | | | |
| Other | | | | | | | |
| Other | | | | | | | |
| **OTHER AREAS** | | | | | | | |
| Heating System | | | | | | | |
| Air Conditioning | | | | | | | |
| Lawn/Garden | | | | | | | |
| Stairs and Hallway | | | | | | | |
| Patio, Terrace, Deck, etc. | | | | | | | |
| Basement | | | | | | | |
| Parking Area | | | | | | | |
| Other | | | | | | | |
| Other | | | | | | | |
| Other | | | | | | | |
| Other | | | | | | | |
| Other | | | | | | | |

☐ Tenants acknowledge that all smoke detectors and fire extinguishers were tested in their presence and found to be in working order, and that the testing procedure was explained to them. Tenants agree to test all detectors at least once a month and to report any problems to Landlord/Manager in writing. Tenants agree to replace all smoke detector batteries as necessary.

# FURNISHED PROPERTY

| | Condition on Arrival | Condition on Departure | Estimated Cost of Repair/Replacement |
|---|---|---|---|
| **LIVING ROOM** | | | |
| Coffee Table | | | |
| End Tables | | | |
| Lamps | | | |
| Chairs | | | |
| Sofa | | | |
| Other | | | |
| Other | | | |
| **KITCHEN** | | | |
| Broiler Pan | | | |
| Ice Trays | | | |
| Other | | | |
| Other | | | |
| **DINING AREA** | | | |
| Chairs | | | |
| Stools | | | |
| Table | | | |
| Other | | | |
| Other | | | |
| **BATHROOM(S)** | Bath 1     Bath 2 | Bath 1     Bath 2 | |
| Mirrors | | | |
| Shower Curtain | | | |
| Hamper | | | |
| Other | | | |
| **BEDROOM(S)** | Bdrm 1   Bdrm 2   Bdrm 3 | Bdrm 1   Bdrm 2   Bdrm 3 | |
| Beds (single) | | | |
| Beds (double) | | | |
| Chairs | | | |
| Chests | | | |
| Dressing Tables | | | |
| Lamps | | | |
| Mirrors | | | |
| Night Tables | | | |
| Other | | | |

| | Condition on Arrival | Condition on Departure | Estimated Cost of Repair/Replacement |
|---|---|---|---|
| Other | | | |
| **OTHER AREAS** | | | |
| Bookcases | | | |
| Desks | | | |
| Pictures | | | |
| Other | | | |
| Other | | | |

Use this space to provide any additional explanation:

_____

_____

_____

_____

_____

_____

_____

_____

_____

_____

_____

_____

Landlord-Tenant Checklist completed on moving in on _____, 199____, and approved by:

_____ and _____
Landlord/Manager                              Tenant

_____
Tenant

_____
Tenant

Landlord-Tenant Checklist completed on moving out on _____, 199____, and approved by:

_____ and _____
Landlord/Manager                              Tenant

_____
Tenant

_____
Tenant

# Move-In Letter

_____
Date

_____
Tenant

_____
Street address

_____
City and State

Dear_____,
                        Tenant

Welcome to _____
_____ (address of rental unit). We hope you will enjoy living here. This letter is to explain what you can expect from the management and what we'll be looking for from you:

**1. Rent:** _____
_____.

**2. New roommates:** _____
_____
_____
_____.

**3. Notice to end tenancy:** _____
_____
_____.

**4. Deposits:** _____
_____
_____.

**5. Manager:** _____
_____
_____.

**6. Landlord-Tenant Checklist:** _____
_____
_____
_____
_____.

**7. Maintenance/Repair Problems:** _____

_____

_____

_____

_____

_____.

**8. Semi-Annual Safety and Maintenance Update:** _____

_____

_____.

**9. Annual Safety Inspection:** _____

_____

_____.

**10. Insurance:** _____

_____

_____

_____

_____.

**11. Moving Out:** _____

_____

_____

_____

_____.

**12. Telephone Number Changes:** _____

_____.

Please let us know if you have any questions.

Sincerely,

_____        _____
Date                             Owner

I have read and received a copy of this statement.

_____        _____
Date                             Tenant

# Termination of Lease

_____ ("Landlord")

and _____

("Tenant") agree that the lease they entered into on _____, for premises at

_____, will terminate

on _____.


_____     _____
Date                        Landlord


_____     _____
Date                        Tenant

# Consent to Assignment of Lease

_____ ("Landlord") and

_____ ("Tenant") and

_____ ("Assignee")

agree as follows:

1. Tenant has leased the premises at _____

_____ from Landlord.

2. The lease was signed on _____, 199____, and will expire on

_____, 199____.

3. Tenant is assigning the balance of Tenant's lease to Assignee, beginning on _____

_____, 199____, and ending on _____, 199____.

4. Tenant's financial responsibilities under the terms of the lease are not ended by virtue of this
   assignment. Specifically, Tenant understands that:

   a. If Assignee defaults and fails to pay the rent as provided in the lease, namely on
      _____, Tenant will be obligated to do so within
      _____ days of being notified by Landlord; and

   b. If Assignee damages the property beyond normal wear and tear and fails or refuses to pay
      for repairs or replacement, Tenant will be obligated to do so.

5. As of the effective date of the assignment, Tenant permanently gives up the right to occupy the
   premises.

6. Assignee is bound by every term and condition in the lease that is the subject of this assignment.


_____        _____
Date                           Landlord


_____        _____
Date                           Tenant


_____        _____
Date                           Assignee

# Letter to Original Tenant and New Co-Tenant

_____

Date


Dear _____ and

     New co-tenant


_____ ,

     Original tenant or tenants


As the landlord of _____

_____ (address) , I am pleased that

_____ (new co-tenant)

has proved to be an acceptable applicant and will be joining _____

_____ (original tenant or tenants) as a co-tenant. Before

_____ (new co-tenant)

moves in, everyone must sign a new lease that will cover your rights and responsibilities. Please

contact me at the address or phone number below at your earliest convenience so that we can

arrange a time for us to meet and sign a new lease. Do not begin the process of moving in until we

have signed a lease.


Sincerely yours,


_____

Landlord


_____

Street address


_____

City and State


_____

Phone

# Resident's Maintenance/Repair Request

Date: _____

Address: _____

Resident's Name: _____

Phone (home): _____ Phone (work): _____

Problem (be as specific as possible): _____

_____

_____

_____

_____

_____

Best time to make repairs: _____

_____

Other comments: _____

_____

_____

_____

I authorize entry into my unit to perform the maintenance or repair requested above, in my absence, unless stated otherwise above.

_____

Resident

. . . . . . . . . . . . . . . . . . . . . . . . . . . . . . . . . . . . . . . . . . . . . .

FOR MANAGEMENT USE

Work done: _____

Time spent: _____ hours

Date completed: _____, 199____

Unable to complete on _____, 199____, because: _____

_____

Notes and comments: _____

_____          _____
Date                                     Landlord/Manager

# Time Estimate for Repair

_____

Date

_____

Tenant

_____

Street address

_____

City and State

Dear_____,
                         Tenant

Thank you for promptly notifying us of the following problem with your unit:

_____

_____

_____

_____

_____

_____

We expect to have the problem corrected on _____, 199____, due to

the following:

_____

_____

_____

_____

We regret any inconvenience this delay may cause. Please do not hesitate to point out any other

problems that may arise.

Sincerely,

_____

Landlord/Manager

# Semi-Annual Safety and Maintenance Update

Please complete the following checklist and note any safety or maintenance problems in your unit or on the premises.

Please describe the specific problems and the rooms or areas involved. Here are some examples of the types of things we want to know about: garage roof leaks, excessive mildew in rear bedroom closet, fuses blow out frequently, door lock sticks, water comes out too hot in shower, exhaust fan above stove doesn't work, smoke alarm malfunctions, peeling paint and mice in basement. Please point out any potential safety and security problems in the neighborhood and anything you consider a serious nuisance.

Please indicate the approximate date when you first noticed the problem and list any other recommendations or suggestions for improvement.

Please return this form with this month's rent check. Thank you.—THE MANAGEMENT

Name: _____

Address: _____

_____

Please indicate (and explain below) problems with:

☐ Floors and floor coverings _____

☐ Walls and ceilings _____

☐ Windows, screens and doors _____

☐ Window coverings (drapes, mini-blinds, etc.) _____

☐ Electrical system and light fixtures _____

☐ Plumbing (sinks, bathtub, shower or toilet) _____

☐ Heating or air conditioning system_____

☐ Major appliances (stove, oven, dishwasher, refrigerator) _____

☐ Basement or attic _____

☐ Locks or security system _____

☐ Smoke detector _____

☐ Fireplace _____

☐ Cupboards, cabinets and closets _____

☐ Furnishings (table, bed, mirrors, chairs) _____

☐ Laundry facilities _____

☐ Elevator _____

☐ Stairs and handrails _____

☐ Hallway, lobby and common areas _____

☐ Garage _____

☐ Patio, terrace or deck _____

☐ Lawn, fences and grounds _____

☐ Pool and recreational facilities _____

☐ Roof, exterior walls, and other structural _____

☐ Driveway and sidewalks _____

☐ Neighborhood _____

☐ Nuisances _____

☐ Other _____

_____

Specifics of problems: _____

_____

_____

_____

_____

Other comments: _____

_____

_____

_____

_____

_____

_____     _____
Date                            Tenant

· · · · · · · · · · · · · · · · · · · · · · · · · · · · · · · · · · · · · · · ·

FOR MANAGEMENT USE

Action/Response: _____

_____

_____

_____

_____

_____

_____

_____

_____

_____

_____     _____
Date                            Landlord/Manager

# Agreement Regarding Tenant Alterations to Rental Unit

_____ (Landlord)

and _____ (Tenant)

agree as follows:

1. Tenant may make the following alterations to the rental unit at _____

_____ :

_____

_____

_____

_____

_____

_____ .

2. Tenant will accomplish the work described in Paragraph 1 by using the following materials and

    procedures: _____

_____

_____

_____

_____ .

3. Tenant will do only the work outlined in Paragraph 1 using only the materials and procedures outlined
   in paragraph 2.

4. The alterations carried out by Tenant _(check either a or b)_:

    ☐ will become Landlord's property and are not to be removed by Tenant during or at the end of the
    tenancy

    ☐ will be considered Tenant's personal property, and as such may be removed by Tenant at any time
    up to the end of the tenancy. Tenant promises to return the premises to their original condition
    upon removing the improvement.

5. Landlord will reimburse Tenant only for the costs checked below:

    ☐ the cost of materials listed in paragraph 2

    ☐ labor costs at the rate of $ _____ per hour for work done in a workmanlike
    manner acceptable to Landlord up to _____ hours.

6. After receiving appropriate documentation of the cost of materials and labor, Landlord shall make any payment called for under paragraph 5 by:

☐ lump sum payment, within _____ days of receiving documentation of costs, or

☐ by reducing Tenant's rent by $ _____ per month for the number of months necessary to cover the total amounts under the terms of this agreement.

7. If under Paragraph 4 of this contract the alterations are Tenant's personal property, Tenant must return the premises to their original condition upon removing the alterations. If Tenant fails to do this, Landlord will deduct the cost to restore the premises to their original condition from Tenant's security deposit. If the security deposit is insufficient to cover the costs of restoration, Landlord may take legal action, if necessary, to collect the balance.

8. If Tenant fails to remove an improvement that is his or her personal property on or before the end of the tenancy, it will be considered the property of Landlord, who may choose to keep the improvement (with no financial liability to Tenant), or remove it and charge Tenant for the costs of removal and restoration. Landlord may deduct any costs of removal and restoration from Tenant's security deposit. If the security deposit is insufficient to cover the costs of removal and restoration, Landlord may take legal action, if necessary, to collect the balance.

9. If Tenant removes an item that is Landlord's property, Tenant will owe Landlord the fair market value of the item removed plus any costs incurred by Landlord to restore the premises to their original condition.

10. If Landlord and Tenant are involved in any legal proceeding arising out of this agreement, the prevailing party shall recover reasonable attorney fees, court costs and any costs reasonably necessary to collect a judgment.

_____     _____

Date                                Landlord


_____     _____

Date                                Tenant

# Disclosure of Information on Lead-Based Paint or Lead-Based Paint Hazards

## *LEAD WARNING STATEMENT*

*Housing built before 1978 may contain lead-based paint. Lead from paint, paint chips and dust can pose health hazards if not managed properly. Lead exposure is especially harmful to young children and pregnant women. Before renting pre-1978 housing, lessors must disclose the presence of known lead-based paint and/or lead-based hazards in the dwelling. Lessees must also receive a federally approved pamphlet on lead poisoning prevention.*

### Lessor's Disclosure

(a) Presence of lead-based paint and/or lead-based paint hazards. Check (i) or (ii) below:

☐ (i) Known lead-based paint and/or lead-based paint hazards are present in the housing (explain):

☐ (ii) Lessor has no knowledge of lead-based paint and/or lead-based paint hazards in the housing.

(b) Records and reports available to the lessor. Check (i) or (ii) below:

☐ (i) Lessor has provided the lessee with all available records and reports pertaining to lead-based paint and/or lead-based paint hazards in the housing (list documents below):

☐ (ii) Lessor has no reports or records pertaining to lead-based paint or lead-based paint hazards in the housing.

### Lessee's Acknowledgment (initial)

___ (c) Lessee has received copies of all information listed above.

___ (d) Lessee has received the pamphlet Protect Your Family From Lead In Your Home.

### Agent's Acknowledgment (initial)

___ (e) Agent has informed the lessor of the lessor's obligations under 42 U.S.Code 4852d and is aware of his/her responsibility to ensure compliance.

### Certification of Accuracy

The following parties have reviewed the information above and certify, to the best of their knowledge, that the information they have provided is true and accurate.

| | | | |
|---|---|---|---|
| Lessor | Date | Lessor | Date |
| Lessee | Date | Lessee | Date |
| Agent | Date | Agent | Date |

# Declaración de Información sobre Pintura a Base de Plomo y/o Peligros de la Pintura a Base de Plomo

## Declaración sobre los Peligros del Plomo

*Se notifica a todo comprador de cualquier interés en propiedad real residencial en la cual fue construida una vivienda residencial antes del año 1978, que dicha propiedad puede presentar una exposición a plomo de la pintura a base de plomo que podría poner a niños jóvenes en situación de riesgo de desarrollar envenenamiento de plomo. El envenenamiento de plomo en niños jóvenes puede producir daños neurológicos permanentes, incluyendo incapacidad para el aprendizaje, cociente de inteligencia reducido, problemas de comportamiento y memoria dañada. El envenenamiento de plomo también representa un peligro especial para las mujeres embarazadas. El vendedor de cualquier interés en una propiedad privada real residencial tiene la obligación de proporcionarle al comprador toda la información que posea sobre los peligros de la pintura a base de plomo que se hayan determinado en evaluaciones o inspecciones de riesgo y de notificarle al comprador sobre cualquier peligro que conozca de la pintura a base de plomo. Se recomienda realizar una evaluación o inspección de posibles peligros de la pintura a base de plomo antes de la compra.*

## Declaración del Vendedor

(a) Presencia de pintura a base de plomo y/o peligros de pintura a base de plomo (marque (i) ó (ii) abajo):

    (i) _____ Confirmado que hay pintura a base de plomo y/o peligro de pintura a base de plomo en la vivienda (explique).

    _____

    (ii) _____ El vendedor no tiene ningún conocimiento de que haya pintura a base de plomo y/o peligro de pintura a base de plomo en la vivienda.

(b) Archivos e informes disponibles para el vendedor (marque (i) ó (ii) abajo):

    (i) _____ El vendedor le ha proporcionado al comprador todos los archivos e informes disponibles relacionados con pintura a base de plomo y/o peligro de pintura a base de plomo en la vivienda (anote los documentos abajo).

    _____

    (ii) _____ El vendedor no tiene archivos ni informes relacionados con pintura a base de plomo y/o peligro de pintura a base de plomo en la vivienda.

## Acuse de Recibo del Comprador (inicial)

(c) _____ El comprador ha recibido copias de toda la información indicada arriba.

(d) _____ El comprador ha recibido el folleto titulado *Proteja a Su Familia del Plomo en Su Casa.*

(e) El comprador ha (marque (i) ó (ii) abajo):

    (i) _____ recibido una oportunidad por 10 días (o un período de tiempo de mutuo acuerdo) para hacer una evaluación o inspección de riesgo de presencia de pintura a base de plomo o de peligros de pintura a base de plomo; o

    (ii) _____ renunciado a la oportunidad de hacer una evaluación o inspección de riesgo de presencia de pintura a base de plomo o de peligros de pintura a base de plomo.

## Acuse de Recibo del Agente (inicial)

(f) _____ El agente le ha informado al vendedor de las obligaciones del vendedor de acuerdo con 42 U.S.C. 4852(d) y está consciente de su responsabilidad de asegurar su cumplimiento.

## Certificación de Exactitud

Las partes siguientes han revisado la información que aparece arriba y certifican que, según su entender, toda la información que han proporcionado es verdadera y exacta.

| Vendedor | Fecha | Vendedor | Fecha |
|----------|-------|----------|-------|
| Comprador | Fecha | Comprador | Fecha |
| Agente | Fecha | Agente | Fecha |

## Are You Planning To Buy, Rent, or Renovate a Home Built Before 1978?

Many houses and apartments built before 1978 have paint that contains lead (called lead-based paint). Lead from paint, chips, and dust can pose serious health hazards if not taken care of properly.

By 1996, federal law will require that individuals receive certain information before renting, buying, or renovating pre-1978 housing:

**LANDLORDS** will have to disclose known information on lead-based paint hazards before leases take effect. Leases will include a federal form about lead-based paint.

**SELLERS** will have to disclose known information on lead-based paint hazards before selling a house. Sales contracts will include a federal form about lead-based paint in the building. Buyers will have up to 10 days to check for lead hazards.

**RENOVATORS** will have to give you this pamphlet before starting work.

**IF YOU WANT MORE INFORMATION** on these requirements, call the National Lead Information Clearinghouse at **1-800-424-LEAD**.

This document is in the public domain. It may be reproduced by an individual or organization without permission. Information provided in this booklet is based upon current scientific and technical understanding of the issues presented and is reflective of the jurisdictional boundaries established by the statutes governing the co-authoring agencies. Following the advice given will not necessarily provide complete protection in all situations or against all health hazards that can be caused by lead exposure.

---

# Protect Your Family From Lead in Your Home

**EPA**
United States Environmental Protection Agency

United States Consumer Product Safety Commission

EPA747-K-94-001
May 1995

U.S. EPA Washington DC 20460
U.S. CPSC Washington DC 20207

## Lead Gets in the Body in Many Ways

People can get lead in their body if they:

◆ Put their hands or other objects covered with lead dust in their mouths.

◆ Eat paint chips or soil that contains lead.

◆ Breathe in lead dust (especially during renovations that disturb painted surfaces).

Lead is even more dangerous to children than adults because:

◆ Babies and young children often put their hands and other objects in their mouths. These objects can have lead dust on them.

◆ Children's growing bodies absorb more lead.

◆ Children's brains and nervous systems are more sensitive to the damaging effects of lead.

1 out of every 11 children in the United States has dangerous levels of lead in the bloodstream.

Even children who appear healthy can have dangerous levels of lead.

---

# IMPORTANT!

## Lead From Paint, Dust, and Soil Can Be Dangerous If Not Managed Properly

FACT: Lead exposure can harm young children and babies even before they are born.

FACT: Even children that seem healthy can have high levels of lead in their bodies.

FACT: People can get lead in their bodies by breathing or swallowing lead dust, or by eating soil or paint chips with lead in them.

FACT: People have many options for reducing lead hazards. In most cases, lead-based paint that is in good condition is not a hazard.

FACT: Removing lead-based paint improperly can increase the danger to your family.

If you think your home might have lead hazards, read this pamphlet to learn some simple steps to protect your family.

## Checking Your Family for Lead

A simple blood test can detect high levels of lead. Blood tests are important for:

◆ Children who are 6 months to 1 year old (6 months if you live in an older home with cracking or peeling paint).

◆ Family members that you think might have high levels of lead.

**Get your children tested if you think your home has high levels of lead.**

If your child is older than 1 year, talk to your doctor about whether your child needs testing.

Your doctor or health center can do blood tests. They are inexpensive and sometimes free. Your doctor will explain what the test results mean. *Treatment can range from changes in your diet to medication or a hospital stay.*

## Where Lead-Based Paint Is Found

Many homes built before 1978 have lead-based paint. The federal government banned lead-based paint from housing in 1978. Some states stopped its use even earlier. Lead can be found:

◆ In homes in the city, country, or suburbs.

◆ In apartments, single-family homes, and both private and public housing.

◆ Inside *and* outside of the house.

◆ In soil around a home. (Soil can pick up lead from exterior paint, or other sources such as past use of leaded gas in cars.)

**In general, the older your home, the more likely it has lead-based paint.**

## Lead's Effects

If not detected early, children with high levels of lead in their bodies can suffer from:

◆ Damage to the brain and nervous system

◆ Behavior and learning problems (such as hyperactivity)

◆ Slowed growth

◆ Hearing problems

◆ Headaches

Lead is also harmful to adults. Adults can suffer from:

◆ Difficulties during pregnancy

◆ Other reproductive problems (in both men and women)

◆ High blood pressure

◆ Digestive problems

◆ Nerve disorders

◆ Memory and concentration problems

◆ Muscle and joint pain

Brain or Nerve Damage

Hearing Problems

Slowed Growth

Digestive Problems

Reproductive Problems (Adults)

**Lead affects the body in many ways.**

## Where Lead Is Likely To Be a Hazard

Lead-based paint that is in good condition is usually not a hazard.

Peeling, chipping, chalking, or cracking lead-based paint is a hazard and needs immediate attention.

Lead-based paint may also be a hazard when found on surfaces that children can chew or that get a lot of wear-and-tear. These areas include:

◆ Windows and window sills.

◆ Doors and door frames.

◆ Stairs, railings, and banisters.

◆ Porches and fences.

Lead dust can form when lead-based paint is dry scraped, dry sanded, or heated. Dust also forms when painted surfaces bump or rub together. Lead chips and dust can get on surfaces and objects that people touch. Settled lead dust can reenter the air when people vacuum, sweep, or walk through it.

Lead in soil can be a hazard when children play in bare soil or when people bring soil into the house on their shoes. Call your state agency (see page 12) to find out about soil testing for lead.

Lead from paint chips, which you can see, and lead dust, which you can't always see, can both be serious hazards

## Checking Your Home for Lead Hazards

You can get your home checked for lead hazards in one of two ways, or both:

◆ A paint inspection tells you the lead content of every painted surface in your home. It won't tell you whether the paint is a hazard or how you should deal with it.

◆ A risk assessment tells you if there are any sources of serious lead exposure (such as peeling paint and lead dust). It also tells you what actions to take to address these hazards.

Have qualified professionals do the work. *The federal government is writing standards for inspectors and risk assessors. Some states might already have standards in place.* Call your state agency for help with locating qualified professionals in your area (see page 12).

Trained professionals use a range of methods when checking your home, including:

◆ Visual inspection of paint condition and location.

◆ Lab tests of paint samples.

◆ Surface dust tests.

◆ A portable x-ray fluorescence machine.

Home test kits for lead are available, but recent studies suggest that they are not always accurate. Consumers should not rely on these tests before doing renovations or to assure safety.

Just knowing that a home has lead-based paint may not tell you if there is a hazard.

## What You Can Do Now To Protect Your Family

**If you suspect that your house has lead hazards, you can take some immediate steps to reduce your family's risk:**

◆ **If you rent, notify your landlord of peeling or chipping paint.**

◆ **Clean up paint chips immediately.**

◆ **Clean floors, window frames, window sills, and other surfaces weekly.** Use a mop or sponge with warm water and a general all-purpose cleaner or a cleaner made specifically for lead. REMEMBER: NEVER MIX AMMONIA AND BLEACH PRODUCTS TOGETHER SINCE THEY CAN FORM A DANGEROUS GAS.

◆ **Thoroughly rinse sponges and mop heads after cleaning dirty or dusty areas.**

◆ **Wash children's hands often, especially before they eat and before nap time and bed time.**

◆ **Keep play areas clean.** Wash bottles, pacifiers, toys, and stuffed animals regularly.

◆ **Keep children from chewing window sills or other painted surfaces.**

◆ **Clean or remove shoes before entering your home to avoid tracking in lead from soil.**

◆ **Make sure children eat nutritious, low-fat meals high in iron and calcium,** such as spinach and low-fat dairy products. Children with good diets absorb less lead.

---

## How To Significantly Reduce Lead Hazards

In addition to day-to-day cleaning and good nutrition:

◆ You can **temporarily** reduce lead hazards by taking actions such as repairing damaged painted surfaces and planting grass to cover soil with high lead levels. These actions (called "interim controls") are not permanent solutions and will need ongoing attention.

◆ To **permanently** remove lead hazards, you must hire a lead "abatement" contractor. Abatement (or permanent hazard elimination) methods include removing, sealing, or enclosing lead-based paint with special materials. Just painting over the hazard with regular paint is not enough.

Always hire a person with special training for correcting lead problems—someone who knows how to do this work safely and has the proper equipment to clean up thoroughly. If possible, hire a certified lead abatement contractor. Certified contractors will employ qualified workers and follow strict safety rules as set by their state or by the federal government.

Call your state agency (see page 12) for help with locating qualified contractors in your area and to see if financial assistance is available.

*Removing lead improperly can increase the hazard to your family by spreading even more lead dust around the house.*

*Always use a professional who is trained to remove lead hazards safely.*

## Remodeling or Renovating a Home With Lead-Based Paint

Take precautions before you begin remodeling or renovations that disturb painted surfaces (such as scraping off paint or tearing out walls):

◆ **Have the area tested for lead-based paint.**

◆ **Do not use a dry scraper, belt-sander, propane torch, or heat gun** to remove lead-based paint. These actions create large amounts of lead dust and fumes. Lead dust can remain in your home long after the work is done.

◆ **Temporarily move your family** (especially children and pregnant women) out of the apartment or house until the work is done and the area is properly cleaned. If you can't move your family, at least completely seal off the work area.

◆ **Follow other safety measures to reduce lead hazards.** You can find out about other safety measures by calling 1-800-424-LEAD. Ask for the brochure "Reducing Lead Hazards When Remodeling Your Home." This brochure explains what to do before, during, and after renovations.

If you have already completed renovations or remodeling that could have released lead-based paint or dust, get your young children tested and follow the steps outlined on page 7 of this brochure.

**If not conducted properly, certain types of renovations can release lead from paint and dust into the air.**

## Other Sources of Lead

◆ **Drinking water.** Your home might have plumbing with lead or lead solder. Call your local health department or water supplier to find out about testing your water. You cannot see, smell, or taste lead, and boiling your water will not get rid of lead. If you think your plumbing might have lead in it:

- Use only cold water for drinking and cooking.

- Run water for 15 to 30 seconds before drinking it, especially if you have not used your water for a few hours.

◆ **The job.** If you work with lead, you could bring it home on your hands or clothes. Shower and change clothes before coming home. Launder your clothes separately from the rest of your family's.

◆ Old painted **toys** and **furniture.**

◆ Food and liquids stored in **lead crystal** or **lead-glazed pottery or porcelain.**

◆ **Lead smelters** or other industries that release lead into the air.

◆ **Hobbies** that use lead, such as making pottery or stained glass, or refinishing furniture.

◆ **Folk remedies** that contain lead, such as "greta" and "azarcon" used to treat an upset stomach.

*While paint, dust, and soil are the most common lead hazards, other lead sources also exist.*

### The National Lead Information Center

Call **1-800-LEAD-FYI** to learn how to protect children from lead poisoning. For other information on lead hazards, call the center's clearinghouse at **1-800-424-LEAD**. For the hearing impaired, call, **TDD 1-800-526-5456** (FAX: **202-659-1192,** Internet: **EHC@CAIS.COM**).

### EPAŌs Safe Drinking Water Hotline

Call **1-800-426-4791** for information about lead in drinking water.

### Consumer Product Safety Commission Hotline

To request information on lead in consumer products, or to report an unsafe consumer product or a product-related injury call **1-800-638-2772.** (Internet: info@cpsc.gov). For the hearing impaired, call **TDD 1-800-638-8270.**

### Local Sources of Information

Some cities and states have their own rules for lead-based paint activities. Check with your state agency (listed below) to see if state or local laws apply to you. Most state agencies can also provide information on finding a lead abatement firm in your area, and on possible sources of financial aid for reducing lead hazards.

| State/Region | Phone Number | State/Region | Phone Number |
| --- | --- | --- | --- |
| Alabama | (205) 242-5661 | Missouri | (314) 526-4911 |
| Alaska | (907) 465-5152 | Montana | (406) 444-3671 |
| Arkansas | (501) 661-2534 | Nebraska | (402) 471-2451 |
| Arizona | (602) 542-7307 | Nevada | (702) 687-6615 |
| California | (510) 450-2424 | New Hampshire | (603) 271-4507 |
| Colorado | (303) 692-3012 | New Jersey | (609) 633-2043 |
| Connecticut | (203) 566-5808 | New Mexico | (505) 841-8024 |
| Washington, DC | (202) 727-9850 | New York | (800) 458-1158 |
| Delaware | (302) 739-4735 | North Carolina | (919) 715-3293 |
| Florida | (904) 488-3385 | North Dakota | (701) 328-5188 |
| Georgia | (404) 657-6514 | Ohio | (614) 466-1450 |
| Hawaii | (808) 832-5860 | Oklahoma | (405) 271-5220 |
| Idaho | (208) 332-5544 | Oregon | (503) 248-5240 |
| Illinois | (800) 545-2200 | Pennsylvania | (717) 782-2884 |
| Indiana | (317) 382-6662 | Rhode Island | (401) 277-3424 |
| Iowa | (800) 972-2026 | South Carolina | (803) 935-7945 |
| Kansas | (913) 296-0189 | South Dakota | (605) 773-3153 |
| Kentucky | (502) 564-2154 | Tennessee | (615) 741-5683 |
| Louisiana | (504) 765-0219 | Texas | (512) 834-6600 |
| Massachusetts | (800) 532-9571 | Utah | (801) 536-4000 |
| Maryland | (410) 631-3859 | Vermont | (802) 863-7231 |
| Maine | (207) 287-4311 | Virginia | (800) 523-4019 |
| Michigan | (517) 335-8885 | Washington | (206) 753-2556 |
| Minnesota | (612) 627-5498 | West Virginia | (304) 558-2981 |
| Mississippi | (601) 960-7463 | Wisconsin | (608) 266-5885 |
| | | Wyoming | (307) 777-7391 |

# Simple Steps To Protect Your Family From Lead Hazards

## If you think your home has high levels of lead:

◆ Get your young children tested for lead, even if they seem healthy.

◆ Wash children's hands, bottles, pacifiers, and toys often.

◆ Make sure children eat healthy, low-fat foods.

◆ Get your home checked for lead hazards.

◆ Regularly clean floors, window sills, and other surfaces.

◆ Wipe soil off shoes before entering house.

◆ Talk to your landlord about fixing surfaces with peeling or chipping paint.

◆ Take precautions to avoid exposure to lead dust when remodeling or renovating (call 1-800-424-LEAD for guidelines).

◆ Don't use a belt-sander, propane torch, dry scraper, or dry sandpaper on painted surfaces that may contain lead.

◆ Don't try to remove lead-based paint yourself.

---

# EPA Regional Offices

Your Regional EPA Office can provide further information regarding regulations and lead protection programs.

## EPA Regional Offices

**Region 1** (Connecticut, Massachusetts, Maine, New Hampshire, Rhode Island, Vermont)
John F. Kennedy Federal Building
One Congress Street
Boston, MA  02203
(617) 565-3420

**Region 2** (New Jersey, New York, Puerto Rico, Virgin Islands)
Building 5
2890 Woodbridge Avenue
Edison, NJ  08837-3679
(908) 321-6671

**Region 3** (Delaware, Washington DC, Maryland, Pennsylvania, Virginia, West Virginia)
841 Chestnut Building
Philadelphia, PA  19107
(215) 597-9800

**Region 4** (Alabama, Florida, Georgia, Kentucky, Mississippi, North Carolina, South Carolina, Tennessee)
345 Courtland Street, NE
Atlanta, GA  30365
(404) 347-4727

**Region 5** (Illinois, Indiana, Michigan, Minnesota, Ohio, Wisconsin)
77 West Jackson Boulevard
Chicago, IL  60604-3590
(312) 886-6003

**Region 6** (Arkansas, Louisiana, New Mexico, Oklahoma, Texas)
First Interstate Bank Tower
1445 Ross Avenue, 12th Floor, Suite 1200
Dallas, TX  75202-2733
(214) 665-7244

**Region 7** (Iowa, Kansas, Missouri, Nebraska)
726 Minnesota Avenue
Kansas City, KS  66101
(913) 551-7020

**Region 8** (Colorado, Montana, North Dakota, South Dakota, Utah, Wyoming)
999 18th Street, Suite 500
Denver, CO  80202-2405
(303) 293-1603

**Region 9** (Arizona, California, Hawaii, Nevada)
75 Hawthorne Street
San Francisco, CA  94105
(415) 744-1124

**Region 10** (Idaho, Oregon, Washington, Alaska)
1200 Sixth Avenue
Seattle, WA  98101
(206) 553-1200

# CPSC Regional Offices

**Eastern Regional Center**
6 World Trade Center
Vesey Street, Room 350
New York, NY 10048
(212) 466-1612

**Central Regional Center**
230 South Dearborn Street
Room 2944
Chicago, IL 60604-1601
(312) 353-8260

**Western Regional Center**
600 Harrison Street, Room 245
San Francisco, CA 94107
(415) 744-2966

## ¿Está Usted Planeando Comprar, Alquilar o Renovar una Casa Construida Antes de 1978?

Muchas casas y apartamentos construidos antes de 1978 tienen pintura que contiene plomo (llamada pintura a base de plomo). El plomo de la pintura, de los pedazos y del polvo pueden representar peligros serios para la salud si no se manejan con cuidado.

Para el año 1996 la ley federal requerir que las personas reciban cierta información antes de alquilar, comprar o renovar casas construidas antes de 1978:

Los **propietarios** tendrán que revelar la información que tienen a sus inquilinos sobre los peligros de la pintura a base de plomo antes que los contratos de arrendamiento (alquiler) entren en vigor.

Los **vendedores** de sus propiedades tendrn que revelar la información que tienen sobre los peligros de la pintura a base de plomo antes de vender una casa. Los contratos de venta incluirn un formulario federal sobre la pintura a base de plomo en el edificio. Los compradores tendrán hasta 10 días para verificar si hay peligros de plomo.

Los **renovadores** tendrn que entregarle a usted este folleto antes de comenzar un trabajo.

Si usted quiere obtener ms información sobre estos requisitos, llame al Centro de Información Nacional para Plomo (National Lead Information Clearinghouse) al **1-800-424-5323.**

---

---

# Proteja a Su Familia del Plomo en Su Casa

**⊕EPA**

Agencia de Protección Ambiental de los Estados Unidos (EPA)

Comisión de Seguridad de Productos de Consumo de los Estados Unidos

EPA747-K-94-001
Agosto 1995

U.S. EPA/CPSC Washington DC 20460
U.S. CPSC Washington DC 20207

# ¡IMPORTANTE!

## El Plomo de la Pintura, el Polvo y la Tierra Pueden Ser Peligrosos Si No Se Manejan Debidamente

**Aviso:** Exponer a los niños o bebes al plomo los puede dañar, incluso antes de nacer.

**Aviso:** Hasta los niños que parecen ser saludables pueden tener niveles peligrosos de plomo en sus cuerpos.

**Aviso:** El plomo puede entrar en los cuerpos de las personas cuando aspiran o tragan polvo de plomo, o si comen tierra o pedazos de pintura que contienen plomo.

**Aviso:** Las personas tienen muchas alternativas para reducir el peligro del plomo. En muchos casos, la pintura a base de plomo que est en buenas condiciones no es un peligro.

**Aviso:** Quitar la pintura a base de plomo incorrectamente puede aumentar el peligro para su familia.

Si usted piensa que su casa puede tener pintura a base de plomo, lea este folleto para conocer unas medidas sencillas que puede tomar para proteger a su familia.

---

## El Plomo Entra en el Cuerpo de Muchas Maneras

**1 de cada 11 niños en los Estados Unidos tiene niveles peligrosos de plomo en su cuerpo.**

### El plomo puede entrar en los cuerpos de las personas si:

◆ Se meten las manos u otros objetos cubiertos de polvo de plomo en la boca.

◆ Comen pedazos de pintura o tierra que contiene plomo.

◆ Aspiran polvo de plomo (especialmente durante renovaciones de superficies pintadas).

### El plomo es aún más peligroso para los niños que para los adultos porque:

◆ Los bebes y los niños pequeños con frecuencia se meten las manos y otros objetos en la boca. Estos objetos pueden tener polvo de plomo.

◆ Los cuerpos de los niños crecen y absorben más plomo que los de los adultos.

◆ Los sistemas nerviosos y los cerebros de los niños son más sensibles a los efectos dañinos del plomo.

## Los Efectos del Plomo

Hasta los niños que parecen ser saludables pueden tener niveles peligrosos de plomo.

Si no se detecta temprano, los niños que tienen alto niveles de plomo en sus cuerpos pueden sufrir de:

◆ Daños al cerebro y al sistema nervioso

◆ Problemas de comportamiento y aprendizaje (tal como hiperactividad)

◆ Crecimiento lento

◆ Problemas para oir

◆ Dolores de cabeza

**El plomo también es dañino para los adultos. Los adultos pueden sufrir de:**

◆ Daño al bebé durante el embarazo

◆ Otros problemas reproductivos (en hombres y mujeres)

◆ Presión alta

◆ Problemas digestivos

◆ Trastornos nerviosos

◆ Problemas de memoria y de concentración

◆ Dolores musculares y de las articulaciones

Daños al Cerebro o a los
Nervios

Problemas
Para Oir

Crecimiento Retardado

Problemas
Digestivos

Problemas de
Reproducción (Adultos)

## Examine a su Familia para Detectar el Plomo

Los exámenes de sangre son importantes para:

◆ Niños que tienen entre 6 meses y 1 año (6 meses si usted vive en una casa o edificio que se está deteriorando, que puede tener plomo en la pintura).

◆ Miembros de la familia que usted cree que pueden tener altos niveles de plomo.

◆ Si su niño(a) tiene **más de 1 año,** hable con su médico sobre si su niño(a) necesita un examen.

**Un examen sencillo de la sangre puede detectar altos niveles de plomo.**

Su médico o centro de salud pueden hacer los exámenes de la sangre. No son caros y a veces se hacen gratis. Su médico le explicará lo que significa el resultado de un examen. El tratamiento puede variar, desde cambios en el ambiente donde vive una persona y de sus hábitos de comer, hasta medicinas o una estencia en un hospital.

## Dónde se Encuentra la Pintura a Base de Plomo

**Muchas casas construidas antes de 1978 tienen pintura a base de plomo. En 1978, el Gobierno Federal prohibió la pintura a base de plomo para viviendas.** Algunos estados ya habían prohibido su uso anteriormente. Se puede encontrar el plomo:

◆ En casas en la ciudad, en el medio rural o en los suburbios.

◆ En apartamentos, casas para una sola familia y en viviendas privadas y públicas.

◆ Adentro y afuera de la casa.

◆ En la tierra alrededor de la casa. (La tierra puede absorber el plomo de la pintura exterior o de otras fuentes como del uso en el pasado de gasolina con plomo en los autos.)

**En general, mientras más antigua sea su casa, mayor será la probabilidad de que tenga pintura a base de plomo.**

## Cómo Verificar si su Casa Tiene Peligros de Plomo

**Usted puede verificar si su casa tiene plomo en una de dos maneras, o ambas:**

◆ Una **inspección** de la pintura le indica el contenido de plomo de todas las superficies pintadas en su casa. No le indicará si la pintura es un peligro ni cómo usted la debería manejar.

◆ Una **evaluación del riesgo** le indica si hay fuentes de exposición seria al plomo (tales como pintura que se está pelando y polvo de plomo). Además, le indica qué acciones pueden ser tomadas para dirigirse a estos peligros.

Haga que inspectores calificados realicen las pruebas. El Gobierno Federal está preparando procedimientos y calificaciones universales para inspectores y evaluadores de riesgo que hacen pruebas de plomo. Posiblemente algunos estados ya tienen estándares vigentes. Llame a su agencia estatal para obtener más información sobre cómo encontrar a profesionales calificados en su área (vea la página 12).

Los profesionales entrenados usan una variedad de métodos cuando llevan a cabo sus pruebas, incluyendo:

◆ Inspección visual del lugar y la condición de la pintura.

◆ Examen de laboratorio de muestras de pintura.

◆ Pruebas del polvo de la superficie.

◆ Una máquina portátil de rayos-x de fluorescencia.

**Hay paquetes de pruebas de plomo para la casa disponibles, pero estudios recientes indican que no siempre son confiables.** Los consumidores no deben confiar en estas pruebas antes de hacer revonaciones o para asegurar que no hay peligro.

**Con sólo saber que una casa tiene pintura a base de plomo no le indica si hay peligro.**

**La pintura a base de plomo es más peligrosa cuando está en la forma de pedazos de pintura, que usted puede ver, o de polvo de plomo, que usted no siempre puede ver.**

---

## Dónde el Plomo Probablemente es un Peligro

**La pintura a base de plomo** que se está en buenas condiciones normalmente no es un peligro.

La pintura a base de plomo que se está pelando, despedazando o quebrando es un peligro y requiere atención inmediata.

La pintura a base de plomo también puede ser un peligro cuando se encuentra en superficies que los niños pueden morder o que tienen mucho uso.

◆ Ventanas y marcos de las ventanas.

◆ Puertas y marcos de las puertas.

◆ Escaleras, barandas y pasamanos.

◆ Portales, terrazas y cercas.

El polvo de plomo se puede formar cuando se raspa o lija en seco o se calienta la pintura a base de plomo. El polvo también se forma cuando las superficies pintadas (como puertas y ventanas) chocan o se juntan. Pedazos de plomo y polvo quedan en superficies que las personas tocan. El polvo de plomo que se acumula puede entrar en el aire cuando se usa una aspiradora o se barre.

El plomo en la tierra puede ser un peligro cuando los niños juegan allí o cuando las personas llevan tierra a la casa en los zapatos. Llame a su agencia estatal (en la lista en la parte de atras de este folleto) para averiguar sobre pruebas de plomo para la tierra.

## Qué Puede Hacer Usted Ahora Para Proteger a su Familia

**Si usted sospecha que su casa tiene peligro de plomo, usted puede tomar algunas acciones inmediatamente para reducir el riesgo para su familia:**

◆ Notifique a su propietario sobre pintura que se esté pelando o quebrando.

◆ Limpie los pedazos de pintura inmediatamente.

◆ Limpie los pisos, molduras y marcos de las ventanas y otras superficies semanalmente. Use un trapeador o una esponja con agua tibia y un detergente corriente o uno especial para plomo. **RECUERDE: Nunca mezcle productos de limpieza de amoníaco y de cloro, porque se produce un gas peligroso.**

◆ Enjuague completamente las esponjas y la cabeza de los trapeadores después de limpiar areas sucias o que tienen polvo. Bote los trapos que fueron usados para limpiar.

◆ **Lávele las manos a los niños frecuentemente, especialmente antes de comer y antes de dormir la siesta y por la noche.**

◆ **Mantenga limpias las áreas de juego.** Limpie las botellas, chupetes, y juguetes periódicamente.

◆ **No deje que los niños muerdan las molduras de las ventanas u otras superficies pintadas.**

◆ **Limpie o quítese los zapatos antes de entrar en su casa para que no entre el plomo de la tierra.**

◆ **Asegúrese que los niños coman comidas nutritivas, bajas en grasa y con alto contenido de hierro y calcio,** tales como espinaca y productos lácteos bajos en grasa. Los niños que tienen buenas dietas absorben menos plomo.

## Cómo Reducir los Peligros del Plomo Significativamente

Siempre consulte a un profesional que esté entrenado para hacer el trabajo debidamente y sin peligro.

Además de la limpieza diaria y la buena nutrición, usted puede considerar otras opciones para reducir los peligros del plomo.

◆ Usted puede reducir **temporalmente** los peligros del plomo tomando acciones como reparar superficies pintadas que han sido dañadas (vea la página siguiente) y sembrando grama o hierba para cubrir la tierra que tiene alto contenido de plomo. Estas acciones (llamadas "controles interinos") no son soluciones permanentes y no eliminarn todos los riesgos de exposición.

◆ Para quitar los peligros **permanentemente,** usted necesitará contratar a un especialista de "supresin" (o eliminación permanente de supresin n (o eliminación permanente de peligro) incluyen quitar, sellar o envolver la pintura a base de plomo con materiales especiales. **Simplemente pintar sobre el peligro con pintura corriente no es suficiente.**

Siempre contrate a una persona que tenga entrenamiento especial para corregir los problemas de plomo, alguien que sepa cómo hacer este trabajo sin peligro y que tenga el equipo necesario para limpiar debidamente después del trabajo. Si fuera posible, contrate a un especialista certificado para la supresión de plomo. Los especialistas **certificados** emplean a trabajadores calificados y cumplen las reglas estrictas de seguridad establecidas por el estado o por el Gobierno Federal.

Llame a su agencia estatal (vea la página 12) para que le ayuden a encontrar especialistas calificados en su área y para ver si hay ayuda financiera disponible.

Quitar el plomo indebidamente puede empeorar el peligro para su familia al regarse aen ms polvo de plomo por toda su casa.

## Cómo Remodelar o Renovar una Casa que Tiene Pintura a Base de Plomo

Tome las precauciones antes de comenzar remodelaciones o renovaciones que puedan mover superficies pintadas (tales como raspar la pintura o quitar paredes):

◆ **Examine el área para ver si hay pintura a base de plomo.**

◆ No use un raspador o una lijadora en seco, soplete de propano o pistola de alta temperatura para quitar la pintura a base de plomo. Estas acciones crean cantidades grandes de polvo de plomo y gases. El polvo de plomo puede quedar en su casa un tiempo largo después que se ha terminado el trabajo.

◆ **Mude temporalmente a su familia** (especialmente a los niños y las mujeres embarazadas) fuera de la casa o del apartamento hasta que se haya terminado el trabajo y limpiado debidamente el área. Si usted no puede mudar a su familia, entonces por lo menos aisle completamente el rea de trabajo.

◆ **Tome otras medidas de seguridad para reducir los peligros del plomo.** Usted puede averiguar sobre otras medidas de seguridad llamando al 1-800-424-5323. Pida el folleto "Cómo Reducir los Peligros del Plomo al Remodelar Su Casa". Este folleto explica qué hacer antes, durante y después de renovaciones para evitar crear peligros basados en el plomo de larga duración.

Si usted ya ha completado renovaciones o remodelaciones que pueden haber soltado pintura o polvo a base de plomo, lleve a sus niños para que les hagan pruebas y siga los pasos indicados en la página 7 de este folleto.

**Si no se hacen debidamente, ciertos tipos de renovaciones pueden soltar al aire el plomo de la pintura y polvo.**

## Otras Fuentes de Plomo

◆ **Agua de beber.** Su casa puede tener tuberías de plomo o soldaduras de plomo. Llame a su departamento de salud local o abastecedor de agua para averiguar sobre cómo hacerle pruebas a su agua. Usted no puede ver, oler ni saborear el plomo, y hervir el agua no le quitará el plomo. Si usted cree que la plomería de su casa puede tener plomo:

- **Use solamente agua fría para beber o cocinar.**

- Deje correr el agua unos minutos antes de beberla, especialmente si usted no ha usado el agua por varias horas.

◆ **En el trabajo.** Si usted trabaja con plomo en su trabajo, usted podría llevar el plomo a su casa en sus manos o en su ropa. Dése una ducha y cámbiese la ropa antes de llegar a su casa. Lave la ropa suya separada a la de su familia.

◆ **Juguetes y muebles viejos pintados.**

◆ Alimentos y líquidos guardados en **cristalería a base de plomo o locería o porcelana con barniz a base de plomo.**

◆ Fábricas de fundición que trabajan con plomo u otras industrias que sueltan plomo en el aire.

◆ **Pasatiempos** que usan plomo, tales como alfarería o vidrios de color, o renovación de muebles.

◆ **Remedios caseros** que contienen plomo, tales como "greta" y "azarcón", que se usan para tratar la descomposición de estómago.

# Para Más Información

### El Centro Nacional de Información Sobre Plomo

Llame al 1-800-532-3394 para obtener información sobre cómo proteger a los niños del envenenamiento de plomo.

Para obtener información adicional sobre peligros del plomo, llame a la oficina del Centro, al 1-800-424-5323, o TDD 1-800-526-5456 para los que tienen problemas para oír. (FAX: 202-659-1192, Internet: EHC@CAIS.COM).

### Teléfono Especial de la EPA para Agua de Beber Segura

Llame al 1-800-426-4761 para obtener información sobre plomo en el agua de beber.

Teléfono Especial de la Comisión de Seguridad de Productos de Consumo

Para pedir información sobre el plomo en productos de consumo, o para reportar que un producto para el consumo es peligroso o una lesión relacionada con un producto, llame al 1-800-638-2772. (Internet: info@cpsc.gov). Las personas que tienen problemas para oir, pueden llamar al 1-800-638-8720.

**Fuentes Locales de Información:**

# Agencias Estatales de Salud y de Protección Ambiental

Algunas ciudades y estados tienen sus propias regulaciones para las actividades relacionadas con pintura a base de plomo. Verifique con su agencia estatal (vea la lista abajo) para ver si hay leyes estatales o locales que le aplican a usted. Las agencias estatales también pueden proporcionar información sobre cómo encontrar una compañía de supresión de plomo en su área, y sobre posibles fuentes de asistencia financiera para reducir los peligros del plomo.

| Estado/Región | Número de Teléfono | Estado/Región | Número de Teléfono |
|---|---|---|---|
| Alabama | (205) 242-5661 | Montana | (406) 444-3671 |
| Alaska | (907) 465-5152 | Nebraska | (402) 471-2451 |
| Arkansas | (501) 661-2534 | Nevada | (702) 687-6615 |
| Arizona | (602) 542-7307 | New Hampshire | (603) 271-4507 |
| California | (510) 450-2424 | New Jersey | (609) 530-8812 |
| Colorado | (303) 692-3012 | New Mexico | (505) 841-8024 |
| Connecticut | (203) 566-5808 | New York | (518) 473-4602 |
| Washington DC | (202) 727-9850 | North Carolina | (919) 715-3293 |
| Delaware | (302) 739-4735 | North Dakota | (701) 328-5188 |
| Florida | (904) 488-3385 | Ohio | (614) 466-1450 |
| Georgia | (404) 657-6514 | Oklahoma | (405) 271-5220 |
| Hawaii | (808) 832-5860 | Oregon | (503) 248-5240 |
| Idaho | (208) 332-5544 | Pennsylvania | (717) 782-2884 |
| Illinois | (800) 545-2200 | Puerto Rico | (809) 766-2823 |
| Indiana | (317) 382-6662 | Rhode Island | (401) 277-3424 |
| Iowa | (800) 972-2026 | South Carolina | (803) 935-7945 |
| Kansas | (913) 296-0189 | South Dakota | (605) 773-3153 |
| Kentucky | (502) 564-2154 | Tennessee | (615) 741-5683 |
| Louisiana | (504) 765-0219 | Texas | (512) 834-6600 |
| Massachusetts | (800) 532-9571 | Utah | (801) 536-4000 |
| Maryland | (410) 631-3859 | Vermont | (802) 863-7231 |
| Maine | (207) 287-4311 | Virginia | (800) 523-4019 |
| Michigan | (517) 335-8885 | Washington | (206) 753-2556 |
| Minnesota | (612) 627-5498 | West Virginia | (304) 558-2981 |
| Mississippi | (601) 960-7463 | Wisconsin | (608) 266-5885 |
| Missouri | (314) 526-4911 | Wyoming | (307) 777-7391 |

# Pasos Sencillos Para Proteger a Su Familia de los Peligros del Plomo

## Si usted cree que su casa tiene altos niveles de plomo:

◆ Lleve a sus niños para que les hagan exámenes para plomo, aunque parezcan saludables.

◆ Lave las manos, botellas y chupetes de los niños frecuentemente.

◆ Asegúrese que los niños coman alimentos sanos y bajos en grasa.

◆ Haga que revisen su casa para ver si hay peligros del plomo.

◆ Limpie los pisos, las molduras de las ventanas y otras superficies frecuentemente.

◆ Quítele la tierra a los zapatos antes de entrar en la casa.

◆ Hable con el propietario que le alquila a usted sobre el arreglo de las superficies que tienen pintura que se esté pelando o quebrando.

◆ Tome precauciones para evitar la exposición al polvo de plomo cuando esté remodelando o renovando (llame al 1-800-424-5323 para obtener orientaciones).

◆ No use una lijadora de cinta, soplete de propano, raspadora en seco o papel de lija en seco en las superficies que pudieran contener plomo.

◆ No trate usted mismo(a) de quitar la pintura a base de plomo.

**Recycled/Recyclable**
Printed on paper that contains at least 20 percent postconsumer fiber.

---

# Oficinas Regionales de la EPA

Su contacto Regional de la EPA puede proporcionar más información sobre regulaciones y programas de envenenamiento de plomo que le afecten a usted.

**Oficinas Regionales de la EPA**

**Región 1** (Connecticut, Massachusetts, Maine, New Hampshire, Rhode Island, Vermont)
John F. Kennedy Federal Building
One Congress Street
Boston, MA 02203
(617) 565-3420

**Región 2** (New Jersey, New York, Puerto Rico, Virgin Islands)
Building 5
2890 Woodbridge Avenue
Edison, NJ 08837-3679
(908) 321-6671

**Región 3** (Delaware, Washington DC, Maryland, Pennsylvania, Virginia, West Virginia)
841 Chestnut Building
Philadelphia, PA 19107
(215) 597-9800

**Región 4** (Alabama, Florida, Georgia, Kentucky, Mississippi, North Carolina, South Carolina, Tennessee)
345 Courtland Street, NE
Atlanta, GA 30365
(404) 347-4727

**Región 5** (Illinois, Indiana, Michigan, Minnesota, Ohio, Wisconsin)
77 West Jackson Boulevard
Chicago, IL 60604-3590
(312) 886-6003

**Región 6** (Arkansas, Louisiana, New Mexico, Oklahoma, Texas)
First Interstate Bank Tower
1445 Ross Avenue, 12th Floor, Suite 1200
Dallas, TX 75202-2733
(214) 665-7244

**Región 7** (Iowa, Kansas, Missouri, Nebraska)
726 Minnesota Avenue
Kansas City, KS 66101
(913) 551-7020

**Región 8** (Colorado, Montana, North Dakota, South Dakota, Utah, Wyoming)
999 18th Street, Suite 500
Denver, CO 80202-2405
(303) 293-1603

**Región 9** (Arizona, California, Hawaii, Nevada)
75 Hawthorne Street
San Francisco, CA 94105
(415) 744-1124

**Región 10** (Idaho, Oregon, Washington, Alaska)
1200 Sixth Avenue
Seattle, WA 98101
(206) 553-1200

# Oficinas Regionales de CPSC

**Centro Regional del Este**
6 World Trade Center
Vesey Street, Room 350
New York, NY 10048
(212) 466-1612

**Centro Regional Central**
230 South Dearborn Street
Room 2944
Chicago, IL 60604-1601
(312) 353-8260

**Centro Regional del Oeste**
600 Harrison Street, Room 245
San Francisco, CA 94107
(415) 744-2966

# Notice of Intent to Enter Dwelling Unit

To:_____
　　Tenant

_____
Street address

_____
City and State

THIS NOTICE is to inform you that on _____,

☐ at approximately _____ AM/PM the landlord, or the landlord's agent, will enter the

premises for the following reason:

☐ To make or arrange for the following repairs or improvements:

_____

_____

_____

_____

_____

☐ To show the premises to:

　　☐ a prospective tenant or purchaser

　　☐ workers or contractors regarding the above repair or improvement

☐ Other: _____

_____

_____

You are, of course, welcome to be present. If you have any questions or if the date or time is

inconvenient, please notify me promptly at _____.
　　　　　　　　　　　　　　　　　　　　　　　　　Phone number

_____　　_____
Date　　　　　　　　　　　　Landlord/Manager

# Amendment to Lease or Rental Agreement

This is an Amendment to the lease or rental agreement dated _____, 199____,

(the Agreement) between _____

(Landlord) and _____

(Tenant) regarding property located at _____

_____ (the premises).


Landlord and Tenant agree to the following changes and/or additions to the Agreement:

_____

_____

_____

_____

_____

_____

_____

_____

_____

_____

_____

_____

_____

_____

_____

_____

_____

_____

_____


| | |
|---|---|
| _____ | _____ |
| Date | Landlord |
| _____ | _____ |
| Date | Tenant |
| _____ | _____ |
| Date | Tenant |
| _____ | _____ |
| Date | Tenant |

# Tenant's Notice of Intent to Move Out

_____

Date

_____

Landlord

_____

Street Address

_____

City and State

Dear_____,

Landlord

This is to notify you that I/we will be moving from _____

_____,

on _____ , _____ from today.

This provides at least _____ written notice as required in our

rental agreement.

Sincerely,

_____

Tenant

_____

Tenant

_____

Tenant

# Move-Out Letter

_____

Date

_____

Tenant

_____

Street address

_____

City and State

Dear_____,

Tenant

We hope you have enjoyed living here. In order that we may mutually end our relationship on a positive note, this move-out letter describes how we expect your unit to be left and what our procedures are for returning your security deposit.

Basically, we expect you to leave your rental unit in the same condition it was when you moved in, except for normal wear and tear. To refresh your memory on the condition of the unit when you moved in, I've attached a copy of the Landlord-Tenant Checklist you signed at the beginning of your tenancy. I'll be using this same form to inspect your unit when you leave.

Specifically, here's a list of items you should thoroughly clean before vacating:

☐ Floors

    ☐ sweep wood floors

    ☐ vacuum carpets and rugs (shampoo if necessary)

    ☐ mop kitchen and bathroom floors

☐ Walls, baseboards, ceilings and built-in shelves

☐ Kitchen cabinets, countertops and sink, stove and oven—inside and out

☐ Refrigerator—clean inside and out, empty it of food, and turn it off, with the door left open

☐ Bathtubs, showers, toilets and plumbing fixtures

☐ Doors, windows and window coverings

☐ Other

_____
_____
_____
_____
_____
_____
_____
_____
_____
_____
_____

If you have any questions as to the type of cleaning we expect, please let me know.

Please don't leave anything behind—that includes bags of garbage, clothes, food, newspapers, furniture, appliances, dishes, plants, cleaning supplies or other items.

Please be sure you have disconnected phone and utility services, canceled all newspaper subscriptions and sent the post office a change of address form.

Once you have cleaned your unit and removed all your belongings, please call me at _____ to arrange for a walk-through inspection and to return all keys. Please be prepared to give me your forwarding address where we may mail your security deposit.

It's our policy to return all deposits either in person or at an address you provide within _____ after you move out. If any deductions are made—for past due rent or because the unit is damaged or not sufficiently clean—they will be explained in writing.

If you have any questions, please contact me at _____.

Sincerely,

_____
Landlord/Manager

# Letter for Returning Entire Security Deposit

_____

Date

_____

Tenant

_____

Street address

_____

City and State

Dear_____,

                         Tenant

    Here is an itemization of your _____ security deposit on the property at

_____,

which you rented from me on a _____ basis on

_____,199____, and vacated on _____, 199____ .

    As you left the rental property in satisfactory condition, I am returning the entire amount of the

security deposit of _____.

Sincerely,

_____

Landlord/Manager

# Security Deposit Itemization
## (Deductions for Repairs and Cleaning)

Date: _____

From: _____

_____

_____

To: _____

_____

_____

Property Address: _____

Rental Period: _____

1. Security Deposit Received      $ _____

2. Interest on Deposit (if required by lease or law):      $ _____

3. Total Credit (sum of lines 1 and 2)      $ _____

4. Itemized Repairs and Related Losses:

_____

_____

_____

_____    Total Repair Cost:   $ _____

5. Necessary Cleaning:

_____

_____

_____

_____    Total Cleaning Cost: $ _____

6. Amount Owed (line 3 minus the sum of lines 4 and 5)

  ☐ a. Total Amount Tenant Owes Landlord:      $ _____

  ☐ b. Total Amount Landlord Owes Tenant:      $ _____

Comments: _____

_____

_____

_____

# Security Deposit Itemization
## (Deductions for Repairs, Cleaning and Unpaid Rent)

Date: _____

From: _____

_____

_____

To: _____

_____

_____

Property Address: _____

Rental Period: _____

1. Security Deposit Received      $ _____

2. Interest on Deposit (if required by lease or law):      $ _____

3. Total Credit (sum of lines 1 and 2)      $ _____

4. Itemized Repairs and Related Losses:

_____

_____

_____

_____ Total Repair Cost: $ _____

5. Necessary Cleaning:

_____

_____

_____

_____ Total Cleaning Cost: $ _____

6. Defaults in Rent Not Covered by Any Court Judgment
   (list dates and rates):

_____

_____

_____

_____ Total Rent Defaults: $ _____

7. Amount of Court Judgment for Rent, Costs, Attorney Fees: $ _____

8. Other Deductions:

   Specify: _____

   _____

   _____          $ _____

9. Amount Owed (line 3 minus the sum of lines 4, 5, 6, 7 and 8)

   ☐  a. Total Amount Tenant Owes Landlord:              $ _____

   ☐  b. Total Amount Landlord Owes Tenant:              $ _____

Comments: _____

_____

_____

_____

_____

_____

_____

_____

_____

_____

_____

_____

_____

_____

_____

_____

_____

_____

# Warning Letter for Lease or Rental Agreement Violation

_____

Date

_____

Tenant

_____

Street address

_____

City and State

Dear_____,

                    Tenant

    This is a reminder that your lease prohibits _____

_____

violation. It has come to my attention that, starting _____, 199____ ,

(date of violation) and continuing to the present, you have broken this condition of your tenancy by

_____

_____

_____ .

    It is our desire that you and all other tenants enjoy living in your rental unit. To make sure this occurs, we enforce all terms and conditions of our leases. So please immediately

_____

_____

_____ .

    If it proves impossible to promptly resolve this matter, we will exercise our legal right to begin eviction proceedings.

    Please contact me if you would like to discuss this matter further and clear up any possible misunderstandings.

Yours truly,

_____

Landlord/Manager

_____

Street address

_____

City and State

_____

Phone

# Index

## BUSINESS

| | | | |
|---|---|---|---|
| ⊙ | The CA Nonprofit Corp Kit (Binder w/CD-ROM) | $39.95 | CNP |
| ▣ | Consultant & Independent Contractor Agreements  (Book w/Disk—PC) | $24.95 | CICA |
| ▣ | The Corporate Minutes Book (Book w/Disk—PC) | $69.95 | CORMI |
| | The Employer's Legal Handbook | $31.95 | EMPL |
| ▣ | Form Your Own Limited Liability Company (Book w/Disk—PC) | $34.95 | LIAB |
| ▣ | Hiring Independent Contractors: The Employer's Legal Guide (Book w/Disk—PC) | $29.95 | HICI |
| ▣ | How to Create a Buy-Sell Agreement and Control the Destiny of your Small Business (Book w/Disk—PC) | $49.95 | BSAG |
| ▣ | How to Form a California Professional Corporation (Book w/Disk—PC) | $49.95 | PROF |
| ▣ | How to Form a Nonprofit Corporation (Book w/Disk —PC)—National Edition | $39.95 | NNP |
| | How to Form a Nonprofit Corporation in California | $34.95 | NON |
| ▣ | How to Form Your Own California Corporation (Binder w/Disk—PC | $39.95 | CACI |
| ▣ | How to Form Your Own California Corporation (Book w/Disk—PC) | $34.95 | CCOR |
| ▣ | How to Form Your Own Florida Corporation (Book w/Disk—PC) | $39.95 | FLCO |
| ▣ | How to Form Your Own New York Corporation (Book w/Disk—PC) | $39.95 | NYCO |
| ▣ | How to Form Your Own Texas Corporation (Book w/Disk—PC) | $39.95 | TCOR |
| | How to Write a Business Plan | $24.95 | SBS |
| | The Independent Paralegal's Handbook | $29.95 | PARA |
| | Legal Guide for Starting & Running a Small Business, Vol. 1 | $24.95 | RUNS |
| ▣ | Legal Guide for Starting & Running a Small Business, Vol. 2: Legal Forms (Book w/Disk—PC) | $29.95 | RUNS2 |
| | Marketing Without Advertising | $19.00 | MWAD |
| ▣ | Music Law (Book w/Disk—PC) | $29.95 | ML |
| | Nolo's California Quick Corp (Quick & Legal Series) | $19.95 | QINC |
| ⊙ | Open Your California Business in 24 Hours (Book w/CD-ROM) | $24.95 | OPEN |
| ▣ | The Partnership Book: How to Write a Partnership Agreement (Book w/Disk—PC) | $34.95 | PART |
| | Sexual Harassment on the Job | $18.95 | HARS |
| | Starting & Running a Successful Newsletter or Magazine | $24.95 | MAG |
| | Take Charge of Your Workers' Compensation Claim (California Edition) | $29.95 | WORK |
| | Tax Savvy for Small Business | $29.95 | SAVVY |
| | Trademark: Legal Care for Your Business and Product Name | $34.95 | TRD |
| | Wage Slave No More: Law & Taxes for the Self-Employed | $24.95 | WAGE |
| | Your Rights in the Workplace | $21.95 | YRW |

## CONSUMER

| | | | |
|---|---|---|---|
| | Fed Up with the Legal System: What's Wrong & How to Fix It | $9.95 | LEG |
| | How to Win Your Personal Injury Claim | $26.95 | PICL |
| | Nolo's Everyday Law Book | $24.95 | EVL |
| | Nolo's Pocket Guide to California Law | $12.95 | CLAW |
| | Trouble-Free Travel...And What to Do When Things Go Wrong | $14.95 | TRAV |

## ESTATE PLANNING & PROBATE

| | | | |
|---|---|---|---|
| | 8 Ways to Avoid Probate (Quick & Legal Series) | $15.95 | PRO8 |
| | 9 Ways to Avoid Estate Taxes (Quick & Legal Series) | $22.95 | ESTX |
| | How to Probate an Estate (California Edition) | $39.95 | PAE |
| | Make Your Own Living Trust | $24.95 | LITR |
| | Nolo's Law Form Kit: Wills | $14.95 | KWL |
| ▣ | Nolo's Will Book (Book w/Disk—PC) | $29.95 | SWIL |
| | Plan Your Estate | $24.95 | NEST |
| | Quick & Legal Will Book (Quick & Legal Series) | $15.95 | QUIC |

## FAMILY MATTERS

| | | | |
|---|---|---|---|
| | Child Custody: Building Parenting Agreements That Work | $26.95 | CUST |
| | The Complete IEP Guide | $24.95 | IEP |
| | Divorce & Money: How to Make the Best Financial Decisions During Divorce | $26.95 | DIMO |
| | Do Your Own Divorce in Oregon | $19.95 | ODIV |
| | Get a Life: You Don't Need a Million to Retire Well | $18.95 | LIFE |
| | The Guardianship Book (California Edition) | $39.95 | GB |
| | How to Adopt Your Stepchild in California | $34.95 | ADOP |
| | How to Raise or Lower Child Support in California (Quick & Legal Series) | $19.95 | CHLD |
| | A Legal Guide for Lesbian and Gay Couples | $25.95 | LG |
| | The Living Together Kit | $29.95 | LTK |
| | Nolo's Pocket Guide to Family Law | $14.95 | FLD |
| | Using Divorce Mediation: Save Your Money & Your Sanity | $21.95 | UDMD |

## GOING TO COURT

| | | | |
|---|---|---|---|
| | Beta Your Ticket: Go To Court and Win! (National Edition) | $19.95 | BEYT |
| | Collect Your Court Judgment (California Edition) | $29.95 | JUDG |
| | The Criminal Law Handbook: Know Your Rights, Survive the System | $24.95 | KYR |
| | Everybody's Guide to Small Claims Court (National Edition) | $18.95 | NSCC |
| | Everybody's Guide to Small Claims Court in California | $18.95 | CSCC |
| | Fight Your Ticket ... and Win! (California Edition) | $19.95 | FYT |
| | How to Change Your Name in California | $34.95 | NAME |
| | How to Mediate Your Dispute | $18.95 | MEDI |

▣   Book with disk      ⊙   Book with CD-ROM

| | | |
|---|---|---|
| How to Seal Your Juvenile & Criminal Records (California Edition) | $24.95 | CRIM |
| How to Sue For Up to $25,000...and Win! | $29.95 | MUNI |
| Mad at Your Lawyer | $21.95 | MAD |
| Represent Yourself in Court: How to Prepare & Try a Winning Case | $29.95 | RYC |

## HOMEOWNERS, LANDLORDS & TENANTS

| | | |
|---|---|---|
| ▣ Contractors' and Homeowners' Guide to Mechanics' Liens (Book w/Disk—PC) | $39.95 | MIEN |
| The Deeds Book (California Edition) | $24.95 | DEED |
| Dog Law | $14.95 | DOG |
| ▣ Every Landlord's Legal Guide (National Edition, Book w/Disk—PC) | $34.95 | ELLI |
| Every Tenant's Legal Guide | $26.95 | EVTEN |
| For Sale by Owner in California | $24.95 | FSBO |
| How to Buy a House in California | $24.95 | BHCA |
| The Landlord's Law Book, Vol. 1: Rights & Responsibilities (California Edition) | $34.95 | LBRT |
| The Landlord's Law Book, Vol. 2: Evictions (California Edition) | $34.95 | LBEV |
| Leases & Rental Agreements (Quick & Legal Series) | $18.95 | LEAR |
| Neighbor Law: Fences, Trees, Boundaries & Noise | $17.95 | NEI |
| Renters' Rights (National Edition—Quick & Legal Series)) | $15.95 | RENT |
| Stop Foreclosure Now in California | $29.95 | CLOS |
| Tenants' Rights (California Edition) | $21.95 | CTEN |

## IMMIGRATION

| | | |
|---|---|---|
| How to Get a Green Card: Legal Ways to Stay in the U.S.A. | $24.95 | GRN |
| U.S. Immigration Made Easy | $44.95 | IMEZ |

## MONEY MATTERS

| | | |
|---|---|---|
| ▣ 101 Law Forms for Personal Use (Quick & Legal Series, Book w/disk—PC) | $24.95 | SPOT |
| Bankruptcy: Is It the Right Solution to Your Debt Problems? (Quick & Legal Series) | $15.95 | BRS |
| Chapter 13 Bankruptcy: Repay Your Debts | $29.95 | CH13 |
| Credit Repair (Quick & Legal Series) | $15.95 | CREP |
| ▣ The Financial Power of Attorney Workbook (Book w/disk—PC) | $24.95 | FINPOA |
| How to File for Chapter 7 Bankruptcy | $26.95 | HFB |
| IRAs, 401(k)s & Other Retirement Plans: Taking Your Money Out | $21.95 | RET |
| Money Troubles: Legal Strategies to Cope With Your Debts | $19.95 | MT |
| Nolo's Law Form Kit: Personal Bankruptcy | $16.95 | KBNK |
| Stand Up to the IRS | $24.95 | SIRS |
| Take Control of Your Student Loans | $19.95 | SLOAN |

## PATENTS AND COPYRIGHTS

| | | |
|---|---|---|
| ▣ The Copyright Handbook: How to Protect and Use Written Works (Book w/disk—PC) | $29.95 | COHA |
| Copyright Your Software | $24.95 | CYS |
| How to Make Patent Drawings Yourself | $29.95 | DRAW |
| The Inventor's Notebook | $19.95 | INOT |
| ▣ License Your Invention (Book w/Disk—PC) | $39.95 | LICE |
| Patent, Copyright & Trademark | $24.95 | PCTM |
| Patent It Yourself | $46.95 | PAT |
| Patent Searching Made Easy | $24.95 | PATSE |
| ⦿ Software Development: A Legal Guide (Book with CD-ROM) | $44.95 | SFT |

## RESEARCH & REFERENCE

| | | |
|---|---|---|
| Legal Research: How to Find & Understand the Law | $24.95 | LRES |
| ⦿ Legal Research Online & in the Library (Book w/CD-ROM—Windows/Macintosh) | $39.95 | LRO |

## SENIORS

| | | |
|---|---|---|
| Beat the Nursing Home Trap | $21.95 | ELD |
| The Conservatorship Book (California Edition) | $44.95 | CNSV |
| Social Security, Medicare & Pensions | $21.95 | SOA |

## SOFTWARE

**Call or check our website at www.nolo.com**

**for special discounts on Software!**

| | | |
|---|---|---|
| ⦿ LeaseWriter CD—Windows/Macintosh | $99.95 | LWD1 |
| ⦿ Living Trust Maker CD—Windows/Macintosh | $79.95 | LTD2 |
| ⦿ Small Business Legal Pro 3 CD—Windows/Macintosh | $79.95 | SBCD3 |
| ⦿ Personal RecordKeeper 5.0 CD—Windows/Macintosh | $59.95 | RKD5 |
| ⦿ Patent It Yourself CD—Windows | $229.95 | PPC12 |
| ⦿ WillMaker 7.0 CD—Windows/Macintosh | $69.95 | WMD7 |

▣ Book with disk ⦿ Book with CD-ROM

**CALL 800-992-6656 OR USE THE ORDER FORM IN THE BACK OF THE BOOK**

# ORDER FORM

| Code | Quantity | Title | Unit price | Total |
|------|----------|-------|------------|-------|
|      |          |       |            |       |
|      |          |       |            |       |
|      |          |       |            |       |
|      |          |       |            |       |
|      |          |       |            |       |
|      |          |       |            |       |
|      |          |       |            |       |
|      |          |       | Subtotal |  |
|      |          | California residents add Sales Tax |  |  |
|      |          | Basic Shipping ($3.95) |  |  |
|      |          | UPS RUSH delivery $8.00–any size order* |  |  |
|      |          | TOTAL |  |  |

Name

Address

(UPS to street address, Priority Mail to P.O. boxes)

\* Delivered in 3 business days from receipt of order.
S.F. Bay Area use regular shipping.

## FOR FASTER SERVICE, USE YOUR CREDIT CARD AND OUR TOLL-FREE NUMBERS

Order 24 hours a day     1-800-992-6656

Fax your order     1-800-645-0895

Online     www.nolo.com

## METHOD OF PAYMENT

☐ Check enclosed

☐ VISA    ☐ MasterCard    ☐ Discover Card    ☐ American Express

Account #        Expiration Date

Authorizing Signature

Daytime Phone

PRICES SUBJECT TO CHANGE.

## VISIT OUR OUTLET STORE!      VISIT US ONLINE!

You'll find our complete line of books and software, all at a discount.

**BERKELEY**
950 Parker Street
Berkeley, CA 94710
1-510-704-2248

on the Internet
**www.nolo.com**

# Take 2 Minutes
# & Give Us Your 2 cents

Your comments make a big difference in the development and revision of Nolo books and software. Please take a few minutes and register your Nolo product—and your comments—with us. Not only will your input make a difference, you'll receive special offers available only to registered owners of Nolo products on our newest books and software. Register now by:

**PHONE**
1-800-992-6656

**FAX**
1-800-645-0895

**EMAIL**
cs@nolo.com

or **MAIL** us
this registration card

**REMEMBER:**
Little publishers have big ears. We really listen to you.

fold here

- - - - - - - - - - - - - - - - - - - - - - - - - - - - - - - - - - - - - - - -

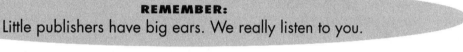

## REGISTRATION CARD

NAME _____ DATE _____

ADDRESS _____

_____

CITY _____ STATE _____ ZIP _____

PHONE _____ E-MAIL _____

WHERE DID YOU HEAR ABOUT THIS PRODUCT? _____

WHERE DID YOU PURCHASE THIS PRODUCT? _____

DID YOU CONSULT A LAWYER? (PLEASE CIRCLE ONE)    YES    NO    NOT APPLICABLE

DID YOU FIND THIS BOOK HELPFUL?    (VERY)    5    4    3    2    1    (NOT AT ALL)

COMMENTS _____

_____

_____

WAS IT EASY TO USE?    (VERY EASY)    5    4    3    2    1    (VERY DIFFICULT)

DO YOU OWN A COMPUTER? IF SO, WHICH FORMAT? (PLEASE CIRCLE ONE)    WINDOWS    DOS    MAC

☐ If you do not wish to receive mailings from these companies, please check this box.

☐ You can quote me in future Nolo.com promotional materials. Daytime phone number _____

ELLI 3.2

**NOLO IN THE NEWS**

"Nolo helps lay people perform legal tasks without the aid—or fees—of lawyers."
**—USA TODAY**

Nolo books are ..."written in plain language, free of legal mumbo jumbo, and spiced with witty personal observations."
**—ASSOCIATED PRESS**

"...Nolo publications...guide people simply through the how, when, where and why of law."
**—WASHINGTON POST**

"Increasingly, people who are not lawyers are performing tasks usually regarded as legal work... And consumers, using books like Nolo's, do routine legal work themselves."
**—NEW YORK TIMES**

"...All of [Nolo's] books are easy-to-understand, are updated regularly, provide pull-out forms...and are often quite moving in their sense of compassion for the struggles of the lay reader."
**—SAN FRANCISCO CHRONICLE**

fold here

- - - - - - - - - - - - - - - - - - - - - - - - - - - - - - - - - - - - - - - - - - - - -

**nolo.com**
**950 Parker Street**
**Berkeley, CA 94710-9867**

**Attn:** | ELLI 3.2 |